Investment Management Regulation

An Introduction to Principles and Practice

Joseph A. Franco
Professor of Law
Suffolk University Law School

Karl-Otto Hartmann
Adjunct Faculty
Suffolk University Law School
CEO and Publisher of 40Act.com

Carolina Academic Press
Durham, North Carolina

ISBN 978-1-61163-717-5
Paperback ISBN 978-1-5310-3488-7
eISBN 978-1-5310-1211-3
LCCN 2018949586

Carolina Academic Press, LLC
700 Kent Street
Durham, North Carolina 27701
Telephone (919) 489-7486
Fax (919) 493-5668
www.cap-press.com

Printed in the United States of America
2025 Printing

Investment Management Regulation

To Brenda, my constant inspiration.
JAF

For Brigitte, my love, for all of her patience and support!
KOH

Contents

Part II
Regulation of Investment Advisers and Private Funds

Part III
Regulation of Registered Investment Companies

Table of Cases

Preface

The subject of investment management regulation is a burgeoning area of law. The business conservatively accounts for $25 trillion in assets under management by money managers in the United States alone, and trillions more internationally. And this number does not even begin to include assets held in accounts that receive investment advice, but are not managed, by market professionals. In 2016, the Investment Company Institute estimated that over 95 million retail investors in the U.S. are directly affected by investments in mutual funds or exchange-traded funds held in individual fund accounts, retail brokerage accounts, or employee retirement accounts. Countless more are indirectly affected by returns from the many varieties of pooled investment vehicles (registered and unregistered) in which institutions (including insurance companies, pension funds, endowments, and foundations) participate.

The enormous economic footprint of the investment management business coupled with the dramatic increase in its size have produced corresponding regulatory changes. Basic animating fiduciary principles have not changed, but their application has had to adapt to new circumstances as the scale of the business has grown, financial strategies have become increasingly complex, and the technical operational aspects of the business have become more interconnected. In addition, legislators and regulators have responded to this changing environment both by extending existing principles to new activities and practices through vigorous enforcement and by introducing new regulatory mandates. Thus, although the basic regulatory pattern was set in 1940 and remains intact, significant legal developments in the ensuing years have made the regulatory scheme more robust and responsive to the financial world of today. Does this mean that the regulatory scheme is adequate to the challenges presented by the financial world of today? No, but the issue of regulatory adequacy or, conversely overreach, is very much fair game for a course on investment management regulation.

This textbook provides students an introduction to investment management regulation as it has evolved. Based on our experience in teaching this course, the authors have deliberately approached the topic differently from the standard legal text to make it more accessible for the typical student. The first major difference for users is that the first five chapters provide a basic primer (an investment management boot camp of sorts) for the uninitiated. Unlike the typical law school subject, we believe students benefit from a preliminary tour of the regulated industry that is the subject of the course and from an understanding of how that industry operates as a business. Investment management, especially its business dimensions, is not intuitive in the way that torts, criminal law, or contracts are. In those subjects, students can draw on their own everyday experience, augmented by popular media, to have a ready intuitive sense of the affected parties' interests. In contrast, the investment management industry is a specialized setting whose workings are largely opaque to the outsider. This primer occupies the first five chapters and resembles more of an undergraduate text than a legal casebook.

The remainder of the book, beginning with Chapter 6, resembles more closely a conventional legal casebook, but also adopts a significantly different presentational style. While the guts of each chapter are excerpts from cases, administrative proceedings, or administrative releases, we use significant framing summaries at the beginning of each chapter and each excerpted item to ensure students understand how topics discussed fit into a broader regulatory tapestry and the purpose of reading the materials that have been selected. There is no attempt to hide the ball. On the contrary, we have selected materials that exemplify current issues and challenges (the majority of the materials excerpted are less than 25 years old). However, the selections are used not merely to illustrate basic legal and regulatory principles, but also to educate students descriptively about the reality and challenges that investment businesses encounter. A good example of this is our reliance on findings from settled SEC administrative proceedings. The administrative orders lack the explicit adversarial dimension typical of adjudicated cases, but invariably they carefully describe the circumstances that serve as a predicate for an order's legal determination. Students, just as practitioners, must derive guidance from these orders regarding conduct that is deemed unlawful. What is left unstated in these administrative orders are the orders' implications for other market participants.

Third, we have consciously designed this book as an introduction to the topic of investment management regulation and have omitted many additional topics that are clearly germane to practitioners. Instead, based in part on our experience, we have tried to create a clear roadmap with respect the basic foundational legal topics in the investment management sphere. Thus, we have limited ourselves to topics that any instructor would surely touch on, even though there are additional, more specialized topics, such as money market funds or capital structure limitations, that we believe are best pursued on a course-by-course basis and possibly in the context of research papers. We have found that an organizational structure tied to foundational simplicity greatly improves overall accessibility of the subject matter for students.

Finally, we have deemphasized to some degree policy analysis in our presentation, not because policy is unimportant, but rather, given its importance, policy analysis is likely to be more sure-footed from a vantage point that reflects the backdrop of legal principles and practice as exemplified by the type of issues and business practices that have arisen. In other words, we don't dwell on the question, "Is there a need for regulation in this area?" The text accepts the policy premise that regulation should work to protect the interests of investors in terms of the specific instances identified, and in the wider sense of creating a framework that allows regulated activities and entities to advance the interests of investors generally. It further assumes that, as a starting point, students should maintain a healthy skepticism simultaneously of both the utility and adequacy of regulatory policies, and also a measure of skepticism regarding the motivations of industry participants. In exploring how regulation in fact operates, however, we leave for the individual course the task of assessing the overall effectiveness of regulation.

The textbook is set forth in 18 chapters divided into three parts. Not all chapters are of equal importance. We have found that chapters 4 and 5 can be relegated to background reading, as can chapter 8, without seriously affecting the text's basic presentation. Two chapters, 9 and 18, took shape in drafting the textbook as indirect regulation of private funds under the Investment Advisers Act developed a momentum of its own (Chapter 9) and the explosive growth of ETFs has injected a disruptive competitive effect on the existing status quo within the investment management business (Chapter 18). These areas promise to be a source of continuing regulatory dynamism in the years to come.

We gratefully acknowledge the research assistance that we received from two law students, Michael Hayes and Taylor Callahan, from the Suffolk Law School Class of 2018.

Joseph A. Franco and Karl-Otto Hartmann
Boston, October 1, 2018

Part I

The Business of Investment Management

Chapter 1

Professional Investment Management

Key Ideas: Professional investment management is the core organizing concept in understanding investment management as a business, and correspondingly, as an area of regulation. The basic idea is simple: investors benefit from having professionals manage their investments. This idea has intuitive appeal to the extent that professional managers possess specialized skills and knowledge regarding investments that can be used for the benefit of clients. The size and breadth of the professional investment management industry underscore that professionals, whether advisors or managers, deliver a range of services and investment styles to serve varied client needs and financial objectives. The distinction between purely advisory services (i.e., merely advising about an investment strategy or product or about a specific investment) and management (i.e., making investment decisions on behalf of a client) is fundamental in thinking about professional investment management. This text gives primary focus to the actual management of client assets by professionals and the substantial legal framework that governs these services. Viewed from a business perspective, the expertise provided by professional investment managers is usually framed in terms of three attributes: (i) superior investment skills in terms of acumen and research (or professional investment management); (ii) ability to provide efficient risk management solutions, such as diversification; and (iii) minimizing transaction costs associated with investment activities (i.e., executing investment strategies in a cost efficient fashion). This chapter offers an introduction to the body of financial terms, concepts, and metrics used to describe and understand how professional investment managers discharge their role and how that role should be evaluated.

Chapter Contents

1.1 Introduction

Professional investment management is the central unifying concept in thinking about investment management as a topic. A broad spectrum of investors, ranging from small retail investors to large institutions, seeks professionals to manage their assets or provide them with investment advice. Firms specialize in providing these services to different categories of clients and they do so in different ways. Two basic themes characterize professional investment management. First, as the term professional implies, these services are delivered as a line of business. The line of business may be the firm's exclusive or primary business, and in other cases, it is packaged with other, typically related, financial services. Managers or advisers generally are well-compensated for their services. Second, professional investment management thrives as a business because investors justifiably believe that investing involves a body of specialized knowledge or skills for dealing with markets and investments. However, the question of whether such knowledge and skills are successful either in generating superior returns for investors or merely in devising sound and appropriate investment solutions for clients is less easily answered. For the most part, this chapter deals with the latter theme, namely what are the basic building blocks in understanding and analyzing the specialized knowledge and factors associated with investing on behalf of clients? The chapter also offers some context in understanding the money management business.

1.2 Professional Money Management as a Business

The business of investment management is best described as eclectic. The industry offers investment management services in many different ways, and the terminology reflects this in confusing ways, unfortunately. For purposes here, a simple but critical practical distinction is between those persons who merely advise clients how to invest their money and money managers (persons who actually are making the investment decisions for their clients based on their understanding of the client's investment objectives and goals). The former activity is non-discretionary, meaning the client retains ultimate authority in determining which investments to pursue. Persons who merely provide advice serve their clients (either individuals or institutions) by recommending investments or by assisting in the selection of a money manager. Money managers, in contrast, invariably formulate investment strategies, but also exercise discretionary authority over the execution of those decisions on behalf of clients within a framework of investment guidelines to which the manager and client have agreed. Later in the text, it will become evident that these two categories of persons (i.e., persons who merely advise and money managers), notwithstanding the inherent dichotomy between their respective activities, are both embraced by the broad definition of "investment adviser" found in the Investment Advisers Act of 1940.

Although a broad range of investment advisory activities are subject to regulation, as this textbook attests, it is possible to make some practical distinctions with respect to similar sounding terminology found in the financial press. The broadest term is "investment adviser," and for purposes of this textbook, it will be used exclusively in its technical legal sense as the foundational definition of the Investment Advisers Act, one of the two statutes that is dealt with in this text. For now, investment advisers can be used generically to refer to anyone who provides advice about securities as part of a business, whether the person exercises discretionary authority over a client's portfolio or acts merely in a non-discretionary advisory sense.

Here is where the confusion begins. "Financial advisor" is a term that is frequently used to refer to market professionals who serve individual clients by working to develop investment strategies and assist in financial planning, such as saving for retirement or children's college tuition. However, financial advisors may or may not be investment advisers in the legal sense. Frequently, financial advisors may work as sales representatives at a brokerage firm and may act purely in a non-discretionary capacity. If the brokerage sales representative provides only non-discretionary advice, the representative's fee structure will likely determine whether the representative is regulated as a broker or an investment adviser. For example, compensation such as commissions based on securities transactions (i.e., purchases and sales) suggests a person is working as a broker. In contrast, fees based on size of an account are characteristic of an investment advisory arrangement. Another type of financial advisor, usually referred to as a "financial planner," primarily generates individualized financial plans for investors supplemented with modest investment recommendations. Such advisors invariably are legally classified as investment advisers because they serve no additional role other than providing financial advice (e.g., they do not engage in trading securities or executing orders for purposes of client trading).

A person having discretionary authority over a client's assets must be an investment adviser for regulatory purposes. Sales representatives that directly manage the assets in an individual client's account at financial services firms (sometimes referred to as "wealth managers") are acting as investment advisers and must be affiliated with an investment advisory firm or securities brokerage firm that is also a registered adviser. Firms that manage the assets of institutional clients such as corporations, banks, pension funds and endowments typically are called "money managers." Institutional money managers may also manage the portfolios of investment companies, such as mutual funds or exchange-traded funds ("ETFs"), hedge funds or even private equity and venture capital funds. Although average retail investors may invest in these funds, e.g., mutual funds and ETFs, the money manger's client in these situations is the fund rather than the retail investors who may own shares of the fund.

1.3 The Building Blocks of Investment Theory

One of the major concerns of investors is how to select or assess the quality of a given investment manager. Not surprisingly, clients and investors seek successful managers, i.e., managers who will provide the best return for the investors' assets. Of course, in the case of investment in a mutual fund, retail investors will look to the fund and its performance in making this determination. As discussed below, the issue of assessment is not straight forward. It involves consideration not just of the manager's potential to generate returns for a client, but also of the levels of risk embedded in the manager's investment strategies. An obvious source of insight about risk and return is the adviser's track record with an important caveat: that **past performance does not guarantee future results.** In the case of advice, it is perhaps possible to reconstruct the advice previously rendered by an adviser to determine whether the adviser's record of advice has been successful in the past. Advisers often will do so for investors as part of their marketing. In the case of money managers, the money manager's record is a very tangible measure of actual performance delivered with respect to the assets under management. This section focuses primarily on factors influencing the reported performance of money managers in order to provide perspective on this seemingly critical dimension in assessing the quality of money managers. As will become evident, there is more to understanding investment performance than may occur to the casual observer on first glance.

1.3.1 Performance and Total Returns

Investors place significant emphasis on performance in selecting a fund or a money manager. The term performance, however, encompasses a central problem for investment management. First there is the problem of how to measure it, and secondly, there is an issue regarding how evidence of past performance relates to future performance.

Performance—the time dimension. Performance is typically measured by returns over a designated period of time. Obviously it would not be very meaningful to compare the performance of one fund against another fund over different periods of time. There are three points relating to comparability of investment performance over time. Such comparisons are an example of comparing apples to oranges. First, the relevant time periods should be of equal duration. After all, if one fund does better over one year rather than another fund over a three year period, a likely explanation is that the different length of time periods may account for widely variant performance results. In addition, however, comparisons should not only be for periods of equal duration but also for corresponding time periods. If one mutual fund's performance was superior in 2016 while another fund's performance was superior in 2017, which is the better fund? If an investor has information only about performance for one fund in 2016 and performance for another fund in 2017, any comparison would be questionable at best as the performance can vary widely from year to year even in the same fund or account. In short, comparing results from 2016 and 2017 will largely reflect random influences rather than being suggestive of skillful management. Performance over comparable time periods makes it possible to compare directly the performance of two different funds or managers while eliminating the potential distortion created by wholly dissimilar market conditions.

Finally, all things being equal, longer periods are likely to be more meaningful in comparing investment track records. Longer investment track records incorporate more information and presumably give more evidence of underlying skill as opposed to the effect of random events or luck. As discussed below, some measures of average performance over a long period smooth out the results from year-to-year variations. However, performance is typically expressed on an annualized basis. For example, performance over three year or even ten year periods will be averaged to reflect annualized performance, e.g., 5% per year over a three year period. However, there are subtle distinctions between simple averaging of annual returns and "average annualized returns" as explained in the section below.

Performance—total returns. Assuming use of comparable periods, the next issue is what is investment performance? If nothing else, performance represents total returns to the investor over a given period of time attributable to the investor's investment in specific securities or assets. In the case of stocks, *total returns* are dividends received (leaving aside any extraordinary distributions) plus any capital appreciation or loss (i.e., whether the price of the stock went up or down in the relevant period) as well as any returns earned on proceeds distributed to the investor during the given period. In the case of a debt instrument, such as a bond, the total return is the amount of interest earned plus any change in the price of the bond over the relevant holding period.

This simple intuition has a couple of important qualifications. Return in any given period may not be realized, that is, it does not result in money paid to or surrendered by the investor. There may be paper profits or losses that can be expected to be realized only when the investments are sold. In other words, if a stock or bond appreciates or loses value, the investor will not enjoy or suffer the consequences of an actual change in the value of a security if they continue to hold the investment. The investor will still have the shares or the bonds, but they will either be more valuable or less valuable depending on the securities' price at the beginning of the relevant period. This paper gain or loss should surely be included in any assessment of performance, even though the investor has not actually realized the gain or loss.

This qualification is potentially less relevant when talking about investments like pooled investment vehicles such as mutual funds. There are two reasons for thinking about investments in pooled investment vehicles differently in this regard. First, the fund may have realized the profit or loss with respect to particular portfolio holdings, even if the fund investor has not realized the gains or losses in its holding of fund shares. Thus, the average investor should look to the return reported by the fund to determine how his or her investment in the fund is doing. Second, fair treatment of investors requires that funds carefully monitor fund performance daily as investors may be buying into a fund or deciding to liquidate (or redeem) their investment on any given day. Because funds are frequently selling new shares to investors while redeeming the shares of others, these transactions should take place at the true current value of the fund's shares which is commonly referred to as the *net asset value* of the fund's shares. Net asset value, as explained in subsequent chapters, is based on the current value of the fund's underlying portfolio of investments which will reflect over time both realized and unrealized gains and losses.

Second, it is important to consider the effect of cost in thinking about returns. The "return" number on a personal investment portfolio generally is not comparable to the return figure used by investment funds because such return figures incorporate investment costs differently. Typically, the raw return number on a personal investment portfolio is not cost adjusted (i.e., it reflects the investments' cost alone and not incidental sales charges or maintenance costs). For the unsophisticated investor, return is simply the sum of the distributions received (interest or dividends) plus the net gain or loss on the value of securities sold or held. In contrast, a fund's total return figure takes into account the costs of managing and administering the investment fund. In other words, fund returns are reported (as it turns out by regulation) on a cost-adjusted basis (i.e., the reported figure is a net return figure) so that the returns reported by different funds are comparable with one another.

For illustration purposes, consider a situation where cost is not incorporated into returns. Suppose money manager A charges 5% annually for managing a fund and generates an annual return of 10%, while a second money manager B charges 1% but only provides an annual return of 9%. Obviously, investors are better off with money manager B because B's return, net of costs, will be 8% annually, while A will return only 5% annually, net of costs.

There is another important adjustment that must be considered in evaluating performance—risk. As discussed in the next couple of sections, risk affects expected return and exposes the investor to outcomes that many would gladly avoid even if it meant reducing expected return. The realities of investment risk are reflected in the marketplace. Accordingly, risky assets that generate a given level of expected return will be valued less than assets that generate the same expected returns but with far less risk. The same point can be stated another way. To the extent that risk and expected return are correlated, one can always boost expected return by taking on additional risk, but with the possibility of an outcome that investors would regard as highly unfavorable. (Think of a roulette wheel in a casino. The payoff for betting on a specific number correctly is stupendous, but betting simply on red or black is much safer!) In comparing investment opportunities, therefore, it is necessary to talk about risk-adjusted performance, i.e., performance that takes into consideration the underlying investment risk.

There is one additional piece of terminology associated with performance that should be discussed. Performance can be viewed either *relative* to a benchmark or in *absolute* terms. This distinction can be illustrated by considering the following propositions: (i) "this fund seeks to outperform the total return of the S&P 500 (an equity index of the 500 largest issuers across economic sectors) over the next year";

and (ii) "regardless of whether S&P 500's total return is positive or negative in the coming year, this fund seeks to provide a positive rate of return of 6% annually." The former assertion involves relative performance which necessarily presupposes a reference benchmark, in this case the S&P 500. In contrast, the latter assertion seeks absolute return regardless of which direction the benchmark moves. As it turns out, most actively managed mutual funds are focused on relative return (i.e., whether the fund outperforms its benchmark) while hedge funds are a classic form of investment vehicle premised on delivering absolute return.

Calendar Year Annual Returns versus Annualized Rates of Total Return

Performance is typically expressed in terms of some form of an annualized return. However there is a difference between an actual annual return, and the annualized rate of return, i.e., the type of return that represents the common form of mandated disclosure return. In the fund world, a fund's annualized total return performance might be reported as follows: 7%—YTD (year-to-date); 11%—1 yr; 6%—5 yr; and 4.9%—10 yr. In contrast, the calendar year return is the actual return achieved in a particular calendar year without any averaging. What that means is that for the calendar year to date, the fund's total return is 7%; for the past fiscal year the total return is 11% (no averaging necessary); for the past five fiscal years the total return has averaged 6% per year; and over the past 10 fiscal years, it averaged 4.9%.

In most cases, the one year return varies year to year. So, for example, it could be 10% in year 1 and 5% in year 2 and 15% in year 3. The average annual calendar return in this example is 10%, i.e., the arithmetic average over the three years. However, the average *annualized* return for the same three years would be approximately 9.7%. Unlike the average annual calendar return each year over three years, the average annualized return reflects the rate of return over the three years while accounting for the effect of compounded returns, i.e., the return in subsequent years from return earned in earlier years. Although the annualized rate of return involves a slightly more sophisticated calculation, it produces a number that is easier to compare with the total return results of other funds and more meaningful from a financial perspective. Nevertheless, annualized return ignores the effects of volatility (reflective of risk), and volatility is clearly a factor that investors do and should care about. In other words, return figures are useful and may provide some basis for comparison, but it is also important to remember that simple uncritical comparisons may obscure important qualifications.

1.3.2 Risk (Part 1): Risk and Diversification

As mentioned in the preceding section, accounting for risk is necessary in order to evaluate performance. Wholly apart from that, however, it is a concern for every investor, and investors will differ in their tolerance for risk. In the world of investments, one measure of risk (or volatility in returns) is variance in returns from year to year. Put simply, the more variance historically, the more risk.

Historically, investors and commentators recognized that one way to reduce risk was to diversify investments in an investment portfolio. In the past 75 years, financial economics has produced a rigorous analytical model for understanding the principles of diversification and their contribution to risk in the context of investment portfolios. Portfolio theory provides a more rigorous way of thinking about the sources of risk in investment portfolios by using a mean-variance approach in analyzing returns. There are several very powerful conclusions flowing from modern portfolio theory.

First, is the concept of *diversification,* which in its simplest form suggests that an investor may be able to reduce risk of investing by spreading his or her bets. To illustrate: the simplest form of diversification would be to invest in several stocks rather than just one, thereby reducing the risk that an adverse event for any one stock will impact the value of all of them. Portfolio theory refines the basic diversification principle by considering correlation among investments. The theory suggests that it is possible to reduce risk for a given level of return by combining assets in a portfolio containing riskier and less risky assets as long as the returns of the assets are not perfectly correlated. This is the essence of diversification. Indeed, such diversification reduces risk precisely because risks across assets are not perfectly correlated. The less correlation in return across assets, the easier it is to reduce risk through diversification. Second, assets (or for these purposes, securities) whose returns are less than perfectly correlated, including assets whose returns are uncorrelated, can be used to construct portfolios that will minimize overall risk for a given level of expected return. In other words, diversification allows for the construction of efficient portfolios, those that optimize return for a given level of risk. Finally, it is not possible to diversify away from all types of market risk to the extent that the returns of most assets are positively correlated in some respect. This type of risk is sometimes referred to as *non-diversifiable risk.* Not surprisingly, this type of risk stands in contrast to the type of risk that can be essentially eliminated through diversification, so-called *diversifiable risk.* If investors seek to be compensated through higher returns for assuming greater risk, then it is perhaps easy to understand that the compensation for greater risk actually relates solely to non-diversifiable risk, precisely because the other type of risk can be eliminated through diversification without any additional compensation.

Hedging is a related concept which arises when the returns of two assets are negatively correlated. A *hedge* is a strategy seeking a return that offsets the return realized from another asset. For example, if an investor owns a stock, he or she generally does so in hopes of profiting from an increase in the stock's market value or price. If the investor is worried that the price may drop, she can sell the stock. That could cost the investor capital gains taxes on her profits. Alternatively, the investor could purchase instruments which move inversely in price to the stock, offsetting potential losses. This is a classic type of hedge. By providing an offsetting exposure on an investment position, a hedge provides a method of shifting or eliminating risk. Hedging works because the return associated with the hedge is inversely correlated with the investment risk that would otherwise exist. As another example, if a company operates a trucking business whose expenses are directly tied to the price of diesel fuel, then buying an inventory of diesel fuel means that the risk of escalating diesel prices is eliminated (or hedged).

Derivatives, such as options and futures contracts, are attractive as financial instruments precisely because they represent an efficient way to shift (or hedge) investment risk. *Derivatives* are simply instruments that derive their value from the performance of an underlying asset like a stock, precious metal, or even oil. Thus, in the preceding example, the trucking firm could also go out and purchase a futures contract that locks in the price of the diesel fuel for a designated period going forward. The firm could then continue to purchase diesel fuel on the spot market (e.g., at the gas pump or the wholesaler), but any increases in operating costs from higher fuel prices would be offset by increases in the value of the futures contract.

Diversification — Is It Ever Possible to Get Too Much of a Good Thing When It Comes to Funds?

Because diversification is generally perceived as beneficial by risk-sensitive investors, one could easily speculate that more and more diversification is always better than less. However, there are obvious limits to this principle. It turns out that the principles already described imply that risk-reduction through diversification increases at a decreasing rate as the number of assets in a portfolio increases. Put differently, each new portfolio position reduces the portfolio's diversifiable risk by smaller and smaller amounts until there is only a very small incremental effect in terms of risk reduction from adding an additional asset to the portfolio.

What about diversification by means of acquiring many different funds? For example, suppose someone sought a diversified portfolio of stocks by buying numerous actively managed equity mutual funds. Does such a strategy make sense? Almost surely not. The reason is that as one continues to add to the number of funds held (in the belief this will produce more diversified aggregate holdings), the investor has changed the investment character of the individual fund holdings into something that in aggregate will begin to resemble a broad-based market basket of stocks. Even though the resulting aggregate holdings may indeed be more diverse, the portfolio will begin to perform roughly similar to the market as a whole.

By itself, there is nothing wrong with trying to get an investment position that mimics the market. But herein lies the rub. It is fairly easy and cheap to purchase a fund that mimics the total market's performance. Such passive strategies are packaged in broad-based index funds and are very cheap in terms of the management fees paid by investors. But the example posed was very different. It hypothesized that an investor went out and bought many actively-managed funds on the theory that such a strategy in aggregate would diversify overall returns relative to the returns of the individual funds. In the hypothetical, the investor selects from a number of individually actively-managed funds (i.e., funds that charge high management fees on the theory that the manager's research and expertise will lead to a fund that outperforms the market). However, once a number of actively-managed funds are combined in an aggregate portfolio, the resulting portfolio will, as noted, begin to look like the broad-based index fund. Wouldn't it be better to purchase the low-cost broad-based index fund at the outset rather than reaching the same result by purchasing a series of relatively expensive actively-managed funds?

1.3.3 Risk (Part 2): Quantifying Risk

Given the important role of risk, one challenge for investors is understanding its role in performance. That is, how does one determine the extent to which the observed performance is merely a consequence of the underlying risk or a reflection of superior investment skills over and above the investment's underlying risk profile?

Some measures of risk are designed to give an adjusted expected return for some investment which in turn can be used to measure unexpected returns or underperformance. Other measures provide other ways of thinking about risk to ensure comparability in evaluating investment performance. Two measures derived from a financial economic approach known as the *Capital Asset Pricing Model* ("CAPM") are widely used: *beta* and *alpha*.

Conceptually, the CAPM provides a systematic and simplified (perhaps overly) way of understanding how risk affects expected returns for an investment. CAPM posits that the expected rate of return of a security or a portfolio should equal the return on a risk-free security plus an additional return for relative market risk. In short, in a world where the CAPM theory and assumptions strictly held, securities (or portfolios) with above-average market risk would yield a return greater than the market. Conversely, securities with below-average market risk should yield less than the broad market return on securities of the same category (such as common stocks or bonds), but still greater than the riskless rate of return (which is nothing more than the time value of money). The same basic concept can be expressed slightly differently. A good proxy for the riskless rate of return is the return provided by short-term U.S. government securities, such as the 90 day Treasury bill rate. If an investor wanted to have a risk-free investment, he or she would invest in the 90 day Treasury bill. However, if seeking a greater expected return, the investor might turn to corporate bonds or an even riskier asset category, such as common stocks.

A key dimension of the CAPM theory concerns risk of the security (or portfolio) relative to market risk, since the model posits that return will depend on greater or lesser amounts of risk relative to market. This is where the concept of "beta" comes into play. Beta is a measure of relative market risk. Essentially, beta reflects how risky an investment is compared to overall market risk and is a function of the volatility of the investment and the market, as well as the correlation between the two. For stocks, the market is usually represented in terms of capitalization weighted indices, such as the S&P 500 index or more general market indices, such as the Russell 1000.

As a practical illustration, if a stock has a beta of 1.0, its performance correlates precisely to the market index or a measure like the S&P 500. If the stock has a beta of 0.5, then it would be expected to have half the volatility of the market index. And if the stock has a beta over 1.0, then it would be expected to rise and fall more than the index.

Betas can be estimated for any single security and a portfolio of securities, but there is no guarantee that betas remain stable over time or that other assumptions underlying the idealized CAPM are entirely valid. Leaving aside the underlying mathematics, CAPM and beta provide useful tools for thinking about how certain forms of risk influence return. At the very least, CAPM demonstrates intuitively why very different portfolio returns may say very little about the skill of the investment manager. Managers who load up on riskier investments should deliver a higher return than managers of portfolios that follow a more conservative investment strategy.

In addition, when viewed in hindsight, expected return will likely deviate from actual return, and the difference between the actual return and the expected return is referred to as "alpha." In some sense, alpha is a measure of whether a manager's portfolio did better or worse than was expected. Obviously, alpha can also be affected by random chance or statistical noise. However, over time, statistical error or noise should cancel out. "Sustained alpha," i.e., alpha which continues over time, is sometimes used as an indirect proxy of skill. If a portfolio always performs better than expected, that means the manager contributes positive alpha to the portfolio's return. Investors seek, and managers try to deliver, positive alpha in their portfolio returns. On the other hand, alpha can be negative, i.e., performance is below expected return. Understandably, investors should shun negative alpha, i.e., an investment manager who provides worse than expected risk-adjusted return.

There are other widely-used measures of risk in the investment management world. Many of these measures are based on the central insights of the CAPM and provide different ways of thinking about risk and portfolio return. For example, the *Sharpe ratio* seeks a risk-adjusted measure of return by calculating the ratio of the premium return earned over a corresponding benchmark return, all relative to the level of additional risk assumed over the benchmark portfolio. In other words, did the manager get a lot of bang for the buck in terms of return for each unit of additional risk that was assumed? There are other measures which provide alternative ways of assessing whether an investment offers an attractive tradeoff between risk and return. While the CAPM approach to risk is widely employed, there are other approaches to risk based on multifactor models and different modeling assumptions (such as assumptions about the underlying probability distributions for expected returns). For present purposes, it is not necessary to go into the differences among the various ways of quantifying risk. These many models underscore two important points—first, risk is inextricably linked to return (and investment performance), and second, because risk is inherently complex, it can be measured and quantified in different ways.

1.3.4 Expenses

As noted above, investment returns must be assessed with respect to the costs (or expenses) in generating those returns. Obviously, if expenses are abnormally high, one would expect superior performance to offset the abnormally high expenses incurred in generating those results. Lesser performance will be further impeded by high expenses. In contrast, low expenses can make up for lesser performance or enhance superior performance. For individual securities such as stocks, understanding expenses is usually quite simple. A flat brokerage fee (or commission) may be assessed for purchases and sales. Generally, these charges are reflected on the transaction confirmation statement sent to investors. In some cases, brokers do not charge a per transaction fee, but rather charge a fee based on a percentage of the value of assets held in an account, such as an annual 1% fee. For managed portfolios and investment funds, management fees of the latter sort are the norm. However, there are a variety of additional expenses which investors take into consideration, including the fees and expenses paid by funds to administer the fund, to maintain shareholder records, and to provide for safekeeping of the fund's assets. These fees and expenses are discussed more extensively in Chapter 4.

1.4 Selected Conceptual Issues Relating to Professional Investment Management

The basic features of risk, return and expenses provide the groundwork for key debates regarding the purpose of investment managers and the goals of investors. While there are many potential topics, three issues are highlighted below because of their importance in understanding the investment product landscape and competing contentions regarding the nature of the services provided by investment managers.

1.4.1 Active versus Passive Management

One of the most pressing debates in the investment management industry concerns benefits and costs of active management strategies relative to passive management strategies. Active investment managers try to outperform the market, i.e., produce a better return on managed assets than would be achieved by merely adhering to passive strategies by holding a portfolio that mimics the returns of the market or some segment of the market. Active managers are arguably able to deliver superior returns based on superior investment skills and superior financial research and analysis. In essence, active managers claim that they will perform above average over the long haul (that is, will be able to select securities that on average return a higher percentage of winners and a lower percentage of losers relative to the market). In the terms discussed above, active managers strive to provide positive alpha.

Passive managers adhere to a different philosophy. They do not try to outperform the overall market's return, rather they try to strictly mimic market performance or, more accurately, the performance of the relevant segment of the market that they intend to track. Unlike active managers, passive managers measure their performance by how well their portfolios are able to match (or as it is more commonly phrased, "track") the designated measure of market performance. Securities indexes are the means by which the market performance of a given basket of securities is measured and, of course, the relevant basket can be assembled in different ways including by company size, sector, and different weighting schemes (e.g., Apple common stock could be given a weight of 5% in a particular equity index or merely 1% in another index). To illustrate, perhaps one of the most famous indexes of equity performance is the "S&P 500 index." That index is a proprietary index formulated by Standard & Poor's (the so-called "index provider"). It is designed to calculate and represent the combined performance of the common stocks of 500 largest U.S. public stock issuers. The index is "capitalization weighted" (i.e., proportionate to the market capitalization of each issuer in the index) and balanced to be "sector neutral" (i.e., representative of the U.S. economy in terms of the weight for sectors in the index such as financial companies, consumer durable sellers, technology, health, and medical products). Of course, there are numerous other securities indexes such as equity indexes based on company size or economic sector and bond indexes tied to the type of bond issuer (government or corporate) or the maturity of the bonds held in the portfolio (short, medium, or long-term). Indexes easily number in the hundreds, if not more.

One of the hottest topics in the investment world is whether active managers that seek to outperform given market benchmarks can provide investors with superior cost-adjusted performance. In other words, do active managers deliver added investment performance commensurate with the management fees they charge? The answer to this question turns on a number of subsidiary issues. Most directly, do active managers on average actually outperform the market average? Unless active managers can on average outperform the market, there would be little sense in using active managers, since an investor could always opt for a passive strategy that will match the market's return.

Advocates of passive management strategies argue that it makes little sense for investors to seek strategies that outperform the market, because on average, the performance of money managers will on average be average. Moreover, theories of market efficiency argue that securities markets already incorporate most public information and so it is hard to envision how any manager would consistently be able to anticipate which securities are likely to enjoy abnormal returns.

Active managers frequently point out that if all money managers were entirely passive in their approach, "price discovery" (the market process that leads each security to move towards its correct market price) would be stunted, which might create new opportunities for active managers to exploit temporary mispricing of securities. Another argument for active managers is sometimes expressed in terms of "capture ratios." Capture ratios focus on the possibility that the returns for a given strategy relative to a passive market benchmark are not always symmetrical: on the upside, a given strategy might outperform the market when it is going up, and on the downside, the same strategy may sustain smaller losses. If this is in fact true for some active strategies, then this asymmetric capture ratio should show up as greater returns over time and possibly a better risk-adjusted rate of return. The claim effectively restates the idea that the active manager is providing a better risk-adjusted rate of return.

There is another important consideration in the debate between active and passive management strategies: costs. Active money management costs more than passive money management in terms of management fees and portfolio management expenses. Active managers invest greater resources in analysis and research of securities and pay more for portfolio managers. In contrast, the principal challenge facing a passive investment manager is to match the performance of the benchmark index, either by owning all of the securities in the index in precisely the right amount (i.e., by "replication" of the index) or through sophisticated statistical techniques that are designed to simulate the movement of the index without holding each and every security in the index (i.e., a selective "sampling" methodology). Because active management is costly, and certainly more costly than passive management, it follows that an active manager will not only have to beat the market benchmark, but beat it by a sufficient amount so that its cost-adjusted performance is still superior to the cost-adjusted performance of a passive manager (which delivers the average market performance at a very low cost).

These considerations have led one of the most influential figures in money management, John Bogle, to cheekily coin a theory dubbed the "Cost-Matters Hypothesis." Bogle was the founder of what we know today as the Vanguard Group, the second largest money manager in the U.S., with over several trillion dollars under management. According to Bogle, it is axiomatic that money managers collectively will perform only as well as the average and an index fund can always guarantee the average performance if run properly. However, costs will be a steady drag on performance, and it will be a much bigger drag on the performance of active managers because their actively managed funds have expense ratios that can easily be anywhere from two to five times more expensive than a passively-managed fund. Since active managers will only on average do no better than the market over time, they will obviously do worse as the added expense creates a significant drag on reported performance. At an intuitive level, there is much appeal to the basic logic of this argument. However, there is still an empirical possibility, even if uncommon, that some managers can consistently outperform the market on a cost-effective basis. Nevertheless, financial economists have offered significant empirical research that corroborates Bogle's basic point: active managers generally underperform the benchmark index after taking account of costs over long periods of time.

Not surprisingly, in recent years, there has been a massive shift of investor assets toward passive over active strategies. Statistics from the Investment Company Institute indicate that nearly one-quarter of all assets under management are passively managed, and the expectation is that this fraction will continue to increase.

Closet Indexing — Why Active Managers Shun the Label

A common complaint heard about some active funds is that the manager is a closet indexer or, in other words, is engaged in "closet indexing." What does closet indexing mean? Essentially it means the manager's portfolio approximately replicates the investment performance of a benchmark index (this aspect is the indexing part of "closet indexing") while the manager is representing to investors that it is executing an active strategy (this aspect is the closet aspect of "closet indexing").

The phrase closet indexer carries a pejorative connotation, and so the next issue is to understand why? After all, low-cost index strategies are increasingly popular among average retail investors and many investment professionals tout the virtues of relying on index strategies to guide investments. Accordingly, the problem with closet indexing is not that the closet indexer is not in replicating the performance of a given index, but that the manager is engaged in using an index strategy when it represents to investors that it is doing something else, namely executing an active strategy that relies on the manager's acumen to beat the market. There is another disheartening feature to the closet indexer from the perspective of the retail investor. Who charges more—an active manager or a passive manager? Clearly the former. This fact is the source of the chief complaint of investors with respect to closet indexing. They are being charged a premium active rate for management services, and they are receiving only a passive type of performance that matches the chosen benchmark (or more precisely, they are getting no better than average performance while paying a premium active management fee). In short, investors wind up overpaying the closet indexing manager for the advisory services provided.

While it may seem obvious why retail investors in an active fund would be disappointed by a manager that uses a closet indexing strategy, it is less clear why a manager might succumb to closet indexing. Presumably, active managers seldom deliberately try to replicate the performance of a benchmark index. However, managers may nevertheless approximate the performance of a benchmark with some deviations here or there, either consciously or unconsciously.

What causes portfolio managers to veer toward higher degrees of closet indexing? In some cases, it's the result of a fund having grown so large in terms of assets that its portfolio starts to resemble the comparative index in terms of performance. In other cases, it's the result of well-intentioned but misguided managers. A truly active manager's return will undoubtedly diverge from the benchmark for good or ill, precisely because the obvious and, indeed, necessary condition for outperformance is selecting a portfolio that differs from the benchmark in the weighting of its component securities within any sector and among securities in different sectors of the economy. However, truly active management is potentially a scary proposition for the portfolio manager, as deviation can lead to significant outperformance or severe underperformance. Timid active managers may select a portfolio that minimizes the likelihood that the portfolio's performance seriously underperforms the benchmark index. Accordingly, they are less likely to make significant active bets (i.e., investments that significantly deviate from the benchmark's component and sector weightings). In baseball parlance, they may be content to try and hit investment singles rather than swinging for the fences. This strategy may be particularly pronounced if portfolio manager compensation is heavily weighted toward merely exceeding the benchmark rather than significantly rewarding outsized performance.

Perhaps the most difficult question posed by closet indexing is whether a money manager is in fact a closet indexer. Financial economists use different metrics to determine whether an actively managed portfolio is really a form of closet indexing. Three different metrics are frequently mentioned: active share, R-squared and tracking error. Financial economists look for a so-called high "active share" fraction for a portfolio to identify true active managers, meaning the managed portfolio's component weightings within and across sectors materially differ from the benchmark index. Low active share suggests the possibility of closet indexing. "R-squared" looks at the correlation between the active portfolio performance and index portfolio performance over short periods of time such as daily or weekly. High correlation is indicative of closet indexing. Finally, "tracking error" looks at the differential between the return of the active portfolio and the passive index, again over short periods of time. A small tracking error (i.e., lockstep movements between an index and an actively managed portfolio) is an indicator of closet indexing. *See generally* K.J. Martins Cremers & Quinn Curtis, *Do Mutual Fund Investors Get What They Pay For? Securities Law and Closet Index Funds*, 11 Va. L. & Bus. Rev. 31 (2016).

1.4.2 Skill versus Luck

Understanding the difference between skill and luck in investment performance is closely related to the debate over active versus passive management. Merely because a money manager outperforms the market or its benchmark index in a particular year does not mean that the money manager is more skillful than other investment managers. The reason is obvious: an investment manager's performance in any given period may be a product of random factors (i.e., luck) rather than skill. One can look at luck as a statistical fluke. A person just happened to bet the right way, just as someone might win money in Las Vegas by betting on red at the roulette wheel or putting their money in a slot machine that just happens to pay out on the next pull of its lever. Over time, however, the laws of probability tend to eliminate the transient effects of luck. This fact is incredibly important in understanding any assessment of investment performance. Over shorter periods of time, luck has a significant potential to distort inferences that can be drawn from performance results. For this reason, investment performance over a longer period of time is a better indicator of investment acumen than short-term skill.

Of course, the difficulty in distinguishing between luck and skill raises additional considerations. First, even if luck and skill can be distinguished by sophisticated observers with sufficient data, are average retail investors likely to be able to differentiate skill and luck when looking at composite performance results? If not, that would appear to be an argument suggesting that average retail investors should avoid active strategies, even if some active strategies outperform the market. Why? Because even though some active strategies may be effective, retail investors are unlikely to be able to identify those that are genuinely the result of skill as opposed to those that merely appear skillful but which are in fact a product of luck.

There are other confounding effects that make it hard to determine whether superior performance is likely to persist. For example, a skillful manager may be more skillful in some market situations than others. In addition, luck and skill are not mutually exclusive, and so while it may be easy to distinguish pure luck from pure skill, it will be relatively difficult to determine subtle gradations in skill. Finally, markets and trading are dynamic, and strategies themselves may not be scalable. In other words, even if a particular active strategy may have provided genuinely superior performance in the past, there is no guarantee that the strategy will continue to be successful in the future, especially as that strategy is copied by others, or that a money manager will adapt quickly enough to changing market opportunities. However, this consideration may also create new possibilities. For example, as the use of passive strategies for assets under management increases, it is quite possible that this may create new opportunities for successful active strategies.

Nevertheless, the fundamental point remains. Regardless of where one comes out on the active versus passive strategy debate, mere knowledge that active strategies in theory may provide superior performance does not mean that average retail investors will be in a position to apply that knowledge usefully in selecting money managers.

1.4.3 Asset Allocation, Securities Selection, and Timing

Financial economists usually isolate three factors in the decision making of investment managers that contribute to reported performance and may be a source of skill: asset allocation, securities selection, and market timing. "Asset allocation" refers to the skill in picking among asset classes as a source of risk-adjusted investment performance. If stocks outperform bonds (leaving risk aside), presumably investment portfolios that focus on stocks over bonds will exhibit a higher return. In other words, a good portion of the reported performance of any investment portfolio will reflect the return experiences for that portfolio's representative class of assets. Typically, investment managers of funds are constrained in their choice of asset allocation. A fund's strategies will focus on a particular asset class to the exclusion of others. Hence, in such situations, the asset class serves as a benchmark for evaluating the manager's skills with respect to securities selection or market timing.

However, there are investment advisers who do focus on choosing asset classes, and the choices typically are designed to focus on both maximizing performance and balancing risk. A financial adviser for an individual (or wealth manager) will typically talk about the weighting of the individual's entire investment portfolio (something like 50% domestic stocks, 10% international stocks, and 40% bonds). This weighting most likely will change as the individual gets closer to retirement to reflect changes in the individual's investment horizon which may also reflect relative risk tolerance. Similarly, a pension fund or endowment typically will deliberately weight its portfolio to get exposure to different asset classes. To some extent, the weighting across asset classes reflects a diversification strategy to reduce risk. Moreover, as different asset classes perform differently, it will be necessary to "rebalance" the portfolio to reestablish the original weightings or, if implementing a new weighting strategy, to change the portfolio's allocation of assets among asset classes.

Asset allocation is typically regarded as the most important determinant of investment performance, but the other two factors are important as well. "Securities selection" refers to the skill brought to bear in selecting among securities within a given asset class. For example, one issuer's stock may outperform another issuer's stock over time even though the issuers come from the same asset class. This may reflect that one company is better than another company in terms of its products, earnings prospects and financial health. The investment manager's skill in securities selection derives from fundamental research and analysis regarding the different issuers.

Finally, some element of return comes from the "timing" associated with investments. Did the investment manager sense when the market was getting ready to move up or go down or for that matter when a particular stock was cheap relative to other stocks? One could imagine two investment managers with roughly similar investment portfolios, but one might do better solely based on the timing of its investments. The skill of the more successful investment manager is in sensing when to buy and when to sell (or in common parlance, it's the consistent ability to "buy low and sell high" as the market moves up and down). Needless to say, this skill seems most at odds to notions of efficient markets affected by random noise. While undoubtedly good timing will positively affect returns, it is something that seems more akin to luck than skill.

Chapter 2

The Basics of Investment Accounts and Products

Key Ideas: Investment advisers, as the label would imply, give advice about investments and more specifically, for purposes of this textbook, investments in securities. An important distinction for investment advisers is whether the adviser acts in a discretionary or non-discretionary capacity. When acting in a discretionary capacity, the adviser makes investment decisions on behalf of the client. In other words, the adviser or money manager will make all decisions of whether and when to buy or sell securities for the client whether an individual, an institution, or a fund. In contrast, non-discretionary advice is advice that the client is free to accept or reject and frequently is, but need not be, personalized with respect to a client's account. Managing a client's assets entails more significant responsibilities than merely non-discretionary advisory services, such as executing trades and administering assets.

Discretionary advisory arrangements can take a number of forms ranging from separate accounts to funds. This textbook focuses primarily on investment advisers acting in a discretionary role managing a client's assets, especially in the context of investment products in which the so-called client is an investment vehicle used to pool the assets of many investors (i.e., a fund). These managers may manage registered and unregistered funds. Funds with managed portfolios could not function unless an investment professional is making decisions on behalf of the fund. This chapter provides a brief working introduction to various investment products which, in the case of registered funds, include mutual funds, exchange-traded funds ("ETFs"), closed-end funds, and unit investment trusts ("UITs"). Unregistered funds include hedge funds, private equity funds, venture capital funds, and collective trusts.

Chapter Contents

2.1 Introduction

The investment management industry manages client or investor assets in the tens of trillions of dollars. Money managers not only invest client assets, which involves buying and selling securities and the timing of those activities, but also monitor and administer those assets, meaning they oversee the safekeeping of the assets and make sure that there are orderly records of account relating to each client's assets. How the assets are managed depends in part on the type of investment arrangement. Professional investment management services can be geared to individual accounts, in which case the relationship will typically take the form of a bilateral arrangement between the client and the investment manager. Other investment arrangements (and by far the more significant in terms of assets under management) take the form of investment vehicles in which the assets of many investors are pooled. These arrangements usually are referred to as funds, and there are a number of different types of funds. Funds are unabashedly marketed as investment products. This chapter provides a survey of these products that introduces students to the basic nomenclature of funds and the funds' basic economic attributes.

2.2 Retail Discretionary Accounts versus Non-Discretionary Accounts

The most basic investment management arrangements are bilateral individual arrangements. These arrangements can take essentially two forms: retail or institutional. In the case of a retail relationship, the investment manager is undoubtedly managing the accounts of many individual clients. As discussed in Chapter 1, a key distinction among retail relationships is between situations where an investment manager has been given discretionary authority and situations where a financial adviser acts solely in a non-discretionary advisory capacity. In the discretionary relationship situation, the wealth manager actually controls the client's account in the sense of making all investment decisions. In addition to making the investment decisions, the manager discharges other responsibilities such as overseeing the execution of the investment decisions made, ensuring the safekeeping of client assets, and overseeing administrative tasks that are necessary to managing clients' assets. The manager may not itself perform these ancillary functions but will at the very least need to coordinate with other services providers. When acting in a purely advisory capacity, an account representative (such as a sales representative or a financial advisor at a brokerage firm) is not actually managing the client's money, but merely providing advice which the client may accept or reject. In a retail environment, it is possible that an adviser acts in more than one capacity, and it will depend on the account. Brokerage accounts tend to be non-discretionary, but in some cases, retail clients use registered investment advisers to manage their brokerage account. Some brokerage customers may be fairly self-sufficient on their own and will not rely on the brokerage firm for personalized advice. These investors are sometimes referred to as "self-directed" investors or accounts.

The basic distinction between discretionary management and non-discretionary advice is less relevant in an institutional setting, only because money managers invariably act in a discretionary capacity. Of course, institutional clients, such as pension funds, may also use investment advisers which are not money managers to assist them, for example, in selecting a money manager to manage fund assets.

2.3 Separately Managed Accounts

Separately managed accounts, or colloquially "separate accounts," are investment arrangements used in both the retail and institutional settings. In either setting, separate accounts represent a classic bilateral arrangement in which an investment manager agrees to manage client assets in a separate account for that client—hence the name separate account. There are two points worth emphasizing. First, separate accounts typically involve large account minimums. For wealthy individuals, the minimum can be several million dollars. Institutional money managers may insist on even larger account minimums for institutional investors, such as $25 or $100 million, in order to provide an investment strategy customized for the client. So, for example, an institutional investor may establish a separate account with a money manager of $100 million with a directive that it be focused on domestic equity with a social investing tilt that emphasizes ESG ("Environmental, Social, and Governance") values. Second, separately managed accounts typically involve a clear investment management mandate that addresses investment strategies and guidelines as provided in the written investment advisory agreement or incorporated by reference therein. A key element of this type of arrangement is its bilateral nature, i.e., the terms of the arrangement

Figure 2A — Separate Account: an account managed by a professional money manager with a mutually agreed investment objective

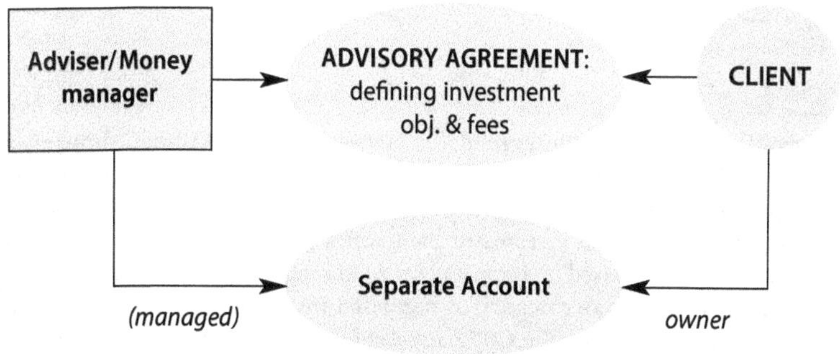

can have customized features as reflected in the terms of the investment advisory agreement. For wealthy individuals of the smaller variety, the investment objectives are usually standardized. For institutional clients, the parties will customize the arrangement as necessary. The agreement will clearly set forth the fees associated with the account. The diagram on the previous page illustrates the basics of this type of arangement.

The diagram captures the salient features. The assets of the client are not pooled with other investors, and the account is managed in accordance with the mandate set forth in the investment advisory agreement. Note: For clarity's sake, it is important to distinguish the term "separate account" as used here from the type that is used in the insurance industry to describe an unrelated type of insurance account for the benefit of a specific class of policyholders whose assets are segregated from other insurance company and policyholder assets.

2.4 Registered Investment Companies — The Four Types (Mutual Funds, Closed-End Funds, UITs, and ETFs)

This textbook, as noted, focuses primarily on investment management as it relates to pooled investment vehicles which are referred to as funds. Registered investment companies (sometimes referred to as "RICs"[1]) are funds that must be registered under the Investment Company Act of 1940 (the "Company Act"). Among funds found in the registered space, mutual funds and exchange-traded funds deservedly garner the most attention because of the amount of assets managed by such vehicles, which is roughly $22 trillion as of end of year 2017 (according to the Investment Company Institute), mutual funds represented 85% of that amount and ETFs about 15%. In addition to these categories of registered funds, closed-end funds and unit investment trusts ("UITs") represent two other well-known types of RICs. The focus in this chapter is largely on the basic functional business characteristics of these types of RICs and not with their technical legal classification under the Company Act. In addition, there are unregistered funds which share a fundamental characteristic of RICs, namely they are pooled investment vehicles. However, they differ from RICs in that they are not sold in public offerings pursuant to the registration requirements of the Securities Act. As a result, they are not subject to registration as investment companies under the Company Act.

---

1. The acronym RIC is also sometimes rendered as a regulated investment company, a term that is used in Subchapter M of the Internal Revenue Code, to identify funds that are entitled to favorable tax treatment. In practice, registered investment companies under the Investment Company Act are the major sub-category of regulated investment companies under the Internal Revenue Code and, thus, the term RIC is sometimes used in a non-tax sense to refer to registered investment companies rather than the slightly broader tax category of regulated investment company. In this textbook, registered investment company under the Company Act and RIC will be used interchangeably.

From a functional perspective, funds have two defining features: first, funds pool the assets of multiple investors in contrast to a separately managed account; and second, they collect the assets of many investors through offerings of securities (shares or units of ownership in a fund). If a fund's shares are offered to the public, the fund must be a RIC. On the other hand, a fund might offer shares in a private or exempt offering, in which case it could operate as an unregistered fund if other conditions are met.

As reflected in the figure below, this basic structure is replicated in the several investment products, and several different variations are discussed in this chapter.

Figure 2B — Basic Investment Company Diagram (subject to many variations)

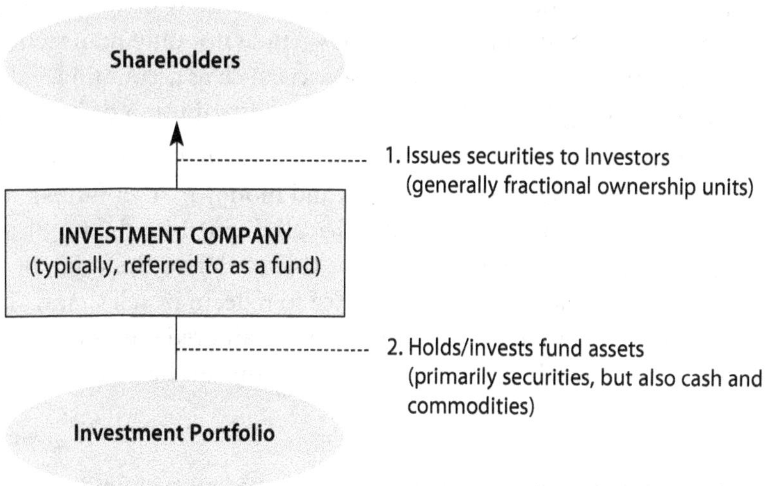

One basic feature of an investment company arrangement is the presence of securities at two different levels of the arrangement. The fund from the perspective of shareholders is represented by an investment company, and the investment company is an issuer of securities. Shareholders of a fund are the fund's investors and the beneficial owners of the fund's capital. A fund's capital in turn will be invested in the securities of other issuers. These securities constitute the fund's portfolio of securities. These two different levels of securities activities give rise to two different issues. On the one hand, the fund must deal with its own shareholders as an issuer of securities which involves at the very least matters of disclosure, e.g., the fund must disclose its investment objectives and policies. With respect to the portfolio of securities held by the fund (that is, its investment of client assets), the fund is responsible for managing the portfolio in a way that comports with fiduciary standards of conduct and ensures financial integrity. Obviously, the relative success of the fund in managing its securities portfolio will determine the return to the fund's shareholders.

2.4.1 Mutual Funds

Without doubt, mutual funds are the largest category of RIC in terms of assets under management ("AUM"), accounting in the U.S. for roughly $18.5 trillion dollars in AUM. As will be clear from the figures that accompany this chapter, mutual funds exhibit the basic structure of any investment company arrangement: a business entity that holds itself out as engaging in the business of investing, holding, or trading securities and that derives its capital (assets) from investors. Mutual funds are notable in one particular respect: they issue redeemable securities. Specifically, mutual fund investors have the right to redeem their shares daily from the fund at the per share net asset value (less possible sales charges) (the "NAV"). In addition, most mutual funds typically have no employees, and if they do, they have very few. Instead most funds rely on external service providers essentially to outsource all their operational functions. In other words, today most funds are "externally managed," although there are some important exceptions in which funds are "internally managed." In an externally-managed fund, the outsourced functions include not only management of the fund's portfolio, but the fund's administrative services such as accounting and valuation of its assets, recordkeeping for its shareholders, and distribution of its shares.

Three key features follow from this basic structure. First, shares are bought and sold (leaving aside any applicable sales charges and money market funds) at net asset value, i.e., a fund's assets minus fund liabilities all divided by the number of fund shares outstanding. Second, the fund must be able to derive the value of its shares (i.e., NAV) daily or it will not know at what price to redeem or sell shares. Therefore, and third, as a practical matter, fund share purchases and redemptions are processed only at the end of the day when a definitive calculation can be made.

Figure 2C — Structure of stand-alone externally managed mutual fund

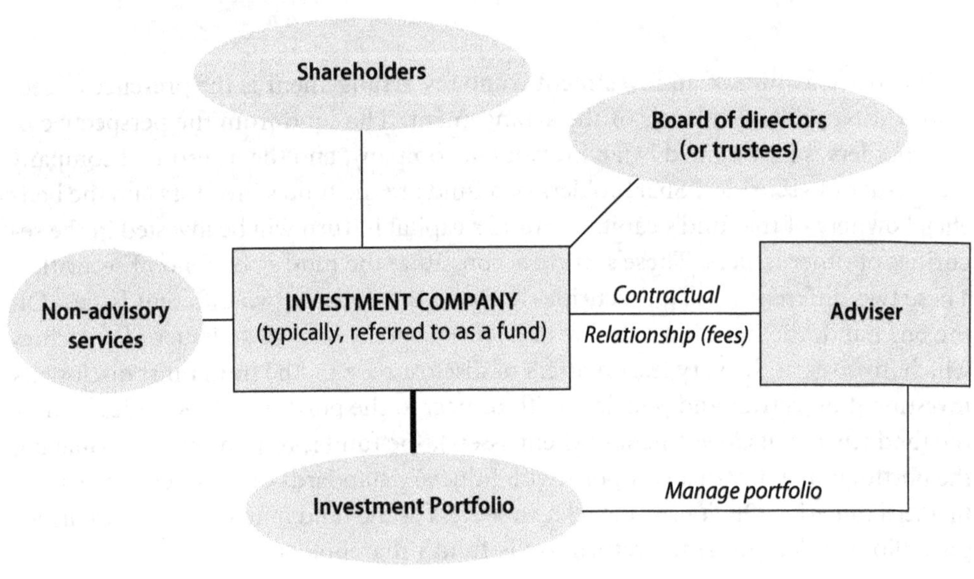

2.4.2 Closed-End Funds

Closed-end funds differ from their mutual fund cousins in a fundamental respect. Closed-end funds do not issue redeemable shares. In other words, shareholders do not have a right to present their shares to the fund at the end of the day and receive the corresponding NAV of those shares. Typically, most closed-end funds have but one public sale of their shares. That is, they do not offer their shares to investors continuously the way that most mutual funds do. In order to permit investors to buy and sell shares after the initial offering, closed-end fund shares trade in secondary markets, e.g., over the counter or listed on exchanges. As a result, the market price of the shares may vary from the shares' NAV. In other words, although closed-end fund shares, just like their mutual fund cousins, will have a determinable net asset value per share, the price of those shares on the secondary market may trade at a discount or premium to their net asset value since the fund itself is not obligated to repurchase (i.e., redeem) the shares at net asset value. Typically, though not invariably, shares trade at a discount to NAV, reflecting some impairment to the value of the shares such as the potential lack of liquidity.

Historically, in the early days of the U.S. fund industry, closed-end funds were the original and dominant form of RIC. After the 1929 stock market crash and the subsequent Great Depression, closed-end funds lost appeal for investors. After enactment of the Company Act and over time, mutual funds became the dominant form of fund, with closed-end funds being only a small fraction of fund industry AUM (less than $300 billion of the $22+ trillion in registered funds). The primary reason for the relative decline in the fortunes of closed-end funds appears to be the fact that mutual funds offer the ability to redeem shares at their NAV versus the uncertainty associated with fluctuating discounts to NAV in the pricing of closed-end fund shares.

Figure 2D — Closed-end investment company

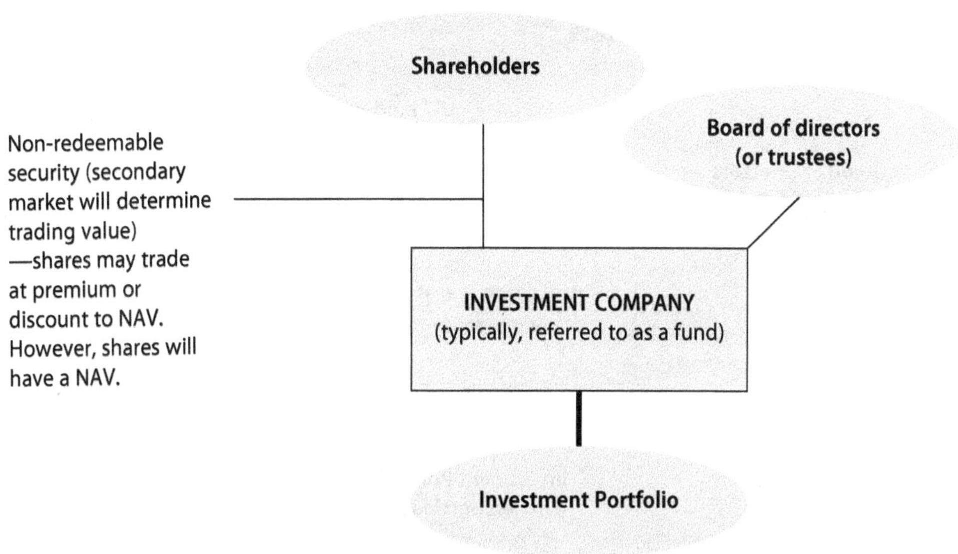

2.4.3 Unit Investment Trusts

Both mutual funds and closed-end funds are managed in the sense that the composition of their portfolio of assets can change daily as a result of the portfolio management activities of the investment managers. A unit investment trust ("UIT") represents a different approach to the constitution of the registered investment company form. Traditional unit investment trusts have unmanaged investment portfolios and no investment advisers. UITs are created by sponsors (often investment management firms) who select a portfolio of securities which generally will not change over the life of the trust. UITs typically have pre-determined termination dates at which time their portfolios are liquidated and the proceeds are distributed to the unit holders. In most cases, the fixed composition of the trust portfolio is specified prior to soliciting investors. For example, a UIT may be formed to administer a portfolio consisting of a million shares each of Alphabet, Facebook, IBM, Merck, and GE. The fixed portfolio dispenses in large measure with the investment management and governance functions associated with mutual funds and closed-end funds. UITs appeal to investors who want to know exactly in which securities a fund invests; for their relatively low costs (no management fees and few portfolio trading costs); and for their predictable distributions since limited portfolio trading means there's usually no capital gains to be distributed.

During the life of the UIT, its units or shares will be redeemable like a mutual fund at NAV. However, investors in some circumstances may also sell their units back to the sponsor, which may resell them. Alternatively, investors may hold the units until the trust is liquidated. On rare occasions, a secondary market may develop for units, allowing them to be traded. This generally happens only with respect to very popular and hard to create portfolios or hard to purchase underlying securities. As a result, there is a reason for shares to trade in the secondary market rather than be redeemed at NAV.

Figure 2E — Unit investment trust

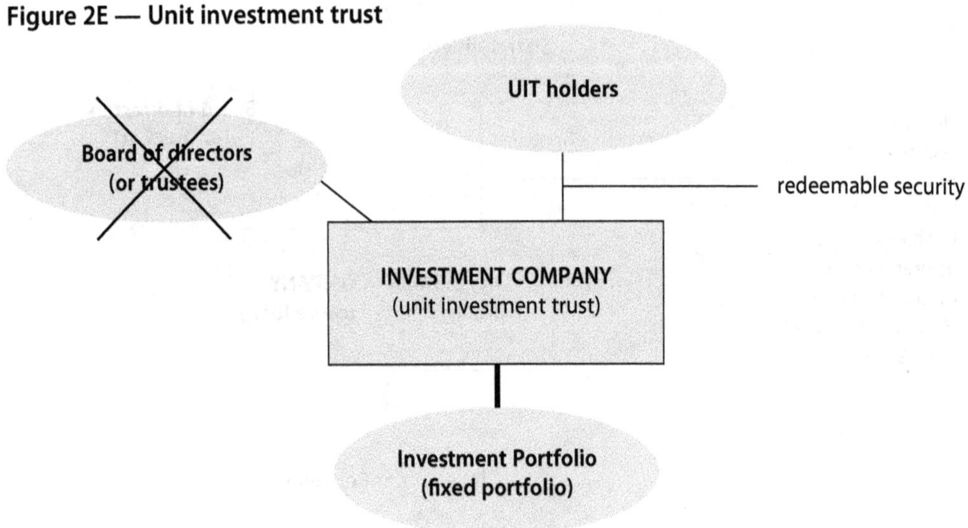

UITs are a relatively small segment of the investment management market (less than $100 billion of the $22+ trillion in registered funds) and will not figure prominently in this text. Nevertheless, the UIT structure was one of the fundamental forms of RICs defined in the Company Act when enacted and should be understood definitionally and conceptually.

2.4.4 Exchange-Traded Funds

Exchange-traded funds ("ETFs") are a hybrid form of registered investment company. Unlike mutual funds, closed-end funds, and UITs, ETFs are not explicitly recognized in the Company Act as a form of investment company. Rather, they came into being only fairly recently and are permitted by means of regulatory relief granted by the SEC. ETFs combine features characteristic of other RICs. The ETF is similar to a mutual fund in that it issues redeemable securities in the form of *creation units*, and the mutual fund template is the most common means of organizing an ETF. However, ETFs are fundamentally different from mutual funds, because they employ a mechanism that allows for trading of shares of the ETF (or more precisely, shares derived from the creation units) on stock exchanges continuously at prices that closely approximate NAV. This aspect of ETF shares makes them similar to closed-end fund shares, although the ETF shares will not trade at significant discounts or premiums to NAV.

Chapter 18 delves more deeply into the unique multi-tiered unit/share structure of ETFs. Basically, while the ETF format has variants, the defining feature is the same among exchange-traded products. Redeemable creation units are sold to a very limited number of large market participants known as "authorized participants." The auth-

Figure 2F — Exchange Traded Fund Structure

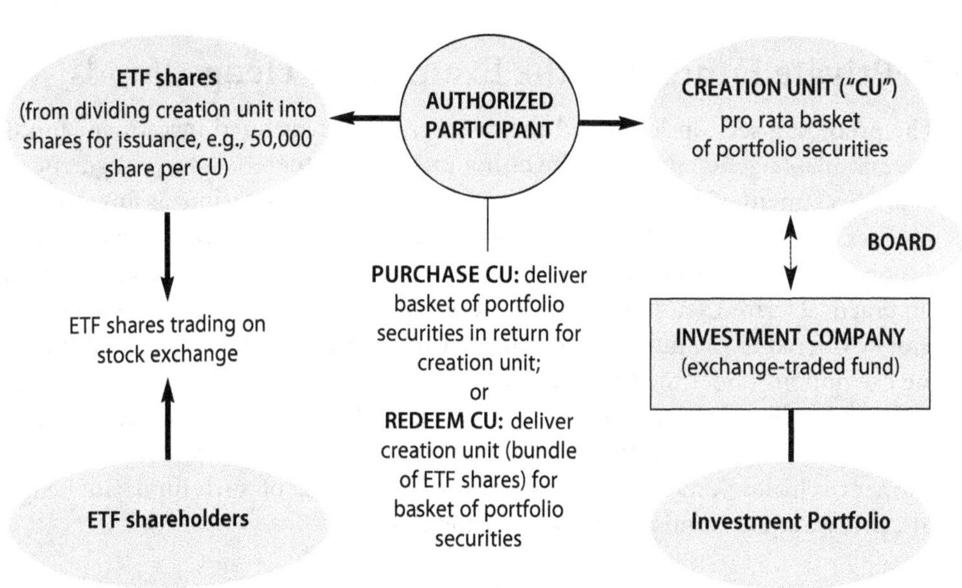

orized participants in turn can subdivide each creation unit into a fixed number of shares, e.g., 50,000 or 100,000 shares. These shares are listed for trading on the stock exchange and are available to investors.

This two-tiered structure yields a unique combination of features: near-NAV pricing and intraday trading. The fact that creation units can be purchased at NAV *and* redeemed at NAV (by gathering up shares in the marketplace to reconstitute the 50,000 or 100,000 block of shares and then tendering them for redemption), creates a fairly direct arbitrage mechanism which in turn ensures shares trading on a stock exchange routinely trade fairly close to their NAV. Because the shares can be bought and sold during the day, investors have ready access to intraday—rather than end-of-day—liquidity.

ETFs have become enormously popular with retail and institutional investors and, as of the end of 2017, represent roughly $3.5 trillion dollars in AUM, marking an incredible growth of assets since being introduced almost three decades ago. They have become the second largest form of RIC in the U.S. During this period, assets under management for EFTs have been growing much faster relatively than assets of mutual funds, and, moreover, in absolute terms, assets in ETFs have grown faster than mutual funds over the past several years.

Up to this point, ETFs have been largely used to implement passive or index investment strategies (i.e., where the composition of the fund portfolio is determined by a pre-announced rule or formula). There is much industry activity intended to try to expand investor interest in so-called "actively managed ETFs" (i.e., where the portfolio manager has the discretion to construct a customized portfolio within the parameters of broad investment objectives and strategies). However, investors have been slow to adopt the limited offerings of such ETFs so far. Moreover, the process for product development in this space has been slowed by numerous regulatory obstacles.

2.5 Private Funds and the Example of Hedge Funds

The preceding section identified the main types of registered investment funds that are available generally to the investing public. But there is a large segment of pooled investment vehicles that are not subject to registration as investment companies. As discussed in Chapters 9 and 10, such funds are structured to fit within exclusions from the legal definition of investment companies. Therefore, such entities are in practical terms exempt from registration as investment companies. Such funds cannot be offered to the public, but rather must be privately offered pursuant to offering exemptions under the Securities Act. In practice, this means that participation in such funds will only be available to certain types of investors, e.g., institutional or wealthy accredited investors. Private funds represent a major category of unregistered investment vehicle. Some of the most common examples of such funds are hedge funds, private equity funds, and venture capital funds.

For now, it is useful to look at just one type of private fund: hedge funds. Several features distinguish hedge funds from registered investment companies. First, hedge funds have fewer regulatory restrictions on their capital structure and as a result have much more latitude in using leverage (borrowing) as an integral component of their investment strategy. Second, hedge funds may use performance fees (which are prohibited in the case of RICs) to provide more generous compensation for their managers. Third, hedge funds are far more likely to use hedging (hence the origin of the label) in their investment strategy than RICs, meaning that such funds are more likely to use long positions (owning securities) and short positions (selling securities that they do not own) together as part of their investment strategy. (Of course, today, derivatives can be used for the same purpose as easily as long-short hedging strategies.) As a result, unlike mutual funds that are typically described as having investment strategies that emphasize relative performance, hedge funds typically have investment strategies that seek "absolute returns," i.e., positive returns regardless of markets or benchmarks moving up or down. Fourth, because of these various attributes, hedge funds are typically structured differently as entities than most RICs—as limited partnerships or limited liability companies—structures that offer more flexible tax treatment. Finally, the ownership units sold to investors invariably have contractually established limitations on redemption of such units to prevent disruption to the complex investment strategies that hedge funds may pursue.

Figure 2G — Hedge Fund Structure

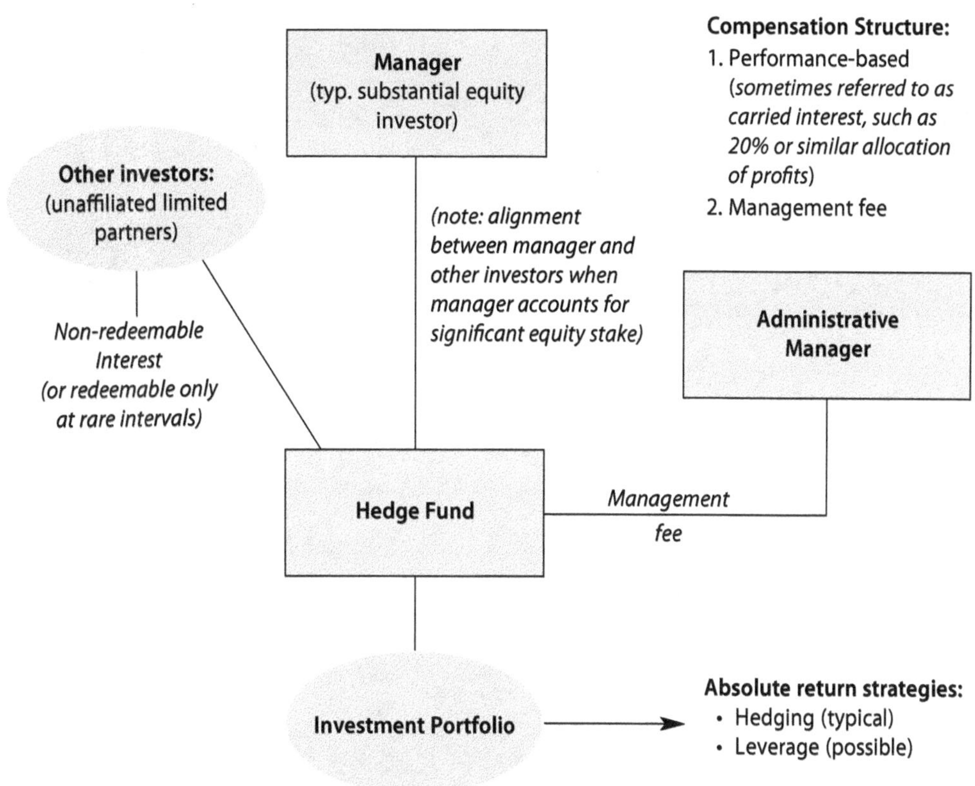

Hedge funds have proven to be extremely popular over the last few decades as investors seek funds which promise to provide positive returns despite volatile markets. However, as with other types of investments, there is often a disconnect between objectives and results. In other words, hedge funds have found it very difficult consistently to provide the positive absolute returns that investors have sought, and typically, hedge funds with poor records can face severe contraction as their demanding investors will withdraw their money once a redemption window opens.

Chapter 3

Fund Formation and a Fund's Core Functions

Key Ideas: Funds may be formed as separate business entities or as independent series within a larger entity composed of multiple fund series. In the latter case, each series is managed solely for the benefit of shareholders of that series/fund. Shareholders are the owners of funds, holding shares or units which represent their ownership interest in a fund. Funds are formed by sponsors and the sponsor typically will work closely with the board of an existing investment company or a newly established investment company vehicle. Although other significant functions of, and service providers to, funds are discussed in Chapter 4, three core functions are addressed in this chapter: governance, investment management, and distribution. With respect to governance, the affairs of most funds (mutual funds, ETFs, and closed-end funds) are overseen by boards of trustees or directors. Fund boards almost invariably have a majority, and often a supermajority of, independent trustees.

As to the investment management functions, funds are typically externally managed, meaning that their investment adviser's relationship with the fund is contractual and approved by the fund's board and its shareholders. The investment adviser is responsible for managing the fund's portfolio, and the adviser's portfolio managers and staff have primary authority in managing the fund's operations and day-to-day affairs, supplemented by other service providers.

Distribution constitutes the third core function. Funds gather assets for the fund by selling shares to investors. In the case of mutual funds, the funds' shares are redeemable, and therefore the size of the fund is subject to contractionary pressures which can be offset by new sales (i.e., the distribution function). Fund distributors oversee the underwriting, marketing, and sales of fund shares and are frequently affiliates of the investment adviser or a third party that specializes in fund distribution. In order to sell shares, the fund distributor may use a variety of distribution channels. The most important distribution channels are: brokerage firms (broker-sold funds); funds sold through affiliated brokers (direct-sold funds) or through self-directed brokerage platforms (so-called "fund supermarkets"); funds sold by banks or registered investment advisers; and funds sold through retirement plans, such as 401(k) plans.

Chapter Contents

3.1 Introduction

Creating and managing funds is a complex process, integrating multiple functions and operations, not unlike producing a movie. Many consumers go to movies and, of course, they recognize their favorite actors. But beyond what the moviegoer actually sees on screen, there is an elaborate production crew necessary in the making of the movie (set designers, make-up artists, special effects people, a director—and usually many assistant directors—a cinematographer, editors, producers, administrative personnel), and a whole distribution network that gets the film on-screen for the moviegoer to see. Similarly, funds have significant production casts to make their investment products available and this chapter, as well as the following chapter, provide an overview of what is entailed.

At the outset, issues of fund formation must be addressed. These issues precede any discussion of functioning of the fund. In short, funds are formed typically either as stand-alone business entities or as a separate component (or series) of a business entity composed of multiple funds, each of which is a series. Note that the terms "fund" and "series" are often used interchangeably. A sponsor is invariably involved in initiating the process and is typically the fund's investment adviser or an affiliate of the adviser. In the case of a new stand-alone fund or series of funds, the sponsor must attend to a number of organizational and housekeeping details. To launch sub-

Figure 3A — Core investment company services: governance, management, and distribution (typically from third party)

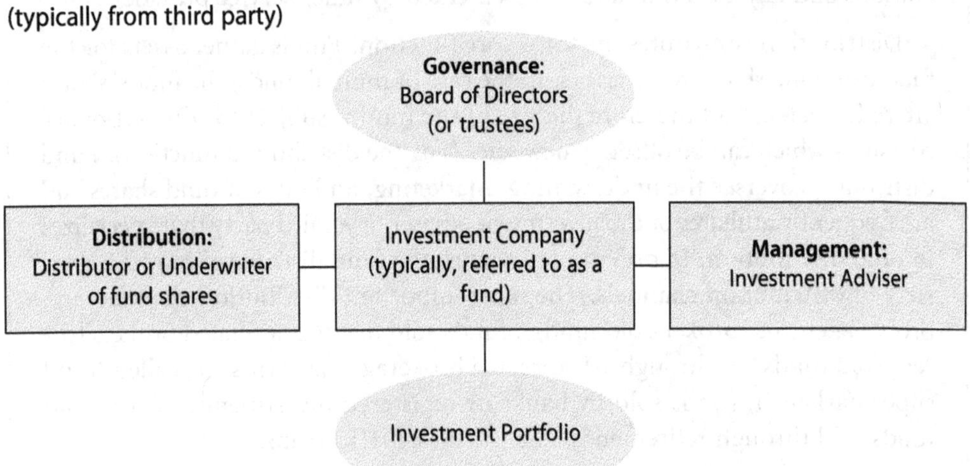

sequent funds in an existing fund series, or a part of a family of funds, the adviser will play a critical role as sponsor but will also work closely with the existing board of the entity in which the fund will be created, with the existing board reviewing and approving all key agreements, investment policies, and operations of the new fund.

The balance of this chapter focuses on the basics of three key functions in funds: governance by a board of directors or trustees; management of the fund's investment portfolio; and distribution. The next chapter focuses on how funds arrange other core operations, which vary depending upon the fund structure and whether key services are performed by affiliates of the adviser or outsourced to third-party service providers. This basic scheme is illustrated in Figure 3A.

3.2 Fund Formation

Who creates funds and why? While the person creating a fund is designated the "sponsor," this by itself would be circular. It is the why that gives substance to the designation. Sponsors, as the Company Act refers to them, do so, presumably, because creating a fund will eventually allow the sponsor, or a sponsoring affiliate, to directly or indirectly reap economic benefits. Not surprisingly, sponsors are generally investment advisers or affiliates of advisers or distributors of funds. Why? Because they will earn fees, i.e., make money, if the fund proves successful. In some cases, the rationale is slightly more nuanced. The fund may appeal to investors with diverse needs and therefore the sponsor may create a fund to better serve existing clients. For example, some insurance clients who are interested in annuities may want the option to purchase variable annuities, or some investors may seek a greater variety of fund options within a single family of funds. In these cases, the expanded range of fund products becomes a way to attract or retain additional assets from investors.

Invariably, there is some type of investment or product thesis behind any fund's creation: (i) the sponsor may have developed a new type of investment strategy for a fund; (ii) the sponsor may believe that it can do a better job executing an investment strategy already existing in the marketplace; (iii) the sponsor may wish to duplicate a fund investment strategy that already exists in the marketplace that is seemingly successful in attracting investor assets; or (iv) the sponsor may seek to offer a fuller stable of funds to appeal to its existing investors in a family of funds.

Fund sponsors are responsible for a broad range of tasks in creating a fund from conceptualization of the fund's purpose to registering the fund with the SEC. For wholly new funds, the process is a bit more complicated, while this is less so in the case for funds being organized within an existing fund organization. Once an idea for a fund has been conceptualized, i.e., its investment thesis and portfolio strategy are designed, the sponsor needs to organize an entity, under state law, for operating the fund. The sponsor will also likely recruit an initial slate of independent directors, ones who are not affiliated with the sponsor, adviser or distributor, to serve as the board of directors. Finally, a new fund requires seed capital of $100,000 under the Company Act. Typically, the sponsor/adviser provides the "seed" capital as an initial investment in the fund's shares.

Simultaneously, the sponsor, if not itself an investment adviser, will work with the adviser to provide the hands-on management of the fund. Typically, investment adviser personnel will be used to provide the fund with officers to oversee the day-to-day operations of the fund, and the sponsor or the investment adviser will provide for the board one or more individuals to serve as "interested" directors or trustees, i.e., those who work for or are significantly connected with the sponsor or adviser. The sponsor or investment adviser will also arrange for other services providers required for the fund's operation. Finally, the sponsor/adviser must register the fund with the SEC as a RIC under the Company Act and register the fund's shares for sale to the public under the Securities Act of 1933. The latter requirement is a topic discussed in subsequent chapters. All of these organizational steps will be ratified by the board at an initial organizational meeting upon the board's election by the sponsor/adviser who will invariably be the sole initial shareholder.

Once a fund family or a group of affiliated funds exists, sponsorship of additional funds results in a simplified process for creating additional funds. Typically, there is no need to form an entirely new legal entity, establish a new board, or recruit new service providers. However, registration is still necessary, and the sponsor/adviser will need to work with and obtain approval from the board for the existing funds.

The preceding exposition describes the basic organizational steps, but it is necessary to look more closely at the type of entity that is likely to be used to house the fund. Recall the basic RIC structure diagram in Chapter 2 (i.e., Figure 2B—Basic Investment Company Structure). In a basic stand-alone fund structure, the fund and the investment company business entity will be one and the same. The business entity (i.e., the investment company) will issue shares or units to investors (i.e., the shareholders) and, in turn, the fund agrees to manage the pool of assets obtained from shareholders in accordance with the fund's investment objectives and strategies.

Typically, an investment company or fund is organized as a corporation or business trust. Limited liability companies and limited partnerships are rarely used, because they do not provide any special tax benefits and introduce some governance issues that must be reconciled with the Company Act. Business trusts have long occupied a leading role as a go-to model structure for mutual funds and ETFs. In part, this may be a historical accident, since the first U.S. mutual funds were organized in Mas-

Consider: if you were to buy shares in a mutual fund called the Pegasus Fund, what are you getting?

Since it's a mutual fund, you'd get a proportionate interest or "share" in the net assets (investments) of the Fund. For example, if you invested $1000 and the Fund had $1,000,000 in net assets, your proportionate ownership interest would be 1/10th of 1% of the Fund. However, shares are typically expressed in dollar terms based on the value of the Fund's assets divided by the number of shares that have been issued. In this example, if each share was worth $10, you'd receive 100 shares ($10 x 100).

sachusetts in the 1920s as Massachusetts business trusts. However, their popularity grew because business trusts allowed a great deal of flexibility in governance compared to many corporate law statutes. According to Investment Company Institute statistics, the most popular forms of organization at the end of 2017 were: 40% Delaware statutory (business) trusts, 35% Massachusetts business trusts, 16% Maryland corporations and 9% other corporations and entities.

As noted in Chapter 2, the units of ownership given to investors purchasing interests in a fund are generally called *shares*. More accurately, they represent shares of stock for corporate entities or shares or units of beneficial interest for trusts.

It's relatively rare to see a stand-alone fund. Generally, funds come in clusters or families. A "fund family" is a group of funds advised and/or sponsored by the same adviser. Fund families or complexes dominate the fund industry. Some of the most notable names in U.S. financial services are fund complexes, e.g., Fidelity, Vanguard, Blackrock, American Funds, and PIMCO. Most families are organized by an investment adviser as sponsor. In some cases, a brokerage firm, such as Charles Schwab, sponsors a fund family and establishes an investment adviser to manage the funds.

These "fund families" can be made up of several separate business entities (trusts or corporations), but it is also possible to use a single business entity (e.g., one trust or corporate entity) which may be subdivided into segregated units or series where each unit or series is a different fund. These are known as "series" funds and are extremely common for reasons of simple economy. The separate series within the business trust or corporation are reflected in different series of shares that give the shareholder economic ownership rights only to the segregated assets and performance of that particular series.

Diagrammatically, a series fund with two series would look something like this and, of course, there is no limit on the number of series that may be added to the investment company vehicle:

Figure 3B — Basic Investment Company for Two Fund Series

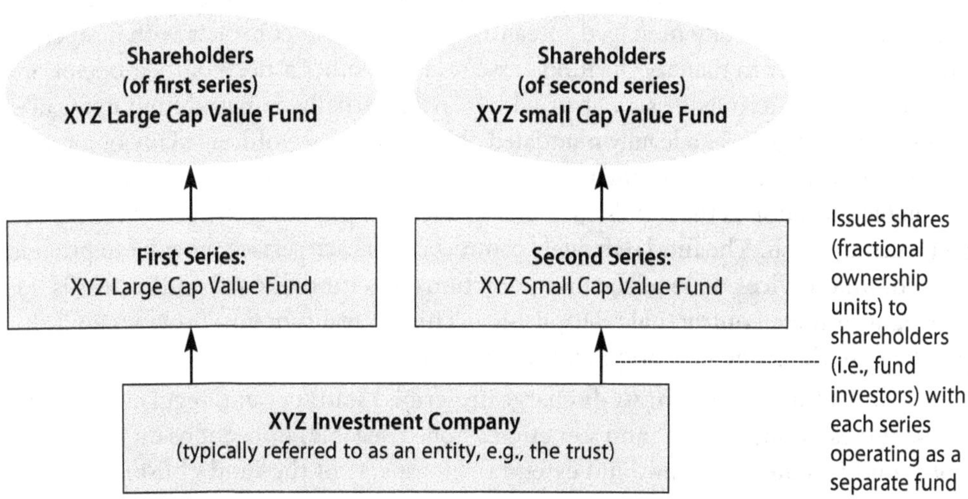

The diagram on the previous page illustrates a simple two fund family or complex. In practice, large complexes such as Fidelity or American Funds have multiple corporations and trusts with dozens of funds. In the case of the American Funds, they've used all of the top three entity types: Delaware statutory trust, Massachusetts business trust, and Maryland corporation, reflective of what was perceived to be the best form of entity at the time of its organization, i.e., best in terms of tax and corporate law. Each of the investment company trusts or corporations may have several funds/series.

3.3 Fund Governance

Regardless of the entity's structure, the Company Act requires almost all registered investment companies to have boards of trustees or directors to oversee governance and operation of the fund. Only UITs are exempt from this requirement given their unique structure, as noted in Chapter 2. Boards may be composed of directors (in the case of corporate entities) or trustees (in the case of business trusts). In practice, the terms "director" and "trustee" are interchangeable and are used in this fashion throughout this text.

Trustees act in the interests of the shareholders and, technically, are elected by them, although initially this may mean only that the sponsor voted for each nominee. Unlike most corporations, most investment companies do not have an annual election of directors and, as a result, there is significant continuity to investment company boards. Shareholders do get a chance to vote on trustees when there is significant turnover of trustees as a result of out of the ordinary events such as resignations, retirement, or death. As fiduciaries, board members owe the duties of due care and loyalty to the fund. The board also formally appoints officers to manage and oversee the day-to-day operations of the funds. The officers are typically from the adviser, distributor, or fund administrator.

While the role of trustees essentially parallels the role of ordinary corporate directors, the context for the fund board is fundamentally different than the ordinary corporation in two respects. First, unlike a conventional corporation, funds typically have few or no employees. Generally, funds such as mutual funds, closed-end funds, and ETFs, are externally managed, meaning that the fund contracts with a separate investment adviser to manage the fund's assets, and all other aspects of their operations will be delegated to outside service providers. An externally managed fund may have, at most, one employee, a legally mandated chief compliance officer. Many of a fund's service providers are often affiliated with each other and with the sponsor/adviser. A notable exception is the fund's custodian, which has physical control over the fund's securities and cash. The fund separately contracts with each service provider to provide the required services. One of the main functions of a fund's board of directors is the oversight of these contractual relationships. This critical function provides an independent check on the operation and management of a fund.

Second, a fund's board must discharge prescribed statutory and regulatory duties. These duties impose added (and sometimes non-delegable) obligations on the board, not found in state entity law, and extend to all aspects of the fund's business. These statutory and regulatory mandates frequently impose special obligations on so-called "independent" trustees as an added check on the fund's affairs. Independent trustees are essentially individuals who have no financial, ownership, or other pecuniary interest in the fund's adviser, distributor, or affiliates of them.The strong regulatory mandate for independence on fund boards stems from the obvious potential for conflicts between the economic interest of funds in minimizing costs and the interests of a fund's adviser and distributor in generating fees and other economic benefits. The distinction between independent trustees and so-called "interested" trustees is spelled out in statutes and regulations, but for now, it is sufficient to note the distinction.

As noted, boards are fiduciaries charged with acting in the best interests of shareholders. The statutory and regulatory mandates effectively give the independent trustees the power to control approval of key contracts and fees paid by a fund. Contracts such as those with a fund's adviser and distributor must be approved by a majority of the independent trustees in addition to receiving approval of the full board. Most boards meet at least quarterly (and for large or complex funds, some boards meet monthly) to review various fund operations, in addition to reviewing and renewing contracts annually. The board routinely reviews the performance of the adviser in managing the fund portfolio, the fund's compliance program, and its operations.

3.4 The Investment Adviser

The second core aspect of any fund is the investment management function. Most funds are managed portfolios, meaning that someone must implement the fund's stated investment objectives and strategies. In this respect, advisers, especially advisers of actively managed portfolios, are the movie stars of money management operations. When people think of hedge funds or mutual funds, they often think of the name personalities or companies actually managing the assets. As noted, the vast majority of mutual funds, ETFs and closed-end funds have third party managers, i.e., they are "externally managed." External management means that the fund's relationship with the investment adviser or manager is contractual in nature, that is, a relationship that results from a bargaining process between the fund and the adviser. Because the adviser's services are contracted for, the board can seek to influence aspects of its relationship with the company but it does not directly control the hiring and firing of the adviser's personnel. Another implication of this contractual relationship is that externally managed funds are, as a practical matter, fully dependent on the adviser and other third-party contractual service providers for fund operations. Fund advisers are profit-seeking companies and, while they indirectly benefit from fund performance, their profits are derived from charging the fund a management fee. In this sense, the advisers' interests will not directly align with the funds' interests in all matters. This external management model was previously illustrated in Figure 2C—Structure of Stand-Alone Externally Managed Mutual Fund.

Although most funds are externally managed, there are a small number of funds that are internally managed, i.e., operations are sponsored and managed by officers and employees of the fund or a management/administrative company owned by the fund. The prime example of this is certain funds of the Vanguard Funds family, which has one of the largest fund operations in the U.S. The management structure in many ways resembles that of mutual insurance companies and credit unions, where the insureds and depositors, respectively, are the owners of the operation. Similarly, with internally managed funds, the shareholders effectively own the operations. Functionally, with this type of fund or family of funds, there is no profit seeking sponsor or adviser directing or managing the funds. As a result, employees, operations, costs, and expenses are shared amongst the funds in the complex.

At the heart of an externally managed fund operation is the fund's investment adviser. As noted in Chapter 2, the basis for the relationship is an investment advisory agreement. The advisory agreement defines the duties and responsibilities of the adviser as well as the fees to be paid to the adviser. Such agreements generally are subject to annual review by the fund's directors, who have to meet in person to consider the approval or renewal of the agreement. Initially, agreements must be submitted to the fund's shareholders for approval and, in forming a fund, typically the sponsor will be the sole shareholder as noted earlier.

The management or advisory fee is the fee paid to the investment adviser for its services under the advisory agreement. Since advisory fees are typically the largest expense for a fund and relate to the fund's overriding purpose, the advisory relationship merits close scrutiny by the fund's directors. The board's review generally entails a review of fund performance, overall management, and fee appropriateness. Over the years, extensive litigation has provided clarity as to the factors considered and processes used by boards in determining appropriate fee levels. This will be discussed in detail later in the text.

As noted, for publicly traded funds, advisory fees are usually calculated as a percentage of AUM. Index funds (and generally ETFs) tend to have much lower management fees because they are passive strategies and are heavily driven by quantitative metrics. Annual management fees can be as low as .03% (3 basis points) up to .3% (30 basis points) for relatively straightforward index strategies. Actively managed mutual funds have uniformly higher fees. Annual management fees may range from .5% (or 50 basis points) of a fund's AUM to as high as 2.00% (or 200 basis points).

Performance is the goal and the measuring stick for any type of fund and its investment adviser. Whether investing in stocks, bonds, or any other types of securities, a fund portfolio manager is involved in a constant cycle of research, analysis, decision-making, trading, and reporting the results of his or her activities, i.e., "portfolio management."

Typically, the portfolio manager or PM is thought of as the person who does it all. But that's only true of small investment advisers. Generally, the portfolio manager is the point person for a team of people performing the management function. In the case of passively managed or index funds, the focus of portfolio management tends to be heavily quantitative, and the chief skill of the manager is efficiently tracking the benchmark index. While passive managers engage in many of the same activities as active managers, active management typically entails a more robust process that includes:

- **Research**—for any type of prospective investments, examining their merits. This is most easily understood regarding investments in stocks of companies. In that case, the research function will entail reading about, reviewing prospectuses, financial statements, making site visits, and interviewing company management and industry specialists regarding the prospects for the company.
- **Analysis**—Often research and analysis are performed together, but in large management companies, you have separate individuals or teams collecting the research data which is then reviewed and analyzed by analysts. What do they analyze? They may be performing simple analyses of dividend growth, i.e., is the company's dividend growing consistently? Or they may be performing complex calculations based on various company and industry financial/performance data.

  The expressions, "bottoms up" and "top down" are frequently used in describing the manager's investment analysis style. "Bottoms up" relates to doing careful and detailed research and analysis of company fundamentals and using that analysis to make investment decisions. "Top down" refers to the style of analysis which focuses on macro-economic issues first, e.g., using that analysis to select industries in which to invest. Then additional analysis may be performed to select companies within the macro-selected industries.
- **Decision-making**—The goal of research and analysis is to help the portfolio managers make decisions regarding which investments to buy or sell. Some investment advisers allow individual PMs to make investment decisions. In other organizations, decision-making is a committee process. In any event, the number of "names" or positions in a fund portfolio provides an approximation of the complexity of the decision-making process.
- **Trading**—Once an investment decision is made, the next step is executing that decision. Again, for small advisers and funds, the PM him or herself will proceed to work with a broker to buy or sell the investments. In larger organizations, there are specialized employees who execute trades. They have familiarity with the various brokers and markets where the investments are traded and can make decisions that seek to get the best prices and execution of their trade orders. Often this operation is called the "trade desk," and the people working there are called the "traders." Increasingly, traders have access to electronic algorithms and different electronic trading venues to optimize trade executions.
- **Reporting of performance**—The portfolio management process doesn't stop with trade execution. Each trade may generate a gain or loss for the fund. As trading activity occurs, another form of analysis takes place, the reporting process. Basically, it amounts to compiling the performance of the trading activity of the fund and reporting the results for shareholder and regulatory purposes. There are also deeper forms of analysis relating to the effectiveness and efficiencies of the trades; the effectiveness of the research and analysis techniques; tax strategies; and other aspects of managing the fund. For registered funds like mutual

funds, the PM reports quarterly results to the fund's board of directors, who also need to review and consider performance annually as part of the annual review process. In addition, results need to be explained to fund shareholders, typically in the form of a shareholder report at least semi-annually. Finally, performance information needs to be included in funds disclosure documents, such as the prospectus.

3.5 Fund Sales and Distribution

Whether it's a hedge fund, ETF, or mutual fund, the lifeblood of the adviser's fees is the growth in fund assets. Since markets rise and fall (and the value of a fund's assets along with such changes), the surest way to garner more fees is to sell more shares of the fund. This follows from the basic formula: greater assets under management (AUM) generate more advisory fees. Like the character Ray (Kevin Costner) in *Field of Dreams* (incidentally based on the W.P. Kinsella novel, *Shoeless Joe*, for those with a more literary bent), many advisers enter the industry hoping that if they build it (their fund), investors will come! Unlike the Field of Dreams mantra of "if you build it, they will come," mutual funds do not effortlessly garner investor interest. The reality is that like any other product, funds have to be sold to investors. Indeed, this reality is memorialized in the oft-repeated bromide: "funds are sold, not bought."

Because mutual funds offer redeemable shares and are thereby subject to the risk of contraction, they typically engage in on-going (or continuous) sales operations. Closed-end funds do not redeem shares the way that mutual funds do. As a result, closed-end funds usually sell their shares in more traditional underwritings, meaning that they have discrete offerings of shares and do not continue to sell shares after the offering is completed. ETFs generally are a variant of the mutual funds' continuous offering process. Finally, hedge funds have a completely different process, usually selling partnership or LLC interests through private placements and offering only limited redemption opportunities.

Distribution of mutual funds is illustrative of the broad array of practices that have evolved to facilitate the distributional objectives of funds. Indeed, mutual fund distribution dwarfs distribution of all other registered investment company products. The legal and business model is compellingly simple: The fund advertises publicly to generate interest in the fund. Interested investors can request a prospectus to read and understand how the fund operates and has performed historically. If an investor is persuaded to invest, she can fill out an application and submit money to invest or seek the assistance of market professionals to facilitate this process.

Not surprisingly, sales processes typically involve several layers of marketing and sales efforts and vary, legally, with the type of fund interest being sold. Perhaps these different layers are easier to conceptualize as a somewhat simplified dichotomy between marketing (i.e., informational issues involving disclosure and sales literature) and the mechanics of distribution (i.e., the persons and process for actually selling fund shares and the charges and fees used to compensate the market participants in the distribution process).

Four factors are the key drivers of fund sales from a marketing perspective: asset class/investment objective, fund performance, and advertising. In addition, increasingly, investors appear to be becoming more cognizant of and sensitive to fund expenses. Some of the legal issues relating to marketing are addressed in Chapter 13 relating to securities disclosure. In brief, some relevant concepts are as follows:

Asset class/investment objective. Investors typically understand that different asset classes have different risk and return profiles. Conservative investors tend to look for funds with conservative investment objectives, such as capital preservation or income, that generally emphasize fixed income securities over stock (e.g., highly rated bonds). Aggressive investors seek growth which, typically translates into equity funds of varying degrees of speculation. Investors who are neither conservative nor aggressive may seek a mix of asset classes and objectives in their investment portfolio.

Performance. Nothing gets attention like tremendous performance. Every investor loves to make money. And so does every portfolio manager. When a fund's performance is much better than its peers and competitors, it will get free press and attention. In addition, despite warnings to the contrary that past success is not indicative of future results, investors seem programmed to chase success. So, top performers will often tout their performance in ads and marketing materials.

Clearly, success may drive mutual fund sales: good performance sells. A prime example was the technology and internet boom of the late 1990s and early 2000s. Stocks of such companies soared, as did mutual funds investing in them. Both retail and institutional investors made enormous investments in the best performing equity funds. Sadly, those late to the action got burned when the stock prices collapsed and the funds with them. More recently, in 2014 and early 2015, Chinese equities were hot, as were funds investing in them. Again, money poured into the funds only to be disappointed when Chinese stocks faltered in later in 2015 and early 2016.

A whole industry of data analyzers, consultants, magazines, and on-line services exists to provide investors small and large with performance comparisons. A firm, Morningstar, popularized a system of 5-star ratings, which measures risk-adjusted performance of funds and compares them to each other. Studies have shown that achieving a 5-star Morningstar rating is a key way to generate sales of a fund's shares.

Advertising. Given these investment considerations, a question arises as to how investors make decisions among similar types of funds. The answer is at the very heart of distribution. A fund's distributor must effectively find investors to whom the fund appeals and will seek to accomplish this task through use of different channels of distribution discussed below.

Appearing in print, television, radio, and various internet sites, advertising is used by funds and their sponsors to support both direct sales and intermediary sales. Advertising may stimulate sales of fund shares, like many other products and services. While highly regulated, fund advertising is nonetheless a multi-million dollar business designed to build brand image and promote funds. According to industry studies, advertising works. Consider the fact that with thousands of funds available, how does a fund make its name known? Advertising? Performance record? Someone promotes or sells the fund?

Expenses. Increasingly, investors appear more sensitive to shareholder expenses incurred in owning different funds. Some investors, as discussed in Chapter 1 in connection with the Cost-Matters Hypothesis, seek average performance from an asset class at the lowest possible cost (e.g., the fund with the lowest shareholder expenses). Index funds perfectly capture this approach and appeal to such investors. However, at the very least, some investors will want to compare actively-managed funds in terms of their respective costs. In short, information about expenses is vital to the investment decisions of many investors.

Notwithstanding the influence of these individual factors in shaping investor decisions, and the importance of advisers and portfolio managers as the most visible representatives of a fund, an equally important aspect is how the mechanics of distribution is structured. Distribution in this context can be viewed from the perspective of three issues. First, consider who is buying fund shares: retail buyers (e.g., individuals) or institutions (e.g., pension funds). Second, each of these groups has multiple ways that shares can be sold to them, called "distribution channels." Why are there different distribution channels? Finally, there's the matter of compensating sales people who are selling fund shares, i.e., brokers and financial advisers, and funding the method of distribution. In short, when considering distribution channels it boils down to a simple question: who pays for distribution and is it affected by the type of distributional channel?

Most mutual funds are sold through brokers, advisers and other intermediaries. According to Investment Company Institute studies, up to 60% of fund share sales can be attributed to some form of advice or recommendation. Without a doubt, recommendations and advice by intermediaries are critical to investors' investment decisions. As a result, a significant portion of fund sales are structured to compensate intermediaries for providing advice to investors and guiding them to the fund in the form of fees and/or commissions. In addition to advice from advisers of varying kinds, some investors are self-directed, seeking guidance from internet sites, publications, social media, or investing seminars. Not surprisingly, the costs of sales to self-directed investors are generally smaller and are paid differently.

Sales of shares will be made directly through the fund (or rather its agents). For legal purposes, most RICs have a third party distributor or underwriter. The distributor is usually registered as a broker-dealer and provides the formal, legal share underwriting function. The goal for the distributor is to see to it that a fund's shares are offered through a variety of distribution channels.

Until the 1980s, funds were generally offered and sold in two ways: either directly to the public or through full-service brokers. Legal developments around this time coupled with the effects of technological change fundamentally altered the landscape, resulting in a proliferation of different distribution channels. Distribution channels include heavy use of intermediaries (who must be compensated) such as traditional stock brokers like Merrill Lynch; discount brokers like Fidelity and Charles Schwab (including fund supermarket platforms maintained by many broker-dealers); retirement plans; insurance companies; investment advisers and financial planners; and many more. Finally, there are some funds which sell their shares directly to the public.

While a bit simplified, Figure 3C illustrates eight key distribution channels for mutual funds (most of which involve the use of intermediaries)

Figure 3C — Examples of principal distribution sales channels for fund shares. Flowing between the parties are varying amounts of advice, fees and commissions, and the investors' money and shares. By law, a fund generally contracts with a distributor to serve as the fund's underwriter. Conceptually, the distributor is an entity which can provide access to all of the distribution channels, but not all of them are necessarily used by each fund. Investors generally use only one of the channels, depending on how they obtain investment advice and guidance, if at all.

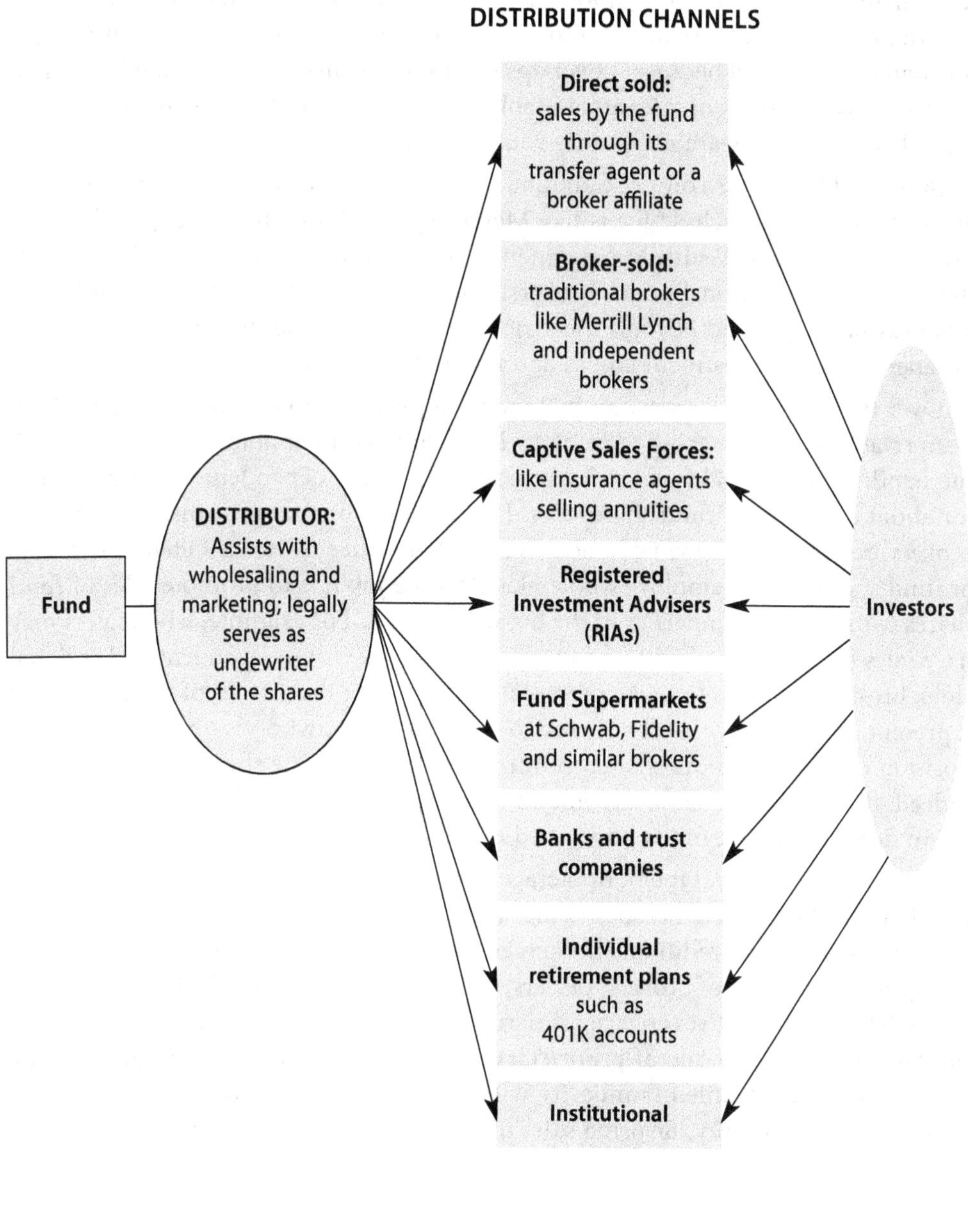

Direct-sold. A distribution channel that has become increasingly important over time is direct-sold funds. Originally these funds were identified as no-load funds, i.e., they did not impose any sales charges. As sales charge arrangements have evolved, this label is less distinctive, but certainly the current leader is Vanguard Funds, followed by such firms like Fidelity and T. Rowe Price. Obviously, direct-sold fund families, which traditionally relied on the mail, telephone, and newspapers, have been fundamentally transformed by the internet and the ability to be in virtually constant contact with retail investors. While these direct-sold, no-load funds and families have grown in recent years, so too have no-load classes of funds sold through other channels involving intermediaries, most notably brokers and RIAs (see below). The sales of these no-load classes of shares is driven by the use of accounts where the fees are levied based on asset-based charges on accounts (as opposed to sales for funds) and retirement plans that afford employees a menu of funds from which to select. (And it is the growth of this segment which has completely obscured the relative sales through each channel because it overlaps several segments; therefore making it hard to identify the amount of sales attributable to each channel. Some estimates are provided below, but they are necessarily rough estimates.)

Broker-sold. Brokers comprise about a fifth of those funds sold through intermediary channels and include firms like Merrill Lynch, Morgan Stanley, Wells Fargo Advisors, and UBS Wealth Management. These are firms that are still popularly thought of as "traditional" stock brokers, but as discussed in Chapter 6, this line of business has expanded beyond the strict confines of brokerage and encompasses broader forms of investment advice and financial planning.

Over the past two decades, an increasing number of small brokerage firms have been established. Advancing technology has facilitated their ability to compete with the handful of national full-service brokerage firms. Independent brokers account for about a quarter of fund share sales. Like national brokerage firms, independent brokers are subject to the same standards in dealing with customers. Often distributors or fund sponsors will employ "wholesalers," whose job it is to promote sales of fund shares within their channels or in the broader market. For example, wholesalers may have sales territories, and within their territories, they visit independent and regional stock brokerage offices to make presentations extolling the virtues of the funds they represent. The analogy is often made to soap salesmen, who visit grocery stores to position their soap products and optimize their space on the shelves of the grocers. Indeed, the term "shelf space" is sometimes used in the broker-sold distribution channel to describe getting funds positioned on brokerage firms' platforms.

Captive sales force. A type of brokerage sales channel that has lost significant market share in the last few decades is the "captive sales force." Historically, insurance companies and large traditional brokerages have used their own sales representatives or captive sales forces of brokers, dealers, or insurance agents to sell affiliated mutual funds. The representatives engage primarily or exclusively in selling the affiliated proprietary funds. While sale of proprietary funds might benefit from a captive sales force in terms of detailed familiarity with the funds and the ability to cultivate a sense of investor loyalty, favoring sales of proprietary funds for reasons other than their investment merit for customers is potentially problematic. As a result of the perceived conflicts of interest in such situations, most firms have reduced or eliminated compensation incentives favoring their proprietary products. In the insurance context, the funds typically are mutual funds sold with an insurance policy, the combination being called "variable annuity funds."

Registered investment advisers (RIAs). As brokerage personnel leave traditional brokers, some establish very small RIA businesses to serve their existing clients instead of seeking broker qualification. It is estimated that about a fifth of mutual fund sales are attributable to this intermediary channel. As noted in Figure 3C, RIAs are registered investment advisers and are subject to different registration requirements, fiduciary standards, and other standards than traditional broker-only sales representatives.

Banks and trust companies. Banks and trust companies make up a surprisingly large intermediary channel, specifically over a third of mutual fund share sales. In addition to checking and savings accounts, many banks, more specialized trust companies, and even credit unions offer clients asset management and/or brokerage options. Investors appear to be comfortable shopping for funds where they bank.

Discount brokers and Fund Supermarkets. Until 1975, commissions charged by securities brokers were fixed by law. After deregulation of commissions, a whole new and burgeoning industry developed: the discount broker, including firms like Charles Schwab, eTrade, TD Ameritrade, and Fidelity. They offer services which differ from traditional brokers and usually charge commissions and fees lower than traditional brokers. In 1984, Charles Schwab pioneered the concept of a "fund supermarket," which is designed to let investors shop and select from a large selection of mutual funds, ETFs, and other investments. In some ways, the supermarket model smashes the fund family concept, since it permits you to mix and match funds from many advisers and sponsors rather than just one family. Firms such as Schwab have negotiated with fund sponsors to facilitate discounted or free ("No Transaction Fee") purchases and sales of fund shares. A rule change in 1980 smoothed the way for this channel by allowing fund payment of certain distribution fees and expenses, which payments are otherwise prohibited under the Company Act. Funds adopting plans under the rule, called "12b-1 Plans" (named after the rule), are able to make payments from fund assets to brokerages like Schwab to facilitate fund share sales. Rule 12b-1 and such plans will be discussed in greater detail in Chapter 17.

Retirement plans. Over the last generation, many, if not most, private employers have abandoned traditional defined-benefit plans in favor of defined-contribution plans where employers make a contribution to an account established for each employee in which the employee directs where the funds should be invested from a menu of pre-selected mutual funds. Sales pursuant to the most common employer retirement plans (such as 401(k)s or 403(b)s) are particularly attractive for funds and their sponsors. Over time, investors regularly increase their investments into the fund (e.g., monthly or bi-monthly). In addition, investments in funds selected for a 401(k) plan tend to be "sticky"—assets once invested tend to stay invested longer in that particular fund selected by the employee.

Institutional. While the retail channels discussed above contribute about 90% of fund sales, institutions also are active buyers of funds. Institutional buyers often demand extremely low sales charges or none at all.

The various types of distribution channels may entail different types of charges used to pay for distribution. Traditionally, most funds were sold at the time of purchase with a sales-load (a so-called front-end sales load, e.g., a sales charge based on the amount invested, such as 5%). The conventional sales load was the primary means of compensating the broker. The allowance of a wide range of sales charges other than sales loads represented a significant legal evolution in the 1980s, aspects of which remain controversial today. The evolution was marked by the introduction of "deferred sales loads" (paid upon sale of the shares), "contingent deferred sales load" (paid upon sale but the size of which diminishes over holding period of the shares), "Rule 12b-1 fees" (paid out of the fund's assets), and combinations that mix and match sales charges and fees.

Perhaps these charges would be easier to understand if each fund only used one type of charge. Unfortunately, for purposes of exposition and understanding, the fund industry evolved into funds using multiple classes of shares for marketing and distribution purposes. Each class is designed to allow different types of compensation structures for distribution (i.e., use of different sales charges sold through different distribution channels).

A simple two series, three class structure would look like the following:

Figure 3D — Two fund series investment company with three share classes for each fund (each class marketed through different distribution channels using different types of sales charges)

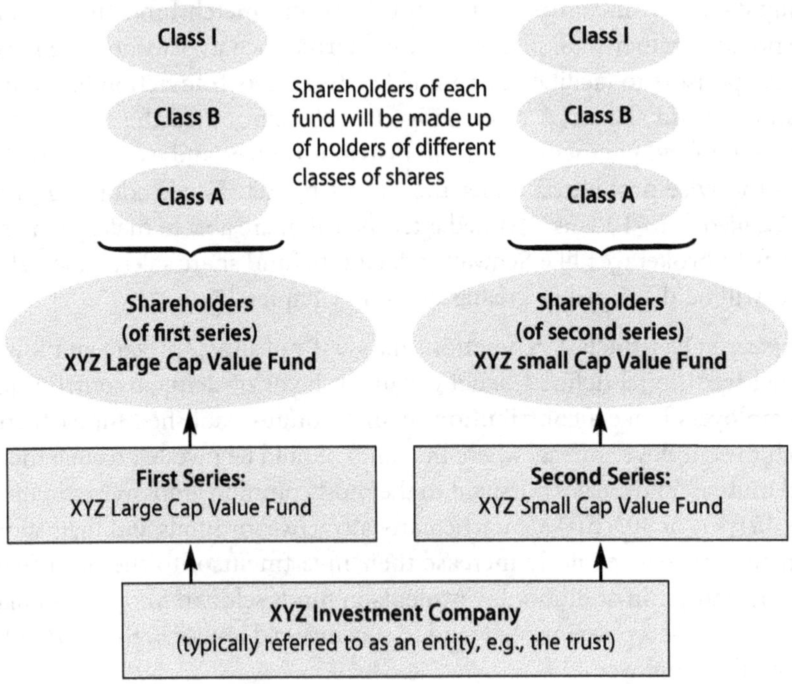

As you can see, the combination of possibilities are numerous, and typically a function of the needs of the adviser and/or distributor of a fund family. Indeed, while three to five classes are common, some funds may have up to a dozen classes of shares for distribution purposes. The legal dimensions of distribution are discussed in detail in Chapter 17.

In light of this discussion, the central questions on distribution posed at the outset begin to have meaning: "Who pays for distribution and how is it paid for?" The true answer all depends on the distribution channel and the charges levied on shares associated with the particular distribution channel. Table 3E offers a highly simplified summary that is developed further in Chapter 17.

Table 3E — Fees associated with distribution

TYPE OF FEE	WHO PAYS THE FEE?	WHO IS COMPENSATED WITH THE FEE?
Sales Load	Investor (at purchase)	Broker
Deferred Sales Load	Investor (at sale)	Fund Distributor who has previously paid broker
Rule 12b-1	Fund (annually)	Varies: fund distributor, fund supermarket (discount brokerage platform), broker
Commission [ETF]	Investor	Broker

Having surveyed aspects of fund formation, fund governance, investment management, and distribution of shares, the next chapter turns to less visible fund operations

Chapter 4

Fund Operations and Service Providers

Key Ideas: In addition to governance, investment management, and distribution, the day-to-day operations of funds involve a host of non-advisory services to support fund activities in carrying out its purpose as an investment vehicle. These non-advisory services are less visible to the average investor, but are vitally important to the fund's ability to conduct business. Non-advisory fund activities are discharged by supporting personnel and service providers. These personnel and service providers include: the fund's officers, the fund's custodian (responsible for the custody and safekeeping of the fund's assets), and fund accounting, administration, and transfer agency operations (shareholder recordkeeping).

In addition, two topics are unusually significant and figure prominently in subsequent chapters: pricing of fund shares (an operation which is primarily addressed in fund accounting) and compliance. Mutual fund, UIT and ETF shares generally must calculate the net asset value of their shares (i.e., the proportionate value of each share of the fund's net assets) at least daily on any business day. This function is critical to the daily process by which fund shares are purchased by investors and sold back to a fund (i.e., redeemed by shareholders) since the relevant price for this subscription and redemption process will be the NAV as calculated by the fund after the order is received.

Every fund must have written policies and procedures and a chief compliance officer charged with overseeing and assessing the implementation of those policies and procedures. This compliance function is of vital importance to fund boards in assuring the integrity of funds' activities and operations consistent with regulatory obligations and each fund's disclosures to investors.

Both advisory and non-advisory services are costly. Funds typically bear the direct expenses associated with front- and back-office services (generally exclusive of distribution expenses) and are paid from fund assets. These fund expenses are ultimately borne pro rata by shareholders indirectly; when the fund pays expenses, the NAV for each share is reduced. Shareholders also may incur expenses associated with distribution directly in the form of sales charges or indirectly through so-called "Rule 12b-1" fees paid out of fund assets.

Chapter Contents

4.1 Introduction and Overview of Fund Operations

Chapter 3 focused on the governance, investment management and distribution operations of funds. These are core functions representing essential features of any registered pooled investment vehicle arrangement. They also are the portion of a pooled investment vehicle's operations that are most visible to investors and the public. In the industry, they are often called the "front office" functions. Less visible are the vital "back office" operations (non-advisory functions) discussed in this chapter. The primary non-advisory service providers that support the activities of the fund are: the custodian (responsible for the custody and safekeeping of the fund's assets), the fund accountant, the fund administrator, and the transfer agent (responsible for shareholder recordkeeping). All of these services must be seamlessly integrated with the other operations, most particularly the investment management functions and the other core functions identified in Chapter 3, in order for the fund to function properly. These various functions are rendered diagrammatically in Figure 4A.

Most back office operations are provided by third party service providers for many funds. However, it is important to realize that fund advisers and fund groups have a broad variety of ways of organizing their operations. On one end of the spectrum are the large fund groups which often have a number of the core operations functions under one roof, e.g., investment management, distribution, fund administration, fund accounting and transfer agency. In other words, the various services are provided by affiliates of the investment adviser. On the other end of the spectrum, there are small funds which may be completely outsourced to third parties that are unaffiliated with the adviser. Often, funds start outsourced when they are small, and the adviser in time will internalize some of these operations for reasons of control and improved oversight as the fund family grows. Between the ends of the spectrum are a large variety of ways of outsourcing and of internalizing operations.

Figure 4A — Principal service providers to investment company (typically from third party)

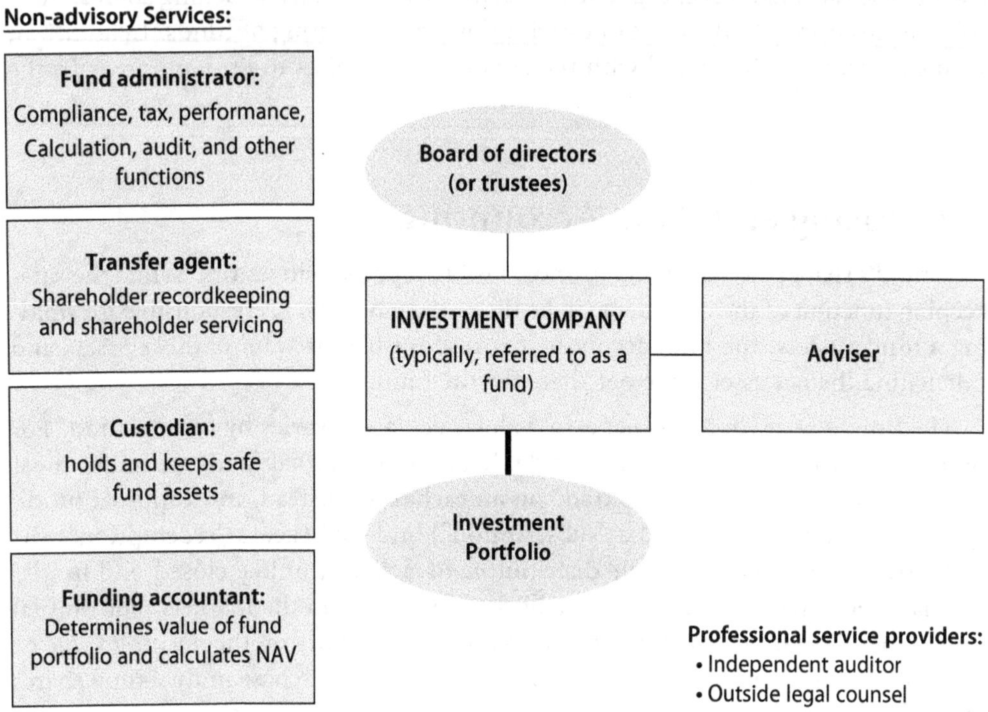

As discussed below, two back office functions will be highlighted: (i) fund accounting and its role in pricing; and (ii) compliance. Fund accounting is important as it relates directly to establishing the price at which investors purchase and sell shares of funds. Central to that operation is the process by which the value of the fund's investments is established on a (business) daily basis. While seemingly simple, this process, called "valuation," is a challenging and potentially error prone process. Compliance policies and procedures and compliance personal ensure applicable legal requirements are met and the fund operates in accordance with its disclosure to investors. Over the last two decades, compliance policies and procedures have become critical to the board's oversight of activities and operations of the fund which extends to the compliance policies and procedures of its adviser and service providers.

The chapter concludes with a brief overview of fund fees and expenses. Advisory and non-advisory activities are costly and result in expenses either for the fund (which are borne indirectly by shareholders) or directly for shareholders. The costs of advisory and non-advisory services (exclusive of distribution expenses with some exceptions) are paid out of the fund assets. However, these expenses are ultimately borne pro rata by shareholders because the expenses reduce net assets and thus ultimately share NAV. Fund expenses are important to investors because high fund costs will inevitably translate into a lower total return on their investment. In addition to the fund expenses indirectly borne by shareholders, shareholders may also directly incur significant costs in the form of sales charges in connection with buying and selling shares. Such costs relate entirely to the costs of distribution and marketing of funds. In addition, such expenses may be shared with the adviser and, subject to limitations, with the fund.

4.2 Pricing and Fund Accounting

A fund's share price is among its most visible aspects to investors. While the safekeeping function of the custodian (to be discussed a bit later) is responsible for holding a fund's assets, the fund accountant is responsible for valuing those assets and calculating the net asset value per share for the fund.

The timing of pricing and net asset value calculation varies by type of fund. For mutual funds and ETFs, it is a daily cycle. In addition, mutual funds are unlike most securities whose shares or units trade on an exchange. Instead, most mutual funds' shares are bought (also called a "subscription") and sold (i.e., a "redemption") directly from the fund itself or its distributor. As a result, unlike closed-end funds, mutual funds' shares values aren't established by traders in the markets. For mutual funds, the subscriptions and redemptions are based directly on the *net asset value* or *NAV* of the funds' shares (as explained below). Investors purchase mutual fund shares at the shares' NAV plus any sales load or commission, which together is called the *offering price.* Share sales or redemptions are made at the NAV less any redemption fees.

One of the key features of mutual funds is the subscription/redemption structure of their shares, and new shares are continuously offered to investors, unless the fund "closes." As a result of the subscription/redemption process, mutual funds' assets are

It's All About the NAV!

The NAV of fund shares is a simple calculation—conceptually that is! Basically, you total the value of the fund's assets, deduct the fund's liabilities and divide by the number of shares issued by the fund.

NAV = (Assets – Liabilities) ÷ # of shares issued and outstanding

For example, a fund with $1 billion in assets and $100 million in liabilities is said to have $900 million in net assets. If it has 100 million shares issued and outstanding, then its NAV is $9.00 per share using the formula.

Fund assets are typically its investments and cash. A fund can also have liabilities as a result of its investment activities; if it borrows money for liquidity or other reasons; and if it accrues fees to pay to its adviser and service providers.

continually growing or shrinking. Indeed, it's the reason that the statutory name for mutual funds is open-end funds. Mutual funds generally calculate their NAVs at the close of business on the New York Stock Exchange, currently 4 pm, each trading day.

Closed-end funds are the opposite of mutual funds. Closed-end funds generally have a set number of shares issued and outstanding, and such shares trade on a securities exchange. As a result, closed-end funds are only required to price their assets and calculate the NAV weekly, although many do it daily as well.

ETFs are hybrids when it comes to pricing. They issue and redeem large units of ownership (called "creation units") that are subject to the redemption and subscription principles governing retail mutual funds. However, creation units are divided into blocks of shares (such as 50,000 or 100,000 shares), and these underlying ETF shares are traded on securities exchanges. Only authorized participants (essentially very large institutional brokers who contract with the ETF) are able to buy and sell ETF creation units from/to the fund. These authorized participants, however, are able to divide creation units into ETF shares for purposes of selling the shares to facilitate market trading, and to aggregate shares into creation units by buying back ETF shares in the market. As a result, ETFs calculate a day-end NAV like mutual funds, but also calculate interim or indicative NAVs all day long to give traders of their shares information regarding the approximate value of the shares throughout the day.

Conceptually simple, the NAV process is actually very complex and keeps the fund accounting staff busy all day in anticipation of their deadline at the end of the day at about 6 pm East Coast time. During the day, fund accountants must review the prior day's purchases and sales that affect the fund's assets; cash holdings; and corporate events (e.g., mergers, bankruptcies, dividends and interest being paid by the stocks and bonds held by the fund, etc.), accrue liabilities, and run trial pricing calculations. Things get especially intense once the stock market closes at 4 pm East Coast time, which is the point in time when a fund's securities positions will be valued. The results have to be reported within two hours in order to be posted on various on-line sites and published in newspapers (for those newspapers still publishing such information). Moreover, the NAV needs to be reported to brokers and other sub-transfer agents which process share trades so that they can process them at the correct price.

The timing of mutual fund pricing merits a few more comments. When an investor buys shares of a mutual fund, he or she must wait until the end of the day (i.e., the 4 pm valuation time) to see what the NAV is for those shares. This is called "forward pricing." Until 1968, funds used "backward pricing," which priced fund share purchases and sales at the most recently calculated NAV (e.g., at yesterday's closing prices). As we will see in a later chapter, backward pricing creates massive opportunities for trading strategies that unfairly game the system and disadvantage the fund and its continuing shareholders.

4.3 Compliance and the Significance of Policies and Procedures

As has been noted, regulated investment companies like mutual funds, ETFs, UITs and closed-end funds are subject to extensive regulations under the Company Act, which establishes a comprehensive scheme for regulation for such companies. In addition, a myriad of other laws and regulations apply to such funds, including laws regulating subjects as diverse as tax, cyber security, privacy, state securities regulation, commodities and futures, brokerage, banking and money transfers, pensions, labor and human relations (if they have staff), and many more. Fund advisers and service providers generally also have a broad variety of regulatory obligations.

As a result, over the last two decades, as regulatory requirements have expanded, the role of compliance officers and the compliance operations have become much more visible and prominent than in prior decades. As will be discussed much more extensively in a later chapter, funds must have robust compliance programs designed, at a minimum, to ensure compliance with applicable federal securities laws. But almost by default, funds have compliance programs with much broader scopes. Critical to compliance are the roles of compliance policies and procedures and of the chief compliance officer in applying and enforcing them.

Significance of policies and procedures. At the heart of a robust compliance program is a comprehensive set of policies and procedures. These are like an operations manual or guide for a fund's compliance program. The process of developing a compliance program can be viewed basically as creating a survey of applicable legal and regulatory obligations applicable to the fund and its service providers. Once such a survey is developed, then appropriate policies are developed which assist fund service providers, officers and others with understanding the regulatory and legal obligations applicable to the fund. In turn, procedures translate policies to actionable steps.

In practice, such a survey and the subsequent policies and procedures do not have to be developed from scratch. A broad variety of forms of policies and procedures and best practice documents are available from law firms, compliance consulting firms and industry trade groups. In addition, regulators such as the SEC often provide guidance on important compliance issues and developments. What is critical, though, is that such documents and information be customized for each fund. In addition, it is important that the policies and procedures be periodically reviewed for effectiveness and continued relevance. A well-run compliance program is continuously evolving and improving. Running such programs generally is the chief compliance officer.

Chief compliance officers. As noted earlier, funds typically have no employees or dedicated staff. Chief compliance officers ("CCOs"), fund officers mandated by the Company Act, are a possible exception. CCOs have an important role overseeing compliance not only with respect to a fund's operations but also in verifying adequate compliance functions at fund service providers. In overseeing compliance for a fund, the CCO will also be intimately familiar with portfolio strategies, trading processes, portfolio pricing and the myriad of other regulatory requirements applicable to fund operations. The role of the CCO is distinct from other fund officers in that the CCO generally is accountable directly to the fund's board of trustees, which is also responsible for setting the CCO's compensation. Boards often rely heavily on the CCO because of his or her theoretical independence from other officers. In reality, the CCO may wear multiple hats, serving as CCO of the adviser or other fund officer functions. Despite such potential conflicts, the CCO function has rapidly become a critical one over the past two decades.

4.4 The Fund's Other Participants and Operations

As noted, front-office functions involving investment management and distribution must be integrated seamlessly with the back-office operations provided either by service providers affiliated with the adviser or third-party service providers. For the most part, these back-office services do not figure directly in this textbook's exposition of the statutory and regulatory requirements. Nevertheless, the brief thumbnail sketches below are designed to demystify the participants in the fund's activities and operations and provide context in understanding the operational problems and challenges that arise in the text's readings.

4.4.1 Executive Oversight: The Role of Officers

In order to conduct business, funds must have officers legally authorized to conduct business on behalf of the fund. Generally the board designates personnel from the investment adviser or administrator to be officers with respect to managing the day-to-day operations of the funds, such as authorizing trading activity in connection with portfolio management. This system of officers provides operational efficiencies between the adviser, administrator and fund. Every fund must designate both a principal executive officer ("PEO") and principal financial officer ("PFO"). Together they are responsible for reviewing and signing-off (legally certifying) the fund's financial statements and internal controls. The PEO is like a chief executive officer: responsible for general management and oversight of the operations of the fund. The PFO, like a treasurer or chief financial officer, is responsible to ensure that the fund's financial and accounting books and records are accurately kept and obligations to fund service providers are paid timely. He or she also arranges for the fund's tax and dividend payments, and, as noted, provides legal certification for the fund's financial statements and internal controls.

4.4.2 Custody and Custodians

Like an investor, a fund needs a checking account and place to hold its assets. This is known as a custody account, and the bank or broker providing the service is called the "custodian." However, unlike the investor, the fund or its adviser may not keep the fund's cash or securities at home or at the office in a vault. Indeed, while the investment adviser may direct and control the investment operations of a fund, it may never exercise physical possession or direct ownership over the fund's assets, namely its cash and securities. Conceptually, the idea is to protect and segregate the fund assets from the adviser's and other service providers' assets and liabilities. Similarly, fund assets must be kept separate from those of the custodian and the custodian's other clients. Although the custodian holds the fund's assets along with the assets of many other clients, it adheres to specific procedures and requirements both in terms of its own finances and how it holds the fund's assets to preserve segregation of assets. As a practical matter, custody operations, especially international ones, are complex and expensive to develop and maintain and have significant economies of scale. As a result, the custody industry is dominated by large banks like Citibank, JPMorgan, State Street Bank, and Brown Brothers Harriman.

Custodians provide a variety of ancillary services including making loans to funds (e.g., credit lines and overdrafts); arranging for funds to lend their securities to others (termed "securities lending") to earn interest; and foreign currency conversions (e.g., when a fund buys and sells securities in foreign markets). In some cases, mostly for holding assets in foreign countries, sub-custodians may be used under the supervision of the custodian.

4.4.3 Fund Administration

The work of the Fund Administrator, "fund administration" is the umbrella term for a broad variety of other important services, including:

- *Legal*—in-house or administrator-provided SEC and regulatory filing services; board of directors and trustees meeting preparation and documentation; general corporate governance.
- *Compliance*—highlighted earlier, compliance is often categorized as an administrative function.
- *Financial reporting*—while the fund accountants calculate a fund's net assets and NAV periodically, a separate team of professionals are responsible for assembling that periodic data into monthly, quarterly, semi-annual and annual reports of various types. These reports include income statements, balance sheets, and portfolio composition reports and are used to update fund portfolio managers, fund management, directors or trustees and, finally, shareholders.
- *Performance reporting*—closely related to financial report production is the translation of the financial results into regulatory-compliant yield and return calculations. Like financial reports, the performance data is included in regulatory filings; reports to management, directors and trustees, and shareholders; and marketing and advertising materials. Investors are heavily influenced by reports of performance. That places a special burden on advisers to maximize fund performance relative to benchmarks and other funds.
- *Tax*—all types of funds have important tax requirements. Most registered funds are known as pass-through entities, meaning that all income and net capital

gains pass through the funds without taxation at the fund level. Shareholders and investors receiving the income and gains are taxed on them. The tax function is responsible for making sure that all pertinent tax requirements to maintain the pass-through status are met.

According to the Investment Company Institute, back-office operations like accounting, fund administration, and transfer agency account for more than 40% of industry employment.

4.4.4 Transfer Agency

Transfer agents, or TAs, provide two important services: customer or shareholder service and shareholder recordkeeping.

Shareholder service. Transfer agents provide a key point of contact with investors with calling centers to assist shareholders with their information and transactional needs. E.g., interested investors may call an 800 phone number and reach the transfer agents' call center where they can request forms and documents like prospectuses and application forms. In addition, shareholders can call a fund's 800 phone number to check account balances, redeem shares, have cash sent to their bank accounts and myriad other transactions. Finally, the transfer agent must be sure to integrate its services with the fund's website and afford investors client service contact through the website.

Shareholder recordkeeping. Once an investor has invested in a fund, he or she becomes a shareholder. The role of the transfer agent is to record on the official books of the fund, the names, addresses, and other important information regarding shareholders. Most importantly, the TA keeps a record of each shareholder's holdings, i.e., number of shares held, the purchase price (known as "basis"), sale price, etc. The role of "sub-transfer agents" or "omnibus recordkeepers" has grown tremendously in the last 25 years. Brokers and retirement account recordkeeping firms have proliferated and keep the detailed records for their investors. In turn they report only high level data to a fund's TA. As an example, a brokerage firm like Charles Schwab might have 5,000 clients holding shares in the fictional Sargent Hall Fund. Schwab will keep detailed records on behalf of their clients and report only the bulk position and sales/purchase activities to the Fund's TA.

4.4.5 Outside Professional Services

As noted in the Introduction, core fund operations can be arranged in a number of ways from internal functions to outsourced services. Several services must be outsourced for legal or practical purposes, including legal, audit and insurance services.

Independent Auditors. While the Fund Administration staff may compile and prepare a fund's financial statements, the laws governing RICs require that independent auditors examine, test and certify the accuracy of the financial statements.

Legal Counsel. Advisers, funds and fund independent trustees all may have outside counsel to advise them, although typically fund counsel will also act as either counsel to the adviser or as counsel to the independent trustee. It is important to consider the potential conflicts of interest that counsel may have when they represent more than one party. For example, no attorney can function as independent counsel to the fund's adviser as well as its independent trustees, because the two clients' interests clearly diverge from one another.

Insurance. Registered funds are required to maintain minimum amounts of insurance as a bond to ensure against larceny and embezzlement by fund officers and agents. As a matter of practice, advisers and funds maintain insurance for errors, omissions, bonding and litigation expense protection. In addition, board members will invariably have insurance as well. All of these policies are typically obtained through independent insurance companies.

4.5 Fund Fees and Expenses

Operating funds is not cheap. The operation of mutual funds and ETFs involves billions of dollars of expenses for the funds. With respect to an investment in a fund, there are two types of expenses: those borne by the fund ("fund expenses") and those borne directly by shareholders ("shareholder expenses"). Of course, fund expenses are borne indirectly by fund shareholders by directly reducing the value of each fund share (i.e., NAV).

Much of the policy discussion regarding fund expenses over the past few decades has focused on two key components: the management (or advisory) fee and the expense ratio. The management fee is the payment made to the investment management firm for managing a fund's assets, of which the most common approach is charging a percentage of assets under management. This approach is typical of investment funds. The number is typically quoted in an annual rate based on assets under management expressed in percentage terms or "basis points" (1/100 of a percentage point). Thus, a management fee of 10 basis points (or 0.1%) on $1 billion would be $1 million on an annual basis. At 75 basis points, the fee would be $7.5 million.

The management fee is a manager's primary source of profits. A major distinction between actively-managed funds and passively-managed (or indexed) funds exists in terms of the relative management fees charged. Put simply, it costs more to actively manage a portfolio of assets as opposed to implementing an index-based strategy. As a result, actively managed portfolios invariably charge a higher fee than index funds for comparable investment styles. However, registered funds as a group charge much lower management fees than private funds, such as hedge funds or private equity funds. This difference is a result of regulatory differences as well as competitive market factors.

The management fee is only one of many fund operating expenses. It is possible to look at all of the expenses incurred in administering a fund on an annual basis. Such expenses would include not merely the management fee, but all fees for the custodian, fund administration, fund accounting, the transfer agent and any taxes (which typically are very low because of the pass-through nature of most funds), but exclude brokerage costs. The total expenses of the fund (excluding brokerage costs) divided by the assets under management is the *expense ratio*.

Expense Ratio Calculation

$$\text{Expense ratio} = \frac{\text{FUND'S TOTAL EXPENSES (including 12b-1 fees* but excluding brokerage expenses)}}{\text{Fund's average net assets (assets minus liabilities)}}$$

Obviously, this figure will be greater than the management fee alone, although in most cases, the management fee is the largest component of a fund's expenses, and this is certainly the case for any actively managed fund. This ratio obviously yields a percentage and for any registered investment company, such as a mutual fund or ETF, that number will be generally considerably less than 2% and typically 1%. More complicated fund arrangements using complex strategies involving, for example, shorting, may be greater. The various fund operating expenses are illustrated in the diagram below.

Figure 4B — Fund Operating Expenses (core components).
Fund operating expenses vary widely depending on their objectives, policies, distribution arrangements, and operations.

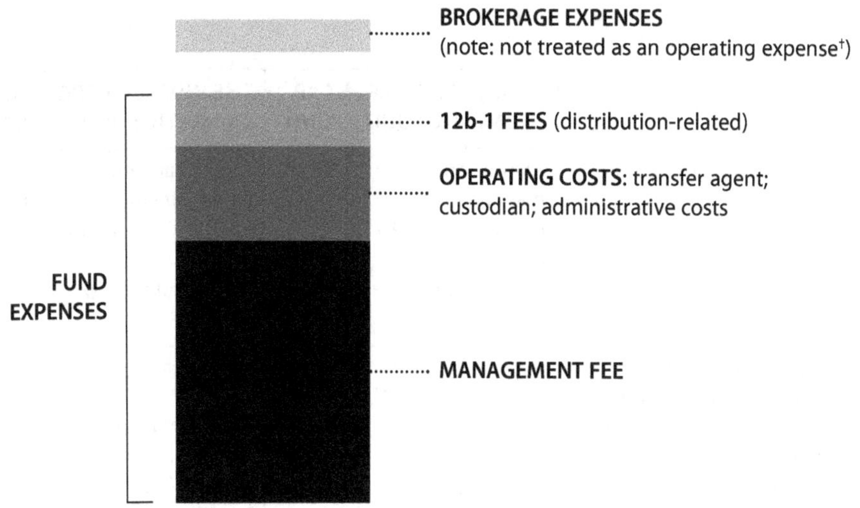

† Portfolio brokerage expenses, while appearing to be a natural type of operating expense, are actually reflected in the calculations of the gains and losses on investments by a fund. As a result, they impact performance and the distributions of the fund to investors and are not included in operating expense calculations.

A final note on fund fees and expenses. This is an area fraught with public policy implications. The fees are ultimately borne by fund shareholders, and so the SEC and investor advocates have long sought to ensure that these fees are not excessive.

* As explained in the illustration above, a 12b-1 fee is a fund asset based fee strictly used to pay for distribution related expenses for a fund. The name derives from the rule, Rule 12b-1, which allows such fees.

An Illustration: A Comparative Look at Fund Operating Expenses

The table below provides a pro-forma illustration of the annual operating expenses for two hypothetical funds: the Active Large Cap Domestic Equity Fund and the Indexed Large Cap Domestic Equity Fund. Both funds have an annual average of $1 billion in assets under management. In addition, the basic investment profile of each fund is similar: each invests in equity (shares of common stock) of U.S. large cap public companies. They differ in management in one critical respect. The Active Domestic Equity Fund is actively managed (meaning the manager engages in research and analysis that will produce outcomes that outperform its benchmark index), while the Indexed Domestic Equity Fund is passively managed (i.e., it merely tries to replicate the performance of a broad-based index, such as the S&P 500). As discussed in Chapter 1, prospective investors want to know whether a particular actively-managed fund and its passively-managed counterpart can consistently outperform the passively-managed fund. One thing is pretty clear: passively-managed funds consistently charge much smaller management fees for comparable fund investment styles and so this illustration shows in concrete terms how that translates directly into the operating expenses of the respective funds.

EXPENSE TYPE	THE ACTIVE LARGE CAP DOMESTIC EQUITY FUND	THE INDEXED LARGE CAP DOMESTIC EQUITY FUND
Investment management fee	Assume an annual management fee of 60 basis points (.6%) of AUM: $6,000,000 [% of fund total expenses: 81.1%]	Assume an annual management fee of 5 basis points (.05%) of AUM: $500,000 [% of fund total expenses: 26.3%]
Non-advisory services (Note: such services include expenses like transfer agent fees; non-marketing shareholder communications; fund accounting and administration; SEC securities registration and other filings; independent auditors fees; fund counsel fees; custody expenses; and trustees' fees and expenses (including fees for independent trustee counsel).)	Assume: annually 14 basis points (.14%) of AUM or $1,4000,000 [% of fund total expenses: 18.9%]	Assume: annually 14 basis points (.14%) of AUM (i.e. roughly the same as the active fund) or $1,4000,000 [% of fund total expenses: 73.7%]
Total expenses	$7,400,000	$1,900,000
Expense ratio	.74 %	.19%

These figures are purely illustrative and will vary across funds and fund styles. Nevertheless this example illustrates some basic features when comparing actively-managed fund expenses and passively-managed fund expenses. The management fee for the passively-managed fund can be significantly lower than the actively-managed fund, whereas the fee for non-advisory services will be roughly the same. Although there may be some variation in expenses for non-advisory services, the overall difference tends to be much smaller. In the actively-managed fund, the management fee will be the lion's share of the fund's total expenses. In contrast, for fairly conventional index strategies, the management fee can be similar to or even less than the total for non-advisory expenses.

In addition, certain qualifications to this simplified pro-forma illustration of fund expenses should be noted. First, brokerage costs are not reflected in the calculation of an expense ratio. Instead those costs are reflected in the net gains or losses on investments. Generally, actively managed funds have greater amounts of trading (as managers try to outperform their benchmark) and, if so, the brokerage expenses experienced by the actively managed funds will be greater (which will cause drag on overall performance). This need not be the case, for example, if the index strategy requires significant portfolio adjustments when the portfolio is rebalanced or new securities are selected for the portfolio index.

Second, this example assumes that fund assets are not used to pay for distribution costs. As will be seen in Chapter 17, this raises a nettlesome issue from a regulatory perspective. Such fees to the extent permitted (known as "Rule 12b-1 fees") are subject to limitations and a host of special requirements. However, if there were such fees, such fees would be reflected as non-advisory fees, and they would increase the expense ratio for any fund that utilizes such fees.

According to the Investment Company Institute ("ICI"), they have been trending downward over the past few decades. The trend is reflective of a number of industry developments: growth in assets under management and related efficiencies of management, development of competitive products and services (most notably ETFs), a changing distribution and sales environment, shareholder fee litigation, and the recent strong trend to passively managed funds and ETFs. However, this does not means, as advocates have pointed out, that they are as low as they should be. This issue will surface in later chapters.

Shareholder expenses is a different way to look at expenses and includes not only the expenses shareholders face indirectly as fund shareholders, but expenses that they bear directly in the form of expenses in purchasing or selling shares of a fund. These sales charges are paid by the investor and are independent of asset-based distribution

Figure 4C — The components of shareholder expenses.

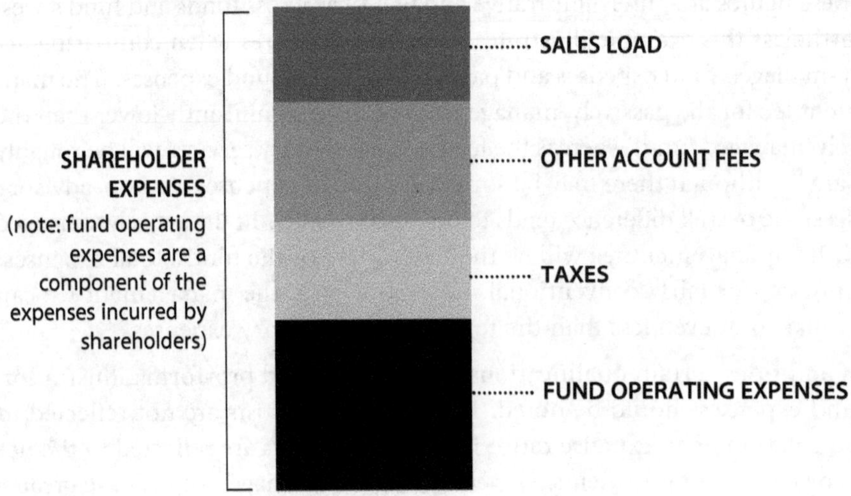

costs which are borne by all shareholders collectively and which are used to calculate the expense ratio. As will be explored in greater depth, such expenses are used to compensate brokers, financial advisers, and investment advisers who may provide investment advice to investors. In addition, there may be other fees for maintaining accounts holding fund shares, such as annual maintenance fees, and taxes which may arise as a result of income distributions or capital gains. As can be seen in Figure 4C, a fund's operating expenses are a significant part of each shareholder's expenses, but these expenses, unlike the others, are paid by the fund directly and not out of the shareholder's pocket. This, in turn, makes Figure 4C potentially misleading if viewed too literally. Although Figure 4C accurately represents all the sources of shareholder expenses, fund operating expenses recur on an ongoing basis, although they are summarized for shareholders on an annual basis. Taxes are usually tied to annual gains and losses realized by the shareholder and are paid directly to the government by the taxpayer, which in most cases will be the shareholder. Account fees are typically paid annually. In contrast, most shareholder charges are typically paid on a one time basis either at the time of purchase or upon sale of the shares.

Chapter 5

The Investment Management Industry and Regulation in Context: Past and Present

Key Ideas: The current investment management industry and current patterns of regulation decisively reflect regulatory responses to industry practices prevailing before the financial collapse accompanying the Great Depression. This context can be viewed in three stages: the industry prior to regulation, the imposition of the basic scheme of regulation in 1940, and investment management post-regulation.

Prior to regulation, investment advisers (or investment counsel) performed a wealth conservation function. Investment trust companies began to appear in the U.S. at the dawn of the twentieth century. Closed-end "investment trusts" dominated the U.S. fund industry in the early part of the twentieth century until the Great Depression, and what are known as mutual funds first appeared in Boston in 1924. The stock market crash of 1929 and the ensuing Depression fundamentally changed the industry. The calamitous losses and abuses of the investment trust era, especially in the area of leveraged closed-end funds, paved the way for regulation.

In 1940, following an exhaustive study of investment trusts by the SEC, Congress enacted two fundamental statutes: the mildly remedial Investment Advisers Act of 1940 and the heavy-handed Investment Company Act of 1940. These statutes, and significant amendments thereto and rules thereunder, still constitute the core of the current regulatory scheme. The almost 80 year period since their enactment has been marked by significant advances in financial innovation and asset accumulation. Mutual funds have emerged as the most popular type of fund. Closed-end funds have become a niche product. New types of funds evolved as well, including money market funds, ETFs, hedge funds, and private equity funds. Together these funds have gathered a staggering $19 trillion in assets under management in the U.S. In addition, financial planners and registered investment advisers have proliferated, and current patterns in retirement savings have moved decisively in the direction of individual retirement accounts which the investment management industry has been well positioned to service with an ever wider array of fund offerings.

Chapter Contents

5.1 Introduction

The world of investment management today reflects the culmination of many different forces: sustained growth of developed economies; a high degree of innovation and sophistication in markets for financial instruments; and a significant dose of democratization of savings in the U.S. In the U.S. alone, financial assets amount to $75 trillion, and pooled investment vehicles represent well over 1/3 of that total. While the U.S. investment company industry has its roots in English and Scottish investment trusts, the U.S. arguably has been the driver of global fund industry growth over the last several decades. At the end of 2017, open-end investment company type funds had over $49 trillion in AUM.

Of course, it is not necessary to understand each step in the history of the investment management industry to understand how the federal regulation of that industry operates. However, the regulatory scheme closely mirrors how the business of investment management operates and, in turn, the business has grown in ways shaped by the regulatory scheme. This chapter offer a panoramic overview of the evolution of the investment management industry and how its regulation provides context for the current scheme of regulation. It is helpful to think about this history in three different stages: the history before federal regulation, the scheme of federal regulation enacted in 1940, and then a brief survey of the history post-regulation. The purpose is not to provide a definitive legal history; rather, it is to contextualize the main features of regulation that are developed in ensuing chapters.

5.2 Fund Industry History—Before Regulation

History has examples of investment vehicles that have had properties that resemble modern pooled investment vehicles, but the lineage most relevant to the U.S. fund industry begins with the English and Scottish investment trusts in the latter half of the nineteenth century. Unlike earlier pooled arrangements in Europe that securitized pools of government bond and diverse colonial investments, the English and Scottish trusts actively managed investor capital by selecting securities for an investment portfolio, including investments in the burgeoning U.S. economy. It is hardly surprising that investment trusts, as an investment concept, soon migrated to the U.S. These investment trust entities functioned in a way similar to today's closed-end funds, i.e., funds which raise a fixed amount of capital and whose shares are themselves traded on public markets.

Investment trusts became popular investment vehicles in the early twentieth century United States, especially during the booming 1920s. The trusts were popular not only with investors, but also sponsors based largely on Wall Street. Four key attributes drove their popularity. First, funds were perceived by retail investors as safer than single-stock equity investments because they represented an interest in a diverse pool of securities and appealed to unsophisticated investors as a way to profit from professional management during the rising stock market era of the 1920s. Second, the funds offered an opportunity for stock brokers to earn retail-fee income: brokers earned commissions by persuading customers to buy shares in an investment trust. Third, some trust managers employed highly leveraged capital structures to enhance the returns of the common shares. Essentially, leveraged funds borrowed money to buy stocks. Trusts borrowed the money they needed by selling bonds and preferred shares, both of which obligated the trusts to make fixed periodic payments. As long as the investment returns exceeded the costs of borrowing, such trusts would be able to boost returns earned by their shareholders. Holders of the trusts' common shares would benefit from the gains in value of portfolio securities held by the trusts as long as the return on the portfolio securities exceeded the interest and coupon payments payable on the trusts' senior securities (the bonds and preferred shares). As a result, the premiums on trust shares would be bid up. Of course, leverage has the opposite effect in terms of magnifying investment losses when portfolio shares decline in value. Fourth, the investment bank and brokerage sponsors occasionally (or perhaps frequently) used their insider roles as fund managers to use fund capital to bid up other securities offerings or to buy unsold offerings sponsored by the same investment bank or brokerage, a process called "dumping."

In his 1929 article *The Era of Investment Trusts*, the great American economist Irving Fisher extolled the benefits of investment trusts because, as he explained, investment trusts provided investors with a way to reduce risks of equity investing economically through diversification and retain the services of professional managers skilled in investing in securities. In addition, he argued that they exercised a moderating effect on markets affected by speculative trading. As the economist John Kenneth Galbraith noted, the rate of creation of investment trusts reached a fever pitch immediately prior to the 1929 Stock Market Crash ("Crash")—185 trusts in 1928 and 265 before October 1929. Rising markets often provide cover for all manner of questionable or risky investment behavior. In the Crash, the perceived advantages of trusts quickly became disastrous. The values of shares of investment trusts dropped much more quickly and precipitously than the overall stock market. Leveraged trusts magnified the effect of the broader market declines leading to faster erosion in the value of the trust's portfolio (i.e., the trust had borrowed money to purchase stocks that were no longer worth what the trust had paid for them). Moreover, instead of premiums, the trusts' share prices were discounted as investors anticipated further declines due to leverage and stock market depreciation. Alas, poor Irving Fisher took his own advice too much to heart and lost most of his family's fortune in the Depression.

Before the 1929 crash, closed-end funds were the dominant form of investment trust. While investment trust sponsors were primarily New York-based investment banks and brokerages, Boston quietly carved out a different role. Boston was the home of the Boston Trustee in the nineteenth century, a genre of private trustee money manager that arose to manage the dynastic fortunes of the great Boston industrial and trading families. The Boston Trustee was associated with progressive money management principles that gave priority to trustee investment discretion guided by prudence. Over time, this class of trustee developed a reputation for trust administration and prudent management of assets informed by investment expertise. In turn, the Boston Trustee concept developed beyond Boston into a new model termed "investment counsel," the forerunner of investment advisers who managed their client's money.

In any event, Boston's role as a center of wealth and wealth management expertise became the foundation for the subsequent creation of mutual funds. The first mutual funds were Boston inventions: Massachusetts Investors Trust and State Street Investors Trust, both formed in 1924, and Incorporated Investors forming a year later. Mutual funds introduced a twist to the traditional investment trust model by issuing shares that were redeemable in theory, if not quite entirely in practice, giving investors a sense of greater liquidity. The use of redeemable shares imposed a significant financial discipline on mutual funds. In order to meet redemption requests, Boston mutual funds favored investment strategies that were fairly conservative relative to their New York cousins and avoided reliance on pyramiding and leverage, a practice which ultimately crushed the New York investment trusts in the Crash. As a result, although mutual funds suffered in the Crash, they were built to be more resilient and managed to grow assets under management during the Depression after the initial precipitous losses.

In 1929, before the stock market Crash, closed-end investment trusts totaled 675 funds managing $7.1 billion, while mutual funds numbered only 19 and managed $140 million. Many closed-end funds closed during the Depression, and the relative pecking order between closed-end and mutual funds was to change in the not too distant future.

5.3 The Federal Scheme of Regulation

The Great Depression was a turning point in the investment management industry in the U.S. and resulted in the central scheme for regulating investment companies and investment advice. Stripped to its essentials, the story is very simple. The Depression wreaked havoc on the then relatively nascent U.S. investment trust industry. While all equity funds were adversely affected, the capital losses at leveraged closed-end funds ran almost 98% (by comparison, non-leveraged closed-end funds experienced losses of 52%). While a number of closed-end trusts suffered spectacular collapses and were forced to cease operations, the small group of mutual funds managed to stabilize their operations. Assets under management shrank in the immediate aftermath of the Crash from the combined effect of declining stock values and investor redemptions, but mutual funds on the whole were able to survive the immediate effects of the economic crisis and slowly rebuild their AUM. Their closed-end cousins suffered a massive decline in assets under management, and the number of investment trusts declined precipitously.

The fund industry was widely perceived as part of the financial shenanigans that accompanied the collapse of the American and global economy. In the first wave of New Deal legislative reforms, Congress focused on securities offerings in the Securities Act of 1933, and then, secondary securities trading and markets, public companies, and establishment of the SEC, all in the Securities Exchange Act of 1934. These two statutes represent the bulwarks of federal securities law regulation. In the Public Utility Holding Company Act of 1935, Congress directed the SEC to prepare a study of investment advisers, trusts and companies in order to establish a regulatory structure for them. The initial installment of the massive report known as the Investment Trust Study was not delivered until in 1939, two years after the statutorily-imposed deadline, and was not fully completed until early 1941.

However, the most significant steps were taken in 1940 when the SEC recommended legislation to provide a regulatory scheme for the investment management industry. The agency's proposals, after significant legislative revisions, eventually led to the passage of the Investment Advisers Act of 1940, providing general oversight of investment advisers, and the Investment Company Act of 1940, providing for a detailed and intrusive regulatory scheme for funds. The process by which the legislation took shape underscores several enduring aspects of the legislation.

First, by design, the Advisers Act and the Company Act were fundamentally different in their regulatory orientation. The Investment Trust Study concluded that investment advisers were not a source of abuse and, accordingly, the SEC recommended only a very modest regulatory scheme, a scheme which through amendment and rulemaking has grown. In contrast, the Investment Trust Study revealed significant abuses in the fund industry, primarily relating to closed-end funds. Accordingly, the SEC recommended a regime that called for massive regulatory oversight. This latter recommendation met with sharp resistance from the industry and produced a temporary legislative stalemate.

What followed next was an unusual resolution. The SEC engaged in intensive well-documented negotiations with the two investment trust groups, closed-end funds (represented by New York counsel) and open-end funds (represented by Boston counsel). Together, the SEC and industry hammered out a mutually agreeable piece of legislation that was submitted to Congress as a compromise and was enacted into law in August 1940.

The "compromise" aspect of the legislation is a second noteworthy feature of the legislation. While the original proposal was stripped of many objectionable features from the industry's perspective, the final legislation remained decidedly heavy handed in its approach toward regulation of investment companies. Does this mean that the industry agreed with all aspects of the legislation or that the SEC was satisfied with the final bill? While it is impossible to determine whether either side was completely satisfied, it is apparent that the result was something that the SEC believed substantially addressed its concerns and was at least workable from the industry's perspective. Indeed, the Company Act potentially affected the respective businesses of closed-end and open-end funds differently. At least one commentator has argued that the closed-end fund industry was motivated to go along to achieve favorable tax treatment that the open-end industry had achieved for its shareholders several years before (mutual funds were treated as pass-through vehicles for tax purposes, provided all gains realized were distributed to investors in the same year). As noted, closed-end funds had more assets under management than open-end companies before the legislation but, post-enactment, that gap disappeared within a few years. Additionally, in the ensuing years, the gap has become dramatically lopsided in favor of mutual funds (open-end companies). In hindsight, it would appear that mutual funds adapted well to the new regulatory scheme, and investors favored the mutual fund's redemption feature after the disastrous consequences produced by leveraged closed-end funds in the Depression.

A third aspect of the legislation is that, as originally conceived, advisers to registered investment companies were not required to register as investment advisers. The Investment Advisers Act, as originally enacted, exempted pure investment company advisers from registration, a provision which was later eliminated only in 1970. Today, the Advisers Act is unequivocal and reflects a complete reversal of position. All advisers to registered investment companies, no matter of what size, must register with the SEC pursuant to the Advisers Act. The result is more than one of idle curiosity. It effectively reordered the relationship between the two statutes. Whereas originally the Company Act was the undisputed legal guidepost for advisers' serving investment companies, and the Advisers Act was primarily directed at all other types of advisers, today, the two statutes perform overlapping roles with respect to advisers to investment companies.

Two Acts, Two Purposes: Comparing the Investment Company Act to the Investment Advisers Act

The Investment Trust Study is nicely summarized in the two Acts' Findings. They are a study in contrasting regulation which has persisted for decades. The Advisers Act relied on Findings of some generality to establish that interstate commerce was implicated (within the reach of Congress's Commerce Clause powers when the scope of the Commerce Clause powers was still being defined). In contrast, the Company Act supplemented its findings with a declaration of policy which is unmistakably proscriptive.

INVESTMENT ADVISERS ACT OF 1940

Section 201. Findings

Upon the basis of facts disclosed by the record and report of the Securities and Exchange Commission made pursuant to section 30 of the Public Utility Holding Company Act of 1935, and facts otherwise disclosed and ascertained, it is hereby found that investment advisers are of national concern, in that, among other things—

(1) their advice, counsel, publications, writings, analyses, and reports are furnished and distributed, and their contracts, subscription agreements, and other arrangements with clients are negotiated and performed, by the use of the mails and means and instrumentalities of interstate commerce;

(2) their advice, counsel, publications, writings, analyses, and reports customarily relate to the purchase and sale of securities traded on national securities exchanges and in interstate over-the-counter markets, securities issued by companies engaged in business in interstate commerce, and securities issued by national banks and member banks of the Federal Reserve System; and

(3) the foregoing transactions occur in such volume as substantially to affect interstate commerce, national securities exchanges, and other securities markets, the national banking system and the national economy.

INVESTMENT COMPANY ACT OF 1940

Section 1. Findings and declaration of policy.

...

(b) Upon the basis of facts disclosed by the record and reports of the Securities and Exchange Commission made pursuant to section 30 of the Public Utility Holding Company Act of 1935, and facts otherwise disclosed and ascertained, it is hereby declared that the national public interest and the interest of investors are adversely affected—

(1) when investors purchase, pay for, exchange, receive dividends upon, vote, refrain from voting, sell, or surrender securities issued by investment companies without adequate, accurate, and explicit information, fairly presented, concerning the character of such securities and the circumstances, policies, and financial responsibility of such companies and their management;

(2) when investment companies are organized, operated, managed, or their portfolio securities are selected, in the interest of directors, officers, investment advisers, depositors, or other affiliated persons thereof, in the interest of underwriters, brokers, or dealers, in the interest of special classes of their security holders, or in the interest of other investment companies or persons engaged in other lines of business, rather than in the interest of all classes of such companies' security holders;

(3) when investment companies issue securities containing inequitable or discriminatory provisions, or fail to protect the preferences and privileges of the holders of their outstanding securities;

(4) when the control of investment companies is unduly concentrated through pyramiding or inequitable methods of control, or is inequitably distributed, or when investment companies are managed by irresponsible persons;

(5) when investment companies, in keeping their accounts, in maintaining reserves, and in computing their earnings and the asset value of their outstanding securities, employ unsound or misleading methods, or are not subjected to adequate independent scrutiny;

(6) when investment companies are reorganized, become inactive, or change the character of their business, or when the control or management thereof is transferred, without the consent of their security holders;

(7) when investment companies by excessive borrowing and the issuance of excessive amounts of senior securities increase unduly the speculative character of their junior securities; or

(8) when investment companies operate without adequate assets or reserves.

It is hereby declared that the policy and purposes of this title, in accordance with which the provisions of this title shall be interpreted, are to mitigate and, so far as is feasible, to eliminate the conditions enumerated in this section which adversely affect the national public interest and the interest of investors.

[***]

Consider the differences between the two Acts' legislative findings. Based on the excerpts above, what type of statute and regulation would follow from each piece of legislation?

5.4 Fund Industry History—Post-Regulation

There is another aspect to the legislation worth pausing over. In 1940, the world of investment management looked very different than it does today. It was clearly a small niche financial services industry in which assets under management at the end of the Depression were less than before the Crash. In 1940, the investment management industry might well have been regarded as a sleepy backwater. However, the events that transpired over the next 75 years transformed this industry into a financial juggernaut. These changes have been driven by two long-term trends. First, financial products involving registered funds and types of funds within the overall category have proliferated. Second, investable savings, including investable savings in the hands of the public, have increased tremendously. Nowhere has this been more evident than in the area of retirement assets.

5.4.1 The Trend Toward Proliferation of Fund Choices

When the Company Act was enacted, the total number of mutual funds barely exceeded 100, if that. Today there are just under 10,000 mutual funds. Assets under management have increased from barely more than a billion to nearly $20 trillion, including ETFs. These changing metrics, of course, are owing to some factors that are unrelated to the investment management industry, things like economic growth of the U.S. economy, inflation, and population growth. However, there is little doubt that the fund industry has dramatically broadened the array of fund products to take advantage of increased investment savings.

Initially, mutual funds were equity focused and exclusively actively managed portfolios. The first balanced fund (a fund that invests in both in equity and fixed income securities) was launched immediately before the Stock Market Crash in October 1929. That fund is now known as the Vanguard Wellington Fund, and its introduction of a portfolio strategy which balanced between debt and equity (instead of a pure equity fund) turned out to be well-timed innovation. The first bond mutual funds were formed in 1932.

By the early 1950s, a few multi-fund families had appeared. By the 1960s, multi-fund families were beginning to be referred to as "mutual fund complexes," and today are commonly referred to as "fund families." The expansion of fund groups by adding more types of funds may appear logical or inevitable, but the development came relatively late to the fund industry and certainly was not a starting premise. Today, large fund groups predominate in assets under management among mutual funds and ETFs—well over 95%—and the stand-alone fund is the exception rather than the rule.

Over the years, a clear pattern has emerged in the fund industry in which the introduction of new types of funds closely followed market trends. In the 1960s, for example, stock markets soared in what has been termed the Go-Go era, and growth stock funds dominated the investment landscape. When the markets slumped in the 1970s, bond funds gathered assets and increased in number.

In addition, the 1970s saw the development of a wholly new type of fund, the money market mutual fund or simply "money market fund." The hallmark of money market funds was maintenance of a stable $1 per share NAV (which allowed investments in funds loosely to resemble deposits in a bank account), rather than fund share prices with fluctuating NAVs like equity and other bond funds. Arising simultaneously from sponsors on the East and West Coasts, money market funds used specialized accounting techniques to achieve the stable $1 NAV with the SEC's approval in the form initially of exemptive relief. In the very high interest rate environment that prevailed in the late 1970s and early 1980s, AUM for money market funds blossomed because, from the public's perspective, they loosely appeared to function like bank accounts, but offered very high interest rates on deposits. As a result, Capital Preservation Fund, the first retail money fund, grew from $50 million AUM in early 1978 to over $3 billion in 1980, meteoric growth for that era.

The primary regulatory challenge posed by money market funds is that in order to maintain stable $1 per share valuation, money market funds used specialized valuation methods in calculating fund share price which, as noted, required SEC exemptive relief. To expedite money market fund development and operation, the SEC adopted Rule 2a-7 in 1983, which standardized specialized pricing procedures in the industry and imposed significant investment restrictions on funds that sought to avail themselves of these pricing procedures. Since then, the rule has been amended several times but remains the regulatory foundation for money market funds and helped popularize them. The popularity of money market funds did not merely invigorate the entire mutual fund industry at a time when asset growth was lagging, it critically exposed a whole class of investors, especially retail investors, to mutual funds overall.

As noted, at its inception, the investment trust fund industry was built on single, actively-managed equity funds. In other words, the fund industry for fifty years was committed to an investment philosophy built around active management, where managers actively research and select investments. This is in contrast to passive or indexed investing, where portfolios are built around an index of securities or other investments. Active management was, and still is, the predominant approach to asset and fund management, but that is changing. In the 1970s, pension funds and Wells Fargo Bank began using index strategies with success. In addition, in the mid-1970s, Vanguard Funds began offering a retail index fund based on the S&P 500 (note: there was only a single index fund as of 1980!). Indexing grew slowly until the 2000s when it started to experience explosive growth. Today almost a third of assets under management in the fund industry are index-based with the largest such fund at about $300 billion—Vanguard's S&P 500 index fund.

The growth and popularity of indexing has been aided, largely, by the development of exchange traded funds ("ETFs") in the early 1990s. Like money market funds, ETFs were the result of extensive regulatory relief permitting a hybrid of features for UITs or mutual funds to trade on stock exchanges in lieu of having retail investor redemption features. While ETFs are discussed in depth in Chapter 18, it is important to note that the growth has been explosive. From just $1 billion ETF AUM in 1993, ETF assets hit $100 billion in 2002, $1 trillion in 2011 and now total roughly $3 trillion. ETFs at this juncture are heavily weighted toward passive index strategies. The number of such strategies (and corresponding indexes) has multiplied greatly. Today it is not uncommon to talk about "smart beta" strategies which may sound more active, but they actually involve the implementation of sophisticated passive rule-based index strategies. Actively managed ETFs are a new and comparatively unexplored frontier that requires removal of certain regulatory obstacles in order to make such ETFs feasible on a larger scale.

One final development should be mentioned, namely the emergence of private unregistered funds such as hedge funds. In 1949, the fund industry largely conformed to the model of funds registered under the Company Act. Alfred Winslow Jones, an editor of Fortune magazine, established what is viewed as the first hedge fund—a partnership which was privately offered to wealthy individuals and was able to engage in strategies such as short selling and use of leverage. Funds configured in this fashion cannot operate within the confines of the Company Act, but are allowed to operate outside the Company Act provided a fund fits within one of the exemptions to the statute's definition of an investment company. Withdrawal rights of investors in such funds is governed by contract, and their advisers are permitted to, and invariably do, charge performance fees. The ability to sidestep the registered fund space enables a variety of private funds (discussed in Chapter 9), including hedge funds, private equity funds, and venture capital funds, to engage in less regulated forms of money management. In order to avoid registration requirements and the regulatory requirements of the Company Act, these funds are not offered publicly, but rather privately, to institutional investors and wealthy individuals. Today, private equity and hedge funds manage roughly $3 trillion in assets. Venture capital funds also manage significant amounts of capital, providing large amounts of money to help young and emerging companies grow.

5.4.2 The Trend Toward Retailization of Funds

The proliferation of new funds has closely matched the interests of an increasingly broad class of investors willing to invest in such products. Experts might debate the merits of which came first in this "chicken or egg" situation, but several factors have undoubtedly contributed to the increasing "retailization" of funds. One contributing factor is a case of unintended consequences. Driven by the need to protect workers' retirement savings, Congress implemented the Employee Retirement Income Security Act in 1974 ("ERISA"). ERISA led directly to the creation of millions of self-directed and advised individual retirement savings accounts which may be invested in mutual funds and other RICs. These include individual retirement accounts ("IRAs"), 401k Plans (employer sponsored retirement investment/savings plans for employee contributions which may be self-directed), and 403b Plans (similar plans for teachers, professors and employees of other non-profit institutions). ERISA plan savings and investments developed into a major AUM source for investment managers and investment companies. At the end of 2014, according to ICI statistics, over $7 trillion of IRA, 401k and 403b plan assets were invested in mutual funds and ETFs. That amounts to about 40% of fund industry AUM.

Funds are also popular with independent financial planners and independent registered advisers whose numbers swelled, in no small measure, because after enactment of ERISA, retirees were (and still are) increasingly faced with managing their own retirement savings instead of relying on a pension plan. Financial advisers brought experience and financial sophistication to the problem of constructing diversified fund portfolios for their clients, which meant a willingness to sift through many fund choices.

In addition, in the mid-1980s, discount brokerage platforms hit upon the idea of fund supermarkets, where suddenly investors had access to hundreds of fund choices, effectively reducing the barriers to access for investors. Familiarity with fund platforms went hand in hand with educating the public about funds and more recently ETFs. Fund supermarkets have proven especially popular in the internet age, where self-directed investors can easily filter through fund choices and move money around with the click of a mouse. Indeed another phenomenon has been the internet giving average investors much greater access to information about investing in funds. Indeed, a recent internet phenomenon has been the advent of robo-advisers, electronic advisory services for individuals based on quantitative algorithms. Robo-advisers can offer customers customized financial planning and fund recommendations based on individual information provided by customers. Funds are financial products ideally suited for robo-advisers, because not only do they offer diversification, but entail predictable profiles that can be reduced to a collection of standardized metrics. In short, the push towards greater investor autonomy and technology that caters to this autonomy has resulted in a golden age for fund investing.

5.4.3 Industry Structure and Competition in an Era of Investor Choice

For most of its existence, the fund industry has been remarkably free of major scandals or meltdowns. This changed in 2003 with revelations regarding late trading and market timing by a significant segment of the industry in violation of pricing and/or disclosure requirements (discussed in Chapter 16). In response to this, compliance standards in the investment management area were significantly enhanced, triggering tightened policies and procedures across the industry. Indeed, today, it would be only a slight exaggeration to say that advisers, funds, and regulators are preoccupied with compliance policies and procedures (a topic that will be discussed in Chapter 15). In response to the Financial Crisis of 2008, funds were surprisingly unaffected from a regulatory perspective, with one or two notable exceptions. Money market funds were subject to extreme stress that nearly led to a meltdown which was averted through government intervention. This event led to a rethinking of money market fund requirements. In addition, disclosure and pricing problems arose with respect to certain funds which had represented to investors that portfolio risk was relatively low, when in fact, as the Crisis revealed, exposure to risk was fairly high.

The picture that emerges is an industry that manages more assets than ever before and that has shown surprising resilience and adaptability to changing economic conditions. Additionally, a few unmistakable patterns have emerged. Investors have embraced passive investment management strategies so that passive strategies are a significant, competitive counterweight to active investment strategies. As a result, costs to investors continue to drop. Industry consolidation is more pronounced in that larger fund firms control a large and increasing percentage of assets under management in the registered space, and the largest registered fund complexes continue to attract the lion's share of new investment cash flows. Firms such as Vanguard and Blackrock have been dominating the new investment flows in the 2000s. Notwithstanding the unavoidable shadow cast by the behemoths, there is a surprising degree

Table 5A — Snapshot of fund assets (number of funds) as of the end of the year

ASSETS UNDER MANAGEMENT (# OF FUNDS) BY YEAR					
	Mutual Funds	Closed-End Funds	ETFs	Money Market Funds	Hedge Funds
1980	$135 billion (564)	+	Did not exist	$76 billion (106)	+
1985	$495 billion (1,528)	+	Did not exist	$244 billion (460)	+
1990	$1,065 billion (3,079)	$59 billion (333)	Did not exist	$489 billion (741)	+
1995	$2,811 billion (5,725)	$143 billion (499)	$1 billion (2)	$753 billion (997)	+
2000	$6,965 billion (8,155)	$143 billion (481)	$66 billion (80)	$1,845 billion (1,039)	$237 billion +
2005	$8,891 billion (7,977)	$276 billion (634)	$301 billion (204)	$2,026 billion (870)	$1,361 billion +
2010	$11,834 billion (7,556)	$238 billion (624)	$992 billion (923)	2,803 billion (652)	$1,694 billion +
2015	$15,650 billion (8,115)	$261 billion (558)	$2,101 billion (1,595)	$2,755 billion (481)	$2,797 billion (8,752)
2017	$18,746 billion (7956)	$275 billion (530)	$3,401 billion (1,831)	$2,847 billion (382)	$3,538 billion (9,007)

+ Consistent, reliable or accurate data not available
Source: Investment Company Institute (all data except hedge fund data); BarclayHedge (hedge fund AUM data); SEC Private Fund Statistics, various dates (hedge fund number of funds data on number of hedge funds reported to SEC)

of access for new entrants as barriers to entry are fairly low. Table 5A illustrates some of these long-term trends clearly.

5.5 The Changing Face of Regulation and Regulatory Considerations

With this history, it is possible to turn to some key structural features that continue to guide the evolution of regulatory policy in the investment management industry. Just as the face of the business evolved over the past 75 years, so too has regulation. Three guideposts are relevant: legislative change, the SEC, and other statutory mandates that indirectly affect the investment management industry.

5.5.1 Legislative Changes

The Investment Company Act and Investment Advisers Act have proven remarkably stable over the last 75 years, but that does not mean that they have remained unchanged. It would not be useful to highlight every statutory change, however, several are worth noting.

The most significant amendments to the Company Act came about in 1970 as it became clear that the fund model envisioned in 1940 did not exactly correspond to fund families in a more modern era. The changes were preceded by two important studies that focused exclusively on the fund industry and were also addressed in the SEC's massive 1963 Report of the Special Study of Securities Markets. The first industry specific study was commissioned by the SEC and prepared by the University of Pennsylvania's Wharton School of Finance. This study known as the Wharton Study Report was completed in 1962 and identified major areas of reform especially associated with the costs to investors of investment company investments. The second report, the Public Policy Implications of Investment Company Growth completed in 1966, built upon the Wharton Report Study and considered, more broadly, a number of features with the benefit of industry input relating to sales costs, advisory fees, and other issues affecting the investment fund industry.

The SEC also prepared extensive legislative recommendations, which in a revised form took several years to become law as the Investment Company Amendments Act of 1970, more commonly known as the "1970 Amendments." The 1970 Amendments were significant in their scope. First, the Amendments imposed a federal fiduciary standard on funds and their advisers with respect to advisory fees paid to advisers. As a result, under the new Section 36(b) of the Company Act, the investors could assert claims in federal court for relief from excessive fees. Second, Section 15 of the Company Act was amended to assign a duty to fund directors, namely to request and evaluate information reasonably necessary to consider the approval of the investment advisory agreement between a fund and its adviser. This laid the foundation for the 15(c) process discussed in Chapter 12. Third, Congress significantly broadened the definition of interested persons in hopes of increasing the independence of fund boards (discussed in Chapter 11). Fourth, all investment advisers to investment companies were required to register with the SEC. Fifth, sales loads and charges were subjected to potential regulation by a self-regulatory authority, now called FINRA (Financial Industry National Regulatory Authority) (discussed in Chapter 17). Sixth, Congress authorized the SEC to adopt rules to regulate personal trading by affiliated fund personnel in securities held or to be acquired by the fund (discussed in Chapter 15). Finally, the 1970 Amendments tightened the anti-pyramiding provisions of the Company Act, i.e., provisions designed to minimize one fund investing in another.

There are also other important amendments, such as the liberalization in 1996 of exemptions from the definition of investment company that greatly facilitated hedge fund formation and the simultaneous bifurcation of the registration of investment advisers into either SEC-registered advisers or state-registered advisers. The recent Dodd Frank Act in 2010 may represent the most significant amendments to the Advisers Act. Those amendments imposed registration and reporting requirements on broad classes of private funds and their advisers, giving the SEC significant authority to regulate the conduct of such advisers.

5.5.2 The Role of the SEC and Regulatory Methods under the Company Act and the Advisers Act

While the statutory framework of the two investment acts is of paramount importance, Congress endowed the SEC with significant power in administering the statutes. This includes extensive rulemaking powers and exemptive authority. It is perhaps useful to summarize briefly the panoply of legal sources that guide application of statutes and regulations in connection with investment management matters. In addition to the statutes themselves, the SEC and courts provide diverse sources of authority in understanding the application of the regulatory scheme. These sources are summarized below and provide a brief introduction to the legal materials encountered in the text.

SEC rulemaking. The Advisers and Company Acts delegate significant rulemaking authority to the SEC. There are circumstances where the agency relies on specific grants of rulemaking authority and other instances where the SEC exercises general rulemaking power. In accordance with the Administrative Procedures Act, SEC rulemaking typically involves notice and commentary periods, meaning the agency will issue a proposing release explaining a proposed rulemaking and soliciting comments. If a rule is adopted, the agency will issue an adopting release that explains its final rationale. These releases are useful not only in describing agency action but also in providing an interpretive gloss for its rules.

SEC exemptive authority (both rule and order). As noted, the Company Act is highly proscriptive, and as a result, there are some provisions that prohibit conduct absent receipt of an order granting exemptive relief from the provision. The SEC has general exemptive authority pursuant to Section 6(c) of the Company Act to promulgate regulations exempting classes of persons or transactions from Company Act requirements where it makes required public interest findings. This exemptive authority gives the SEC considerable discretion in tailoring the application of various statutory provisions. An exemption for a person as opposed to a regulation will result in the issuance of an order if granted. Prior to granting an exemptive order, the SEC invariably publishes a notice of application for an exemption, and the notice will give a preliminary indication of the agency's view but will solicit public comment. Typically, an applicant, if notified of the SEC's intent to deny the application, will withdraw the application prior to the issuance of notice. The casebook offers a few examples of exemptive orders.

Interpretive releases. On occasion, the SEC will issue interpretive guidance regarding statutory or regulatory provisions. As the agency charged with administering the two Acts and promulgating rules, the SEC is entitled to differing degrees of administrative deference, including dispositive deference, with respect to its interpretations.

Staff no-action letters. The SEC has well-developed administrative practices regarding the issuance of so-called SEC staff "no-action letters." A no action letter assures the recipient that the agency will not bring any enforcement action against the recipient in acting in reliance of the staff's no action assurance, provided that the recipient acts in accordance with the letter's conditions. The letter's status is informal and, unless stated otherwise, can only be relied upon by the recipient who sought the no-action letter, but it is not uncommon for others to seek similar relief if their situation is indistinguishable from the original recipient. The staff remains free at any time to withdraw the letter upon notice to the recipient. Such letters tend to be fact-specific, but nevertheless provide an informal understanding of the staff's interpretive views on particular practices. However, the nature of the letters generally indicates some tentativeness in the staff's positions. The tentativeness may arise because the staff is unsure of the full implications of its interpretive position, because it is reluctant to broadly grant relief to a class of persons or transactions, or because the position cannot be squared with the literal language of a statute or rule as written. This casebook offers a few examples of no-action letters, which are a common form of regulatory relief sought by businesses.

Enforcement, administrative actions, and agency adjudicative decisions. The SEC administrative authority extends to enforcement of the federal statutes and rules that it is charged with administering. In short, the SEC brings a range of civil and administrative actions to sanction and remedy violations of statute and rule. Civil actions are, of course, litigated in federal court, and meaningful interpretations of the law will be in the hands of the judiciary. Unlike civil actions, administrative proceedings remain largely within the agency's domain. Administrative actions are tried before administrative judges, and determinations are subject to *de novo* review before the full Commission. The Commission's adjudicative decisions are appealable to a U.S. Court of Appeals. However, the vast majority of administrative proceedings are settled before any administrative hearing and without the involvement of an administrative law judge. Nevertheless, in such matters, the agency will issue a final order and release summarizing its findings of fact and imposing sanctions. These administrative releases are highly instructive to practitioners. The findings of the release, reflecting largely the SEC's version of the facts, are set forth with a brief legal analysis that supports the order's legal conclusion. While some practitioners may question any particular determination, such orders provide unequivocal expressions of the SEC's views with particular factual scenarios. This casebook uses these orders as a major instructional tool not only to illustrate the SEC's legal positions, but also to illustrate potentially problematic business practices that exist in the investment management industry.

Judicial decisions. Courts have a role in overseeing rights and remedies under the Advisers and Company Acts. While each Act affords only limited private rights of action, the express causes of action, coupled with those under other federal securities law statutes, have resulted in decisions that shed light on the obligations of funds and their advisers. In addition, as noted, the SEC may commence proceedings in federal court to redress securities law violations. Final agency action, including rulemakings, may generally be challenged directly in a federal appellate court in a review proceeding, and other forms of administrative challenges can be brought in federal courts pursuant to the Administrative Procedures Act.

FINRA rules. FINRA is a self-regulatory association constituting the sole association of national securities dealers. All broker-dealers, with minor exceptions, must belong to FINRA, and their associated persons must have FINRA licenses. While broker-dealers may appear unrelated to investment advisers or investment companies, in fact there is significant overlap in that some registered investment advisers are also broker-dealers. More importantly, funds are sold through broker-dealers which are under the supervision of FINRA. As a result, FINRA rules have significant effect on the marketing, sale, and distribution of investment funds. Although self-regulatory organizations like FINRA rely on their members firms to formulate rules and adhere to oversight processes, FINRA rulemaking and oversights actions are subject to review by the SEC.

5.5.3 Other Relevant Regulatory Regimes

The Investment Company Act and the Investment Advisers Act are the principal federal securities law statutes with respect to investment companies and investment advisers. That is not to say that other securities law and additional statutes are not relevant. The activities of investment companies and advisers intersect with other broad statutory mandates involving retirement security and taxation, not to mention related securities law statutes that touch both directly and indirectly on the activities of investment companies and advisers. The table below provides an overview of the key laws and regulators affecting money managers and investment companies that are helpful in keeping the specific issues addressed in this casebook in a broader context of relevant legal requirements.

PRINCIPAL LAWS GOVERNING ADVISERS AND INVESTMENT COMPANIES	
Investment Company Act of 1940 ("Company Act," "1940 Act," or "'40 Act")	Addresses the structure, registration, and operations of publicly offered investment companies. The 1940 Act is a detailed and proscriptive act in contrast to the original Advisers Act. The 1940 Act governs investment company disclosure requirements and registration; capital structures and requirements; safekeeping and custody of fund assets; compliance duties; investment activities; conflicts of interest, including transactions with affiliated parties such as a fund's adviser; and governance by a board of directors or trustees.
Investment Advisers Act of 1940 ("Advisers Act")	Regulates investment advisers. Requires large advisers and those advising regulated investment companies to register with the SEC. Originally designed as a "census" regulation to collect basic information on advisers, the Advisers Act has evolved to include a variety of substantive provisions, including recordkeeping, compliance, custody, conflicts of interest, and reporting requirements and responsibilities.
Securities Act of 1933 ("Securities Act," "1933 Act," or "'33 Act")	Addresses the registration of publicly offered securities, including investment company shares. Requires registration of offerings and regulates the public offering process. The 1933 Act's extensive disclosure requirements apply to investment companies, but the application of its provisions is modified regarding dissemination of prospectuses and related documents to investors.
Securities Exchange Act of 1934 ("Exchange Act," "1934 Act," or "'34 Act")	Established the SEC. Governs broker-dealers, which includes investment company securities distributors, requiring them to be registered with the SEC. Regulates the purchase, sale or trading of securities on securities exchanges or otherwise. Governs the activities and registration requirements of securities exchanges, and authorizes the SEC to permit the establishment of self-regulatory authorities such as FINRA to assist in supervising broker-dealers.
Internal Revenue Code ("IRC")	Is the statutory codification of federal tax law. It has provisions specifically relevant to investment companies in Subchapter M. This section of the IRC became law in the Revenue Act of 1936 and exempts most investment income and capital gains from corporate taxation of properly qualified investment companies. This permits mutual funds and, subsequently, closed-end investment companies to pass through dividends, interest and other income to investors without taxation at the fund level provided that they satisfy conditions governing distribution of gains and incomes annually.
Employee Retirement Income Security Act of 1974 ("ERISA")	Regulates pension funds and retirement savings accounts. The Department of Labor ("DOL") is the primary regulator with respect to ERISA.
State Securities Regulations	Particularly for investment advisers, state securities regulations provide oversight and regulatory requirements for state compliance. State regulation is pre-empted substantively for large advisers and registered investment companies.

Part II

Regulation of Investment Advisers and Private Funds

Chapter 6

Investment Adviser Act Status Issues: Investment Advisers Defined and Their Registration Obligations

Key Ideas: The Investment Advisers Act can be divided broadly into two major subjects: status issues and substantive obligations. This chapter addresses the two primary status issues: (i) who is an investment adviser for purposes of the Advisers Act; and (ii) registration of advisers (i.e., which advisers must register and with whom, i.e., whether with state authorities or the SEC, the relevant federal agency). Subsequent chapters address key substantive obligations of investment advisers. Who is an investment adviser under the statute is primarily informed by the two-part statutory definition found in Advisers Act Section 202(a)(11). The first part of the definition contains two broadly inclusive clauses which when parsed give rise to three elements: (1) rendering advice about securities; (2) being in the business of advising; and (3) receipt of compensation for advisory services rendered. The second part of the definition enumerates eight exclusions for persons that might otherwise satisfy the definition's inclusive forepart, but which are statutorily excluded for a variety of policy reasons. The other major status issue—which investment advisers must register and with whom—involves the Adviser Act's intricate registration provisions which combine enumerated federal statutory exclusions and a bifurcated federal and state registration scheme. Registration is governed by two different statutory provisions—Advisers Act Section 203 and Section 203A—and application of these provisions results in a four-tiered scheme: (i) advisers who must register with the SEC; (ii) advisers who are permitted to register with the SEC; (iii) advisers prohibited from registering with the SEC in view of an adequate available state registration scheme; and (iv) advisers exempt from registration regardless of registration status under applicable state law provisions.

Chapter Contents

6.1 Introduction

The conduct of investment advisers is potentially subject to regulatory requirements under several federal securities statutes, as well as additional state and federal law provisions. The Investment Advisers Act and the rules thereunder are the source of a comprehensive federal regulatory scheme with respect to investment adviser activity. This statute operates in tandem with the Investment Company Act in regulating the activities of registered investment company advisers. However, unlike the Company Act, the Advisers Act applies to the full spectrum of investment advisers—those that perform purely advisory functions as well as a wide array of money managers—and not merely to investment advisers of registered investment companies.

The Advisers Act differs from the Company Act in two major respects. As noted above, the former focuses solely on investment advisers rather than investment companies. Because the investment adviser relationship is critical to understanding the structure and management of investment companies, the Advisers Act has clear application to management of investment companies, but extends to a wider range of advisory activities and relationships. Second, a simple comparison of the Advisers Act and the Company Act reveals that the former entails a more limited and less intrusive regulatory scheme. The more limited regulatory focus of the Advisers Act stems from its historical foundation in 1940. The SEC found widespread abuses in the Depression era investment trust industry, but only negligible problems in the investment adviser area. However, notwithstanding this starting point, the scope of regulation under the Advisers Act has grown dramatically in the last 50 years as the number and types of investment advisers has grown.

The Advisers Act can be thought of as creating two distinct categories of regulatory issues: status issues and substantive issues affecting adviser conduct and activities. The status issues can be divided into two central considerations: (i) who is an investment adviser?, a question that turns on the statutory definition of an investment adviser; and (ii) which advisers are required (and/or permitted) to register in the federal scheme (i.e., who are SEC registered advisers)? These two status topics are addressed in this chapter. The definition is important in describing not only who is an investment adviser, but also in providing explicit exclusions from the definition's very broad language. These twin concerns of breadth reveal policy tensions between over- and under-inclusiveness in the definition. Once a market actor's status as an investment adviser is resolved, there remains the separate issue of whether the adviser should be required to register with the SEC. Not all investment advisers are subject to registration requirements, although generally larger institutional advisers are, as well as advisers with multi-state operations. The registration scheme has become increasingly complex in recent years and involves reconciling general registration requirements and exclusions with a bifurcated federal/state registration scheme that relegates smaller and more localized advisers to the state system. The registration scheme has significant consequences, because it establishes a divide between advisers who are subject to mere antifraud regulation (registered and unregistered advisers) from those which are subject to a full array of affirmative reporting and compliance obligations (registered advisers only). Even though it would seem federal regulation involves a greater regulatory burden, many advisers seek federal registration as a form of reputational validation and centralized, rather than fragmented, oversight.

The other issues addressed by the Advisers Act relate to the conduct and activities of investment advisers. These issues will be covered in the next chapter (Chapter 7). There are of course other requirements affecting adviser conduct and activities relating to the terms of fees and agreements (dealt with in Section 205), books and records and disclosure (addressed in Section 204), and custody of client assets. Selected topics of this sort are addressed in Chapter 8.

6.2 Definition of Investment Adviser and Relevant Exclusions

As noted above, the statutory definition of investment advisor can be divided into two parts: (i) the inclusionary clauses found in the forepart of the statutory definition found in Adviser Act Section 202(a)(11); and (ii) the definition's enumerated exclusions. The inclusionary language is addressed first.

6.2.1 The Definition's Inclusive Language and Its Three Elements

Statement of Staff Interpretive Position on the Applicability of the Investment Advisers Act to Financial Planners, Pension Consultants, and Other Persons Who Provide Investment Advisory Services as a Component of Other Financial Services

Investment Advisers Act Release No. 1092 (Oct 16, 1987)

[**Textbook Note:** *This SEC Staff Interpretation (approved somewhat uncharacteristically by a vote of the full Commission) provides a definitive interpretation of the term "investment adviser" found in Section 202(a)(11) of the Advisers Act and identifies three key elements in the definition's application. The* *interpretive position clarifies classification of less conventional types of advisory activities such as financial planners and pension consultants. The staff position also provides insight into the "solely incidental" language underlying some of the definition's exclusions which will be discussed in the next subsection.*]

[***] I. Background

Financial planning typically involves providing a variety of services, principally advisory in nature, to individuals or families regarding the management of their financial resources based upon an analysis of individual client needs. Generally, financial planning services involve preparing a financial program for a client based on the client's financial circumstances and objectives. This information normally would cover present and anticipated assets and liabilities, including insurance, savings, investments, and anticipated retirement or other employee benefits. The program developed for the client usually includes general recommendations for a course of activity, or specific actions, to be taken by the client. For example, recommendations may be made that the client obtain insurance or revise existing coverage, establish an individual retirement account, increase or decrease funds held in savings accounts, or invest funds in securities. A financial planner may develop tax or estate plans for clients or refer clients to an accountant or attorney for these services.

The provider of such financial planning services in most cases assists the client in implementing the recommended program by, among other things, making specific recommendations to carry out the general recommendations of the program, or be selling the client insurance products, securities, or other investments. The financial planner may also review the client's program periodically and recommend revisions. Persons providing such financial planning services use various compensation arrangements. Some financial planners charge clients an overall fee for developing an individual client program while others charge clients an hourly fee. In some instances financial planners are compensated, in whole or in part, by commissions on the sale to the client of insurance products, interests in real estate, securities (such as common stocks, bonds, limited partnership interests, and mutual funds), or other investments.

A second common form of service relating to financial matters is provided by "pension consultants" who typically offer, in addition to administrative services, a variety of advisory services to employee benefit plans and their fiduciaries based upon an analysis of the needs of the plan. These advisory services may include advice as to the types of funding media available to provide plan benefits, general recommendations as to what portion of plan assets should be invested in various investment media, including securities, and, in some cases, recommendations regarding investment in specific securities or other investments. Pension consultants may also assist plan fiduciaries in determining plan investment objectives and policies and in designing funding media for the plan. They may also provide general or specific advice to plan fiduciaries [under the Employee Retirement Income Security Act of 1974 or "ERISA"] as to the selection or retention of persons to manage the assets of the plan. Persons providing these services to plans are customarily compensated for their services through fees paid by the plan, its sponsor, or other persons; by means of sales commissions on the sale of insurance products or investments to the plan; or through a combination of fees and commissions.

Another form of financial advisory service is that provided by persons offering a variety of financially related services to entertainers or athletes based upon the needs of the individual client. Such persons, who often use the designation "sports representative" or "entertainment representative," offer a number of services to clients, including the negotiation of employment contracts and development of promotional opportunities for the client, as well as advisory services related to investments, tax planning, or budget and money management. Some persons providing these services to clients may assume discretion over all or a portion of a client's funds by collecting income, paying bills, and making investments for the client. Sports or entertainment representatives are customarily compensated for their services primarily through fees charged for negotiation of employment contracts but may also receive compensation in the form of fixed charges or hourly fees for other services provided, including investment advisory services.

There are other persons who, while not falling precisely into one of the foregoing categories, provide financial advisory services. As discussed below, financial planners, pension consultants, sports or entertainment representatives or other persons providing financial advisory services, may be investment advisers within the meaning of the Advisers Act, state adviser laws, or both.

II. Status as an Investment Adviser

A. Definition of Investment Adviser

Section 202(a)(11) of the Advisers Act defines the term "Investment adviser" to mean:

> ... any person who, for compensation, engages in the business of advising others, either directly or through publications or writings, as to the value of securities or as to the advisability of investing in, purchasing, or selling securities, or who, for compensation and as part of a regular business, issues or promulgates analyses or reports concerning securities....

Whether a person providing financially related services of the type discussed in this release is an investment adviser within the meaning of the Advisers Act depends upon all the relevant facts and circumstances. As a general matter, if the activities of any person providing integrated advisory services satisfy the elements of the definition, the person would be an investment adviser within the meaning of the Advisers Act, unless entitled to rely on one of the exclusions from the definition of investment adviser in clauses (A) to [(H)] of section 202(a)(11). A determination as to whether a person providing financial planning, pension consulting, or other integrated advisory services is an investment adviser will depend upon whether such person: (1) Provides advice, or issues reports or analyses, regarding securities; (2) is in the business of providing such services; and (3) provides such services for compensation. These three elements are discussed below.

1. Advice or Analyses Concerning Securities

It would seem apparent that a person who gives advice or makes recommendations or issues reports or analyses with respect to specific securities is an investment adviser under section 202(a)(11), assuming the other elements of the definition of investment adviser are met, i.e., that such services are performed as a part of a business and for compensation. However, it has been asked on a number of occasions whether advice, recommendations, or reports that do not pertain to specific securities satisfy this element of the definition. The staff believes that a person who provides advice, or issues or promulgates reports or analyses, which concern securities, but which do not relate to specific securities, generally is an investment adviser under section 202(a)(11), assuming the services are performed as part of a business[1] and for compensation. The staff has interpreted the definition of investment adviser to include persons who advise clients concerning the relative advantages and disadvantages of investing in securities in general as compared to other investments. A person who, in the course of developing a financial program for a client, advises a client as to the desirability of investing in, purchasing or selling securities, as opposed to, or in relation to, any non-securities investment or financial vehicle would also be "advising" others within the meaning of section 202(a)(11). Similarly, a person who advises employee benefit plans on funding plan benefits by investing in, purchasing, or selling securities, as opposed to, or in addition to, insurance products, real estate not involving securities, or other funding media, would be "advising" others within the meaning of section 202(a)(11). A person providing advice to a client as to the selection or retention of an investment manager or managers also, under certain circumstances, would be deemed to be "advising" others within the meaning of section 202(a)(11).[6]

---

1. In this regard, as discussed in detail below, it is the staff's view that a person who gives advice or prepares analyses concerning securities generally may, nevertheless, not be "in the business" of doing so and, therefore, will not be considered an "investment adviser" as that term is used in section 202(a)(11).

6. *See, e. g., FPC Securities Corp.* (pub. avail. Dec. 1, 1974) (program to assist client in selection and retention of investment manager by, among other things, recommending investment managers to clients, monitoring and evaluating the performance of a client's investment manager, and advising client as to the retention of such manager); *William Bye Co.* (pub. avail. Apr. 26, 1973) (program involving recommendations to client as to selection and retention of investment manager based upon client's investment objectives and periodic monitoring and evaluation of investment manager's performance). On occasion in the past the staff has taken no-action positions with respect to certain situations involving persons providing advice to clients as to the selection or retention of investment managers. *See, e. g., Sebastian Associates, Ltd.*, (pub. avail. Aug. 7, 1975) (provision of assistance to clients in obtaining and coordinating the services of various professionals such as tax attorneys and investment advisers, including referring clients to such professionals, in connection with business as agent for clients with respect to negotiation of employment and promotional contracts); *Hudson Valley Planning Inc.* (pub. avail. Feb. 25, 1978) (provision of names of several investment managers to client upon request, without recommendation, in connection with business of providing administrative services to employee benefit plans).

2. The "Business" Standard

Under section 202(a)(11), an investment adviser is one who, for compensation, (1) engages in the business of advising others as to the value of securities or as to the advisability of investing in, purchasing, or selling securities, or, alternatively, (2) issues or promulgates reports or analyses concerning securities as part of a regular business. Each of these two alternatives in the statutory definition of investment adviser contains a business test—one involves "engaging in the business" of advising others while the other involves issuing reports about securities as "part of a regular business." While the "business" standards established under section 202(a)(11) are phrased somewhat differently, it is the staff's opinion that they should be interpreted in the same manner. In both cases, the determination to be made is whether the degree of the person's advisory activities constitutes being "in the business" of an investment adviser. The giving of advice need not constitute the principal business activity or any particular portion of the business activities of a person in order for the person to be an investment adviser under section 202(a)(11). The giving of advice need only be done on such a basis that it constitutes a business activity occurring with some regularity. The frequency of the activity is a factor, but is not determinative.

Whether a person giving advice about securities for compensation would be "in the business" of doing so, depends upon all relevant facts and circumstances. The staff considers a person to be "in the business" of providing advice if the person: (i) Holds himself out as an investment adviser or as one who provides investment advice, (ii) receives any separate or additional compensation that represents a clearly definable charge for providing advice about securities, regardless of whether the compensation is separate from or included within any overall compensation, or receives transaction-based compensation if the client implements in the investment advice, or (iii) on anything other than rare, isolated and non-periodic instances, provides specific investment advice. For the purposes of (iii) above, "specific investment advice" includes a recommendation, analysis or report about specific securities or specific categories of securities (e.g., industrial development bonds, mutual funds, or medical technology stocks). It includes a recommendation that a client allocate certain percentages of his assets to life insurance, high yielding bonds, and mutual funds or particular types of mutual funds such as growth stock funds or money market funds. However, specific investment advice does not include advice limited to a general recommendation to allocate assets in securities, life insurance, and tangible assets.

In applying the foregoing tests, the staff may consider other financial services activities offered to clients. For example, if a financial planner structures his planning so as to give only generic, non-specific investment advice as a financial planner, but then gives specific securities advice in his capacity as a registered representative of a dealer or as agent of an insurance company, the person would not be able to assert that he was not "in the business" of giving investment advice. See discussion of the broker-dealer exception set forth in section 202(a)(11)(C) of the Advisers Act, *infra*. In the staff's view, it is necessary to consider these other financial services activities. Section 208(d) of the Advisers Act makes it illegal for someone to do indirectly under the Advisers Act what cannot be done directly.

3. Compensation

The definition of investment adviser applies to persons who give investment advice for compensation. This compensation element is satisfied by the receipt of any economic benefit, whether in the form of an advisory fee or some other fee relating to the total services rendered, commissions, or some combination of the foregoing. It is not necessary that a person who provides investment advisory and other services to a client charge a separate fee for the investment advisory portion of the total services. The compensation element is satisfied if a single fee is charged for a number of different services, including investment advice or the issuing of reports or analyses concerning securities within the meaning of the Advisers Act. As discussed above, however, the fact that no separate fee is charged for the investment advisory portion of the service could be relevant to whether the person is "in the business" of giving investment advice.

It is not necessary that an adviser's compensation be paid directly by the person receiving investment advisory services, but only that the investment adviser receive compensation from some source for his services. Accordingly, a person providing a variety of services to a client, including investment advisory services, for which the person receives any economic benefit, for example, by receipt of a single fee or commissions upon the sale to the client of insurance products or investments, would be performing such advisory services "for compensation" within the meaning of section 202(a)(11) of the Advisers Act. [***]

* * *

Notes and Applications

Robo-advisers. The SEC has characterized "robo-advisers" as advisory services provided through the use of "online algorithmic-based programs" that "operate under a wide variety of business models and provide a range of advisory services." Division of Investment Management, U.S. Securities and Exchange Commission, *Robo-Advisers*, Guidance Update No. 2017-02 (Feb. 2017). This type of service is well-suited for obtaining and dispensing advice over the internet where a large population of retail clients can input personal information about their financial circumstances and objectives, especially as consumers have become increasingly comfortable with, and increasingly seek the convenience of, website applications. One of the chief benefits of advice delivered in this fashion is that it lends itself to very low-cost advisory models.

Robo-advisers have proliferated in recent years. Early models were nondiscretionary, combining some basic elements of financial planning coupled with advice regarding mutual fund selections. Financialengines.com which was the brainchild of a Nobel laureate economist, William Sharpe, was one of the earliest entrants in this area and was marketed to employers as a tool to help employees manage their self-directed retirement accounts, as well as directly to retail investors. An obvious question is whether financialengines.com and similar services are investment advisers within the meaning of the Advisers Act. The three elements of the definition of an investment adviser are typically satisfied, even in the non-discretionary advice context. The advice clearly encompasses securities and is explicitly marketed to serve the needs of investors for a fee.

More recently, robo-advisers have been used to deliver discretionary advice, i.e., manage client assets. Many national brokerage firms have introduced such platforms and sometimes involve use of robo-advisers supplemented by human interaction. This area in particular has elicited closer regulatory scrutiny regarding the adequacy of client disclosures, suitability determinations and compliance oversight.

Should the use of robo-advisers by retail investors enhance or diminish regulatory concerns? How are robo-advisers likely to benefit retail investors from a policy perspective and in what respects might they be unsatisfactory for retail investors?

6.2.2 The Definition's Exclusions

The definition of investment adviser in Section 202(a)(11) of the Advisers Act specifies eight statutory exclusions:

A. a bank, or any bank holding company as defined in the Bank Holding Company Act of 1956, which is not an investment company, except that the term "investment adviser" includes any bank or bank holding company to the extent that such bank or bank holding company serves or acts as an investment adviser to a registered investment company, but if, in the case of a bank, such services or actions are performed through a separately identifiable department or division, the department or division, and not the bank itself, shall be deemed to be the investment adviser;

B. any lawyer, accountant, engineer, or teacher whose performance of such services is solely incidental to the practice of his profession;

C. any broker or dealer whose performance of such services is solely incidental to the conduct of his business as a broker or dealer and who receives no special compensation therefor;

D. the publisher of any bona fide newspaper, news magazine or business or financial publication of general and regular circulation;

E. any person whose advice, analyses, or reports relate ... [solely to securities issued by the United States or backed by government-sponsored corporations];

F. any nationally recognized statistical rating organization, as that term is defined in section 3(a)(62) of the Securities Exchange Act of 1934, unless such organization engages in issuing recommendations as to purchasing, selling, or holding securities or in managing assets, consisting in whole or in part of securities, on behalf of others;

G. any family office, as defined by rule, regulation, or order of the Commission, in accordance with the purpose of this title; or

H. such other persons not within the intent of this paragraph, as the Commission may designate by rules and regulations or order.

While each exclusion will not be reviewed, several exclusions will be analyzed to provide illustrations of how they work. To start, it is at least worth pausing over the concept of exclusions. The use of exclusions in a statute is an unequivocal indication that the forepart of the definition of investment adviser is too broad. That definition might be too broad either because a subject entity's activities do not implicate the investor protection concerns of the Advisers Act or because the definition would otherwise result in regulation of entities or providers best regulated by other means. It is possible to evaluate each of the enumerated exclusions and offer an explanation for the exclusion along these lines. The final category, namely exclusion (H), gives the SEC substantial discretionary authority in excluding other entities that might fit within the definition but, as the statutory provision states, are not within the definition's intent. In other words, Congress gave the SEC ongoing rulemaking authority to limit the scope of the definition of investment adviser further. The scope of this discretionary authority is discussed in the *Financial Planning Association* decision in subpart (b) below.

a. The Publisher Exclusion

Lowe v. SEC

472 U.S. 181 (1985)

[**Textbook Note:** *In this case, the U.S. Supreme Court weighed in on the publisher's exclusion from the definition of the term investment adviser found in Advisers Act Section 202(a)(11) with a wrinkle. The defendant in this SEC enforcement action raised a First Amendment challenge to the efforts of the SEC to enjoin publication of his investment newsletter. The majority interpreted the publisher's exclusion in a way to avoid possible constitutional issues based on one possible reading of the legislative history. In contrast, the concurring opinion recommended a narrower construction of the exclusion and resolving any constitutional concerns by barring certain types of remedies.*]

Stevens, J [***] The question is whether petitioners may be permanently enjoined from publishing non-personalized investment advice and commentary in securities newsletters because they are not registered as investment advisers under Section 203(c) of the Investment Advisers Act of 1940 (Act).

Christopher Lowe is the president and principal shareholder of Lowe Management Corporation. From 1974 until 1981, the corporation was registered as an investment adviser under the Act. During that period Lowe was convicted of misappropriating funds of an investment client, of engaging in business as an investment adviser without filing a registration application with New York's Department of Law, of tampering with evidence to cover up fraud of an investment client, and of stealing from a bank. Consequently, on May 11, 1981, the Securities and Exchange Commission (Commission), after a full hearing before an Administrative Law Judge, entered an order revoking the registration of the Lowe Management Corporation, and ordering Lowe not to associate thereafter with any investment adviser.

A little over a year later, the Commission commenced this action by filing a complaint in the United States District Court for the Eastern District of New York, alleging that Lowe, the Lowe Management Corporation, and two other corporations, were violating the Act, and that Lowe was violating the Commission's order. The principal charge in the complaint was that Lowe and the three corporations (petitioners) were publishing two investment newsletters and soliciting subscriptions for a stock-chart service. The complaint alleged that, through those publications, the petitioners were engaged in the business of advising others "as to the advisability of investing in, purchasing, or selling securities ... and as a part of a regular business ... issuing reports concerning securities." Because none of the petitioners was registered or exempt from registration under the Act, the use of the mails in connection with the advisory business allegedly violated Section 203(a) of the Act. The Commission prayed for a permanent injunction restraining the further distribution of petitioners' investment advisory publications; for a permanent injunction enforcing compliance with the order of May 11, 1981; and for other relief.

Although three publications are involved in this litigation, only one need be described. A typical issue of the Lowe Investment and Financial Letter contained general commentary about the securities and bullion markets, reviews of market indicators and investment strategies, and specific recommendations for buying, selling, or holding stocks and bullion. The newsletter advertised a "telephone hotline" over which subscribers could call to get current information. The number of subscribers to the newsletter ranged from 3,000 to 19,000. It was advertised as a semimonthly publication, but only eight issues were published in the 15 months after the entry of the 1981 order.

Subscribers who testified at the trial criticized the lack of regularity of publication, but no adverse evidence concerning the quality of the publications was offered.

I

We granted certiorari to consider the important constitutional question whether an injunction against the publication and distribution of petitioners' newsletters is prohibited by the First Amendment. Petitioners contend that such an injunction strikes at the very foundation of the freedom of the press by subjecting it to license and censorship. In response the Commission argues that the history of abuses in the securities industry amply justified Congress' decision to require the registration of investment advisers, to regulate their professional activities, and, as an incident to such regulation, to prohibit unregistered and unqualified persons from engaging in that business.

In order to evaluate the parties' constitutional arguments, it is obviously necessary first to understand, as precisely as possible, the extent to which the Act was intended to regulate the publication of investment advice and the reasons that motivated Congress to authorize such regulation. Moreover, in view of the fact that we should "not decide a constitutional question if there is some other ground upon which to dispose of the case," and the further fact that the District Court and the dissenting judge in the Court of Appeals both believed that the case should be decided on statutory grounds, a careful study of the statute may either eliminate, or narrowly limit, the constitutional question that we must confront. We therefore begin with a review of the background of the Act with a particular focus on the legislative history describing the character of the profession that Congress intended to regulate.

II

As we observed in *SEC v. Capital Gains Research Bureau, Inc.*, the "Investment Advisers Act of 1940 was the last in a series of acts designed to eliminate certain abuses in the securities industry, abuses which were found to have contributed to the stock market crash of 1929 and the depression of the 1930s.

One of the statutory exclusions is for "the publisher of any bona fide newspaper, news magazine or business or financial publication of general and regular circulation." Although neither the text of the Act nor its legislative history defines the precise scope of this exclusion, two points seem tolerably clear. Congress did not intend to exclude publications that are distributed by investment advisers as a normal part of the business of servicing their clients. The legislative history plainly demonstrates that Congress was primarily interested in regulating the business of rendering personalized investment advice, including publishing activities that are a normal incident thereto. On the other hand, Congress, plainly sensitive to First Amendment concerns, wanted to make clear that it did not seek to regulate the press through the licensing of non-personalized publishing activities.

The exclusion itself uses extremely broad language that encompasses any newspaper, business publication, or financial publication provided that two conditions are met. The publication must be "bona fide," and it must be "of regular and general circulation." Neither of these conditions is defined, but the two qualifications precisely differentiate "hit and run tipsters" and "touts" from genuine publishers. Presumably a "bona fide" publication would be genuine in the sense that it would contain disinterested commentary and analysis as opposed to promotional material disseminated by a "tout." Moreover, publications with a "general and regular" circulation would not include "people who send out bulletins from time to time on the advisability of buying and selling stocks," see Hearings on H.R. 10065, at 87, or "hit and run tipsters."[51] *Ibid.* Because the content of petitioners' newsletters was completely disinterested, and because they were offered to the general public on a regular schedule, they are described by the plain language of the exclusion.

---

51. The term "tipsters" is explained in the testimony of Douglas T. Johnston, n. 38, *supra* [omitted] — persons "who through newspaper advertisements offer to send, for a nominal price, a list of stocks that are sure to go up." Justice White is unable "to imagine" any workable definition of the exclusion "that does not sweep in all publications that are not personally tailored to individual clients," *post,* at 2576. The definition Congress actually wrote, however, does not sweep in bulletins that are issued from time to time in response to episodic market activity, advertisements that "tout" particular issues, advertised lists of stocks "that are sure to go up" that are sold to individual purchasers, or publications distributed as an incident to personalized investment service.

These various formulations recast the statutory language without capturing the central thrust of the legislative history, and without even mentioning the apparent intent of Congress to keep the Act free of constitutional infirmities.[53] The Act was designed to apply to those persons engaged in the investment-advisory profession—those who provide personalized advice attuned to a client's concerns, whether by written or verbal communication. The mere fact that a publication contains advice and comment about specific securities does not give it the personalized character that identifies a professional investment adviser. Thus, petitioners' publications do not fit within the central purpose of the Act because they do not offer individualized advice attuned to any specific portfolio or to any client's particular needs. On the contrary, they circulate for sale to the public at large in a free, open market—a public forum in which typically anyone may express his views.

The language of the exclusion, read literally, seems to describe petitioners' newsletters. Petitioners are "publishers of any bona fide newspaper, news magazine or business or financial publication." The only modifier that might arguably disqualify the newsletters are the words "bona fide." Notably, however, those words describe the publication rather than the character of the publisher; hence Lowe's unsavory history does not prevent his newsletters from being "bona fide." In light of the legislative history, this phrase translates best to "genuine"; petitioners' publications meet this definition: they are published by those engaged solely in the publishing business and are not personal communications masquerading in the clothing of newspapers, news magazines, or financial publications. Moreover, there is no suggestion that they contained any false or misleading information, or that they were designed to tout any security in which petitioners had an interest. Further, petitioners' publications are "of general and regular circulation." Although the publications have not been "regular" in the sense of consistent circulation, the publications have been "regular" in the sense important to the securities market: there is no indication that they have been timed to specific market activity, or to events affecting or having the ability to affect the securities industry.

The dangers of fraud, deception, or overreaching that motivated the enactment of the statute are present in personalized communications but are not replicated in publications that are advertised and sold in an open market. To the extent that the chart service contains factual information about past transactions and market trends, and the newsletters contain commentary on general market conditions, there can be no doubt about the protected character of the communications, a matter that concerned Congress when the exclusion was drafted. The content of the publications and the audience to which they are directed in this case reveal the specific limits of the exclusion. As long as the communications between petitioners and their subscribers remain

53. The Commission's focus on the content of the publication to determine whether a publisher is within the exclusion represents a dramatic departure from the objective criteria in the statute itself. As far as content is concerned, the statutory exclusion broadly encompasses every "business or financial publication" but then limits the category by a requirement that it be "bona fide," and a further requirement that it be "of general and regular circulation."

entirely impersonal and do not develop into the kind of fiduciary, person-to-person relationships that were discussed at length in the legislative history of the Act and that are characteristic of investment adviser-client relationships, we believe the publications are, at least presumptively, within the exclusion and thus not subject to registration under the Act.

We therefore conclude that petitioners' publications fall within the statutory exclusion for bona fide publications and that none of the petitioners is an "investment adviser" as defined in the Act. It follows that neither their unregistered status, nor the Commission order barring Lowe from associating with an investment adviser, provides a justification for restraining the future publication of their newsletters. It also follows that we need not specifically address the constitutional question we granted certiorari to decide.

The judgment of the Court of Appeals is reversed.

Justice White (concurring): The issue in this case is whether the Securities and Exchange Commission may invoke the injunctive remedies of the Investment Advisers Act, to prevent an unregistered adviser from publishing newsletters containing investment advice that is not specifically tailored to the needs of individual clients. The Court holds that it may not because the activities of petitioner Lowe (hereafter petitioner) do not make him an investment adviser covered by the Act. For the reasons that follow, I disagree with this improvident construction of the statute. In my view, petitioner is an investment adviser subject to regulation and sanction under the Act. I concur in the judgment, however, because to prevent petitioner from publishing at all is inconsistent with the First Amendment.

....

[The defendant] falls outside the definition of an "investment adviser" only if each of his publications qualifies as a "bona fide newspaper, news magazine or business or financial publication of general and regular circulation." The question is whether the "bona fide publications" exception is to be construed so broadly as to exclude from the definition all persons whose advisory activities are carried out solely through publications offering impersonal investment advice to their subscribers.

It is hardly crystal clear from the face of the statute how the primary definition and the "bona fide publications" exception are supposed to mesh, but the SEC has, since the Act's inception, interpreted the statutory definition of "investment adviser" to cover persons whose activities are limited to the publication of investment advisory newsletters or reports such as those published by petitioner. At the conclusion of the Act's first year of operation, the Commission reported that of the approximately 750 persons and firms registering under the Act, "165 firms indicated that their investment advisory service consisted only of the sale of uniform publications."

Any construction that expands the "bona fide publications" exception beyond the bounds set by the SEC, however, poses great difficulties. If the exception is expanded to include more than just publications that are not primarily vehicles for distributing investment advice, it is difficult to imagine any workable definition that does not sweep in all publications that are not personally tailored to individual clients. Indeed, it appears that this is precisely the definition the Court adopts.[3] But such an expansive definition of the exception renders superfluous certain key passages in the primary definition of an "investment adviser": one who engages in the business of rendering investment advice "*either directly or through publications or writings*" or who "*issues or promulgates analyses or reports concerning securities.*" Had Congress intended the "bona fide publications" exception to encompass *all* publications, it is difficult to imagine why the primary definition of "investment adviser" should have spoken in the disjunctive of those who rendered advice directly and those who rendered it through publications, analyses, or reports. Nor is it clear why Congress would have chosen the adjective "bona fide" had it not intended that the SEC look beyond the form of a publication in determining whether it fell within the exception. The construction of the Act that would exclude petitioner from the category of investment advisers because he offers his advice through publications thus conflicts with the fundamental axiom of statutory interpretation that a statute is to be construed so as to give effect to all its language.

....

The power of government to regulate the professions is not lost whenever the practice of a profession entails speech....

But the principle that the government may restrict entry into professions and vocations through licensing schemes has never been extended to encompass the licensing of speech *per se* or of the press. At some point, a measure is no longer a regulation of a profession but a regulation of speech or of the press; beyond that point, the statute must survive the level of scrutiny demanded by the First Amendment. [***]

* * *

Notes and Applications

1. *Constitutional prohibitions and statutory construction.* The *Lowe* case addresses the intersection of regulation of investment advisers' expressive conduct and the First

3. The Court suggests that "tipsters" and "touts" might not qualify under its reading of the "bona fide publications" exception either because their publications are not sufficiently regular or because their advice is not sufficiently disinterested. Both suggestions seem implausible. As is evident from the Court's conclusion that petitioner's publications meet the regularity requirement, the Court's construction of the requirement adopts the view of our major law reviews on the issue of regular publication: good intentions are enough. Thus, if a "tout" or "tipster" promised to publish his recommendations at more or less regular intervals, he, like petitioner, would meet the regularity requirement. Moreover, a truly "hit and run" practitioner—one who did not even claim an intention of issuing further recommendations—would not fall within the definition of an "investment adviser" because he would not be deemed to "engag[e] in the business" of advising others. *See Applicability of Investment Advisers Act to Certain Publications*, SEC Release No. IA-563, 42 Fed. Reg. 2953 (1977), codified at 17 CFR § 276 (1984). As for the Court's suggestion that "touts" and "tipsters" might not qualify under the exception if their advice was not disinterested, it appears completely unfounded: nowhere in the language or history of the Act is there any suggestion that whether a person is an investment adviser depends on whether his advice is disinterested....

Amendment. One should begin by asking how, if at all, the Advisers Act runs afoul of constitutional prohibitions. Both the majority and concurring opinion appear to agree that the SEC's enforcement action raises potential First Amendment concerns, but each opinion attaches a different judicial implication arising from these concerns. Justice Stevens invokes constitutional avoidance principles in his opinion to shape his construction of the statute, while Justice White would merely limit remedies afforded the SEC for certain violations. Describe the practical consequences in terms of regulatory outcomes that ensue from the two different approaches. For an examination of the problematic potential of constitutional avoidance principles in statutory construction, see Neal Kumar Katyal & Thomas P. Schmidt, *Active Avoidance: The Modern Supreme Court and Legal Change*, 128 Harv. L. Rev. 2109 (2015).

In matters of statutory construction, once the Supreme Court has spoken, it is nearly impossible to revisit the issue judicially. Congress, of course, is free to revise the statute through amendment. However, such a result is rare. As a result, Justice Stevens' construction of the statutory definition has enshrined an interpretation that emphasizes personalized forms of investment advice as of primary interest under the Advisers Act.

2. *The problem of touting.* The case itself arose out of conduct that is highly problematic—a market participant who touts a particular security but whose recommendations may be guided by self-interest rather than the best interests of investors. Touting by unscrupulous investment advisers is a source of recurring concern. Should regulators be interested in this type of problem and, if so, why? Specifically, are market participants in a position not merely to mislead investors, but to profit from the gullibility of these investors? Explain how an investment adviser is able to profit from touting conduct. Although there was no proof that Lowe had a conflict of interest in this case, such a possibility, given the background and facts, would certainly be consistent with such concerns. In order to challenge touting conduct, a threshold issue is whether the person is acting as an investment adviser and therefore even subject to the Advisers Act.

3. *Lowe meets the internet.* Justice Stevens' opinion has posed an enforcement obstacle for the SEC in policing investment advice disseminated over the the internet or mass media. On the internet, an investment adviser can distribute its advice in seemingly "impersonalized" ways to numerous people through blast e-mails, interactive chat rooms, blogs and probably various types of social media. This issue surfaced in the so-called "Toyko Joe Case" in which an individual self-styled on the internet as "Tokyo Joe" developed a menu of member services available to clients through e-mail and internet interfaces that discussed and recommended investments for internet clientele. The SEC brought an enforcement action for failure to register under the Advisers Act. In denying the defendant's motion to dismiss (a motion based on *Lowe* and the absence of personalized advice), the district court concluded that the relevant electronic communications, including e-mails, satisfied the requisite element of personalization. *SEC v. Park*, 99 F. Supp. 2d 899 (N.D. Ill. 2000). The SEC ultimately settled with the defendant. *Yun Soo Oh Park and Tokyo Joe's Societe Anonyme Corp.*,

SEC Litigation Release No. 16925 (March 8, 2001). In other public media outlet cases, the SEC has gone after tipsters and touters on grounds of fraud under Exchange Act Section 10(b) and Rule 10b-5 thereunder free of potential constitutional challenges. *SEC v. Pirate Investors LLC*, 580 F.3d 233 (4th Cir. 2009), *cert. denied*, 561 U.S. 1036 (2010); *Thom Calandra*, Lit. Release No. 19028 (Jan. 10, 2005). Explain why general antifraud prohibitions sidestep the *Lowe* issue.

b. The Broker Exclusion and the Difference between Brokers and Advisers

Financial Planning Association v. SEC

482 F.3d 481 (D.C. Cir. 2007)

[**Textbook Note:** *In this decision, the D.C. Circuit Court of Appeals examined the SEC's authority to exclude certain conduct from the definition of investment adviser, especially where it overlapped with an existing statutory exclusion from the investment adviser definition for persons engaged in broker-dealer activity that is solely incidental to its business and who receives no special compensation for such activity. The SEC's rulemaking activity was motivated by changes in the financial industry, but as the court explains, that does not free the SEC from statutory limitations. The dissenting opinion disputed the meaning affixed by the majority to the broker-dealer exclusion, and moreover, interpreted the SEC's general rulemaking authority expansively to craft additional exclusions from the definition. The issue has wide ranging implications for the differences between broker-dealer and investment advisers which Congress returned to in the Dodd-Frank Act of 2010.*]

Rogers, Circuit Judge ... Brokers and dealers are not subject to the requirements of the Investment Advisers Act ("[Advisers Act]") where their investment advice is (1) "solely incidental to the conduct of [their] business as a broker or dealer," and (2) the broker or dealer "receives no special compensation therefor." 15 U.S.C. Section 80b-2(a)(11)(C) (2000). The Securities and Exchange Commission, acting pursuant to Section 202(a)(11)[(H)] and Section 211(a) of the [Advisers Act], 15 U.S.C. §§ 80b-2(a)(11)[(H)], 80b-11(a), promulgated a final rule exempting broker-dealers from the [Advisers Act] when they receive "special compensation therefor." *See* "Certain Broker-Dealers Deemed Not to be Investment Advisers," 70 Fed. Reg. 20,424 (Apr.19, 2005). The Financial Planning Association ("FPA") petitions for review of the final rule on the ground that the SEC has exceeded its authority. We agree, and we therefore grant the petition and vacate the final rule.

I.

The [Advisers Act] was enacted by Congress as one title of a bill "to provide for the registration and regulation of investment companies and investment advisers." Pub. L. No. 76-768, tit. II, 54 Stat. 847 (1940). The other title was the Investment Company Act ("ICA"). Pub. L. No. 76-768, tit. I, 54 Stat. 789 (1940). These were the last in a series of congressional enactments designed to eliminate certain abuses in the securities industry that contributed to the stock market crash of 1929 and the depression of the 1930s....

"A fundamental purpose, common to these statutes, was to substitute a philosophy of full disclosure for the philosophy of *caveat emptor* and thus to achieve a high standard of business ethics in the securities industry." *SEC v. Capital Gains Research Bureau, Inc.*, 375 U.S. 180, 186, (1963). The [Advisers Act] arose from a consensus between industry and the SEC "that investment advisers could not 'completely perform their basic function—furnishing to clients on a personal basis competent, unbiased, and continuous advice regarding the sound management of their investments—unless all conflicts of interest between the investment counsel and the client were removed.'" *Id.* at 187 (citation omitted). According to the Committee Reports, "[t]he essential purpose of the Advisers Act ... [was] to protect the public from the frauds and misrepresentations of unscrupulous tipsters and touts and to safeguard the honest investment adviser against the stigma of the activities of these individuals by making fraudulent practices by investment advisers unlawful." H.R.Rep. No. 76-2639, at 28 (1940).

> "Virtually no limitations or restrictions exist with respect to the honesty and integrity of individuals who may solicit funds to be controlled, managed, and supervised.... Individuals assuming to act as investment advisers at present can enter profit-sharing contracts which are nothing more than 'heads I win, tails you lose' arrangements. Contracts with investment advisers which are of a personal nature may be assigned and the control of funds of investors may be transferred to others without the knowledge or consent of the client."

S.Rep. No. 76-1775, at 21–22 (1940).

Under the [Advisers Act], investment advisers are required, among other things, to register and to maintain records, 15 U.S.C. § 80b-3(c) & (e); to limit the type of contracts they enter, *id.* § 80b-5; and not to engage in certain types of deceptive and fraudulent transactions, *id.* § 80b-6.

In Section 202(a)(11) of the [Advisers Act], Congress broadly defined "investment adviser" as

> "any person who, for compensation, engages in the business of advising others, either directly or through publications or writings, as to the value of securities or as to the advisability of investing in, purchasing, or selling securities, or who, for compensation and as part of a regular business, issues or promulgates analyses or reports concerning securities...."

15 U.S.C. § 80b-2(a)(11). Carving out [eight] exemptions from this broad definition, Congress determined that an "investment adviser" did not include:

> ....
>
> (C) any broker or dealer [1] whose performance of such services is solely incidental to the conduct of his business as a broker or dealer and [2] who receives no special compensation therefor;

...

[(H)] such other persons not within the intent of this paragraph, as the Commission may designate by rules and regulations or order.

15 U.S.C. Section 80b-2(a)(11). Subsections (C) and [(H)] are at issue in this appeal.

Before enactment of the [Advisers Act], broker-dealers and others who offered investment advice received two general forms of compensation. Some charged only traditional commissions (earning a certain amount for each securities transaction completed). Others charged a separate advice fee (often a certain percentage of the customer's assets under advisement or supervision). *See* 11 Fed. Reg. 10,996 (Sept. 27, 1946). The Committee Reports recognized that the statutory exemption for broker-dealers reflected this distinction; the Reports explained that the term "investment adviser" was "so defined as specifically to exclude ... brokers (insofar as their advice is merely incidental to brokerage transactions for which they receive only brokerage commissions)." S. Rep. No. 76-1775, at 22; H.R. Rep. No. 76-2639, at 28....

The final rule provides, generally, in *Paragraph (a)(1),* on "fee-based programs," that a broker-dealer who (1) receives special compensation will not be deemed an investment adviser if (2) any advice provided is solely incidental to brokerage services provided on a customer's account and (3) specific disclosure is made to the customer. In *Paragraph (a)(2),* on discount brokerage programs, a broker-dealer will not be deemed to have received special compensation merely because it charges one customer more or less for brokerage services than it charges another customer. *Paragraph (b)* lists three non-exclusive circumstances in which advisory services, for which special compensation is received under paragraph (a)(1), would not be performed "solely incidental to" brokerage: when (1) a separate fee or contract exists for advice; (2) a customer receives certain financial planning services; and, (3) generally, a broker-dealer has investment discretion over a client's account. *Paragraph (c)* states a "special rule" that broker-dealers registered under the Exchange Act are investment advisers only for those accounts for which they receive compensation that subjects them to the [Advisers Act]. *Paragraph (d)* defines the term "investment discretion," which appears in paragraphs (a)(1) and (b)(3), to have the same meaning as Section 3(a)(35) of the Exchange Act, 15 U.S.C. Section 78c(a)(35), except for "discretion granted by a customer on a temporary or limited basis."

The FPA petitions for review, challenging the SEC's authority to promulgate the final rule....

III.

The FPA contends that when Congress enacted the [Advisers Act], Congress identified in subsection (C) the group of broker-dealers it intended to exempt, and that subsection [(H)] was only intended to allow the SEC to exempt new groups from the [Advisers Act], not to expand the groups that Congress specifically addressed.... [W]e review the SEC's exercise of its authority pursuant to subsection [(H)] under the familiar two-step analysis of *Chevron, U.S.A., Inc. v. Natural Res. Def. Council, Inc.,* 467 U.S. 837, 842-43(1984). Under step one, the court must determine whether Congress has directly spoken to the precise question at issue. "If the intent of Congress is clear, that is the end of the matter; for the court, as well as the agency, must give effect to the unambiguously expressed intent of Congress." *Id.* Under step two, "if the statute is silent or ambiguous with respect to the specific issue, the question for the court is whether the agency's answer is based on a permissible construction of the statute." *Id.* at 843. In reviewing an agency's interpretation of its authority under a statute it administers, the court will uphold that interpretation as long as it is a reasonable interpretation of the statute.

....

In the final rule, the SEC purports to use its authority under subsection [(H)] to broaden the exemption for broker-dealers provided under subsection (C). The rule is inconsistent with the Advisers Act, however, because it fails to meet either of the two requirements for an exemption under subsection [(H)]. First, the legislative "intent" does not support an exemption for broker-dealers broader than the exemption set forth in the text of subsection (C); therefore, the final rule does not meet the statutory requirement that exemptions under subsection [(H)] be consistent with the "intent" of paragraph 11 of section 202(a). Second, because broker-dealers are already expressly addressed in subsection (C), they are not "other persons" under subsection [(H)]; therefore the SEC cannot use its authority under subsection [(H)] to establish new, broader exemptions for broker-dealers.

....

No other indicators of congressional intent support the SEC's interpretation of its authority under subsection [(H)]. The relevant language in the committee reports suggests that Congress deliberately drafted the exemption in subsection (C) to apply as written. Those reports stated that the "term 'investment adviser' is so defined as specifically to exclude ... brokers (insofar as their advice is merely incidental to brokerage transactions for which they receive *only* brokerage commissions)." S.Rep. No. 76-1775, at 22 (emphasis added); *see also* H.R.Rep. No. 76-2639, at 28. By seeking to exempt broker-dealers beyond those who receive only brokerage commissions for investment advice, the SEC has promulgated a final rule that is in direct conflict with both the statutory text and the Committee Reports.

The text of subsection [(H)] confirms this conclusion by the limiting the SEC's exemption authorization to "other persons." We agree with the FPA that when Congress enacted the [Advisers Act], Congress identified the specific classes of persons it intended to exempt. As to broker-dealers, subsection (C) applied to "*any* broker or dealer." Congress, through the use of contrasting text in subsection [(H)], signaled that it only authorized the SEC to exempt "*other* persons" when consistent with the intent of the paragraph, and thus only when doing so would not override Congress's determination of the appropriate persons to be exempted from the [Advisers Act]'s requirements....

....

In an attempt to overcome the plain language of the statute, the SEC asserts that Congress was also concerned about the regulation of broker-dealers under both the [Advisers Act] and Exchange Act, and that such concern was reflected in the "intent" of the paragraph. *See* 70 Fed. Reg. 20,430; *see also* 64 Fed. Reg. 61,228. The SEC points to no convincing evidence that supports these assertions. At the time Congress enacted the Advisers Act in 1940, broker-dealers were already regulated under the Exchange Act.... The Advisers Act's essential purpose was to "protect the public from the frauds and misrepresentations of unscrupulous tipsters and touts and to safeguard the honest investment adviser against the stigma of the activities of these individuals by making fraudulent practices by investment advisers unlawful." H.R. Rep. No. 76-2639 at 28; *see also id.* at 21. As the FPA emphasizes, there is nothing in the committee reports to suggest that Congress was particularly concerned about the regulatory burdens on broker-dealers....

In light of the context in which Congress drafted subsections (C) and [(H)], we conclude that, as indicated by the structure of Section 202(a)(11) and the problems that Congress addressed in the Advisers Act, as well as the other indicators of Congress's intent, under *Chevron* step one the text of subsections (C) and [(H)] is unambiguous, and that, therefore, the SEC has exceeded its authority in promulgating the final rule.

....

Garland, Circuit Judge, dissenting. The Investment Advisers Act contains [eight] specific exceptions, and urther authorizes the SEC to exempt "such other persons not within the intent of this paragraph, as the Commission may designate by rules." 15 U.S.C. Section 80b-2(a)(11). Unlike my colleagues, I cannot derive an unambiguous meaning from the terms "such other persons" and "within the intent of this paragraph." As required by *Chevron,* I would therefore defer to the SEC's reasonable interpretation of the statute it administers and uphold the Commission's fee-based brokerage rule.

... As the court states, the question before us is whether subsection [(H)] gives the SEC the authority to "except from[Advisers Act] coverage an additional group of broker-dealers beyond the broker-dealers exempted by Congress in subsection (C)." ... The SEC believes that it does. In the Commission's view, although these broker-dealers receive "special compensation" in a technical sense, they provide investment advice in the same manner as those who are exempt under subsection (C), and exempting them would thus serve the same purpose. *See infra* Part III.

....

A

Like my colleagues, I begin with the term "within the intent of this paragraph." Under *Chevron,* a statutory term is unambiguous only if Congress has "directly spoken to the precise question at issue." 467 U.S. at 842-43. The court is obviously correct in stating that "the plain text *of subsection (C)* exempts only broker-dealers who do not receive special compensation for investment advice"—that is, broker-dealers who do not receive compensation other than commissions. Court Op. at 488 (emphasis added). But that is not the precise question before us. That question is whether Congress intended *subsection [(H)]* to permit the SEC to exempt broker-dealers beyond those already exempt under subsection (C).

The court cannot point to any words in paragraph 11, or in any other paragraph of the Act, that suggest a negative answer to that question—or that explain what Congress intended with respect to that question at all. Instead, the court appears to rely on a version of the *expressio unius* canon—the principle that the mention of one thing implies the exclusion of another—by reasoning that the exception for some broker-dealers in subsection (C) means that coverage of all other broker-dealers must be "within the intent of" paragraph 11. But this court has repeatedly held that *expressio unius* is "an especially feeble helper in an administrative setting, where Congress is presumed to have left to reasonable agency discretion questions that it has not directly resolved." *Martini v. Fed. Nat'l Mortgage Ass'n,* 178 F.3d 1336, 1343 (D.C.Cir.1999) (quoting *Cheney R.R. Co. v. ICC,* 902 F.2d 66, 69 (D.C.Cir.1990)) (internal quotation marks omitted); ... *see Texas Rural Legal Aid, Inc. v. Legal Servs. Corp.,* 940 F.2d 685, 694 (D.C.Cir.1991) ("[T]he *expressio* canon is simply too thin a reed to support the conclusion that Congress has clearly resolved the issue."). The canon's negative inference is particularly implausible where—as in subsection [(H)]—Congress has explicitly authorized additional exceptions beyond those specified in the statute.

Turning from the statutory text to the legislative history, the court quotes a committee report stating that the "'term "investment adviser" is so defined as specifically to exclude ... brokers (insofar as their advice is merely incidental to brokerage transactions for which they receive *only* brokerage commissions).'" (quoting S. Rep. No. 76-1775, at 22 (1940)); *see also* H.R. Rep. No. 76-2639, at 28 (1940). This quotation, however, has the same problem identified above. The committee was referring only to the specific exclusion provided by subsection (C), and not to the further exclusions permitted by subsection [(H)]. That is made clear by the sentence that follows the one quoted by the court: "*In addition,* the Commission is authorized by rules and regulations or order, to make certain *further* exceptions according to prescribed statutory standards." S. Rep. No. 76-1775, at 22 (emphasis added); *see also* H.R. Rep. No. 76-2639, at 28. There is nothing in the committee report that explains Congress' intentions with respect to those "further exceptions."

B

The court also perceives clarity in the subsection [(H)] term "such other persons." According to the court, "other persons" excludes any person who is a member of one of the broad categories referenced in paragraph 11's [seven] specific exceptions. Because some broker-dealers are referenced in subsection (C), the court concludes that the subset of broker-dealers covered by the fee-based brokerage rule cannot constitute "other persons" within the meaning of subsection [(H)]. The SEC, by contrast, contends that "other persons" excludes only those persons who actually come within one of the [seven] preceding exceptions. On the SEC's reading, the fee-based brokerage rule is a permissible exercise of the Commission's delegated authority because it exempts broker-dealers other than those exempted by subsection (C)....

III

Under *Chevron* step two, "if the implementing agency's construction is reasonable," a court must "accept the agency's construction of the statute, even if the agency's reading differs from what the court believes is the best statutory interpretation." [*National Cable Telecom. Ass'n v.*] *Brand X*, 545 U.S. at 980, 125 S.Ct. 2688 (citing *Chevron*, 467 U.S. at 843-44 & n. 11).

For the same reasons that I find subsection [(H)]'s use of the term "such other persons" ambiguous, *see supra* Part II.B, I conclude that the SEC's construction of that term is reasonable. There is nothing implausible about interpreting those words to encompass anyone not actually exempt under one of the five preceding exceptions. In so doing, the SEC does not "rewrite the statute." Court Op. at 491. Rather, it gives effect to one of two plausible interpretations of the statutory language.

The reasonableness of the SEC's interpretation of "such other persons" does not end the analysis, of course. Any regulatory exception must also be consistent with "the intent of" paragraph 11. The remaining question, then, is whether an exception for broker-dealers who provide investment advice solely incidental to their business as broker-dealers, but who are paid fee-based rather than commission-based compensation, is consistent with that intent.

The SEC has presented a reasonable case for concluding that it is. The Commission explained that, at the time of the Advisers Act's passage in 1940, broker-dealers were providing investment advice and receiving compensation in only two ways: "as an auxiliary part of the traditional brokerage services for which their brokerage customers paid fixed commissions and, alternatively, as a distinct advisory service for which their advisory clients separately contracted and paid a fee." Certain Broker-Dealers, 70 Fed.Reg. at 20,428. Congress was concerned about the potential for fraud and misrepresentation when advice was provided in the latter form—whether it was provided by broker-dealers charging separately for such advice or by others whose only business was to provide advice for a fee. *See id.* at 20,429–30 & n. 60. In enacting the Advisers Act, however, Congress did not express the same concern about investment advice included within a larger package of brokerage services—as evidenced by the exception contained in subsection (C). [***]

* * *

Notes and Applications

1. *Statutory interpretation.* The *Financial Planning Association* case had significant implications for the way in which registered investment advisers and broker-dealers compete. The case, brought by the Financial Planning Association, challenged the SEC's authority to grant broker-dealers significant regulatory relief in how they structure their fees and, in turn, compete with investment advisers for clients. While the decision implicates the express exclusion found in Advisers Act Section 202(a)(11) clause (C), which is limited to advisory activities of broker-dealers "solely incidental to the conduct of [ ] business" and not involving the receipt of "special compensation,"

the SEC actually used its discretionary powers under clause (H) to expand the scope of the exclusion for broker-dealers in clause (C). The case ultimately turned on the proper reading of the statute's two different clauses together, and the majority and dissenting opinions offer starkly different constructions. The majority opinion emphasizes the plain language of clause (C), while the dissent attempts to view the language of the two clauses contextually in terms of what Congress was attempting to accomplish in 1940 in formulating the exclusions as it did.

2. *Broker-dealer status and broker-dealer conduct.* Although the case turned on narrow issues of statutory construction, the decision focuses on a hotly contested area of market competition between financial advisors who are typically regulated as investment advisers (under the Advisers Act) and broker-dealers who until recently were generally regulated as broker-dealers (under the Exchange Act). Of course, in well-defined circumstances, such as when the broker-dealer (or one of its representatives) exercises discretionary investment authority over an account, the broker-dealer is viewed as acting as an investment adviser (or in the case of the sales representative, a person associated with an investment adviser) and regulated as such. However, in other circumstances, the broker-dealer may be viewed as acting solely in a brokerage capacity, including in circumstances where making non-discretionary investment recommendations.

This distinction is important, because the Advisers Act imposes fiduciary obligations on investment advisers with respect to their clients. The Advisers Act's fiduciary standard is tied to the client's best interests and requires a continuing assessment by the investment adviser. In contrast, broker-dealer conduct is evaluated in terms of a suitability standard and is limited to an assessment at the time when the customer enters into a transaction. *See, e.g., DeKwiatkowski v. Bear Stearns & Co.*, 306 F.3d 1293 (2d Cir. 2002).

The differing conduct standards—one fiduciary and the other based on suitability—raise both a competitive and a policy issue. The competitive issue, very much in the fore of the *Financial Planning Association* case, is whether broker-dealers are free to adopt compensation structures, such as asset-based fees, characteristic of investment advisory relationships, without shouldering the fiduciary obligations of investment advisers. The SEC sought to answer this question in the affirmative by adopting Rule 202(a)(11)-1(a), the rule challenged in *Financial Planning Association*. The SEC's rationale was that brokers' use of asset-based fees was better for broker-dealer customers than commission-based fees. However, the SEC was concerned that treating broker-dealers as investment advisers, merely because they used asset-based fees, would discourage broker-dealers from adopting asset-based client compensation arrangements. The rule foreclosed this potential disincentive. In contrast, the FPA regarded the rule as conferring a potential competitive advantage on brokers because it allowed broker-dealers to use asset-based fees to solicit clients without having to bear the burdensome fiduciary obligations applicable to investment advisers.

The related underlying policy issue is of particular significance: should the two types of market professionals—investment advisers and broker-dealers—be subject to different conduct standards in providing services to clients? This is not merely an issue of fair competition, but also implicates investor protection concerns generally. Is it reasonable to believe that investors understand this distinction? In fairness to both sides of the debate, broker-dealers tend to serve a wide spectrum of clients, including many who are self-directed and do not seek advice, but rather primarily seek low cost trade executions. As a result, the debate is more narrowly focused on the provision of personalized investment services to retail investors.

In 2010, Congress mandated in the Dodd-Frank Act of 2010 that the SEC examine whether the continuation of non-uniform conduct standards as between broker-dealers and investment advisers was warranted. It also amended the Exchange Act to give the SEC rulemaking authority to impose on broker-dealers fiduciary standards comparable to those of investment advisers in providing personalized investment advice to retail investors. The SEC staff issued a report that endorsed rulemaking suggestions to move toward a more uniform set of standards. Staff of the Securities and Exchange Commission, *Study of Investment Advisers and Broker-Dealers* (January 2011). However, after that report was issued, no significant action was taken.

Subsequently, the Department of Labor seized the rulemaking initiative by adopting a Fiduciary Rule standard pursuant to the Employee Retirement Income Security Act (ERISA) to clarify standards governing fiduciary investment advice for retirement accounts subject to ERISA, including individual retirement accounts. The rule required an adviser to put the best interests of its client ahead of the adviser's interests, which effectively discouraged the use of certain compensation arrangements. The rule also contained intricate exemptions. Implementation of the rule was largely deferred with the change of presidential administrations in 2017 and at the behest of the financial services industry. The rule was struck down by a divided U.S. court of appeals panel in *Chamber of Commerce v. U.S. Dept. of Labor*, 885 F.3d 360 (5th Cir. 2018), and the Department of Labor declined to seek further review. As a result, two years after its enactment, the rule is largely a dead letter.

In April 2018, the SEC undertook a broader regulatory initiative to address the duties of investment advisers and broker-dealers in dealing with retail customers or clients. Specifically, the SEC proposed two rules and an interpretation. The first rule ("Regulation Best Interest") would modestly enhance the duties of broker-dealers in dealing with retail customers by requiring broker-dealers to act in customers' best interests in making investment recommendations at the time the recommendation is made. The second rule would require investment advisers and broker-dealers to provide retail investors with a new disclosure document the summarizes the key features of the market professional's relationship to its customer (dubbed "Form CRS") and would restrict broker-dealer personnel's use of titles, such as financial advisor, when acting other than as an investment adviser. Finally, the SEC proposed an interpretation intended to clarify the standard of conduct applicable to investment advisers under the Advisers Act. As of September 2018, the proposed rules and interpretations have not been adopted. Moreover, because the SEC's Commissioners had sharply different views with respect to the proposals, it is difficult to predict what form any final proposals will take and, if finalized, whether, compared to existing regulations, the proposals will yield significant additional investor protections.

3. *The accountants and lawyers exclusion and "solely incidental."* The "professional" exclusion for accountants and lawyers is easily understood at an intuitive level. Accountants and lawyers, especially those specializing in tax or estate planning, are likely to offer legal advice that may be interdependent with investment advice. The nexus between the investment advice provided and the professional advice rendered is the lynchpin of the "solely incidental" condition. In the 1987 staff interpretation relating to financial planners, the staff addressed interpretive advice relating to the exclusions, including the exclusion for accountants and lawyers as follows:

> A person relying on an exclusion from the definition of investment adviser must meet all of the requirements of the exclusion. The staff's view is that the exclusion contained in section 202(a)(11)(B) is not available, for example, to a lawyer or accountant who holds himself out to the public as providing financial planning, pension consulting, or other financial advisory services. In such a case it would appear that the performance of investment advisory services by the person would not be incidental to his practice as a lawyer or accountant.[12]

Just as there are circumstances where supplemental investment advice would not be solely incidental (e.g., an accountant directly managing the client's money account), there are other situations where it would be incidental, such as the accountant or tax lawyer telling the client to invest in tax exempt bonds to minimize taxable gain or to defer selling an asset to take advantage of capital gains treatment. The exclusion covers the latter situation but not the former.

4. *Banks.* Banks is a particularly interesting exclusion from the definition of investment adviser because it reflects a political compromise that recognizes the longstanding divide between the securities industry and the banking industry. The Depression era Glass-Steagall Act mandated a barrier between the business of banks and securities activities associated with investment banks. This separation proved messy in some areas such as broker-dealers and investment advisers, since some traditional banking activities clearly encompassed activities performed by broker-dealers and investment advisers. Prior to 1999, banks and bank holding companies enjoyed

12. "The 'professional' exclusion provided in section 202(a)(11)(B) by its terms is only available to lawyers, accountants, engineers, and teachers. A person engaged in a profession other than one of those enumerated in section 202(a)(11)(B) who performs investment advisory services would be an investment adviser within the meaning of section 202(a)(11) whether or not the performance of investment advisory services is incidental to the practice of such profession. Unless another basis for excluding the person from the definition of investment adviser is available, the person would be subject to the Advisers Act."

a broad exclusion from the definition of investment adviser even though they managed money for institutional and wealthy clients. Banks were similarly excluded from the definition of broker-dealer, notwithstanding creative (and perhaps overly aggressive) efforts to force banks engaged in securities dealing to register as broker-dealers. *American Bankers Ass'n v. SEC*, 804 F.2d 739 (D.C. Cir. 1986). However, banks, but not non-bank affiliates of bank holding companies, were prohibited under the Glass-Steagall Act from advising registered investment companies. *See Investment Company Institute v. Camp*, 401 U.S. 617 (1971); *Board of Governors v. Investment Company Institute*, 450 U.S. 46 (1981).

The Gramm-Leach-Bliley Act of 1999 repealed the Glass-Steagall Act's prohibition on banks engaging in investment banking activity, but reworked the banking exclusion from the definition of investment adviser under the Advisers Act. As amended, the Advisers Act continues the broad exclusion of banks with respect to most banking activity, but specifically includes banks within the definition of investment adviser to the extent that the bank advises registered investment companies. However, the exclusion/inclusion feature is highly nuanced. The bank itself does not necessarily become an investment adviser for purposes of the Investment Advisers Act in its entirety, but merely to the extent that a "separately identifiable department or division" performs "such services or actions." Not surprisingly, banks as entities seek to avoid entanglement with the Advisers Act with respect to their entire operations and so are likely to segregate advisory activities within an affiliate or a bank unit if the activities are provided to a registered investment company. The bank unit's activities do not need to be entirely segregated from bank activities, and bank employees may function in dual capacities within the investment adviser as an adviser to the registered vehicle or in discharging investment advisory duties for traditional banking non-registered investment management services.

5. *Family offices.* The "family office" exclusion was added to the Adviser Act's definition of an investment adviser by the Dodd-Frank Act. The new exclusion was necessitated in part by other amendments under the Dodd-Frank Act which eliminated registration exemptions on which family offices previously relied. Family offices traditionally are companies formed to manage the wealth and service the affairs of the members of a single family, which over the course of several generations could become quite expansive. Family offices were once fairly rare and conjured up the likes of the Rockefeller family. Indeed, the Rockefeller family needs outgrew a conventional family office arrangement and morphed into a low-profile specialized investment manager for very high net worth individuals under the aegis of Rockefeller & Co. and Rockefeller Financial Services. Nevertheless, with increasing instances of fabulous wealth, family offices are no longer as rare as they once were and fulfill the need of a unique client niche. The SEC adopted Adviser Act Rule 202(a)(11)(G)-1 to give some substance to the concept and in particular the permitted clientele of the family office. Some hedge fund managers have also reconstituted their primary investment vehicles as family offices to manage their own immense wealth, and thereby diminish regulatory scrutiny, in response to specific challenges faced by the manager. *See In the Matter of S.A.C. Capital Advisors, L.P., et al.*, Investment Advisers Act Release No.

3864 (June 27, 2014) (noting respondents' undertaking to transfer hedge fund manager operations to new family office). The SEC subsequently agreed that in 2018 the hedge fund manager's principal can reenter the hedge fund business.

6. *Investment advisers under the Advisers Act and the Company Act.* As discussed above, the Advisers Act statutorily contains a definition for investment advisers. The term investment adviser is separately defined under the Investment Company Act to describe a contractual relationship with a registered investment company involving furnishing advice regarding or managing the investment company's investment activities. This definition also encompasses sub-advisers to investment companies (i.e., investment advisers who contract with the investment company's primary investment adviser to furnish such services).

6.3 Registration as an Investment Adviser

The Advisers Act generally requires investment advisers to register with the SEC unless exempted or otherwise excluded from the registration requirements. Registration under the Advisers Act is significant in several respects. First, affirmative registration requirements reflect a regulatory determination that the defined class of market professionals, namely investment advisers, must provide regulators with specific information. In other words, the regulator, in this case the SEC, has a right to obtain basic information about investment advisers required to register. Directly tied to the information-gathering function of registration requirements is a corollary practical compliance imperative for potential registrants: it is a violation of federal law for an investment adviser to engage in the business (or more specifically to use the instrumentality of interstate commerce) and not to register, unless exempt or excluded from the registration requirements.

There is a third important aspect to registration under the Advisers Act. Unlike advisers not required to register, registered investment advisers (including investment advisers who are required to be registered but have not) are subject to variety of additional regulatory requirements relating to client disclosure, recordkeeping, contracting with clients, custody of clients' assets, and compliance policy and procedures. These are discussed in more detail in Chapter 8. However, all investment advisers, registered and unregistered, must adhere to the self-effectuating general antifraud provisions of Advisers Act Section 206. Thus, Section 206's broad prohibitions on fraudulent or deceitful conduct apply to all advisers whether registered or not. There is one major caveat in this regard. Advisers Act Section 206(4) authorizes the SEC to adopt rules to prohibit fraudulent conduct but also rules reasonably designed to prevent fraudulent conduct. Generally the SEC has used its rulemaking authority to regulate only activities of advisers registered or required to be registered. The one exception in this regard is Advisers Rule 206(4)-8. It extends to all advisers, whether registered or unregistered, which seems reasonable in that the rule broadly proscribes advisers from engaging in fraudulent conduct aimed at investors or prospective investors in pooled investment vehicles, including private funds (such as hedge funds) excluded from regulation under the Company Act.

6.3.1 Some History about the Structure of Adviser Registration Requirements

For the reasons described above, it is very important as a matter of practice for investment advisers to know if they are subject to registration and, if so, whether registration is at the federal or state level. Ironically, some investment advisers actually prefer registration at the federal level if the alternative is state registration. At the very least, lawyers advising clients need to be able to navigate through the various registration requirements, which poses technical challenges in terms of reading the statute and the accompanying rules to reach a conclusion. Mastering the technical details is absolutely essential in practice. However, it is not necessarily a good use of time in a survey course. Instead, it makes more sense to understand a bit about the structure of registration requirements and the key elements governing the structural scheme. These elements emerge from a basic narrative describing the evolution of adviser registration requirements which entails three different stages.

When the Advisers Act was enacted, it contained a number of exclusions from registration for investment advisers where regulatory concerns appeared muted. Many of these remain today, such as exclusions for investment advisers who solely advise insurance companies, operate solely intrastate, or who were established to service charitable organizations or collective funds established by charitable organizations. In the years after enactment, the exclusions were extended to advisers who act pursuant to an exclusive arrangement with a Taft-Hartley or tax-qualified defined pension plan.

The Advisers Act used to contain a very important exclusion for advisers with fewer than 15 clients—the so-called "private investment adviser exclusion." The private investment adviser exclusion was relied on widely by hedge funds, private equity funds, and venture capital funds until its repeal in 2010 by the Dodd-Frank Act. The source of the problem with the private investment adviser exclusion arose from a somewhat dated counting rule interpretation by the SEC for purposes of the exclusion. Under the SEC's interpretive counting rule, an adviser's clients were counted in terms of each client entity (such as a limited partnership) advised by the adviser rather than the number of participants in the limited partnership if one "looked through" the entity. In other words, a limited partnership might have ninety limited partners, but it would count as a single client for the private investment adviser exclusion. In 2004, the SEC sought to replace its existing counting approach with a formal rule than eliminated the counting rule's application to hedge funds. The SEC's formal rule was struck down by the United States Court of Appeals in *SEC v. Goldstein*, 451 F.3d. 873 (D.C. Cir. 2006). In 2010, the private investment adviser exclusion was replaced with a more pro-active regulatory approach toward advisers of private funds.

In addition, however, the registration scheme underwent a major transformation in 1996 as part of the National Securities Markets Improvements Act. In that legislation, Congress adopted a registration scheme for investment advisers that separated advisers in terms of whether they should be registered with the SEC or state authorities. The undisputed purpose of Advisers Act Section 203A, as reflected by its structure, was to limit the number of federally-registered investment advisers. As of 2018, there were approximately 12,500 SEC-registered advisers and roughly 3500 reporting exempt advisers. Although the numbers are imprecise, it is estimated that roughly twice as many advisers are registered with state authorities as opposed to the SEC. Under this federalized scheme, the SEC directly regulates the most economically significant investment advisers in terms of assets under management by advisers and also in terms of scope of advisory activities, such as advisers operating across multiple states or advisers discharging non-management advisory functions to clients with substantial assets. This scheme was further modified by the Dodd-Frank Act, expanding the potential class of advisers who will register with state regulators.

Title IV of the Dodd-Frank Act, a mammoth piece of legislation enacted in 2010 in response to the Financial Crisis of 2008, represented the third major stage in bringing about the current approach to adviser registration. It specifically addressed registration of investment advisers, principally registration of investment advisers to hedge funds and other private funds, and also expanded the class of advisers prohibited from registering with the SEC (i.e., the class of state-registered advisers).

The Dodd-Frank Act fundamentally altered the registration treatment of advisers to private funds. Whereas prior to the Dodd-Frank Act, advisers with fewer than 15 clients (which could mean fewer than 15 hedge funds or private funds in aggregate) were exempt from registration, the Dodd-Frank Act eliminated the private adviser exemption and established a different registration scheme for private funds. In place of the private adviser exemption is a series of individual exclusions depending on the type and size of the funds advised by the investment adviser. The original exemption has been replaced by three basic exclusions—for advisers to venture capital funds, for advisers to mid-sized or smaller private funds, and for foreign advisers of private funds having a small number of U.S.-based investors.

Of these, the exclusion to advisers of private funds (other than venture capital funds) is the most intricate. It has two different exemptions tied to a $150 million threshold. The first is for U.S. advisers which exclusively manage private funds having assets in aggregate of less than $150 million. The second relates to non-U.S. advisers, that is, advisers having a place of business outside the U.S., with a qualified private fund or funds resident in the U.S. Such advisers are exempt as long as managed U.S. assets are exclusively held in private funds and the private funds in aggregate hold AUM of less than $150 million from U.S. investors. A remnant of the private adviser exemption survived for foreign private advisers, that is (i) advisers with no place of business in the U.S., and (ii) having fewer than 15 U.S. clients in foreign private funds with less than $25 million in funds attributable to U.S.-based clients or investors.

In addition, the Dodd-Frank Act once again expanded the potential class of advisers excluded from federal regulation by creating a new category—so-called "mid-sized advisers." Under Section 203A, mid-sized advisers must register with the states if they manage less than $100 million in assets, unless (1) they advise a registered investment company or business development company; (2) are not subject to examination by state regulators in their state of principal business; or (3) are not otherwise exempt.

6.3.2 A Practical Guide to the Scheme for Adviser Registration

With this background, it is now possible to try to present the key features of the registration scheme in a schematic form. As is apparent from the preceding discussion, the registration scheme has become increasingly intricate with overlapping classification criteria. To properly analyze any registration issue, it is necessary to consider three additional levels of analysis in addition to the general requirement mandating registration found in Section 203(a): (i) a bifurcated registration classification scheme (in a framework laid out in Section 203A) that essentially requires many small and mid-sized advisers to register only with an appropriate state jurisdiction (if available), while permitting all other investment advisers subject to the general registration requirement to register with the SEC; (ii) rule-based categories created by the SEC pursuant to SEC rulemaking authority under Section 203(c) to expand the class of advisers eligible to register with the SEC that would otherwise be required to register with an available state jurisdiction; and (iii) statutory registration exemptions from the general registration requirement found in Section 203(b). Two statutory provisions are critical to this scheme: Advisers Act Sections 203(b) and 203A. To a lesser extent, the definition of an investment adviser found in Adviser Act Section 202(a)(11) and for foreign private adviser found in Section 202(a)(30) are also relevant.

The results of the basic scheme are summarized in the tables appended to this chapter. Common registration categories are fairly easy to summarize, and practitioners should be aware of the basic framework of the registration scheme. One way to think about the structure created from the combination of statutory and rule-based requirements is as a four-tiered scheme: (i) advisers who must register with the SEC; (ii) advisers who are permitted to register with the SEC; (iii) advisers prohibited from registering with the SEC in view of an adequate available state registration scheme; and (iv) advisers exempt from registration regardless of registration status under applicable state law provisions.

Who must register with the SEC? In some ways, it is easiest to start with the obvious. For example, investment advisers to mutual funds, closed-end funds or exchange-traded funds organized as mutual funds must register with the SEC. This follows from the basic result that any adviser that is an adviser to a registered in-vestment company must registered with the SEC, no matter how small. Similarly, any U.S. investment adviser that manages U.S.-based advisory clients, located either across state lines or that include private funds, with aggregate assets greater than $150 million, must also register with the SEC, with the exception of advisers that solely advise venture capital funds. Finally any interstate investment adviser advising clients in aggregate with more than $100 million in assets under management but in total with less than $150 million in assets, excluding any investment adviser who exclusively advises private funds with less than $150 million in assets, must register. This yields three basic categories that must register. In addition, under the state preemption provision (Section 203A(c)), if an adviser is required to register with the SEC, it cannot be required to separately register with the state (though representatives of the investment adviser in that state may be required to register).

There are others who are required to register, but the requirement turns on a far more detailed analysis. Probably the major stumbling block is understanding the interface between the state registration regime for advisers and the federal scheme administered by the SEC, and so it is necessary to address that category next.

The state-federal registration scheme interface and who is prohibited from registering with the SEC. Section 203A's mandate skews the logic of the statutory registration analysis by framing the registration issue in terms of a prohibition on federal registration. Specifically, Section 203A strictly prohibits federal registration by less economically significant investment advisers who cannot meet certain statutory thresholds. Under the section, nearly two-thirds of U.S. advisers register with states rather than the SEC. Excluding those categories of advisers required to register with the SEC already discussed above, federal law establishes two categories of advisers prohibited from registering with the SEC:

(i) state-registered interstate advisers with less than $25 million in assets under management; and

(ii) state-registered interstate advisers with less than $100 million in assets under management (or such higher threshold prescribed by the SEC) but more than $25 million in assets and who (i) are subject to examination by state authorities; and (ii) would not be required to register with 15 or more states as a result.

Here are several caveats in applying these two basic prohibitions. First, the advisers required to register with the SEC are not subject to these two federal registration prohibitions, for example, advisers to registered investment companies. Second, there are advisers with less than $25 million in assets under management located in states that do not have a registration scheme (e.g., Wyoming), and such advisers by default are subject to SEC registration. Similarly, there are state-registered interstate advisers who manage less than $100 million but where the state either does not conduct examinations of advisers or exempts advisers from examination. Once again, such advisers default into the SEC-administered registration scheme and are required to register with the SEC. Finally, the Advisers Act preempts state registration requirements as to federally-registered advisers.

Other advisers permitted to register with the SEC (i.e., are not subject to the federal registration prohibitions). One of the interesting by-products of state-federal interface effectuated by federal registration prohibitions has been the desire of several different classes of investment advisers to register with the SEC rather than the states. Again this refers only to advisers who would otherwise be required to register at the state level in light of what has already been said. Undoubtedly being an SEC-registered adviser carries with it the reputation effect that the adviser belongs with the better-known and better capitalized advisers. However, reputation considerations alone would hardly lead to a rational bifurcated registration scheme.

Who then are these advisers who actually prefer federal registration rather than state registration? First, there are state-registered investment advisers that may have to register in many states with the attendant administrative difficulties or who are already affiliated with an SEC-registered adviser. Dealing with the SEC as an SEC-registered investment adviser largely means one-stop shopping on substantive regulatory issues. Second, there are advisers that are engaged in very sophisticated advisory businesses that do not actually manage assets. Under the asset-based thresholds, these advisers may seem economically small, when in fact they may have dozens or even hundreds of employees.

Congress recognized the need for some flexibility in the bifurcated scheme, and therefore granted rulemaking authority to the SEC to enlarge the class of advisers that may register under the federal registration scheme. The SEC in turn has exercised this authority to exempt certain types of advisers from the federal registration prohibitions. The principal exemptions are set forth in Advisers Act Rule 203A-2 and include: (a) major pension consultants; (b) investment advisers affiliated with SEC-registered advisers; (c) advisers registering in anticipation of satisfying the SEC registration requirements within 120 days (i.e., newly-formed advisers who are gathering assets for management); (d) investment advisers who would otherwise be required to register with 15 or more states; and (e) internet advisers.

And what of foreign-based advisers? One final category of potential registrant should be noted: non-U.S. based investment advisers. Obviously a purely non-U.S. investment adviser is not subject to U.S. registration in the case that it does not conduct business in the United States. Servicing U.S. based clients can trigger domestic registration at the state or federal level of non-U.S. advisers, including advisers with no office or personnel in the United States. The more interesting situations are when non-U.S. investment advisers (who may have a non-primary place of business in the U.S.) and foreign private advisers (who do not have a place of business in the U.S.) are subject to domestic U.S. registration. Put simply, they are subject to registration when they have U.S. clients with the exception of two specific exemptions. Non-U.S.-based advisers are exempt from U.S. registration provided the U.S. advised clients consist solely of private funds having less than $150 million in assets in aggregate. Foreign private advisers are exempt from registration as long as they are non-U.S. based and serve no more than 15 U.S. clients (including investors in non-U.S. based private funds) and the investors account for less than $25 million in assets under management (or such higher amount as determined by the SEC).

Exempt advisers. The final category to be aware of are advisers expressly exempt from the registration requirements. As noted, in some cases, foreign private advisers and non-U.S. based advisers advising U.S. private funds with less than $150 million in assets. A similar exemption exists for U.S. advisers advising private funds with less than $150 million in assets. In addition, advisers who advise solely venture capital funds are exempt from registration. There are other exemptions summarized in the tables below, but one additional distinction should be noted. Although an adviser may be exempt from registration, there may nevertheless be some exempt advisers who are subject to specific SEC reporting obligations. Advisers in this category are referred to as *exempt reporting advisers.* Exempt reporting advisers (especially large venture capital advisers or modest sized U.S. private fund advisers) may be subject to reporting select information on Form ADV discussed below.

6.3.3 The Practicalities of Registering as an Adviser

How to register is frequently nothing more than an afterthought in academic explorations of investment adviser registration requirements, but it is the kind of subject that has ministerial significance in ordinary practice. An investment adviser that is subject to registration cannot engage in business until registered. Both federal and state investment adviser registrants use a uniform registration process. Prospective registrants register by filing electronically Form ADV (consisting of Parts 1 and 2A & B) through the Investment Advisory Depository System (IARD), an electronic system maintained by FINRA (the Financial Industry Regulatory Authority).

The Form ADV is the adviser registration form developed by the SEC. Part 1 provides the regulator with confidential information relating to the investment adviser's business and operations in a basic check-the-box and fill-in-the-blank format. Part 2 is closely tied with Advisers Act Rule 204-3 which requires delivery of a brochure consisting in form or substance of all information found in Part 2A and all relevant information from Part 2B. In other words, Part 2 of Form ADV is a disclosure statement for advisory clients. Part 2A provides information about firm business practices, fees and conflicts of interest. Part 2B, referred to as a brochure supplement, requires information about firm personnel providing investment advice to clients. A firm must deliver firm supplements to clients only about firm personnel relevant to the particular client. To some extent, state requirements vary from federal requirements relating to brochure rule disclosures.

Within 45 days of a registration filing, the SEC must either grant or deny the registration. The system is not based on investment qualifications but rather is purely disclosure and information driven. Once registered, an investment adviser remains an investment adviser unless the registration is revoked by the SEC or the adviser files for withdrawal and the SEC approves the filing. The adviser's Form ADV must be updated annually. Associated persons of the investment advisers, such as officers or employees, are not required to separately register through the IARD system.

As part of the Dodd-Frank Act, the SEC was given rulemaking authority to require systemic risk reporting by certain investment advisers. Pursuant to Advisers Act Rule 204(b)(1), non-exempt private funds are required to make confidential reports on Form PF. Large private fund advisers are subject to fairly extensive reporting requirements (both Sections 1 and 2), while less extensive requirements apply to smaller private fund advisers (Section 1 only).

Table 6A — Summary of Adviser Registration Requirements

	SEC REGISTRATION REQUIRED		
	Category	**Nature or Qualifications**	**Statutory or Rule Basis**
1.	**Advisers to "registered investment companies" ("RIC Adviser")**		General registration requirement and express non-applicability of prohibition on registration with SEC (IAA Section 203A(a)(1))
2.	**Large advisers (without any specific exclusion)**	Generally, any adviser that manages more than $100 million AUM with some exemptions for venture capital and private fund advisers	General registration requirement and express non-applicability of prohibition on registration with SEC (IAA Section 203A(a)(2))
3.	**Large private fund advisers**	Investment adviser that (1) manages from a U.S. principal office exclusively private funds in aggregate with more than $150 million in AUM; or (2) manages exclusively from a principal office outside the U.S. with the private funds located in the U.S. that in aggregate have more than $150 million in AUM	General registration requirement + (1) negative implication of IAA Section 203(m) and Rule 203(m)–1(a); (2) negative implication of Section 203(m) and Rule 203(m)-1(b)
4.	**Certain small investment advisers** (essentially small Wyoming-based advisers)	Non-RIC investment adviser that has less than $25 million in AUM whose principal place of business is in a state that does not require registration of investment advisers (e.g., Wyoming) and is not otherwise exempt	IAA Section 203A(a)(1)
5.	**Certain mid-sized advisers not fully regulated by state**	Adviser which manages less than $100 million in AUM with principal place of business is in a state that does not examine investment advisers registered in the state.	IAA Section 203A(a)(2)

Table 6A, continued

	SEC REGISTRATION PERMITTED BY RULE (EVEN IF STATE REGISTRATION AVAILABLE)		
	Category	**Nature or Qualifications**	**Statutory or Rule Basis**
1.	**Pension consultants**	Pension consultant to at least $200 million of advised assets	IAA Rule 203A-2(a) + general registration requirement + IAA Section 203A(c)
2.	**Affiliated investment advisers to SEC registered investment advisers**	1. affiliation by any of 3 types of controlling relationship 2. share same principal place of business as registered adviser	IAA Rule 203A-2(b) + general registration requirement + IAA Section 203A(c)
3.	**Multi-state investment advisers**	Adviser which would otherwise be required to register as an investment adviser in 15 or more states	IAA Rule 203A-2(d) + general registration requirement + IAA Section 203A(c)
4.	**Internet investment advisers**	(1) Adviser which provides advice exclusively over interactive website, except advice permitted to 15 or fewer non-internet clients; (2) maintains record of eligibility; and (3) is not in a control affiliation with an adviser that seeks to use the internet adviser as the basis for registration.	IAA Rule 203A-2(e) + general registration requirement + IAA Section 203A(c)
5.	**Prospectively eligible advisers**	Must have reasonable expectation of eligibility within 120 days	IAA Rule 203A-2(c) + general registration requirement + IAA Section 203A(c)

	EXEMPTIONS FROM SEC REGISTRATION		
	Category	**Nature or Qualifications**	**Statutory or Rule Basis**
1.	**Intrastate investment adviser**	Adviser the principal office of which is located in the same state as all of its clients and does not advise any private funds	IAA Section 203(b)(1)
2.	**Investment advisers which solely service insurance companies**		IAA Section 203(b)(2)
3.	**Foreign private investment advisers**	Adviser with no place of business in the U.S. nor holds itself out in the U.S. as an investment adviser and has 15 or fewer investors or clients in private funds advised by the adviser and the U.S. investors hold in aggregate less than $25 million in AUM	IAA Section 203(b)(3), Section 202(a)(30) & Rule 202(a)(30)-1
4.	**Investment advisers to charitable companies or religious retirement plans**		IAA Section 203(b)(4) & (b)(5)
5.	**Commodity futures trading advisers which dispense incidental investment advice**		IAA Section 203(b)(6)
6.	**Investment advisers which solely advise small business investment companies**		IAA Section 203(b)(7)

Table 6A, continued

	SEC REGISTRATION PROHIBITED (i.e., State-Registered Advisers)		
	Category	**Nature or Qualifications**	**Statutory or Rule Basis**
1.	**Advisers with less than $25 million in AUM**	1. State of principal place of business permits registration 2. Does not advise a RIC 3. Not a BDC 4. SEC registration not permitted by rule	IAA Section 203A(a)(1)
2.	**Advisers with less than $100 million in AUM**	1. State of principal place of business permits registration and *conducts examinations* 2. Does not advise a RIC 3. Not a BDC 4. SEC registration not permitted by rule	IAA Section 203A(a)(2)

	STATE REGISTRATION PREEMPTION		
	Category	**Nature or Qualifications**	**Statutory or Rule Basis**
1.	**Advisers registered with the SEC under IAA Section 203**		IAA Section 203A(b)(1)(A)
2.	**Advisers excepted from the federal definition of investment adviser under IAA Section 202(a)(11)**	Significantly, this provision excludes from state registration (i) bank advisory activities outside the scope of the investment adviser status; (ii) credit rating agencies; and (ii) family offices	IAA Section 203A(b)(2)(B)

Chapter 7

Fiduciary and Antifraud Obligations of Investment Advisers

Key Ideas: The Investment Advisers Act contains substantive requirements that regulate the conduct and activities of investment advisers, whether registered or unregistered. These substantive requirements include both affirmative obligations for advisers (covered in Chapter 8) as well as conduct requirements (covered in this chapter). In addition, Chapter 9 provides an overview of how regulators use the Advisers Act to police the activities of private funds, including hedge funds, through oversight of their advisers. Section 206 and the rules thereunder are the source for the Act's antifraud provisions and other conduct restrictions. Section 206 contains four subsections, two of which are of unusual significance in understanding the Act's profound effect in regulating adviser conduct—subsections 206(2) and 206(4). Section 206(2) prohibits advisers from conduct and dealings that involve undisclosed conflicts of interest with clients. This simple principle applies to a potentially vast range of adviser activities, especially when applied to the affairs of pooled investment vehicles. Moreover, this principle imparts a fiduciary cast to the role of advisers under federal law, thereby extending the scope of regulation beyond mere fraud. Section 206(4) authorizes the SEC to adopt rules that are designed to prevent fraud, and thus, permits the SEC to fill in gaps in statutory protections with rules designed to police conduct that is not intrinsically fraudulent. Sections 206(1) and (3) are nevertheless important. The former prohibits fraudulent conduct and practices, while the latter provides special protections with respect to the adviser's trading activity on behalf of or with a client. Although investment clients may be injured by conduct in violation of Section 206 or the rules thereunder, the Act does not afford investors a private remedy for damages for such adviser misconduct.

Chapter Contents

7.1 Introduction

As noted, the Advisers Act addresses two broad categories of regulatory issues: (i) status issues relating to the definition of investment advisers and registration requirements; and (ii) issues relating to restrictions and requirements on the conduct and activities of investment advisers, either as a whole or, in some cases, solely those who are registered. This chapter and Chapters 8 and 9 deal with the latter category involving substantive regulation of adviser activity and conduct. This chapter addresses fiduciary and antifraud prohibitions found in Section 206 of the Advisers Act, which covers a wide range of investment advisers' conduct, including fraudulent practices and undisclosed conflicts of interest, rather than affirmative obligations relating to fees, disclosure and safekeeping of client assets.

The Advisers Act's general antifraud provision is compact and so it is perhaps easiest to begin with the statute's text. Section 206 contains four clauses:

> It shall be unlawful for any investment adviser, by use of the mails or any means or instrumentality of interstate commerce, directly or indirectly—
>
> (1) to employ any device, scheme, or artifice to defraud any client or pros-pective client;
>
> (2) to engage in any transaction, practice, or course of business which op-erates as a fraud or deceit upon any client or prospective client;
>
> (3) acting as principal for his own account, knowingly to sell any security to or purchase any security from a client, or acting as broker for a person other than such client, knowingly to effect any sale or purchase of any security for the account of such client, without disclosing to such client in writing before the completion of such transaction the capacity in which he is acting and obtaining the consent of the client to such transaction. The prohibitions of this paragraph (3) shall not apply to any transaction with a customer of a broker or dealer if such broker or dealer is not acting as an investment adviser in relation to such transaction; or
>
> (4) to engage in any act, practice, or course of business which is fraudulent, deceptive, or manipulative. The Commission shall, for the purposes of this paragraph (4) by rules and regulations define, and prescribe means reason-ably designed to prevent,

such acts, practices, and courses of business as are fraudulent, deceptive, or manipulative.

While the four clauses seem to overlap one another, they each serve slightly different purposes with respect to imposing restrictions on the conduct and activity of investment advisers. By taking some liberties with the text, this four-tier prohibitory provision can be summarized as follows:

(1) Prohibition of fraud (essentially a classic formulation of a general antifraud provision).

(2) Prohibition of practices that are deceitful, i.e., practices that are in breach of a fiduciary duty owed to clients, including undisclosed conflicts of interest.

(3) Prohibition of particular types of trading involving client accounts in the absence of the client's prior informed consent.

(4) Grant of rulemaking authority to the SEC to adopt rules that either define fraudulent conduct or prescribe means reasonably designed to prevent fraud.

In a survey text, there is not much to add to the obvious need for prohibiting fraudulent conduct. However, in a casebook such as this one, these provisions merit closer inspection. The Adviser Act's prohibition is consonant with antifraud provisions under the other federal securities law statutes, which prohibit fraud broadly, although each statute is designed to protect slightly different classes of investors (i.e., offerees and purchasers of securities in the Securities Act, investors purchasing or selling securities in the Exchange Act, or clients of investment advisers in the Adviser Act). The Advisers Act's protection of the adviser's "client" clearly encompasses fraudulent misstatements, but also extends more naturally than other instances of antifraud principles to practices that are fraudulent from a relational perspective (e.g., the failure to act to protect a client from disclosure that over time becomes misleading).

Section 206(2) is of particular note, not merely because it expands the scope of conduct subject to regulatory sanction to non-fraudulent conduct (Sections 17(2) and (3) of the Securities Act do, too), but to conduct implicating fiduciary obligations. As a result, the subsection establishes a higher standard of conduct for investment advisers than currently prevails for broker-dealers under the Exchange Act. This particular issue is a source of some controversy, an issue previously noted in connection with the broker-dealer exclusion from the definition of an investment adviser. However, the controversy is not that investment advisers are subject to a higher duty, but rather that broker-dealers and their associated persons are not when acting in very similar situations.

Section 206(3) is not discussed in this chapter, because of its more specialized focus. However, it is notable among the antifraud provisions of Section 206 because it imposes an even higher fiduciary standard with respect to securities trading involving client assets. Specifically, it imposes flat prohibitions, absent prior written approval of the client, on an adviser trading as a principal with its client (i.e., as the counterparty in the client's transaction) or in facilitating cross-trading among clients. The SEC has provided some relief from these flat prohibitions by rule, but they are extremely limited. In the area of trading, the statute goes beyond mere disclosure and requires affirmative client consent.

Finally, Section 206(4), which is sometimes referred to as the "great coat hook," gives the SEC significant administrative latitude in governing advisory practices that the agency has determined to be problematic (i.e., conduct that is not itself necessarily fraudulent, but might lead to fraudulent practices). Technically, from an administrative law perspective, the provision is a grant of rulemaking authority that permits the SEC to adopt rules designed to prevent fraud by prohibiting certain practices and conduct. However, for purposes here, the provision's relevance is that it has been used by the SEC to impose affirmative obligations on investment advisers to root out certain conduct and clearly identify prospective practices that are sources of recurring problems that may lead to fraudulent practices. The takeaway from this four-tiered prohibitory structure is that the IAA creates more exacting standards for the conduct and practices of investment advisers than would exist with only a general antifraud provision.

This chapter is arranged in three key substantive parts. The first of the three sections focuses on Sections 206(1) and (2), and in particular, undisclosed conflicts of interests of investment advisers. The next section broadly describes the SEC's rulemaking powers to police areas of potential misconduct by advisers and specifically highlights their application to advertising and marketing relating to representations regarding adviser performance, an area of recurring problems. Finally, the text addresses the issue of whether the Adviser Act creates implied rights of private action for investors that have been harmed.

7.2 Fraud and Undisclosed Conflicts of Interest

Section 206(1) prohibits fraud by an investment adviser. Such a general prohibition is important, but also unsurprising. It represents the bare minimum in terms of investor protection. A regulatory scheme that would permit fraud is difficult to imagine. Section 206(2) uses additional language to also prohibit advisers from "engag[ing] in any transaction, practice, or course of business which operates as a fraud or deceit upon any client or prospective client." Obvious questions arising from this language are whether this prohibition goes beyond mere fraud, and if so, how far? The Supreme Court's answer to these questions has radically shaped the obligations owed by investment advisers to their clients under federal law.

7.2.1 Fraud versus Breach of Fiduciary Duty

SEC v. Capital Gains Research Bureau, Inc.

375 U.S. 180 (1963)

[**Textbook Note**: *The significance of this Supreme Court decision construing the scope of Section 206(2) cannot be overstated. It is easily the single most important decision presented in this casebook. At its heart, the Court's decision ex-*

amines whether the Act was intended to, and in fact did, expand normal antifraud principles at common law to encompass a broader range of adviser activities. The case arises out of a controversial practice commonly known as touting, which also was the backdrop for the SEC's concerns in Lowe v. SEC *addressed in Chapter 6.*]

Justice Goldberg. We are called upon in this case to decide whether under the Investment Advisers Act of 1940 the Securities and Exchange Commission may obtain an injunction compelling a registered investment adviser to disclose to his clients a practice of purchasing shares of a security for his own account shortly before recommending that security for long-term investment and then immediately selling the shares at a profit upon the rise in the market price following the recommendation. The answer to this question turns on whether the practice—known in the trade as "scalping"—"operates as a fraud or deceit upon any client or prospective client" within the meaning of the Act. We hold that it does and that the Commission may "enforce compliance" with the Act by obtaining an injunction requiring the adviser to make full disclosure of the practice to his clients.

... Respondents publish two investment advisory services, one of which—"a Capital Gains Report"—is the subject of this proceeding. The Report is mailed monthly to approximately 5,000 subscribers who each pay an annual subscription price of $18. It carries the following description:

> *An Investment Service devoted exclusively to (1) the protection of investment capital. (2) The realization of a steady and attractive income therefrom. (3) The accumulation of CAPITAL GAINS thru the timely purchase of corporate equities that are proved to be undervalued.*

Between March 15, 1960, and November 7, 1960, respondents, on six different occasions, purchased shares of a particular security shortly before recommending it in the Report for long-term investment. On each occasion, there was an increase in the market price and the volume of trading of the recommended security within a few days after the distribution of the Report. Immediately thereafter, respondents sold their shares of these securities at a profit. They did not disclose any aspect of these transactions to their clients or prospective clients.

On the basis of the above facts, the Commission requested a preliminary injunction as necessary to effectuate the purposes of the Investment Advisers Act of 1940. The injunction would have required respondents, in any future Report, to disclose the material facts concerning, inter alia, any purchase of recommended securities "within a very short period prior to the distribution of a recommendation...," and "(t)he intent to sell and the sale of said securities ... within a very short period after distribution of said recommendation...."

....

The decision in this case turns on whether Congress, in empowering the courts to enjoin any practice which operates "as a fraud or deceit upon any client or prospective client," intended to require the Commission to establish fraud and deceit "in their technical sense," including intent to injure and actual injury to clients, or whether Congress intended a broad remedial construction of the Act which would encompass nondisclosure of material facts. For resolution of this issue we consider the history and purpose of the Investment Advisers Act of 1940.

I.

The Investment Advisers Act of 1940 was the last in a series of Acts designed to eliminate certain abuses in the securities industry, abuses which were found to have contributed to the stock market crash of 1929 and the depression of the 1930's. It was preceded by the Securities Act of 1933, the Securities Exchange Act of 1934, the Public Utility Holding Company Act of 1935, the Trust Indenture Act of 1939, and the Investment Company Act of 1940. A fundamental purpose, common to these statutes, was to substitute a philosophy of full disclosure for the philosophy of caveat emptor and thus to achieve a high standard of business ethics in the securities industry. As we recently said in a related context, "It requires but little appreciation ... of what happened in this country during the 1920's and 1930's to realize how essential it is that the highest ethical standards prevail" in every facet of the securities industry.

....

[Congress'] concern was not limited to deliberate or conscious impediments to objectivity. Both the advisers and the Commission were well aware that whenever advice to a client might result in financial benefit to the adviser—other than the fee for his advice—"that advice to a client might in some way be tinged with that pecuniary interest [whether consciously or] subconsciously motivated...." The report quoted one leading investment adviser who said that he "would put the emphasis ... on subconscious" motivation in such situations. It quoted a member of the Commission staff who suggested that a significant part of the problem was not the existence of a "deliberate intent" to obtain a financial advantage, but rather the existence "subconsciously [of] a prejudice" in favor of one's own financial interests. The report incorporated the Code of Ethics and Standards of Practice of one of the leading investment counsel associations, which contained the following canon:

> '[An investment adviser] should continuously occupy an impartial and disinterested position, as free as humanly possible from the *subtle* influence of prejudice, *conscious or unconscious*; he should scrupulously avoid any affiliation, or any act, which subjects his position to challenge in this respect." (Emphasis added.)

....

One activity specifically mentioned and condemned by investment advisers who testified before the Commission was "trading by investment counselors for their own account in securities in which their clients were interested...."

....

... The broad proscription against "any ... practice ... which operates ... as a fraud or deceit upon any client or prospective client" remained in the bill from beginning to end. And the Committee Reports indicate a desire to preserve "the personalized character of the services of investment advisers," and to eliminate conflicts of interest between the investment adviser and the clients as safeguards both to "unsophisticated investors" and to "bona fide investment counsel." The Investment Advisers Act of 1940 thus reflects a congressional recognition "of the delicate fiduciary nature of an investment advisory relationship," as well as a congressional intent to eliminate, or at least to expose, all conflicts of interest which might incline as investment adviser—consciously or unconsciously—to render advice which was not disinterested. It would defeat the manifest purpose of the Investment Advisers Act of 1940 for us to hold, therefore, that Congress, in empowering the courts to enjoin any practice which operates "as a fraud or deceit," intended to require proof of intent to injure and actual injury to clients.

This conclusion moreover, is not in derogation of the common law of fraud, as the District Court and the majority of the Court of Appeals suggested. To the contrary, it finds support in the process by which the courts have adapted the common law of fraud to the commercial transactions of our society....

....

Nor is it necessary in a suit against a fiduciary, which Congress recognized the investment adviser to be, to establish all the elements required in a suit against a party to an arm's-length transaction. Courts have imposed on a fiduciary an affirmative duty of "utmost good faith, and full and fair disclosure of all material facts," as well as an affirmative obligation "to employ reasonable care to avoid misleading" his clients. There has also been a growing recognition by common-law courts that the doctrines of fraud and deceit which developed around transactions involving land and other tangible items of wealth are ill-suited to the sale of such intangibles as advice and securities, and that, accordingly, the doctrines must be adapted to the merchandise in issue. The 1909 New York case of *Ridgely v. Keene,* 134 App. Div. 647, 119 N.Y.S. 451, illustrates this continuing development. An investment adviser who, like respondents, published an investment advisory service, agreed, for compensation, to influence his clients to buy shares in a certain security. He did not disclose the agreement to his client but sought "to excuse his conduct by asserting that ... he honestly believed, that his subscribers would profit by his advice...." The court, holding that "his belief in the soundness of his advice is wholly immaterial," declared the act in question "a palpable fraud."

We cannot assume that Congress, in enacting legislation to prevent fraudulent practices by investment advisers, was unaware of these developments in the common law of fraud. Thus, even if we were to agree with the courts below that Congress had intended, in effect, to codify the common law of fraud in the Investment Advisers Act of 1940, it would be logical to conclude that Congress codified the common law "remedially" as the courts had adapted it to the prevention of fraudulent securities transactions by fiduciaries, not "technically" as it has traditionally been applied in damage suits between parties to arm's-length transactions involving land and ordinary chattels.

....

II.

We turn now to a consideration of whether the specific conduct here in issue was the type which Congress intended to reach in the Investment Advisers Act of 1940. It is arguable—indeed it was argued by "some investment counsel representatives" who testified before the Commission—that any "trading by investment counselors for their own account in securities in which their clients were interested" creates a potential conflict of interest which must be eliminated. We need not go that far in this case, since here the Commission seeks only disclosure of a conflict of interests with significantly greater potential for abuse than in the situation described above. An adviser who, like respondents, secretly trades on the market effect of his own recommendation may be motivated—consciously or unconsciously—to recommend a given security not because of its potential for long-run price increase (which would profit the client), but because of its potential for short-run price increase in response to anticipated activity from the recommendation (which would profit the adviser). An investor seeking the advice of a registered investment adviser must, if the legislative purpose is to be served, be permitted to evaluate such overlapping motivations, through appropriate disclosure, in deciding whether an adviser is serving "two masters" or only one, "especially ... if one of the masters happens to be economic self-interest." Accordingly, we hold that the Investment Advisers Act of 1940 empowers the courts, upon a showing such as that made here, to require an adviser to make full and frank disclosure of his practice of trading on the effect of his recommendations.

III.

Respondents offer three basic arguments against this conclusion. They argue first that Congress could have made, but did not make, failure to disclose material facts unlawful in the Investment Advisers Act of 1940, as it did in the Securities Act of 1933, and that absent specific language, it should not be assumed that Congress intended to include failure to disclose in its general proscription of any practice which operates as a fraud or deceit. But considering the history and chronology of the statutes, this omission does not seem significant. The Securities Act of 1933 was the first experiment in federal regulation of the securities industry. It was understandable, therefore, for Congress, in declaring certain practices unlawful, to include both a general proscription against fraudulent and deceptive practices and, out of an abundance of caution, a specific proscription against nondisclosure.... In light of this, and in light of the evident purpose of the Investment Advisers Act of 1940 to substitute a philosophy of disclosure for the philosophy of caveat emptor, we cannot assume that the omission in the 1940 Act of a specific proscription against nondisclosure was intended to limit the application of the antifraud and antideceit provisions of the Act so as to render the Commission impotent to enjoin suppression of material facts. The more reasonable assumption, considering what had transpired between 1933 and 1940, is that Congress, in enacting the Investment Advisers Act of 1940 and proscribing any practice which operates "as a fraud or deceit," deemed a specific proscription against nondisclosure surplusage.

....

Respondents argue, finally, that their advice was "honest" in the sense that they believed it was sound and did not offer it for the purpose of furthering personal pecuniary objectives. This, of course, is but another way of putting the rejected argument that the elements of technical common-law fraud—particularly intent—must be established before an injunction requiring disclosure may be ordered. It is the practice itself, however, with its potential for abuse, which "operates as a fraud or deceit" within the meaning of the Act when relevant information is suppressed. The Investment Advisers Act of 1940 was "directed not only at dishonor, but also at conduct that tempts dishonor." Failure to disclose material facts must be deemed fraud or deceit within its intended meaning, for, as the experience of the 1920's and 1930's amply reveals, the darkness and ignorance of commercial secrecy are the conditions upon which predatory practices best thrive. To impose upon the Securities and Exchange Commission the burden of showing deliberate dishonesty as a condition precedent to protecting investors through the prophylaxis of disclosure would effectively nullify the protective purposes of the statute. Reading the Act in light of its background we find no such requirement commanded.... It misconceives the purpose of the statute to confine its application to "dishonest" as opposed to "honest" motives. As Dean Shulman said in discussing the nature of securities transactions, what is required is "a picture not simply of the show window, but of the entire store ... not simply truth in the statements volunteered, but disclosure." The high standards of business morality exacted by our laws regulating the securities industry do not permit an investment adviser to trade on the market effect of his own recommendations without fully and fairly revealing his personal interests in these recommendations to his clients.

....

Justice Harlan, dissenting.... [The Court of Appeals' *en banc* opinion] recognized that "federal securities laws are to be construed broadly to effectuate their remedial purpose." 306 F.2d, at 608. It did not hold or intimate that proof of "intent to injure and actual injury to clients" was necessary to make out a case under these sections of the statute. Rather it explicitly observed: "Nor can there be any serious dispute that a relationship of trust and confidence should exist between the advisor and the advised," thus recognizing that no such proof was required. In effect the Court of Appeals simply held that the terms of the statute require, at least, some proof that an investment adviser's recommendations are not disinterested.

I think it clear that what was shown here would not make out a case of fraud or breach of fiduciary relationship under the most expansive concepts of common law or equitable principles. The nondisclosed facts indicate no more than that the respondents personally profited from the foreseeable reaction to sound and impartial investment advice. [***]

* * *

Notes and Applications

1. *What does* Capital Gains *stand for in practice? Capital Gains* addresses a fundamental question. Under federal law, can investment advisers be sanctioned for non-fraudulent conduct not otherwise in violation of any affirmative obligation imposed by statute or rule? A majority of the Supreme Court answered in the affirmative. To put this in sharp relief, one should ask oneself whether the Capital Gains Bureau improperly enriched itself or even caused clients to lose money? The answer, at least according to Justice Harlan's opinion, is that there were no allegations to that effect. These considerations suggest a series of policy issues:

- In the absence of client loss, why should the SEC be concerned with the conduct at issue in *Capital Gains*?
- Specifically, should the SEC care if an adviser makes recommendations provided the recommendations are bona fide when made?
- Assuming we want advisers to share "well-thought out recommendations," is the SEC's position really proposing that advisers always be sanctioned for sharing recommendations to purchase stock that the adviser might own?
- What would be the effect of requiring, as Justice Harlan urges, the SEC to prove that an investment adviser's recommendations are not disinterested? How would the SEC establish a lack of disinterest?

2. *The scope of the adviser's fiduciary duty under the Advisers Act.* It is well-established that the fiduciary duty recognized in *Capital Gains* encompasses undisclosed conflicts of interest and probably any form a conduct that entails a breach of loyalty. It is less clear how its fiduciary principle applies to breaches of the duty of care. For example, what if an adviser gives lousy advice, is that actionable under Section 206(2)? The SEC indicated in certain circumstances that the answer may be in the affirmative in an enforcement proceedings excerpted in Chapter 9—*In the Matter of Hennessee Group LLC and Charles J. Gradante*, Investment Advisers Act Release No. 2871 (April 22, 2009). For an interesting historical discussion of whether *Capital Gains*' fiduciary principle is properly viewed as grounded in the Advisers Act or rather state law, see Arthur B. Laby, *SEC v. Capital Gains Research Bureau and the Investment Advisers Act of 1940*, 91 B.U. L. Rev. 1051 (2011). Are there reasons for not federalizing breaches of the duty of care by advisers under the Advisers Act? What effect would a new and evolving federal law due care standard have on existing state law due care standards?

7.2.2 Preferring the Interests of the Adviser over the Client: The Case of Trade Errors

Undisclosed conflicts of interest can take many forms, and therefore it is important to internalize the core concern rather than try to understand the concept as a series of enumerated conflicts. Nevertheless, the types of conflicts fall into two major categories: (i) conflicts in which the adviser's immediate economic interests are put ahead of its client's; and (ii) conflicts in which the adviser favors the interests of one client over another. The first type of conflict is perhaps the easiest to sense intuitively. An adviser owes its client a fiduciary duty and necessarily cannot seek to profit at a client's expense or take advantage of its client. The other type of conflict of interest is less obvious because it may not appear that the adviser is enriching itself at the clients' expense. However, an adviser typically favors one client over another because the adviser values the favored client for reasons tied to that client relationship and the potential benefits derived therefrom. This section of the casebook and the next provide illustrations of each type of conflict with situations and practices that frequently arise in the investment management industry.

In the Matter of Michael T. Jackson

Investment Advisers Act Release No. 2374 (Apr. 6, 2005)

[**Textbook Note:** *This SEC administrative action involves a common situation, namely trade errors caused by the investment adviser. When a trade error results in losses, the question invariably is who should suffer or "eat" the losses generated by the error—the client or the adviser? In this case, the trade error worked to the disadvantage of the client. In a case where a trade error works to the client's disadvantage, ignoring the error favors the adviser's interest. But trade errors can also generate windfalls for clients. One could equally ask in such situations who should get the benefit of the error? The SEC imposed sanctions in this action, based on the agency's view that Section 206(2) provides clear guidance on how losses (and presumably gains) arising from errors should be allocated, absent any agreement.*]

[* * *] 3. Michael T. Jackson, 68, is a resident of Belvedere, California. Jackson founded EGM Capital in 1987, and served as its Chief Executive Officer, Chairman of the Board, and majority shareholder during the relevant period.

4. EGM Capital, incorporated in California in 1991, was an investment adviser registered with the Commission beginning in 1987 (when it was known as Emerging Growth Management) until June 2003. EGM Capital's principal place of business was San Francisco, California. As of November 2000, EGM Capital had assets under management of $1.1 billion, including both individually managed accounts and investment limited partnerships (hedge funds). EGM Capital provided investment management services to individuals as well as entities such as corporations and qualified retirement accounts. In April 2003, EGM Capital sold its assets to EGM Capital, LLC, a separate entity which is not involved in this proceeding, and in June 2003 withdrew its registration as an investment adviser. Jackson is no longer involved in the operations or investment decisions of EGM Capital, LLC.

Facts

5. In mid-November 2000, the portfolio managers responsible for managing certain EGM Capital client accounts made a determination to liquidate their clients' holdings

of Ivax Corporation, a biotechnology stock. At the time, a total of approximately 122,000 shares of the stock were held by four EGM Capital hedge funds and two individually managed hedge fund accounts.

6. On November 21 and 22, 2000, pursuant to the instructions of the portfolio managers, the senior trader at EGM Capital's trading desk sold all 122,000 shares of Ivax. Due to human or possibly computer error, a second trader at EGM Capital's trading desk failed to realize that the position had been liquidated. Between November 24 and November 27, 2000, the second trader sold an additional 100,000 shares of Ivax. These sales resulted in an unintended short position of 100,000 shares spread over the four EGM Capital hedge funds and two individual hedge fund accounts.

7. By November 28, 2000, personnel in EGM Capital's operations department discovered the trade error. EGM Capital's trading desk covered the short position. Because the price of Ivax shares had increased in the interim, a loss of approximately $404,000 was incurred.

8. The inadvertent oversell of Ivax shares was brought to Jackson's attention. EGM Capital had no policy or procedure specifying how trade errors were to be handled. Nonetheless, it was known to EGM Capital and Jackson that, consistent with industry practice and an investment adviser's fiduciary duty to its clients, losses caused by an investment adviser's own trade error were the responsibility of the adviser and should not be borne by clients. Jackson, however, took the position internally that the accounts in which the shares were oversold should bear the losses incurred by covering the inadvertent short position. Based on his recommendation, EGM Capital treated the erroneous trade as a normal transaction, and assigned the loss to the EGM Capital hedge fund accounts and the individual client hedge fund accounts that held the Ivax stock.

9. In order to conceal the trade error, EGM Capital created records that gave the false impression that the firm had intentionally sold Ivax short on behalf of its clients. EGM Capital personnel prepared trade tickets backdated to November 24 and November 27, 2000, purporting to show that the portfolio managers had instructed the trading desk to sell the stock short on those dates. In reality, as described above, the portfolio managers had provided no such instructions to the trading desk on those dates.

10. Of the $404,000 loss the trade error caused, the net loss to EGM Capital clients was $326,000. During the course of an inquiry into these events by the Commission staff, EGM Capital repaid the full $326,000 lost by its clients, plus interest.

Legal Discussion

11. Section 206 of the Advisers Act provides, in pertinent part, that "[i]t shall be unlawful for any investment adviser ... to employ any device, scheme, or artifice to defraud any client or prospective client" or "engage in any transaction, practice or course of conduct, which operates as a fraud or deceit upon any client or prospective client." Under the Advisers Act, investment advisers owe a fiduciary duty of good faith to their clients.

12. As a result of the conduct described above, EGM Capital willfully violated Sections 206(1) and (2) of the Advisers Act, and Jackson willfully aided and abetted and was a cause of EGM Capital's violations of Sections 206(1) and 206(2) of the Advisers Act. [* * *]

* * *

Notes and Applications

1. *Trade errors generally.* Trading errors are pervasive in the investment management industry, not due to frequent carelessness but rather the inevitability of errors when there are hundreds of thousands of transactions (if not more) each day. Quite simply, trade errors of one sort or another are a fact of life. These errors can take the form of (to name just a few): (i) the purchase or sale of the wrong amount of securities; (ii) incorrect coding of trades for execution or assignment to accounts; and (iii) making investments that violate client investment restrictions or client objectives with respect to a class of securities (and this type of error is sometimes described as an "investment error"). What is interesting for purposes of this discussion is not that they occur, but rather what is the investment adviser's responsibility when they do occur? The investment adviser has a fiduciary duty to make good on the error, but this can be difficult since errors inevitably give rise to trading gains or losses as a direct consequence of any trading error itself. Thus, the investment adviser is frequently faced with the issue of how to correct the consequential gains or losses arising from the original trading error.

2. *Correction of errors.* The investment adviser's fiduciary duty to correct the error should have been fairly obvious in the *Michael T. Jackson* action. An adviser cannot conceal or lie about a trade error that results in injury to the client. In other words, Section 206(2) ensures that an adviser cannot favor its own interest in ignoring the consequences to its clients of its own mistakes relative to the client's interest in recouping the losses it suffered. However, remediation issues are not always entirely clear cut. For example, suppose a trade error creates a windfall for the client. In theory, the client has not been harmed and the gains should be returned to the adviser. But the adviser's duty is greater than merely being seemingly fair. The investment adviser must have the consent of the client before reversing any accidental windfalls that have accrued to clients. It is not uncommon that these issues might be addressed contractually in the context of the adviser-client relationship. In this regard, common contractual provisions involve netting of gains and losses within any time period arising from errors or even disregarding *de minimis* errors. As an attorney, how would you explain such language in an investment advisory agreement to your client if it is (i) an adviser or (ii) an institutional investor? How would you respond to one-sided arrangements, i.e., clients bear the risk of loss occasioned by errors by the adviser, but the adviser, in its discretion, may retain the gains arising from any errors? Do you think disclosure should be part of any such error allocation provision?

3. *Technology errors.* With greater reliance on technology in implementing quantitative strategies, it was inevitable that investment errors would arise from improperly

programed computer algorithms. As with conventional trading error situations, an investment adviser violates its fiduciary duties to clients by concealing errors made by computer programs once they become known to the adviser. In addition, however, the SEC has also suggested that advisers' policies and procedures should address the risk of such errors. *See In the Matter of AXA Rosenberg Group LLC*, Investment Advisers Act Release No. 3149 (Feb. 3, 2011), and the related, *In the Matter of Barr M. Rosenberg*, Investment Advisers Act Release No 3285 (Sept. 22, 2011).

4. *Processing errors—a different sort of error.* In some cases, errors can arise from professionals other than the investment adviser that are involved in serving the adviser's clients. Suppose a transfer agent delays by several days placing funds received from a defined contribution plan into the relevant investment funds, resulting in millions of dollars in foregone gains? *See SEC v. Karnig H. Durgarian*, et al., SEC Litigation Release No. 19517 (Jan. 3, 2006) (commencing a civil action against former officers of transfer agent). The result in that action proved mixed from an enforcement perspective. While some officers subsequently settled the enforcement actions, others successfully sought dismissal of the charges on grounds that, as pled by the SEC, the alleged concealment of the error (a disclosure omission) did not aid or abet fraudulent disclosure. *SEC v. Papa*, 555 F.3d 31(1st Cir. 2010).

7.2.3 Preferring the Interests of One Client over Another: The Case of Hot IPO Allocations

While in the *Michael T. Jackson* enforcement action, the adviser was found to have breached its fiduciary duties by putting its own financial interests ahead of its clients' interests, another interesting conflict of interest arises where one client's interests are put ahead of another's. The following administrative action illustrates such a scenario.

In the Matter of Account Management Corporation

Investment Advisers Act Release No. 1529 (Sept. 29, 1995)

[**Textbook Note:** *This settled SEC administrative action is typical of an entire genre of cases arising under Section 206(2) that involve the allocation of favorable trading opportunities among clients of investment advisers. This case involved a "hot IPO," an opportunity to buy shares in an initial public offering where the demand is so great that the newly issued shares begin trading in the secondary market at a significant premium to the offering price. The opportunity to buy shares at the offering price in a hot IPO, by definition, will virtually guarantee that the investor profits in the short term.*]

[* * *] 1. Respondents

a. AMC has been registered with the Commission as an investment adviser since 1964 (File No.801-3548). It is located in Boston, Massachusetts, and is jointly owned and controlled by de Roetth and Albright. As of June 30, 1994, AMC had approximately $95 million under management.

b. De Roetth, a resident of Boston, Massachusetts, has been continuously associated with AMC since 1964, serving as its president.

c. Albright, a resident of Wayland, Massachusetts, has been continuously associated with AMC since 1964, serving as its vice president.

2. AMC's Business

a. Clients

During the relevant period [January1992 through June 1993], AMC had sixty-five client accounts under management. Forty-five of AMC's client accounts, holding approximately $93.5 million, were assessed an annual management fee of from 1% to 1.5% of client assets under management (the "fee-paying clients"). These accounts ranged in size from $100,000 to $34 million in assets under management. Most of these clients had been with AMC for twenty years or longer. The remaining twenty client accounts, holding in the aggregate approximately $1.4 million, were not assessed a management fee (the "gratis clients"). For the most part, these clients were close friends of either de Roetth or Albright, most of whom opened accounts with assets averaging less than $5,000.

b. Investment Strategies

AMC's primary investment strategy was to buy and hold small capitalization stocks to achieve long-term appreciation. In its form ADV, AMC described its " timing of purchases and sales" as, "[t]ypically ... a long per1od of accumulation, often 6–12 months or more, followed by a holding period of several years (preferably 5 to 10) and then a gradual distribution...." AMC executed this strategy, in part, by reviewing planned initial public offerings ("IPOs") of common stock and by purchasing a substantial number of shares issued in connection with select IPOs in which AMC could obtain a substantial number of shares at a price AMC considered attractive.

In addition to this long-term strategy, and as a result of its search of the IPO market for long-term investment opportunities, AMC occasionally purchased and sold securities on a short-term basis. Primarily, such short-term trading involved "hot IPOs" in which AMC had no long-term investment interest. In significant part because of its ongoing presence as a buyer of IPOs for long-term investment, selling syndicate members would offer AMC an opportunity to purchase shares in certain "hot IPOs." It was AMC's practice to flip the "hot IPOs" on the same day or within two or three days of the purchases for a short-term profit.[3]

c. AMC's Inadequate Disclosure of Its Allocation Policy

During the relevant eighteen month period, AMC bought and promptly sold thirty-four "hot IPOs" thereby generating short-term trading profits of approximately

3. "Flipping" is the practice of buying a "hot issue" and then selling it within a short period of time into a rising market, earning a quick profit on the transactions.

$337,000.[4] These short-term investment opportunities were allocated among AMC's clients exclusively according to the discretion of de Roetth and Albright. De Roetth and Albright did not seek over time to distribute the shares of "hot IPOs" equitably to all eligible accounts.[5] Instead, de Roetth and Albright intentionally favored a small group of accounts, predominantly gratis clients. For example, AMC participated in over forty IPOs with the expectation that the issue would be "hot." All but three were profitable as anticipated. Of the profits earned in these issues, approximately 65%, or $218,460, was generated for the accounts of gratis clients. While only twenty of the thirty-three eligible fee-paying clients were given investment opportunities in twenty-one of the forty "hot IPOs" AMC participated in, the gratis clients participated in all of such "hot IPOs." De Roetth and Albright determined which gratis clients would receive shares of a "hot IPO" based on their subjective judgment as to which of those clients needed money at the time.

AMC did not adequately disclose its policy for allocating shares of "hot IPOs." The "hot IPOs" were scarce investment opportunities that could not be purchased in sufficient quantity for all eligible accounts. When allocating shares of a "hot IPO," de Roetth and Albright did not consider the appropriateness of the IPO for each eligible account. Although it referred to the discretionary exercise of investment power for clients, AMC's Form ADV did not describe the factors that de Roetth and Albright employed in exercising their discretion to allocate investment opportunities, including "hot IPOs," among AMC's clients.

B. LEGAL ANALYSIS

1. Violations of Section 206(2) of the Advisers Act

Section 206(2) of the Advisers Act makes it unlawful for any investment adviser, by use of the mails or any means or instrumentality of interstate commerce, directly or indirectly, to engage in any transaction, practice or course of business which operates as a fraud or deceit upon any client or prospective client. Section 206 of the Advisers Act establishes a statutory fiduciary duty for investment advisers to act for the benefit of their clients. *In the Matter of Chancellor Capital Management. Inc.*, Investment Advisers Act Rel No. 1447 (October 18, 1994) citing *Transamerica Mortg. Advisors. Inc. v. Lewis*, 444 U.S. 11, 17 (1979). Advisers, as fiduciaries, have an affirmative duty to exercise the utmost good faith in dealings with clients. *SEC v. Capital Gains Research Bureau*, 375 U.S. 180, 194 (1963). This duty includes a duty of loyalty to each client.

---

4. AMC purchased shares issued in 40 "hot IPOS," 34 of which were promptly sold for a profit, three of which were sold somewhat later for a loss, and three of which were held for long-term investment.

5. "Eligible accounts" as used in this Order means those AMC accounts which, in light of their investment objectives, legal restrictions, instructions to AMC or other relevant considerations, were eligible to purchase "hot IPOs." Twelve AMC customer accounts (all members of the same family), which in the aggregate held more than half of the assets under AMC's management, were not eligible to invest in "hot IPOs."

Section 203(e) of the Advisers Act authorizes the Commission to sanction any investment adviser who "has willfully violated any provisions of the Securities Exchange Act of 1934 ... [the Advisers Act] ... the rules or regulations under any of such statutes ... [and] has willfully aided, [and] abetted ... the violation by any other person of any provision of the Securities Exchange Act of 1934 [and the Advisers Act]...."

....

De Roetth and Albright, AMC's principals, established AMC's allocation practices and were responsible for its disclosure concerning those practices. De Roetth and Albright thereby substantially assisted AMC's violation of Section 206(2) of the Advisers Act. By their actions, de Roetth and Albright willfully aided and abetted AMC's violation of Section 206(2) of the Advisers Act by directing allocations of "hot IPOs" to a limited group of eligible accounts, without adequate disclosure. [* * *]

* * *

Notes and Applications

While it should be obvious that a fiduciary should not be able to take advantage of the person to whom the fiduciary owes an obligation of trust and confidence, it is perhaps less obvious on first impression why a fiduciary cannot advantage one client over another. After all, on its face, the fiduciary is not profiting from any difference in the way it treats clients, or is it? For example, does the fiduciary possibly benefit indirectly? Normally one might suspect that the adviser might choose to prefer a more profitable client over a less profitable one. Here, however, the adviser favored *gratis* clients over paying clients. It turned out in this case that one of the *gratis* clients was a very powerful national politician. Even apart from personal considerations that may affect a fiduciary's judgment, shouldn't we expect impartiality and disinterest from a fiduciary among clients in discharging his or her responsibilities, unless told otherwise?

The other issue raised by the *Account Management* case is what does Section 206(2) require of advisers in this situation if a potential conflict of interest exists? Typically advisers managing separate accounts will oversee many different accounts. Is it realistic or even possible to treat all accounts exactly alike with respect to every investment decision, especially if some of the decisions involve limited (or scarce) opportunities? Take the example of shares in a hot IPO. A firm may be allocated only so many shares in the IPO—for example, 5000 shares in the hot IPO. Do the shares have to be divvied up among the accounts equally? What about accounts, as was the case in *Account Management*, where accounts may have investment restrictions precluding investments in hot IPOs? The SEC does not endorse a hard and fast rule requiring equal treatment in all circumstances, but rather suggests that as a default position. How does the SEC's approach differ from an approach mandating strict equal treatment of clients, and based on that approach, what means or methodologies could an adviser adopt to be fair to clients and avoid sanctions?

7.3 Rules-Based Obligations to Prevent Fraud

Under Section 206(4), Congress granted the SEC authority to adopt rules that "define, ad prescribe means reasonably designed to prevent" fraudulent or deceptive acts or practices. Such a rulemaking grant goes beyond practices that are fraudulent or deceptive and encompasses a range of practices that may contribute to or are necessary to prevent fraudulent or deceptive conduct. *See U.S. v. O'Hagan*, 521 U.S. 642, 666-77 (1997) (discussing construction of similar language found in Section 14(e) of the Securities Exchange Act). The SEC has used its rulemaking authority to adopt seven rules (one previously adopted rule has been repealed which accounts for the numbering of eight rules of which seven remain in force) each of which could be examined in greater detail. Instead, a simple summary is provided in the next subsection, and the second subsection addresses a specific and contested area—performance advertising.

7.3.1 The SEC's Fraud Deterrence Rules

Although all rules under Section 206(4) are couched in terms of a prohibition on fraudulent or deceptive practices, they actually fall into two categories: rules that impose substantive affirmative obligations on investment advisers regarding specific areas of adviser activity, and rules that target specific areas of abusive conduct and practices. The three rules in the first category provide guidance how, given that many advisers will necessarily need to address the sort of activities addressed in the rule, to engage operationally in such activities. Specifically, the rules establish minimum standards regarding custody of client assets (Rule 206(4)-2), proxy voting procedures (Rule 206(4)-6), and compliance policies and procedures (Rule 206(4)-7). The mandates in these rules effectively require that the affected adviser operations be structured to meet the rules' requirements. Chapter 8 in part addresses the issue of custody of client assets.

The remaining four rules target specific areas of abusive conduct and practices. Two rules relate directly to the marketing of services. Rule 206(4)-1, known as the "advertising rule," identifies a broad multi-part standard for what constitutes fraudulent or deceptive practices with respect to advertisements by advisers covering testimonials, past recommendations, and any untrue statements of material facts. Rule 206(4)-1(a)(5)—the rule's catchall provision—specifically prohibits materially misleading statements in advertising and provides an excellent illustration of the breadth of SEC authority under such a broad anti-deceit provision. Advisers frequently face issues of potential misrepresentation with respect to representations about the performance achieved by the adviser's clients. The next subsection addresses two such cases.

The other conduct-based rules are directed at: cash payments for client solicitations (Rule 206(4)-3); political contributions to candidates from persons associated with the advisory firm that can influence the awarding of public contracts to advisory firms (Rule 206(4)-5); and the making of materially false or misleading statements to investors in pooled investment vehicles advised by the adviser (Rule 206(4)-8). This last rule is notable, because investors in pooled investment vehicles technically are not the adviser's clients, but are merely investors in the adviser's client (i.e., the pooled investment vehicle). However, even though the investors may not be in legal privity with the adviser, they are directly affected by the adviser's management of the pooled investment vehicle and the adviser's disclosures regarding the pooled investment vehicle. Although there is insufficient space to address each of these rules, it is worth remembering that these rules target activities where the risk of fraud and deception to clients is readily apparent and are largely designed to strictly curb the potential for abusive practices. In the case of cash payments to solicitors and political contributions, the rules strive for some flexibility for such activities and practices deemed non-abusive.

7.3.2 The Advertising Rule and Its Interpretive Gloss: Performance Disclosure in Advertisements

The advertising rule covers various aspects of advertising conduct by registered advisers that can lead to abuse or misleading disclosure. It flatly prohibits testimo-nials concerning the investment adviser and also prohibits, directly or indirectly, selective references to past specific recommendations. These prohibitions have been interpreted as precluding dissemination of client lists that are not generally representative, but rather compiled to highlight clients with favorable results. These specific prohibitions speak to concerns about the use of advertising to burnish an adviser's reputation by projecting messages that provide a poor means of assessing true adviser quality.

As noted, Rule 206(4)-1(a)(5) is of particular importance in policing advertising, because it is a catchall anti-deceit provision and moreover allows for very direct oversight of an area with great potential for abuse, namely representations relating to performance of an adviser's client accounts. Misleading representation of past performance achieved for clients is a source of recurrent problems in the investment management area and is closely regulated in the context of registered investment companies. Rule 206(4)-1(a)(5), however, is the principal means for regulating performance assertions by advisers overseeing separate account or unregistered pooled investment vehicles. Although this section addresses misconduct of advisers in performance representations, related issues arise with respect to the representation of performance by funds, which will be discussed in later chapters. The conduct can be addressed through general statutory antifraud prohibitions found in both the Advisers and the Company Act, but it can also give rise to liability, including private liability for damages, under the more familiar securities law antifraud provision, Section 10(b) of the Exchange Act and Rule 10b-5 thereunder in the context of securities transactions. Advisers Act Rule 206(4)-1(e) also addresses such behavior.

Investors place incredible reliance on performance representations, even though financial experts uniformly caution that past performance is not a reliable indicator of future results. Investors are prone to "chase performance," meaning that they are frequently tempted to place undue weight on immediate performance figures without considering the many factors that may contribute to performance. The SEC staff has provided guidance regarding the presentation of actual and model performance returns in a series of no-action letters. In addition to this guidance, SEC enforcement proceedings provide a catalogue of various types of performance misrepresentations. The two actions highlighted in the text evidence how two factors contribute to the recurrent problems with performance advertising. First, marketing incentives fuel exaggerated performance claims as well as strategies to obscure instances of underperformance. Second, performance results are inherently contextual and therefore subject to framing bias and manipulation. As the following cases demonstrate, there are infinite ways to alter and massage results. Generally, the SEC has sought to discourage gaming tactics through enforcement actions while simultaneously encouraging reliability in performance presentations.

ZPR Investment Management Inc. v. SEC

861 F.3d 1239 (11th Cir. 2017)

[**Textbook Note:** *This decision is an appeal seeking review of an SEC decision. The SEC regularly sits in an adjudicatory capacity with respect to administrative actions brought by its Division of Enforcement and tried before an administrative law judge. One issue addressed concerns a basic issue of advertising performance results: even if the results presented are literally accurate, what kinds of circumstances can render them contextually inaccurate? In this case, widely-used voluntary industry practices designed to promote standardization in the presentation of performance reporting were subverted. Consider why standardization and investors' understanding of those standardization conventions are important. Here, the court considered several different Adviser Act violations, and the references to violations of Section 206(4) are in fact references to violations predicated on violations of Rule 206(4)-1(a)(5) thereunder.*]

Martin, Circuit Judge: Max Zavanelli and his investment firm, ZPR Investment Management, Inc. ("ZPRIM"), are before us seeking review of a final order of the Securities and Exchange Commission ("SEC" or the "Commission")....

1. Mr. Zavanelli and ZPRIM

In 1994, Mr. Zavanelli founded ZPRIM, an investment firm registered as an "investment adviser" with the SEC. Mr. Zavanelli was ZPRIM's president and sole shareholder. As such, he "had ultimate authority over all aspects of ZPRIM's advisory business, including its advertising." ZPRIM employed Ted Bauchle as its operations manager from 1999 until early 2013. According to Mr. Bauchle, Mr. Zavanelli was ZPRIM's "boss man." Mr. Zavanelli "made all the decisions" and "was difficult to disagree" with "because he was under the impression that the company should be run his way and that he was always correct."

2. Global Investment Performance Standards

The Global Investment Performance Standards ("GIPS") are "universal, voluntary standards to be used by investment managers for quantifying and presenting investment performance that ensure fair representation, full disclosure, and apples-to-apples comparisons." GIPS has two related components, which are the performance standards and the advertising guidelines. The performance standards establish how a firm should calculate and present its investment performance. As you might have guessed, those firms that comply with the GIPS performance standards may represent themselves as being "GIPS-compliant." It is generally understood that compliance with GIPS "provides a level of credibility" to the firm's performance results and gives prospective clients "a greater level of confidence" in the firm's performance presentations.

Under GIPS, if a firm chooses to advertise that it is GIPS compliant, that firm must also comply with the GIPS advertising guidelines.[2] The advertising guidelines require any advertisement claiming GIPS compliance to disclose specific information about the firm's investment returns. Specifically, the firm must provide: "(1) period-to-date composite performance results and (2) either one-, three-, and five-year cumulative annualized composite returns or five years of annual composite returns."

3. ZPRIM Began Claiming It Was GIPS Compliant

Mr. Zavanelli knew that GIPS compliance was "very important" for marketing to institutional clients and he wanted ZPRIM to have those "bragging rights." To that end, ZPRIM hired a GIPS verification firm, Ashland Partners & Company LLP ("Ashland"), to help bring ZPRIM into compliance. In January, February, and April 2008, ZPRIM placed advertisements in financial magazines claiming it was GIPS compliant. Together with the claim of GIPS compliance, and in keeping with GIPS advertising guidelines, the ads included period-to-date returns and at least five years of annual returns.

4. In Fall 2008, ZPRIM Published Ads Omitting Information Required Under GIPS

In the fall of 2008, ZPRIM published three more magazine ads claiming GIPS compliance. But these ads had no period-to-date performance results, nor did they include either one-, three-, and five-year annualized results or five years of annual results. One effect of leaving out this GIPS-required information was that the ads hid ZPRIM's recent poor performance. Had ZPRIM shown its investment returns over the time periods required by GIPS, the ads would have revealed that the firm's performance lagged behind ZPRIM's benchmark index by as much as ten percentage points. Instead of disclosing the called-for returns with the unflattering information, ZPRIM showed its returns over a longer period of time during which ZPRIM outperformed its benchmark index.

Mr. Bauchle testified that before these ads were published, he told Mr. Zavanelli they didn't meet the GIPS requirements for showing investment return information.

2. The GIPS rules say: "[S]hould a GIPS-compliant FIRM choose to advertise performance results, the FIRM MUST apply … the GIPS Advertising Guidelines in order to include a claim of compliance with the GIPS standards."

But Mr. Zavanelli dismissed Mr. Bauchle's concerns, saying it wasn't necessary to put the information in the ads because ZPRIM would give it to prospective clients before they invested. Mr. Zavanelli "wanted to run those ads," so ZPRIM published them even though they did not comply with the GIPS advertising guidelines. Although Ashland had reviewed and approved ZPRIM's earlier ads, ZPRIM never asked Ashland to review the fall 2008 ads.

....

6. The SEC Notified ZPRIM of False Claim of GIPS Compliance

In January 2010, the SEC sent ZPRIM a letter. The letter noted that, while ZPRIM's December 2008 advertisement "claimed compliance" with GIPS, "the [SEC's] examination found that it did not comply with GIPS advertising guidelines." The letter told ZPRIM that "[a]s a result, ZPR[IM] may have violated Section 206 of the Advisers Act and Rule 206(4)-1, thereunder."

ZPRIM responded that it "did not intend to mislead with this ad." Beyond that, ZPRIM assured the SEC that "[w]e have changed our ads" going forward to comply with the GIPS advertising guidelines by including the "1–3–5 year annualized returns" as a "[c]orrective action[ ]."

In August 2010, the SEC sent ZPRIM another letter notifying the firm that the SEC was "conducting an investigation" into ZPRIM.

....

8. In Spring 2011, ZPRIM Published Additional Ads Omitting Information Required Under GIPS

Despite ZPRIM's assurances to the SEC that it would change its ads to comply with the GIPS advertising guidelines, ZPRIM published three more ads—in February, March, and May 2011—claiming GIPS compliance but failing to include the returns required by the GIPS advertising guidelines. Mr. Zavanelli testified that he conceived of and approved these ads.

....

Petitioners challenge the Commission's order.... More specifically, they say substantial evidence does not support the Commission's findings that: (1) the false claims of GIPS compliance in ZPRIM's advertisements were material; ...

Discussion

A. Materiality of ZPRIM's Advertisements

1. The Materiality Requirement

A false or misleading statement by an investment adviser violates the antifraud provisions of the Advisers Act only if the fact misrepresented or omitted is "material." See *SEC v. Capital Gains Research Bureau, Inc.*, 375 U.S. 180, 200–01, 84 S.Ct. 275, 287, 11 L.Ed.2d 237 (1963); [*Steadman v. SEC*,] *Steadman I*, 603 F.2d at 1129–34. An "omitted fact is material if there is a substantial likelihood that a reasonable [investor] would consider it important." *Basic Inc. v. Levinson*, 485 U.S. 224, 231, 108 S.Ct. 978, 983, 99 L.Ed.2d 194 (1988) (quotation omitted). "[T]here must be a substantial likelihood that the disclosure of the omitted fact would have been viewed by the reasonable investor as having significantly altered the 'total mix' of information made available." *Id.* at 231–32, 108 S.Ct. at 983 (quotation omitted).

2. Materiality as to ZPRIM's Advertisements

ZPRIM published ads claiming GIPS compliance but omitted the investment return information required by the GIPS advertising guidelines. ZPRIM's claim of GIPS compliance was therefore false, and petitioners do not say otherwise. Rather, they argue their omission of the GIPS-required information was not material. We conclude to the contrary. Substantial evidence showed that reasonable investors would find it important that ZPRIM's ads did not actually comply with GIPS even while they claimed compliance.

To begin, the evidence showed that the status of being "GIPS compliant" is important to investors. Mr. Zavanelli himself testified that being able to market oneself as GIPS compliant "is very important" for attracting institutional clients. Mr. Bauchle explained that institutional clients "screen[]" for GIPS compliance and will not even consider firms that are not compliant. Given the significance of GIPS compliance as a marker in the industry, reasonable investors would have wanted to know that ZPRIM's claim of GIPS compliance was false.

Beyond the value of the label itself, the false claim of GIPS compliance was also material because it caused prospective clients to wrongly believe the performance results in ZPRIM's ads adhered to the GIPS advertising guidelines. As the Commission explained, the purpose of the advertising guidelines is to give investors the assurance that any GIPS-compliant firm will present its performance data in a way that is "complete, fair[], and comparable to those of other firms." The guidelines' requirements for presenting performance data provide "uniformity and comparability among investment managers." That meant investors looking at the ZPRIM ads could have believed they were looking at the uniform, standardized set of returns required by GIPS, when in fact ZPRIM was deviating from the standardized presentation and putting its investment performance in a more favorable light. ZPRIM presented its numbers as an "apples-to-apples comparison" with the data posted by other GIPS-compliant firms, when its numbers were not actually comparable. This discrepancy is something a "reasonable [investor] would consider [] important." *Basic*, 485 U.S. at 231, 108 S.Ct. at 983 (quotation omitted).

For the ads published in fall 2008, the showing of materiality was even stronger. If ZPRIM had listed its investment returns in those ads as required by GIPS, the information would have revealed that ZPRIM was significantly underperforming its benchmark. Certainly, a prospective investor would have wanted to know about those undisclosed, negative results. See *SEC v. Merch. Capital*, LLC, 483 F.3d 747, 769 (11th Cir. 2007) (holding that defendants made material omissions by marketing interests in their company to investors "without disclosing the poor performance of the interests that had already been sold").

Petitioners argue that ZPRIM's failure to disclose the GIPS-required information in its ads was not a material omission because the firm provided the information later. Petitioners say ZPRIM sent a fact sheet that disclosed the performance data required by GIPS to every prospective client who responded to a ZPRIM ad. Petitioners also point to data the firm posted on its website. Because ZPRIM eventually gave prospective clients the GIPS-required information, petitioners say that information *was* "part of the total mix of information provided," and therefore its omission from the ads was not material. See *Basic*, 485 U.S. at 231–32, 108 S.Ct. at 983.

These after-advertisement disclosures do not carry the day. Materiality is "determined in light of the circumstances existing *at the time* the alleged misstatement occurred." *Ganino v. Citizens Utils. Co.*, 228 F.3d 154, 165 (2d Cir. 2000) (emphasis added); see also *SEC v. Morgan Keegan & Co.*, 678 F.3d 1233, 1253 (11th Cir. 2012) (per curiam) (holding that disclosures made "after the alleged oral misrepresentations" do not render the misrepresentations immaterial). Because our inquiry is limited to what investors knew at the time the false statements were made, ZPRIM's later disclosures cannot negate the materiality of the earlier misrepresentations.[6] See *Morgan Keegan*, 678 F.3d at 1253.

Focusing the materiality inquiry on the time when the misrepresentations were made is especially important where, as here, the context of the false statements is advertising to attract new investors. A later disclosure would not have cured the misrepresentation that already occurred at the advertising stage because, again, many institutional investors "screen[ ]" for GIPS compliance. ZPRIM's false claims of GIPS compliance likely resulted in interest from investors who would not otherwise have considered or contacted ZPRIM. As the Commission explained, "[t]he adviser's false statement has succeeded because it has garnered interest, regardless of whether the adviser later provides enough information for an astute individual to detect its misstatement." The problems caused by a false ad cannot be cured by passing along corrected information to the very customers the company attracted through the misinformation in the first place. See *id.* at 1252 (holding that "adequate written disclosures" provided after a false statement did not render the false statement immaterial because the disclosure was "given to customers only upon a customer's request"). [* * *]

* * *

---

6. It could be argued that ZPRIM's publishing of the GIPS-required information on its website was not a subsequent disclosure, since the website was available at the same time as the ads. But, even assuming that ZPRIM put the correct information on its website, that would not render immaterial the false claims of GIPS compliance in ZPRIM's ads. That is because the ads never alerted investors that they needed to look to ZPRIM's website for the GIPS-required disclosure; neither did the website alert investors that it contained the GIPS-required information omitted from ZPRIM's ads. See *Morgan Keegan*, 678 F.3d at 1252 (finding disclosure of accurate information on firm's website did not render immaterial earlier misrepresentations where there was "no evidence that brokers directed customers" to the information on the web page).

Notes and Applications

1. *The utility of GIPS.* As the decision above points out, GIPS standards are voluntary, and if figures identified as GIPS-compliant figures are used in advertisements, there are additional guidelines that the user must follow. Note that GIPS are not promulgated by the SEC and therefore do not have the force of law. However, if an adviser chooses to identify its performance figures as GIPS compliant, it cannot misrepresent that fact if, as the court concluded, that fact is material. Is the court's explanation of its conclusion persuasive? It would appear that ZPRIM could easily have ducked any problem by merely omitting any assertion that its performance figures complied with GIPS. Why do you think instead, it chose to voluntarily make a false representation that its figures were GIPS complaint?

2. *Verification of GIPS.* Use of a third-party verifying agent, as noted in this case, is an additional GIPS feature. What purpose does the presence of a verifying agent serve for investors? For other advisers that self-identify as GIPS compliant?

In the Matter of Alpha Fiduciary, Inc.

Investment Company Act Release No. 4283 (Nov. 30, 2015)

[**Textbook Note:** *In this settled administrative proceeding, the SEC imposed sanctions on an adviser for violations of the advertising rule involving recurrent issues: misuse of backtesting in performance presentations and selective use of performance results of non-representative clients or recommendations. Backtesting refers to the practice of testing new investment strategies against historical data to determine the hypothetical results that would have been achieved if such a strategy had been used from an earlier point in time. The key is that the results are purely hypothetical (i.e., what might have been achieved) as opposed to actual results (i.e., results from strategies that were in fact implemented without the benefit of hindsight). The presentation of results based on backtesting raises a host of issues. The SEC has permitted the use of backtested performance results under appropriate circumstances, but only if fully and adequately disclosed to clients. The performance representations in this proceeding illustrate how such results might be used by the adviser in a highly misleading fashion.*]

[* * *] Summary

1. From at least August 2010 until March 2013, Respondents and AFI's former vice president and business development director created and distributed to clients and prospective clients performance advertising that failed to disclose with sufficient prominence and detail that AFI's Global Tactical Multi Asset Class Strategies' ("GTMACS") advertised performance was hypothetical rather than actual. Doglione created the GTMACS' performance data by back-testing static models dating back to 1999 and consisting of indices that generated minimized volatility and maximized returns, before either AFI or the GTMACS existed. While AFI provided several pieces of performance advertising generally disclosing its use of "certain hypothetical performance and portfolio

information," that disclosure was imprecise, often not on the same page as the hypothetical performance data, and contrary to other statements indicating that the GTMACS' performance data represented actual rather than hypothetical returns. AFI's former vice president and business development director also created performance advertising without any disclosure language and distributed it to a limited number of prospective clients. In addition, AFI's advertising included examples of favorable investment decisions showing returns of up to 58.62% without providing or offering to provide all the firm's investment decisions, and select client portfolios showing over 28% in annualized gains without determining whether those gains represented all AFI clients.

2. AFI also failed to implement written compliance policies and procedures reasonably designed to prevent its employees from presenting performance advertising to clients or prospective clients that violated the Advisers Act and its rules.

Respondents

3. Alpha Fiduciary, Inc. (SEC File No. 801-68218) is an Arizona corporation based in Phoenix, Arizona. AFI has been registered with the Commission as an investment adviser since 2007. As of May 29, 2015, AFI had $737 million in assets under management held in 731 accounts.

4. Arthur T. Doglione, age 53, is a resident of Scottsdale, Arizona. Doglione is the majority owner, managing member, and president of AFI, and until April 2014, its chief compliance officer.

Background

5. Doglione formed AFI in November 2006 and registered it as an investment adviser with the Commission in August 2007. In 2010, AFI began marketing its GTMACS as an investment strategy designed to reduce portfolio volatility and enhance returns by investing in seven to ten global, diversified asset classes.

6. Beginning in 2010, Respondents designed models for the Balanced, Conservative, Growth, and Income GTMACS consisting of seven to nine equity, bond, commodity, and hedge fund indices representing ten asset classes. Respondents created the GTMACS' hypothetical performance by selecting a static allocation of seven to nine indices to maximize returns and minimize volatility when back-tested to 1999. The static GTMACS' model portfolios never represented the holdings of any AFI account, nor could they. Many of the indices comprising the models had no corresponding tracking product like a mutual fund or exchange-traded fund, making replication of the back-tested holdings impossible.

7. Respondents included the hypothetical performance of the GTMACS in charts and tables in AFI's various advertising pieces, such as two-page executive summaries, 25-page firm profiles, 60-page presentations, and website. Respondents and/or AFI's former vice president and business development director periodically updated the GTMACS' performance data to the then most recent quarter, with comparisons to the performance of the S&P 500 index. For example, AFI's advertising materials presented

that the GTMACS' Balanced model returned 163.34% from January 1999 through September 2012, compared to a 17.20% return by the S&P 500 during that same period.

8. AFI's executive summaries, firm profiles, and presentations disclosed that they contained "certain hypothetical performance and portfolio information," but did not disclose that all of the GTMACS' performance data was completely hypothetical. In AFI's firm profiles and presentations, the disclosure language did not appear on the same page as the hypothetical performance data, but at or near the end of a 25 or 60 page document.

9. In fact, AFI's advertising materials contained statements suggesting that the GTMACS' hypothetical performance data represented actual returns. For example, AFI's firm profile stated "[s]ince January 1999 our Balanced GTMAC Strategy Index has produced a 6.98% annualized rate of return." Similarly, AFI's presentation invited prospective clients to "Try it on!" and indicated that "if you would have invested with Alpha Fiduciary over the last ten years," a one million dollar investment would have increased to almost $2.4 million, representing a 119.61% rate of return.

10. AFI employees knew that the GTMACS' performance data was hypothetical and based on a static, back-tested allocation of seven to nine indices. Nevertheless, AFI's former vice president and business development director emailed a handful of clients and prospective clients the GTMACS' hypothetical performance data without including even the disclosure about "certain hypothetical performance and portfolio information." In several e-mails to prospective clients, AFI's former vice president and business development director also made misleading statements suggesting the hypothetical GTMACS' model performance data represented actual past performance.

11. AFI's advertising materials also contained examples of investment decisions made using the GTMACS in 2009 and 2010 generating realized or unrealized gains of 5.51% to 58.62%. All of the advertised investment decisions were profitable, yet some of AFI's investment decisions during those two years were not profitable. AFI never provided, or offered to provide, a list of all its profitable and unprofitable investment decisions during that time period to prospective clients.

12. AFI, through its former vice president and business development director, also provided prospective clients with a redacted report of an existing client's portfolio, one of which, for example, presented a 14.4% return net of fees over a six-month period. Respondents selected the sample client portfolio without considering whether it was representative of the performance of other AFI clients.

....

Violations

14. As a result of the conduct described above, AFI willfully violated Section 206(2) of the Advisers Act, which prohibits an investment adviser from engaging "in any transaction, practice, or course of business which operates as a fraud or deceit upon any client or prospective client." Proof of scienter is not required to establish a violation of Section 206(2) of the Advisers Act, but may rest on a finding of simple negligence.

SEC v. Steadman, 967 F.2d 636, 643 n.5, (D.C. Cir. 1992) (citing *SEC v. Capital Gains Research Bureau, Inc.*, 375 U.S. 180, 195 (1963)).

15. As a result of the conduct described above, AFI willfully violated Section 206(4) of the Advisers Act and Rules 206(4)-1(a)(2) & (5) thereunder. Section 206(4) prohibits any investment adviser from engaging in "any act, practice, or course of business which is fraudulent, deceptive, or manipulative," and authorizes the Commission to prescribe rules designed to prevent such conduct. Rule 206(4)-1(a)(2) makes it a fraudulent, deceptive, or manipulative act, practice, or course of business for a registered investment adviser to publish, circulate, or distribute any advertisement which refers, directly or indirectly, to past specific recommendations of such investment adviser which were or would have been profitable to any person without offering to furnish a list of all recommendations made by such investment adviser within the immediately preceding period of not less than one year. Rule 206(4)-1(a)(5) makes it a fraudulent, deceptive, or manipulative act, practice, or course of business for a registered investment adviser to publish, circulate, or distribute any advertisement which contains any untrue statement of a material fact, or which is otherwise false or misleading. [***]

* * *

Notes and Applications

1. *The problem of backtested results.* There are a number of enforcement actions involving the improper use of backtested results. The SEC sharply distinguishes between actual results and results from backtesting. Why? Assuming the backtested results reflect the results that would have been achieved based on actual past market data, is there any reason to accord greater weight to actual results as opposed to backtested results? Most financial economists would agree with the SEC. Backtesting is different from achieving investment results in real time. In real time, an investment adviser is committing real investment resources to get actual results and, thus, there is an added element of validation that the adviser has perhaps considered many strategies, but has selected one as superior to the rest based in part on hypothetical testing but also probably on conceptual analysis. In backtesting, there is a considerable hindsight bias entangled with constructing the strategy. An adviser can search through many possible strategies and pick the one that is best based entirely on hindsight without the added element of professional judgment of having selected a strategy prospectively that has produced observable results in the future. Of course, it could be asked, if there is a potential for hindsight bias, why ever allow advisers to present backtested results? In other words, is the SEC saying that backtested results are of no informational value?

2. *Backtesting and hypothetical results.* Backtested results are clearly a form of hypothetical performance results, but hypothetical results go beyond mere backtested results. In a highly colorful example of "backtesting" in action (that eventually was vacated on other grounds by the Supreme Court and is awaiting retrial as of the writing of this textbook) the SEC in 2005, in a divided opinion, decided the use of

the phrase "backtested" in a presentation of performance results implies that the speaker is indeed presenting results using actual past data, rather than a blend of actual data and disclosed hypothetical assumptions. *See In the Matter of Raymond J. Lucia Companies, Inc.*, Investment Advisers Act Release No. 4190 (SEC Decision Sept. 3, 2015), *aff'd, Raymond J. Lucia Companies, Inc. v. SEC*, 832 F.3d 277 (D.C. Cir. 2016), *aff'd by an equally divided court*, 868 F.3d 1021 (D.C. Cir. 2017) (*en banc*), *reversed on other grounds*, 585 U.S. ___ (2018). The *Lucia* matter arose from a radio adviser personality's power point marketing presentations at a Marriott hotel which featured the adviser's Buckets-of-Money strategy. The strategy advised prospective clients to divide their assets into three buckets, buckets with safe only, moderately safe, and risker growth assets. Under the strategy, the investor would use the assets from the safe bucket to finance current needs and over time constantly rebalance ("re-bucketize") the assets. His presentation purported to show the superiority of the strategy based on backtested results that were not strictly based on historical data. Among other issues addressed in the SEC decision is whether power points slides are "advertisements" subject to the advertising rule. The SEC had little trouble in concluding that they were indeed advertisements based on the extremely broad definition of advertisements contained in Rule 206(4)-1(b).

3. *And who is responsible for checking the backtested results?* Without a doubt, an adviser who produces the backtested results is responsible for ensuring their accuracy. However, what if an adviser uses performance results obtained from a sub-adviser in the adviser's own marketing materials? The SEC sanctioned an adviser who blindly relied on a seemingly trustworthy sub-adviser's fabricated backtested results in *Matter of Virtus Investment Advisers, Inc.*, Investment Advisers Act Release No. 4266 (Nov. 16, 2016). Is it reasonable and cost-effective as a matter of policy to force advisers to look over the shoulders of their sub-advisers in verifying backtested performance results? This problem is less likely to occur with actual results in that there are other sources of information available to the adviser (e.g., from other service providers, such as the custodian) in ascertaining actual results of a sub-adviser.

7.4 Implied Private Rights of Action under the Investment Advisers Act

Exchange Act Rule 10b-5 is the general antifraud provision of the federal securities laws. From longstanding judicial interpretation, the rule has been read as conferring an implied private right of action on investors injured by a defendant's fraudulent conduct, even though the Exchange Act conferred no such express cause of action. The issue of whether Section 206 of the IAA could be read as also implying a remedy for injured advisory clients took many years to reach the Supreme Court, and by the time that it had, the Court's view on implying private causes of action under federal law had become stricter. In the following case, the Court considered implied private rights of action under the IAA using this more restrictive judicial approach toward implied private rights of action.

Transamerica Mortgage Advisors v. Lewis

444 U.S. 11 (1979)

[**Textbook Note:** *In this case, the Supreme Court addressed whether the Investment Advisers Act creates an implied right of action for private plaintiffs under Section 206 of the Advisers Act, given that the provision itself does not contain an express private right of action. The case was based on alleged misconduct of the adviser involving several violations of Section 206, but also sought remedial relief under Section 215. The topic of implied rights of action (i.e., the right of private parties to bring damages claims for redress under a statute that does not expressly authorize such lawsuits) is well-known in federal jurisdiction courses. Following the Supreme Court's decision in* Cort v. Ash, *422 U.S. 66 (1975), the modern judicial approach implies private rights of action only in a very narrow range of cases. In this decision, the Court's holding distinguishing between damage and equitable remedies is not a total surprise. Of course, some private claims involving violations of Section 206 may be actionable for damages under Exchange Act Rule 10b-5.*]

Justice Stewart: The Investment Advisers Act of 1940, 15 U.S.C. § 80b-1 et seq., was enacted to deal with abuses that Congress had found to exist in the investment advisers industry. The question in this case is whether that Act creates a private cause of action for damages or other relief in favor of persons aggrieved by those who allegedly have violated it.

The respondent, a shareholder of petitioner Mortgage Trust of America (Trust), brought this suit in a Federal District Court as a derivative action on behalf of the Trust and as a class action on behalf of the Trust's shareholders. Named as defendants were the Trust, several individual trustees, the Trust's investment adviser, Transamerica Mortgage Advisors, Inc. (TAMA), and two corporations affiliated with TAMA, Land Capital, Inc. (Land Capital), and Transamerica Corp. (Transamerica), all of which are petitioners in this case.

The respondent's complaint alleged that the petitioners in the course of advising or managing the Trust had been guilty of various frauds and breaches of fiduciary duty. The complaint set out three causes of action, each said to arise under the Investment Advisers Act of 1940. The first alleged that the advisory contract between TAMA and the Trust was unlawful because TAMA and Transamerica were not registered under the Act and because the contract had provided for grossly excessive compensation. The second alleged that the petitioners breached their fiduciary duty to the Trust by causing it to purchase securities of inferior quality from Land Capital. The third alleged that the petitioners had misappropriated profitable investment opportunities for the benefit of other companies affiliated with Transamerica. The complaint sought injunctive relief to restrain further performance of the advisory contract, rescission of the contract, restitution of fees and other considerations paid by the Trust, an accounting of illegal profits, and an award of damages.

....

The Investment Advisers Act nowhere expressly provides for a private cause of action. The only provision of the Act that authorizes any suits to enforce the duties or obligations created by it is [Section] 209, which permits the Securities Exchange Commission (Commission) to bring suit in a federal district court to enjoin violations of the Act or the rules promulgated under it. The argument is made, however, that the clients of investment advisers were the intended beneficiaries of the Act and that courts should therefore imply a private cause of action in their favor....

The question whether a statute creates a cause of action, either expressly or by implication, is basically a matter of statutory construction....

... It is asserted that the creation of a private right of action can fairly be inferred from the language of two sections of the Act. The first is [Section] 206, which broadly proscribes fraudulent practices by investment advisers, making it unlawful for any investment adviser "to employ any device, scheme, or artifice to defraud ... [or] to engage in any transaction, practice, or course of business which operates as a fraud or deceit upon any client or prospective client," or to engage in specified transactions with clients without making required disclosures. The second is § 215, which provides that contracts whose formation or performance would violate the Act "shall be void ... as regards the rights of" the violator and knowing successors in interest.

It is apparent that the two sections were intended to benefit the clients of investment advisers, and, in the case of [Section] 215, the parties to advisory contracts as well. As we have previously recognized, [Section] 206 establishes "federal fiduciary standards" to govern the conduct of investment advisers. Indeed, the Act's legislative history leaves no doubt that Congress intended to impose enforceable fiduciary obligations. See H.R. Rep. No. 2639, 76th Cong., 3d Sess., 28 (1940); S. Rep. No. 1775, 76th Cong., 3d Sess., 21 (1940); SEC, Report on Investment Trusts and Investment Companies (Investment Counsel and Investment Advisory Services), H.R. Doc. No.477, 76th Cong., 2d Sess., 27-30 (1939). But whether Congress intended additionally that these provisions would be enforced through private litigation is a different question.

On this question the legislative history of the Act is entirely silent — a state of affairs not surprising when it is remembered that the Act concededly does not explicitly provide any private remedies whatever....

In the case of [Section] 215, we conclude that the statutory language itself fairly implies a right to specific and limited relief in a federal court. By declaring certain contracts void, [Section] 215 by its terms necessarily contemplates that the issue of voidness under its criteria may be litigated somewhere. At the very least Congress must have assumed that [Section] 215 could be raised defensively in private litigation to preclude the enforcement of an investment advisers contract. But the legal consequences of voidness are typically not so limited. A person with the power to void a contract ordinarily may resort to a court to have the contract rescinded and to obtain restitution of consideration paid.

For these reasons we conclude that when Congress declared in [Section] 215 that certain contracts are void, it intended that the customary legal incidents of voidness would follow, including the availability of a suit for rescission or for an injunction against continued operation of the contract, and for restitution. Accordingly, we hold that the Court of Appeals was correct in ruling that the respondent may maintain an action on behalf of the Trust seeking to void the investment advisers contract.

We view quite differently, however, the respondent's claims for damages and other monetary relief under [Section] 206. Unlike [Section] 215, [Section] 206 simply proscribes certain conduct, and does not in terms create or alter any civil liabilities. If monetary liability to a private plaintiff is to be found, it must be read into the Act. Yet it is an elemental canon of statutory construction that where a statute expressly provides a particular remedy or remedies, a court must be chary of reading others into it....

... But what evidence of intent exists in this case, circumstantial though it be, weighs against the implication of a private right of action for a monetary award in a case such as this. Under each of the securities laws that preceded the Act here in question, and under the Investment Company Act of 1940 which was enacted as companion legislation, Congress expressly authorized private suits for damages in prescribed circumstances. For example, Congress provided an express damages remedy for misrepresentations contained in an underwriter's registration statement in [Section] 11(a) of the Securities Act of 1933, and for certain materially misleading statements in [Section] 18(a) of the Securities Exchange Act of 1934. "Obviously, then, when Congress wished to provide a private damages remedy, it knew how to do so and did so expressly." The fact that it enacted no analogous provisions in the legislation here at issue strongly suggests that Congress was simply unwilling to impose any potential monetary liability on a private suitor.

....

For the reasons stated in this opinion, we hold that there exists a limited private remedy under the Investment Advisers Act of 1940 to void an investment advisers contract, but that the Act confers no other private causes of action, legal or equitable. Accordingly, the judgment of the Court of Appeals is affirmed in part and reversed in part, and the case is remanded to that court for further proceedings consistent with this opinion.

Justice White dissenting. [***] The purposes of the Act have been reviewed extensively by the Court in *SEC v. Capital Gains Research Bureau, Inc.*, 375 U.S. 180 (1963). A meticulous review of the legislative history convinced the Court that the purpose of the Act was "to prevent fraudulent practices by investment advisers." *Id.* at 195. The Court concluded that "Congress intended the Investment Advisers Act of 1940 to be construed like other securities legislation 'enacted for the purpose of avoiding frauds,' not technically and restrictively, but flexibly to effectuate its remedial purposes." *Ibid.* (footnote omitted).

Implication of a private right of action for damages unquestionably would be not only consistent with the legislative goal of preventing fraudulent practices by investment advisers, but also essential to its achievement. While the Act empowers the SEC to take action to seek equitable relief to prevent offending investment advisers from engaging in future violations, in the absence of a private right of action for damages, victimized clients have little hope of obtaining redress for their injuries.... Moreover, the SEC candidly admits that, given the tremendous growth of the investment advisory industry, the magnitude of the enforcement problem exceeds the Commission's limited examination and enforcement capabilities. The Commission maintains that private litigation therefore is a necessary supplement to SEC enforcement activity. [***]

* * *

Notes and Applications

1. *Separating the relevant issues relating to private rights of action.* The topic of implied rights of action extends far beyond the particulars of the Advisers Act. The larger issue for the Court is when, as a general matter, is it appropriate to imply a private right of action when Congress did not expressly so provide? As noted, the clear recent judicial trend has been to reject implied rights of action, and this approach is reflected in the majority's decision. Undoubtedly, this sea change in the Court's jurisprudence gained considerable traction from the fact that Congress in recent times has created more and increasingly detailed statutes which, if rights of action were freely implied, would require courts to be more actively involved in a quasi-legislative function of defining those rights and the elements of such claims.

However, there is a separate policy issue of whether Congress should have created a private right of action for damages under Section 206. This is the theme that resonates in the dissenting opinion. What purpose does a private right of action serve that is not fulfilled by government enforcement actions alone? If such actions might lead to more effective enforcement of statutory provisions, why would Congress withhold the creation of corresponding express private rights of action?

2. *Implied rights of action and the Investment Company Act.* A similar issue relating to implied private rights of action arises under the Investment Company Act. Recent decisions of the U.S. courts of appeals have repeatedly rejected implied rights of action in that context as well, especially in the wake of the *Alexander v. Sandoval*, 532 U.S. 275, 286-87 (2001), a more recent Supreme Court decision reflecting a general and emphatic reluctance to imply private rights of action. *See Laborers' Loc. 265 Pension Fund v. iShares Trust*, 769 F.3d 399, 406 (6th Cir. 2014) (rejecting implied right of action under ICA § 36(a)), *cert. denied*, 135 S. Ct. 1500 (2015); *Northstar Fin. Advisors, Inc. v. Schwab Invs.*, 615 F.3d 1106, 1122 (9th Cir. 2010) (rejecting implied right of action under ICA § 13(a)); *Bellikoff v. Eaton Vance Corp.*, 481 F.3d 110, 117 (2d Cir. 2007) (rejecting implied rights of action under §§ 34(b), 36(a), & 48(a)); *Olmsted v. Pruco Life Ins. Co.*, 283 F.3d 429, 435 (2d Cir. 2002) (rejecting implied rights of action under ICA §§ 26(f) & 27(i)). For an earlier case that found an implied

right of action under the Company Act, see *Meyer v. Oppenheimer Mgmt. Co.*, 764 F.2d 76, 86-88 (2d Cir. 1985) (holding implied right of action under ICA § 15(f)).

* * *

The types of adviser conduct that may violate Section 206 antifraud provisions and the rules thereunder are numerous. Many, as noted, are recurring in the investment management industry. However, the more important takeaway is that this fairly succinct provision affects a vast range of conduct and practices by advisers, and the underlying principles are sufficiently flexible to address new types of conduct and practices that potentially harm advisory clients. Chapter 9 returns to Section 206 as applied to unregistered investment vehicles, such as hedge funds and private equity funds.

Chapter 8

Additional Substantive Obligations of Investment Advisers

Key Ideas: In addition to the antifraud and fiduciary obligations of investment advisers discussed in the preceding chapter, the Advisers Act and rules thereunder impose additional substantive obligations on advisers. Indeed, since its enactment in 1940, the Advisers Act and its rules have blossomed into a more robust regulatory framework. This chapter focuses on four types of requirements that significantly shape the adviser-client relationship. The first group of requirements relate to the advisory agreement. The actual requirements are minimal, but a key feature is that the adviser cannot lock the client into a long-term (and potentially disadvantageous) relationship. A second set of requirements relates to fees and, in particular, significant limitations on the ability of an adviser to receive so-called "performance fees" (i.e., fees the amount of which is contingent on the success of an investment strategy). These requirements are particularly important since they divide the world of registered funds where performance fees are generally prohibited and the world of unregistered funds where fees are largely unregulated. A third set of requirements concerns disclosures required to be made to clients and, to a lesser degree, reporting by large advisers. Basic client disclosure protections, including disclosures relating to fees, are provided under Section 204 and especially Rule 204-3—the so-called "Brochure Rule." A final area concerns highly technical issues relating to the custody and handling of assets, which is governed by Rule 206(4)-2—a rule designed to deter potentially fraudulent practices. Perhaps most important in this regard is the concept of independent safekeeping of clients' assets, which acts as a separate check on malfeasance by or shoddy internal procedures of advisers. As discussed in prior chapters, there are other requirements relating to advisers, but these four areas, as supplemented by antifraud considerations, serve an important investor protection function for investors.

Chapter Contents

8.1 Introduction

The Advisers Act originated as a census and anti-fraud law regarding advisers. Over time, a variety of additional rules and requirements have evolved, mostly focused on protection of investors and their assets. This chapter focuses on several areas of substantive adviser regulation which serve to protect investors: agreements, fees, advisers' brochures and disclosures, and custody of client assets.

8.2 Advisory Agreements

At the heart of the relationship between an adviser and its clients is the advisory agreement, which governs the relationship. Attorneys and students are often surprised at how lightly the Advisers Act regulates advisory agreements' terms. Indeed, the Act allows advisers and their clients great flexibility with respect to establishing the terms of their advisory agreements. However, it is important to note that, while the Advisers Act imposes certain minimal requirements, advisory contracts are governed by standard state contract common law principles. In other words, the federal rationale for the Advisers Act's advisory agreement requirements co-exist with the basic contract law precepts embodied in state law.

Section 205 of the Advisers Act lays out important, but fairly minimal, affirmative requirements relating to advisory agreements if entered into by investment advisers registered with, or required to be registered with, the SEC. Although Section 205 deals with the topic explicitly, antifraud and other principles under the Act also come into play. For purposes of this discussion, five key aspects of advisory contracts need to be considered: (i) the absence of a writing requirement, (ii) assignments, (iii) termination provisions, (iv) standards of care and liability and exculpatory provisions, and (v) fee limitations. The topic of fees will be dealt with alone in a following section.

First it is important to understand that the Advisers Act does *not require* that advisory agreements be in writing. However, it is virtually unheard of in practice that an advisory agreement would not be reduced to writing. Consider for a moment the potential for confusion and second-guessing that could, and likely would, ensue in the absence of a written agreement. In a retail setting, written agreements are a sensible practice for market professionals. Invariably, the professional will have a basic template for a client agreement which is likely to be drafted with the professional's interest in mind and to avert misunderstandings down the road. Interestingly, the

Company Act *requires* that registered investment company advisory agreements be in writing, as will be discussed later in the text, because of the higher degree of formality associated with such arrangements.

Secondly, Section 205(a)(2) of the Advisers Act effectively requires that advisory agreements contain provisions prohibiting their assignment without consent of the clients. This provision recognizes the investor's interest in retaining its relationship with the adviser it hired and not having a change of advisers imposed on it. The restriction is intended not merely to address concerns about imposing involuntary advisory relationships on clients, but also to prevent advisers from marketing or trading on client relationships for their own personal benefit. Quite simply, from the perspective of the Advisers Act, an adviser's clients are not assets of the adviser. If it were otherwise, there would be heightened conflicts of interest associated with any change of control of the adviser.

Section 205(a)(2) refers to the definition of "assignment." Under Section 202(a)(1), the definition of assignment "includes any direct or indirect transfer ... of an advisory contract by [an adviser] or of a controlling block of [an adviser's] outstanding voting securities...." In other words, the sections work together to restrict both direct assignments of advisory agreements and indirect assignment, e.g., through sale of an adviser, without the consent of the adviser's clients. Neither the Act nor the rule defines what constitutes client consent. The SEC has suggested that client consent may be either written or oral, and in some instances, even a "negative consent" may suffice. The latter is the situation where consent may be inferred if an adviser provides at least 60 days' prior notice of an assignment to its clients who do not object.

These express requirements with respect to advisory agreements are supplemented by SEC interpretations of the Act's antifraud provisions that recognize additional limitations. A good example relates to termination provisions and specifically termination penalties for terminating the advisory relationship early. The SEC's staff takes the position that termination penalties may be inconsistent with the adviser's fiduciary duties and therefore may violate Section 206. Under this approach, an adviser in receipt of advance payment of fees may be required to provide a *pro rata* refund of unearned pre-paid fees upon termination of an advisory agreement. *See, e.g., Robert D. Brown Investment Counsel*, SEC Staff No-Action Letter (July 19, 1984). Such a requirement is expressly provided in Section 15(a) of the Company Act with respect to the advisory fees of a registered investment company. In addition, clients should receive adequate prior disclosure of the terms of the termination provisions. *See, e.g., BISYS Fund Services, Inc.*, SEC Staff No-Action Letter (Sept. 2, 1999).

Similar reasoning informs the SEC staff's views regarding standards of care and liability and exculpatory provisions. Obviously, an adviser's advice given in good faith should not expose it to liability for any losses arising from such advice. After all, investments can be risky and advisers are not guarantors for their clients' investments. Nevertheless, investment advisers are professionals and have a duty to provide their services consistent with the care that would be exercised by a reasonably prudent adviser.

However, under these circumstances, advisers understandably may seek to protect or exculpate themselves in certain situations. Such limitations of liability have been the cause of substantial review and analysis by the SEC as well as the securities bar.

One area of concern has been the use of "hedge clauses". Hedge clauses are contractual provisions stating that the investment adviser has no liability to, or that the client will not seek legal action against, the adviser if the adviser violates a provision of the Advisers Act. Such clauses are problematic, because Section 215(a) of the Advisers Act essentially voids any terms of an agreement that attempts to waive compliance with any provisions of the Advisers Act. In a long held view, the SEC staff takes the position that "the anti-fraud provisions of the SEC statutes are violated by the employment of any ... hedge clause ... which is likely to lead an investor to believe that he has in any way waived any right of action he may have...." *See Opinion of the General Counsel Relating to the Use of Hedge Clauses etc.*, Investment Advisers Act Release No. 58 (April 10, 1951). In other words, if an adviser includes a hedge clause in a client's advisory agreement, it arguably may mislead its client by having it believe that it has no legal right or remedy under the Advisers Act, an action which may be fraudulent.

What are the policy reasons for the SEC's views, i.e., how are the interests of an investor protected by the SEC staff's interpretation of Section 215(a)? Basically, there are two considerations. First, as noted above, Section 215(a) effectively does not allow any person to waive compliance with the Act and its rules as a condition of entering into a contract by voiding such agreements. Congress has determined that the requirements of the Act itself are not waivable and are not subject to bargaining between the adviser and the client. Secondly, the SEC's interpretation addresses situations in which a hedge clause provision might lead a client to believe erroneously that it can agree to surrender the protections of the Advisers Act. Misleading characterizations of adviser liability and the protections under the Advisers Act from the staff's perspective is itself potentially fraudulent.

Thus, an issue arises regarding how to balance the interests of clients in seeking to hold advisers accountable and the interests of advisers in not being exposed to liability for client losses arising from normal market forces or otherwise beyond the scope of the Advisers Act. Advisers typically seek to limit liability exposure for conduct outside the purview of the Advisers Act. A common approach used by advisers is to condition the provisions of a hedge clause with an additional clause (so-called "non-waiver disclosure") like: "except as may be otherwise provided by applicable provisions of state or federal law...." Although the exception eliminates any direct conflict with the Act's anti-waiver provision, the SEC has expressed reservations regarding such clauses, even in instances where the adviser seeks only to limit its liability to acts involving gross negligence or willful malfeasance. *See, e.g., Auchincloss & Lawrence Inc.*, SEC Staff No-Action Letter (Feb. 8, 1974).

Given the SEC's historical anathema to hedge clauses and advisers' attempts to limit their liability, what's an adviser to do? In a fairly recent no-action letter (*Heitman*

Capital Management, LLC, et al., SEC Staff No-Action Letter (Feb. 12, 2007)), the SEC staff signaled some flexibility in its prior positions with respect to sophisticated clients. Specifically, the staff indicated that depending on the facts and circumstances relating to particular sophisticated clients, hedge clauses that purport to limit adviser's liability to acts involving gross negligence or willful misfeasance, coupled with non-waiver disclosure, may not violate the Advisers Act anti-fraud provisions under sections 206(1) and 206(2). In short, advisers have more leeway using such clauses with sophisticated investors than with the typical unsophisticated investor.

8.3 Advisory Fees

The Advisers Act does not give the SEC authority to regulate advisory fees rates directly. Nevertheless, Section 205 contains a significant prohibition on use of performance fees. However, Section 205 also contains a number of express exclusions from this prohibition. The starting point for this discussion is an overview of basic fee arrangements.

8.3.1 Basic Fee Arrangements

There are many types of investment advisers and, as a result, many types of fee arrangements, both as to the amount of compensation and the form of compensation. Typically, the fees an adviser may charge may be a function of the services it provides. Thus, an adviser providing a newsletter type service may charge a yearly subscription fee. In contrast, advisers providing more involved services may decide on one or more of several types of fee structures.

The simplest fee structure is a "fixed fee," e.g., $100 for a financial plan or $1000 for a year of financial advice. Generally, a fixed fee structure is used by advisers providing only financial planning services. "Hourly fees" or billing by the hour for investment and financial advice is another common practice, primarily amongst financial planners, attorneys and accountants.

Getting more complex, some advisers may employ an "asset-based" fee, i.e., an annual fee based on average assets held in an account. Such a fee arrangement is common for advisers who have discretion to manage a client's account and even for some non-discretionary wealth management accounts. Note that such fees apply whether a client loses or gains money in the account. For example, a 2% per year fee is simply calculated by taking the average dollar value of the client's account and multiplying it by 2% to derive the fee. Recall also that there is a dichotomy between investment advisers and brokers. For brokers, a common compensation method is commissions and fees on securities transactions. Thus, a broker recommending the purchase of AT&T would receive a commission based on the number of shares purchased by the client.

Finally, asset-based fees are the basis (or at least a component) of fee arrangements with respect to advisers of pooled investment vehicles and large institutional separate accounts. Such fees are calculated as a percentage of assets under management ("AUM"). Asset-based fees are virtually the only type of advisory fee in mutual funds and ETFs. Mutual funds often have fees which decline as funds' AUM get bigger. For example, a fund may pay a composite fee of 0.75% of AUM on the first $1 billion of AUM, plus 0.70% on the next billion, and 0.65% on AUM thereafter. The various points where the fees step down are called "break points." Such fee structures are generally premised on the belief that as advisers realize economies of scale from managing more assets in a fund, such economies should be shared with investors through lower fees.

A separate issue is the layering of fees. Investors and advisers should be sensitive to issues arising when a client pays advisory fees on accounts that invest in funds that charge advisory fees, especially if the adviser collects both fees. The antifraud provisions of Section 206 can be violated if the adviser "double dips," i.e., charges an advisory fee on an asset allocation account and a fee on the underlying mutual funds in which the account invests. In the SEC's view, such a combination of fees may be excessive in light of the services being provided. The SEC has generally required an adviser managing such an account to offset the mutual fund fees against the asset allocation advisory fee. In some limited cases, the SEC has permitted double fees. For example, an adviser is generally permitted to invest client assets in an affiliated money market fund.

Fees that an adviser charges its clients must be disclosed to the SEC (and, thus, generally the public) and to clients. Form ADV mandates disclosure of fees. In addition, the *SEC v. Capital Gains Research Bureau* case, previously discussed in Chapter 7, makes clear that as fiduciaries, advisers have the obligation to fully and fairly disclose fees. Moreover, it is a best practice to include clear fee provisions in advisory agreements.

The SEC has suggested that in some circumstances fees are subject to the antifraud provisions of Section 206. As was noted in a no-action letter many years ago: "[w]e interpret the antifraud provisions to apply to advisory fee arrangements, and any investment adviser who charges excessive fees may violate Section 206 of the Act." *See Financial Counseling Corporation*, SEC Staff No-Action Letter (Dec. 7, 1974). One may ask on what is that premised and how does a high fee work as a fraud on clients? Recall, that advisers are fiduciaries, and as such they have a duty of undivided loyalty to their clients and must deal fairly and honestly with them. Thus, by the SEC's reasoning, articulated in several no-action letters, a high fee is essentially unfair, unless the adviser discloses to existing and prospective clients that such a fee is higher than that charged by other advisers that provide the same or similar services. *See, e.g., Equitable Communications Company*, SEC Staff No-Action Letter, *(Feb. 26, 1975); Financial Counseling Corporation*, SEC Staff No-Action Letter (Dec. 7, 1974); *John G. Kinnard & Co., Inc.*, SEC Staff No-Action Letter (Nov. 30, 1973). These 1970s era letters suggested that 2% of total AUM may be excessive.

8.3.2 Performance Fee Arrangements

A *performance fee* is a fee charged by an investment adviser based upon a share of the capital gains or other appreciation of a client's account. In other words, the fee is success driven: the better the performance of the client's account, the higher the fee for the adviser. For example, a common performance fee charged by private funds advisers is 20% of a fund's capital gains. Thus, if a hedge fund enjoys capital gains of $1 million in a year, the fund's manager may collect a fee of 20% of the gains, or $200,000. Performance fees which purport to be a function of client gains are more problematical than basic fees simply based on AUM. For example, notwithstanding sharing in the gains, advisers rarely share in client losses.

Section 205(a) of the Advisers Act flatly prohibits performance fees by prohibiting advisers from entering into or performing advisory agreements that contain such provisions. Congress and the SEC have expressed concerns that performance fees may encourage undue speculation with clients' investments. Nevertheless, Congress also recognized that performance fees should not be prohibited in all circumstances, and accordingly, established in Section 205(b) exceptions to the prohibition for certain funds and investors, in circumstances where Congress deemed that there are sufficient investor protections.

The exceptions for registered investment companies are extremely limited. For example, under Section 205(b)(1), funds may charge a standard asset-based fee with respect to assets under management, including accretions to assets under management from the fund's total returns—which technically is a type of performance fee. Similarly, registered investment companies can employ a "fulcrum fee," which is also based on AUM over a specified period, but is enhanced or diminished based on exceeding or falling short of a benchmark. However, the key with a fulcrum fee is that it be a symmetrical performance fee, it must increase or decrease proportionately with the investment performance of funds under management in relation to an appropriate index of securities prices. In other words, an adviser is penalized for bad performance to the same extent as it is rewarded for good performance. As an example, if an adviser receives a base fee of 1% of AUM of a $100 million fund, then the adviser's annual base fee is $1 million. If the contract also has a 10% fulcrum fee based on the fund's performance relative to the S&P 500, then in a year in which the fund outperforms the S&P 500, the fee may be increased by 10% to $1.1 million. In contrast, in a year in which the fund underperforms the S&P 500, the fee may be reduced by 10% to $900,000.

Outside of registered investment company contexts, investment advisers and brokers are constantly testing fee alternatives to determine market receptivity and to gain marketing advantages. Part of that evolutionary process is ensuring that new concepts are compliant with existing law. In circumstances where there may be some ambiguity or concern that the SEC could bring enforcement actions, attorneys typically advise their clients to seek no-action relief.

Amerivest Investment Management, LLC

Investment Advisers Act of 1940—Section 205(a)(1) (August 19, 2014)

[**Textbook Note:** *This no-action letter is reflective of the potential complexities of performance fees. The Applicant, Amerivest, sought assurances from the SEC's staff that it would not take action against Amerivest if it implemented a rebate scheme to refund advisory fees in the event of poor performance, i.e., that the performance fee is contingent on certain occurrences. By way of background, prior to this letter, in 1980, the SEC provided interpretive guidance in* Contingent Advisory Compensation Arrangements, *Investment Advisers Act Release No. 721 (May 16, 1980). In the Release, the SEC staff took the position that Advisers Act Section 205(a)(1)'s prohibition of investment advisory contracts that contain performance fees applies to advisory agreements that provide for "contingent fees." As described in the Release, a contingent fee is "an advisory fee [that] will be waived or refunded, in whole or in part, if a client's account does not meet a specified level of performance" or that is contingent on the investment performance of the assets of advisory clients. In designing a program like this, Amerivest is clearly seeking to gain client favor by limiting some client investing risk. Although it successfully persuades the SEC to grant relief, Amerivest is subject to substantial compliance conditions, presumably designed among other things to blunt the potential conflicts of interest inherent in the arrangement.*]

Response of the Chief Counsel's Office

Division Of Investment Management

No-Action Letter, IM Ref. No. 20144101037

Your letter dated August 18, 2014 requests our assurance that we would not recommend enforcement action to the Securities and Exchange Commission (the "Commission" or "SEC") under Section 205(a)(1) of the Investment Advisers Act of 1940 (the "Advisers Act") against Amerivest Investment Management, LLC ("Amerivest"), an investment adviser that is an affiliate of TD Ameritrade, Inc. ("TD Ameritrade") and is registered with the Commission under the Advisers Act, if Amerivest offers to certain clients an advisory fee rebate (the "Proposed Fee Arrangement") in the manner described in your letter and summarized below.

Background

You state the following:

Amerivest currently offers a discretionary advisory service known as Amerivest Portfolios, which is made available to retail brokerage clients of TD Ameritrade (the "Service"). Under the Service, Amerivest serves as the investment adviser to the clients and is responsible for implementing the asset allocation models and corresponding mutual fund and exchange-traded fund investment recommendations provided by Morningstar Associates, LLC ("Morningstar Associates"). Morningstar Associates serves as an investment adviser and independent consultant to Amerivest with respect to the Service, but does not enter into an investment advisory agreement with Amerivest's clients. Amerivest vets and implements Morningstar Associates' investment recommendations in their entirety, subject to non-investment related factors such as tax considerations and any reasonable restrictions a client may impose.[1] Morningstar Associates is compensated by Amerivest based on a fee schedule that includes an asset-based fee component and a licensing fee component. Accordingly, Morningstar Associates does not receive performance-based compensation.

Under the Proposed Fee Arrangement, Amerivest would continue to charge a quarterly asset-based advisory fee in advance. However, Amerivest would rebate investment advisory fees for eligible clients who are invested in a model portfolio that experiences two consecutive discrete calendar quarters of negative performance (before advisory fees) during a twelve-month period (a "Term"). The amount of the rebate would be equal to 100% of the advisory fees paid by each eligible client for the two calendar quarters in which the performance composite for the model portfolio corresponding to the client's account experienced negative performance. To determine whether performance was negative, each calendar quarter would be measured independently; the performance for multiple quarters would not be aggregated. Amerivest will fully and clearly disclose the rules governing eligibility for the Proposed Fee Arrangement and the methodology for calculating the composite performance (together, the "Rebate Terms") to all clients participating in the Service. Amerivest will follow the Rebate Terms and apply them fairly and consistently. In the event that Amerivest decides to change the Rebate Terms in a manner that would disadvantage participating clients, Amerivest will notify participating clients of the change, and no such change will become effective prior to the commencement of the next subsequent Term.

The Proposed Fee Arrangement will not contain any "catch up" or other provision that would allow Amerivest to recapture foregone fees through future appreciation. Amerivest will not deviate from or otherwise seek to influence Morningstar Associates' investment recommendations for the purpose of avoiding payment of any fee rebate under the Proposed Fee Arrangement. Amerivest may deviate from Morningstar Associates' recommendations solely: (i) for non-investment and non-performance related reasons such as tax considerations or reasonable client restrictions; or (ii) to the extent so required to fulfill its fiduciary duty to clients. Amerivest will make and keep true,

1. You state that Amerivest's vetting process is designed to consider whether the asset allocations and securities recommendations provided by Morningstar Associates are reasonable in relation to the investment mandate and risk/return characteristics of each model portfolio and the overall operation of the Service. You state further that Amerivest may choose not to implement a recommendation provided by Morningstar Associates based on non-investment related considerations that might adversely impact client accounts (e.g., the tax ramifications of substituting one ETF for another). You represent that the mere fact that Amerivest has deviated from or declined to implement a recommendation of Morningstar Associates will not—in and of itself—cause a client to be ineligible for the rebate.

accurate and current records detailing any such deviation and explaining why such deviation was necessary. There will be no contract, arrangement, or other understanding, explicit or tacit, by and between Amerivest and Morningstar Associates or any principals thereof, such that Morningstar Associates' compensation or continued engagement would be affected by the payment or non-payment by Amerivest of any fee rebate pursuant to the Proposed Fee Arrangement.

The Proposed Fee Arrangement would be implemented for (i) all new discretionary client accounts, and (ii) all existing discretionary client accounts with a new deposit of $25,000 or higher, provided that the new deposit represents net new assets to Amerivest. Clients would not have to elect to participate in the Proposed Fee Arrangement or request a fee rebate. The fee rebate would automatically apply in the event of two consecutive calendar quarters of negative performance. To be eligible for the Proposed Fee Arrangement, an account must participate in the Service for a minimum of two consecutive calendar quarters during the Term, and during such participation the client must not withdraw more than the required deposit of $25,000 to remain eligible for subsequent quarters. Amerivest would reserve the right to extend the Term for additional twelve-month periods or to discontinue the Proposed Fee Arrangement upon ninety (90) days advance written notice to clients.

Subject to enforcing the requirements set forth in the preceding paragraph, Amerivest will not take any action for the purpose of negating or compromising a client's eligibility for the rebate, including, without limitation, any action that would result in a client no longer participating in the Service.

Analysis

Section 205(a)(1) of the Advisers Act generally prohibits registered investment advisers from entering into, extending, renewing or performing any investment advisory contract that provides for compensation to the investment adviser on the basis of a share of capital gains or capital appreciation in a client's account or any portion thereof. Section 205(a)(1) is designed, among other things, to eliminate "profit sharing contracts [that] are nothing more than 'heads I win, tails you lose' arrangements," and that "encourage advisers to take undue risks with the funds of clients," to speculate, or to overtrade.[22]

You argue that Section 205(a)(1) does not, on its face, extend to fee waivers or rebates that are contingent on negative performance. You acknowledge, however, that the SEC staff in Investment Advisers Act Release No. 721 (May 16, 1980) ("Release

22. Trainer, Wortham & Co., et al., SEC Staff No-Action Letter (Dec. 6, 2004) ("*Trainer*") at 7, *citing* S. Rep. No. 1775, 76th Cong., 3d Sess. 22 (1940), H.R. Rep. No. 2639, 76th Cong., 3d Sess. 29 (1940), and Securities and Exchange Commission, *Investment Counsel, Investment Management, Investment Supervisor and Investment Advisory Services*, H.R. Doc. 477, 76th Cong., 2nd Sess. at 30 (1939).

721")[3] stated that the concerns animating the performance fee ban "are as apposite to advisory fees which are contingent upon an advisory account obtaining a certain level of performance as they are to fees which vary directly with capital gains or appreciation."

You note that the SEC staff has nonetheless provided no-action assurances in situations where fees are contingent on performance, but the conflicts of interest associated with performance fees are not present or are substantially mitigated.[5] In particular, you state that in Trainer the SEC staff took the position that although a general satisfaction guarantee supported by the offer of a full refund was a contingent fee arrangement squarely within the scope of Release 721, it was "structured in a manner that would greatly reduce any incentive on the part of the [a]dvisers to take undue risks, speculate, or overtrade[]" and "could serve to encourage the [a]dvisers to develop a strong culture of client service and responsiveness."

While you acknowledge that the Proposed Fee Arrangement represents a contingent fee arrangement of the kind prohibited by Section 205(a)(1) for the reasons discussed in Release 721, you argue that several aspects of the Proposed Fee Arrangement make it highly unlikely that Amerivest would attempt to avoid the rebate by taking undue risks, timing transactions in a client's account or over-trading. In particular, you argue that Amerivest would not be in a position to directly affect the value of a client's account because Morningstar Associates, an investment adviser that is independent from Amerivest, would be responsible for security selection and asset allocation recommendations with respect to the model portfolios. Moreover, you believe that any incentive that Amerivest might have to override Morningstar Associates' asset allocation recommendations in order to invest in more speculative investments is mitigated by the inability to recapture waived or rebated fees. You argue that the Proposed Fee Arrangement is designed to further align Amerivest's interests with those of its clients because Amerivest does not make money if an eligible client does not make money. You contend that the Proposed Fee Arrangement is the opposite of the "heads I win, tails you lose" approach that Section 205(a)(1) was designed to prevent.

We believe that certain aspects of the Proposed Fee Arrangement—particularly the role of Morningstar Associates in selecting securities and making asset allocation recommendations and the limited discretion Amerivest would have to deviate from such recommendations—help to alleviate the concerns that form the basis of Section 205(a)(1). Based on the facts and representations in your letter, we would not

3. *Contingent Advisory Compensation Arrangements*, Investment Advisers Act Release No. 721 (May 16, 1980).

5. In addition, the SEC staff has stated that Section 205(a)(1) does not prohibit a voluntary refund of advisory fees by an investment adviser, provided that there is no contractual provision or other understanding between the adviser and the client regarding a fee refund or waiver related to investment performance. Investment Advisers, Interpretive Matters (George Coleman), SEC Staff No-Action Letter (Jul. 18, 1995).

recommend enforcement action to the Commission under Section 205(a)(1) of the Advisers Act against Amerivest if Amerivest enters into the Proposed Fee Arrangement as described in your letter and summarized above.

Our position is based particularly on your representations that: (1) Amerivest will fully and clearly disclose the Rebate Terms to all clients participating in the Service, and will follow the Rebate Terms and apply them fairly and consistently; (2) in the event that Amerivest decides to change the Rebate Terms in a manner that may disadvantage participating clients, Amerivest will notify participating clients of the change, and no such change will become effective prior to the commencement of the next subsequent Term; (3) the Proposed Fee Arrangement will not contain any "catch up" or other provision that would allow Amerivest to recapture foregone fees through future appreciation; (4) Amerivest will not deviate from or otherwise seek to influence Morningstar Associates' investment recommendations for the purpose of avoiding payment of any fee rebate under the Proposed Fee Arrangement; (5) Amerivest may deviate from Morningstar Associates' recommendations solely: (i) for non-investment and non-performance related reasons such as tax considerations or reasonable client restrictions; or (ii) to the extent so required to fulfill its fiduciary duty to clients; (6) Amerivest will make and keep true, accurate and current records detailing any such deviation and explaining why such deviation was necessary; (7) the mere fact that Amerivest has deviated from or declined to implement a recommendation of Morningstar Associates will not—in and of itself—result in a loss of eligibility for the rebate; (8) there will be no contract, arrangement, or other understanding, explicit or tacit, by and between Amerivest and Morningstar Associates or any principals thereof, such that Morningstar Associates' compensation or continued engagement would be affected by the payment or non-payment by Amerivest of any fee rebate pursuant to the Proposed Fee Arrangement; and (9) subject to enforcing certain eligibility requirements, Amerivest will not take any action for the purpose of negating or compromising a client's eligibility for the rebate including, without limitation, any action that would result in a client no longer participating in the Service. [***]

* * *

Notes and Applications

1. *Unregistered funds and performance fees.* Section 205(b)(4) provides a significant exception to the prohibition of performance fee agreements which applies to certain types of unregistered funds, such as hedge funds or private equity funds. Such funds, which are not registered under the Company Act, generally qualify because they are offered only to wealthy or sophisticated investors. Such funds, which include numerous hedge funds, typically rely on Section 3(c)(7) of the Company Act for exemption from registration as investment companies, which is discussed in greater detail in Chapter 9.

2. *Qualified clients and performance fees.* In addition, advisers are generally permitted to enter into performance fee arrangements with wealthy investors. Advisers Act Rule 205-3 permits certain "qualified clients" to enter into performance fee arrange-

ments with advisers on the premise that such clients have the sophistication and wealth to understand and negotiate such fees. Under the rule, a *qualified client* is (1) an individual or company that will have at least $1 million AUM with the adviser; (2) an individual or company that the adviser reasonably believes has a net worth of at least $2 million at the time of contracting, or is a *qualified purchaser* under the Company Act Section 2(a)(51) (which has even higher thresholds of wealth); or (3) an individual who has served in an official capacity (e.g., partner, officer, director, etc.) of the adviser for at least 12 months. The statutory assumption appears to be that wealthy clients can better fend for themselves and, moreover, may seek advisory services that command premium compensation schemes.

8.4 Affirmative Disclosure Obligations and the Brochure Rule

As discussed in Chapter 6, an investment adviser that is required to register with the SEC must initially file a registration statement on Form ADV and periodically update its filing to keep the disclosures in its registration statement current. While Form ADV typically is not a publicly used or available document, certain parts of the Form ADV, i.e., Parts 2A and 2B, have affirmative client disclosure requirements and may be used to serve as the adviser's client disclosure document. Part 2A is known as the brochure ("Brochure") and Part 2B as the brochure supplement ("Brochure Supplement").

Brochure Rule and the Brochure. A registered adviser must prepare and deliver to clients a plain English, narrative Brochure that contains all information required by Part 2A of Form ADV. Some advisers prepare separate Brochures for delivery to clients and prospective investors, while others use their Part 2A as filed. The Brochure requirement of Rule 204-3 mandates disclosure of, among other things, the adviser's business practices, investment strategies, fees, conflicts of interest, and disciplinary information. An adviser's Brochure must be delivered to a client before or at the time of entering into an advisory contract with the client. The Brochure must be updated annually and delivered to the client, and the update must contain or be accompanied by a summary of material changes, or a summary of material changes with an offer to deliver the updated Brochure upon the client's request. The Brochure is typically the primary disclosure document that investment advisers provide to their clients.

Explanation: About "Plain English"

In recent decades, the SEC has required certain documents targeted to retail investors to be written in "plain English," i.e., in a way which is easily understood by non-experts. In 1998, the SEC prepared its own manual of style, which explains Plain English as follows:

"Plain English means analyzing and deciding what information investors need to make informed decisions, before words, sentences, or paragraphs are considered. A plain English document uses words economically and at a level the audience can understand. Its sentence structure is tight. Its tone is welcoming and direct. Its design is visually appealing. A plain English document is easy to read and looks like it's meant to be read." (See, *A Plain English Handbook: How to Create Clear SEC Disclosure Documents*, Office of Investor Education and Assistance, U.S. Securities and Exchange Commission (August 1998), p.5.)

In other words, according to the *Handbook*, a plain English document should be:

- "Succinct and readable"
- "[U]se short sentences; definite, concrete, everyday words; and the active voice."
- "Avoid legal jargon or highly business terms" unless you explain them simply or believe that all of your clients will understand them.
- Don't use "legalese," i.e., legal jargon.

An example:

- **Complex English version:** "XYZ Investment Securities LLC provides investment advisory services to clients, and, therefore, charges fees based on assets that are being held under management."
- **Plain English version:** "The firm charges a fee for its services. Such fees are based on the amount of money you have invested with us."

Form ADV's requirements for Part 2A (the Brochure). In preparing their Brochure, advisers must respond to each of the separate required items of disclosure in a predetermined order and label each item with the mandated headings. In the instructions to the Form ADV regarding the Brochure section, the SEC emphasized the importance of full and fair disclosure:

> Under federal and state law, you are a fiduciary and must make full disclosure to your *clients* of all material facts relating to the advisory relationship. As a fiduciary, you also must seek to avoid conflicts of interest with your clients, and, at a minimum, make full disclosure of all material conflicts of interest between you and your clients that could affect the advisory relationship. This obligation requires that you provide the client with sufficiently specific facts so that the client is able to understand the conflicts of interest you have and the business practices in which you engage, and can give informed consent to such conflicts or practices or reject them. To satisfy this obligation, you therefore may have to disclose to clients information not specifically required by Part 2 of Form ADV or in more detail than the brochure items might oth-

> erwise require. You may disclose this additional information to clients in your brochure or by some other means.... All information in your brochure and brochure supplements must be true and may not omit any material facts.

General Instructions for Part 2 of Form ADV, Item 3, Form ADV (Paper Version) Uniform Application for Investment Adviser Registration, SEC Website (accessed Jan. 21, 2018).

An adviser is allowed to tailor its Brochures for different markets, i.e., it may prepare separate Brochures with respect to clients for whom it provides substantially different advisory services. It is important to note that under the anti-fraud provisions of the Advisers Act, simple delivery of a compliant Brochure may not necessarily satisfy an adviser's full disclosure obligations. As a result, it is customary for advisers to include additional information in their Brochures and Form ADV's. There are a variety of additional rules regarding Brochure delivery to small clients, private funds, and by sub-advisers which are beyond the scope of this discussion. However, one notable rule to note is that advisers may deliver Brochures to their clients electronically, if the clients consent to such delivery.

Chapters 6 and 7 laid out the basics of registration, disclosure, and antifraud regulations applicable to advisers. The following case presents an interesting amalgam of such issues, notably under the Brochure rule, Form ADV, fee requirements, and registration requirements.

In the Matter of Noonan Capital Management, LLC

Investment Advisers Act of 1940 Release No. 3609 (May 17, 2013)

> [**Textbook Note:** *This case settlement presents several issues of what can go wrong or be mishandled respecting disclosures and fees. It also reflects a deliberate attempt by the adviser to circumvent the bar to federal registration as an adviser prior to the Dodd-Frank Act which further tightened the federal registration thresholds.*]

[***] Respondents

1. **Noonan Capital, LLC** is a Commission-registered and Georgia-based investment adviser. Noonan Capital has been operating since in or about February 2009 and has been registered with the Commission since March 2009. While Noonan Capital represented in its initial Form ADV (filed on February 27, 2009) and in its most recently amended Form ADV (filed on July 13, 2009) that it was a Georgia limited liability company, it did not and has not taken the necessary legal steps required to become such an entity. In its July 13, 2009 amended Form ADV, Noonan Capital also represented that it provided advisory services to twenty-three accounts with $39.4 million in assets under management ("AUM"). Noonan Capital's client accounts were custodied at Charles Schwab and Co., Inc. ("Schwab") from the time Noonan Capital first began operations to in or about early 2011. Noonan Capital is presently non-operational and based on its sworn Statement of Financial Information has practically no assets.

2. **Timothy George Noonan**, age 54, has been, for all relevant times, the sole owner, chief compliance officer, manager and employee of Noonan Capital.....

Noonan Capital Misappropriated Client Assets by Charging Excessive "Advisory Fees"

3. In Noonan Capital's Form ADV, Part 2, Fee Schedule filed with the Commission on March 9, 2009 and, then again, on March 12, 2009 ("Fee Schedule"), Noonan Capital represented that its advisory fees from its clients' accounts were to be payable quarterly and in advance based on the value of the accounts' portfolio on the last business day of the prior quarter. The Fee Schedule provided for fees ranging from 1.0 to 1.5% based on the AUM held in the clients' accounts.

4. Noonan did not provide written advisory agreements to Noonan Capital clients. Although Noonan Capital and Noonan did not provide Part 2 of the Form ADVs to clients, Noonan Capital and Noonan represented to clients that they would be charged advisory fees at the rates set forth in those filings. Additionally, Noonan Capital and Noonan represented to and agreed with one of Noonan Capital's largest clients—who had accounts containing approximately $1 million in AUM—that Noonan Capital would not charge any advisory fees until that client's accounts grew by approximately 50%, an event that never occurred.

5. Based on the Fee Schedule and/or Noonan's oral representations to clients, Noonan Capital should have charged the twenty-two clients a total of $92,212 between April 2009 and January 2011. Instead, Noonan Capital and Noonan charged these clients advisory fees totaling $183,908, resulting in total overcharges of approximately $91,696 in advisory fees. In at least some client accounts, the improper fee requests resulted in the sale of money market funds to satisfy the requests.

6. As a result of these misappropriations, on an annualized basis, some clients paid "fees" of up to 7%, which was far in excess of the 1.0 to 1.5% they should have been charged.

Noonan Capital and Noonan Misrepresented Noonan Capital's Assets under Management and Failed to Withdraw Its Registration from the Commission

7. Noonan Capital and Noonan misrepresented Noonan Capital's AUM in the Form ADV filed with the Commission. In its initial Form ADV filed with the Commission on February 27, 2009, Noonan Capital invoked Rule 203A-2(d), a registration prohibition exemption, thereby effectively representing that the firm expected to have $25 million in assets under management within 120 days. On March 12, 2009, Noonan Capital filed an amended Form ADV again representing that the firm expected to have $25 million in assets under management. And, on July 13, 2009, Noonan Capital filed an amended Form ADV in which the firm claimed that it was eligible to remain registered with the Commission because it had $39.4 million in assets under management, comprised of $9.4 million in twenty-two discretionary accounts and $30 million in one non-discretionary account.

8. In fact, Noonan Capital never had more than approximately $9 million in AUM. Noonan Capital's and Noonan's representations concerning its AUM in its July 2009 Form ADV were false at the time it was submitted.

9. At no time did Noonan Capital file any amendment to its Form ADV reflecting a corrected AUM of under $25 million or seek to withdraw from registration. Noonan Capital further failed to file its required annual amendments to its Form ADV for the fiscal years ending December 31, 2009, 2010, and 2011.

Noonan Capital Failed to Create or Maintain Proper Books and Records and Failed to Provide a Brochure or Part 2 of Its Form ADV to Its Clients

10. Noonan Capital did not create or maintain required balance sheets, income statements, and supporting documents as required under certain rules of the Advisers Act.

11. Neither Noonan Capital nor Noonan ever provided to any client Part 2 of Form ADV or any brochure containing the information required by Part 2.

Violations

....

13. As a result of the conduct described above, Noonan Capital and Noonan willfully violated Sections 206(1) and 206(2) of the Advisers Act, which prohibit fraudulent conduct by an investment adviser.

14. As a result of the conduct described above, Noonan Capital willfully violated, and Noonan willfully aided and abetted and caused Noonan Capital's violation of Section 203A(a)(1)(A), which, during the relevant time, generally prohibited an adviser regulated or required to be regulated in the state in which it had its principal office and place of business from registering with the Commission, unless it had assets under management in excess of $25 million or advised a registered investment company.

15. As a result of the conduct described above, Noonan Capital and Noonan willfully violated Section 207 of the Advisers Act, which makes it "unlawful for any person willfully to make any untrue statement of a material fact in any registration application or report filed with the Commission ... or willfully to omit to state in any such application or report any material fact which is required to be stated therein."

16. As a result of the conduct described above, Noonan Capital willfully violated, and Noonan willfully aided and abetted and caused Noonan Capital's violation of Section 204(a) of the Advisers Act and Rules 204-1(a)(1), 204-2(a)(6), 204-3(a), and 204-3(b)(1) and (2) thereunder. Section 204 of the Advisers Act requires every registered investment adviser to make and keep "such records ... as the Commission, by rule, may prescribe as necessary or appropriate in the public interest or for the protection of investors." Such records are subject to periodic examinations by the Commission. Rule 204-1(a)(1) requires registered investment advisers to amend their Form ADV "at

least annually, within 90 days of the end of [its] fiscal year." Rule 204-2(a)(6) requires registered investment advisers to make and keep true, accurate, and current certain books and records relating to its investment advisory business, including, trial balances, financial statements, and internal audit working papers relating to the business of the investment adviser. Rule 204-3(b)(1) requires delivery of the current brochure to a client or prospective client before or at the time the investment adviser enters into an investment advisory contract with the client. Rule 204-3(b)(2) requires an adviser to deliver to each client annually, if there are material changes in the brochure, a current brochure or the summary of material changes to the brochure. [***]

* * *

8.5 Safekeeping and Custody of Client Assets

The topics covered so far in this chapter are representative of the numerous substantive requirements applicable to investment advisers. The requirements flow from several sources, including the general fiduciary duties of advisers, requirements imposed by the Advisers Act, and regulation under other laws. A final example to be reviewed is the possession, security, or safekeeping of client assets and money, which is at the heart of the fiduciary relationship. This is known as *custody.* Given the complexities of custody and the custody rule under the Advisers Act, Rule 206(4)-2, most advisers do *not* maintain custody of their clients' assets. Rather such assets are generally held by a bank or broker-dealer, which are the typical third-party custodians. For example, despite the various compliance violations outlined in the *Noonan* case, the SEC affirmatively found that Noonan maintained third-party custody of client assets with the brokerage firm Charles Schwab.

The custody rule, Rule 206(4)-2, was first adopted in 1963 and amended in 2003 and 2009 to reflect the increasing complexity of custody. The Rule has four key requirements:

1. Maintenance of custody of client assets and money with a qualified custodian;
2. Client notification of where custody is maintained;
3. Quarterly account statements must be sent by the custodian to clients; and
4. Annually, there needs to be a surprise verification of the assets held by the custodian.

The critical point is that advisers must take specific, affirmative actions to protect client assets from loss or theft.

On its face, custody would seem to be an easy subject to deal with: an adviser either holds its clients' assets or it doesn't. And that's the threshold issue regarding custody: under what circumstances is an adviser deemed to have custody?

Information for Newly-Registered Investment Advisers: Requirements for Investment Advisers That Have Custody or Possession of Clients' Funds or Securities

(SEC website—accessed March 14, 2018)

[**Textbook Note:** *The SEC's webpage contains useful informal information including, for example, information regarding investment advisers' legal and compliance requirements. This document provides a clear explanation of the custody requirements. As the document notes, there are numerous ways custody can be inferred or construed. It's not just simply holding the cash and securities of a client. It is this complexity which has led to several enforcement actions and, in some cases, large losses of client assets by advisers. The SEC continues to identify troubling situations where an adviser may have constructive custody and provides periodic updates via a Q&A document on the SEC's site and occasional IM Guidance Updates.*]

[***] "Custody" is defined as "holding, directly or indirectly, client funds or securities, or having any authority to obtain possession of them." This includes situations in which you:

- have physical possession of client funds or securities, even temporarily;
- enter into arrangements (including a general power of attorney) authorizing you to withdraw funds or securities from the client's account (note that if you are authorized to deduct your advisory fees or other expenses directly from clients' accounts, you have custody); and
- serve in a capacity that gives you or a supervised person legal ownership or access to client funds or securities (note that if you are a general partner to a privately-offered pooled investment vehicle, you have custody).
- If you are a trustee, you may have custody.

If you have custody, with limited exceptions, you must maintain these client funds and securities at a "qualified custodian." Generally, qualified custodians include most banks and insured savings associations, SEC-registered broker-dealers, Commodity Exchange Act-registered futures commission merchants, and certain foreign financial institutions. With a limited exception, for client accounts over which you have custody, you must have a reasonable basis, after due inquiry, for believing that the client (or a designated representative) receives periodic reports *directly from the custodian* that contain specific information with respect to the funds and securities in custody. With respect to pooled investment vehicles over which you have custody, the qualified custodian must send account statements for the pooled vehicle directly to each investor.

If you have custody of client funds or securities that are held at an unrelated, independent qualified custodian, then you must have a "surprise verification" by an independent public accountant. The independent public accountant must verify the funds and securities in your custody or possession at least once each calendar year, and must then promptly file a "certificate of accounting" with Form ADV-E electronically through IARD. [IARD is the electronic filing system for advisers.]

If you have custody of client funds or securities that you or a related person maintains as a qualified custodian, then you must also have an internal control report completed by an independent public accountant registered with, and subject to regular inspection by, the Public Company Accounting Oversight Board. [***]

* * *

Especially difficult is the recognition by an adviser of situations *where it effectively holds assets*. The SEC in an information and guidance document, *Significant Deficiencies Involving Adviser Custody and Safety of Client Assets*, 2013 National Exam Program Risk Alert, Vol. III, Issue 1 (March 4, 2013), noted the following situations as examples where an adviser effectively has custody of client assets and, thus, must comply with the custody rule requirements:

- **The Role of Employees or Related Persons:** The adviser's personnel or a "related person" serve as trustee or have been granted power of attorney for client accounts.
- **Bill-Paying Services:** The adviser provides bill-paying services for clients and, therefore, is authorized to withdraw funds or securities from the client's account.
- **Online Access to Client Accounts:** The adviser manages portfolios by directly accessing online accounts using clients' personal usernames and passwords without restrictions and, therefore, has the ability to withdraw funds and securities from the clients' accounts.
- **Adviser Acts as a General Partner:** The adviser serves as the general partner of a limited partnership or holds a comparable position for a different type of pooled investment vehicle.
- **Physical Possession of Assets:** The adviser has physical possession of client assets, such as securities certificates.
- **Check-Writing Authority:** The adviser or a related person has signatory and check writing authority for client accounts.
- **Receipt of Checks Made to Clients:** The adviser received checks made out to clients and failed to return them promptly to the sender.

Given the complexities, advisers often try to avoid having custody of client assets. A typical way for advisers to delegate custody to a third-party custodian is to have their clients open accounts with a brokerage firm such as Charles Schwab or Fidelity. The clients then execute trades in those accounts in accordance with the adviser's advice. On the other hand, many clients prefer to give trading discretion to the advisers, which can lead to complications as illustrated by the *GW & Wade* case, discussed below. Even with recent rule enhancements and attempts by the SEC to educate advisers, legal counsel, and compliance personnel, problems continue.

Custody issue: safekeeping stock certificates. In one case, *In the Matter of Knelman Asset Management Group, LLC, and Irving P. Knelman,* Investment Advisers Act Release No. 3705 (October 28, 2013), the SEC had previously warned the firm of weaknesses in its custody procedures, including the adviser holding stock certificates for the funds it managed. The adviser attempted to remedy the violations by putting the stock certificates in a safe deposit box in the funds' names (but adviser personnel had access to the safe deposit box). That technically left custody of the stock certificates in the adviser's control. A better practice would be to hire a third-party custodian bank or broker to hold the certificates in the relevant funds' name. In addition, in a follow-up examination, the SEC found that the adviser's funds were not subject to annual surprise examinations and certain clients did not receive quarterly account statements from a qualified custodian. Such statements are useful compliance controls validating third-party custody. The SEC's narrative also detailed other violations of the securities laws, including improper discretionary cash distributions to certain investors, failure to adopt and implement controls designed to safeguard client assets, and failure to conduct annual compliance reviews. Finally, as a small firm, with about $100 million AUM, the owner performed multiple roles, including serving as CEO and chief compliance officer. The SEC questioned his qualifications as such.

It's hard to set up and operate a small investment adviser: The requirements are complex and numerous. It can be expensive to hire the right experts to help. Yet one must do so as the *Knelman* case clearly illustrates.

Custody issue: Letters of Authorization. Another illustration of the challenges of custody rule compliance is the case of *GW & Wade, LLC* which was announced the same day that the *Knelman* case. *In the Matter of GW & Wade, LLC,* Investment Advisers Act Release No. 3706 (October 28, 2013). In the *GW & Wade* case, the firm was a $5 billion investment adviser and broker-dealer which provided high-quality concierge services to wealthy clients. Unlike Knelman, the firm had qualified compliance and legal staff, but nonetheless ran afoul of the regulations. Custody of client assets and funds were maintained at GW & Wade's own brokerage operation or at a variety of banks and other brokers. Among GW & Wade's services was one which enabled GW & Wade staff to transfer or send client funds on a client's behalf via a pre-authorized transfer form, a Letter of Authorization. Having pre-signed forms in the office enabled the firm to accommodate requests without having to get signed forms every time, a convenience feature for the client ... and, as it turns out, thieves.

GW & Wade's Letter of Authorization practices contributed to a large client loss in 2012 when someone hacked the client's email account and sent a withdrawal request. The request directed funds to be sent to a bank account in Singapore. While the GW & Wade staff tried to validate the request, they were unsuccessful but believed it to be genuine. In the end, several transfers were made totaling $290,000 all of which were sent to a foreign bank and stolen.

On examination, the SEC found that the Letter of Authorization process was effectively custody by GW & Wade. As a result, the adviser was found to have violated the custody rule, compliance rule, disclosure requirements, and books and records requirements just like Knelman.

* * *

The topics covered in this chapter are representative of affirmative regulatory requirements applicable to investment advisers beyond those covered in Chapter 7. While these requirements all flow from the Advisers Act, other statutes contain additional requirements bearing on investment advisers. These include privacy laws designed to protect the privacy of client information, identity theft regulations to protect clients, beneficial ownership and institutional investor reporting requirements under the Exchange Act, and broker-dealer registration for advisers serving in a dual capacity.

Chapter 9

Regulating Private Funds through Regulation of Advisers

Key Ideas: Private funds (such as hedge funds, private equity funds, and venture capital funds) and other forms of unregistered pooled vehicles (such as collective trusts) present a regulatory challenge. Like registered investment companies, these unregistered vehicles are pooled investment vehicles, but in contrast to registered investment companies, these funds are eligible for exclusion from the Company Act's definition of investment company, and therefore are not subject to registration or any of the Company Act's mandates. The relevant exclusions from the Company Act are discussed in the next chapter. However, given the large number of unregistered vehicles and assets excluded from the Company Act in this fashion, it is necessary to address how the activities of such funds and their managers are regulated. Under recent legislative and rule changes, the activities of unregistered funds are subject to indirect regulation under the Advisers Act because the advisers to these funds are typically required to register under the Advisers Act (as discussed in Chapter 6). Therefore, such advisers and their conduct with respect to client-unregistered funds are subject to the substantive requirements of the Advisers Act (as discussed in Chapters 7 and 8). In this regard, private funds and other unregistered pooled vehicles face many of the same practical challenges faced by registered investment companies in terms of fair treatment of investors, custody and safekeeping of fund assets, pricing and valuation of assets, and sales and marketing practices. However, these issues must be evaluated from the perspective of the adviser's role, rather than in terms of the affirmative requirements under the Company Act imposed on registered funds, such as mutual funds. There is a second less obvious regulatory hook with respect to the activities of private fund sponsors. Sales of unregistered securities are nevertheless subject to the antifraud provisions of the Securities Act of 1933 and the Securities Exchange Act of 1934 and Rule 10b-5 thereunder. In addition, a private fund sponsor must also be careful to adhere to broker-dealer requirements that may govern the marketing of participation units in the unregistered fund.

Chapter Contents

9.1 Introduction

This chapter addresses a topic that falls between the Investment Advisers Act, which has been addressed in the preceding several chapters, and the Investment Company Act, which will be discussed throughout the next nine chapters. Specifically, it discusses regulation of advisers to unregistered investment vehicles, in particular advisers to well-known types of private funds, such as hedge funds, private equity funds, and venture capital funds, that manage roughly five trillion dollars in assets. The regulatory story of why the investment vehicles themselves are not regulated, while their advisers generally are, is a twisting narrative that involves a combination of unanticipated consequences and political inertia over decades.

Prior to 1940, the world of investment funds in terms of number and types was drastically simpler than the investment world of today: most funds were offered to the public. The legislative and regulatory focus in 1940 was largely limited to these publicly offered investment vehicles, such as closed-end funds and mutual funds, while a limited carve-out was created for collective arrangements that were not offered to the public, presumably in the belief that non-public vehicles did not present significant concerns. Over time, and especially toward the end of the 20th century, unregistered funds (i.e., hedge funds, private equity funds and venture capital funds) began to accumulate hundreds of billions of dollars in assets. The funds, known as "private funds" because of their reliance on specific exclusions from the Company Act, substantially augmented existing unregistered pooled investment vehicles, such as collective trusts overseen by trust banks.

While private funds remained virtually unregulated, that all began to change in the early 21st century as the size of this sector became impossible to ignore and investor protection and other regulatory issues began to mount. The spectacular collapse of a large hedge fund (known as Long Term Capital Management) in 1998 shook the banking world. In the early 2000s, the SEC began to raise concerns about the unregulated nature of this segment of funds, but were stymied in efforts to exercise direct regulation over such entities. The Financial Crisis of 2008–2009 had little to do with private funds, but it ushered in the sweeping Dodd-Frank Act of 2010 which also substantially altered the regulatory landscape for private funds. Under the Dodd-Frank Act, private funds do not need to register, but for the first time, many advisers to such funds do. As discussed in Chapter 6, Dodd-Frank extended the Adviser Act's registration requirements to encompass many advisers of unregistered private funds. Quite simply, the regulatory objectives realized by regulation of the advisers of private funds do not directly implicate the status of the funds as unregulated vehicles under the Company Act.

In many ways, focusing on Advisers Act issues affecting unregistered funds repeats some of the issues addressed in Chapters 7 and 8 in a different context. However, because of the increasing economic importance of such funds and unique features in how they are structured, the discussion of regulation of advisers as it pertains to their management of unregistered vehicles is sufficiently important to warrant a separate context-specific discussion. The discussion begins with a fuller description of the principal types of private funds. The chapter then explores two types of issues that arise with some frequency: (i) issues relating to sales and marketing of interests in unregistered vehicles; and (ii) conflicts of interest of different shapes and variety that can spring up in this area. Thinking about indirect regulation of unregistered vehicles through regulation of advisers will serve as excellent preparation for the other side of the coin, namely intensive regulation of registered investment vehicles.

9.2 Private Funds—An Overview

While the term phrase "private funds" is commonly used to refer to hedge funds, venture capital funds, and private equity funds, this term has a very precise legal meaning. Private funds must be understood in reference to the correlative term "investment company" under the Company Act and the statutory phrase "registered investment companies," since under the Company Act, any investment company must in fact be registered to conduct business in the United States. As explained in Chapter 10, the statutory definition of investment company excludes a variety of pooled investment vehicles, and the specific exclusions relied upon by hedge funds, venture capital funds, and private equity funds are known as the "private funds exclusions." This distinction is carried over and codified under the Advisers Act where the definition of *private funds* was added to the Advisers Act in 2010 by the Dodd-Frank Act. Section 202(a)-29 specifically uses those Company Act exclusions—Company Act Section 3(c)(1) and, more importantly, Section 3(c)(7)—to define the universe of private funds for purposes of the Advisers Act.

As noted in Chapter 6, the adviser registration provisions require a domestic private fund adviser (other than one that exclusively advises a venture capital fund) to register if it advises qualifying private funds with regulatory assets under management of greater than $150 million. There is a corollary provision for non-U.S. advisers of U.S. based private funds that also relies on the $150 million threshold. In addition, advisers to private funds that are not exempt from registration are subject to enhanced confidential reporting requirements on Form PF. Pursuant to IAA Rule 204(b)(1), registered advisers of private funds with aggregate assets of $150 million or more must complete sections of Form PF based on their size. All such regulated private fund advisers must complete Section 1 of Form PF containing less extensive general reporting requirements. However, large private advisers, depending on the types of private fund and collective assets among the funds advised, must complete detailed portfolio data collection reporting requirements: hedge funds ($1.5 billion), liquidity funds ($1 billion), and private equity funds ($2 billion). These reporting requirements give regulators a sense of total portfolio exposures in these private funds.

The Company Act exclusions for private funds require that ownership units in the private funds not be publicly offered nor sold to investors, but rather pursuant to qualified purchaser or private placement exemptions under the Securities Act. As a result, the universe of participants, as a practical matter, is limited to institutional investors and wealthy investors (who at the very least qualify as "accredited investors") and, indeed, the vast majority of substantial private funds will be even more selective in their targeting only certain potential investors (i.e., investors that are extremely well-funded investors who can make minimum investments that can easily exceed $5 million).

The remainder of this section provides a brief overview of the three basic business categories of private funds (hedge funds, venture capital funds, and private equity funds) and their respective structures.

9.2.1 Hedge Funds

The first hedge fund was founded by an Australian turned New York journalist for Fortune magazine in 1949. Alfred Winslow Jones, frequently identified as the father of the hedge fund industry, started what he called a "hedged fund." At the time, mutual funds did not hedge their investments by selling stock short and, under the Company Act, their use of leverage was severely limited. Besides hedging, Jones' fund featured a number of additional aspects still used in hedge funds today, including a tax-advantaged limited partnership structure and performance fees that would not be permitted for registered funds. His fund, which started with $100,000, enjoyed good success through the 1950s, prompting others to establish similar funds in the 1960s, and the industry was born. In 1997, hedge funds held just over $100 billion in net assets. In 2004, they crossed the trillion dollar mark and, by 2018, managed a little over $3 trillion in assets (excluding so-called funds of funds, i.e., hedge funds that hold a portfolio of hedge funds) comprising somewhere between six to ten thousand funds.

While they are generally structured as partnerships or LLCs and do not have governance structures characteristic of mutual funds, among other types of private funds, hedge funds bear the greatest similarity to mutual funds. Hedge funds invariably are based on investment strategies that involve active trading of investments whether securities or commodities. These trading strategies can be fairly conventional, such as buy and hold strategies, but hedge funds are best known for aggressive and not infrequently complex trading strategies that involve the use of large trading positions, leverage and hedging through the use of short selling or derivatives. Because hedge funds engage in trading strategies, their investment horizons tend to be shorter, and typically investors in such funds are sensitive to annual performance. Hedge funds also differ from mutual fund trading strategies in that they are most interested in absolute return strategies, that is strategies that provide positive returns regardless of market conditions rather than relative return strategies in which the manager seeks to outperform the relevant market return (i.e., earn more than the market rate of return when the market is up and lose less when the market is down). In addition to hedged equity and fixed income strategies, hedge funds pursue specialized trading styles and strategies, such as strategies involving merger arbitrage, emerging markets, or macro themes (a trading strategy which seeks to benefit from valuation discrepancies that can crop up between markets internationally).

Figure 9A illustrates the basic structure of a hedge fund, a model which shares some features with private equity and venture capital funds. (These funds differ significantly from hedge funds in one significant respect: they do not seek to profit from trading strategies and thus, unlike hedge funds, they do not use prime brokers nor maintain internal trading desks.) A hedge fund itself is generally a limited partnership or limited liability company which permits pass-through tax treatment. Investors receive limited partnership interests (or ownership units) as their investments. As a limited partnership, the fund is required to have a general partner, which is either the adviser or an affiliate of the adviser. The adviser provides advice regarding investment selection and management as well as operations and administrative oversight. It is not unusual to see firms where the advisory business is separated legally from the other management or administrative functions. A custodian or prime broker (which is essentially a broker providing trading services, custody, and loans to the fund) holds the investments made by the fund.

Figure 9A — Core model of venture capital, private equity, and hedge funds

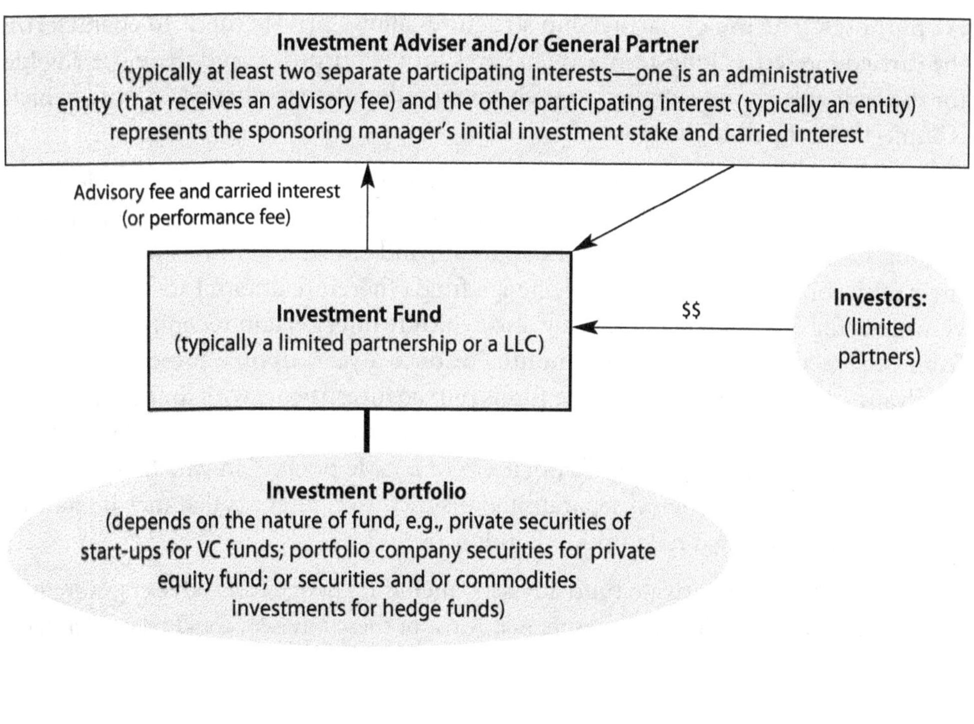

An important factor in these funds is the stake of the fund sponsor, which invariably is the adviser. While a detailed discussion is beyond the scope of this chapter, a brief note is important. Typically, the adviser will have a significant ownership stake in the fund (i.e., the adviser has "skin" in the game) which may represent an initial capital contribution or profits derived from managing the funds. As noted in Figure 9A, these funds generally pay the adviser or affiliates of the adviser both an AUM-based percentage fee and a performance fee (sometimes called a profit allocation). These fees are quite steep relative to registered investment companies. Until recently, many hedge fund managers could command a so-called "2/20 fee" structure, i.e., a 2% annual for administering and managing the fund and an additional performance fee of 20% of fund profits for the relevant accounting period. Most funds also have a minimum investment return threshold that must be achieved before the adviser can collect the performance fee. This is known as the "hurdle rate," which requires a return threshold to be able to start collecting performance fees. In other words, unless a fund meets or exceeds the minimum investment return threshold or hurdle rate, the adviser cannot collect a performance fee. In addition, a "high water mark" is another common provision designed to ensure that the adviser only collects the performance fee for gains in net asset value above the highest net asset value previously attained at the end of any prior fiscal year. Accordingly, if an investor suffers a period of loss regarding his or her investment in the fund, that loss must first be recouped before the adviser is entitled to any performance fees.

The adviser's share of the profits of an investment or gains in a private fund that are paid to the adviser in excess of the amount that it contributed to the fund is called the "carried interest" or "carry." This carry typically represents not only the return on the sponsor's or adviser's stake, but the allocation of profits attributable to its performance fee. Hedge funds, and indeed all private funds, are carefully structured for tax purposes. The use of partnership structures allows private funds to characterize the carried interest as long-term capital gains for tax purposes (and therefore eligible for the favorable tax rate applied to such gains) rather than as current income, which is subject to a much higher rate of taxation.

Hedge fund interests, unlike mutual funds shares, are not freely redeemable at the discretion of the hedge fund investor. This allows hedge funds to engage in riskier trading strategies that would be difficult to unwind efficiently if investors could pull their money out of the fund. While hedge funds therefore attempt to "lock-up" investments for extended periods, they also typically offer certain redemption periods from time to time, e.g., every six months or once a year, upon a prescribed period of advance notice. Sometimes hedge funds pursue investments with limited liquidity. In such circumstances, the fund adviser typically retains the authority to isolate those investment positions in the fund's portfolio to a "side pocket" in which all fund investors hold a *pro rata* interest separate and distinct from interests that may be subject to redemption during a redemption window period.

In early 2000, most private fund advisers, including hedge fund advisers, were not required to register under the Advisers Act. Most of these advisers could take advantage of a statutory registration exception under the Advisers Act (which has since been eliminated) for advisers providing advice to fewer than 15 clients in any 12 month period. Hedge funds were able to use this exception based on an older SEC interpretation which interpreted clients of a hedge fund adviser as the fund rather than the investors in the fund. Already regulatory concerns had arisen in 1998 when financial derivatives markets were pushed to the brink of a massive meltdown in the wake of the collapse of Long-Term Capital Management, a huge hedge fund run by Nobel economic laureates that is reported to have controlled $100 billion in assets. *See* Report of the President's Working Group on Financial Markets, *Hedge Funds, Leverage, and the Lessons of Long-Term Capital Management* (April 1999). The events of the Long-Term Capital Management debacle are recounted in Roger Lowenstein's best-seller, WHEN GENIUS FAILED (2000). In its 2003 report on *Implications of the Growth of Hedge Funds*, the SEC voiced a number of concerns relating to the unregulated nature of the hedge fund industry. Shortly thereafter, it adopted a rule that would have changed this interpretation for hedge funds (but not for private equity or venture capital funds). That rule, however, was successfully challenged as beyond the SEC's authority in *SEC v. Goldstein*, 451 F.3d 873 (D.C. Cir. 2006).

As a result, the SEC's effort to exert more regulatory authority over hedge funds appeared stymied but for legislative action, and Congress did not appear inclined to make any changes. The Financial Crisis of 2008 led to a broad rethinking of financial regulation and, as noted, the Dodd-Frank Act of 2010 in connection with a host of significant legislative initiatives amended the Advisers Act by eliminating the 15 client registration exception, instead substituting in its place a complex scheme of registration that dealt expressly with registration of advisers to hedge funds, private equity funds, and venture capital funds discussed in Chapter 6. These changes had several effects: (i) the SEC gained current access to financial information in this sector; (ii) it made all large advisers in this sector subject to the substantive standards of the Advisers Act; and (iii) resulted in a more pro-active enforcement stance (i.e., the agency was better positioned to identify and pursue conduct problems). It is fair to say that the resulting regulatory framework has produced an environment with more robust compliance and other regulatory safeguards.

9.2.2 Private Equity Funds

The other main categories of private funds (although there are other categories) are private equity and venture capital funds. Unlike hedge funds, private equity funds are not organized to engage in active trading of securities or commodities. Instead, they are typically formed as funds of limited duration (such as 10 years) to acquire or recapitalize mature businesses. The idea is to commit capital to portfolio companies for a period that will permit those businesses to reach some sort of transformative stage, such as going public or being sold to another large operating business, rather than to become permanent long-term investors.

The private equity category is sufficiently broad that it encompasses the kinds of activities performed long ago by merchant banks. However, what is known as private equity today is typically associated with a style of dealmaking that emerged in the early stages of the merger and acquisitions field of the 1980s. A few firms emerged that specialized in large takeover transactions packaged as leveraged buy-outs, that is, acquisitions financed with significant amounts of debt. For an accessible discussion of these developments through the Financial Crisis and contractual aspects of private equity acquisition transactions, see Steven M. Davidoff, *The Failure of Private Equity*, 82 S. Cal. L. Rev. 481 (2009). These firms, coupled with increasingly aggressive willingness of investment banks and money center banks to extend financing for such transactions, gave birth to an industry that in 2017 is estimated to account for an estimated $2.5 trillion dollars in fund assets. Today, private equity funds are an integral part of the world of mergers and acquisitions and restructurings.

Private equity funds frequently invest in securities of publicly traded companies, but they can just as easily focus on buy-outs of private companies. Offerings of private funds, including private equity as well as venture capital and hedge funds, are generally made in personal presentations supported by a "private placement memoranda" ("PPMs" or "offering circulars") which are similar to prospectuses of registered funds and other documentation. These documents spell out the intent and objective of the fund as well as detailed information on how the fund operates. The underlying limited partnership agreement is the key document which addresses various aspects of the sponsor's managerial discretion, fees that the sponsor can earn, and the rights and obligations of the investor.

The partnership interests may be structured as an initial capital contribution and an ongoing commitment to supply additional capital as investment transactions are identified and need to be funded. The manager has the ability to call for capital based on these commitments over a period of time called the "investment period." The failure of a limited partner to meet such a "capital call" typically results in a severe financial penalty for the investor in terms of diluted or forfeited capital stakes. After 2000, the emergence of multi-billion dollar private equity funds became commonplace, although private equity firms specialize in all segments of the market: large, mid-market, or small acquisitions.

Private equity funds, and for that matter venture capital funds, are distinct from hedge funds in the way they are liquidated or wrapped up. Typically, private equity and venture capital funds do not permit redemptions or a return until portfolio investments are liquidated, meaning that the portfolio company goes public, is sold, or the funds' investment in the company is otherwise wrapped up. As the portfolio liquidation process continues, investor money (and profits, hopefully) are returned to investors. As a result, the entire process inevitably takes years from start to finish.

As noted in Chapter 6, the adviser registration provisions require a domestic private fund adviser (other than one that exclusively advises a venture capital fund) to register if it advises qualifying private funds with regulatory assets under management of greater than $150 million. There is a corollary provision for non-U.S. advisers and advisers to private funds of less than $150 million triggered by features of advisory regulation in the states applicable to mid-sized advisers. The key point here is advisers who exclusively advise venture capital funds have, as discussed below, a much broader registration exception. Of course, many asset managers operate a mix of private equity, hedge, and venture capital funds.

9.2.3 Venture Capital Funds

Venture capital investing can be traced back to a corporation that engaged in this investment strategy long before funds came to be the dominant method of venture capital investing. American Research and Development Corporation ("ARD") was formed in 1946 by a former Harvard Business School professor, Georges Doriot, along with two other like-minded investors to invest in new research and development enterprises in the New England area. ARD made a huge windfall by investing in a technology company called Digital Equipment Corporation, which eventually went public and was subsequently acquired by a much larger technology company. Although it made many other investments, ARD was the first institutional investor to become famous by investing in a pre-IPO company that subsequently went public yielding returns of enormous multiples on its investment. Although ARD was a trailblazer in this style of investing, it was not structured in the later common fund form for venture investing.

In many respects, venture capital funds are a sub-category of the much broader private equity category. Like private equity funds, they seek to acquire significant stakes in portfolio companies and typically envision capital commitments of significant duration. Unlike private equity funds, venture capital funds invest in start-up and young companies. Once a fund has been raised, its adviser spends much of its time examining potential investment opportunities by reviewing business plans, listening to pitches, and reviewing financial and market data. An adviser may select only one or two companies out of dozens that are reviewed. Of these investments, many will either fail or be only marginally successful. The venture capital investor, however, seeks to recoup its capital and enjoy significant profits from the few investments that yield rich returns (think Google—now Alphabet—and Facebook).

Initial investments in start-ups are often small, sufficient only to demonstrate the viability of a concept or business. Once there has been a proof of concept, then larger investment rounds may be made. Venture capital firms often team up to jointly fund companies in "rounds" of funding, and these different rounds are frequently designated with letters, A, B, C (which is a naming convention that refers to different series of preferred stock issued by the portfolio company) or referred to in terms of the different stages in the investment process—seed, early stage, mezzanine, or late stage. While investments are being made, the adviser may also provide (or arrange for) managerial assistance to portfolio companies or participate in their governance. The goal is to coach portfolio companies along to a successful "exit strategy," typically a sale of the company or public offering of its stock. Successful exits are the profits for the VC fund, and the venture capital adviser may be entitled to a performance fee on the fund's overall success.

The investing economics of a venture capital fund differs from the private equity fund. Venture capital funds tend to be much smaller than the average private equity fund and in total may account for investments in the tens of billions of dollars in contrast to the trillions under investment in the mainstream private equity sector. Similarly, the venture capital sector is populated by hundreds of funds rather than the thousands that populate the private equity sector. In addition, unlike private equity funds, venture capital funds typically do not seek or obtain a controlling stake in the start-ups in which they invest. Moreover, they provide infusions of capital that do not involve the use of leverage or borrowing, in contrast to the typical pattern of investment involving private equity funds. Venture capital fund investments typically take the form of different series of convertible preferred stock issued by start-ups or emerging companies. Venture capital firms are very focused on anti-dilution provisions with respect to future rounds of financing and exit rights, both of which are spelled out in the terms of each series.

As noted, venture capital fund advisers are subject to a much broader exemption from registration than advisers of other private funds, provided the adviser solely advises venture capital funds. See Advisers Act Section 203(l). Unlike the private fund adviser exemption, this exemption is not contingent on size of the fund. Rule 203(l)-1 under the Advisers Act defines a *venture capital fund* as a private fund that holds itself out as pursuing a venture capital strategy, that seeks equity participation primarily through qualifying investments, and whose capital structure involves low levels of leverage.

9.3 Disclosure and Marketing of Private Funds

As discussed in Chapter 6, representations about performance, in this case of a private fund, may easily be found to be misleading, and the financial incentives to certain persons associated with the adviser to frame performance figures unduly favorably or even overstate them may be overwhelming. In the case of marketing of interests to prospective investors and disclosure to existing investors, such conduct may run afoul of the antifraud provisions of the Securities Act or the Exchange Act's Rule 10b-5. In addition, the antifraud provisions of the Advisers Act may be implicated.

In the Matter of Oppenheimer Asset Management Inc.

Investment Advisers Act Release No. 3566 (March 11, 2013)

[**Textbook note:** *This settlement resulted from misrepresentations to prospective and existing investors regarding the performance of the major asset of a private fund. The misconduct involved use of performance calculations employing a methodology that was inconsistent with the valuation methodologies that investors were told were being used and the only ones authorized to be used by the adviser's compliance personnel. The SEC found violations of general antifraud provisions of the Securities Act and other violations of the Advisers Act rules designed to deter conduct by an adviser to a pooled investment vehicle that defrauds the fund's holders. Notably, the adviser had compliance policies and procedures* *designed to prevent some forms of misconduct, but those proved ineffective in preventing the misconduct that manifested itself, indicating that perhaps they were not suitably designed.*]

[***] SUMMARY

1. This matter concerns registered investment advisers Oppenheimer Asset Management Inc.'s ("OAM") and Oppenheimer Alternative Investment Management, LLC's ("OAIM") misrepresentations and omissions to investors and prospective investors about the asset value of a fund of private equity funds vehicle they managed, Oppenheimer Global Resource Private Equity Fund I, L.P. ("OGR"). OAM's and OAIM's written policies and procedures did not contain provisions reasonably designed to prevent violations of the Advisers Act and the rules adopted thereunder. While the policies and procedures required the compliance department to review and approve marketing materials, those procedures did not require a review of portfolio manager valuations and were not reasonably designed to ensure that valuations were determined in a manner consistent with written representations to investors.

2. From October 2009 through 2010, Respondents disseminated marketing materials to prospective investors and quarterly reports to existing investors that contained material misrepresentations and omissions concerning Respondents' valuation policies and OGR's performance. Respondents stated in the marketing materials and quarterly reports to investors that OGR's asset values were "based on the underlying managers' estimated values" when that was not the case with respect to one of the assets in OGR's investment portfolio. Beginning in October 2009, while OGR was being marketed to new investors, OGR's portfolio manager ("Portfolio Manager") changed the value of OGR's largest holding, Cartesian InvestorsA, LLC ("Cartesian"), using a different valuation method than that used by Cartesian's underlying manager. The Portfolio Manager did not inform, and caused Respondents not to inform, investors either of this change or of the fact that the new valuation method resulted in a significant increase in the value of Cartesian over that provided by Cartesian's underlying manager.

3. Additionally, former employees overseeing OAIM's investments misrepresented and caused Respondents to misrepresent to potential investors that: (i) the increase in Cartesian's value was due to an increase in Cartesian's performance when, in fact, the increase was attributable to the Portfolio Manager's new valuation method; (ii) a third party valuation firm used by Cartesian's underlying manager wrote up the value of Cartesian when that was not true; and (iii) OGR's underlying funds were audited by independent, third party auditors when, in fact, Cartesian was unaudited. Former employees overseeing OAIM's investments and the Respondents marketed OGR using the marked-up value of the Cartesian investment from October 2009 through June 2010 and succeeded in raising approximately $61 million in new investments in OGR during that period.

4. These misrepresentations and omissions were made possible, in part, by Respondents' failure to adopt and implement written policies and procedures reasonably designed to prevent violations of the Advisers Act and the rules adopted thereunder....

BACKGROUND

8. In 2007, Respondents formed OGR, a private equity fund of funds vehicle that began admitting limited partners in April 2008. As of September 30, 2009, OGR made commitments to four investment vehicles, including Cartesian, a vehicle managed by Cartesian Capital Group, LLC ("Cartesian Capital"). Cartesian was formed by Cartesian Capital in June 2008 for the purpose of purchasing shares of S.C. Fondul Proprietatea S.A ("Fondul"), and Fondul is Cartesian's only holding. Fondul, in turn, is a holding company set up by the Romanian government to compensate citizens whose property was seized by the communist regime. Upon adjudication of a citizen's claim for restitution and an assessment of the value of the seized property, the Romanian government issued an equivalent value of shares of Fondul at 1 RON per share (also referred to as the "par value" of the Fondul shares).

9. From at least October 2009 through June 2010, the Portfolio Manager and his group marketed OGR to investors, primarily institutions such as pensions, foundations and endowments, as well as high net worth individuals and families. The Portfolio Manager found prospective investors through Oppenheimer's network of financial advisors and through independent consulting firms ("consultants") that provided investment advice to institutional investor clients.

10. Respondents and the Portfolio Manager distributed pitch books to consultants and investors that summarized the performance of OGR's investments as of a particular quarter. Respondents and the Portfolio Manager also responded to consultants' questionnaires and other requests for information, and their communications and documents contained representations concerning OGR's valuation policies and performance.

11. Investors in OGR received quarterly reports that contained summaries of the performance of OGR's investments as of a particular quarter. The performance summaries also contained representations concerning OGR's valuation policies and performance.

MISREPRESENTATIONS AND OMISSIONS

12. By October 2009, OGR had raised approximately $70 million in capital commitments — approximately one-third of the goal of $200 million — and the Portfolio Manager had succeeded in securing an extension of the fund's closing date.

13. As of Thursday, October 22, 2009, Respondents' compliance department had approved an OGR pitch book that was to be used to market OGR. Pursuant to Respondents' practice, compliance assigned to the pitch book a compliance code, which is an alphanumeric code that is unique to each compliance-approved document.

14. The pitch book that was approved by compliance on October 22, 2009 stated that OGR's asset values were "based on the underlying managers' estimated values." The asset values of the underlying funds — including Cartesian — were in fact based upon the values provided by the underlying managers, as had been OGR's valuation practice since inception. However, the approval process did not contain a provision to ensure that the valuations were based on the values provided by such managers.

15. On or about October 22, 2009, the Portfolio Manager declined to value Cartesian using the methodology adopted by Cartesian Capital, the manager of Cartesian, and instead valued OGR's investment in Cartesian himself. Rather than relying on Cartesian's valuation methodology, the Portfolio Manager valued OGR's investment in Cartesian at "par value"—that is, the price at which the Romanian government issued shares to claimants. Use of the par value of Fondul to value OGR's investment in Cartesian resulted in a material increase in the value of OGR's Cartesian investment and, because it was OGR's largest holding, in OGR's performance.

16. Immediately after Respondents' compliance department approved the OGR pitch book on October 22, the Portfolio Manager instructed members of his team to incorporate the higher par value of Fondul in any document that included performance numbers for Cartesian. Over the weekend of October 23–25, 2009, the Portfolio Manager, with the assistance of members of his team, revised OGR marketing materials (including the pitch book) to reflect his higher par value valuation. After revising these documents, no one resubmitted the pitch book to Respondents' compliance department for review, as required by Respondents' policies. Moreover, the Portfolio Manager and his team left the same compliance code that was affixed to the October 22 presentation on the revised presentation, thus creating the appearance that the revised presentation had been approved by Respondents' compliance department.

17. By no longer using Cartesian Capital's valuation, the presentation's performance table footnote, which stated that the asset values were based on the underlying managers' values, was no longer accurate.

18. The Portfolio Manager never subsequently informed compliance that he had changed the valuation of one of OGR's investments so as to deviate from the policy stated in the footnote to the performance table, which stated that the values were based on values provided by the underlying managers. Because Respondents did not verify that the asset values were in fact based on values provided by the underlying managers, the misleading footnote continued to appear in later versions of the pitch book that compliance did approve.

19. The Portfolio Manager incorporated the new valuation into performance summary tables in pitch books and quarterly reports that were used to market OGR to prospective investors from October 26, 2009 through June 2010.

20. The performance summary tables in the pitch books and quarterly reports used with prospective investors contained explanatory footnotes stating that OGR's asset values were "based on the underlying managers' estimated values" as of a particular quarter. For the October 2009 through December 2010 period during which the Portfolio Manager valued OGR's Cartesian investment using his par value rather than adopting Cartesian Capital's value, these statements about valuation policy were false and misleading.

21. The Portfolio Manager's use of par value rather than Cartesian Capital's value resulted in a material increase in both the value and internal rate of return ("IRR") of OGR's Cartesian investment. As Cartesian was OGR's largest holding, the change in

Cartesian's IRR had a significant impact on the IRR of OGR. For example, for the quarter ended June 30, 2009, the Portfolio Manager's mark-up of the Cartesian investment changed OGR's IRR from approximately 3.8% to 38.3%.[3]

22. During their marketing efforts, the Portfolio Manager and others in his group touted the performance of Cartesian and OGR to prospective investors, pointing to OGR's high IRR. No one told investors and prospective investors that the reported increase in OGR's performance was a result of the Portfolio Manager's change in valuation method and that, if OGR had used Cartesian Capital's value, as OGR had done in the past and as was stated in the quarterly statements and pitch books, the performance numbers would have been materially lower.

23. The former employees overseeing OAIM's investments made additional misrepresentations in connection with the marketing of OGR. They represented that: (i) the increase in Cartesian's value was due to an increase in performance when, in fact, the increase was attributable to the Portfolio Manager's new valuation method; (ii) a third party valuation firm used by Cartesian's underlying manager wrote up the value of Cartesian when that was not true; and (iii) OGR's underlying funds were audited by independent, third party auditors when, in fact, Cartesian was unaudited....

VIOLATIONS

25. As a result of the conduct described above, Respondents willfully violated Section 17(a)(2) of the Securities Act, which prohibits any person in the offer or sale of securities from obtaining money or property by means of any untrue statement of a material fact or any omission to state a material fact necessary in order to make the statements made, in light of the circumstances under which they were made, not misleading.

26. As a result of the conduct described above, Respondents willfully violated Section 17(a)(3) of the Securities Act, which prohibits any person in the offer or sale of securities from engaging in any transaction, practice, or course of business which operates or would operate as a fraud or deceit upon the purchaser.

27. As a result of the conduct described above, Respondents willfully violated Section 206(4) of the Advisers Act and Rule 206(4)-8 thereunder, which prohibits any fraudulent, deceptive, or manipulative act, practice, or course of business by an investment adviser to any investor or prospective investor in a pooled investment vehicle.

28. As a result of the conduct described above, Respondents willfully violated Section 206(4) of the Advisers Act and Rule 206(4)-7 thereunder, which requires, among other things, that registered investment advisers adopt and implement written policies

---

3. Internal Rate of Return is a metric commonly used to compare the profitability of various investments. The IRR of an investment is the discount rate at which the net present value of costs (negative cash flows) of the investment equals the net present value of the benefits (positive cash flows) of the investment. The market value of each investment at the end of each quarter is also included in the IRR computation. IRR is expressed as a percentage and essentially measures the rate of growth of an investment.

and procedures reasonably designed to prevent violation, by the investment adviser and its supervised persons, of the Advisers Act and its rules. [***]

* * *

Notes and Applications

1. *The interplay between compliance policies and procedures and misleading representations.* The topic of compliance is addressed formally in Chapter 15. However, this case demonstrates the interplay between the conduct of private fund advisers and the adviser's compliance policies and procedures. Here, there were clearly policies and procedures that were designed to guard against potentially misleading misrepresentations, but they proved ineffective. Why? Perhaps the explanation has something to do with one or more of the following factors: the timing of the compliance review in relation to the misconduct, the depth of the compliance review, and the ability of advisory personnel to circumvent the review procedures in place. Try to explain which of these factors was most important in this settled proceeding.

2. *Hedge fund disclosure.* Disclosure, and specifically fraudulent disclosure, by hedge funds was an area of pronounced concern prior to the Dodd-Frank Act in 2010. Although some hedge fund advisers were registered with the SEC, other large advisers could escape registration and thus remain below the regulatory radar screen and operate without substantial compliance infrastructure. The concerns were a consideration in the SEC's 2004 rulemaking effort to require hedge fund adviser registration. The instances of fraud did not always arise from outright scams, but from trading strategies that went awry. In these cases, the lack of reliable safeguards encouraged the adviser to try to correct and cover up the problems with even riskier trading strategies. For example, in one case, hedge fund investors lost $300 million when an unregistered hedge fund adviser misrepresented and manipulated the valuation of securities held by a core master hedge fund (drawing investor monies from three feeder funds) to conceal losses in trading volatile mortgage-backed securities, losses that were compounded by doubling down on ill-timed trading strategies that bet on interest rates rising as interest rates fell. *SEC v. Beacon Hill Asset Management LLC, et al.*, SEC Litigation Release No. 18950 (Oct. 28, 2004). The asset managers in that case also sought to eliminate losses sustained in institutional managed accounts by a familiar strategy of selling securities in the separate institutional accounts at inflated values to the master hedge fund.

3. *The role of broker-dealer requirements.* The sales and marketing activities of private funds and their placement agents present challenges for private fund sponsors and advisers. Sales of interests in a fund (as is the case with securities in generally) must be conducted through a broker-dealer, unless the seller falls within the so-called "issuer exemption" pursuant to Exchange Act Rule 3a4-1. That rule authorizes associated persons of an issuer to make sales without use of a broker-dealer subject to certain conditions, the most important being that the sales person does not receive transaction-based compensation for the sales. This means in the private fund context that personnel for the adviser who are also officers or directors of the fund may make

sales that qualify for the issuer exemption provided that they do not receive transaction-based compensation. However, advisers frequently enlist the assistance of finders that have existing relationships with institutional investors that are being solicited. In *In the Matter of Ranieri Partners LLC*, Investment Advisers Act Release No. 3563 (March 8, 2013), an investment adviser to a couple of private funds engaged the services of an independent consultant to help market investments in the funds managed by the affiliates' investment advisers. The unsupervised consultant's conduct crossed the line between merely acting as an information conduit for the funds and actively soliciting investors, a regulated broker-dealer activity that requires registration as a broker-dealer. Although "finders" and "consultants," are commonly used by private fund sponsors to find appropriate investors without actually soliciting sales or making offers, it is easy to see how, without close supervision, the activitiy of finding investors can easily slide into the activity of soliciting investors.

In some cases, investment advisers are retained by clients to evaluate the honesty and reliability of private funds and their advisers. The next case addresses a situation where the investment adviser did not do a very good job on behalf of its clients.

In the Matter of Hennessee Group LLC

Investment Advisers Act Release No. 2871 (April 22, 2009)

[**Textbook note:** *The adviser in this settled proceeding held itself out as an expert in evaluating hedge funds and provided clients with advice based on its evaluations. This case was based on its recommendation to clients relating to investment in a hedge fund that turned out to be nothing more than a fraudulent Ponzi scheme. The adviser failed to apply its own due diligence and screening tools for investments. Had it done so, it may have prevented the disastrous consequences for its clients that invested in the funds. The SEC found that the adviser breached its fiduciary duties to its clients in failing to undertake the elaborate screening and due diligence steps that it had represented to its clients that the firm provided as part of its services.*]

[***] A. RESPONDENTS AND OTHER RELEVANT ENTITIES

Respondents

Hennessee Group LLC is an investment adviser registered with the Commission pursuant to Section 203(a) of the Advisers Act, and is a New York limited liability company with its principal place of business in New York City. Hennessee Group is a hedge fund consultant that provides a range of hedge fund investment advisory services for its clients, which consist largely of qualified individual investors and family groups as well as foundations, endowments, and similar institutions. In 2005, Hennessee Group had approximately 100 clients and $1.35 billion in client assets under management.

Charles J. Gradante ("Gradante"), age 63, resides in New York City. From 1997 through the present, Gradante has served as president, chief executive officer, chief investment officer, and a managing principal of Hennessee Group, which he co-founded with his spouse. At all relevant times, Gradante was a principal, agent, and control person of Hennessee Group and an investment adviser to Hennessee Group's clients. Gradante supervised all aspects of Hennessee Group's due diligence evaluation concerning the Bayou hedge funds and ultimately was responsible for Hennessee Group's decision to recommend investments in the funds to its clients.

Other Relevant Individuals and Entities

Bayou Fund LLC was a Stamford, Connecticut hedge fund formed in 1996 that was directed, managed, and controlled by an investment adviser, Bayou Management, LLC, that, in turn, was directed, managed, and controlled by Samuel Israel III, Daniel E. Marino, and, from 1996 through October 2001, James G. Marquez ("Marquez"). In January 2003, Bayou Management reorganized Bayou Fund into four successor funds: Bayou Superfund, LLC; Bayou Accredited Fund, LLC; Bayou Affiliates Fund, LLC; and Bayou No Leverage Fund, LLC. The successor funds are collectively referred to as the "Bayou Funds" and, for ease of reference, the Bayou Fund, the successor Bayou Funds, and Bayou Management, LLC are collectively referred to herein as "Bayou." Neither the Bayou Funds nor Bayou Management was registered with the Commission in any capacity.

Samuel Israel III ("Israel"), age 49, was the owner and managing member of Bayou Management from the time of its inception in 1996 until it ceased operation as a hedge fund in late 2005.

Daniel E. Marino ("Marino"), age 48, was the chief operating officer and chief financial officer of Bayou Management from the time of its inception in 1996 until it ceased operation as a hedge fund in late 2005.

B. SUMMARY

Hennessee Group is a hedge fund consultant and investment adviser that recommends hedge funds for client investment and monitors those investments on its clients' behalf. In the course of soliciting clients, Hennessee Group, by and through its principal, Charles Gradante, made numerous representations concerning the quality and rigor of its due diligence process for evaluating hedge funds. Hennessee Group also routinely represented to clients and prospective clients that it would not recommend investments in hedge funds that did not satisfy all phases of its due diligence. Hennessee Group's services in this regard were particularly important to its clients when, as was the case with Bayou, information regarding a fund's trading strategies, solvency, and management was not publicly available. With regard to Bayou, Hennessee Group, at Gradante's direction, did not perform several key elements of its advertised due diligence practices.

From February 2003 through August 2005, approximately forty clients of Hennessee Group invested a total of over $56 million in the Bayou funds after receiving Hennessee Group's recommendations. Most of those monies were lost and dissipated by Bayou's principals, who defrauded their investors by fabricating Bayou's performance in client account statements, periodic newsletters, and year-end financial statements that included a phony audit opinion fabricated by one of Bayou's principals.

Hennessee Group and Gradante, in their capacities as investment advisers, owed fiduciary duties to their clients to perform the services that they represented they would provide and to disclose all material departures from the representations that they made to their clients. Despite their representations about their services, with regard to the Bayou Funds and the funds' management, Hennessee Group and Gradante did not perform two of the five elements of the due diligence evaluation that they had represented to their clients they would undertake. In addition, Hennessee Group and Gradante failed to adequately respond to information that they received that suggested that the identity of Bayou's outside auditor was in doubt and that there existed a potential conflict of interest between one of Bayou's principals and its purported outside auditor.

As a result of the conduct described above, Hennessee Group and Gradante willfully violated Section 206(2) of the Advisers Act, which prohibits any transaction, practice, or course of business which operates as a fraud or deceit upon any client or prospective client, and Gradante caused Hennessee Group's violations of Section 206(2) of the Advisers Act.

C. FACTS

Background — The Bayou Fraud

In 1996, Israel, Marino, and Marquez founded the Bayou Fund as a hedge fund or private investment pool. Israel and Marquez were Bayou's portfolio managers and Marino served as chief financial officer and chief operating officer. Marquez resigned from the Bayou entities in October 2001, and Israel and Marino continued to operate Bayou Fund and its four successor funds through 2005.

Bayou's purported investment strategy was day trading — buying and selling stocks throughout the day in an attempt to capture profits from market momentum. Israel represented to investors that he had developed a unique trading system and technical analysis that enabled him to trade profitably regardless of market conditions. Bayou also represented that, in order to maintain liquidity and minimize overnight exposure, virtually all of Bayou's securities positions were converted into cash at the close of each trading day.

Almost from its inception, the Bayou Fund lost money from trading. By 1997, Bayou devised and implemented a scheme to defraud investors and prospective investors by fabricating the fund's performance in monthly client account statements, periodic newsletters, and year-end financial statements. In 1998, realizing that the funds could not withstand an independent audit, Bayou's principals dismissed the funds' then-auditor, Grant Thornton LLP ("Grant Thornton"), and Marino fabricated "independent" audited financial statements and a phony auditor opinion letter. The bogus opinion letter was written on the stationery of a purported accounting firm named "Richmond-Fairfield Associates" ("Richmond-Fairfield"). From 1996 through mid-2005, Bayou attracted over $400 million in investor capital by concealing trading losses and giving investors the misleading impression that the funds achieved modest and steady profits. The fraud unraveled in August 2005, after Bayou issued worthless redemption checks to certain investors from overdrawn bank accounts and began shutting down its operations.

Hennessee Group's Hedge Fund Consulting Services

Gradante managed Hennessee Group as an independent hedge fund consulting firm since its founding in 1997. Hennessee Group and its principals held themselves out as "Pioneers in Hedge Fund Consulting" with years of experience helping clients achieve "higher investment returns with lower risk" by recommending "a customized portfolio of hedge funds, properly diversified and managed." Hennessee Group's client relationships typically began with a meeting with the prospective client during which Gradante and others described Hennessee Group's services and provided a written presentation outlining its hedge fund evaluation and selection process and containing sample portfolios of hedge funds. If the prospective client wished to retain Hennessee Group, the parties executed an advisory agreement. Hennessee Group's advisory fee was one percent or less of the value of the assets that a client invested in hedge funds based on the firm's recommendation.

From 2002 through 2005 (the "relevant period"), Hennessee Group promoted its process for evaluating and selecting hedge funds as the "Five Level Due Diligence Process." Hennessee Group represented to clients and prospective clients that it would not recommend investment in hedge funds that did not satisfactorily complete all five levels of its due diligence evaluation. As explained to clients and prospective clients, that process included:

(i) a request for general information and data on "historical returns" from the hedge fund;

(ii) a face-to-face initial interview with the fund manager that covered numerous topics such as the background of the fund manager, the fund's "portfolio construction and attributes" and "risk management" principles, and the name and contact information of the fund's outside audit firm;

(iii) a detailed review and analysis of the fund's investment portfolio, trading practices, and risk management discipline, generally based on prime brokerage reports sufficient to reflect the fund's actual activity over a given period;

(iv) an on-site visit to the fund's offices to meet and interview key personnel such as the portfolio manager and head trader, examine the fund's "technology and systems," discuss the results of the Level III portfolio/trading analysis, and address any remaining issues from Hennessee Group's earlier due diligence; and

(v) a reference and background check on the fund's manager, consisting primarily of "utiliz[ing] the principals' contacts to verify [the] reputation of [the] portfolio manager," and a "review of all audited financial statements," as well as a review of the fund's offering memorandum and "subscription documents."

Hennessee Group's marketing materials, its website, and its oral and written presentations described or referred to this "Five Level Due Diligence Process." Hennessee Group routinely touted the excellence and rigor of the process.

Hennessee Group had an Investment Committee, chaired by Gradante and comprised of the firm's research staff, that met each month to review the status of each fund then undergoing the due diligence process and determine whether to proceed to the next level of evaluation of a particular fund. After recommending an investment in a hedge fund to its clients, Hennessee Group committed to monitor the fund for its clients on a monthly basis. Hennessee Group made monthly requests to funds for performance data, and conducted periodic meetings or conference calls with the fund manager to inquire about the manager's current market views and concerns, the fund's portfolio structure, the manager's expectations for the fund, and any organizational changes.

Hennessee Group's Recommendation of Bayou

In April 2002, a Hennessee Group client suggested that Hennessee Group review Bayou and several other funds with a view toward possibly recommending investments in Bayou to Hennessee Group's clients. Hennessee Group contacted Bayou to initiate review and Bayou agreed to begin the process shortly thereafter. Hennessee Group began recommending Bayou to its clients in December 2002. Thereafter, Hennessee Group conducted ongoing monitoring of Bayou, which consisted of inquiries about the manager's current market views and concerns, the fund's portfolio structure, the manager's expectations for the fund, and any organizational changes, and continued recommending client investments in Bayou from January 2003 through July 2005, when Bayou announced that it would be liquidating the funds.

During the relevant period, Hennessee Group collected over $500,000 in advisory fees for referring approximately forty clients to the Bayou Funds. By mid-2005, just prior to the public disclosure of Bayou's failure, Hennessee Group clients had placed over $56 million in capital contributions into Bayou.

Hennessee Group Did Not Conduct a Due Diligence Evaluation of Bayou Consistent With its Representations to Clients and Prospective Clients

With regard to Bayou, Hennessee Group, at Gradante's direction, failed to perform two elements of the due diligence evaluation that Hennessee Group had told its clients and prospective clients that it would do: (1) a portfolio/trading analysis; and (2) a verification of Bayou's relationship with its purported independent auditor. By not conducting the entire due diligence evaluation that it had advertised, and by failing to disclose to clients that its evaluation of Bayou deviated from its prior representations, Hennessee Group and Gradante rendered the prior representations about the due diligence process materially misleading and breached their fiduciary duties to Hennessee Group's clients.

A. Hennessee Group Did Not Conduct a Portfolio/Trading Analysis on the Bayou Funds

Hennessee Group maintained detailed procedures on how the five levels of due diligence that were described in its marketing materials and website were to be conducted. Hennessee Group's evaluation purportedly included a detailed review and analysis of a fund's portfolio and trading records (also known as a "Level III review"). The promotional materials that Hennessee Group distributed to clients and prospective clients created the impression that the portfolio/trading analysis was Hennessee Group's specialty and a core element of its due diligence process, stating, for example, that investors "need to see more than just the returns; [they] should be able to understand how the returns were achieved and what factors affected them."

In order to conduct its portfolio/trading analysis, Hennessee Group sought prime brokerage reports either directly from a fund or from the fund's prime broker, consisting of a "portfolio snapshot" of a fund's investments at a given time and "trading activity reports" (also known as "realized and unrealized gain/loss reports"). Hennessee Group purportedly used the data in the reports to evaluate a manager's risk management discipline, hedging strategies, stop losses, distribution of returns by security, pricing of securities, and other trading practices. Although Hennessee Group often was unable to obtain such reports from funds, the firm failed to disclose to its clients that it did not conduct a portfolio/trading analysis under such circumstances.

In the fall of 2002, Bayou refused to provide Hennessee Group with the prime brokerage reports that Hennessee Group had requested. However, instead of insisting that Bayou provide the reports as a condition of potentially being recommended, Hennessee Group proceeded to the next phases of due diligence. Gradante decided that a portfolio/trading analysis was irrelevant for a day-trading fund like Bayou, which stated in marketing materials that it held securities positions for brief periods of time and converted positions to cash prior to each day's market closing.

As a result, Hennessee Group did not obtain or evaluate any quantitative information about Bayou's portfolio characteristics, investment and trading strategies, or risk management discipline. Instead of confirming Bayou's results and processes through an analysis of Bayou's historical trading data to determine whether the fund was, in fact, executing its purported "high-velocity" day-trading strategy and utilizing appropriate risk management techniques, Gradante and Hennessee Group relied entirely on Bayou's uncorroborated representations and purported rates of return that Bayou had provided during its initial information-gathering phases.

Hennessee Group never told the clients to whom it recommended Bayou that it had not conducted a portfolio/trading analysis on the funds. By failing to disclose this information in connection with its recommendation of Bayou, Hennessee Group left those clients with the misleading impression that it had conducted a portfolio, trading, and risk management evaluation of Bayou and that Bayou had satisfied Hennessee Group's purported standards. In so doing, Hennessee Group and Gradante breached their fiduciary duties to Hennessee Group's clients.

B. Hennessee Group Failed to Verify Bayou's Relationship with its Independent Auditor

Hennessee Group told many of the clients to whom it recommended an investment in Bayou, that as part of its review of a fund's audited financial statements, Hennessee Group verified the fund's relationship with its purported independent auditor and that the audit firm had actually conducted the audit. Hennessee Group's staff frequently made this representation to prospective clients. In reality, Hennessee Group's "Verify Auditor" procedure consisted only of confirming that a fund's financial statements contained an unqualified audit opinion letter.

In mid-2002, Bayou provided Hennessee Group with copies of its three most-recent annual financial statements, for fiscal years 1999 through 2001. Those financial statements were presented on Richmond-Fairfield stationery and included unqualified audit opinions purportedly issued by Richmond-Fairfield, but in fact were drafted by Marino and signed by him in the firm's name. Bayou also told Hennessee Group numerous times during the due diligence process that the funds had "outgrown" Richmond-Fairfield and had selected another accounting firm, Hertz, Herson & Co., LLP ("Hertz Herson"), to serve as its new auditor beginning with the 2002 annual audit. However, despite having represented to prospective clients that it verified a fund's audit relationship, Hennessee Group took no steps during the initial evaluation to contact either Hertz Herson, which was an actual accounting firm, or Richmond-Fairfield to confirm whether either had an audit relationship with Bayou.

Auditor verification was particularly warranted with regard to Bayou. Hennessee Group had no prior dealings with and was unfamiliar with Richmond-Fairfield and Hertz Herson. Of the approximately 150 hedge funds that Hennessee Group monitored on behalf of its clients, none other than Bayou had ever used Hertz Herson or Richmond-Fairfield as its outside auditor.

Hennessee Group Disregarded Red Flags During its Due Diligence Review and Subsequent Monitoring of Bayou

Hennessee Group also failed to adequately investigate and reconcile certain negative and contradictory information about Bayou that Hennessee Group had a duty to investigate by virtue of its representations to its clients that it would conduct on-going monitoring of the clients' investments.

Although Hennessee Group reviewed audited financial statements of the Bayou funds, Hennessee Group failed to reconcile Bayou's conflicting claims about its auditor's identity, and accepted without the requisite skepticism or searching inquiry Bayou's claim that it had changed outside auditors several times. During the due diligence process, Bayou provided Hennessee Group with several contradictory responses regarding the identity of its auditor. In June 2002, Bayou informed Hennessee Group that its auditor was Grant Thornton. During the fall of 2002, Bayou gave Hennessee Group three different marketing documents, two identifying Hertz Herson as Bayou Fund's auditor, and the third identifying Grant Thornton as Bayou Fund's auditor. In fact, Grant Thornton had not audited Bayou since fiscal year 1997, and Hertz Herson had never been retained to audit the hedge fund.

In September 2002, Israel and Marino told Gradante that, while Bayou's original auditor had been Grant Thornton, "bad service" had prompted Bayou to switch to the "more client friendly" Richmond-Fairfield in 1999. At that time, Israel and Marino also told Gradante that Bayou had "outgrown" Richmond-Fairfield and had selected Hertz Herson to be its new auditor. Marino later provided Hennessee Group with the name of the purported engagement partner at Hertz Herson. Hennessee Group did not attempt to investigate this inconsistent information to determine whether Hertz Herson had in fact been retained to conduct the audit of Bayou Fund for 2002. In fact, Hertz Herson had not been retained to conduct the 2002 audit of the Bayou Fund. In addition, Hennessee Group also failed to contact Richmond-Fairfield or Grant Thornton to verify those past relationships and obtain their perspectives on whether and why Bayou had terminated them. In the spring of 2003, after Hennessee Group had already begun recommending investments in Bayou, Bayou sent Hennessee Group two marketing documents that identified Hertz Herson as Bayou's auditor. One of those documents further stated, "In 2002, *Hertz Herson conducted a first time audit* for the Bayou Fund LLC. Previous auditor for the Bayou Fund LLC was Richmond Fairfield." (Emphasis added.) As noted above, Bayou previously had told Hennessee Group during the due diligence process in 2002 that it had outgrown Richmond-Fairfield and retained Hertz Herson as its new auditor.

Shortly thereafter, in May of 2003, Hennessee Group received a copy of Bayou Fund's audited financial statements for fiscal year 2002, presented on Richmond-Fairfield stationery, which included an audit opinion from Richmond-Fairfield, rather than Hertz Herson. Gradante and a Hennessee Group research analyst both reviewed Bayou's audit report as part of the firm's routine monitoring process, and noted the discrepancy in the information that Bayou had provided concerning the identity of its outside auditor, but made no effort to inquire into Bayou's prior representations about having retained Hertz Herson.

The following year, in June 2004, Hennessee Group received a copy of the Bayou Funds' audited financial statements for fiscal year 2003, which again purportedly had been prepared and certified by Richmond-Fairfield, not Hertz Herson. Despite this, Hennessee Group and Gradante took no action to investigate this inconsistency in Bayou's representations regarding its auditor, and relied solely on an explanation from Bayou.

In late April 2005, Marino told Hennessee Group that "[t]he audit for 2004 was recently completed by Hertz Herson and he anticipates it being sent out in the next week or two." However, Hennessee Group did not actually receive Bayou's fiscal year 2004 audit until mid-July 2005. As with the 2002 and 2003 audits, Bayou's 2004 audit purportedly had been conducted and certified by Richmond-Fairfield, instead of Hertz Herson. One week after Hennessee Group received the 2004 audit report, Bayou announced that it was liquidating the funds. Hennessee Group and Gradante did not disclose to any of their clients the contradictory information that Bayou had provided over several years concerning the identity of its auditor.

Hennessee Group and Gradante Failed to Investigate a Rumor That Marino was Affiliated With Bayou's Outside Auditing Firm

Hennessee Group also failed to investigate a rumor concerning Marino's connection to Richmond-Fairfield. On Friday, January 14, 2005, a client of Hennessee Group who had invested in Bayou sent an email to Hennessee Group stating:

> I am told the head of back office for Bayou is also a principal in the firm that does their annual audit; also that there have been discrepancies in K-1's put out by Bayou. Seems like a lot of smoke. For a 12 to 15% return fully taxed at

> ordinary rates, I'm thinking I shouldn't take a chance on another implosion. When will your next due diligence take place on Bayou and will it cover such things as the fact it appears the head of back office (Marino or some name like that) is auditing himself by being a principal of the outside audit firm?

On January 19, four days after Hennessee Group received the investor's email, Gradante sent an email to Israel and Marino titled "RUMOR WITH POTENTIALLY DAMAGING IMPACT ON BAYOU" that stated:

> A CLIENT of hennessee and bayou has heard that dan marino is a principal or has an economic interest in your accounting firm.... i know you guys are always doing the right thing so i wouldn't be surprised if this is a stretch of the truth.... can you go on the record for me so i can help us all "NIP THIS IN THE BUD."[2]

Marino called Gradante in response to the email and told Gradante that, before joining Bayou in 1999, he had been associated with Bayou's audit firm, but that he had severed all ties with the audit firm when he joined Bayou. Gradante accepted Marino's explanation and requested that Marino put a statement of denial in an email or letter. Marino agreed to provide an email by January 21 that would give "a full explanation" of his resume and background.

On January 25, 2005, Marino sent an email to Gradante in which he represented that from 1991 through 1998, Marino operated his own accounting practice at a firm known as "Marino & Group, CPA"; in 1997, Marino began providing accounting and tax advice for the Bayou entities; in 1998, Marino began performing audit work for the Bayou Fund; and in January 1999, Marino sold his share of the accounting firm and accepted Israel's offer to join Bayou full time to manage operations and the back office, and had served as Bayou's chief financial officer and chief operating officer since that time.

Marino's assertions in the email, however, conflicted with information that Bayou had provided to Hennessee Group during the previous three years. For example, at least two Bayou marketing documents provided to Hennessee Group in early 2003 contained biographical information about Marino that stated, "*In 1996*, Mr. Marino joined Mr. Israel as part of the original management team at Bayou as CFO and COO, and *has performed these functions for Bayou since its inception*." (Emphasis added.) These earlier disclosures directly contradicted Marino's assertion in the email to Gradante that he had joined Israel at Bayou in January 1999 as chief financial officer and chief operating officer. In addition, at that time, Hennessee Group's due diligence file and materials on Bayou already contained several statements from Marino that Bayou had switched auditors from Grant Thornton to "a more client friendly" Richmond-Fairfield in 1999, which directly conflicted with Marino's claim in the email that "Marino & Group, CPA" had begun performing audit work for Bayou in 1998.

2. At some point, Hennessee Group received information suggesting that the source of the rumor may have been an individual affiliated with a rival hedge fund consulting group that had advised its clients to withdraw all of their money from Bayou.

Gradante read Marino's email shortly after it was received. Although Hennessee Group had information in its files that directly contradicted Marino's explanation, the firm made no effort to verify the assertions Marino made in his email. Gradante took no other steps to verify Marino's claims, such as contacting Richmond-Fairfield or conducting internet and/or public records searches on Richmond-Fairfield or Marino. In fact, Marino was listed as Richmond-Fairfield's registered agent in New York State public records. Publicly-available state accountancy board records disclosed that Richmond Fairfield had been registered with New York State in October 2000 under Marino's name and personal address.

Shortly thereafter, Gradante told the investor that the rumor was false and that Marino had provided a full explanation.

D. VIOLATIONS

Hennessee Group and Gradante, in their capacities as investment advisers, owed fiduciary duties to their clients to not misrepresent the services that they were providing and to disclose all material departures from the representations that they made to their clients. With regard to the Bayou Funds and the funds' management, Hennessee Group and Gradante failed to conduct two of the five elements of the due diligence review that they had represented to their clients they would undertake. In addition, Hennessee Group and Gradante failed to adequately respond to information that they received that suggested that the identity of Bayou's outside auditor was in doubt and that there existed a potential conflict of interest between one of Bayou's principals and the purported outside auditor of Bayou. Hennessee Group and Gradante breached their fiduciary duties to their investment advisory clients.

As a result of the conduct described above, Hennessee Group and Gradante willfully violated Section 206(2) of the Advisers Act, which prohibits any transaction, practice, or course of business which operates as a fraud or deceit upon any client or prospective client, and Gradante caused Hennessee Group's violations of Section 206(2) of the Advisers Act. [***]

* * *

Notes and Applications

1. *Oops and the occasional scandals.* The Bayou Funds scandal was easily the largest of the hedge fund Ponzi scheme scandals where the hedge fund sponsor gathered investor money and misappropriated the funds. The Bayou Funds lost tens of millions of dollars in their first year of operation, and the principals quickly converted the operation into a wholesale fraud. Of the $400 million that was deposited, there was only about $150 million in Bayou Management's hands by 2005 when the SEC took action. Although rumors had surfaced in the close knit hedge fund world, as noted in the order, everything came to a head in 2005 when a disgruntled investor visited the firm and found a tell-all premature confession/suicide note from Marino (who is currently alive and well serving a 20 year term in a federal penitentiary). His confederate Israel pled guilty and then staged a phony suicide while on his way to prison

to begin serving his jail sentence. The sensational details made the newspapers and network news magazines (including America's Most Wanted). Mr. Israel's auto was found on a deserted stretch of an interstate highway bridge over the Hudson River with the words "Suicide is Painless" spelled out on the dusty hood of his SUV. He spent the next month holed up with his girlfriend in an RV parked in a campground in Massachusetts before ultimately surrendering to authorities. Abha Bhattarai & Nelson Schwartz, *Fund Manager Who Faked His Suicide Surrenders*, N. Y. Times electronic ed. (July 3, 2008). The incident also tarnished the reputation of E. Lee Hennessee, a pioneering woman in the world of hedge funds and now deceased, her namesake firm, and Gradante, her husband, for having been taken in.

2. *Fiduciary duties and Section 206(2).* The SEC's order also broke new ground in elaborating a theory of liability under Section 206(2) of the Advisers Act. Chapter 7 noted that undisclosed conflicts of interest of an investment adviser having a fiduciary duty to its client has become a well-established basis for liability under Section 206(2). This order is not premised on any undisclosed conflict of interest. Although arguably based on misleading representations about services provided by the adviser at the time the representations were made to clients, another reading of the facts would suggest that the order is premised on a duty to update clients to whom a fiduciary duty is owed and a breach of the duty of care of the adviser in discharging its fiduciary obligations. Is there a difference between a failure to update theory (e.g., clients are not updated to the fact that the adviser is not doing its job as represented) and a breach of the duty of care theory? If the latter is a viable theory, why would investment advisers be potentially concerned? In particular, in what other kinds of situations involving an adviser's activities might duty of care arise? Is it fair to characterize "disregarding red flags" as a duty of care theory?

9.4 Conflicts of Interest in Private Funds

The administration of private funds or other unregistered pooled investment vehicles can lead to unfair treatment among investors or deliberate investor abuses. Both cases below involve private funds. The proceedings involve different types of misconduct: (a) a range of practices that allowed the adviser to pocket fees or opportunities without sufficient candor to investors; and (b) inadvertence that resulted in unfair treatment of investors in one private fund relative to investors in another private fund. These forms of misconduct are potential problems for private funds.

9.4.1 Fees and Self-Dealing by Private Fund Advisers

In the Matter of Blackstreet Capital Management, LLC

Investment Advisers Act Release No. 4411 (June 1, 2016)

[**Textbook note:** *In recent years, the SEC has expressed concerns regarding the fees obtained by, and the dealings of, private equity advisers with the private equity funds that they manage. The following settled action illustrates a range* *of problems involving a relatively small private equity investment adviser with respect to different aspects of the way in which the adviser managed the relevant funds' affairs with respect to fees charged, use of assets, and side arrangements with limited partnership and other related investors. Not surprisingly, the SEC found that the series of one-off issues evidenced a severely deficient compliance structure for managing conflicts.*]

[***]SUMMARY

1. These proceedings arise from violations by registered private equity fund adviser BCM and its principal, Gunty, relating to: (i) the receipt of transaction-based compensation for the provision of brokerage services in connection with the acquisition and disposition of portfolio companies,[2] while not being registered as a broker; (ii) the collection and receipt of certain unauthorized and inadequately disclosed fees in one of the BCM-advised funds; (iii) the unauthorized use of fund assets; (iv) the unauthorized purchase of portfolio company interests; and (v) the purchase of limited partnership interests. In addition, BCM failed to adopt and implement reasonably designed compliance policies and procedures to prevent violations of the Advisers Act and its rules arising from the foregoing conduct.

....

RESPONDENTS

9. **Blackstreet Capital Management, LLC ("BCM")** is a Delaware limited liability company with its principal place of business in Chevy Chase, Maryland. BCM was originally formed in 2002 as MMP Capital Management. In 2007, MMP Capital Management changed its name to Blackstreet Capital Management. BCM is an investment adviser that has been registered with the Commission since August 2005. BCM provides advisory and management services to private equity funds. According to its most recent Form ADV, filed in March 2016, BCM had more than $156.3 million in assets under management.

10. **Murry N. Gunty ("Gunty")** ... founded MMP Capital Management, which became BCM. Gunty has been the managing member and principal owner of BCM since May 2005.

OTHER RELEVANT ENTITIES

11. **Blackstreet Capital Partners ("Fund I")**, formerly known as MMP Capital Partners, is a private equity fund comprised of two related Delaware limited partnerships, Blackstreet Capital Partners (AI), L.P. and Blackstreet Capital Partners (QP), L.P. The two entities are identical except that one consists of accredited investors, and the other

2. As part of its investment strategy, BCM first formed an acquisition vehicle, which BCM referred to as a portfolio company. The portfolio company then purchased a controlling interest in the actual operating company. This Order uses the term "portfolio company" when referring to the acquisition vehicle and/or operating company.

consists of qualified purchasers. Both entities make the same investments on a side-by-side basis, oftentimes through the same special purpose vehicle, and are collectively referred to as "Fund I." Fund I primarily invests in leveraged buyouts of businesses primarily located in the Eastern United States and with revenues typically between $20 million and $100 million.

12. **Blackstreet Capital Partners II ("Fund II")** is a private equity fund comprised of two related Delaware limited partnerships, Blackstreet Capital Partners (AI) II, L.P. and Blackstreet Capital Partners (QP) II, L.P. The two entities are identical except that one consists of accredited investors, and the other consists of qualified purchasers. Both entities make the same investments on a side-by-side basis, oftentimes through the same special purpose vehicle, and are collectively referred to as "Fund II." Fund II primarily invests in leveraged buyouts of businesses primarily located in the Eastern United States and with revenues typically between $20 million and $100 million.

13. **Blackstreet Capital Advisors, LLC ("BCA")** is a Delaware limited liability company with its principal place of business in Chevy Chase, Maryland. BCA is an investment adviser that has been registered with the Commission since January 2006. BCA is the general partner of Fund I. According to its most recent Form ADV, filed in March 2016, BCA had more than $42.9 million in assets under management.

14. **Blackstreet Capital Advisors II, LLC ("BCA II")** is a Delaware limited liability company with its principal place of business in Chevy Chase, Maryland. BCA II is an investment adviser that has been registered with the Commission since January 2009. BCA II is the general partner of Fund II. According to its most recent Form ADV, filed in March 2016, BCA II had more than $113.4 million in assets under management.

FACTS

A. Background

15. BCM provides investment advisory and management services to Fund I and Fund II (collectively, the "Funds"). The Funds are each governed by an Agreement of Limited Partnership ("LPA") that sets forth the terms and operation of the fund. Pursuant to each LPA, BCA and BCA II, as general partners, are responsible for management of their respective funds, but each is permitted to, and did, appoint BCM to serve as manager.

16. The Funds invest primarily in undervalued portfolio companies that are mismanaged, unprofitable, orphaned by a parent conglomerate, or have limited earnings potential in a declining market. The Funds call capital from their respective LPs, which may be used to fund the acquisition of the portfolio companies, including related turnaround fees and other transaction fees and costs, or to pay "Partnership Expenses," which include management fees and all fund costs and expenses (as distinctly defined in each LPA). LPs failing to satisfy capital calls may be defaulted, subjecting them to possible forfeiture of their interests in the fund.

17. BCM earns a management fee equal to 2% of the aggregate capital commitment, which is then reduced by .2% per year following expiration of the commitment period.

BCM also is entitled to a "carry" of 20% of the sum of all distributions in excess of the sums contributed by the LPs in Fund I and up to 25% in Fund II.

B. Unregistered Broker-Dealer Activity

18. Although the LPAs expressly permitted BCM to charge transaction or brokerage fees, BCM has never been registered with the Commission as a broker nor has it ever been affiliated with a registered broker. Rather than employing investment banks or broker-dealers to provide brokerage services with respect to the acquisition and disposition of portfolio companies, some of which involved the purchase or sale of securities, BCM performed these services in-house, including soliciting deals, identifying buyers or sellers, negotiating and structuring transactions, arranging financing, and executing the transactions. BCM received at least $1,877,000 in transaction-based compensation in connection with providing these brokerage services.

C. Undisclosed OPO Fees

19. In 2011 and 2012, BCM charged two Fund I portfolio companies at least $450,000 in OPO [operating partner oversight] fees. These fees were paid directly to BCM pursuant to a written agreement between BCM and the portfolio companies for various BCM employees to provide certain senior-level operating and management services to these companies in circumstances where the companies were having difficulty recruiting suitable talent to work directly for them. The fees were intended to remain in place until the portfolio companies were able to attract suitable personnel to perform these services. The OPO fees resulted in a conflict of interest between the fund and BCM because BCM used the fund's assets to compensate itself and BCM employees. Fund I's LPA did not expressly address OPO fees or specifically authorize BCM to charge these fees to the portfolio companies (and, indirectly, to the fund). BCM did not disclose the OPO fees to the fund's LPs until after the LPs committed capital and the fees were being charged.

D. Unauthorized Use of Fund Assets

20. In several instances between 2005 and 2012, BCM used fund assets for purposes that were not expressly authorized by the Funds' LPAs. In particular, the LPAs did not address using fund assets to pay for political contributions, charitable contributions, and entertainment expenses.

....

24. Although BCM disclosed to the Funds' LPs that fund assets had been used to make political and charitable contributions, and to pay entertainment expenses, the disclosures were not made until after the LPs committed capital and until after the contributions were made and the expenses were incurred. BCM neither sought nor obtained appropriate consent for these expenditures.

E. Purchase of Portfolio Company Interests

25. BCM provided incentive-based compensation to employees assigned to perform services on behalf of portfolio companies. Such incentives included the opportunity

to invest alongside the Funds and purchase shares in the portfolio companies. In those instances, the employees signed share purchase agreements that granted the portfolio companies exclusive rights to repurchase the employees' shares at fair market value in the event of the employees' departure or termination.

26. Despite that term of the share purchase agreements, in 2010, BCM purchased a departing employee's incentive-based shares in Fund I portfolio companies. By acquiring the shares, BCM engaged in a conflicted transaction because it purchased shares in portfolio companies owned by Fund I without disclosing its financial interest or obtaining appropriate consent to engage in the transaction. BCM later transferred the shares and associated distributions, plus interest, to Fund I.

F. Acquisition of LP Interests

27. Between 2010 and 2012, Gunty, through an entity he controlled, acquired interests in Fund II from two defaulted LPs and from six LPs who were seeking to sell their interests and exit the fund.

28. As to the two defaulted LPs, Fund II's LPA permits the general partner—BCA II—to require defaulted LPs to forfeit all but one dollar of their interests, and then the general partner shall purchase the defaulted partner's remaining interest for one dollar. Gunty, however, paid only one dollar to acquire each defaulted LP's entire forfeited interest for himself rather than forfeiting all but one dollar of their interests to the fund. Gunty later relinquished to Fund II the forfeited interests that he acquired. As to the six LPs who sought to sell their interests and exit the fund, Gunty and the LPs agreed on a negotiated price at which Gunty would pay for their interests.

29. Fund II's LPA states that anyone who acquires the interest of another LP assumes that LP's obligation to make future capital contributions. Despite this disclosure, BCA II, at Gunty's direction, waived Gunty's obligation to make future capital calls on any new investments that would have been associated with the interests he purchased from the two defaulted LPs and the other six LPs. The waivers of Gunty's obligation to make future capital calls on new investments were not disclosed to the Fund II LPs. Accordingly, BCM's failure to disclose the waivers rendered the LPA's disclosures concerning LPs' obligations to make future capital calls materially misleading.

30. Although Gunty did not participate in the gains resulting from new investments made in Fund II subsequent to acquiring the defaulting and non-defaulting LP interests, his failure to make future capital calls reduced the capital available for investment opportunities and increased the pro rata share of future capital calls borne by the remaining LPs.

G. Failure to Adopt and Implement Policies and Procedures Reasonably Designed to Prevent Violations of the Advisers Act and its Rules

31. As a registered investment adviser, BCM was subject to the Advisers Act's rule requiring it to adopt and implement written policies and procedures reasonably designed to prevent violations of the Advisers Act and its rules.

32. BCM adopted and implemented written policies and procedures in the form of its Investment Adviser Supervisory Procedures and Compliance Manual. BCM, however, did not adopt or implement any policies and procedures designed to prevent violations of the Advisers Act or its rules arising from the improper use of fund assets, undisclosed receipt of fees, or purchase of LP interests. Furthermore, despite BCM's policies and procedures designating Gunty as BCM's "Designated Supervisor" responsible for ensuring compliance with BCM's policies and procedures and the federal securities laws, BCM failed to adopt and implement any policies and procedures designed to address conflicts of interest arising from Gunty's supervisory role. Thus, BCM's policies and procedures were not reasonably designed to prevent the violations of the Advisers Act and its rules described herein.

VIOLATIONS

33. Section 15(a)(1) of the Exchange Act makes it unlawful for any broker or dealer to use the mails or any other means of interstate commerce to "effect any transactions in, or to induce or attempt to induce the purchase or sale of, any security" unless that broker or dealer is registered with the Commission in accordance with Section 15(b) of the Exchange Act. "Broker" is defined in Section 3(a)(4) of the Exchange Act as "any person engaged in the business of effecting transactions in securities for the account of others." As a result of the conduct described above, BCM willfully violated, and Gunty caused BCM's violations of, Section 15(a) of the Exchange Act.

34. Section 206(2) of the Advisers Act prohibits investment advisers from directly or indirectly engaging "in any transaction, practice, or course of business which operates as a fraud or deceit upon any client or prospective client." A violation of Section 206(2) of the Advisers Act may rest on a finding of simple negligence.... Proof of scienter is not required to establish a violation of Section 206(2) of the Advisers Act. As a result of the conduct described above, BCM willfully violated, and Gunty caused BCM's violations of, Section 206(2) of the Advisers Act.

35. Section 206(4) of the Advisers Act and Rule 206(4)-8 thereunder make it unlawful for any investment adviser to a pooled investment vehicle to "[m]ake any untrue statement of a material fact or omit to state a material fact necessary to make the statements made, in the light of the circumstances under which they were made, not misleading, to any investor or prospective investor in the pooled investment vehicle" or "engage in any act, practice, or course of business that is fraudulent, deceptive, or manipulative with respect to any investor or prospective investor in the pooled investment vehicle." As a result of the conduct described above, BCM willfully violated, and Gunty caused BCM's violations of, Section 206(4) of the Advisers Act and Rule 206(4)-8 thereunder. [***]

* * *

Notes and Applications

1. *Advisers Act Rule 206(4)-8.* Following the decision of the D.C. Circuit in *SEC v. Goldstein* mentioned above and the court's construction of the Advisers Act, an

issue emerged whether a private fund adviser who engaged in conduct that defrauded the investors of a hedge fund was liable for that conduct since the investors were not the adviser's client—only the fund was. The SEC adopted Advisers Act Rule 206(4)-8 in 2007 to address this concern by expressly prohibiting adviser conduct that had the effect of defrauding investors of pooled investment vehicles. In other words, Rule 204(4)-8 made clear that advisers were liable for conduct that defrauded investors of funds, even if the investors themselves were not clients of the adviser.

2. *Adviser fees and opportunities.* The *Blackstreet Capital* proceeding is one of several cases where the SEC shone a spotlight on practices in the private equity world that fall short of the stringent fiduciary requirements of the Advisers Act. If nothing else, it illustrates the potential for opaque fees, especially in the context of complex limited partnership agreements. In the wake of this and other proceedings, sponsors have become more attentive in describing fees to investors that are available to the sponsor. In part, there are inherent challenges associated with the private equity structure. The manager oversees a long-term investment where circumstances may require new business strategies. For example, suppose the manager was expecting to earn fees over several years from managing a portfolio company's business and a determination is made that it would be better for the fund to sell its stake. Do you think the adviser should be able to recover management fees that would have been earned had the asset not been sold, if the LP agreement authorized the recovery of such fees? More importantly, is this an issue that should be resolved by the adviser's obligations under the Advisers Act or subject to private ordering in relevant partnership agreements?

3. *A new kind of broker-dealer issue.* As in the *Ranieri* matter referred to above, the SEC found that Blackstreet had violated the securities laws by acting as an unregistered broker-dealer. However, unlike the consultant in *Ranieri*, the violation was not based on selling interests in the fund but rather in connection with Blackstreet's activities in selling portfolio companies owned by the fund. The area has been a closely watched issue for private equity firms. The issuer exemption probably applies if there is no transaction-based compensation, and possibly even applies if any transaction-based fees directly offset the fund's advisory fee (on the theory that the transaction-based fees are merely an alternative way of paying the advisory fee). However, in this proceeding, there were transaction-based fees and no record of an advisory fee offset. Are there meaningful distinctions here that justify forcing private equity firms to register as broker-dealers for the protection of investors?

* * *

In *In the Matter of State Street Bank and Trust Company,* Securities Act Release No. 9107 (Feb. 4, 2010), the SEC sanctioned State Street Bank for providing divergent disclosure to investors of funds which may have been private funds or collective investment trusts [a type of pooled investment vehicle that is not an investment company under the Company Act]. The relevant funds invested in a range of mortgage-backed securities, including securities backed by sub-prime mortgages. In the early stages of the Financial Crisis, the supposedly safe funds faced imminent and mounting losses. They engaged in various types of communications with outside investors as well as State Bank personnel making investments on behalf of accounts that they managed. Investors were frequently serviced by different sales teams at the Bank, and the sales teams had access to different information which in some cases they communicated to investors who happened to call in or whom they contacted on their own initiative. Such conduct would be highly problematic for an adviser with respect to investors in a registered investment company. Essentially all shareholders should be on common footing. The *State Street Bank* matter extended this approach to investors in unregistered pooled investment vehicles.

The SEC's theory of liability, however, was somewhat unconventional. The Bank was sanctioned for violations of Sections 17(a)(2) and (3) of Securities Act of 1933 rather than for violations of the Advisers Act. The excerpt from the Commission's order below sheds some light on this enforcement strategy:

[***] Summary

1. During the subprime mortgage crisis in 2007, State Street engaged in a course of business that misled investors about the extent of subprime mortgage-backed securities held in certain unregistered funds under its management. As a result of State Street's conduct, investors in State Street's funds lost hundreds of millions of dollars during the subprime market meltdown in mid-2007.

2. State Street offered investments in certain collective trust funds to institutional investors, including pension funds, employee retirement plans, and charities. These funds included two substantially identical funds—referred to together as the Limited Duration Bond Fund (the "Fund")—made available to different categories of investors. Other actively-managed bond funds and a commodity futures index fund managed by State Street ("the related funds") also invested in the Fund. State Street established the Fund in 2002 and marketed the Fund by saying it utilized an "enhanced cash" investment strategy that was an alternative to a money market fund for certain types of investors. By 2007, however, the Fund was almost entirely invested in or exposed to subprime residential mortgage-backed securities ("subprime investments"). Nonetheless, State Street continued to describe the Fund to prospective and current investors as having better sector diversification than a typical money market fund, while failing to disclose the extent of its exposure to subprime investments.

3. When the subprime market collapsed in mid-2007, many investors in the Fund and the related funds were unaware that the Fund had such significant exposure to subprime investments. In fact, the Fund's offering materials, such as quarterly fact sheets, presentations to current and prospective investors, and responses to investors' requests for proposal, contained misleading statements and/or omitted material information about the Fund's exposure to subprime investments and use of leverage. As a result, many investors either had no idea that the Fund held subprime investments and used leverage, or believed that the Fund had very modest exposure to subprime investments and used little or no leverage.

4. Beginning on July 26, State Street sent a series of shareholder communications concerning the effect of the turmoil in the subprime market on the Fund and the re-

lated funds that misled investors and continued State Street's failure to disclose the Fund's concentration in subprime investments. At the same time, State Street provided certain investors with accurate and more complete information about the Fund's subprime concentration. These other investors included clients of State Street's internal advisory groups, which provided advisory services to some of the investors in the Fund and the related funds. During 2007, State Street's advisory groups became aware, based on internal discussions and internally available information, that the Fund was concentrated in subprime investments. Prior to July 26, 2007, at least one internal advisory group also learned that State Street was going to sell a significant amount of the Fund's distressed assets to meet significant anticipated redemptions. State Street's internal advisory groups subsequently decided to redeem or recommend redemption from the Fund and the related funds for their clients. State Street Corporation's pension plan was one of those clients. State Street sold the Fund's most liquid holdings and used the cash it received from these sales to meet the redemption demands of these better informed investors, leaving the Fund with largely illiquid holdings.

Respondent

5. **State Street**, a subsidiary of publicly-traded State Street Corporation, is a Massachusetts trust company and a bank that is a member of the Federal Reserve System. The principal place of business of State Street and State Street Corporation is Boston, Massachusetts. Because State Street is a bank, it relies on the exclusion from the definition of investment adviser contained in Section 202(a)(11) of the Investment Advisers Act of 1940. The unregistered collective trust funds State Street advises, such as the Fund and the related funds, similarly rely on the exclusion from the definition of investment company under Section 3(c)(11) of the Investment Company Act of 1940. [***]

* * *

However, the outcome in *State Street* potentially may have direct implications for advisers subject to the Advisers Act. If an investment adviser engaged in similar conduct, could that adviser be charged with violations of the Advisers Act and rules thereunder? If so, which provisions are implicated? It is useful to consider why a large money manager might have these problems, namely a potential to provide different disclosure to investors at different times. What kinds of steps would be necessary to mitigate this problem?

There is another aspect of this administrative proceeding which will be addressed in Chapter 13. The SEC simultaneously commenced administrative proceedings against two individual officers of State Street Bank on similar theories related to specific disclosures made by the two officers to investors. The proceedings against the two individuals were originally dismissed by the administrative law judge. This result was reversed on appeal to the SEC sitting in its adjudicative capacity, and the SEC entered an order imposing sanctions. The SEC's order in turn was reversed on appeal by a U.S. court of appeals. *See Flannery v. SEC*, 810 F.3d 1 (1st Cir. 2015). That decision provides some illumination regarding the disclosure obligations arising under both the Securities Act and the Exchange Act.

9.4.2 Unfair Treatment of Investors in Different Private Funds

In the Matter of Lincolnshire Management, Inc.

Investment Advisers Act of 1940 Release No. 3927 (September 22, 2014)

[**Textbook note:** *This settled administrative action explores another aspect of conflicts of interest and fair treatment of clients in a private equity fund context—an adviser acting on behalf of more than one fund. A key issue in this case is the integration of operations between portfolio companies of two private equity funds, with distinct sets of investors, advised by the same adviser. The integration of operation may well have been in the economic interests of each fund's investors. However, in this case, the SEC found there were problems in how the integration was handled in practice.*]

[***]SUMMARY

1. These proceedings arise from a breach of fiduciary duty by private equity fund adviser Lincolnshire Management, Inc. ("LMI"). Beginning in 2001, LMI integrated two portfolio companies owned by different LMI-advised funds and managed them as one company. The two companies—Peripheral Computer Support, Inc. ("PCS") and Computer Technology Solutions Corp. ("CTS")—were owned by separately advised LMI private equity funds with distinct sets of investors and LMI owed a fiduciary duty to each LMI fund. As part of this integration, the companies utilized a joint management team and developed an expense allocation policy that required each portfolio company to pay a certain percentage of various operating and administrative expenses. The expense allocation policy was not followed in certain instances, however, which resulted in one portfolio company paying more than its share of certain expenses that benefitted both companies. This constituted a breach of LMI's fiduciary duty to the funds and violated Section 206(2) of the Advisers Act.

2. LMI separately violated Section 206(4) of the Advisers Act and Rule 206(4)-7 thereunder by failing to adopt and implement written policies and procedures reasonably designed to prevent violations of the Advisers Act arising from integrating two portfolio companies owned by separately advised LMI private equity funds.

RESPONDENT

3. **Lincolnshire Management, Inc. ("LMI")** is a privately held Delaware corporation that was formed in 1986 and has been registered with the Commission as an investment adviser since March 28, 2012. During the relevant time period, LMI served as the investment adviser for Lincolnshire Equity Fund, L.P. and Lincolnshire Equity Fund II, L.P. LMI's principal place of business is in New York, New York.

OTHER RELEVANT ENTITIES

4. **Lincolnshire Equity Fund, L.P. ("LEF")** is a Delaware limited partnership and private investment fund formed in 1993 to make private equity investments in middle market companies.

5. **Lincolnshire Equity Fund II, L.P. ("LEF II")** is a Delaware limited partnership and private investment fund formed in 1999 to make private equity investments in middle market companies.

FACTS

A. Background

6. LMI is a New York-based private equity fund adviser with approximately $1.7 billion in assets under management. LMI was formed to make private equity investments in leveraged buyouts and recapitalizations.

7. During the relevant time period, LMI advised multiple private equity funds, including LEF and LEF II. LEF and LEF II had separate Limited Partnership Agreements ("LPA") and distinct sets of limited partner investors. The LPA for each fund governs the rights and obligations of its limited partners, including their obligations to pay advisory and other fees and expenses to LMI pursuant to a separate management agreement between each fund and LMI.

8. In April 1997, LMI caused LEF to acquire PCS through a $5 million equity investment. PCS was a California-based company that primarily serviced and repaired computer hard disk drives.

9. In September 2001, LMI caused LEF II to acquire CTS through an $8.5 million equity investment. CTS was a Texas-based company that primarily serviced and repaired laptop computers and handheld devices.

10. The investment opportunity in CTS was brought to LMI's attention by PCS management. The LMI investment committee believed PCS and CTS would have valuable synergies and that each company would complement the other. However, by 2001, LEF's commitment period was closed and it could not call capital to make a new acquisition. Therefore, LMI caused LEF II to acquire CTS with the intention of integrating PCS and CTS where possible and ultimately marketing the two companies for a combined sale. In connection with the 2001 acquisition of CTS, LMI disclosed to LEF's and LEF II's limited partners its intention to integrate and jointly sell the two portfolio companies. In quarterly fund disclosures thereafter, LMI provided regular updates to LEF's and LEF II's limited partners on the operations of the respective portfolio companies, together with additional information regarding the progress toward integration and plans to sell the two companies together.

11. From at least July 2009 to January 2013, PCS was the only portfolio company held by LEF.

12. LMI entered into consulting agreements with each portfolio company that was owned by an LMI-advised fund. Pursuant to the terms of the consulting agreements, LMI charged each portfolio company an annual fee in exchange for rendering con-

sulting and advisory services concerning the portfolio company's financial and business affairs, its relationships with lenders, and the operation and expansion of its business. With regard to LEF II, a percentage of any consulting fees paid to LMI, as well as certain other fees charged by LMI, were used to offset the limited partners' share of the management fees owed to LMI under the LPA.

13. LMI entered into consulting agreements with PCS and CTS in April 1997 and-September 2001, respectively. CTS paid LMI $250,000 annually under its consulting agreement; $125,000 of the $250,000 was used to offset management fees owed to LMI. PCS also paid LMI $250,000 annually during the relevant period, but was unable to pay its consulting fee from 2001 through 2004 based on its financial condition. No portion of PCS's $250,000 annual consulting fee was used to offset management fees.

B. The Integration of PCS and CTS

14. Although LEF could not purchase CTS because its commitment period had closed, LMI believed that owning both PCS and CTS together would create value for each set of limited partners in LEF and LEF II. Accordingly, in September 2001, LMI caused LEF II to purchase CTS.

15. At the time LEF II purchased CTS, in 2001, LMI disclosed to the limited partners of both LEF and LEF II that it believed there were synergies between PCS and CTS that would provide customers with a single venue to support their personal computing and mobile device support needs. LMI believed that these synergies would allow the companies to compete more effectively in the industry and would add value to both companies. LMI further disclosed its intention to exit the PCS and CTS investments by combining both companies and selling them together. As contemplated, the management of PCS and CTS—at LMI's direction—took various steps to integrate certain operations of the two companies.

16. By 2005, PCS and CTS had integrated their financial accounting systems, and a number of business and operational functions, including all payroll and 401(k) administration, and substantial portions of their respective human resources, marketing, and technology.

17. PCS and CTS also integrated their financing needs. For example, the two companies entered into a line of credit on a joint and several basis.

18. The integration of PCS and CTS operations extended to subsidiaries outside the United States. For example, a wholly owned subsidiary of PCS in Singapore supplied various parts and labor to CTS at cost. Likewise, CTS sold parts to various PCS subsidiaries at cost.

19. By March 2009, to further streamline operations and costs, LMI helped recruit a joint management team for PCS and CTS, including a joint chief executive officer and chief financial officer. Additionally, PCS and CTS shared a joint head of sales and controller.

20. From at least March 2009 to January 2013, the two separately owned companies had a joint "PCS CTS" logo that was used in marketing, advertising, and on employees' business cards.

21. From at least 2005 to January 2013, PCS and CTS were integrated and, in certain respects, operating as one company, although they remained two separate legal entities with separate audited financial statements.

22. During the relevant period, LMI made three separate efforts to sell the two companies jointly. In 2003 and later in 2007, LMI retained investment banks who developed marketing materials aimed at selling the two companies as a single entity under the joint "PCS CTS" marketing logo. While these two efforts were unsuccessful, in January 2013, PCS and CTS were sold together to a single buyer.

C. Expense Allocation Policy

23. Although certain operations of PCS and CTS were integrated, they were owned by separately advised LMI funds—LEF and LEF II, respectively—and LMI owed a fiduciary duty to each fund.

24. From at least 2005 until January 2013, PCS and CTS generally allocated expenses that benefitted both companies based on the proportion of each company's revenue to the combined revenue of PCS and CTS. For example, in 2011, the combined revenue of PCS and CTS was approximately $120 million, with approximately $22 million (or 18%) attributable to PCS. Under the expense allocation policy, PCS was required to pay 18% of any relevant shared expense.

25. There was no written guidance or detail that accompanied this expense allocation policy. While the expense allocations were documented in the CTS and PCS financial records and subject to review during the respective annual audits, neither CTS nor PCS had any written agreements relating to sharing or allocating expenses. There were no documents setting forth the parties' respective rights and obligations toward each other.

26. The shared expenses of PCS and CTS related to administrative fees associated with: payroll and 401(k) benefits; information technology; sales and marketing; and corporate management.

D. Misallocated Expenses

27. From at least 2005 to January 2013, PCS and CTS shared numerous annual expenses. While generally the shared expenses were properly allocated and documented in certain instances, a portion of the shared expenses was misallocated and went undocumented, which resulted in one portfolio company paying more than its share of expenses that benefitted both companies.

28. Prior to the integration of PCS and CTS, PCS utilized administrator services to assist with payroll and 401(k) benefits. PCS paid these administrators a fee for the services they provided.

29. After PCS and CTS were integrated, management decided to use PCS's third-party administrators to provide payroll services, and to administer the 401(k) programs for both PCS's and CTS's employees. Notwithstanding the fact that the related administrative expenses covered CTS employees, PCS paid all of the administrative expenses for at least eight years and did notreceive any reimbursement from CTS. During this

eight-year period, the estimated administrative expenses paid by PCS averaged approximately $25,000 annually.

30. In addition to these administrative expenses, there were several employees who performed work that benefitted both PCS and CTS, but their salaries were not allocated between the two companies, as required under the policy.

31. PCS's wholly owned Singapore subsidiary performed services for, and sold supplies and parts to, CTS at cost. For example, in 2011 PCS Singapore sold approximately $150,000 in supplies and parts to CTS at cost. However, CTS did not contribute to the general overhead costs of running the Singapore subsidiary. Notably, there were PCS Singapore employees devoted solely to performing work for CTS. CTS reimbursed PCS for the salaries of those specific employees but did not pay any of the costs associated with their office space, their computers, or the local business licenses that PCS had to maintain in order to do business in Singapore.

32. When PCS and CTS were sold in January 2013, PCS's and CTS's then-existing executives were paid transaction bonuses. LEF, which owned PCS, paid 10% of the transaction bonuses of two executives who were solely CTS employees....

VIOLATIONS

37. As a result of the conduct described above, LMI violated Section 206(2) of the Advisers Act by breaching its fiduciary duty owed to LEF and LEF II. LMI's breach of fiduciary duty resulted in one portfolio company (and, indirectly, the fund that owned it) paying more than its share of certain expenses that benefitted both companies. [***]

* * *

Notes and Applications

Potential conflicts arising from advising multiple co-investing private funds. It is not uncommon for a single investment adviser to oversee more than one private fund as was the case in *Lincolnshire.* In such circumstances, the private funds may join together in a transaction or possibly engage in related transactions where one fund sells securities to another related fund as purchaser or one fund invests in the same company but on a different basis (such as providing debt financing rather than equity). These situations are rife with conflicts for an adviser acting for co-investing funds. Investing is frequently a zero sum game, and to the extent that the funds do not share equally in an opportunity or actually are opposing participants in a transaction, a question necessarily arises as to whose interests the adviser is representing, private fund A or private fund B? Given what happened in this matter, should private equity sponsors necessarily avoid joint undertakings and transactions among different funds? Are there steps that the adviser could take to avoid the type of conflict that arose? Another recently concluded proceeding, *In the Matter of Kohlberg Kravis Roberts & Co.*, Investment Advisers Act Release No. 4131 (2015), identified problems encountered by an adviser in fairly disclosing its practices to different fund participants with respect

to allocating broken deal expenses (i.e., expenses incurred by the adviser in reviewing many, many deals for possible investment, but that do not result either in a bid or a successful investment transaction) among multiple co-investing or affiliated private funds advised by the same adviser. Recall the hot IPO enforcement action addressed in Chapter 7. Are there similarities in the issues presented?

Part III

Regulation of Registered Investment Companies

Chapter 10

Definition of Investment Company

Key Ideas: The Investment Company Act imposes significant requirements on the governance and operation of investment companies and also authorizes the SEC to adopt regulations in furtherance of the Act's objectives. The threshold issue under the Company Act concerns definition of the term "investment company." The definition is set forth in Section 3, and this definition is fundamental to understanding the statute's application. Quite simply, an entity is either an investment company subject to the Act's requirements or the entity is not an investment company in which case the Act does not apply.

The definition has three subsections. Subsection (a) defines which entities are presumptively investment companies. An entity is presumptively an investment company if it holds itself out as being in the business of investing or trading securities (typically, referred to as an "orthodox investment company") or if its asset structure fails the "40% test" (i.e., more than 40% of the entity's total assets are investment securities). In this latter situation, the entity is categorized as a "prima facie" or an "inadvertent" investment company. Subsection (b) establishes an important set of exclusions for companies that are inadvertent investment companies. In essence, although holding investment securities amounting to more than 40% of their total assets, many inadvertent investment companies may, under subsection's (b)'s second-level analysis, be excluded from the definition if they are primarily engaged in a non-investment business through wholly-owned subsidiaries, or are found to be primarily engaged in non-investment businesses through majority-owned or controlled subsidiaries.

Subsection (c) establishes another set of exclusions for companies that might otherwise be classified as investment companies. While these companies, including pooled investment vehicles, may be engaged in a business that invests in securities, subsection (c) enumerates a series of exclusions, notwithstanding the investment activities of such companies. Congress appears to have concluded that Company Act regulation of certain investment entities and funds is unnecessary as a policy matter, either because alternative schemes of regulation exist, or because the investors are not in need of the Company Act's regulatory protections. These exclusions encompass entities such as banks, insurance companies, broker-dealers, many pension funds, and of particular importance, private funds, such as hedge, venture capital, and private equity funds.

Chapter Contents

10.1 Introduction

The definition of an investment company is to the Company Act what the definition of an investment adviser is to the Advisers Act: it determines the statute's regulatory scope. The Company Act only applies to entities that are investment companies within the statute's definition and not to similar entities that are excluded by statute or by rule promulgated by the SEC. This formalistic rendering, however, frames a basic policy issue underlying the Company Act. Certain business that are engaged in investing the assets of investors should be subject to heightened regulatory scrutiny while excluding from regulation (i) entities that hold investment securities, but are really not in an investment business, and (ii) other entities that are engaged in investment businesses, but in investment businesses not appropriately regulated under the Company Act. Section 3 represents a legislative effort to distinguish between entities targeted for regulation and entities, though structurally similar, that should be excluded from the Company Act's regulatory scheme.

Section 3's definition of an investment company is structured similarly to the shorter definition of investment adviser found in the Advisers Act. Both definitions begin with over- inclusive language (i.e., language that would make the definition too broad in its coverage if not modified by significant exclusions). The latter portion of each definition attempts to carve out exclusions to avoid overbreadth. This chapter explores the different parts of the investment company definition in the next three subsections. Section 10.2 discusses the basic core of the definition and the exclusion from the definition of many types of holding companies. Section 10.3 looks at the definition from a slightly different perspective, namely can an investment company exist, even if there is no stand-alone "entity," but rather merely an "account" that holds collectively assets of many investors? Section 10.4 discusses the exclusions found in Section 3(c) for entities engaged in investment businesses that are nevertheless excluded from the investment company definition for other reasons. Section 10.5 moves beyond the definition of investment company to the Company Act's classification of investment companies. Investment company classification is a bridge between the Company Act's threshold definition which determines which entities are covered by the statute and the different types of investment companies operating under the statute.

10.2 The Basic Definition and the Holding Company Exclusions

The Company Act's investment company definition is multi-layered. In order to fully evaluate the statute's definition, it is necessary to understand how the basic definition operates in tandem with the accompanying exclusions. This section considers the basic definition and the exclusions applicable to holding company structures. Section 3(a)(1) establishes an over-inclusive definition of investment company while subsequent sections exclude a variety of businesses that would otherwise be swept into the overly inclusive definition found in Section 3(a)(1).

10.2.1 The Basic Definition: Orthodox & Prima Facie Investment Companies

Section 3 is titled: "Definition of Investment Company." Section 3(a)(1) set forth the basic definition in two clauses: clause (A) [that is, Section 3(a)(1)(A)], sometimes referred to as the orthodox investment company test, and clause (C), known as the prima facie or inadvertent investment company test. The statute provides:

> (1) When used in this subchapter, "investment company" means any issuer which—
>
> > (A) is or holds itself out as being engaged primarily, or proposes to engage primarily, in the business of investing, reinvesting, or trading in securities;
> >
> > ....
> >
> > (C) is engaged or proposes to engage in the business of investing, reinvesting, owning, holding, or trading in securities, and owns or proposes to acquire investment securities having a value exceeding 40 per centum of the value of such issuer's total assets (exclusive of Government securities and cash items) on an unconsolidated basis.

On their face, clauses (A) and (C) appear to be similar. They differ, however, in two important respects. First, the analytical focus of each clause is different; clause (A) is said to be a subjective test while clause (C) is objective in nature. Clause (A) focuses on the way in which a fund intends the public to perceive its activities. It encompasses each entity that "hold[s] itself out" as being in the business of investing in securities such as mutual funds, closed-end funds and exchange traded funds. The definition's application with respect to clause (A) is largely unremarkable. Not surprisingly, there is little controversy to the statute's classification as investment companies of thousands of funds that hold themselves out as mutual funds, closed-end funds, and exchange-traded funds. Indeed, the vast majority of all registered investment companies are investment companies in this sense.

In contrast, clause (C) categorizes entities as investment companies based on the objective composition of the company's assets. Any company where more than 40% of the company's assets are investment securities is a prima facie investment company. The application of the 40% test is heavily dependent on the definition of "investment securities" found in Section 3(a)(2). This clause, based on asset composition alone, is the principal source of the definition's potential for overbreadth as many companies who fail the 40% test (i.e., exceed the 40% threshold) do not intend to be or hold themselves out as investment companies.

Second, the prima facie investment company category reaches a broader range of investment activities than those associated with orthodox investment companies. The prima facie clause relates to companies' "engag[ing] in the business of investing, reinvesting, owning, holding, or trading in securities" while orthodox investment companies are those in the "business of investing, reinvesting, or trading in securities." Again, the inclusion of "owning and holding" as investing activities for prima facie investment companies expands the category of companies to which the 40% test applies.

Application of the 40% test is easy to grasp by looking at a few examples. Figure 10A illustrates an obvious situation involving a prima facie investment company. The assets of the parent consist entirely of its holding of non-majority equity ownership stakes in the common stock of five subsidiaries. How does this flunk the 40% test? Under Section 3(a)(c)(1), the issue is simple: are more than 40% of the parent's total assets, so-called investment securities? The definition of investment securities (Section 3(a)(2)) companies includes equity stakes in non-majority owned subsidiaries. Since

Figure 10A — Prima facie investment company: holding only investment securities

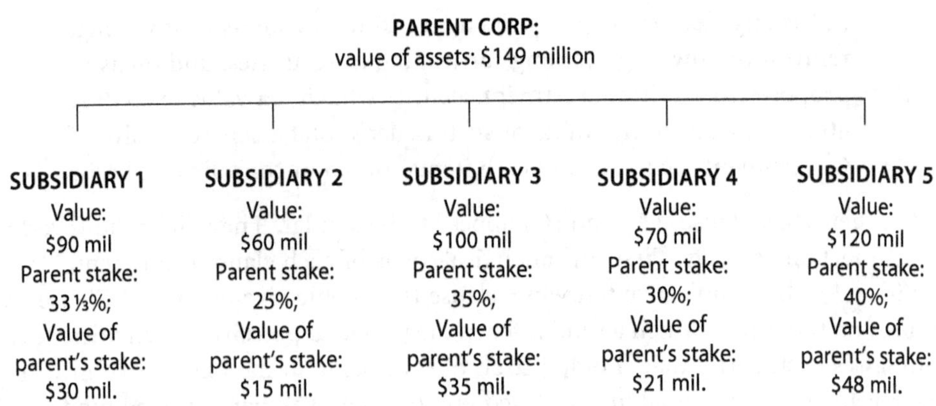

all of the assets of the parent company in Figure 10A are securities of that type, 100% of the parent's total assets are investment securities.

The assumed circumstances of the illustration are altered in Figure 10B, but the result is the same. Once again, the parent company's assets consist entirely of equity stakes in subsidiaries, and it is necessary to categorize the parent company's stakes in the subsidiaries as either investment securities or non-investment securities. Figure 10B differs from Figure 10A in that the parent company in Figure 10B has a majority stake in Subsidiary 5. As a result, that position is excluded from the definition of an investment security. However, the equity stake in the remaining subsidiaries as a percentage of the parent company's total assets is still over 50%, and therefore, the parent company still flunks the 40% test.

Figure 10B — Prima facie investment company: holding both investment and non-investment securities, but investment securities exceed 40% of total assets

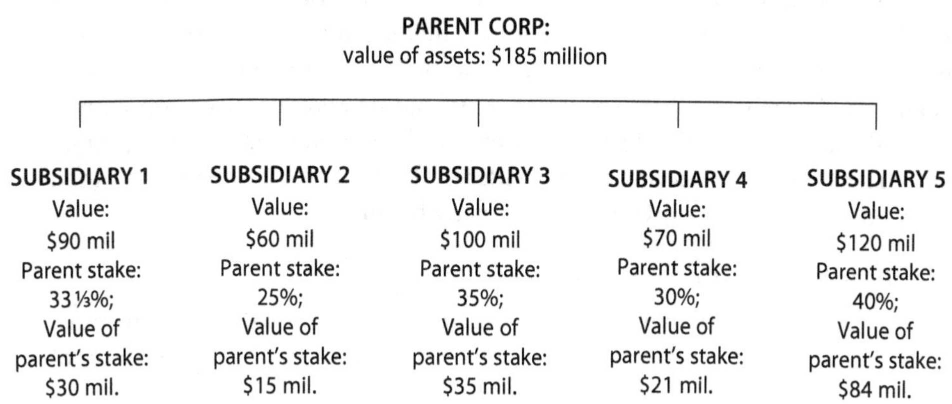

Figure 10C — Prima facie investment company: holding both investment and non-investment securities, but investment securities less than 40% of total assets

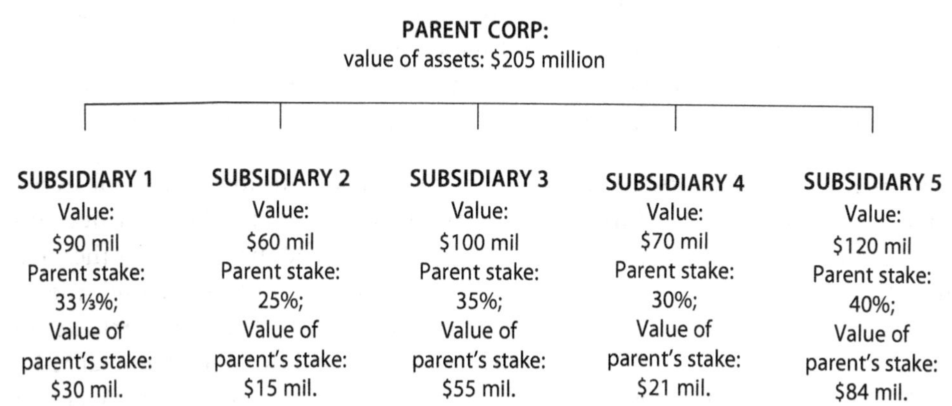

Figure 10C entails the same type of analysis, but the underlying assumptions have sufficiently been altered so that the result is now different. The parent company is not a prima facie investment company. In Figure 10C, the equity stakes in both subsidiary 3 and subsidiary 5 are disregarded in determining the parent's investment securities. Why? Because the equity stakes are majority stakes and therefore are no longer classified as investment securities. As a result, the ratio of investment securities to total assets is less than 1/3 (or 66/205 to be more precise), well below the 40% trigger.

10.2.2 The Holding and Operating Company Exclusions

Because of the breadth of the prima facie investment company category, there are just too many companies that potentially satisfy this standard that are not appropriate for regulation under the Company Act. Understandably, Congress created specific exemptions to constrain the overbreadth. In addition, the SEC has used its rulemaking power to add to exemptions that address other scenarios where the clause's overbreadth is either apparent or presumptively established.

In particular, subsection (b) of Section 3 contains broad exemptions from the definition of investment company found in subsection (a). The most important exclusions are set forth in subsections (b)(1) and (b)(2). These exemptions are primarily designed to deal with the problem created by holding and operating company structures and corporate families. Specifically, even if the holding and operating companies flunk the 40% test, subsection (b) provides exemptions for companies deemed primarily engaged in a non-investment company business.

> (b) **Exemption from provisions**
>
> Notwithstanding paragraph (1)(C) of subsection (a) of this section, none of the following persons is an investment company within the meaning of this subchapter:
>
> (1) Any issuer primarily engaged, directly or through a wholly-owned subsidiary or subsidiaries, in a business or businesses other than that of investing, reinvesting, owning, holding, or trading in securities.
>
> (2) Any issuer which the Commission, upon application by such issuer, finds and by order declares to be primarily engaged in a business or businesses other than that of investing, reinvesting, owning, holding, or trading in securities either directly or (A) through majority-owned subsidiaries or (B) through controlled companies conducting similar types of businesses.

There are two quick observations relating to these exemptions. First, subsection (b)(1) focuses only on holding company structures involving wholly-owned subsidiaries that collectively show that the company is engaged in a business other than "investing, reinvesting, owning, holding, or trading in securities." Second, the exclusion afforded by subsection (b)(1) is self-executing. In other words, reliance on the subsection does not require any formal notice to the SEC or any additional action by SEC to provide formal relief. In contrast, subsection (b)(2) is not self-executing.

A company relying on the exclusion afforded by subsection (b)(2) must apply to the SEC for and obtain exemptive relief. Moreover, the focus of inquiry is on whether the applicant is engaged in a business other than "investing, reinvesting, owning, holding, or trading in securities" through its majority-owned and controlled subsidiaries, rather than merely through its wholly-owned subsidiaries.

Although both subsections rely in part on determining that a prima facie investment company is indeed engaged primarily in a business other than holding or investing in securities, the meaning of the primarily engaged standard is not apparent on the face of the statute. As is discussed in the first case below, the SEC long ago addressed this issue interpretively in the so-called "*Tonapah* factors," factors used to evaluate whether an entity is primarily engaged in a non-investment business.

10.2.3 The Definition's Application

A number of definitional issues arises from entities that do not wish to be classified as investment companies. Such situations predictably arise with respect to entities that satisfy the definition of a prima facie investment company found in Section 3(a)(1)(C). If the standard for a prima facie investment company is met, the next question will be whether the putative prima facie investment company satisfies one of the exclusions found in Section 3(b).

SEC v. National Presto Industries, Inc.

486 F.3d 305 (7th Cir. 2007)

[**Text note:** *This decision arose from a truly muddled situation. The SEC believed that National Presto Industries was operating as a prima facie investment company and brought an injunctive action to compel compliance—either through registration or possibly by forcing the company to change the composition of its assets. While the company appeared willing to take such steps, it was nevertheless compelled by a district court to actually register as an investment company, a result that the SEC and National Presto had worked to avoid. On appeal, however, the SEC had to defend the proposition that National Presto technically was obligated to register while National Presto argued against that result. The appellate decision provides an exposition of the ins and outs of the definition and its application that is not without its own problems.*]

Easterbrook, Chief Judge. Most mutual funds and other investment companies come within the scope of the Investment Company Act of 1940 because they hold themselves out "as being engaged primarily, or propos[ing] to engage primarily, in the business of investing, reinvesting, or trading in securities." 15 U.S.C. § 80a-3(a)(1)(A). But firms can be dragged within the Act's coverage kicking and screaming, even though they depict themselves as operating businesses rather than as managing other people's money. Any issuer that owns "investment securities" worth 40% of its total assets is an investment company under § 80a-3(a)(1)(C) unless some other provision of the Act takes it outside the definition. For this purpose, however, "Government securities and cash items" are omitted from both the numerator and the denominator.

National Presto Industries, a seller of both consumer goods (cookware, diapers, and other household items) and munitions, used to make everything it sold. During the 1970s it began to divest its manufacturing facilities and to contract production to third parties. In 1993 the Department of Defense closed a facility that Presto had used to make artillery shells. Presto was left with a pile of cash, most of which it retained with a long-term plan to acquire other businesses, and a shrunken book value of operating assets. Financial instruments were 86% of its total assets by 1994 and 92% in 1998. Since 2000 Presto has purchased two manufacturers of military supplies and two makers of diapers and puppy pads. But in 2003 financial instruments still represented 62% of its physical and financial assets. Intellectual property, although of considerable value to Presto, is not carried on corporate books at its full economic value, so this ratio overstates the significance of its portfolio of securities, but Presto does not argue that it could come under the 40% ratio by marking its patents and trademarks to current market value.

All of Presto's consumer products other than absorbent products are made by subcontractors, so although it has a substantial operating *income* it does not have operating *assets* to match—and the Investment Company Act's main test is asset-based. The SEC concluded that Presto was well past the 40% trigger. When the firm refused to register as an investment company—and make the changes to its corporate structure, management, and financial reporting required of investment companies—or request an administrative exemption, the SEC filed this suit to seek an injunction that would require compliance. After preliminary maneuvering vindicated the SEC's choice of forum, the district court granted summary judgment in the agency's favor, and issued an injunction requiring Presto to register under the 1940 Act. The firm has complied pending appeal.

After suffering defeat on the merits, Presto replaced enough of its existing portfolio with "Government securities and cash items" to bring investment securities under the 40% threshold. The SEC had proposed an injunction that would have allowed Presto the opportunity to do this (or to seek an administrative exemption) in lieu of registration; the firm thought to avail itself of the opportunity even before the injunction was entered.

Without inviting comment from the parties, however, the district judge deleted these options from the SEC's draft and entered an injunction unconditionally requiring Presto to register as an investment company. The judge did not explain why. The result was a regulatory mismatch: a firm that is today required (by statute) to be organized and to report its financial position as an operating company is required (by injunction) to be organized and report its financial position as an investment company. Instead of doing this, the district court would have been well advised to craft an injunction commanding registration only if Presto should revert to its old portfolio design; obliging it to register as an investment company even when its investments do not require this is hard to fathom except as a form of punishment for Presto's conduct in past years, and civil injunctions are not supposed to punish litigants.

The unconditional injunction has caused considerable trouble. Investment companies are subject to many governance requirements that do not apply to operating companies. Presto's auditor, Grant Thornton, resigned because the SEC questioned its certification of Presto's financial statements as those of an operating company. Now that Presto is officially an investment company, Grant Thornton has refused to allow the statements it certified to be used for any purpose. This has disabled Presto from complying fully with *either* the Investment Company Act or the Securities Exchange Act of 1934. Without the financial statements, it is unable to file quarterly and annual reports. It has hired another auditor, but recreating and re-certifying financial statements for many past years is expensive and time consuming. Meanwhile stock exchanges have threatened to delist its stock because Presto is out of compliance with both statutory and exchange-based financial-reporting requirements.

At oral argument we inquired whether Presto's financial rearrangement has made the case moot. Now that it has complied with the injunction by registering as an investment company, can't it deregister and go back to its preferred status as an operating company, subject to registration under the Securities Exchange Act, no matter what happens on appeal? Deregistration requires the consent of the SEC, however, and although Presto filed the appropriate papers with the agency in January 2006 the SEC has failed to act on them.

One senses from this prolonged silence, and the tenor of the SEC's brief and oral argument, that the agency (or its senior staff) is in a snit because Presto declined to do what many other firms with excess liquid assets have done — apply to the agency for an exemption. See 15 U.S.C. § 80a-3(b)(2). (Microsoft, for example, holds more than 40% of its assets in the form of investment securities but received permission to operate outside the 1940 Act.) The agency's counsel implied at oral argument that an exemption would have been forthcoming if sought. Yet a firm's refusal to kowtow to an agency is not a good reason to force its investors to bear unnecessary costs — for it is the investors who must pay to recreate the financial statements, though *they* did not contribute to this imbroglio — and keep a firm inappropriately registered, as Presto now is. Why is the SEC bent on grinding down a corporation that it appears to acknowledge would not mislead or otherwise injure investors by using the governance and reporting devices appropriate to an operating company?

Because Presto remains registered as an investment company while the SEC sits on its hands, there is a live case or controversy, because a remedy is possible: we could end its registration forthwith. Moreover, if we hold that Presto's former portfolio does not bring it within the Investment Company Act, it will be free to rejigger its investments; the old investments likely had a higher rate of return, which is why Presto switched only after the district court's opinion.

Let us begin, then, with Presto's argument that even before the recent changes to its portfolio, enough of its investments were "Government securities and cash items" to keep its "investment securities" under the 40% trigger.

"Government securities" is a defined term. The phrase "means any security issued or guaranteed as to principal or interest by the United States, or by a person controlled or supervised by and acting as an instrumentality of the Government of the United States pursuant to authority granted by the Congress of the United States; or any certificate of deposit for any of the foregoing." 15 U.S.C. § 80a-2(a)(16). According to Presto, pre-refunded municipal bonds ("refunded bonds" for short) fit this definition. Presto held these instruments in quantity.

A refunded bond is a bond backed by U.S. securities as well as the credit of the issuer. Suppose that a municipality issues long-term bonds for a project (say, an airport) and that the market rate of interest later falls. The issuer would like to take advantage of the lower rate, but the bonds lack a call feature. The municipality can issue new bonds at the current lower rate and use the proceeds to buy Treasury bonds with the same maturity as the original issue of municipal bonds. The Treasury securities are held in trust to pay interest and principal on the original issue. The municipality pays the interest on the new issue; the Treasury securities may cover the old issue, and if not the municipality can chip in the difference. Refinancing in this way works because municipal bonds are not subject to federal taxes, so they often pay lower interest rates than Treasury securities. Bonds that can be bought with the proceeds of the new municipal issue may produce enough interest by themselves to cover the interest on the old issue.

The Treasury bonds held in trust lead Presto to call the refunded bonds themselves "Government securities." It should be apparent, however, that they do not fit the statutory definition. Refunded municipal bonds are still municipal bonds, exactly as they were before the refunding transaction. Municipal bonds are neither issued nor guaranteed by the national government or any federal instrumentality. If the municipality defaults, or a local employee reaches into the till and makes off with the Treasury securities, the national government will not cover the loss. The bonds in trust make the municipal bonds safer, but 15 U.S.C. § 80a-2(a)(16) does not include in the category of "Government securities" everything that a company deems "almost as safe as" Treasury securities.

The argument "X has the same economic attributes as Y, so X must have the same legal attributes as Y" has a history in securities law. It was the basis of the sale-of-business doctrine that many courts accepted before *Landreth Timber Co. v. Landreth*, 471 U.S. 681(1985). The idea was that someone who bought all of the stock in a closely-held corporation was buying the corporation's assets, as an economic matter, so the transaction should not be governed by the securities laws. *Landreth Timber* held, however, that someone who wants the legal treatment of an asset acquisition must buy the assets rather than the stock; people may choose between transacting in securities and transacting in assets, and the law follows the form — not only because that is what the statute says, but also because trying to determine, one case at a time, when a transaction "really" has the economic attributes of a different form would lead to a great deal of uncertainty for little purpose. *Landreth Timber* represents the norm in securities law. Stock or bonds in a company that invests the proceeds in land, or gold, or art, are still regulated as securities rather than as land, or gold, or art. Pooled interests in orange groves are regulated as investment contracts rather than as oranges. *See SEC v. W.J. Howey Co.*, 328 U.S. 293 (1946). And municipal bonds issued by a city that plans to repay using U.S. bonds are still municipal bonds.

Securities laws regulate the form of financial transactions, rather than looking through form to substance. *See Reves v. Ernst & Young*, 494 U.S. 56 (1990) (demand notes are regulated as securities even though they have many economic attributes of exempt instruments). True enough, § 80a-2 begins, as several other definitional clauses in the securities laws do, with the phrase, "unless the context otherwise requires." The Supreme Court used this in *Marine Bank v. Weaver*, 455 U.S. 551 (1982), to hold that a one-off transaction—a 50% interest in a neighbor's farm in exchange for a short-term loan, the sort of investment that could not even in principle be traded among anonymous investors—should not be treated as a security....

... The Investment Company Act has been with us for 67 years without giving problems through the definition of "Government securities." And even if there were some wriggle room via the context clause, Presto has not established that refunded bonds are the economic equivalent of Treasury bonds. A report in the record from Morgan Stanley shows that the yield for Treasury bonds maturing in 2006 was 4.95%, while the taxable equivalent yield for refunded bonds was 6.1% for taxpayers in the 38% bracket. That's a 23% premium over Treasuries, which must reflect extra risk. (The nominal interest rate for refunded bonds is below that for Treasury bonds, because of the tax subsidy for municipal securities; an adjustment must be made to find real returns and implicit risks.)

Mutual funds may treat refunded bonds as if they were "Government securities" for the purpose of 15 U.S.C. § 80a-5, which says how an investment company's portfolio must be structured if it calls itself "diversified." See 17 C.F.R. § 270.5b-3(b). How can refunded bonds be "Government securities" for one purpose but not the other? Presto asks. Yet treating A as if it were B for one purpose does not imply that A *is* B for every purpose. The regulation on which Presto relies governs how investment companies describe their portfolios; that's a very different subject from whether something is an investment company in the first place. Equating refunded bonds with Treasury securities for the purpose of diversification allows mutual funds to offer tax advantages (which refunded bonds supply) without any change in the covariance of risk across a fund's assets. Denying investors that opportunity would injure them; it's sensible for the SEC to look at the economic attributes of instruments when determining what counts as diversification (another economic inquiry) while insisting that the statutory definition be used to determine what entities are covered by the statute in the first place.

"Cash items" also are excluded when calculating the 40% ratio, and Presto maintains that "variable-rate demand notes" should be treated as "cash items." A variable-rate demand note is an instrument (usually a bond or debenture) whose rate of interest is updated weekly (if not more often) based on some index, such as the London Interbank Offering Rate. Whenever the interest rate changes, the note's holder is entitled to redeem at par. Usually this transaction is handled by a remarketing agent, who buys the note from the holder and resells it in the secondary market to another investor; the note's issuer is involved only if the note is trading for less than par.

In contrast to the detailed statutory definition of "Government securities," the Investment Company Act does not define "cash items." Presto maintains that variable-rate demand notes are equivalent to cash because of the weekly opportunity to sell the instruments at par for cash. If liquidity were enough, however, one would treat all shares of stock in large issuers, and many bonds, as "cash items" because they can be sold on liquid markets in a matter of minutes. The reason that such investments are not treated as cash or its equivalent, however, is that the market price the instrument will fetch when sold is variable. Presto thinks that the "redeem at par" feature of the variable-rate demand note insulates them from that sort of risk, but that's not true. The investor is entitled to *demand* redemption at par, but whether the issuer will comply depends on its financial health. A business reverse (or, for a municipal issuer, a shortfall of taxes) will mean no redemption, or redemption at a discount. That's a kind of risk an investor takes with any stock or bond—but does not take with cash.

Although the statute does not define "cash item," the SEC gave this definition when adopting a safe-harbor rule (17 C.F.R. § 270.3a-1):

> For purposes of determining compliance with the proposed rule, cash, coins, paper currency, demand deposits with banks, timely checks of others (which are orders on banks to immediately supply funds), cashier checks, certified checks, bank drafts, money orders, traveler's checks and letters of credit generally would be considered cash items. Certificates of deposit and time deposits typically would not be considered cash items absent convincing evidence of no investment intent.

Certain Prima Facie Investment Companies, Investment Company Act Release No. IC-10937 (Nov. 13, 1979), at n. 29; regulation adopted in final form 46 Fed. Reg. 6879 (Jan. 22, 1981). This definition applies only to Rule 3a-1, but Presto does not contend that we should ignore it—or that it is arbitrary or capricious. Agencies are entitled to add detail to the statutes they administer, and their resolution of ambiguities is entitled to respect. *See Chevron U.S.A. Inc. v. Natural Resources Defense Council, Inc.*, 467 U.S. 837 (1984).

A variable-rate demand note does not fit this definition. Presto chose to invest in variable-rate demand notes rather than, say, money-market funds (which are diversified portfolios of safe and liquid investments) because the notes have higher rates of return. The higher return stems from higher risk, which explains why the notes differ from "cash items." (Presto does observe that many variable-rate demand notes are backed by letters of credit, which the SEC is willing to treat as "cash items," but that's a replay of the argument that refunded bonds are "Government securities" because they are secured by Treasury bonds.) Presto was making an *investment* in these notes, along the lines of "time deposits" (which are "cash items" only with "convincing evidence of no investment intent"), rather than holding them for liquidity.

Presto therefore comes within the 40% test and is an investment company unless one of the (many) statutory exceptions applies. The one on which Presto relies is § 80a-3(b)(1): "Any issuer primarily engaged, directly or through a wholly-owned subsidiary or subsidiaries, in a business or businesses other than that of investing, reinvesting, owning, holding, or trading in securities." Presto is actively engaged in several businesses. A visitor to its web site for consumers ... will find sales promotions, warranty information, and instruction manuals for pizza ovens and coffee makers but nary a hint that someone would want to buy Presto's stock as a means to own a derivative interest in refunded municipal bonds or variable-rate demand notes. But is Presto "primarily" engaged in selling pressure cookers, deep fryers, popcorn poppers, diapers, and ordnance rather than the business of holding securities? The statute is unhelpful; "primarily" is not a defined term. No regulation fills the gap.

Sixty years ago the SEC announced that it would consider five factors to decide whether a firm that sold off its operating assets and chose not to distribute the proceeds to its stockholders had become what people today call an "inadvertent investment company." *In re Tonopah Mining Co.,* 26 S.E.C. 426 (1947). See also Sydney H. Mendelsohn, Mark B. Goldfus & Mark J. Mackey, *Status Seeking: Resolving the Status of Inadvertent Investment Companies,* 38 Bus. Law. 193 (1982); Edmund H. Kerr, *The Inadvertent Investment Company: Section 3(a)(3) of the Investment Company Act,* 12 Stan. L.Rev. 29 (1959).

According to *Tonopah,* what matter are the company's history, the way the company represents itself to the investing public today, the activities of its officers and directors, the nature of its assets, and the sources of its income. Of these, all but the fourth favor Presto. Founded in 1905, Presto was an active manufacturer of industrial, consumer, and military products until the 1980s, when it started to subcontract manufacturing activities. It remains an active manufacturer of absorbent goods and military ordnance and sells a line of kitchen goods under its own trademarks.

As far as we can see, this is the first time that the SEC has argued that a firm with such a substantial ongoing presence in product markets is an inadvertent investment company. The model inadvertent investment company—of which Tonopah Mining is the initial exemplar and Fifth Avenue Coach Lines is perhaps the best-known, see *SEC v. Fifth Avenue Coach Lines, Inc.,* 289 F.Supp. 3 (S.D.N.Y.1968), affirmed, 435 F.2d 510 (2d Cir.1970)—is one in which the firm has sold all or almost all of its assets, reduced its operations to a skeleton staff (Tonopah Mining was down to one unprofitable mine and Fifth Avenue Coach Lines to no busses at all), and purports to be looking for acquisitions but never seems to find them. Perhaps one could have applied the "purports to be looking for acquisitions" label to Presto in the 1980s and 1990s, but one could *not* say that Presto had withdrawn from active business operations in the meantime. It continued selling both consumer and military products. It changed from a manufacturer to a firm that was (principally) a designer and marketer of products assembled by others, but this did not make Presto less an operating enterprise. Many other firms have made a similar transition (Apple comes to mind) without being thought to have evolved into mutual funds.

Presto presents itself to the public (and to investors) as an operating company. That's how its web site, its annual reports, and its publicity all depict it. The contrast with Tonopah Mining and Fifth Avenue Coach Lines is stark. An investor in the market for a mutual fund, a hedge fund, or any other investment pool would not dream of turning to Presto, whose net income can increase or decrease substantially as a result of business successes or reverses. The price of Presto's stock moves in response to changes in its operating profits rather than the slight annual changes in its investment income. The SEC has not identified even one confused investor who bought stock in Presto thinking that he was making an investment in a closed-end mutual fund whose assets were the securities that Presto holds.

"Activities of Officers and Directors," the third factor in *Tonopah,* likewise favors Presto. Directors and senior managers at Tonopah Mining and Fifth Avenue Coach Lines spent most of their time managing the firms' investment portfolios. Presto estimates that 95% of its managers' time is devoted to running its consumer-products and military-ordnance businesses. The SEC has not offered any contrary evidence. Cf. *First National Bank & Trust Co. v. Beach,* 301 U.S. 435 (1937) (a firm is "primarily engaged in farming" under the Bankruptcy Code if its officers and directors devote most of their time to farming).

As for the fifth factor, income, *Tonopah* looked at both gross and net figures, as well as at the firm's expenditures to produce income. (Looking at both gross and net is essential; otherwise an operating loss, with negative net income, would turn a firm into an "investment company".) Gross income at Presto is dominated by receipts from its consumer and military sales. More than 90% of Presto's gross receipts for every year covered by the record (1994 through 2003) comes from its sales of products. In 2003, for example, Presto recorded about $125 million in sales, yielding a net profit of $18.9 million; total receipts from investment securities that year were $4.2 million.

Only net income helps the SEC's position: the agency calculates that, over the decade covered by the record, 50.22% of Presto's net profits were derived from investments in securities. Presto's calculations show that operating profits exceed investment profits for the decade as a whole. The SEC acknowledges that, in each of the three years immediately preceding the district court's injunction requiring Presto to register as an investment company, investments produced less than 40% of Presto's net profit. So even if we take the view most favorable to the SEC, that a firm is "primarily" engaged in a business other than investment management only if more than half of its net profits come from non-investment sources, Presto was "primarily" an operating business when the injunction issued. Whatever classification may have been appropriate in the 1990s (when more than half of net profits came from investments) cannot support an injunction issued in 2005, when at least 60% of net profit was coming from consumer and military sales. In *Tonopah,* by contrast, "the company's only source of net income consists of interest, dividends and profits on the sale of securities;

and we find nothing to indicate that this situation will be changed substantially in the foreseeable future." 26 S.E.C. at 431.

This leaves the fourth *Tonopah* factor, the nature of Presto's assets. Here the picture at last favors the SEC, for more than 60% of Presto's assets were investment securities during every year covered by the record. In full flight from the Commission's multi-factor approach in *Tonopah,* the SEC's lawyer in this court urges us to give little weight to any consideration other than Presto's asset structure. Yet looking primarily at accounting assets has a potential to mislead. Imagine a firm that owns substantial assets such as patents and trademarks that do not show up on its balance sheet as assets, and that operates a business from a leased headquarters where it designs, contracts for, and sells products. Such a firm could have annual sales exceeding $100 million, and profits exceeding $10 million as Presto does, with book-value assets of only $1 million in office furniture. If that firm stored even 10% of two years' profits in refunded bonds, as a hedge against business reverses (or to finance expansion), instead of distributing all profits to investors in dividends, it would become an investment company under the approach the SEC urges in this litigation. Yet no investor would perceive such a firm as a substitute for a closed-end mutual fund; its stock returns would continue to depend on its operating profits and losses.

According to the SEC's brief, *Tonopah* deemed assets the "most important" of the five considerations. It would be surprising if that were so, because it would make the exclusion in § 80a-3(b)(1) unavailable as a practical matter. The only reason one turns to this exclusion is that the 40% asset test has been satisfied. If subsection (b)[(1)] does nothing except raise the 40% test to 50% as a definition of the firm's "primary" engagement, it is an odd statutory provision indeed. What sense would it make to enact a law using 40% as the threshold in subsection (a)(1)(C), and convert the "real" rule to 50% in subsection (b)(1) by using words rather than numbers? Subsection (b)(1) has to be about considerations other than assets (or at least in addition to assets). And that's what the SEC said in *Tonopah:* "More important ... [is] the nature of the assets and income of the company, disclosed in the annual reports filed with the Commission and in reports sent to stockholders, was such as *to lead investors to believe* that the principal *activity* of the company was trading and investing in securities." 26 S.E.C. at 430 (emphasis added). In other words, the Commission thought in *Tonopah* that what principally matters is the beliefs the company is likely to induce in investors. Will its portfolio and activities lead investors to treat a firm as an investment vehicle or as an operating enterprise? The Commission has never issued an opinion or rule taking a different view, and its lawyers cannot adopt a new approach by filing briefs. Only the Commission's members may change established norms, and they must do so by rulemaking or administrative adjudication.... Reasonable investors would treat Presto as an operating company rather than a competitor with a closed-end mutual fund. The SEC has not tried to demonstrate anything different about investors' perceptions or behavior. It follows that Presto is not an investment company. [***]

* * *

Notes and Applications

The first part of the *National Presto* decision illustrates how in real terms the 40% test operates mechanically. It turns on a close analysis of asset composition. It also attests to the practical issues faced by companies that are exiting from one business and that have not fully decided how to redeploy their assets on a permanent basis. There are other cases in this vein. *See, e.g.*, *SEC v. Fifth Avenue Lines*, 435 F.2d 510 (2d Cir. 1970); *Moses v. Black* [1981 Transfer Binder] Fed. Sec. L. Rep. (CCH) ¶ 97,866 (S.D.N.Y. 1981). The SEC adopted a rule to provide guidance as to the definition's application in this sort of situation that can arise from time to time. *See* Company Act Rule 3a-2 (relating to so-called transient investment companies).

However, the court's analysis of how the (b)(1) exclusion's primarily engaged standard operates represents a non-textual gloss on the statutory language. Needless to say, the *National Presto* court's interpretation is at odds with the SEC's approach. According to the court, "what principally matters is the beliefs the company is likely to induce in investors." While such an approach might be a reasonable policy choice, and arguably would be easier to apply, it does not appear to account for the intended difference between the subjective (orthodox) and objective (prima facie) disjunctive prongs of subsection (a)(1), namely clauses (A) and (C). Specifically, why have an objective test if the ultimate test for exclusion will turn on whether potential investors are subjectively confused regarding the Company Act's applicability or the entity's true nature? At the very least, the case represents a skeptical view of an overly narrow application of subsection (b)(1).

* * *

Yahoo! Inc.: Notice of Application

Investment Company Act Release No. 24459 (May 18, 2000)

[**Text note:** *This Notice of Application is instructive in two respects. First, it provides a concrete example of the means by which a party that arguably satisfies the definition of a prima facie investment company can seek relief from the Commission. Typically, the applicant will file an application which provides the basis for its request for relief and the staff will publish receipt of the application and provide a preliminary indication of its view. Absent an objection or request for a hearing, the Commission will likely ratify its preliminary views. Second, and more relevant substantively, this application shows how the novel structure of high technology companies can easily trigger the definition of a prima facie investment company inadvertently because the value of such companies is frequently derived from intangible, rather than operating, assets. This particular order shows a creative perspective on the underlying facts relating to "controlled companies" that eschews a mechanical reading of the relevant statutory provisions.*]

[***] 1. Yahoo!, a Delaware corporation, was formed in 1995. Yahoo! states that it is a global Internet new media company that offers a branded network of media, commerce and communication services. Yahoo! develops, operates and markets advertis-

ing-supported online properties, including *Yahoo!*, a branded Internet navigational service that is among the most widely used and recognized search guides on the World Wide Web. Yahoo! states that it conducts its Internet and new media business directly and through wholly-owned and majority-owned subsidiaries and Yahoo! Japan, a company that it controls within the meaning of section 2(a)(9) of the Act.[1] Yahoo! states that it is not in the business of investing, reinvesting or trading in securities.

2. Yahoo! has expanded its Internet and new media business to Japan through Yahoo! Japan, which, unlike Yahoo!'s other international subsidiaries, is not majority-owned or wholly-owned by Yahoo!. Yahoo! states that Yahoo! Japan was created in 1996 as a joint venture between Yahoo! and Softbank Corp. to establish and manage a Japanese version of the Yahoo! directory service, develop related Japanese online navigational services and conduct other related businesses. Yahoo! states that it currently owns 34% of the outstanding voting securities of Yahoo! Japan and Softbank Corp. owns 51%. Yahoo! states that Yahoo! Japan currently is a publicly traded company with shares listed on the Tokyo Stock Exchange. Yahoo! represents that Yahoo! Japan is not an investment company and is not relying on section 3(c)(1) or 3(c)(7) of the Act. As of December 31, 1999, Yahoo! states that the fair market value of Yahoo!'s interest in Yahoo! Japan was approximately $8.4 billion, accounting for over 90% of the value of Yahoo!'s total assets (exclusive of government securities and cash items) on an unconsolidated basis.

3. Yahoo! represents that it maintains a large cash position to help fund operations, research and development, and to take advantage of acquisition opportunities as they arise. Yahoo!'s cash position is currently invested in cash and government securities; Yahoo! plans to invest part of its cash position in higher-yielding corporate bonds and other high-quality debt securities that are consistent with the goal of capital preservation. Yahoo! represents that it has adopted a Corporate Investment Policy to ensure that its cash management investments consist of only certain high-quality predominately short-term debt instruments (together with cash items and government securities, "Cash Management Investments"). Yahoo! represents that it needs sufficient cash for bona fide business purposes, such as funding operations, funding research and development and improvements to its network, and funding strategic acquisitions. Yahoo! also states that it does not engage in speculative short-term trading with its Cash Management Investments.

4. Yahoo! states that it makes certain small strategic, non-controlling investments in companies that can complement or enhance Yahoo!'s Internet and new media business ("Strategic Investments"). Yahoo! states that it carries these investments on its balance sheet as "long-term" assets and does not invest or trade in such securities for short-term or speculative purposes. As of December 31, 1999, the value of the Strategic Investments was less than 5% of the value of Yahoo!'s total assets (exclusive of gov-

---

1. Section 2(a)(9) of the Act defines "control" as the power to exercise a controlling influence over the management or policies of a company. That section creates a presumption that an owner of more than 25% of the outstanding voting securities of a company controls the company.

ernment securities and cash items) on an unconsolidated basis. Yahoo! states that it does not hold Strategic Investments because of the possibility of gain resulting from an increase in the market price of the securities, but primarily as a means to enter into or solidify business relationships with companies to expand Yahoo!'s business lines. Yahoo! further states that it uses Strategic Investments as a way of outsourcing research and development instead of developing technology internally.

Applicant's Legal Analysis:

1. Yahoo! seeks an order under section 3(b)(2) of the Act declaring that it is primarily engaged in a business other than that of investing, reinvesting, owning, holding or trading in securities, and therefore not an investment company as defined in the Act.

2. Under section 3(a)(1)(C) of the Act, an issuer is an investment company if it is engaged or proposes to engage in the business of investing, reinvesting, owning, holding or trading in securities, and owns or proposes to acquire investment securities having a value in excess of 40% of the value of the issuer's total assets (exclusive of government securities and cash items) on an unconsolidated basis. Section 3(a)(2) of the Act defines "investment securities" to include all securities except government securities, securities issued by employees' securities companies, and securities issued by majority-owned subsidiaries of the owner which (i) are not investment companies, and (ii) are not relying on the exclusions from the definition of investment company in section 3(c)(1) or 3(c)(7) of the Act.

3. Yahoo! states that its interest in Yahoo! Japan represents over 90% of its total assets (exclusive of government securities and cash items) on an unconsolidated basis. Yahoo! states that it cannot rely upon rule 3a-1 under the Act because, although it owns over 25% of the outstanding voting securities of Yahoo! Japan, it does not primarily control Yahoo! Japan because another entity owns a larger percentage of voting securities.[2] If the interest in Yahoo! Japan is deemed to be an "investment security" (as that term is defined in section 3(a)(2) of the Act), Yahoo! may be deemed to be an investment company within the meaning of section 3(a)(1)(C) of the Act.

4. Yahoo! states that it views its controlling interest in Yahoo! Japan as an operating asset. Yahoo! represents that it plays a significant role in the management of Yahoo! Japan and is fully involved both directly and indirectly, in the operations of Yahoo! Japan. Yahoo! states that it directly oversees the operations of Yahoo! Japan through its involvement with the board of directors of Yahoo! Japan. Yahoo! further states that Yahoo! Japan operates under various agreements with Yahoo! that give Yahoo! significant power to direct the operations of Yahoo! Japan, including a licensing agreement that, among other things, sets minimum content specifications and subjects Yahoo! Japan to an international pricing policy designed by Yahoo! to allocate sales revenue involving more than one Yahoo! entity. Yahoo! argues that these facts demon-

---

2. Rule 3a-1 provides an exemption from the definition of investment company if no more than 45% of a company's total assets consist of, and not more than 45% of its net income over the last four quarters is derived from, securities other than government securities and securities of majority-owned subsidiaries and companies primarily controlled by it.

strate not only that Yahoo! controls Yahoo! Japan, but also that it is involved in the management and operations of Yahoo! Japan.

5. Section 3(b)(2) of the 1940 Act provides that, notwithstanding section 3(a)(1)(C) of the Act, the Commission may issue an order declaring an issuer to be primarily engaged in a business or businesses other than that of investing, reinvesting, owning, holding, or trading in securities either directly, through majority-owned subsidiaries, or controlled companies conducting similar types of business. Yahoo! requests an order under section 3(b)(2) of the Act declaring that it is primarily engaged in a business other than that of investing, reinvesting, owning, holding or trading in securities, and therefore not an investment company as defined in the Act.

6. In determining whether a company is primarily engaged in a non-investment company business under section 3(b)(2), the Commission considers: (a) the applicant's historical development; (b) its public representations of policy; (c) the activities of its officers and directors; (d) the nature of its present assets; and (e) the sources of its present income.[3]

a. *Historical Development.* Yahoo! states that since its inception in 1995, it has considered itself to be a company engaged in the Internet and new media business of developing and providing Internet-related products and services. Yahoo! represents that its business strategy has not changed since it outlined its business plan in its prospectus for the initial public offering of its securities in 1996. Yahoo! has used its revenue and raised capital to expand its operations into foreign countries, to expand its product and service lines and to acquire companies with complementary products or services.

b. *Public Representations of Policy.* Yahoo! states that it has never represented that it is involved in any business other than the Internet and new media business that develops and provides Internet-related products and services. Yahoo! asserts that it has consistently stated in its reports to stockholders, press releases and periodic reports filed with the Commission that it is an Internet and new media company. Yahoo! states that it emphasizes operating results and has never emphasized either its investment income or the possibility of significant appreciation from its Cash Management Investments or Strategic Investments as a material factor in its business or future growth.

c. *Activities of Officers and Directors.* Yahoo! states that its board of directors and its officers spend almost all of their time on Yahoo!'s Internet and new media business. The board of directors' activities with respect to Yahoo!'s Cash Management Investments is minimal, limited to its adoption of the Corporate Investment Policy and periodically receiving reports. Yahoo! also states that only two of its approximately 2,000 employees spend any time with respect to its Cash Management Investments, and those employees spend only approximately 20% of their time in this manner. Yahoo! states that the amount of time that the board of directors dedicates to the Strategic

---

3. *Tonopah Mining Company of Nevada*, 26 SEC 426, 427 (1947).

Investments is small relative to the amount of time dedicated to Yahoo!'s business activities.

d. *Nature of Assets.* Yahoo! states that as of December 31, 1999, exclusive of cash items and government securities, over 90% of Yahoo!'s total assets, on an unconsolidated basis, was attributable to direct non-investment security assets and Yahoo!'s interests in wholly- and majority-owned subsidiaries and Yahoo! Japan. As of December 31, 1999, Yahoo represents that less than 5% of its total assets (exclusive of cash items and government securities), on an unconsolidated basis, were attributable to Strategic Investments. Yahoo further represents that Cash Management Investments comprised less than 10% of its total assets, as of December 31, 1999.

e. *Sources of Income.* Yahoo! states that for the year ended December 31, 1999, Yahoo!'s investment income comprised approximately 37% and its operating income comprised approximately 63% of Yahoo!'s gross income. Yahoo! further states that for the quarter ended March 31, 2000, Yahoo!'s investment income comprised approximately 44%, and operating income comprised approximately 57% of Yahoo!'s gross income. Moreover, Yahoo! states that 70% of the approximately $57 million of investment income it reported in the quarter ended March 31, 2000, resulted from the consolidation of certain joint venture operations following Yahoo!'s acquisitions of Geocities and broadcast.com, not from speculation in securities. Yahoo! notes that in the past its income from operations has fluctuated widely and Yahoo! has incurred substantial non-recurring costs in connection with acquisitions and product development. Yahoo! notes that the composition of its income, at times, is not representative of Yahoo!'s activities as an operating company. Yahoo! believes that the sources of its revenue are more representative of Yahoo!'s activities as an operating company. Yahoo states that as far back as 1996, Yahoo! generated 83% of its total revenue from sales of advertisements and 14% from investment income. For the year ended December 31, 1999, Yahoo states that it generated 94% of its total revenue from operating activities and the remaining 6% from investment income. Yahoo! expects that in the future the percentage of its total revenues derived from operating activities will ordinarily be over 90%.

7. Yahoo! thus asserts that it satisfies the standards for an order under section 3(b)(2) of the Act.

Applicant's Conditions:

Applicant agrees that the order granting the requested relief will be subject to the following conditions:

1. Yahoo! will continue to allocate and utilize its accumulated cash and Cash Management Investments for bona fide business purposes.

2. Yahoo! will refrain from investing or trading in securities for short-term speculative purposes.

For the Commission, by the Division of Investment Management, pursuant to delegated authority.

* * *

Notes and Applications

1. *Incubating venture investments.* The Division of Investment Management, acting for the Commission in the matter, concluded that Yahoo was "engaged in a business other than that of investing, reinvesting, owning, holding, or trading securities" and accordingly granted the application. *See In the Matter of Yahoo! Inc.*, Investment Company Act Release No. 24494 (July 13, 2000). The Yahoo application illustrates a problem that entrepreneurial new economy companies have encountered in staying outside the purview of the Company Act. The Company Act results in highly restrictive regulatory oversight that would not be suitable for most firms that engage in some form of venture investing. However, as in the case of Yahoo, venture investing by a public operating company whose assets are largely intangible may lead to small equity stakes in one or more wildly successful new ventures. The value of resulting successful seeded ventures may potentially eventually exceed that of assets in public company's operating assets which in turn is likely to trigger classification as a prima facie investment company. Faced with this type of scenario, Yahoo had to argue in its (b)(2) application that it actually exercised control over Yahoo! Japan's business. In what sense did it control and in what sense did it not strictly control Yahoo! Japan? Which sense of control is relevant for purposes of subsection (b)(2)?

2. *Other rule-based exclusions.* The SEC has adopted a series of rules that augment the exclusions from the definition of investment company excluding particular types of businesses from classification as an investment company. These rules are codified sequentially under Section 3(a) of the Company Act. The first of these, Rule 3a-1, was specifically designed to address the overbreadth of the 40% test for prima facie investment companies. The SEC's rule supplements the 40% investment securities test with a modified bifurcated 45% test (essentially a company's investment securities are 45% or less of total assets and net income from such holdings is 45% or less of the company's net income after taxes). Rule 3a-2 for transient investment companies was mentioned above. Rule 3a-7 carves out a significant class of securitized investment vehicles (i.e., investment vehicles that issue asset-backed securities). The text separately discusses Rule 3a-4 below.

3. *Research and development companies.* One of the rule exclusions, Rule 3a-8, is worth pausing over because it further illustrates situations where changing business models have indicated a need to relax the investment company definition's exclusions to further accommodate the realities of new economic models for businesses. In 2003, the SEC adopted this rule to exclude R & D companies that are not uncommon in high technology fields such as biotech or pharmaceuticals from classification as an investment company. These companies may raise a significant amount of capital with the plan of using the capital to fund research over many years. The initial capital is frequently invested in income generating securities, other than treasury securities, to generate additional funding for continued research over the R&D project's life cycle. Typically, such companies spend down (or burn through) their capital (which is frequently held in the form of financial assets) over several years on research. Their

total assets early on may be heavily weighted toward investment securities (which might be the financial assets that offer the highest low-risk return). The rule establishes an elaborate set of conditions to enable companies to avoid classification as an investment company, while ensuring that the company is primarily engaged in bona fide research and development activities rather than the business of either holding or trading securities. These conditions ensure that research and development efforts, rather than investment activities, are the company's primary focus.

10.3 Pooled Investment Accounts Marketed to the Public

The language of Section 3(a)(1), read casually, would seem to suggest that only companies or entities should be treated as investment companies for purposes of the Investment Company Act. But this casual observation must be examined more closely in light of the statute's actual language. Section 3(a)(1) is framed in terms of "any issuer" engaged in investment activities. This basic concept appears to establish three requirements, none of which strictly require a stand-alone entity: (1) there must be an issuer; (2) the issuer must issue securities; and (3) depending on the relevant clause of Section (a)(1), the issuer must either (i) engage in a business involving securities activities and hold investment securities that represent more than 40% of its total assets, or (ii) be or hold itself out as being engaged primarily in the business of investing, reinvesting, or trading securities.

10.3.1 Informal Investment Companies

While these requirements are formally satisfied, for example, by a stand-alone mutual fund organized as a business trust, there are in fact numerous investment arrangements that arguably satisfy these elements informally. The case below extends the basic investment company analysis to variable annuity policies issued by Prudential Insurance. Variable annuities are a hybrid investment insurance product sold by insurance companies which pays a stream of regular benefits to the annuitant, the exact amount depending (or variable) on the success of the insurance company's investment return on the policy premiums received from the policy holder. This determination requires an analysis of the attributes of the insurance product against the requisite elements of the Company Act's definition of an investment company.

Prudential Insurance Company v. SEC

326 F.2d 383 (3d Cir. 1964)

[**Textbook Note:** *In this matter, the SEC had entered an order compelling Prudential Insurance Company to register a variable annuity fund as an investment company. The result is seemingly puzzling since insurance companies are expressly excluded from the definition of an investment company under Section 3(c)(3). Notwithstanding that a variable annuity is a product sold by insurance companies,*

Prudential Insurance faced two challenges: first, trying to establish that the variable annuity product did not exhibit the three necessary elements of an investment company; and second, even assuming that the policies' underlying investment of proceeds met the requisite elements, whether the policies and associated investment funds satisfied one of the Company Act's many express exclusions. The decision not only provides a lesson in how to read the statute's various definitions, but also explains how a range of informal (non-incorporated) investment arrangements might well be classified as investment companies in their own right.]

Staley, *Circuit Judge*.... The narrow but provocative question posed by this case is whether the Investment Company Act of 1940, 15 U.S.C. § 80a applies to the Investment Fund resulting from the sale of variable annuity contracts to members of the public by The Prudential Insurance Company of America. The Securities and Exchange Commission answered this question in the affirmative, rejecting the view of Prudential that the Act exempts such a program because the contracts are offered and sold by an insurance company. The case is before us on the petition of Prudential for review of the order of the Commission entered pursuant to that determination.

Though there are variations in the form of the variable annuities which Prudential proposes to sell, their salient characteristics are not disputed and their nature has been concisely summarized by the Commission in its opinion in this case:

> 'In substance, the variable annuity contracts which Prudential proposes to sell to individuals provide that the purchaser will make monthly purchase payments of fixed amounts over a period of years (the 'pay-in' period), the proceeds of which, after certain deductions, will be invested in a portfolio of securities. The purchaser will be credited monthly with 'units' representing his proportionate interest in this fund. The value of these units will fluctuate, essentially depending upon the investment results of the fund. During the annuity, or 'pay-out' period, Prudential guarantees that the purchaser will receive in cash the varying value of a fixed number of units as monthly annuity payments.
>
> 'Specifically the payments made by the purchasers will be placed in a 'Variable Contract Account' which will be managed by Prudential and be subdivided into two accounts. The first, the 'Investment Fund' account, will have its assets invested primarily in common stocks and will constitute the fund in which the purchasers hold units; this account will be dedicated solely to the variable annuity contract holders and its assets will not be subject to claims of any other contract or policyholder of the company. The second, the 'Other Assets' account, an administration account, will receive the amounts deducted from the purchase payments to cover administration expenses, sales commissions, and certain taxes, and to provide a surplus or reserve for the obligations to purchasers contained in the contracts. Transfers will be made periodically from the Other Assets account to the Investment Fund account to meet the contractual requirements that the assets of the latter be equal to the company's existing obligations under the variable contracts. Any excess over the amounts estimated to be needed for the foregoing purposes

may be declared as so-called 'dividends' which will provide additional fund units or cash payments for the contract holders; it will also be available to support the guarantees on contracts administered by Prudential's other operations. Any deficiency resulting from lower mortality than assumed, for example, will be met out of the general surplus of Prudential.

'During the pay-in period a purchaser will have the right to terminate the contract and receive the value of all units credited to his account, less certain termination charges. If a purchaser should die during the pay-in period, the contract is automatically terminated and his beneficiary is paid the greater of (i) the value of all units credited to the purchaser's account or (ii) an amount equal to the total of all purchase payments made.

Prudential concedes that such contracts have been held to be 'securities' within the meaning of the Securities Act of 1933, *Securities and Exchange Commission v. Variable Annuity Life Insurance Co.* (hereinafter called '*VALIC*'), 359 U.S. 65 (1959), and it is willing to register them under that Act. Prudential argues, however, that the Investment Company Act of 1940 specifically excludes insurance companies from its scope.[2] The Commission acknowledged that Prudential is excluded from the Act, but held that the fund created by the sale of the contracts, which is to be used for investment purposes, gives rise to a separate investment company within the coverage of the statute. The Commission concluded that Prudential is not itself an investment company but is the creator of one, and proposes to be its investment adviser and principal underwriter.

In this court, Prudential, premising its argument on the insurance company exclusion, asserts that this construction of the statute is inordinately complicated, abstruse, and without basis in law. It asserts that the statute is plain and forecloses Commission jurisdiction in this case. However, since it is conceded that Prudential is excluded from the Act, the issue is narrowed to the question of whether the Commission made a permissible interpretation in concluding that the variable annuity program results in the creation of a separate, non-exempt investment company.

Of course, in resolving this issue we start with the premise that securities legislation must be broadly construed in order to insure the investing public a full measure of protection. The parties agree that the statutory definitions contained in the Investment Company Act of 1940 are cast in broad terms. The critical term is 'company', which, so far as relevant to our discussion, is defined as 'a trust, a fund, or any organized group of persons whether incorporated or not.' 15 U.S.C. § 80a-2(a)(8).

On this score Prudential argues that the Act regulates only identifiable business entities with some sort of internal organization, and that it is the only such entity involved in this program. Thus, it is asserted that the purchasers cannot be described

2. Insurance companies are excluded from the definition of 'investment company' by 15 U.S.C. § 80a-3(c)(3). An insurance company is earlier defined as 'a company which is organized as an insurance company, whose primary and predominant business activity is the writing of insurance or the reinsuring of risks underwritten by insurance companies, and which is subject to supervision by the insurance commissioner or a similar official or agency of a State * * *.' 15 U.S.C. § 80a-2(a)(17).

as an 'organized group of persons'; that the plan has no elements of a common-law trust; and that the 'fund' referred to in the Act means a mutual fund or any other similar entity, but not Prudential's Investment Fund. But, as Mr. Justice Brennan has cogently observed, the regulatory provisions of the Act 'are of particular relevance to situations where the investor is committing his funds to the hands of others on an equity basis, with the view that the funds will be invested in securities and his fortunes will depend on the success of the investment.' *VALIC*, 359 U.S. at 79 (concurring opinion). Furthermore, a study of the legislative history of the Act shows that Congress intentionally drafted the statutory definitions in general terms in order to control such situations regardless of the legal form or structure of the investment enterprise.

Initially, it must be noted that the Committee reports of both the House and the Senate state that the legislation was drafted principally on the basis of reports submitted by the Securities and Exchange Commission following an extensive study of investment trusts and investment companies undertaken at the direction of Congress. H.R.Rep.No.2639, 76th Cong., 3rd Sess. 5-6 (1940); S.Rep.No. 1775, 76th Cong., 3rd Sess. 1, 5 (1940). The Act itself contains a similar acknowledgment. 15 U.S.C. § 80a-1. The significance of such reports in ascertaining the intent of Congress in enacting securities legislation was recently underscored by the Supreme Court in *Securities and Exchange Commission v. Capital Gains Research Bureau, Inc.*, 375 U.S. 180 (1963).

Among the various types of investment companies referred to in the exhaustive report of the Commission were those involving 'an agency relationship between the individual contributors to the fund and the management upon whom they confer substantially a power of attorney to act as agent in the investment of the moneys contributed. The group of individual investors is not a legal entity but rather constitutes in essence a combination of distinct individual interests.' H.R.Doc.No.707, 75th Cong., 3rd Sess. 24 (1939). Additionally, the report made specific reference to an investment company known as the 'Alexander Fund' which it described as 'merely a descriptive name given to the commingled funds of numerous investors who employed W. Wallace Alexander as their agent to invest such funds.' *Id.* at 46. Similarly, in describing the nature of the investment enterprises which Congress was seeking to control, the House Report quotes from the testimony of Commissioner Healy who stated that 'Essentially these organizations are large liquid pools of the public's savings entrusted to managements to be invested.' H.R.Rep.No.2639, 76th Cong., 3rd Sess. 6 (1940).

In these circumstances we reject Prudential's argument that the broad statutory phrase 'a trust, a fund, or any organized group of persons whether incorporated or not' refers only to recognizable business entities. On the contrary, the legislative history compels the conclusion that Prudential's Investment Fund is a 'fund' as that term is used in the statute. As we have previously seen, the Investment Fund is a completely segregated account, devoted to investing in securities. The cash for these investments is derived from payments made by the purchaser of the variable annuity contract. Though the proceeds of the fund are held for the sole benefit of the annuitant, it is this fund, and no other entity, in which he has an interest. Thus, the fund is separable from the insurance company which, as the Supreme Court noted in *VALIC*, 'guarantee(s) nothing to the annuitant except an interest in a portfolio of common stocks or other equities- an interest that has a ceiling but no floor.' 359 U.S. at 72. The restricted interest of the annuitant is perhaps best expressed in the Court's pithy observation that he 'gets only a pro rata share of what the portfolio of equity interests reflects—which may be a lot, a little, or nothing.' 359 U.S. at 71.

It follows from this that the Investment Fund, and not Prudential, is the 'issuer' of these securities for the purposes of the Investment Company Act of 1940. As the Commission observed, 'Prudential would in fact be the writer of the contracts—the insurance and annuity promises and the obligation to set up the investment fund. But the investment fund, the 'company' to which the investment interests relate, is the 'issuer' of those interests.'[6]

One of the principal arguments of Prudential in favor of exclusion is that the existence of adequate state regulation was the basis for the exemption of insurance companies. But this line of argument was conclusively rejected by the Supreme Court in *VALIC* for the reason that variable annuities are 'securities' and involve considerations of investment not present in the conventional contract of insurance. Prudential attempts to distinguish *VALIC* on the grounds that the company there involved was not, on the basis of the Court's decision, primarily or predominantly engaged in the business of writing insurance. But regardless of the merits of this distinction, that case holds unequivocally that adequate state regulation of insurance is immaterial when variable annuity contracts are being considered under a Federal statute.

Prudential also asserts that the specific exemption provided for the common trust funds of banks shows that regulation under the Act was imposed on an institutional rather than on a functional basis. It is pointed out that this exemption is provided in addition to the general exemption for banks. Prudential declares that such common trust funds are functionally indistinguishable from investment companies, but were excluded from the Act 'because they were in fact part of the banking business and intended to be covered by the broad exemption for banks.' We think that this specific exemption leads to the opposite conclusion, for as the Commission reasoned:

> '... Obviously, if as Prudential argues, the exemption of banks and insurance companies had been intended to include an exemption of funds set up by such companies, there would have been no need to provide for the additional specific exemption of funds set up by banks. Congress thus viewed such funds, even though usually maintained as departments of the bank, as separate from the banking business. It rested this exemption on the special considerations that the funds were used for bona fide fiduciary purposes rather than as a medium for general public investment and had only a limited impact in the investment fund picture.'

6. The mere fact that Prudential is the obligor of certain of the insurance and annuity features of the contract is not significant, for the annuitant's investment participation is measured solely by the Investment Fund.

Considerations of logic and policy provide further support for our conclusion. The Investment Company Act of 1940 contains significant safeguards for the protection of those who, like the purchasers of variable annuities, invest in 'securities.' These safeguards, characterized by the Commission as insuring 'corporate democracy,' include disclosure of investment policy and operating practices, and the regulation of fees, trading practices, and changes in investment policy. See *VALIC*, 359 U.S. at 79. The mere fact that the investment program in the case at bar is under the aegis of an insurance company ought not to negate compliance with these controls in the absence of compelling circumstances. We find no such circumstances here. [***]

* * *

After reading the case, it is useful to enumerate exactly how each of the three elements were met by the variable annuity. Who was the issuer? What security did the issuer issue? Did the issuer engage in the business of investing, reinvesting, trading, holding and owning securities and if so how?

10.3.2 Retail Advisory Programs and the Wrap Fee Exclusion

Prudential Insurance demonstrates that the definition of an investment company may be triggered by an investment arrangement, even though the arrangement is not formally a stand-alone business entity in its own right. The definition extends to funds, trusts or, in theory, accounts in which investors' assets are commingled. This has potential implications for retail programs that attempt to service the needs of a number of retail investors collectively. Therein lies a potential policy tension: the need for prohibitively expensive regulation as an investment company if an arrangement rises to the level of an investment company versus low-cost investment programs that may unwittingly expose investors to managerial and operational risks that arise from the informality of particular investment arrangements. This is precisely the policy conundrum that the SEC faced in determining how to treat so-called wrap fee programs offered to retail investors: programs that offer small retail investors a low management fee for participation in an investment program designed to meet the needs of small retail investors collectively. The first reading conveys the potential risks that investors face in such programs and the second reading shows how the SEC tried to deal with the situation through an exemptive rule in which the SEC sought to resolve the conflicting policy implications.

In the Matter of Clarke Lanzen Skalla Investment Firm, Inc.

Investment Advisers Act Release No. 1501 (1995)

[**Textbook Note:** *This settled administrative proceeding resulted in the imposition of sanctions against an investment adviser for operating an unregistered investment company. To find that the program operated by this investment adviser was in fact an investment company, the SEC was required to find that the three requisite elements were satisfied: (i) there was an issuer; (ii) securities being issued to investors by the issuer; and (iii) the issuer invested in securities for its* *investors. The administrative order does not attempt to explain why the investment adviser in this matter chose to configure the program in the way that it did, but at least implies that a desire to offer cost-savings to clients and unawareness of overlapping Company Act considerations may have been factors.]*

[***] A. SUMMARY

This matter involves the offering of an investment program, the Managed Asset Allocation Program ("MAAP II"), that was promoted and administered by CLS, a registered investment adviser, and its principals, Clarke, Lanzen and Schaap. In essence, MAAP II was an investment program by which discretionary advisory accounts were pooled and invested in a substantially similar manner exclusively in shares of registered investment companies ("mutual funds"). The pool of nominally separate MAAP II accounts constituted a de facto unregistered investment company. In addition, MAAP II constituted a "fund of funds" by purchasing shares of other investment companies in excess of statutory limits. Moreover, by failing to register the interests in MAAP II, MAAP II offered and sold unregistered securities in violation of the Securities Act.

B. FACTS

....

2. MAAP II

Beginning in approximately March 1991 until mid-1992, CLS, under control of its three principals, Clarke, Lanzen and Schaap, offered MAAP II. During this period, CLS established approximately 360 MAAP II accounts with an approximate aggregate market value of $24 million. In approximately May 1992, CLS ceased to offer MAAP II.

Under MAAP II, CLS directed the allocation and investment of clients' monies in no-load mutual funds specializing in securities of varying risk. The clients were presented with a choice of six different investment strategies—aggressive, progressive, moderate, balanced, conservative and defensive—each with a predetermined investment formula. Once each client chose an investment strategy, the client's assets were invested identically with all the assets of other clients who had chosen the same strategy. When the CLS principals determined to change the mix of mutual funds in which MAAP II clients who had chosen a given strategy were invested, that decision was made simultaneously for all clients invested in that strategy. Assets of clients who had chosen different strategies could and frequently did invest in shares of the same mutual funds. The CLS principals were vested with investment discretion and they made all investment decisions for MAAP II clients.

3. Custodial Services

CLS utilized one custodian to handle the assets of MAAP II clients. Upon the opening of a MAAP II account, the client's assets were sent to the custodian which deposited the assets into a common, omnibus account, which was accounted for by the custodian. After one day, the assets were swept into a cash account to earn interest, payable to the client, while the client's check cleared.

The custodian opened one omnibus account in its name with each mutual fund. Seven to ten omnibus accounts were established in this manner. Once a client's check cleared, CLS directed the custodian to wire available monies to designated mutual funds. The procedure for all MAAP II client assets was identical. The custodian registered the shares purchased in the name of the custodian "for the benefit of CLS," not in the names of individual clients. The mutual funds had no knowledge of the clients; thus, a client could not discuss his or her account in any way with the funds.

4. Recordkeeping by CLS and the Custodian

The custodian maintained records of each client's account, and provided the client with quarterly statements and certain tax-related information. CLS similarly sent each client a quarterly account statement showing the client's account information. MAAP II clients did not receive confirmations of investment transactions as they occurred or even monthly. Confirmation of each investment transaction was shown only on the custodian's and CLS' quarterly statements. These statements indicated the purchases and sales of mutual fund shares and the client's current position with each fund.

5. Client Contact

Clarke, Lanzen and Schaap shared responsibility for MAAP II client contacts. Clients were interviewed concerning their resources and investment objectives before opening a MAAP II account. As noted, clients received account statements from the custodian; CLS mailed quarterly information statements and other correspondence. Each quarterly statement from CLS explained that "If there is a significant discrepancy on your statement please notify us as soon as possible." There was no request for clients to contact CLS to discuss changes in investment needs or goals.

Clarke, Lanzen and Schaap had many duties in addition to those related to MAAP II. Some clients had personal meetings or telephone contacts with Clarke, Lanzen or Schaap. However, there were no records in client files or otherwise which established that clients in the MAAP II program were contacted periodically during each year to ascertain whether investments in each client's MAAP II account continued to meet the client's individualized investment needs or goals.

6. Management and Custodial Fees

From the omnibus account described above, CLS' annual advisory fee (between one and two percent of assets under management) and a one-time, one percent of assets under management "set-up" fee for each account were paid to a CLS account or directly to CLS. In addition, each MAAP II account paid the custodian an annual fee equal to .30 percent of assets under custody.

7. Delivery of Mutual Fund Prospectuses, Proxy Statements and Periodic Reports

At the time each account was opened, CLS provided MAAP II clients with prospectuses of the mutual funds in which the MAAP II clients would immediately invest. Thereafter, MAAP II clients did not receive prospectuses of the mutual funds in which their assets were subsequently invested nor did they receive proxies or semi-annual and annual reports, directly or indirectly, from the mutual funds or from the custodian. The custodian received annual reports from the mutual funds, but did not forward them to the MAAP II clients. Under MAAP II, the owner of record of the mutual fund shares was the custodian "for the benefit of CLS." Accordingly, the mutual funds could not have known to send proxies, prospectuses and annual and semi-annual reports to the individual MAAP II clients. None of the agreements obligated CLS to forward such documents to MAAP II clients. However, the custodial agreement entered into between the custodian and each MAAP II client provided that the custodian forward all proxies and proxy-soliciting material, but not prospectuses or periodic reports, to the MAAP II client.

8. Clients' Rights to Pledge their Shares, Impose Restrictions on or Withdraw Funds from MAAP II

Under MAAP II, clients could not pledge, hypothecate or unilaterally request (from the mutual funds) the withdrawal of the mutual fund shares in their MAAP II accounts. MAAP II clients had no contractual right to instruct CLS to refrain from purchasing shares of particular mutual funds which the clients did not wish to own, although the clients retained the authority to instruct the custodian directly regarding the changing of an investment strategy or liquidation of their shares. None of the agreements between CLS, the custodian and the MAAP II clients expressly permitted the pledging of mutual fund shares by MAAP II clients or the imposition of any restrictions on investments by MAAP II clients.

C. VIOLATIONS

MAAP II violated Section 7(a) of the Investment Company Act because it was operated as, and offered interests in, an investment company without being registered as an investment company. MAAP II also violated Section 12(d)(1)(A) of the Investment Company Act because, as an unregistered investment company, MAAP II purchased securities issued by registered investment companies, the aggregate value of which, immediately thereafter, exceeded ten percent of its total assets.[1] ...

1. MAAP II was an Unregistered Investment Company

If clients of a managed discretionary account program, such as MAAP II, do not receive individualized advisory services and do not retain sufficient indicia of rights traditionally associated with individual ownership of the securities purchased for their accounts, the pool of nominally separate client accounts in the program may be an investment company. Whether a particular managed discretionary account program is an investment company depends upon the particular features of the program. MAAP II, as operated, fell within the statutory definition of an investment company.

Section 7(a) of the Investment Company Act provides that "[n]o investment company ... unless registered under Section 8, shall directly or indirectly—offer for sale, [or] sell ... any security...." MAAP II operated as an "investment company" as defined

---

1. The Commission recognizes that there are managed discretionary account programs which do not impermissibly pool the investments of their investors. In such instances, there is no common enterprise and, therefore, the programs are not issuing securities. Because they are not "issuers,"

under Section 3(a) of the Investment Company Act. It offered, sold or redeemed securities without registering as an investment company under Section 8 of the Investment Company Act. Accordingly, MAAP II violated Section 7(a) of the Act.

MAAP II met the "issuer" requirement of Section 3(a) because it issued investment contracts, a type of security,[3] to MAAP II clients. The Supreme Court has defined an investment contract to be: 1) an investment of money, 2) in a common enterprise, 3) with an expectation of profits to come solely from the efforts of a promoter or third party. *SEC v. W.J. Howey Co.*, 328 U.S. 293 (1946). The first element of the test is established because numerous persons placed money in MAAP II. The common enterprise element was met because investors' monies were pooled in the purchase of mutual funds. In addition, because advisory fees were based on a percentage of assets under management with CLS, gains in a MAAP II client's account would also result in a corresponding increase in advisory fees to CLS. The third element is established because MAAP II clients expected to gain profits solely through the efforts of CLS in choosing mutual funds consistent with MAAP II's six investment strategies. The profits earned by the MAAP II clients depended solely upon the expertise of CLS in determining which funds to purchase. Thus, MAAP II was issuing securities to MAAP II clients.

Under Section [3(a)(1)(A)], MAAP II operated as an investment company because it was engaged primarily in "the business of investing, reinvesting, or trading in securities." Assets invested in MAAP II were not earmarked for any purpose other than to invest in mutual funds according to the discretion of CLS. MAAP II also met the definition of "investment company" under Section 3(a)(3) because it owned investment securities having a value greater than 40 percent of the value of its total assets. In fact, because the only assets of MAAP II were mutual fund shares, the value of the investment securities owned by MAAP II was 100 percent of the value of its total assets.

MAAP II was an issuer of securities representing interests in a pool of securities. In addition, investors in MAAP II retained few indicia of rights in the mutual fund shares purchased by the program traditionally associated with individual ownership. As noted, because MAAP II was not registered with the Commission as an investment company and offered and sold interests in MAAP II without registration under the Investment Company Act, MAAP II violated Section 7(a) of the Act.

MAAP II was an issuer of securities representing interests in a pool of securities. In addition, investors in MAAP II retained few indicia of rights in the mutual fund shares purchased by the program traditionally associated with individual ownership. As noted,

---

these programs are also not investment companies under Section 3(a) of the Investment Company Act. Certain of these programs are popularly styled as "wrap-fee programs." ...

3. Section 2(a)(36) of the Investment Company Act defines a security to include an "investment contract." The definition of "security" under Section 2(1) of the Securities Act also includes an "investment contract." Under Section 2(a)(22) of the Investment Company Act, an issuer is "every person who issues or proposes to issue any security, or has outstanding any security which it has issued." Section 2(a)(28) of the Investment Company Act defines "person" as "a natural person or a company." Section 2(a)(8) defines "company" to include "a fund, or any organized group of persons whether incorporated or not,...."

because MAAP II was not registered with the Commission as an investment company and offered and sold interests in MAAP II without registration under the Investment Company Act, MAAP II violated Section 7(a) of the Act. [***]

* * *

As in *Prudential Insurance*, a good first step in understanding this proceeding is to clarify the three elements in the SEC's analysis: (1) who is the issuer? (2) what securities have been issued to investors? and (3) does the issuer invest in securities? Obviously, the SEC concluded that an investment company was present. What kinds of investor protection concerns does an unregistered investment company pose? In particular, what are the risks faced by investors in Clarke, Lanzen's program.

Figure 10D — Basic structure of wrap fee investment advisory program

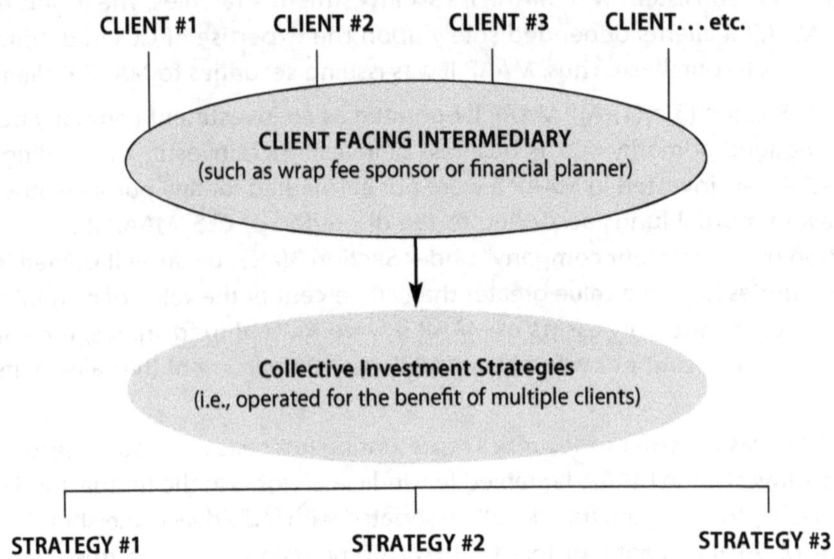

In the wake of this proceeding, the SEC moved to provide regulatory guidance to the industry regarding advisory programs designed to serve the needs of adviser's clients on a collective basis. These programs are known as wrap fee programs. There are different ways to structure wrap fee programs. However, Figure 10D provides a simple illustration of the basic features: many retail clients, one or more advisers serving the needs of the clients, and a sponsored program overseen by an adviser implementing a common strategy for many clients. After *Clarke, Lanzen*, sponsors understandably sought bright-lines to determine whether a particular wrap fee program could be deemed an investment company. In response, the SEC adopted a safe-harbor rule to clarify advisory arrangements that would not be deemed investment companies.

Status of Investment Advisory Programs under the Investment Company Act of 1940

Investment Company Act Release No. 22579 (1997)

[**Textbook Note:** *The following excerpt is from the adopting release promulgated by the SEC in connection with its adoption of a final rule under the Company Act, Rule 3a-4. The rule establishes a so-called non-exclusive safe harbor from the statutory definition of an investment company. As the release makes clear, no one is required to adhere to the terms of a non-exclusive safe harbor, but it provides bright-line assurances to parties that their arrangements will not be challenged as an informal investment company (i.e., that the arrangement is not subject to requirements found in the Company Act). The terms of the rule correlate directly with the concerns highlighted by the Commission in the* Clarke, Lanzen *order above. In some ways they are contextual bookends—*Clarke, Lanzen *shows the potential enforcement issue for those who fail to heed the terms of Section 3 in such retail arrangements, while Rule 3a-4 provides a regulatory blueprint for avoiding the issue in similar retail contexts. The rule's conditions are critical to structuring a program that avoids classification as an investment company.*]

[***] EXECUTIVE SUMMARY

The Commission is adopting rule 3a-4 under the Investment Company Act to provide a nonexclusive safe harbor from the definition of investment company for certain investment advisory programs. These programs typically are designed by investment advisers or other money managers seeking to provide the same or similar professional portfolio management services on a discretionary basis to a large number of advisory clients having relatively small amounts to invest. Under rule 3a-4, any investment advisory program organized and operated in accordance with the rule's provisions is deemed not to be an investment company within the meaning of the Investment Company Act. In addition, a preliminary note to rule 3a-4 states that there is no registration requirement under section 5 of the Securities Act of 1933 ("Securities Act") with respect to investment advisory programs that are organized and operated in compliance with the provisions of the rule.

The rule provides that: (i) each client's account must be managed on the basis of the client's financial situation and investment objectives, and in accordance with any reasonable restrictions imposed by the client on the management of the account; (ii) the sponsor of the program must obtain sufficient information from each client to be able to provide individualized investment advice to the client; (iii) the sponsor and portfolio manager must be reasonably available to consult with each client; (iv) each client must have the ability to impose reasonable restrictions on the management of the client's account; (v) each client must be provided with a quarterly account statement containing a description of all activity in the client's account; and (vi) each client must retain certain indicia of ownership of all securities and funds in the account. The rule is intended to be a nonexclusive safe harbor; a program that is not organized and operated in a manner consistent with the rule does not necessarily meet the Investment Company Act's definition of Investment Company....

I. BACKGROUND

In recent years, the number of investment advisory programs that are designed to provide professional portfolio management services on a discretionary basis to a large number of clients has increased greatly. These programs historically have been offered typically to clients who are investing amounts of money less than the minimum investments for individual accounts otherwise required by participating investment advisers, but significantly more than the minimum account sizes of most mutual funds.

These investment advisory programs typically are organized and administered by a sponsor, which provides, or arranges for the provision of, asset allocation advice and administrative services.[2] In some programs, the sponsor or its employees also provide portfolio management services, including the selection of particular securities, to the program's clients. In other programs, the sponsor selects, or provides advice to clients regarding the selection of, another investment adviser (which may or may not be affiliated with the sponsor) to act as the client's portfolio manager. In these programs, the sponsor generally is responsible for the ongoing monitoring of the management of the account by the manager or managers selected. The sponsor, rather than the portfolio manager, often serves as the primary contact for the client in connection with the program. Sponsors and portfolio managers usually meet the definition of "investment adviser" under the Investment Advisers Act of 1940 ("Advisers Act"), and may be required to register under that Act. Included among investment advisory programs developed in the recent past are those commonly referred to as "wrap fee programs." In a wrap fee program, the client typically is provided with portfolio management, execution of transactions, asset allocation, and administrative services for a single fee based on the size of the account. At year-end 1995, assets in wrap fee programs totaled approximately $101.6 billion, an increase of over 30 percent in one year.

Under wrap fee and other investment advisory programs, a client's account typically is managed on a discretionary basis in accordance with pre-selected investment objectives. Clients with similar investment objectives often receive the same investment advice and may hold the same or substantially the same securities in their accounts. In light of this similarity of management, some of these investment advisory programs may meet the definition of investment company under the Investment Company Act, and may be issuing securities for purposes of the Securities Act.

---

2. The sponsor often is a money management firm, a broker-dealer, a mutual fund adviser or, in some instances, a bank. See, e.g., Wall Street Preferred Money Managers, Inc. (pub. avail. Apr. 10, 1992) (broker-dealer); United Missouri Bank of Kansas City, n.a. (pub. avail. May 11, 1990, as modified Jan. 23, 1995) (bank); Strategic Advisers Inc. (pub. avail. Dec. 13, 1988) (mutual fund adviser). The sponsor or one of its affiliates also may execute some or all of the transactions for client accounts.

In 1980, the Commission sought to address certain issues presented by investment advisory programs by proposing rule 3a-4 under the Investment Company Act, which would have provided a safe harbor from the definition of investment company for investment advisory programs operating in the manner described in the rule....

II. DISCUSSION

The Commission is adopting rule 3a-4 under the Investment Company Act. Like the proposed and revised proposed rules, rule 3a-4 provides a nonexclusive safe harbor from the definition of Investment Company for investment advisory programs that are organized and operated in the manner described in the rule. The rule's provisions have the effect of ensuring that clients in a program relying on the rule receive individualized treatment, including the opportunity to place investment restrictions on the management of their accounts and the right to receive disclosure documents in connection with securities held in their accounts. Moreover, if an advisory program were operated by an investment adviser registered under the Advisers Act, clients of the program would receive the protections of that Act. The safe harbor thus is designed to provide an exemption for certain investment advisory programs without undermining the protection of investors who participate in those programs.

....

C. Provisions Designed to Ensure that Each Client Receives Individualized Treatment

Revised proposed rule 3a-4 contained four provisions relating to the individualized treatment received by clients in investment advisory programs covered by the rule....

1. Individualized Management of Client Accounts

Paragraph (a)(1) of the revised proposed rule provided that a client's account must be managed on the basis of the client's financial situation, investment objectives and instructions. The July Release noted that this provision was designed to delineate a key difference between clients of investment advisers and investors in investment companies. A client of an investment adviser typically is provided with individualized advice that is based on the client's financial situation and investment objectives. In contrast, the investment adviser of an investment company need not consider the individual needs of the company's shareholders when making investment decisions, and thus has no obligation to ensure that each security purchased for the company's portfolio is an appropriate investment for each shareholder.

2. Initial and Ongoing Client Contact

Paragraph (a) (2) of revised proposed rule 3a-4 reflects the view that providing individualized investment advice contemplates an adviser having sufficient contact with a client to elicit the information necessary to provide the advice. In particular, under paragraph (a)(2), a program relying on the rule must provide that the sponsor or a person designated by the sponsor ("designated person") contact and solicit information from the client. Such a program also must provide for the sponsor and the portfolio manager to be reasonably available to consult with the client concerning the management of the client's account.

Under paragraph (a)(2) of the revised proposed rule, an advisory program intended to qualify for the safe harbor set out in the rule would have needed to require that the sponsor or a designated person: (1) obtain information from the client concerning the client's financial situation and investment objectives (including any restrictions that the client may wish to impose regarding the management of the account) at the time the client opens the account; (2) contact the client at least annually to determine whether there have been any changes in the client's financial situation or investment objectives, or whether the client wishes to impose any reasonable restrictions on the management of the account or modify an existing restriction in a reasonable manner; and (3) notify the client in writing at least quarterly that the sponsor or designated person should be contacted if there have been any changes in the client's financial situation or investment objectives, or if the client wishes to impose or modify any restrictions on the management of the account....

3. Reasonable Management Restrictions

The ... ability of a client in an investment advisory program to place reasonable restrictions on the management of his or her account is a critical factor in determining whether individualized treatment is provided under the program. Paragraph (a)(3) of the revised proposed rule, therefore, would have provided that a program relying on the rule must include a requirement that each client have the ability to impose reasonable restrictions on the management of his or her account. Such restrictions were described to include, for example, prohibitions with respect to the purchase of particular securities or types of securities. This provision of the rule is being adopted as reproposed, except that language has been added to the provision to clarify that a program relying on rule 3a-4 need not provide clients with the right to direct the manager to purchase specific securities or types of securities.

As noted in the July Release, whether a particular restriction would be reasonable depends on an analysis of the relevant facts and circumstances. In general, a restriction would be unreasonable if it is clearly inconsistent with the portfolio manager's stated investment strategy or philosophy or the client's stated investment objective,[47] or is fundamentally inconsistent with the nature or operation of the program.[48] Other

---

47. ... The exclusion of individual stocks or stocks from a particular country, for example, would appear to be a reasonable restriction under ordinary facts and circumstances. A general restriction on the purchase of the securities of foreign issuers may be unreasonable, however, if the manager's investment strategy is to invest exclusively or primarily in foreign securities. Under those circumstances, it may be necessary for the client and the sponsor to reassess the choice of manager or the client's investment objective or strategy.

48. ... While rule 3a-4 generally contemplates that clients in mutual fund asset allocation programs should have the ability to exclude specific funds from their accounts, under some circumstances a restriction on the purchase of a fund included in the program may be inconsistent with the operation of the program. This could be the case, for example, when there is only a single fund with a specified investment objective available in the program, and that fund plays a necessary role in the overall investment strategy determined to be appropriate for the client. See *Benson White & Company, supra*

factors that bear on whether a particular restriction is reasonable are the difficulty in complying with the restriction,[49] the specificity of the restriction and the number of other restrictions imposed by the client.[50] A restriction would not be unreasonable, however, simply because it placed administrative burdens on the manager, or could affect the performance of the account.

4. Quarterly Account Statements

Paragraph (a) (4) of the revised proposed rule stated that each client in a program covered by the rule must be provided quarterly with a statement describing all activity in the client's account during the preceding quarter, including all transactions made on behalf of the account, all contributions and withdrawals made by the client, and all fees and expenses charged to the account. The Commission therefore is adopting this provision substantially as proposed, with one modification clarifying that statements may be sent more often than quarterly.

5. Minimum Account Size

The Commission has concluded that a particular account size is not a necessary element to ensure that clients are provided with individualized investment management services. The Commission recognizes, however, that the smaller the minimum account size of an investment advisory program, the more likely that clients would not have the ability to demand and receive individualized treatment in the program. In assessing the status under the Investment Company Act of a program that does not qualify for the safe harbor under rule 3a-4, therefore, the Commission will consider a relatively large minimum account size as evidence that individualized treatment is being provided to clients of the program. [***]

* * *

As the release explains, the adopted rule represented the SEC's second attempt over a period of many years to clarify which individualized investment advisory programs are not de facto investment companies (and by implication, those that might be). Rule 3a-4 has great practical significance in the brokerage and advisory industry regarding the structuring of wrap fee programs, arrangements used pervasively in structuring advisory client relationships. A primary focus of industry practice is to

---

note 12 [omitted] (program under which client assets are allocated among four mutual funds based upon the client's age need not give clients the opportunity to place restrictions on the purchase of any of the funds).

49. In the context of a mutual fund asset allocation program, for example, compliance with restrictions based on the securities held by a fund in which program assets are invested (i.e., a restriction that would require a manager to monitor the fund's portfolio securities) may be so burdensome as to be unreasonable.

50. The restrictions that a client seeks to impose on his or her account could be unreasonable when considered in the aggregate, even though each restriction may be reasonable when considered separately, or if the client alters them or imposes new restrictions with excessive frequency. Paragraph (a)(2)(iii) of the rule, which contemplates that a sponsor notify each client at least quarterly to contact the sponsor if the client wishes to modify restrictions concerning the management of the account, is not intended to imply that it necessarily would be reasonable for a client to change his or her investment restrictions on a quarterly basis.

ensure satisfaction of the safe harbor rule's four critical conditions. Which condition do you think imposes the greatest difficulty for advisers in seeking to satisfy the safe harbor's conditions? The failure of an investment advisory program to meet the safe harbor's conditions does not automatically mean that the program is an investment company, but at the very least, the sponsor is on notice that the SEC is likely to raise questions regarding the status of such a program under the Company Act.

10.4 Section 3(c) Exclusions

Section 3(c) contains a number of exclusions from the definition of investment company, most of which are important in understanding why a number of investment entities are not treated as investment companies. Section 3(c) exclusions are different in this respect from the primary Section 3(b) exclusions. While Section 3(b) is intended to exclude companies that are not primarily investment businesses (and their subsidiaries) from the definition of investment company, Section 3(c) is designed to exclude from the definition of investment company entities that are manifestly investment oriented businesses that regularly engage in securities transactions because the particular type of investment business (i) does not raise the same type of regulatory concerns characteristic of investment companies marketed to public investors; or (ii) is subject to other kinds of regulatory schemes.

Although the thirteen enumerated categories involve investment funds or businesses that significantly engage in trading and holding securities, they are also subject to substantial forms of alternative regulation, most notably banks and insurance companies (Section 3(c)(3)), broker-dealers (Section 3(c)(2)), and eligible pension funds (Section 3(c)(11)). Congress also excluded charitable endowments (Section 3(c)(10)) and retirement plans for religious orders (Section 3(c)(14)), because these investment vehicles are not representative of the kinds of issues to which the Company Act is directed. In addition, investment products that are typically associated with banks such as common trust funds (Section 3(c)(3)) and collective trusts (Section 3(c)(11)) are excluded from the Company Act's definition of an investment company, because those products were seen as different from the kinds of investment arrangements that gave rise to the concerns motivating the Company Act and operated within the confines of banking. In addition, the exclusions also address specialized finance arrangements involving lending, factoring or real estate finance arrangements (Sections 3(c)(4), (5), and (6)); oil and gas properties holding arrangements (Section 3(c)(9)), and voting trusts (Section 3(c)(12)). Again, the Company Act is not regarded as providing an appropriate regulatory framework for these specialized investment arrangements, at least as long as such specialized arrangements remained separate and distinct from retail-oriented investment arrangements. This textbook does not attempt to explore these specialized categorical exclusions. However, there is an important remaining category of exclusions that have immense significance for the investment management industry because of their outsized influence in money management circles and close interconnection and overlap with advisory issues affecting registered investment companies—the exclusions for private investment companies.

Private investment companies are investment companies formed in reliance on the exclusions found in Section 3(c)(1) and, even more importantly, Section 3(c)(7). Today, these exclusions are regularly used by practitioners to create investment vehicles free of the restrictions of the Company Act relating to fees, governance and capital structure that would largely curb the customary business operations of private funds. As discussed in Chapter 9, these arrangements instead are regulated in terms of the activities of the managers who, if sufficiently large, are subject to registration as investment advisers under amendments to the Advisers Act as part of the Dodd-Frank Act of 2010.

10.4.1 Private Funds (1): Section 3(c)(1)—Funds with Limited Number of Investors

One of the private fund exclusions under the Company Act, and indeed one that dates to enactment of the Company Act, concerns investment vehicles who have not made a public offering of securities and whose securities are owned by 100 or fewer investors. The original basis for Section 3(c)(1) was to permit formation of investment clubs which in a bygone era were viewed as benign arrangements. Section 3(c)(1), however, proved to be sufficiently elastic to enable new types of pooled investment vehicles in the form of hedge funds and other forms of private investment funds. This exclusion became increasingly important as a means of organizing large investment vehicles while remaining outside the purview of the Company Act. However, as a result, until 1996, hedge funds could have no more than 100 investors.

The strict 100 investor limit, although objective in nature, has posed two challenges in practice. The first issue concerns how to compute the number of beneficial owners and specifically whether to look through business entities that were beneficial owners of the private 3(c)(1) fund and count only the direct owners of each of those shareholding entities toward the 100 investor threshold. The so-called "look-through" issue is easily illustrated. Consider a private fund Alpha that has 79 investors consisting of 78 natural persons and one business entity, Beta, that itself has 90 investors. This situation is illustrated in Figure 10E.

Figure 10 E—The Look-Through Provision of Section 3(c)(1)

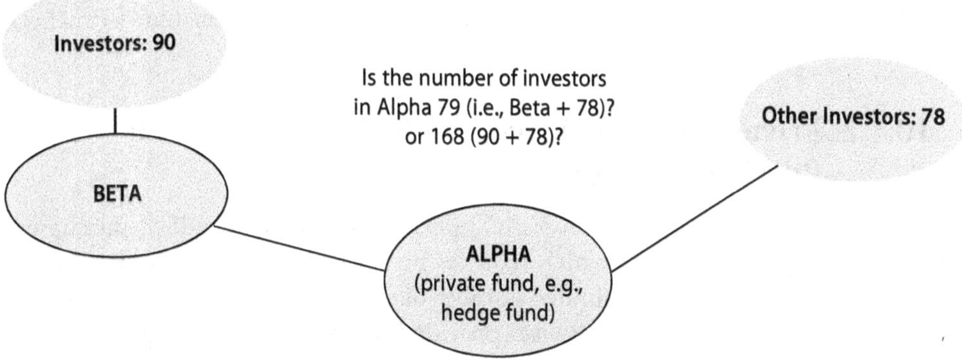

An obvious question posed by this situation is whether the private fund Alpha has 79 investors (if we count only direct shareholders) or 168 investors (the 78 natural persons plus the 90 beneficial owners of Beta)? The statutory provision was amended in 1996 to make clear how the look through issue should be analyzed. Under the statute as amended, the answer turns on the size of Beta's ownership and Beta's character as a business entity. Beta's shareholders are counted only if two conditions are satisfied: (1) the entity beneficial owner owns 10% or more of the 3(c)(1) private fund; *and* (2) the 10% holder must itself be a private investment company under either Section 3(c)(1) or (c)(7). In our example, Beta's beneficial shareholders would be disregarded for purposes of computing Alpha's beneficial owner if either Beta owns less than 10% of Alpha or Beta is not a private investment company. Thus, for example, if Beta were a hedge fund (organized as a Section 3(c)(1) private fund) and owned 20% of Alpha, Beta's shareholders would be counted towards Alpha's shareholders for purposes of Section 3(c)(1). The two "look-through" conditions make intuitive sense. Essentially, the statute precludes circumvention of the 100 person shareholder limit by means of pyramiding ownership stakes of other private investment companies in a single private fund. In all other circumstances, the statute disregards the beneficial owners of direct shareholders.

The other potential circumvention issue inherent in Section 3(c)(1) is addressed by integration concepts under the Company Act. Under this circumvention strategy, a sponsor might create multiple private funds of 99 investors, all with the same investment strategy. Regulators engrafted a concept analogous to integration of private offerings under the Securities Act to sort out this issue, namely whether multiple 3(c)(1) funds are in fact distinct from one another or whether the funds should be integrated for determining compliance with the 100 beneficial owner limit. If integrated, the 3(c)(1) funds likely will violate the beneficial owner limit because the number of beneficial owners will be aggregated across funds. Although the SEC has brought at least one administrative action involving parallel 3(c)(1) funds with a common investment adviser and in aggregate more than 100 beneficial owners (*Gerald Klein & Associates*, Investment Company Act Release No. 26986 (2005)), this issue is of less importance today. In 1996, Congress enacted a new exclusion to the definition of an investment company which is not tied to the number of investors but rather the type of investor—namely, "qualified purchasers." As a result, sponsors of private funds who might have been constrained by the 100 beneficial owner limit have other means for qualifying for an exclusion, unrelated to the number of the fund's beneficial owners.

10.4.2 Private Funds (2): Section 3(c)(7)—Qualified Purchaser Funds

The exclusion found in Section 3(c)(7) permits so-called "qualified purchaser" funds. Unlike Section 3(c)(1) which requires no more than 100 investors, 3(c)(7) funds in theory may have an unlimited number of investors (although other unrelated legal limitations may dictate otherwise) provided the investors are all qualified purchasers. Qualified purchaser is a defined term under the Company Act (and supplemented by rules thereunder) and generally means investors (either natural persons or companies) with investments of not less than $5 million as well as other trusts or investment professionals that meet analogous requirements. However, like Section 3(c)(1), Section 3(c)(7) funds cannot make a public offering to investors. Rather than focusing on the number of investors, the Section 3(c)(7) creates an exclusion for fund vehicles limited to either wealthy or institutional participants. Moreover, unlike 3(c)(1), Section 3(c)(7) does not entail the same kind of look-through or integration concerns. Indeed Section 3(c)(7) funds are subject to an express anti-integration provision with a similar 3(c)(1) fund managed by the same sponsor.

For major players in the hedge fund, private equity and venture capital space, Section 3(c)(7) offers much greater practical latitude in structuring such funds, especially for larger funds that typically solicit large institutional investors. The strict investor limit in 3(c)(1) funds artificially constrained the size of hedge funds and other private funds. In contrast, Section 3(c)(7) greatly expands the number of investors who may participate in a fund, provided the investors meet the relevant qualification standard. Congress determined that a high qualification standard for investors seemed to provide an appropriate trade-off to obtain relief from the artificial 100 investor cap. Clearly facts have borne out the benefits of the trade-off for private funds. Not only have Section 3(c)(7) funds proliferated, but clearly 3(c)(7) funds predominate in assets under management among private funds.

The other defining feature for private investment funds is that they are not permitted to make public offerings. In other words, such funds can only offer securities by means of an exempt offering. Invariably, fund sponsors rely on the Rule 506 offering exemption of Regulation D under the Securities Act. Following the Jumpstart Our Business Start-ups (JOBS) Act of 2012, Rule 506 was sub-divided into two exemptions. Rule 506(b) is the old exemption and applies to sales to not more than 35 non-accredited investors who meet the rule's sophistication requirement and Regulation D's general solicitation prohibition. Rule 506(c) permits sales to verified accredited investors by means of general solicitations and therefore potentially eases the offering process for fund sponsors who choose to avail themselves of the exemption.

10.5 Classification of Investment Companies: Company Act Sections 4 and 5

The chapter's preceding sections dealt with the definition of an investment company. There is a related, but distinct, aspect of the statute's treatment of investment companies. Essentially it classifies investment companies into two basic categories and then again into two subsidiary categories. The two basic categories are unit investment trusts ("UITs") and management companies (Section 4 of the Company Act). UITs have portfolios whose composition is fixed. Because such a structure lacks the need for a dedicated governance function, UITs do not have a governing boards.

Management companies are defined as any investment company other than a unit investment trust or face-amount certificate company (a rare bird in the investment management world that will be passed over). Management companies, unlike unit investment trusts, are investment companies that have governing boards. Under Section 5 of the Investment Company Act, investment companies are divided into two categories: open-end and closed-end. Open-end management companies are better known in common parlance as mutual funds. The key difference between an open-end and closed-end investment company is that the former issues redeemable securities (meaning that the investment company must redeem shares at each share's net asset value upon request from the shareholder) while closed-end funds do not. This distinction also explains the naming convention; by issuing redeemable securities, the number of shares outstanding is subject to daily variation (i.e., open-ended), while in a closed-end fund, equity capital is committed, at least for some period of time. Since closed-end fund shares are not redeemable as of right by shareholders, shareholders achieve liquidity for their investments by trading shares on a stock exchange at prices that most frequently are at a discount to net asset value (but can sometimes be at a premium). Mutual funds shares do not trade on secondary markets, although there have been some recent rumblings in that direction which are taken up in Chapter 18.

Section 5 also classifies management companies as diversified or non-diversified. The Company Act's legal diversification standard is not the same as a strict standard of economic diversification, but the practical effect of the requirement is to require greater diversification of securities portfolio holdings of investment companies denominated as diversified, even if the technical requirements do not always insure such a result.

Chapter 11

Organization and the Governance of Investment Companies

Key Ideas: Although some aspects of an investment company's organization as an entity are controlled by the Company Act, investment companies, like all business entities, are creatures of state law. State law is the source of law in forming business entities used in organizing funds, including the basic features of governance. The choice of entity is left up to the sponsor, but a recent industry survey showed that 90% of all funds are in one of three business entity types: a Massachusetts common law business trust, a Delaware statutory trust, or a Maryland corporation (with its special provisions for registered investment companies). In addition, although funds can be organized as stand-alone entities (i.e., the fund is the entity and the entity is a fund), it is far more common today for funds to be organized as one of several distinct series within a single series entity, such as a trust (e.g., a single trust may house many different funds, each of whose assets and liabilities are separate and distinct from other funds). The role of shareholders is essential for some matters, but shareholder votes are needed only occasionally and indeed years can pass between shareholder votes. At the federal level, the Company Act prescribes certain structural governance requirements, but for the most part, these formal requirements are modest in nature: funds other than UITs must have a governing board and shareholders must elect the board with some exceptions in filling vacancies. If there is a conflict between federal and state law governance requirements, then federal law preempts state law. Conversely, however, in the absence of a conflict with the Company Act, state entity law controls. Federal regulation, however, imposes significant affirmative responsibilities on boards over and above fiduciary duties that also exist pursuant to state law, and these enumerated augmented duties on independent directors will be discussed in subsequent chapters. In addition, the Company Act imposes requirements regarding board independence. Depending on the circumstances, a certain percentage of directors or trustees must be independent (or alternatively, "non-interested" or "disinterested"), which is governed by detailed statutory definitions. For some situations and types of funds, the SEC has, with some success, pushed to raise the threshold well above a majority of directors (and augmented independence in fund governance in other ways), but has also encountered challenges to its efforts.

Chapter Contents

11.1 Introduction

Much of the attention of the business participants in setting up investment companies is on activities like developing fund investment strategies, preparing an offering strategy to secure assets, and setting up service provider arrangements. However, lawyers initially focus on the mechanical issues of establishing an operating legal infrastructure for the fund, which means focusing on creating an entity to house the fund and the processes and resources to govern it. In the first instance, the legal mechanics of governance are discussed, including entity selection, the role of shareholders and establishing a board. These issues are closely tied to the fundamental role of state law in organizing investment companies and the potential for tension between state law and federal law governance requirements. Aside from the legal mechanics, there is the role of the board in governance and the special role carved out by the statute and the SEC for independent directors. Determining independence can be deceptively challenging: A person's status as independent is governed by statutorily defined terms regarding interested persons (Section 2(a)(19), affiliated persons (Section 2(a)(3), and control (Section 2(a)(9)). Not only do independent directors serve in the customary capacity of directors bound by state law fiduciary obligations to the fund and its shareholders, but they also discharge enumerated responsibilities under the Company Act and the rules thereunder. Most managed funds are externally managed, meaning that the adviser's relationship is contractual. For those funds especially, independent directors exercise an integral role in overseeing the contractual relationships and outside service providers. The SEC has sought to use its rulemaking powers to increase the independence of fund boards in terms of composition and process. These efforts have met with some, but not uncontested, success. Developments in this area have raised policy issues both in terms of the SEC's legal authority, but also in practical terms regarding the ultimate effect enhanced board independence has had for fund shareholders. This chapter begins with the legal mechanics of fund organizational form and then turns to the issue of board independence in overseeing the fund's activities.

11.2 Choice of Entity and Other Entity Formalities

Investment companies are formed according to one of two basic models: (i) a sponsor for the first time seeks to organize one or more funds (the new entrant model) or (ii) a sponsor seeks to sponsor additional funds within an existing family of funds (the existing entrant model). The existing entrant model is probably responsible for the creation of more funds year in and year out. However, the new entrant model is useful as a starting process to understand the fund formation. Typically, working with the client sponsor, a securities attorney will have already discerned that the client seeks to offer an investment vehicle to the public that involves a securities-based investment strategy. A number of legal and business considerations go into the creation of a fund to provide this investment strategy to prospective investors. Generally, the client sponsor will have already decided where in the fund space it seeks to operate, either as a mutual fund, an ETF, or some other type of fund offering. Necessary legal considerations include entity selection and formation, board member selection, registration and disclosure documents preparation, contract negotiations, and development of compliance programs. On the business side, the sponsor must consider distribution strategies, third party vendor arrangements, and marketing plans. Once again, within an existing fund family, these issues and relationships have already been worked out, thereby substantially simplifying the process of forming a new fund.

The most basic legal issue for a fund is entity selection. Although a fund's operations are heavily regulated under federal law (e.g., the Company Act), the fund as an entity is a creature of state entity law. If the fund is organized as a stand-alone vehicle, then the fund is the entity and the entity is the fund. The stand-alone configuration represents the historically accepted means of organizing a fund as pictured in Figure 11A. Funds look to state law for traditional forms of limited liability vehicles and

Figure 11A — Stand-alone externally managed mutual fund

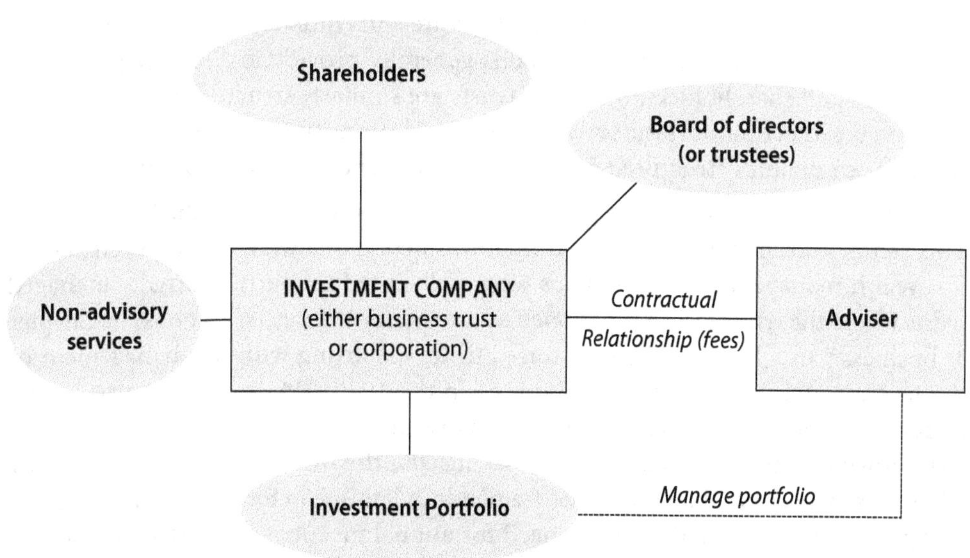

principles insulating directors and trustees from personal liability. While there are numerous organizational forms available for creation of investment companies, the industry tends to focus on just a handful—Massachusetts common law business trusts, Delaware statutory business trusts, and Maryland corporations.

This remarkable consensus as to entity type and jurisdiction stems from a relatively limited number of business planning considerations affecting choice of entity and organizational jurisdiction. The two most important considerations are the ability to minimize shareholder meetings (and dispense with annual director elections) and minimizing franchise taxes incurred in issuing and redeeming shares. Business and statutory trusts, as well as Maryland investment company corporations, meet these objectives.

Somewhat less obvious is the lack of interest in other forms of limited liability vehicles. Part of the reason may be historical. The fund industry was established before the advent of limited partnerships or limited liability partnership cousins thereof, and well before limited liability companies. Such vehicles are common for hedge funds and other types of private funds where considerations of tax and customized organizational features favor use of such vehicles. Limited partnerships or LLCs provide no apparent tax advantages for registered investment companies because special tax provisions (Subchapter M of the Internal Revenue Code) afford RICs the benefits of pass-through treatment. In addition, the Company Act's requirements regarding governance by a board of directors or trustees makes partnerships and LLCs unnecessarily cumbersome.

When organized as a business trust, an investment company is established and governed by a declaration of trust and, occasionally, by-laws. Legal title to the trust's assets is held by the trustees. The ownership interests or beneficial interest in the trust is divided into units often called shares of beneficial interest. These shares are transferable and proportionate interests in the trust. Beneficiaries of a trust for these purposes are typically called investors or shareholders. In Massachusetts, a pattern of common law recognition of the trust structure and enforcement of the declaration of trust provisions arose. Such provisions generally provide for liability protection of trustees and shareholders. Statutory trusts are similarly structured, including the additional protection of statutory provisions and protections regarding liability. Investment companies structured as business trusts function like corporations.

As noted, business trusts are perhaps the most common legal vehicles for funds. This stems from historical reasons in that business trusts were a recognized vehicle for wealth management and perhaps were well suited for early internally managed trusts where the trustees also functioned as the money managers. As noted in Chapter 3, business trusts have a long and storied history, starting with the management of the first mutual funds formed in the U.S. in the 1920s. Massachusetts was long a leader in business trusts at common law, but over the past 20 years, Delaware adopted a statutory business trust code. In Massachusetts, the business trust is functionally a business association that is afforded tremendous latitude in formulating its structure and governance. Hence there is no need for annual meetings by trust shareholders. This feature is carried over in Delaware statutory trust law.

Figure 11B — Externally managed series trust with multiple funds

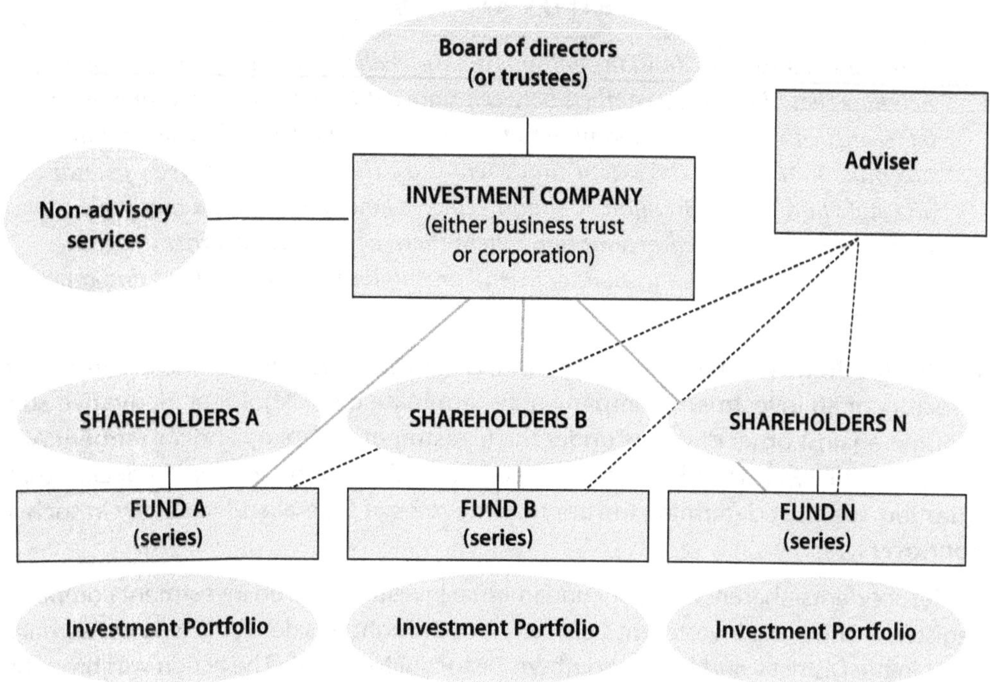

In addition, and more characteristic of contemporary business planning strategies, all three entity choices permit organization in series form. The series structure allows a single business entity to house many funds and each fund represents a different series in the entity (trust or corporation). In theory, a single trust could have an unlimited number of funds, and it is not unheard of for some trusts to have more than a dozen funds. The assets and liabilities of each series of the trust are segregated from other series in the trust and, of course, since the individual series within the trust are publicly offered, the shareholders of each series are invariably distinct from shareholders in the other series. For purposes of the Company Act, the trust is a registered investment company as is each series in the trust. This organizational configuration is illustrated in Figure 11B and differs from the stand-alone configuration in that the trust's shareholders collectively comprise shareholders of each series in aggregate and so each fund's shareholders are a subset of the trust's aggregate shareholders.

11.3 The Relationship between the Investment Company Act and State Entity Law

While investment companies are generally structured as business trusts or corporations under state law, their activities are directly governed by a federal statute, the Company Act. While direct conflicts between federal and state law must, under the U.S. Constitution, be resolved in accordance with federal law, it is less clear in other cases where state law does not directly conflict with the Company Act.

Burks v. Lasker

441 U.S. 471 (1979)

[**Textbook Note:** *This decision confronts a basic challenge posed by the Company Act: how should potential conflicts between state entity governance requirements be reconciled with the Company Act's federal law mandates? While federal law preempts state law to the extent that there is a direct conflict between federal and state law, Justice Brennan's opinion explores how courts should analyze potential issues of implied preemption where there is no direct conflict. In doing so, it illuminates the implications of federal preemption doctrine in the Company Act context.*]

Mr. Justice Brennan. The question presented in this case is whether the disinterested directors of an investment company may terminate a stockholders' derivative suit brought against other directors under the Investment Company and Investment Advisers Acts of 1940, 15 U.S.C. § 80a-1 *et seq.;* 15 U.S.C. § 80b-1 *et seq.* To decide that question, we must determine the appropriate roles of federal and state law in such a controversy.

Respondents, shareholders, of Fundamental Investors, Inc., an investment company registered under the Investment Company Act, brought this derivative suit in February 1973 in the District Court for the Southern District of New York. The action was brought against several members of the company's board of directors and its registered investment adviser, Anchor Corp. The complaint alleged that the defendants had violated their duties under the Investment Company Act (ICA), the Investment Advisers Act (IAA), and the common law in connection with the 1969 purchase by the corporation of $20 million in Penn Central Transportation Co. commercial paper.[3] In response to the suit, Fundamental's board of directors determined that the five of its members who were neither affiliated with the investment adviser [4] nor defendants in the action would decide what position the company should take in the case. On the basis of outside counsel's recommendation and their own investigation, the five, acting as a quorum pursuant to the company's bylaws, concluded that continuation of the litigation

---

3. The complaint alleged, *inter alia*, that "Anchor breached its statutory, contractual and common law fiduciary duties by relying exclusively upon the representations of Goldman, Sachs & Co. (a seller of commercial paper), rather than independently investigating the quality and safety of the Penn Central 270-day notes purchased by the Fund. It is further alleged that the defendant directors knew or should have known of Anchor's failure to meet its responsibility; that they violated their ... duties ... by as corporate fiduciaries acquiescing in Anchor's omissions; that the financial condition of the Penn Central steadily worsened during the period from November 28, 1969 to June 21, 1970, the date that it filed for reorganization; and that during this period of decline all of the defendants failed to investigate and review the financial condition of the Penn Central and the quality and safety of its commercial paper." 426 F.Supp. 844, 847 (SDNY1977).

4. The five were "disinterested" within the meaning of the ICA.... Of the remaining six directors, five were defendants in the suit, and one was a director of the investment adviser. 404 F.Supp. 1172, 1175 (1975).

was contrary to the best interests of the company and its shareholders and moved the District Court to dismiss the action.

I

A fundamental issue in this case is which law—state or federal—governs the power of the corporation's disinterested directors to terminate this derivative suit. The first step in making that determination is to ascertain which law creates the cause of action alleged by the plaintiffs. Neither the ICA nor the IAA—the plaintiff's two federal claims—expressly creates a private cause of action for violation of the sections relevant here.... [W]e shall assume without deciding that respondents have implied, derivative causes of action under the ICA and IAA.

II

The fact that "the scope of [respondents'] federal right is, of course, a federal question" does not, however, make state law irrelevant. It is true that in certain areas we have held that federal statutes authorize the federal courts to fashion a complete body of federal law. Corporation law, however, is not such an area.

A derivative suit is brought by shareholders to enforce a claim on behalf of the corporation. See Note, *The Demand and Standing Requirements in Stockholder Derivative Actions*, 44 U.Chi.L.Rev. 168 (1976). This case involves the question whether directors are authorized to determine that certain claims not be pursued on the corporation's behalf. As we have said in the past, the first place one must look to determine the powers of corporate directors is in the relevant State's corporation law. "Corporations are creatures of state law," *ibid.,* and it is state law which is the font of corporate directors' powers. By contrast, federal law in this area is largely regulatory and prohibitory in nature—it often limits the exercise of directorial power, but only rarely creates it. In short, in this field congressional legislation is generally enacted against the background of existing state law; Congress has never indicated that the entire corpus of state corporation law is to be replaced simply because a plaintiff's cause of action is based upon a federal statute.

Federal regulation of investment companies and advisers is not fundamentally different in this respect. Mutual funds, like other corporations, are incorporated pursuant to state, not federal, law. Although the Court of Appeals found it significant that "nothing in ... the legislation regulating investment companies and their advisers ... suggests that ... disinterested directors ... have the power to terminate litigation brought by mutual fund stockholders...," 567 F.2d, at 1210, such silence was to be expected. The ICA does not purport to be the source of authority for managerial power; rather, the Act functions primarily to "impos[e] *controls and restrictions* on the internal management of investment companies."

The ICA and IAA, therefore, do not require that federal law displace state laws governing the powers of directors unless the state laws permit action prohibited by the Acts, or unless "their application would be inconsistent with the federal policy underlying the cause of action...." Although "[a] state statute cannot be considered 'inconsistent' with federal law merely because the statute causes the plaintiff to lose the litigation," *Robertson v. Wegmann,* [436 U.S. 584 (1978),] *supra,* at 593, federal courts must be ever vigilant to insure that application of state law poses "no significant threat to any identifiable federal policy or interest...." ...

III

The foregoing indicates that the threshold inquiry for a federal court in this case should have been to determine whether state law permitted Fundamental's disinterested directors to terminate respondents' suit. If so, the next inquiry should have been whether such a state rule was consistent with the policy of the ICA and IAA. Neither the District Court nor the Court of Appeals decided the first question, apparently because neither considered state law particularly significant in determining the authority of the independent directors to terminate the action. And in that circumstance, neither court addressed the question of inconsistency between state and federal law. At least implicitly, however, the Court of Appeals did make a related determination. Its holding that nonfrivolous derivative suits may never be terminated makes manifest its view that no other rule—whether state or federal—would be consistent with the ICA. We disagree.

... A mutual fund is a pool of assets, consisting primarily of portfolio securities, and belonging to the individual investors holding shares in the fund. *Tannenbaum v. Zeller,* 552 F.2d 402, 405 (CA2 1977). Congress was concerned because

> "[m]utual funds, with rare exception, are not operated by their own employees. Most funds are formed, sold, and managed by external organizations, [called 'investment advisers,'] that are separately owned and operated.... The advisers select the funds' investments and operate their businesses.... Since a typical fund is organized by its investment adviser which provides it with almost all management services..., a mutual fund cannot, as a practical matter sever its relationship with the adviser. Therefore, the forces of arm's-length bargaining do not work in the mutual fund industry in the same manner as they do in other sectors of the American economy."

S.Rep.No. 91-184, p. 5 (1969); U.S.Code Cong. & Admin.News 1910, pp. 4897, 4901.

As a consequence, "[t]he relationship between investment advisers and mutual funds is fraught with potential conflicts of interest," *Galfand v. Chestnutt Corp.,* 545 F.2d 807, 808 (CA2 1976). See generally S.Rep.No. 91-184, *supra,* at 5; H.R.Rep.No. 2337, 89th Cong., 2d Sess., 9, 45–46, 64 (1966); H.R.Doc.No. 136, 77th Cong., 1st Sess., 2485–2490, 2569, 2579–2580, 2775 (1942); Hearings before a Subcommittee of the House Committee on Interstate and Foreign Commerce on H.R. 10065, 76th Cong., 3d Sess., 58–59 (1940); Securities and Exchange Commission, Report on Investment Trusts and Investment Companies, pt. 3, pp. 1–49 (1940); 15 U.S.C. § 80a-1(b) (findings and declaration of policy). Yet, while these potential conflicts may justify some restraints upon the unfettered discretion of even disinterested mutual fund directors, particularly in their transactions with the investment adviser, \\lthey hardly justify a flat rule that directors may never terminate non-frivolous derivative actions involving co-directors. In fact, the evidence is overwhelming that Congress did not intend to require any such absolute rule.

The cornerstone of the ICA's effort to control conflicts of interest within mutual funds is the requirement that at least 40% of a fund's board be composed of independent outside directors. 15 U.S.C. § 80a-10(a). As originally enacted § 10 of the Act required that these 40% not be officers or employees of the company or "affiliated persons" of its adviser. 54 Stat. 806. In 1970, Congress amended the Act to strengthen further the independence of these directors adding the stricter requirement that the outside directors not be "interested persons." See 15 U.S.C. §§ 80a-10(a), 80a-2(a)(19). To these statutorily disinterested directors, the Act assigns a host of special responsibilities involving supervision of management and financial auditing. They have the duty to review and approve the contracts of the investment adviser and the principal underwriter, 15 U.S.C. § 80a-15(c); the responsibility to appoint other disinterested directors to fill vacancies resulting from the assignment of the advisory contracts, 15 U.S.C. § 80a-16(b), and are required to select the accountants who prepare the company's Securities and Exchange Commission financial filings, 15 U.S.C. § 80a-31(a).

Attention must be paid as well to what Congress did *not* do. Congress consciously chose to address the conflict-of-interest problem through the Act's independent-directors section, rather than through more drastic remedies such as complete disaffiliation of the companies from their advisors or compulsory internalization of the management function. See Report of the SEC on the Public Policy Implications of Investment Company Growth, H.R. Rep. No. 2337, 89th Cong., 2d Sess., 147–148 (1966). Congress also decided *not* to incorporate into the 1940 Act a provision, proposed by the SEC, that would have forced investment companies to seek court approval before settling claims against "insiders" that could be the target of derivative suits. See S. 3580, 76th Cong., 3d Sess. § 33(a) (1940); *Wolf v. Barkes,* 348 F.2d 994, 997 n. 4 (CA2 1965). And when Congress did intend to prevent board action from cutting off derivative suits, it said so expressly. Section 36(b), 84 Stat. 1428, 15 U.S.C. § 80a-35(b)(2), added to the Act in 1970, performs precisely this function for derivative suits charging breach of fiduciary duty with respect to adviser's fees. No similar provision exists for derivative suits of the kind involved in this case.

Congress' purpose in structuring the Act as it did is clear. It "was designed to place the unaffiliated directors in the role of 'independent watchdogs,' " *Tannenbaum v. Zeller,* 552 F.2d, at 406, who would "furnish an independent check upon the management" of investment companies, Hearings on H.R. 10065 before a Subcommittee of the House Committee on Interstate and Foreign Commerce, 76th Cong., 3d Sess., 109 (1940). This "watchdog" control was chosen in preference to the more direct controls on behavior exemplified by the options not adopted. Indeed, when by 1970 it appeared that the "affiliated person" provision of the 1940 Act might not be adequately restraining conflicts of interest, Congress turned not to direct controls, but rather to stiffening the requirement of independence as the way to "remedy the act's deficiencies." S.Rep.No. 91-184, pp. 32-33 (1969); U.S.Code Cong. & Admin.News 1970, p. 4927. Without question, "[t]he function of these provisions with respect to unaffiliated directors [was] to supply an independent check on management and to provide a means for the representation of shareholder interests in investment company affairs." *Id.,* at 32; U.S.Code Cong. & Admin. News 1970, p. 4927.

In short, the structure and purpose of the ICA indicate that Congress entrusted to the independent directors of investment companies, exercising the authority granted to them by state law, the primary responsibility for looking after the interests of the funds' shareholders. There may well be situations in which the independent directors could reasonably believe that the best interests of the shareholders call for a decision not to sue—as, for example, where the costs of litigation to the corporation outweigh any potential recovery. See Note, 47 Ford.L.Rev. 568, 580 (1979); Note, 44 U.Chi.L.Rev., at 196. See, *e. g., Tannenbaum v. Zeller, supra,* at 418; *Cramer v. General Tel. & Electronics Corp.,* 582 F.2d 259, 275 (CA3 1978). In such cases, it would certainly be consistent with the Act to allow the independent directors to terminate a suit, even though not frivolous. Indeed, it would have been paradoxical for Congress to have been willing to rely largely upon "watchdogs" to protect shareholder interests and yet, where the "watchdogs" have done precisely that, require that they be totally muzzled.

IV

We hold today that federal courts should apply state law governing the authority of independent directors to discontinue derivative suits to the extent such law is consistent with the policies of the ICA and IAA. [***]

* * *

Notes and Applications

1. *Shareholder meetings.* The analysis in *Burks* carries beyond derivative actions. Prior to 1986, funds often held annual shareholder meetings on the theory that such a requirement was implicit in the Company Act. In that year, however, the staff reached a different interpretive position in *John Nuveen & Co., Inc.*, SEC No-Action Letter (Nov. 18, 1986). Company Act Section 16(a) imposes no condition with respect to annual shareholder meetings and, indeed, its construction supports a different inference by suggesting that an election of directors by shareholders is a requirement only under certain circumstances. Thus, the staff reasoned that the issue was controlled entirely by state law (or, by extension, the entity's own organizational documents in the absence of a specific statutory mandate) since federal law did not impose an express conflicting requirement. Business trusts are not required to hold annual shareholders meetings for the election of directors, and the same is true for corporations that are investment companies in several states. As a result, annual meetings are rarely, if ever, required for mutual funds or ETFs organized as mutual funds. Should investment companies have annual shareholder meetings or are fund sponsors correct in arguing that such meetings are an unnecessary expense?

Notwithstanding the absence of requirements relating to annual shareholder meetings in the Company Act, the Act contains other provisions where a need for a shareholder meeting (i.e., a shareholder vote) may be triggered, for example, to approve certain actions for the fund or, in certain circumstances, to elect new members to the board. In other cases, federal law requirements expressly pre-empt state law. For example, other than with respect to the application of fraud prohibitions or notice requirements, state law securities disclosure and offerings requirements for registered investment companies and their securities are expressly pre-empted pursuant to Securities Act Section 18(a)(2) which pre-empts state law securities requirements relating to issuers of covered securities.

2. *Derivative actions.* Derivative actions, that is actions brought by individual shareholders in the name of business entity for injuries to the entity, have significance beyond their implications for preemption analysis under the Company Act. Derivative actions are a judicial mechanism whereby shareholders seek to wrest control over the litigation of claims by an entity's board to vindicate the rights of the entity and indirectly shareholders. In the fund context, most derivative claims involve putative misconduct of the investment adviser or its affiliates. State law is uniformly deferential to the board's authority to control the prosecution of derivative actions as evidenced by the demand requirement which requires that the plaintiff shareholder must first seek the permission of the board to bring such an action. Typically, the board will reject the demand and either prosecute the action itself or, as is more likely, abandon it usually after determining that the merits of the claim are doubtful. Although the plaintiff may seek to by-pass the demand requirement under a well-recognized futility exception, the exception's application is not frequently sustained. In most cases, the independent directors of a fund are well-positioned to withstand challenges to their authority to control litigation on behalf of the fund. Thus, strict state law standards on derivative actions frequently have the effect of foreclosing a potential class of claims against investment advisers which has led some commentators to argue that derivative actions are not a terribly effective check on the conduct of fund boards. *See* Donald C. Langevoort, *Private Litigation to Enforce Fiduciary Duties in Mutual Funds, Derivative Suits, Disinterested Directors and the Ideology of Investor Sovereignty*, 83 Wash. U. L.Q. 1017 (2005).

To get around the constraining effect of the derivative action's demand requirement, some fund shareholders have sought to frame the asserted claim as direct rather than derivative. A direct claim seeks redress for injury suffered by the shareholder in the shareholder's individual capacity in an action brought by the shareholder. The distinction between direct and derivative actions is not an easy one. In determining whether a claim is direct or derivative, a widely-cited Delaware standard looks to who suffered the harm (the entity or the shareholder) and whether the entity or the shareholder would receive the benefit of any recovery or remedy. Most actions by shareholders against a fund's investment adviser under state law (in contrast to actions under Company Act Section 36(b) discussed in Chapter 12) have been viewed as derivative rather than direct. *See, e.g., Hastel v. Vanguard Group, Inc.*, No. Civ. A. 5394-VCP, 2011 WL 2421003 (Del. Ch. June 15, 2011). A recent Ninth Circuit decision, however, represents a controversial one in which the court agreed that certain shareholder claims were direct, although the case was subsequently dismissed on other grounds. *See Northstar Financial Advisors v. Schwab Investments*, 779 F.3d 1036 (9th Cir.), *cert denied*, 136 S. Ct. 240 (2015); *see also Strougo v. Bassini*, 282 F.3d 162 (2d

Cir. 2002) (holding that non-participating shareholders in a rights offering conducted by a closed-end fund had standing to assert a direct action because their injury differed from mere pro rata dilution in share price suffered by all shareholders).

3. *Umbrella trusts.* Umbrella trusts mark an interesting development. Many investment company trusts operate series funds. For example, it is fairly commonplace for fund families to use trusts to house many series of funds. However, fund families typically operate under a common name and typically have a single investment adviser (although the adviser may be assisted by sub-advisers). There are trusts willing to house many different fund series, and the individual series in the trust are sponsored by different investment advisers. In such a situation, the trust is described as an "umbrella trust" or alternatively as a "shared series trust." One might ask who would sponsor a shared series trust to house individual fund series with unrelated investment advisers? The individual investment advisers would have little incentive to sponsor the trust to service the needs of funds sponsored by other unaffiliated advisers. Indeed, the sponsor of umbrella trusts typically seek to induce advisers to sponsor a fund series within the trust by openly touting the fact that there is no need for the adviser to get involved in sponsoring a trust or worry about its governance. Consider whether some other participant might have a financial incentive to sponsor the trust. Frequently, funds within a series trust share common service providers, such as a fund administrators or providers of compliance services. Would it be surprising to find that such service providers might be willing to sponsor a shared series trust?

11.4 Investment Company Governance

Funds, either as stand-alone entities or as a series within an entity containing multiple series (i.e. multiple funds), generally must have a board of directors or trustees under state law, but except for unit investment trusts, the Company Act requires all registered investment companies to have governing boards. (Note: the terms directors and trustees are used interchangeably throughout this text because the relevant entities may be either corporations or trusts). In other words, mutual funds, closed-end funds and virtually all ETFs (namely, ETFs that are organized analogously to mutual funds) have boards. Like directors of any business entity, directors have fiduciary obligations of care and loyalty and are guided by those obligations in the discharge of their duties. Presumably, students have previously addressed such issues in a business associations course and, thus, those issues as they arise under state law are not addressed here.

The Company Act contains a number of provisions the shape governance by the board in a registered investment company, but the effect of the Company Act requirements operate in tandem with state law requirements. The prevailing state law norm is that there is no need to hold annual meetings and, as a result, there is a business planning advantage for the sponsor in selecting the original board. One might be tempted to think that at its inception the board will be elected by a diverse body of shareholders, but that is not the case. Typically, when formed, the sole shareholder of the investment company will be the sponsor, who will then elect the board. The board in theory remains in place until there is a need for a new election.

Although the Company Act does not impose any requirements regarding the need for annual shareholders meetings, Section 16(a) does require that shareholders have elected a majority of the board and, moreover, precludes the board itself from filling vacancies if doing so would reduce the number of shareholder elected board members to less than two-thirds. This provision preserves only a very modest role for shareholders in exercising any control over the board of trustees because there is no statutory requirement for an election unless (1) the remaining members elected by shareholders drops below a majority; or (2) in filling the vacancy by the board, the remaining number of members elected by shareholders would be less than two-thirds. Even then, shareholders may only have an opportunity to vote on vacancies where a shareholder vote is required. As a result, once elected by the sponsor, a fund board (or the board for a series of funds) can remain intact for years until retirement or death of enough elected trustees to trigger the need for a shareholder election. The requirements (discussed below) relating to board independence may also make it more likely that there will need to be a shareholder election, since those requirements may require new board members while also satisfying conditions (1) and (2) above. In any event, the role of shareholders in affecting board membership is severely muted relative to conventional public company counterparts. To be sure, this result implicates significant public policy concerns.

Wholly apart from the lack of meaningful shareholder control of the board, the Company Act imposes a significant number of governance requirements regarding board composition and the allocation of affirmative duties within the board. Many of these requirements are focused on the role of independent directors (or trustees) in overseeing the affairs of the registered investment company. The discussion and materials below explore different aspects of fund governance by trustees: (1) the role of independent trustees in fund oversight; (ii) the statutory analysis that determines which trustees are interested and by implication those that are non-interested (or independent); and (iii) the SEC's relatively recent efforts to bolster the structural role of independent trustees in overseeing the affairs of fund companies.

11.4.1 Independent Trustees and Their Special Role on Fund Boards

As discussed above, the role of directors or trustees of a fund is functionally equivalent to directors under corporate law. They are bound by general state law fiduciary standards relating to duties of care and loyalty and must act in good faith in serving the interests of the business entity and its shareholders. The Company Act assigns the board specific statutory obligations, such as approving the fund's advisory agreement, its principal underwriting agreement, and the selection of the fund's independent auditor. In addition, however, the Company Act and its rules give independent directors an enhanced role in the oversight of fund affairs. A majority of independent directors must approve the fund's advisory and principal underwriter agreements, the fund's code of ethics, and the fund's compliance policies and procedures, including its valuation policies.

The independent trustee mandate is further enhanced by requiring that independent directors constitute a high percentage of the board's composition. The first board composition requirements were set forth in the Company Act itself. Section 10 requires at least 40% of the board be non-interested persons (i.e., independent) in most circumstances. By rule, as discussed below, the practical threshold is now above 50%, with many funds observing a 75% threshhold on independent directors.

A trustee's status as independent is governed by the definition of interested person found in Section 2(a)(19) of the Company Act and related statutory definitions concerning *affiliated person* and *control*, which are incorporated concepts with Section 2(a)(19). If someone is interested, that person will be deemed not independent. In other words, independent trustees may not satisfy any of the various criteria contained in Section 2(a)(19) that determine whether a person is interested. Although the actual analysis for each trustee is detailed in nature, it underscores a pronounced legislative policy that in general, a significant portion of fund directors should be facially independent as measured by fairly exacting objective standards. However, the definition does not entirely prohibit indirect relationships based on, for example, business relationships attenuated by connection or time.

Turning to Section 2(a)(19)'s definition of interested person of an investment company, it contains two operative sub-sections: (A) relating to interested persons of an investment company; and (B) relating to interested persons of an investment adviser. The two sub-sections relate directly to one another because an interested person of the investment adviser is deemed an interested person of the investment company as well pursuant to Section 2(a)(19)(A)(iii). Thus, in order to be a non-interested person of an investment company, the person cannot be either an interested person of the investment adviser (or its principal underwriter) as determined by Section 2(a)(19)(B), or fit within any of the other interested person criteria for investment companies found in Section 2(a)(19)(A).

Analysis under Section 2(a)(19) is very methodical and answers very practical questions. Thus, can a partner in a law firm that represents an investment adviser serve as an independent trustee on a fund managed by the investment adviser? What about the partner's spouse? What about the partner in a law firm to an investment adviser that serves as a sub-adviser with respect to the fund's portfolio? And so on and so on. Company Act lawyers engage in this form of analysis routinely to ensure that putatively independent board members are in fact independent when elected to the board and continue to remain independent when this issue is reviewed annually. Obviously it is important that such review be systematic and rigorous. What methods could a law firm use to make these determinations in an orderly fashion? Following the reading below is an exercise that discusses determining exactly who is a disinterested (that is, independent) board member.

Interpretive Matters Concerning Independent Directors of Investment Companies

Investment Company Act Release No. 23083 (October 14, 1999)

[**Textbook Note:** *The role of independent directors has been of growing importance and interest since 1999. In this interpretive release, the SEC endorses the views of its staff explaining the importance of independence in fund governance. In addition, the release discusses at length the type of material business relationships between a person and fund affiliates that it regards as disabling from an independence perspective. Certain aspects of the SEC's approach were subsequently codified in amendments to Section 2(a)(19).*]

[***] Executive Summary

Management investment companies are governed by a board of directors, at least 40% of whom must not be "interested persons" of the company under section 2(a)(19) of the Investment Company Act of 1940 (the "Act") (i.e., "independent directors"). Independent directors of registered investment companies ("investment companies" or "funds") play a critical role in overseeing the funds' operations and protecting the interests of their shareholders.... [T]he Commission is publishing this release, which contains the views of its staff concerning a number of interpretive issues under the Act that relate to independent directors, and briefly describes the role of the Commission in connection with certain disputes between independent fund directors and fund management.

I. Background

A. The Role and Independence of Independent Directors

The critical role of independent directors of investment companies is necessitated, in part, by the unique structure of investment companies. Unlike a typical corporation, a fund generally has no employees of its own. Its officers are usually employed and compensated by the fund's investment adviser, which is a separately owned and operated entity. The fund relies on its investment adviser and other affiliates—who are usually the very companies that sponsored the fund's organization—for basic services, including investment advice, administration, and distribution.

Due to this unique structure, conflicts of interest can arise between a fund and the fund's investment adviser because the interests of the fund do not always parallel the interests of the adviser. An investment adviser's interest in maximizing its own profits for the benefit of its owners may conflict with its paramount duty to act solely in the best interests of the fund and its shareholders.

In an effort to control conflicts of interest between funds and their investment advisers, Congress required that at least 40% of a fund's board be composed of independent directors. Congress intended to place independent directors in the role of "independent watchdogs," who would furnish an independent check upon the management of funds and provide a means for the representation of shareholder interests in fund affairs.

Independent directors play a critical role in policing the potential conflicts of interest between a fund and its investment adviser. The Act requires that a majority of a fund's independent directors: approve the fund's contracts with its investment adviser and principal underwriter; select the independent public accountant of the fund; and select and nominate individuals to fill independent director vacancies resulting from the assignment of an advisory contract. In addition, rules promulgated under the Act require independent directors to: approve distribution fees paid under rule 12b-1 under the Act; approve and oversee affiliated securities transactions; set the amount of the fund's fidelity bond; and determine if participation in joint insurance contracts is in the best interest of the fund. Each of these duties and responsibilities is vital to the proper functioning of fund operations and, ultimately, the protection of fund shareholders.

In addition to the requirements of federal law, directors must abide by standards of care prescribed by state statutory and common law. Specifically, directors are subject to state law duties of care and loyalty. The duty of care generally requires that directors act in good faith and with that degree of diligence, care and skill that a person of ordinary prudence would exercise under similar circumstances in a like position. The duty of loyalty generally requires that directors exercise their powers in the interests of the fund and not in the directors' own interests or in the interests of another person or organization.

B. Improving Fund Governance

The role of independent fund directors, and proposals to enhance their independence and effectiveness, have been the subject of a number of initiatives since the Act was enacted in 1940. For example, the Wharton School, at the request of the Commission, began a detailed study of the fund industry in the late 1950s. At that time, any person who was not an officer, employee or investment adviser of a fund, or an affiliated person of the investment adviser, could serve as an independent director of the fund. Under this standard, the Wharton study questioned the "extent to which reliance can be placed on the independent directors to safeguard adequately the rights of shareholders in negotiations between the [fund] and the investment adviser." The Commission followed the Wharton study with its own study, which agreed that the then-current standard for director independence was inadequate. Subsequently, Congress enacted an amendment to the Act in 1970 which required that independent directors not be "interested persons" of a fund under new section 2(a)(19) of the Act. The amendment substantially limited the categories of persons who could serve as independent directors for funds.

The Commission staff revisited the issue of the effectiveness of fund directors in the early 1990s, which culminated in a published report in 1992.[20] The staff concluded

20. Division of Investment Management, SEC, Protecting Investors: A Half Century of Investment Company Regulation, Ch. 7 (1992).

that the governance model embodied in the Act was sound, but suggested a number of changes designed to improve the effectiveness of fund directors. One of these recommendations was to increase the minimum percentage of independent directors on fund boards from 40% to greater than 50%. In addition, the staff suggested that a fund's independent directors be allowed to choose the persons who would fill independent director vacancies and that the independent directors be given the express authority to terminate advisory contracts.

Fund governance has recently returned to the forefront. The press has questioned the effectiveness of independent directors and, in a number of instances, independent directors have come under fire by fund management and been replaced with directors who were nominated by management. Private litigants have challenged independent directors' independence, and the Commission has instituted enforcement actions against independent directors for failing to fulfill their legal obligations. The prominence of these developments has been magnified by the extraordinary growth of the fund industry....

II. Interpretive Guidance

A. Commission Orders under Section 2(a)(19) of the Act

Sections 2(a)(19)(A)[(vii)] and (B)[(vii)] of the Act authorize the Commission to issue an order finding that a person is "interested" by reason of a material business or professional relationship with certain persons and entities. The Commission and the staff have not publicly provided guidance concerning these sections for a significant period of time. The staff believes that it would be useful to provide additional guidance about the types of professional and business relationships that may be considered to be material for purposes of sections 2(a)(19)(A)(vi) and (B)(vi). This guidance should be particularly useful because the staff understands that many fund groups will not nominate an individual as an independent director if they identify a material business or professional relationship that the individual has with a Specified Entity (as defined below) due to concerns that the Commission may commence proceedings under section 2(a)(19).

The Commission has the authority to issue an order under section 2(a)(19) of the Act when it finds that a person has or had a "material business or professional relationship" with certain specified persons and entities, including some fund affiliates ("Specified Entities").[32] Section 2(a)(19) does not define a "material business or professional relationship." The legislative history, however, indicates that a business or professional relationship would be material if it "might tend to impair the independence of [a] director." The legislative history also states that "[o]rdinarily, a business or professional relationship would not be deemed to impair independence where the

32. Those entities include the fund, its principal executive officer, the investment adviser and principal underwriter of the fund, the principal executive officer of the investment adviser or principal underwriter, or any controlling person of the investment adviser or principal underwriter, any other fund with the same investment adviser or principal underwriter, and the principal executive officer of such other fund. *See* Sections 2(a)(19)(A)(iv) and (B)(vi) [15 U.S.C. §§ 80a-2(a)(19)(A)(vi), (B)(vi)].

benefits flow from the director of an investment company to the other party to the relationship. In such instances the relationship is not likely to make the director beholden to that party."

The staff believes that issues arising under sections 2(a)(19)(A)[(vii)] and (B)[(vii)] must be analyzed based on the particular facts of each case to determine whether a director's interests and relationships might tend to impair his or her independence. The staff also believes, however, that it would be useful to provide guidance about the types of professional and business relationships between a director and a Specified Entity that may be considered to be material. In particular, this section of the release describes how the staff will analyze whether a person should be treated as "interested" by virtue of (1) holding or having held certain positions with a Specified Entity, and (2) engaging or having engaged in certain material transactions with a Specified Entity.

Positions as Material Business or Professional Relationships

The staff believes that a fund director may be treated as "interested" if he or she currently holds or held, at any time since the beginning of the last two completed fiscal years of the fund (the "two-year period"), certain positions with a Specified Entity. The staff would consider a position that a director holds with a Specified Entity as a "material business or professional relationship" if it would tend to impair a director's independence by providing incentives for the director to place his or her own interests over the interests of fund shareholders. The key factors in evaluating whether a director's position with a Specified Entity would tend to impair his or her independence include the level of the director's responsibility in the position and the level of compensation or other benefits that the director receives or received from the position.

For instance, the staff would consider an individual who served as the fund's portfolio manager during the two-year period to have had a material business or professional relationship with the fund and its investment adviser. The staff previously has informally advised certain funds of this position on several occasions. The staff believes that a fund's former portfolio manager must be viewed as having had a material business or professional relationship with the fund and its adviser because he or she would have had significant responsibilities with the fund and the adviser, and likely would have received substantial compensation and other benefits from the adviser and/or the fund. Indeed, the staff would view the former portfolio manager's position as material due to the manager's responsibility in the position even if the manager had not received substantial compensation from adviser or the fund. Similarly, the staff believes that former directors, officers, and employees of the fund's investment adviser or principal underwriter could be viewed as having had a material business or professional relationship with a Specified Entity, depending on the facts and circumstances.

In addition, a fund director who at any time during the two-year period also was a director, officer or employee of a current or former holding company of the fund's investment adviser may be treated as interested by reason of a material business or professional relationship with the controlling person of the fund's adviser (a Specified Entity). As described above, the staff's analysis of the materiality of the relationship would focus on, among other things, the level of the director's responsibility with the holding company and the level of compensation or other benefits that the director received from the position.

The staff believes that not every position that a director holds or held with a Specified Entity would be deemed to impair his or her independence. For example, a director of a fund who also is a director of another fund managed by the same adviser generally would not be viewed as an interested person of the fund under section 2(a)(19) solely as a result of this relationship.

Material Transactions as Material Business or Professional Relationships

The staff believes that a fund director may be treated as "interested" if he or she has, at any time during the two-year period, directly or indirectly engaged (or proposed to engage) in any material transactions (or proposed material transactions) with a Specified Entity. Such a relationship could result from a single transaction or from multiple transactions. These transactions may be structured as service arrangements, including legal, investment banking, and consulting services, or other business transactions, such as business and personal loans, and real estate purchases. In addition, a material business or professional relationship with a Specified Entity may result from a fund director's position with, or ownership interest in, an entity that engages in material transactions with a Specified Entity.

For example, the staff believes that a fund director may be treated as "interested" if the fund's investment adviser manages or managed for the director, at any time during the two-year period, an advisory or brokerage account, and the adviser favors, or creates the expectation that it will favor, the account over the other accounts that it manages. In the staff's view, a director would receive favored treatment, for instance, if the adviser charged the director no fees or fees that were lower than the fees that it charged for similar types of accounts, or accorded the director's account special treatment regarding portfolio management decisions or securities allocations. By favoring the director's account over other accounts that it manages, the adviser may create an incentive for the director to act in a manner that will preserve or increase the favorable treatment. In this instance, significant economic benefits from the relationship between the director and the adviser would flow to the director, or the director may have the expectation that significant economic benefits would flow in the future to the director.

The staff believes that a fund director who serves as a chief executive officer of any company for which the chief executive officer of the fund's adviser serves as a director also may be treated as "interested." The relationship between the fund director and the adviser's chief executive officer may tend to impair the director's independence because the adviser's chief executive officer has the power to vote on matters that affect the director's compensation and status as chief executive officer of the company. In this instance, the fund director may act with respect to fund matters in a manner to preserve his or her relationship with the company and with the adviser's chief executive officer, rather than in the interest of the fund's shareholders.

A fund director may be deemed to have indirectly engaged in a material transaction with a Specified Entity through his or her interest in a company that conducted business with the Specified Entity. In determining whether the director would have a material business or professional relationship with a Specified Entity due to his or her interest in the company and the company's transaction with the Specified Entity, the staff would look to the nature and significance of the director's interest in the company and the company's interest in the transaction. In particular, the staff would focus on the significance of any economic or other benefit that would flow to the director. For example, a fund director who had a controlling interest in a company that conducted material business with a fund would likely receive significant economic benefits, either directly or indirectly, as a result. Such a director may be treated as interested because the director may have a material business or professional relationship with the fund as a result of having indirectly engaged in a material transaction with the fund.

A material relationship resulting from a *proposed* material transaction with a Specified Entity might include the negotiation of a service contract between a company controlled by the director and the Specified Entity. During the negotiation of such a contract (and even if such contract is never finalized), the director may be concerned about interests other than those of the fund and its shareholders. As a result, the process of negotiating a material transaction may tend to impair the director's independence, and thus may itself create a material business or professional relationship with a Specified Entity for purposes of section 2(a)(19). [* * *]

* * *

Notes and Applications

1. *Making fact-specific determinations.* The determination of independence is fact-specific and requires consideration of the relevant standards set forth in Section 2(a)(19). Consider how the definition would be applied in the case of the following hypothetical:

Suppose we have a fund family, consisting of three equity funds—the Bacchus Growth Fund, the Bacchus Death Spiral Fund and the Bacchus Wimp Fund. The investment objectives and styles of the funds respectively are capital appreciation (Growth Fund), aggressive capital appreciation through investments in securities of distressed issuers (Death Spiral), and value orientation with an eye to capital preservation (Wimp). The funds are all advised by Bacchus Advisors and distributed by an affiliate, Bacchus Fund Distributors, the principal underwriter.

> Bacchus Advisers and Bacchus Fund Distributors are directly owned by a huge financial services firm, Pacific Capital Corporation. Pacific Capital has two major lines of businesses: asset management services and a multi-billion dollar commercial lending business.

a. The president of Pacific is Mary Wary.

   (i) If Mary Wary were on the board of Bacchus Wimp Fund, would she be considered an interested person? Using Section 2(a)(19), explain why.

   (ii) Suppose Mary Wary's husband were asked to sit on the board of Bacchus Wimp Fund. Would the result be different? Explain.

b. Bacchus Advisors up until a year ago was represented by Marsha Doodle. Ms. Doodle retired last year from Hack, Saw & Ripp LLP, a firm that continues to represent Bacchus Advisors. Ms. Doodle was recently named to the board of the Bacchus Death Spiral Fund. Using Section 2(a)(19), discuss whether Ms. Doodle is an interested person.

c. Anthony Brush Jr. is the co-trustee of a $30 million trust established by his father for the benefit of his father's grandchildren, including Junior's children. The trust holds 10,000 shares of Pacific Capital worth approximately $1 million. Can Anthony Brush serve as a non-interested person on the board of the Bacchus Fund?

Based on the plain language of Section 2(a)(19), each of the individuals would be an interested person. Of course, it is easy to tweak the facts in each case to make the outcome far less obvious. Nevertheless, these examples illustrate the basic mode of analysis that must be used to reach a determination.

As noted, "who is an interested person?" is an inherently fact-specific analysis and in practice is invariably made in advance of considering a candidate for nomination to the board, and thereafter annually. Instead of collecting information in an unstructured format and having the attorney determine whether the facts suggest a potentially disqualifying relationship, these determinations are typically made through use of an elaborate questionnaire for board members or potential board members in which the respondent is methodically surveyed on each part of the statutory definition to reveal possible relationships that would be germane to determining the relevant person's independence.

2. *The potential fuzziness of material business relationships.* Item (vii) of Section 2(a)(19)(A) & (B) focuses on material business relationships with the investment company, affiliated investment companies, the investment adviser or the principal executive officer of any such entity. This topic is the subject of extensive discussion in the SEC's staff interpretation regarding independence. Unlike the other standards in the statutory definition, it technically requires a determination from the SEC that the relationship is indeed disqualifying. Of course, the fund and its counsel are unlikely to risk a finding that a trustee is not independent if there appears to be a material business relationship. Thus, a trustee questionnaire will attempt to ferret out material business relationships in advance. In some circumstances, fund counsel might seek clarification from the staff regarding a potentially material disqualifying relationship through a no-action letter regarding the staff's views regarding whether a particular business relationship is indeed material.

3. *Independence outside the Company Act and unitary boards.* Many fund families use either a "unitary board" (i.e., a single board for all funds) or a cluster board (i.e., splitting the funds into several groups with each group subject to its own board). The Company Act makes no mention of unitary boards or cluster boards, but the statutory definition of interested person makes clear that serving on the investment company's board or on the board of affiliated investment companies shall not be a factor in determining whether a person is interested. Thus, being a board member on a fund family alone does not make the board member interested for purposes of the Company Act. Indeed, a particular person might serve on the board of dozens of affiliated investment companies without being rendered interested.

Being non-interested under the Company Act would not necessarily render a person disinterested or independent under state law. This seemingly technical distinction is not without practical significance. In theory, a board member who sits on the board of several affiliated investment companies might be regarded as interested (or non-independent) under state law, even though independent under the Company Act. Such a situation arose in *Strougo v. Scudder, Stevens & Clark, Inc.*, 964 F. Supp. 783 (S.D.N.Y. 1997), where a district court determined, not without considerable controversy, that a plaintiff was excused from making a demand in bringing a derivative action against a Maryland closed-end fund because all but one of the board's putatively independent directors served on boards of affiliated investment companies for which they received separate and additional compensation. The investment company industry sought to undo this result and persuaded the legislatures of Maryland and Massachusetts to adopt statutory provisions that precluded a finding of non-independence merely by virtue of an investment company director serving on the board of related investment companies.

11.4.2 Enhancing the Role of Independent Trustees in Fund Governance

In connection with its interpretive guidance, the SEC proposed new requirements to strengthen the hand of independent directors and trustees in fund governance matters. Instead of trying to tighten the definition of independent director even further, the SEC sought to enhance board independence in terms of board composition and have boards adopt practices that would promote greater independence in the way independent directors acted. The SEC rulemaking exceeded the statutory independence requirements of the Company Act and necessarily triggered questions regarding the source of the agency's authority in connection with the agency's rulemaking.

Role of Independent Directors of Investment Companies

Investment Company Act Release No. 24816 (Jan. 2, 2001)

[**Textbook Note:** *In 2001, the SEC adopted new regulatory definitions of the term "independent legal counsel" (Company Act Rule 0-1(a)(6)) and "fund governance standards" (Company Act Rule 0-1(a)(7)). These definitions impose specific and exacting requirements on board composition in terms of independent* *trustees and independence requirements for counsel to the fund's independent trustees. On first inspection, the rules seem like a potential regulatory overreach because the Company Act nowhere authorizes the SEC to impose such requirements on investment companies. Nevertheless, on closer inspection, the rules themselves (couched as definitions) do not impose a flat mandate on funds, although most mutual funds and ETFs adhere to them. Thus, it is useful to ascertain the basis for the SEC's asserted authority as explained below in the adopting release.*]

I. BACKGROUND

Mutual funds are organized as corporations, trusts, or limited partnerships under state laws, and thus are owned by their shareholders, beneficiaries, or partners. Like other types of corporations, trusts, or partnerships, a mutual fund must be operated for the benefit of its owners. Unlike most business organizations, however, mutual funds are typically organized and operated by an investment adviser that is responsible for the day-to-day operations of the fund. In most cases, the investment adviser is separate and distinct from the fund it advises, with primary responsibility and loyalty to its own shareholders. The "external management" of mutual funds presents inherent conflicts of interest and potential for abuses that the Investment Company Act and the Commission have addressed in different ways.

One of the ways that the Act addresses conflicts between advisers and funds is by giving mutual fund boards of directors, and in particular the disinterested directors, an important role in fund governance. In relying on fund boards to represent fund investors and protect their interests, Congress avoided the more detailed regulatory provisions that characterize other regulatory schemes for collective investments. The Commission has similarly relied extensively on independent directors in rules we have adopted that exempt funds from provisions of the Act.

Millions of Americans are today invested in mutual funds, which have experienced a tremendous growth in popularity over the past twenty years. In light of this growth, and our growing reliance on independent directors to protect fund investors, last year we undertook a review of the governance of investment companies, the role of independent directors, our rules that rely on oversight by independent directors, and the information that funds are required to provide to shareholders about their independent directors.

II. DISCUSSION

A. Amendments to Exemptive Rules to Enhance Director Independence and Effectiveness

We are amending ten rules that exempt funds and their affiliates from certain prohibitions of the Act (the "Exemptive Rules").[17] As discussed further below, the amend-

---

17. The Exemptive Rules are:
Rule 10f-3 (permitting funds to purchase securities in a primary offering when an affiliated broker-dealer is a member of the underwriting syndicate);
Rule 12b-1 (permitting use of fund assets to pay distribution expenses);
Rule 15a-4(b)(2) (permitting fund boards to approve interim advisory contracts without shareholder

ments add conditions to the Exemptive Rules to require that, for funds that rely on the rules, (i) independent directors constitute a majority of the board, (ii) independent directors select and nominate other independent directors, and (iii) any legal counsel for the independent directors be an independent legal counsel.

1. Independent Directors as a Majority of the Board

....

We are amending the Exemptive Rules to require that the boards of funds relying on the rules have a majority of independent directors. A majority requirement will permit, under state law, the independent directors to control the fund's "corporate machinery," i.e., to elect officers of the fund, call meetings, solicit proxies, and take other actions without the consent of the adviser. As a result, independent directors who comprise the majority of a board can have a more meaningful influence on fund management and represent shareholders from a position of strength. In short, a board with a majority of independent directors can be more effective in representing investors than a board with a majority of "inside" directors. Commenters were supportive of this proposal....

2. Selection and Nomination of Independent Directors

We are adopting, as a condition of the Exemptive Rules, a requirement that the independent directors of funds relying on those rules select and nominate any other independent directors. Commenters supported the proposal, and many specifically agreed that the self-selection and self-nomination of independent directors fosters an independent-minded board that focuses primarily on the interests of a fund's investors rather than its adviser.

Several commenters asked that we clarify the extent to which fund shareholders or a fund's adviser may participate in the selection and nomination process under the amendments. Control of the selection and nomination process at all times should rest with a fund's independent directors. These amendments are not intended to supplant or limit the ability of fund shareholders under state law to nominate independent directors. The adviser may suggest independent director candidates if the independent directors invite such suggestions, and the adviser may provide administrative assistance

---

approval where the adviser or a controlling person receives a benefit in connection with the assignment of the prior contract);
Rule 17a-7 (permitting securities transactions between a fund and another client of the fund's adviser);
Rule 17a-8 (permitting mergers between certain affiliated funds);
Rule 17d-1(d)(7) (permitting funds and their affiliates to purchase joint liability insurance policies);
Rule 17e-1 (specifying conditions under which funds may pay commissions to affiliated brokers in connection with the sale of securities on an exchange);
Rule 17g-1(j) (permitting funds to maintain joint insured bonds);
Rule 18f-3 (permitting funds to issue multiple classes of voting stock); and
Rule 23c-3 (permitting the operation of interval funds by enabling closed-end funds to repurchase their shares from investors).

in the selection and nomination process. Independent directors, however, should not view participation by shareholders and investment advisers in this process as precluding or excusing the independent directors from the responsibility to canvass, recruit, interview, and solicit independent director candidates.

3. Independent Legal Counsel

We are adopting amendments to each of the Exemptive Rules to require that any legal counsel for the fund's independent directors be an "independent legal counsel." We believe that the conflicts involved in the transactions and arrangements permitted by the Exemptive Rules make it critical that independent directors, when they seek legal counsel, be represented by persons who are free of significant conflicts of interest that might affect their legal advice.

The Commission received many comments on this proposal. Most fund management companies, and a number of independent directors and their lawyers, opposed the proposed amendments. Many argued that the selection of counsel was a matter that should be left to independent directors. Some argued that the bar association rules of professional conduct are adequate to assure independence of counsel. Others argued that imposing the independent counsel requirement could deny independent directors competent counsel from larger law firms with many potential conflicts.

Given the vital role of independent directors in the resolution of conflicts between the fund and its investment adviser, it is important that they have access to counsel who is free from conflicting loyalties. This is particularly true when directors are called upon to exercise judgment in certain key areas of their responsibilities such as approving the advisory contract or a distribution plan, approving a merger, monitoring the allocation of fund brokerage, or valuing fund securities. Yet, as we observed in the Proposing Release, some independent directors have relied on counsel who has simultaneously represented the fund's adviser, or who does substantial legal work for the adviser or its affiliates. We continue to be concerned by these conflicts and how they affect the ability of directors to carry out their responsibilities under the Act and the Exemptive Rules.

Funds also should be concerned when counsel to the independent directors have these types of conflicts of interest. The appearance of a conflict undermines the confidence investors have in the independence of their fund's directors to represent investors' interests. Directors who accept these conflicts strengthen the argument that more drastic changes are necessary in the way mutual funds are governed. Fund advisers also should be concerned when independent directors engage counsel with substantial conflicts, because the adviser and the funds may be denied a significant defense in any lawsuit charging that its advisory fee or other payments or transactions are excessive or inappropriate.

While we are persuaded that Commission rulemaking is necessary, we appreciate the concerns that the independent directors expressed in their comment letters on the proposed amendments. Many were concerned that the proposal did not afford them sufficient flexibility in selecting counsel. Some misunderstood our proposal as permitting counsel to have conflicts that are only extremely small or remote. That was not our intention, which we have clarified in revising the proposed amendments.

Under the final rule amendments, reliance on each of the Exemptive Rules would be conditioned on any legal counsel for a fund's independent directors being an "independent legal counsel." A person is considered an independent legal counsel if (i) the independent directors determine that any representation of the fund's investment adviser, principal underwriter, administrator (collectively "management organizations") or their control persons during the past two fiscal years is or was sufficiently limited that it is unlikely to adversely affect the professional judgment of the person in providing legal representation, and (ii) the independent directors have obtained an undertaking from the counsel to provide them information necessary for their determination, and to update promptly that information if the counsel begins, or materially increases, the representation of a management organization or control person.

The final amendments rely on the independent directors to determine whether a person is an independent legal counsel. They must make this determination no less frequently than annually, and the basis for the determination must be recorded in the board's meeting minutes. If the independent directors obtain information that their counsel has begun to represent a management organization or control person, they must determine whether this new representation — together with any other representations of management organizations and control persons — is unlikely to adversely affect the counsel's professional judgment. In order to prevent the fund from losing the availability of the exemptions in these circumstances, the rule provides that counsel can still be considered "independent legal counsel" for up to three months, which will provide time for the independent directors to make a new determination about the counsel or to hire a new independent legal counsel.

In determining whether a counsel is an "independent legal counsel" under the rule, the judgment of the directors is not unbounded; it must be reasonable. The independent directors should consider all relevant factors in evaluating whether the conflicting representations are "sufficiently limited." For example, independent directors should consider (i) whether the representation is current and ongoing; (ii) whether it involves a minor or substantial matter; (iii) whether it involves the fund, the adviser, or an affiliate, and if an affiliate, the nature and the extent of the affiliation; (iv) the duration of the conflicting representation; (v) the importance of the representation to counsel and his firm (including the extent to which counsel relies on that representation economically); (vi) whether it involves work related to mutual funds; and (vii) whether the individual who will serve as legal counsel was or is involved in the representation. Applying these factors, we do not believe that independent directors could ordinarily conclude that a lawyer whose firm simultaneously represents the fund's adviser and independent directors in connection with matters as important to fund shareholders as the negotiation of the advisory contract or distribution plan, or other key areas of conflict between the fund and its adviser, is an "independent legal counsel."

We admonish directors to consider that your decision in selecting an independent counsel is not merely a matter of personal preference (as some commenters suggested), but an important exercise of your business judgment as an independent director. The final rule makes it clear, however, that you are entitled to rely on information provided by counsel in forming your judgment. [***]

* * *

Notes and Applications

So just how many counsel are there? The independent counsel rule (codified at 17 C.F.R. § 270.0-1(a)(6)) reinforced what had become an emerging best practice in the industry—the use of separate counsel for independent trustees, that is counsel independent of the investment adviser. What incentives does the definition of independent legal counsel create for independent trustees to obtain independent legal counsel? The effect of the SEC's governance rulemaking has virtually assured that there will be at least two different sets of attorneys in addressing fund matters—one the adviser's counsel and the other independent trustees' counsel. This leaves open the question of who is counsel to the fund itself? As it turns out, fund counsel is seldom a third attorney at the table. Rather, typically either adviser's counsel or the trustee's counsel will also serve as fund counsel. Does representing the fund compromise the independence of trustees' counsel? Few would disagree that the answer is no, but in order to assure the independence of trustees' counsel, counsel must ensure that their role as fund counsel does not involve any form of representation of the adviser that might be construed as material. Of course, adviser's counsel could instead act as fund counsel, in which case, trustees' counsel would solely represent the independent trustees. What is the practical significance of whether adviser's counsel or trustees' counsel represent the fund? Obviously, it will affect the remuneration of the respective counsel as the fund itself is a source of significant legal work. Arguably counsel that represents the fund will have somewhat greater influence in terms of controlling the legal agenda of fund affairs. Nevertheless, both counsel will ultimately have to sign off on fund matters and will need to forge a constructive relationship. Moreover, since experienced Company Act counsel is confined to a fairly small number of firms, it is not unlikely that adviser's counsel and trustees' counsel for one fund family will find their roles reversed in connection with another fund family.

* * *

In the fall of 2003, a huge scandal erupted in the mutual fund industry regarding trading practices known as late trading and market timing. A significant aspect of the scandal involved how advisers in overseeing fund affairs allowed certain outside investors in funds, such as hedge funds, to employ trading practices in the mutual fund's shares that were clearly detrimental to the funds' other shareholders. In response, the SEC enacted a wide-ranging set of new compliance requirements. In addition, the SEC in a 2004 rulemaking further enhanced the role of independent trustees in governing fund affairs.

Chamber of Commerce v. SEC

412 F.3d 133 (D.C. Cir. 2005)

[**Textbook Note:** *In 2004, the SEC amended the fund governance standards (Company Act Rule 0-1(a)(7)) to require funds seeking to satisfy the fund governance standards have a board consisting 75% of independent members and an independent chair person. The Chamber of Commerce challenged the SEC's authority to adopt such rule amendments and the agency's rationale for doing so. The D.C. Circuit, while affirming the SEC's authority to adopt such rule amendments, indicated that the SEC nevertheless was required to carefully consider additional factors affecting implementation costs in connection with the rulemaking process.*]

Ginsburg, Chief Judge. The Chamber of Commerce of the United States petitions for review of a rule promulgated by the Securities and Exchange Commission under the Investment Company Act of 1940(ICA), 15 U.S.C. § 80a-1 *et seq.* The challenged provisions of the rule require that, in order to engage in certain transactions otherwise prohibited by the ICA, an investment company—commonly referred to as a mutual fund—must have a board (1) with no less than 75% independent directors and (2) an independent chairman. The Chamber argues the ICA does not give the Commission authority to regulate "corporate governance" and, in any event, the Commission promulgated the rule without adhering to the requirements of the Administrative Procedure Act, 5 U.S.C. § 551 *et seq.*

We hold the Commission did not exceed its statutory authority in adopting the two conditions, and the Commission's rationales for the two conditions satisfy the APA. We agree with the Chamber, however, that the Commission did violate the APA by failing adequately to consider the costs mutual funds would incur in order to comply with the conditions and by failing adequately to consider a proposed alternative to the independent chairman condition. We therefore grant in part the Chamber's petition for review.

I. Background

A mutual fund, which is "a pool of assets ... belonging to the individual investors holding shares in the fund," *Burks v. Lasker*, 441 U.S. 471, 480 (1979), is operated by an "investment company" the board of directors of which is elected by the shareholders. Although the board is authorized to operate the fund, it typically delegates that management role to an "adviser," which is a separate company that may have interests other than maximizing the returns to shareholders in the fund. In enacting the ICA, the Congress sought to control "the potential for abuse inherent in the structure of [funds]" arising from the conflict of interests between advisers and shareholders, *id.;* to that end, the ICA prohibits a fund from engaging in certain transactions by which the adviser might gain at the expense of the shareholders. *See generally* 15 U.S.C. § 80a-12(a)-(g).

Pursuant to the Commission's long-standing Exemptive Rules, however, a fund that satisfies certain conditions may engage in an otherwise prohibited transaction. *See, e.g.,* Rule 10f-3, 17 C.F.R. § 270.10f-3 (2004) (when conditions are satisfied, fund may purchase securities in primary offering although adviser-affiliated broker-dealer is member of underwriting syndicate).

Early in 2004 the Commission proposed to amend ten Exemptive Rules by imposing five new or amended conditions upon any fund wishing to engage in an otherwise prohibited transaction. *See* Investment Company Governance, Proposed Rule, 69 Fed.Reg. 3472 (Jan. 23, 2004). Although the Commission had amended the same ten rules in 2001 to condition exemption upon the fund having a board with a majority of independent directors (that is, directors who are not "interested persons" as defined in § 2(a)(19) of the ICA), *see* Role of Independent Directors of Investment Companies, Final Rule, 66 Fed.Reg. 3734 (Jan. 16, 2001), by 2004 the Commission had come to believe that more was required. "[E]nforcement actions involving late trading, inappropriate market timing activities and misuse of nonpublic information about fund portfolios" had brought to light, in the Commission's view, "a serious breakdown in management controls," signaling the need to "revisit the governance of funds." 69 Fed.Reg. at 3472. Accordingly, the Commission proposed to condition the ten exemptions upon, among other things, the fund having a board of directors (1) with at least 75% independent directors and (2) an independent chairman. *Id.* at 3474.

After a period for comment and a public meeting, the Commission unanimously adopted three of the proposed new conditions and, by a vote of three to two, adopted the two corporate governance conditions challenged here. *See* Investment Company Governance, Final Rule, 69 Fed.Reg. 46,378 (Aug. 2, 2004). The Commission majority adopted those two conditions in light of recently revealed abuses in the mutual fund industry, reasoning that the Exemptive Rules rely on the independent judgment and scrutiny of directors, including independent directors, in overseeing activities that are beneficial to funds and fund shareholders but that involve inherent conflicts of interest between the funds and their managers.... These further amendments provide for greater fund board independence and are designed to enhance the ability of fund boards to perform their important responsibilities under each of the rules. *Id.* at 46,379. Raising the percentage of independent directors from 50% to 75%, the Commission anticipated, would "strengthen the independent directors' control of the fund board and its agenda," *id.* at 46,381, and "help ensure that independent directors carry out their fiduciary responsibilities," *id.* at 46,382. The Commission justified the independent chairman condition on the ground that "a fund board is in a better position to protect the interests of the fund, and to fulfill the board's obligations under the Act and the Exemptive Rules, when its chairman does not have the conflicts of interest inherent in the role of an executive of the fund adviser." *Id.*

The dissenting Commissioners were concerned the two disputed conditions would come at "a substantial cost to fund shareholders," and they believed the existing statutory and regulatory controls ensured adequate oversight by independent directors. 69 Fed.Reg. at 46,390. Specifically, they faulted the Commission for not giving "any real consideration to the costs" of the 75% condition, *id.* at 46,390–46,391; for failing adequately to justify the independent chairman condition, *id.* at 46,391–46,392; and for not considering alternatives to that condition, *id.* at 46,392–46,393. The Chamber timely petitioned for review, asserting an interest in the new conditions both as an investor and as an association with mutual fund advisers among its members.

II. Analysis

The Chamber makes two arguments on the merits: The Commission had no authority under the ICA to adopt the two conditions; and the Commission violated the APA in the rulemaking by which it promulgated the conditions....

B. The Commission's Authority under the ICA

The Chamber maintains the Commission did not have authority under the ICA to condition the exemptive transactions as it did. First the Chamber observes rather generally that "matters of corporate governance are traditionally relegated to state law"; and second, it maintains these particular conditions are inconsistent with the statutory requirement that 40% of the directors on the board of an investment company be independent, *see* 15 U.S.C. § 80a-10(a). The Commission points to § 6(c) of the ICA, 15 U.S.C. § 80a-6(c), as the source of its authority.* That provision conspicuously confers upon the Commission broad authority to exempt transactions from rules promulgated under the ICA, subject only to the public interest and the purposes of the ICA.

In *Business Roundtable v. SEC,* 905 F.2d 406, 416–17 (1990), we held the Commission did not have authority under the 1934 Act to bar a stock exchange from listing common stock with restricted voting rights. The Commission had invoked the provision of that Act authorizing it to make rules "otherwise in furtherance of the purposes" of the Act. *Id.* at 410. Reasoning that "unless the legislative purpose is defined by reference to the *means* Congress selected, it can be framed at *any* level of generality," and the means the Congress selected in the 1934 Act was disclosure, *id.,* we vacated the rule because it went beyond disclosure to regulate "the substance of what the shareholders may enact," *id.* at 411.

Business Roundtable is of little help to the Chamber because, as the Commission documents, the purposes of the ICA include tempering the conflicts of interest "inherent in the structure of investment companies," *Burks,* 441 U.S. at 480; *see also* 15 U.S.C. § 80a-1(b) ("policy and purposes of [ICA] ... shall be interpreted ... to eliminate" conflicts of interest); and regulation of the governance structure of investment companies is among the means the Congress used to effect that purpose. *See Burks,* 441 U.S. at 479, 99 S.Ct. 1831 (ICA "functions primarily to impose controls and restrictions

* The Commission, by rules and regulations upon its own motion, or by order upon application, may conditionally or unconditionally exempt any person, security, or transaction, or any class or classes of persons, securities, or transactions, from any provision or provisions of this [Act] or of any rule or regulation thereunder, if and to the extent that such exemption is necessary or appropriate in the public interest and consistent with the protection of investors and the purposes fairly intended by the policy and provisions of this [Act].

on the internal management of investment companies") (emphases removed); *id.* at 484, 99 S.Ct. 1831 (in enacting ICA Congress "place[d] the unaffiliated directors in the role of independent watchdogs ... who would furnish an independent check upon the management of investment companies"). Moreover, the Commission's effort to enlarge the role of independent directors on the boards of investment companies accords with "the structure and purpose of the ICA [both of which] indicate that Congress entrusted to the independent directors ... the primary responsibility for looking after the interests of the funds' shareholders." *Id.* at 484–85.

In *Teicher v. SEC*, 177 F.3d 1016, 1019–20 (1999), we held a provision of the 1934 Act authorizing the Commission to "place limitations on the activities or functions" of a person convicted of securities fraud in the broker-dealer industry did not authorize it to place limitations upon the activities or functions of that person in an industry regulated under a different "occupational licensing regime" administered by the Commission. The Commission's authority, we reasoned, must be read with "some concept of the relevant domain" in mind; even the Commission did not "suggest that [provision] allows it to bar one of the offending parties from being a retail shoe salesman, or to exclude him from the Borough of Manhattan." *Id.* at 1019. The present case is different from *Teicher* because here the Commission did not exercise its regulatory authority to effect a purpose beyond that of the statute from which its authority derives.

The Chamber's second contention is that the conditions conflict with the intent of the Congress, expressed in § 10(a) of the ICA, that 40% of the directors of an investment company be independent. *See Chevron, U.S.A., Inc. v. NRDC*, 467 U.S. 837, 842–43 (1984) ("If the intent of Congress is clear, that is the end of the matter; for the court, as well as the agency, must give effect to the unambiguously expressed intent of Congress"). Section 10(a), however, states only that a fund may have "no more than" 60% inside directors, 15 U.S.C. § 80a-10(a), which necessarily means at least 40% must be independent and strongly implies a greater percentage may be; it speaks not at all to authority of the Commission to provide an incentive for investment companies to enhance the role of independent directors and, as the Commission is keen to point out, the challenged conditions apply only to funds that engage in exemptive transactions.

C. The Requirements of the APA

The condemnation of the APA extends to any rule that is "arbitrary, capricious, an abuse of discretion, or otherwise not in accordance with law." 5 U.S.C. § 706(2)(A). Although the "scope of review under the 'arbitrary and capricious' standard is narrow and a court is not to substitute its judgment for that of the agency," we must nonetheless be sure the Commission has "examine[d] the relevant data and articulate[d] a satisfactory explanation for its action including a rational connection between the facts found and the choice made." *Motor Vehicle Mfrs. Ass'n v. State Farm Mutual Auto. Ins. Co.*, 463 U.S. 29, 43 (1983); *see also Pub. Citizen v. Fed. Motor Carrier Safety Admin.*, 374 F.3d 1209, 1216 (D.C.Cir.2004).

The Chamber argues the Commission violated the APA because it (1) failed to show the connection between the abuses that prompted the rulemaking and the conditions newly included in the Exemptive Rules; (2) did not comply with its obligation under the ICA to consider whether those conditions "will promote efficiency, competition, and capital formation," 15 U.S.C. § 80a-2(c); *see Pub. Citizen*, 374 F.3d at 1216 (rule is "arbitrary and capricious" if agency fails to consider factors "it must consider under its organic statute"); and (3) did not consider reasonable alternatives to the independent chairman condition.

1. Justification for the Rulemaking

The Chamber maintains the "rulemaking is flawed for the elementary reason that the Commission amended ten separate and distinct pre-existing rules [by imposing the two challenged conditions] without any meaningful consideration of them." Similarly, the Chamber argues the Commission did not adequately explain why the conditions it added were necessary in light of the conditions previously contained in the Exemptive Rules. The Commission answers that its stated justification for amending the Exemptive Rules satisfies the standards of the APA. We agree.

In the wake of recent revelations of certain abuses in the mutual fund industry, the Commission was concerned about what it diagnosed as "a serious breakdown in management controls." *See* 69 Fed.Reg. at 46,378–46,379; 69 Fed.Reg. at 3472. Although it is true, as the Chamber repeatedly notes, that none of the documented abuses involved a transaction covered by the Exemptive Rules, the Commission, as we have said, thought it prudent to amend those rules because the particular abuses that had come to light revealed a more general problem with conflicts of interest than it had previously suspected and portended further abuses if that perceived problem was not addressed. The Commission thus viewed strengthening the role of independent directors in relation to exemptive transactions as a prophylactic measure, not a response to a present problem involving abuse of the Exemptive Rules. *See* 69 Fed.Reg. at 46,379.

The Chamber claims the Commission's decision was unreasonable because the conditions for engaging in exemptive transactions had already been tightened in 2001. But that begs the question whether the conditions of 2001 were adequate in view of the new evidence that some boards were failing to prevent egregious conflicts of interest involving late trading and market timing. Might not they also fail to police sufficiently the conflicts of interest inherent in the exemptive transactions? That those transactions were already subject to some regulation does not render unreasonable the Commission's judgment that additional regulation was called for as a prophylactic.

Finally, the Chamber argues the "actual terms" of the conditions were not reasonable in light of "the problems [the Commission] claimed justified the rulemaking." Those problems all trace to the failure of investment company boards, for whatever reason, to guard against advisers' conflicts of interest. *See* 69 Fed.Reg. at 3473 ("boards may have simply abdicated their responsibilities, or failed to ask the tough questions of advisers; in other cases, boards may have lacked the information or organizational structure necessary to play their proper role"). So that boards are apprised of the activities of their fund's adviser, the Commission, in a separate proceeding first required funds to designate a chief compliance officer charged with bringing relevant information to the board. *See* Compliance Programs of Investment Companies and Investment Advisers, 68 Fed.Reg. 74,714 (Dec. 24, 2003). The Commission then undertook in the present rulemaking to ensure that independent directors would be in a position to put such information to good use.

To that end, the Commission reasonably concluded that raising the minimum percentage of independent directors from 50% to 75% would "strengthen the hand of the independent directors when dealing with fund management, and may assure that independent directors maintain control of the board and its agenda." 69 Fed.Reg. at 46,382. Similarly, the Commission concluded that having an independent chairman would be beneficial because the chairman plays "an important role in setting the agenda of the board[,] ... in providing a check on the adviser, in negotiating the best deal for shareholders when considering the advisory contract, and in providing leadership to the board that focuses on the long-term interests of investors." 69 Fed.Reg. at 46,383. We have no basis upon which to second-guess that judgment.

In sum, the Chamber points to nothing in the ICA to suggest the Congress restricted the authority of the Commission to make "precautionary or prophylactic responses to perceived risks," *Certified Color Mfrs. Ass'n v. Mathews,* 543 F.2d 284, 296 (D.C.Cir.1976); and the Commission's effort to prevent future abuses of exemptive transactions was not arbitrary, capricious, or in any way an abuse of its discretion, in violation of the APA.

2. Consideration of Costs

The ICA mandates that when the Commission "engage[s] in rulemaking and is required to consider or determine whether an action is consistent with the public interest [it] shall ... consider ... whether the action will promote efficiency, competition, and capital formation." 15 U.S.C. § 80a-2(c). The Chamber argues the Commission violated this mandate, and hence the APA, by failing (1) to develop new, and to consider extant, empirical data comparing the performance of funds respectively led by inside and by independent chairmen; and (2) to consider the costs of the conditions it was imposing, which costs in turn impede efficiency, competition, and capital formation. The Commission denies the charges.

The particulars of the Chamber's first contention are that the Commission should have directed its staff to do a study of the effect of an independent chairman upon fund performance and that when such a study, commissioned by Fidelity Investments, was presented during the comment period, the Commission gave it short shrift. 69 Fed.Reg. at 46,383 n.52; *see* Geoffrey H. Bobroff and Thomas H. Mack, Assessing the Significance of Mutual Fund Board Independent Chairs (Mar. 10, 2004). As to the former point, although we recognize that an agency acting upon the basis of empirical data may more readily be able to show it has satisfied its obligations under the APA, *see Nat'l Ass'n of Regulatory Util. Comm'rs v. FCC,* 737 F.2d 1095, 1124 (D.C.Cir.1984) (in informal rulemaking it is "desirable" that agency "independently amass [and] verify the accuracy of" data), we are acutely aware that an agency need not—indeed cannot—base its every action upon empirical data; depending upon the nature of the problem, an agency may be "entitled to conduct ... a general analysis based on informed conjecture." *Melcher v. FCC,* 134 F.3d 1143, 1158 (D.C.Cir.1998); *Nat'l Ass'n of Regulatory Util. Comm'rs,* 737 F.2d at 1124 (failure to conduct independent study not violative of APA because notice and comment procedures "permit parties to bring relevant information quickly to the agency's attention"); *see also a0 FCC v. Nat'l Citizens Comm. for Broad.,* 436 U.S. 775, 813–14, 98 S.Ct. 2096, 56 L.Ed.2d 697 (1978) (FCC, in making "judgmental or predictive" factual determinations, did not need "complete factual support" because "a forecast of the direction in which future public interest lies necessarily involves deductions based on the expert knowledge of the agency").

Here the Commission, based upon "its own and its staff's experience, the many comments received, and other evidence, in addition to the limited and conflicting empirical evidence," concluded an independent chairman "can provide benefits and serve other purposes apart from achieving high performance of the fund." 69 Fed.Reg. at 46,383–46,384. The Commission's decision not to do an empirical study does not make that an unreasoned decision. *See BellSouth Corp. v. FCC,* 162 F.3d 1215, 1221 (D.C.Cir.1999) ("When ... an agency is obliged to make policy judgments where no factual certainties exist or where facts alone do not provide the answer, our role is more limited; we require only that the agency so state and go on to identify the considerations it found persuasive").

Nor did the Commission violate the APA in its consideration of the Fidelity study. Although Chairman Donaldson did, as the Chamber points out, betray a dismissive attitude toward the value of empirical data, SEC Open Meeting, 57–58 (June 23, 2004) ("there are no empirical studies that are worth much. You can do anything you want with numbers and we've seen evidence of that in a number of our submissions"), the Commission did not reject the Fidelity study or decline to do its own study upon that basis. Rather, the Commission concluded the Fidelity study was "unpersuasive" because, as the authors acknowledged, it did not rule out "other important differences [than independence of the chairman] that may have impacted performance results," 69 Fed.Reg. at 46,383 n.52 (quoting study), and because it did not use a reliable method of calculating fund expenses, *id.* The Commission also noted that other commenters reviewing the Fidelity study had concluded funds with an independent chairman did "slightly better in terms of returns, but at lower cost." *Id.* Although a more detailed discussion of the study might have been useful, the Commission made clear enough the limitations of the study, and we have no cause to disturb its ultimate judgment that the study was "unpersuasive evidence." *Cf. Hüls Am. Inc. v. Browner,* 83 F.3d 445, 452 (D.C.Cir.1996) (court owes "extreme degree of deference to the agency when it is evaluating scientific data within its technical expertise").

We reach a different conclusion with regard to the Commission's consideration of the costs of the conditions. With respect to the 75% independent director condition, the Commission, although describing three methods by which a fund might comply with the condition, claimed it was without a "reliable basis for determining how funds would choose to satisfy the [condition] and therefore it [was] difficult to determine the costs associated with electing independent directors." 69 Fed.Reg. at 46,387. That particular difficulty may mean the Commission can determine only the range within which a fund's cost of compliance will fall, depending upon how it responds to the condition but, as the Chamber contends, it does not excuse the Commission from its statutory obligation to determine as best it can the economic implications of the rule it has proposed. *See Pub. Citizen,* 374 F.3d at 1221 (in face of uncertainty, agency must "exercise its expertise to make tough choices about which of the competing estimates is most plausible, and to hazard a guess as to which is correct, even if ... the estimate will be imprecise").

With respect to the costs of the independent chairman condition, counsel maintains the Commission "was not aware of any costs associated with the hiring of staff because boards typically have this authority under state law, and the rule would not require them to hire employees." The Commission made that observation, however, in regard not to the independent chairman condition but to a condition not challenged here, and we cannot therefore consider counsel's rationalization for the regulation under review. *See Motor Vehicle Mfrs. Ass'n,* 463 U.S. at 50, 103 S.Ct. 2856 ("courts may not accept appellate counsel's *post hoc* rationalizations for agency action"). In any event, the argument is a *non sequitur;* whether a board is authorized by law to hire additional staff in no way bears upon the contention that, because of his comparative lack of knowledge about the fund, an independent chairman would in fact cause the fund to incur additional staffing costs.

What the Commission itself did was acknowledge in a footnote that an independent chairman "may choose to hire [more] staff" but it stopped there because, it said, it had no "reliable basis for estimating those costs." 69 Fed.Reg. at 46,387 n.81. Although the Commission may not have been able to estimate the aggregate cost to the mutual fund industry of additional staff because it did not know what percentage of funds with independent chairman would incur that cost, it readily could have estimated the cost to an individual fund, which estimate would be pertinent to its assessment of the effect the condition would have upon efficiency and competition, if not upon capital formation. And, as we have just seen, uncertainty may limit what the Commission can do, but it does not excuse the Commission from its statutory obligation to do what it can to apprise itself—and hence the public and the Congress—of the economic consequences of a proposed regulation before it decides whether to adopt the measure.

In sum, the Commission violated its obligation under 15 U.S.C. § 80a-2(c), and therefore the APA, in failing adequately to consider the costs imposed upon funds by the two challenged conditions.

3. Consideration of Alternatives

Finally, the Chamber argues the Commission gave "inadequate consideration" to suggested alternatives to the independent chairman condition, citing as an example—the only significant one, it seems to us—the proposal, endorsed by the two dissenting Commissioners, that each fund be required prominently to disclose whether it has an inside or an independent chairman and thereby allow investors to make an informed choice. Commission counsel responds by noting generally that the agency is "not required to discuss every alternative raised" and that it did consider the "major alternatives" proposed by commenters, adding more specifically that it had no obligation to consider the dissenters' disclosure alternative because the "Congress rejected a purely disclosure-based approach to regulating conflicts of interest under the [ICA]."

We conclude the Commission's failure to consider the disclosure alternative violated the APA. To be sure, the Commission is not required to consider "every alternative ... conceivable by the mind of man ... regardless of how uncommon or unknown that alternative" may be. *Motor Vehicle Mfrs. Ass'n,* 463 U.S. at 51, 103 S.Ct. 2856. Here, however, two dissenting Commissioners raised, as an alternative to prescription, reliance upon disclosure, *see* 69 Fed. Reg. at 46,393—a familiar tool in the Commission's tool kit—and several commenters suggested that the Commission should leave the choice of chairman to market forces, making it hard to see how that particular policy alternative was either "uncommon or unknown."

The Commission would nevertheless be excused for failing to consider this alternative if it were, for whatever reason, unworthy of consideration. Commission counsel accordingly suggests one such reason, namely, that in the ICA the Congress rejected a "purely disclosure-based approach." *See also SEC v. Variable Annuity Life Ins. Co.,* 359 U.S. 65, 78, 79 S.Ct. 618, 3 L.Ed.2d 640 (1959) (ICA "passes beyond a simple 'disclosure' philosophy"). Counsel's statement is true but irrelevant; that the Congress required more than disclosure with respect to some matters governed by the ICA does not mean it deemed disclosure insufficient with respect to all such matters. On the contrary, the ICA requires funds to make extensive disclosures. *See, e.g.,* 15 U.S.C. § 80a-8(b) (fund must file registration statement with Commission); *id.* § 80a-29(e) (fund must send semiannual report to shareholders); *id.* § 80a-44(a) (fund must make available to public all documents filed with Commission); *see also* Mary M. Frank et al., *Copycat Funds: Information Disclosure Regulation and the Returns to Active Fund Management in the Mutual Fund Industry,* 47 J.L. & Econ. 515 (2004) ("[ICA] regulates information disclosure by mutual funds"). Indeed, the Commission augmented the disclosure requirements of the ICA even as it was considering the independent chairman condition. *See* Final Rule, Shareholder Reports and Quarterly Portfolio Disclosure of Registered Management Investment Companies, 69 Fed. Reg. 11,244, 11,245 (Mar. 9, 2004).

In sum, the disclosure alternative was neither frivolous nor out of bounds and the Commission therefore had an obligation to consider it. *Cf. Laclede Gas Co. v. FERC,* 873 F.2d 1494, 1498 (D.C.Cir.1989) ("where a party raises facially reasonable alternatives ... the agency must either consider those alternatives or give some reason ... for declining to do so") (emphases removed). The Commission may ultimately decide the disclosure alternative will not sufficiently serve the interests of shareholders, but the Commission—not its counsel and not this court—is charged by the Congress with bringing its expertise and its best judgment to bear upon that issue. *See SEC v. Chenery Corp.,* 332 U.S. 194, 196–97 (1947); *see also Motor Vehicle Mfrs. Ass'n,* 463 U.S. at 54. [* * *]

Notes and Applications

The SEC attempted to cure the deficiencies in its 2004 rulemaking identified in the court's decision, but those efforts too were found wanting by the D.C. Circuit. *Chamber of Commerce v. SEC*, 443 F.3d 890 (D.C. Cir. 2006). The D.C. Circuit's decisions were a stinging defeat for the SEC. As a result, the rule amendments relating to board composition and board chair, as codified in the Code of Federal Regulations, are not technically binding, although other amendments that were not challenged, are. The failure of the board composition amendments means that the board composition requirement (i.e., the requirement that 50% or more of the board members be independent as codified in 2001) remains binding, not the 75% threshold. Nevertheless, according to the Investment Company Institute, industry best practices have moved decidedly in the direction of the requirements as codified in 2004 in terms of increased membership of independent trustees on most boards (more than 80% of fund boards have more than 75% of their members who are independent) and a majority have independent board chairs. Thus, in some sense, the SEC could be said to have lost the battle, but won the war.

Chapter 12

The Advisory Relationship and Advisory Fees

Key Ideas: The advisory relationship, that is the relationship between a fund and its investmentƒ adviser, is the defining relationship for most registered investment companies, whether mutual funds, ETFs or closed-end funds. In addition to its critical role in managing the fund's assets, the investment adviser generally coordinates the roles of the funds' many ancillary service providers. Most investment companies retain an external investment adviser (which frequently is the fund sponsor). Section 15(a) of the Company Act contains specific requirements for investment advisory agreements that require regular periodic board approval and at least initial approval by shareholders. Section 15(c) establishes a separate role for independent trustees in overseeing the contract review and approval process, including information gathering, and imposes information-sharing duties on the adviser as part of this process. These provisions also have implications for termination of advisory relationships.

Among the additional statutory and regulatory safeguards that govern the advisory relationship, perhaps none is more important than Section 36(b) of the Company Act in focusing attention on the management fee received by a fund's investment adviser for managing fund assets. The management fee is generally the largest and most significant fee incurred by funds on an annual basis. Section 36(b) imposes a fiduciary obligation on investment advisers with respect to an adviser's receipt of management fees from a fund. Specifically, the provision creates a direct private cause of action that allows shareholders to seek recovery for the fund of any amounts deemed excessive. In 2010, the Supreme Court in *Jones v. Harris*, 559 U.S. 335 (2010), endorsed a well-established judicial standard for this fiduciary principle—the "*Gartenberg* Standard"—pursuant to which a finding of breach would be warranted only if the investment adviser receives a fee that is so disproportionately large that it bears no reasonable relationship to the services rendered and would not have resulted if there had been arm's-length bargaining. Finally, although generally not explicitly prescribed by statute, boards typically, either directly or indirectly, scrutinize and approve the funds' contractual relationships with the fund's other service providers.

Chapter Contents

12.1 Introduction

The early chapters of this textbook focused on a high-level understanding of the structure of the industry and fund operations. The last chapter, Chapter 11, discussed formation and governance of funds in more detailed terms. In this chapter, the discussion continues into a deeper understanding of the legal requirements relating to the advisory and other service relationships needed to operate a fund. Central to any discussion of the legal aspects of fund management and advisory agreements is understanding the nature of the advisory arrangements and basic features of the fund fee and expense arrangements. The business aspects of these issues were introduced in Chapters 3 and 4 and in this and subsequent chapters, the legal aspect of these issues within the context of the Company Act are explored.

The investment advisory function of a fund can be configured in one of two ways: internally or externally. An internally managed fund is one managed by the fund's employees or by an entity owned by the fund. Internally managed funds were not uncommon during the early years of the fund industry, but today they are rare numerically. One of the most celebrated exceptions to this trend is the Vanguard funds, which collectively own Vanguard Group, which in turn manages most, but not all, of the Vanguard funds, one of the largest fund families with a collective AUM in the trillions of dollars in assets. In contrast, most investment companies contract with a legally distinct investment adviser and are referred to as "externally managed funds." Externally managed funds rely on the investment adviser to not only manage the funds' investment portfolios, but also to oversee and/or provide non-advisory services through third-party service providers or affiliates of the investment adviser.

Although investment advisers' relationship with a fund may be contractual, it is seldom arm's length. The investment adviser almost invariably sponsors the formation of the fund. In other words, the investment adviser is not a stranger to the fund it advises or merely an unrelated third party. It is this aspect of the relationship that is of fundamental significance in understanding the Company Act's legal framework for addressing the advisory relationship, and especially the externally managed advisory relationship. Under the Company Act, the fund's board, and more specifically its independent trustees, are charged with providing a counterweight to the investment adviser in its dealing with the fund. The board's role as counterweight is closely tied to the economic aspect of the advisory relationship, most notably determination of the management fee and ongoing evaluation of the quality of services rendered by the adviser.

Although management fees command significant attention, the board also oversees non-advisory expenses incurred by the fund as well as shareholder charges (i.e., costs borne directly by shareholders, including sales loads or commissions paid to buy shares of a fund). In either case, the board is charged with acting for the benefit of shareholders. Non-advisory fund expenses include a variety of operating expenses ranging from the costs of fund administration to legal, tax and regulatory costs. They may also include some fund expenses (asset-based charges) to facilitate distribution, but use of fund assets for such purposes is severely limited by Rule 12b-1. The board also reviews other shareholder charges used to pay for distribution of a fund's shares (i.e., compensate brokers, financial advisers and investment advisers who may provide investment advice to investors). These fund expenses and sales charges tied to distribution are no less subject to the board's purview than the management fee. However, the management fee, that is the fee paid to the investment adviser for managing the fund, is typically the most significant component of a fund's operating expenses.

As discussed in this chapter, the Company Act seeks to ensure accountability with respect to the board's role in reviewing, approving and overseeing the advisory arrangement, including the processes used by the board in discharging its responsibilities. It also separately makes advisers directly accountable for the fees that they receive. In many ways, these requirements result from bargaining dynamics that leave funds without competitive market alternatives to an existing advisory relationship, thereby arresting the operation of market forces with respect to the determination of management fees.

While this chapter gives significant attention to the board's role in approving fees, it also addresses another statutory check on advisory fees. Company Act Section 36(b) imposes a fiduciary duty on investment advisers with respect to the receipt of fees from a fund. More importantly, it also creates a right of action that empowers shareholders to seek recoupment on behalf of the fund of any excessive fees paid to the adviser. Not surprisingly, courts have been called upon to give meaning to this remedy.

12.2 The Advisory Agreement

Externally managed funds are unlike most business organizations in that their day-to-day operations are entrusted to an external investment adviser (which is frequently the fund sponsor) and other third-party service providers. The adviser is in business for its own shareholders (which could either be private owners or public shareholders), and its interests are in conflict with those of fund shareholders when it comes to the management fee. One approach would be for a fund and its shareholders to seek the lowest cost provider of investment advice, but such a strategy is rarely, if ever, embraced by a fund board. If true, does that fact necessarily represent a breach of the board's fiduciary duties to the fund and its shareholders? Why? Assuming that a fund is not necessarily required to seek the adviser who charges the lowest management fee, the fund's board should in theory at the very least seek the optimal mix of quality relative to cost. In contrast, an adviser will seek the highest fee the market will bear. The advisory agreement memorializes their negotiated arrangement.

The key legal requirements relating to a registered investment company's advisory agreement and to the board's central role in selecting and overseeing the fund's adviser are set forth in Section 15(a) and (c) of the Company Act.[1] Just as Section 205(a) of the Advisers Act establishes the minimum requirements for investment advisory agreements of registered investment advisers, Section 15(a) of the Company Act establishes the minimum requirements for an investment advisory agreement for an externally managed investment company. The formal aspects of the contract are threefold: (i) the contract must be in writing, (ii) it must precisely describe the compensation arrangement (and is necessarily constrained by the performance fee prohibitions in Section 205(b) of the Advisers Act); and (iii) it must contain termination provisions that allow termination by the fund on not more than 60 day notice and for automatic termination upon assignment. More importantly, Section 15(a) establishes a process governing the advisory agreement's approval and renewal. The contract must initially be approved by a vote of the majority of the fund's outstanding shares and may not continue beyond two years without being formally renewed. Unlike the initial approval, the contract's continuance can be renewed annually thereafter, either with the approval of the board or with a majority vote of the shareholders.

The initial investment advisory agreement will almost certainly be executed before shares are sold to the public. In that situation, the only shareholder will be the fund sponsor, which in all likelihood will be the investment adviser. The process effectively leaves the sponsor in control of the initial investment advisory relationship. It is true that the fund's board will also be involved before the agreement is submitted to shareholders, but once again, the investment adviser will most likely have selected the board as well. As noted, after the initial two year period, the fund will shift to an annual renewal process. Not surprisingly for reasons of efficiency and expense, funds invariably choose to rely on board, rather than shareholder, approval action in con-

1. The Company Act is also undeniably aimed at providing a check on the role of the fund's principal underwriter and imposes similar responsibilities on the board with respect to the principal underwriting agreement. Specifically, Section 15(b) imposes analogous requirements to Section 15(a) in that regard. For expositional reasons, it is simpler to focus exclusively on the investment adviser agreement. While historically there were strong reasons to equate board oversight of these twin functions, this equivalence is less true in practice today. Typically, an affiliate of the adviser or a specialized third-party provider acts as the principal underwriter. The principal underwriter no longer garners significant fees relative to the adviser in its current role and as a result has been given less attention here. There is some discussion of principal underwriters in Chapter 17, although the focus there is more on fees used to support different distribution channels.

nection with annual renewals of the investment advisory agreement. Nevertheless, the need for shareholder approval can be triggered in the future if the investment adviser changes or, more likely, there is an assignment of the investment advisory agreement by virtue of change in control of the adviser.

Section 15(c) supplements the role of the board by requiring that the terms of any advisory contract, and any renewal thereof, be approved by a vote of the majority of the independent (or disinterested) trustees. Significantly, Section 15(c) also requires a fund's trustees to request and evaluate, and an investment adviser to a fund to furnish, such information as may reasonably be necessary to evaluate the terms of any advisory contract. The review process is often referred to as the "15(c) review" or "15(c) due diligence." The information exchange features of Section 15(c) were added to the Company Act in 1970, amendments which also saw the addition of Section 36(b) to the Company Act. That section imposes a fiduciary duty on advisers with respect to the receipt of management fees. As discussed below, the factors use to evaluate whether management fees are excessive under Section 36(b) are also the factors most relevant to independent trustees' evaluation of the investment advisory contract in connection with the board's Section 15(c) process. Why is this not surprising?

Notes and Applications

Sub-advisers. Sub-advisers as the name would imply are investment advisers who assist the investment advisers in managing an investment portfolio and are frequently used in managing all or some portion of a fund's investment portfolio. The definition of investment adviser for purposes of the Company Act encompasses sub-advisers. Sub-advisers are typically used in one of two ways. A portfolio's assets may be divided among several different managers, in which case each manager would be a sub-adviser for the portion of the portfolio allocated to that manager. This approach is sometimes referred to as a multi-manager or manager-of-managers approach. In another approach, a sub-adviser which has been selected by the investment adviser, may function as the sole manager of a portfolio. The investment adviser in this context functions purely in a capacity of selecting and monitoring the sub-adviser while the sub-adviser performs the day-to-day portfolio management (single-manager sub-advised funds).

A sub-advisory arrangement is subject to the requirements of Sections 15(a) & (c), even though the sub-adviser agreement is typically between the investment adviser and the sub-adviser. Thus, absent exemptive relief, the sub-advisory arrangement must be approved initially by shareholders and be renewed annually by the board after the initial two-year period. While this makes good sense at the inception of the entire investment advisory arrangement, it seems less appropriate as time goes on because the investment adviser may wish to replace the sub-adviser based on its oversight role. Indeed, one purpose of the primary investment adviser is to "manage" the sub-adviser. Of course, shareholder involvement would be required if, as a result of a change in sub-advisers, the total management fee increased. But this is seldom the case. Instead, the management fee is unchanged and the investment adviser and the new sub-adviser negotiate over how the fee should be apportioned. As a result, the

SEC has a well-developed practice of granting manager-of-managers exemptive orders subject to conditions designed to protect the interests of investors. These orders dispense with the need for a shareholder vote in the event of a mere substitution of a sub-adviser, but retains board oversight and review of any substitution. The SEC proposed a rule (Company Act proposed Rule 15a-5 some years ago) that would have codified this exemptive relief, but decided not to go forward with the rule.

Another aspect of the sub-advisory arrangement is the apportionment of fees between the primary adviser and the sub-adviser. In practice, the primary investment adviser receives more than half the fee, which might appear surprising since the sub-adviser appears to be making and executing the day-to-day investment decisions. Why is this the case? The apportionment perhaps reflects the relative bargaining power of the two participants. The sub-adviser's bargaining power derives from being a provider of actual investment management services, while the primary adviser derives its bargaining power from its de facto control over the fund's assets under management. Does the apportionment reveal lurking fiduciary issues for the primary investment adviser or the fund's board?

12.2.1 Obligations of Advisers Regarding Approval of Advisory Agreements

While Section 15(c) requires fund boards to request information needed to evaluate advisory contracts and fees, it also requires advisers to provide such information. Cases or administrative proceedings exploring the fabric of the information exchange requirement are relatively few and raise questions regarding the nature of the adviser's obligations. Do advisers need to provide any information that independent trustees request? When do advisers need to volunteer information? How far can advisers go in massaging the data provided to make their negotiating position more favorable? In short, how transparent must an adviser be? The following case is illustrative of the challenges and issues.

In the Matter of New York Life Investment Management LLC

Investment Company Act Release No. 28747(May 27, 2009)

[**Textbook Note:** *This settled administrative proceeding addresses the obligations of the investment adviser under Section 15(c) to provide independent trustees with meaningful and complete information regarding the advisory relationship. The fund at the center of this proceeding was an investment option for variable annuity insurance contracts. Such insurance products provide purchasers with regular distributions for income during a purchaser's retirement. The size of the distributions is based on the performance of the underlying mutual funds. Among the features of this particular product was a guarantee, assuring investors that they would receive back at least the amount of their investment, regardless of market performance. The finding of a violation of Section 15(c) here was one* *of several intertwined violations (some of which have been omitted from this excerpt). Consider to what extent, if at all, the SEC's findings evidence application of a standard between fund and adviser that exceeds an arms-length negotiation standard.*]

[***] Summary

This matter concerns multiple violations of Section 206(2) of the Advisers Act and Sections 15(c) and 34(b) of the Investment Company Act by NYLIM in connection with a mutual fund it advised, the MainStay Equity Index Fund ("Equity Index Fund"), during the period from early 2002 through June 30, 2004 (the "relevant period"). The Equity Index Fund is an open-end investment company that seeks to replicate the movements of the S&P 500 index before expenses.

During the relevant period, the disinterested members of the Board of Trustees and the Board of Trustees of The MainStay Funds, approved the renewal of three investment advisory contracts between NYLIM and the Equity Index Fund. For each contract renewal process, commonly known as the "15(c) process," the Board of Trustees received information showing that the management fees NYLIM charged to the Equity Index Fund were among the highest of the Equity Index Fund's peer-group of mutual funds. NYLIM urged the Board of Trustees to consider the "Guarantee" feature of the Equity Index Fund in evaluating the management fees NYLIM proposed, but, in violation of Section 206(2) of the Advisers Act and Section 15(c) of the Investment Company Act, failed to provide the Board of Trustees information reasonably necessary to evaluate the cost of the Guarantee.[2] Moreover, at the same time that NYLIM was claiming that the Guarantee should be considered to justify the Equity Index Fund's management fees, it was filing with the Commission, in violation of Section 34(b) of the Investment Company Act, prospectuses, annual reports, and registration statements in which it misrepresented that there was "no charge" to the Equity Index Fund or its shareholders for the Guarantee.

Respondent

1. **NYLIM** is a registered investment adviser and an indirect wholly-owned subsidiary of New York Life Insurance Company. It is the investment adviser to the Equity Index Fund, which is a series of The MainStay funds, a load family of open-end investment companies, which was, during the relevant period, primarily distributed by registered representatives of NYLIFE Securities, Inc., an affiliate of NYLIM.

---

2. Pursuant to the Guarantee, a NYLIM affiliate, NYLIFE LLC, agreed to make up any shortfall if the value of a shareholder's investment in the Equity Index Fund on the tenth anniversary of his or her investment was less than his or her original investment, provided the shareholder remained in the Equity Index Fund for the entire period and reinvested all distributions. The only payouts under the Guarantee have occurred recently. As a result of the recent stock market decline, since October 2008, NYLIFE LLC has paid approximately $8,920,751 to shareholders of the Equity Index Fund under the terms of the Guarantee.

Other Relevant Parties

2. **New York Life Insurance Company** is the largest mutual life-insurance company in the United States and one of the largest life insurers in the world. New York Life affiliates provide an array of securities products and services including institutional and retail mutual funds.

3. **The Equity Index Fund** is an open-end investment company that seeks to replicate the movements of the S&P 500 index before expenses. The Equity Index Fund was closed to new share purchases and new investors effective January 1, 2002.

4. **NYLIFE LLC** is a wholly-owned subsidiary of New York Life Insurance Company.

5. **The Board of Trustees** of The MainStay Funds was comprised of up to eleven members, consisting of four affiliated trustees and at least six independent trustees during the relevant period.

6. **Independent Trustees** (also referred to as the "disinterested members of the Board of Trustees") are the members of the Board of Trustees of The MainStay Funds who are not affiliated with NYLIM.

Facts

7. The Equity Index Fund was opened in 1990, when NYLIM proposed to the Board of Trustees of The MainStay Funds (the "Board") that NYLIM offer an S&P 500 index fund to investors as part of the MainStay family of funds.

8. According to the Equity Index Fund's initial prospectus, the Equity Index Fund came with an unconditional guarantee (the "Guarantee") from NYLIFE LLC (originally NYLIFE Inc., until its merger with NYLIFE LLC on September 30, 1999) stating that: "If on the business day immediately after ten years from your date of purchase (the 'Guarantee Date'), the net asset value of a Fund share, plus the value of all cumulative reinvested dividends and distributions paid on the share during the ten-year period, is less than the price you initially paid for the Fund share, NYLIFE will pay you the difference between the price you paid and the net asset value of a Fund share as of the close of business on the Guarantee Date."

9. From the Equity Index Fund's inception through June 30, 2004, every prospectus, registration statement, and annual report NYLIM filed with the Commission included a statement that, "[t]here is no charge to the [Equity Index] Fund or its shareholders for the Guarantee."

10. Section 15(c) of the Investment Company Act requires the investment adviser to a mutual fund "to furnish, such information as may reasonably be necessary to evaluate the terms of any contract whereby [it] undertakes regularly to serve or act as investment adviser ..." to the fund. Section 15(c) of the Investment Company Act requires, among other things, that a majority of a fund's disinterested directors/trustees approve the advisory contract between the investment adviser and the fund.

11. Before the 2000 advisory contract renewal process, NYLIM was the Board's sole source of information in the 15(c) process concerning the Equity Index Fund's costs of operation, profitability, and peer-group fee comparisons. For the 15(c) process for

the years from 2000 through 2003, however, the Independent Trustees of the Board also engaged a series of outside consultants to provide information about peer-group fee comparisons for The MainStay Funds, including the Equity Index Fund. The Independent Trustees also were advised by their own independent legal counsel at all times relevant to this matter.

12. The Board met on March 13, 2000 to consider the Equity Index Fund's advisory contract renewal for its 2000 contract period. For the meeting, the Board was provided with an independent consultant's report, which showed the Equity Index Fund's management fees were the highest in its peer-group. The Board was also provided with information that showed that NYLIM generated a 91% profit margin from the Equity Index Fund. The Board approved the contract as NYLIM proposed.

13. The Board met on March 12 and 13, 2001, to consider the Equity Index Fund's advisory contract renewal for the one-year period beginning on May 1, 2001. By then a new independent consultant had been hired to provide a peer-group fee comparison report for the 15(c) process. However, this report was not completed by the March 2001 meeting but was instead provided for a June 11, 2001 Board meeting after the Equity Index Fund's advisory contract had been renewed for 2001. At the March meeting, NYLIM presented information showing that the Equity Index Fund's management fees were the highest in its peer-group. NYLIM also provided the Board with information showing that NYLIM generated a 9% profit margin from the Equity Index Fund. At the June 11, 2001 meeting, the new consultant's report was provided to the Board. That report showed that the Equity Index Fund's total expense ratio (total expenses for the fund as a percentage of average net assets) was the highest in its peer-group. Again, the contract was approved as proposed.

14. During the spring and summer of 2001, in light of changing market conditions, New York Life Insurance Company for the first time began to analyze the financial exposure of providing the Guarantee.

15. The Board met on September 10, 2001. At the meeting, the Board voted to close the Equity Index Fund on or about January 1, 2002. The Equity Index Fund was then closed to new share purchases and new investors effective January 1, 2002.

16. On January 14, 2002, as a result of the risk analysis done in 2001, NYLIFE LLC established for the first time a reserve of $2 million related to the Guarantee on its 2001 year-end financial statements.

17. The Board met on March 12, 2002 to consider the Equity Index Fund's advisory contract renewal for the one-year period beginning on May 1, 2002. For the meeting, in addition to an internal NYLIM profitability analysis, which reflected a 7% profit margin, the Board obtained a report from a third independent consultant. The report showed that the Equity Index Fund had the highest management fees in its peer-group. As part of the 15(c) process, NYLIM urged the Board to consider the Guarantee in evaluating the management fees NYLIM proposed to charge the Equity Index Fund, but failed to provide the Board information reasonably necessary to evaluate the proper level of such fees. No information was given to the Board regarding either the

estimated financial cost or value of the Guarantee or the fact that NYLIFE LLC had established a reserve for the Guarantee. The Board approved the contract as NYLIM proposed.

18. On June 10 and 11, 2002, the Board met again to consider the renewal of the Equity Index Fund advisory contract (the contract renewal period having been changed to begin August 1 each year). The reports provided to the Board at the June 2002 meeting, including the report of the third independent consultant, were substantially the same as the March 2002 reports. Again, no information was given to the Board regarding the estimated cost or value associated with the Guarantee or the fact that NYLIFE LLC had established a reserve for the Guarantee. The Board again approved the contract as NYLIM proposed.

19. In January 2003, NYLIFE LLC recorded a reserve of $11.9 million related to the Guarantee in its 2002 year-end financial statements.

20. The Board met on June 9 and 10, 2003 to consider the Equity Index Fund's advisory contract renewal for the one-year period beginning on August 1, 2003. As part of the 15(c) process, NYLIM presented the Equity Index Fund's management fees as being 28 basis points higher than the selected peer-group median and the second most "unfavorable" of its funds. The explanation NYLIM gave to the Board for the unfavorable comparison was the Equity Index Fund's "unique guarantee." As part of the 15(c) materials, the Board was provided an independent consultant's report and a profitability analysis. The independent consultant's report showed the Equity Index Fund's management fees and total fees were both the highest in its peer-group. The independent consultant concluded: (1) "[h]igh expenses are the main reason this fund ranks worst among its index-fund peers for the one-, three-, and five-year periods;" (2) the "main culprit" for the Equity Index Fund's poor peer-group comparison was a management fee "that is more than twice the peer-group average;" and (3) the Guarantee, although "unique," was "of somewhat limited value." The report also questioned if the Guarantee had any cost associated with it at all "given how unusual it would be for the S&P 500 to lose money over such a long period (and the guarantee is good only on one specific day, the 10-year anniversary of the investor's purchase date) ... and [n]ow that the fund is closed to new investors, it would seem the liability for the guarantee would be shrinking."

21. NYLIM's profitability analysis for the Equity Index Fund included in the 2003 15(c) materials reflected a negative 103% profit margin, due to the inclusion of a $9.9 million expense for a reserve for the Guarantee. NYLIM however did not explain the expense represented an increase in the estimate of the reserve for the Guarantee, that the reserve for the Guarantee represented the present value of all future payments related to the Guarantee, or that the cost of the Guarantee to NLYIM could have been spread over future years. Moreover, NYLIM did not provide the Board with information concerning the assumptions used to calculate the reserve or explain why NYLIM believed the full amount of the increase to the reserve should be included in the analysis of the profitability of the Equity Index Fund. The increase to the reserve was simply shown as a line item on the Equity Index Fund's profitability analysis,

without which the Equity Index Fund would have shown a profit margin of 31%. The Board approved the contract as NYLIM proposed.

22. The Board met on June 14 and 15, 2004 to consider the Equity Index Fund's advisory contract renewal for the one-year period beginning on August 1, 2004. The independent consultant retained by the Board submitted a report showing that the Equity Index Fund's management fees were 21 basis points higher than the selected peer-group median. NYLIM's profitability analysis for the Equity Index Fund included in the 2004 15(c) materials reflected net income of $9.8 million, resulting in a 163% profit margin, due to the release of $8.3 million of the reserve into income. NYLIM explained in the analysis that this income resulted from a significant reversal in the amount of the reserve for the Guarantee on NYLIFE's financial statements. Moreover, the internal reports NYLIM provided for the meetings stated that the Independent Trustees had specifically asked NYLIM to focus on the Equity Index Fund and its "above average Net Management Fees." For the first time, NYLIM provided the Board with information concerning the assumptions used to calculate the reserve and explained why NYLIM believed the reserve should be included in the analysis of the profitability of the Equity Index Fund. Also, in response to written questions on behalf of the disinterested members of the Board of Trustees, NYLIM provided information concerning the estimated cost of the guarantee. Moreover, in providing information to the Board concerning the guarantee, the independent consultant indicated that the cost of protecting an original investment over a set time period could be estimated by pricing a put option and estimated that the cost of a 10-year put option on the S&P 500 would range between 31 and 64 basis points per year.

23. NYLIM continued to assert at the June 14 and 15 meetings that the Guarantee feature of the Equity Index Fund justified the higher fees for the Equity Index Fund. In the materials for these meetings, NYLIM asked the Board to "consider ... that the MainStay Equity Index Fund's total operating expenses are comparable to the total expenses of other types of principal protected funds."[3] Yet during the same meetings, NYLIM provided other materials to the Board stating that the Guarantee was provided to the shareholders at "no cost." The Board did not approve the contract renewal during these meetings.

24. On June 30, 2004, NYLIM amended the prospectus for the Equity Index Fund to inform investors for the first time that the Guarantee was taken into account in setting the management fees for the Equity Index Fund, stating that "For the services that NYLIM and its affiliates provide to the Fund, they receive the fees described in the prospectus. Neither NYLIM nor its affiliates receive a separate fee for providing the Guarantee, although the Guarantee has been considered in connection with the annual renewal of the management fee."

3. Other types of funds had features like the Equity Index Fund's that served to protect investors from losing their principal investment.

25. In July 2004, as part of the contract renewal approval process, the Board voted to lower the management fee of the Equity Index Fund from 50 basis points to 30 basis points and to cap the Equity Index Fund's expense ratio at 80 basis points.

26. During the relevant period, as a result of its conduct, NYLIM received management fees from the Equity Index Fund in excess of the peer median of approximately $3,950,075.

....

Violations of Law

A. NYLIM Violated Section 15(c) of the Investment Company Act

27. Section 15(c) of the Investment Company Act requires the investment adviser to a mutual fund "to furnish, such information as may reasonably be necessary to evaluate the terms of any contract whereby [it] undertakes regularly to serve or act as investment adviser...." to the fund. Section 15(c) of the Investment Company Act requires, among other things, that a majority of a fund's independent directors/trustees approve the advisory contract between the investment adviser and the fund.

28. By virtue of the foregoing, NYLIM willfully violated Section 15(c) of the Investment Company Act in 2002 and 2003. During the 2002 and 2003 15(c) processes NYLIM explained the fee being sought by reference to the Guarantee feature of the Equity Index Fund while failing to provide information necessary for the Board to evaluate the Guarantee's true cost or value. Prior to the 2004 Board meeting, NYLIM did not provide the Board with information concerning the assumptions used to calculate the reserve or explain why NYLIM believed the reserve should be included in the analysis of the profitability of the Equity Index Fund.

B. NYLIM Violated Section 206(2) of the Advisers Act

29. Section 206(2) of the Advisers Act prohibits an investment adviser from engaging "in any transaction, practice or course of business which operates as a fraud or deceit upon any client or prospective client" and imposes on investment advisers a fiduciary duty to their clients to act in "utmost good faith," fully and fairly disclose all material facts, and use reasonable care to avoid misleading clients. *SEC v. Capital Gains Research Bureau, Inc.*, 375 U.S. 180, 191, 194 (1963). Proof of scienter is not required to establish a violation of Section 206(2). *SEC v. Steadman*, 967 F.2d 636, 643 n.5 (D.C. Cir. 1992); *Steadman v. SEC*, 603 F.2d 1126, 1134–35 (5th Cir. 1979), *aff'd*, 450 U.S. 91 (1981).

30. NYLIM willfully violated Section 206(2) of the Advisers Act in 2002 and 2003 by not disclosing all material facts to the Board during the 15(c) processes for the Equity Index Fund. NYLIFE LLC established a reserve for the Guarantee in its financial statements on January 14, 2002, but in the 2002 15(c) process, NYLIM provided no information to the Board regarding either the estimated cost or value of the Guarantee or the fact that NYLIFE LLC had even established a reserve for the Guarantee in its financial statements. For the 2003 15(c) meeting, NYLIM provided a profitability report to the Board that reflected a $9.9 million expense for the reserve for the Guarantee. NYLIM however did not explain that the expense represented an increase in the estimate of

the reserve for the Guarantee, that the reserve for the Guarantee represented the present value of all future payments related to the Guarantee, or that the cost of the Guarantee to NYLIM could have been spread over future years. Moreover, NYLIM did not provide the Board with information concerning the assumptions used to calculate the reserve or explain why NYLIM believed the full amount of the increase to the reserve should have been included in the analysis of the profitability of the Equity Index Fund. [* * *]

* * *

It is clear that Section 15(c) alters the bargaining playing field between the fund and its independent trustees on the one hand and the adviser on the other. The adviser cannot conceal material information from the independent trustees relevant to the determination of an appropriate management fee.

12.2.2 Information Gathering and Evaluation Obligations of Independent Trustees

Section 15(c) has implications not only for the adviser, but also for independent trustees in terms of the independent trustees' obligations to approve the advisory relationship and document their deliberations in connection with the renewal process. As noted earlier, funds' independent trustees have an obligation to obtain and evaluate information relevant to the Section 15(c) process. The form and nature of the 15(c) review process has been shaped by years of litigation regarding excessive fees under Section 36(b), which is discussed later in the chapter. To the extent a board authorizes an excessive management fee, the adviser's receipt of the fee would be actionable under Section 36(b). However, what if the board merely does its job badly without any showing that it has resulted in excessive fees? Understandably the SEC, as the regulator, seeks to have independent trustees discharge their fiduciary obligations proactively as the best safeguard against excessive management fees. The following case illustrates different aspects of the board's Section 15(c) review process and obvious deficiencies that accompanied it in this case.

In the Matter of Northern Lights Compliance Services, LLC

Investment Company Act Release No. 30502 (May 2, 2013)

[**Textbook Note:** *The board's deficiencies in this matter led to administrative sanctions against the trustees (including independent trustees) and the affiliated service providers of an umbrella trust. Although not explicit in this order, the SEC's regulatory scrutiny in this case may have been particularly intensive because of the lurking perception that the business model for umbrella trusts (a term discussed in Chapter 11) might lead to perfunctory oversight by the board. Notwithstanding the concerns expressed as to the review process itself, the SEC did not impose sanctions on the independent trustees under Section 15(c). How-*

ever, the SEC did sanction the board and its service providers for their failure to faithfully observe the requisite disclosure and recordkeeping requirements associated with the board's 15(c) approval process. The SEC also found a variety of compliance violations which have been omitted from this excerpt.]

[***] Summary

This proceeding relates to certain disclosure, reporting, recordkeeping and compliance violations associated with the turnkey operations of Northern Lights Fund Trust and Northern Lights Variable Trust, two series trusts registered with the Commission as open-end investment companies (collectively, the "Trusts"). During the period January 2009 through December 2010 (the "relevant period"), the Trusts collectively included up to 71 series, most of which were managed by different, unaffiliated advisers and sub-advisers. During this same time, the Trusts utilized, on behalf of each series, the administrative services of Gemini Fund Services, LLC ("GFS"), the chief compliance officer ("CCO") services of Northern Lights Compliance Services, LLC ("NLCS") and shared a common board of five trustees (the "Trustees"). As more fully described below, NLCS, GFS and the Trustees were a cause of certain series' violations of the federal securities laws.

Section 15(c) of the Investment Company Act imposes a duty on the directors of a registered investment company to request and evaluate, and a duty on an adviser to furnish, such information as may reasonably be necessary for the directors to evaluate the terms of an advisory contract. In accordance with fund filing disclosure requirements, a relevant fund's next shareholder report must discuss, in reasonable detail, the material factors and conclusions that formed the basis for the directors' approval or renewal of that contract. Boilerplate disclosure of the evaluation process for advisory contracts does not provide meaningful disclosure. However, on certain occasions during the relevant period, disclosures included in shareholder reports concerning the Trustees' evaluation process filed by certain series of the Trusts contained boilerplate disclosures that were materially untrue or misleading in violation of Section 34(b) of the Investment Company Act. GFS made these disclosures in the fund shareholder reports based on board minutes reviewed by the Trusts' outside counsel, and then reviewed and approved by the Trustees. The Trustees therefore were a cause of these violations. In addition, GFS failed to ensure that certain shareholder reports contained the required disclosures concerning the Trustees' evaluation process and failed to ensure that certain series within the Trusts maintained and preserved their Section 15(c) files in accordance with Investment Company Act recordkeeping requirements. Accordingly, GFS caused those series' violations of Sections 30(e) and 31(a) of the Investment Company Act and Rules 30e-1 and 31a-2(a)(6) thereunder.

Respondents

1. Northern Lights Compliance Services, LLC ("NLCS"), a Nebraska limited liability company based in Omaha, Nebraska and Hauppauge, New York, is an affiliate of GFS and provides CCO services to investment companies. NLCS has provided its CCO services to the Trusts and their respective series since the Trusts' inception.

2. Gemini Fund Services, LLC ("GFS"), a Nebraska limited liability company based in Omaha, Nebraska and Hauppauge, New York, is a full-service mutual fund administrator, providing comprehensive services to mutual funds for fund administration, fund accounting, transfer agent services, and custody administration. GFS has acted as the fund administrator to the Trusts and their respective series since the Trusts' inception.

[**Ed. Note**: the order went on to identify individually the trustees, including independent trustees.]

Other Relevant Entities

8. Northern Lights Fund Trust ("NLFT"), a Delaware statutory trust with its principal place of business in Omaha, Nebraska, has been registered with the Commission as an open-end management investment company since January 2005. NLFT operates as a series company and was comprised of up to 64 series during the relevant period.

9. Northern Lights Variable Trust ("NLVT"), a Delaware statutory trust with its principal place of business in Omaha, Nebraska, has been registered with the Commission as an open-end management investment company since February 2006. NLVT, a variable insurance trust, operates as a series company and was comprised of up to 7 series during the relevant period.

Facts

The Trusts, Third-Party Service Providers and the Trustees

10. The Trusts are registered open-end series investment companies that were formed to allow advisers that are unaffiliated with each other to manage the portfolios of one or more mutual fund series. Specifically, by utilizing the administrative services of GFS, among other third-party service providers, and a common board of trustees and officers, the Trusts are marketed as a turnkey investment company platform to advisers who want to manage small to mid-size mutual funds (each a series of the Trust) without having to administer the day-to-day operations of a fund, including the management of corporate, board and regulatory governance. During the relevant period, NLFT and NLVT were comprised of up to 64 and 7 series, respectively, many of which were managed by different advisers and sub-advisers.

11. NLCS, an affiliate of GFS, is a company that was formed in 2004 to provide CCO services to mutual funds in light of the Commission's adoption of Rule 38a-1 under the Investment Company Act in 2003. NLCS provides its CCO services to the Trusts and their respective series, and is also paid for its services out of fund assets based on a contract approved by the independent Trustees.

12. GFS is a full-service mutual fund administrator that provides comprehensive services to the Trusts and their respective series for fund administration, fund accounting, and transfer agent services based on a contract approved by the independent Trustees. GFS is affiliated with other service providers of the Trusts, excluding advisers. Each series within the Trusts pays for GFS's services out of fund assets.

13. During the relevant period, the Trusts' boards of trustees consisted of five individuals, four of whom were not an "interested person" of the Trusts as that term is defined under Section 2(a)(19) of the Investment Company Act. They included Miola, the sole interested trustee and chairman of the Trusts, and Bryan, Hertl, Lanzen and Taylor, the not interested trustees.

Section 15(c) of the Investment Company Act and the Related Fund Filing Reports and Disclosures

The Requirements of the Investment Company Act and the Rules Thereunder

14. The Investment Company Act assigns specific responsibilities upon the directors of a mutual fund for the protection of its shareholders, including the duty to evaluate the terms of a fund's advisory contract when approving the contract. Specifically, Section 15(c) of the Investment Company Act makes it unlawful for a fund to enter into or renew any advisory contract unless the terms of the contract are approved by a majority of the fund's independent directors. As part of the approval process, Section 15(c) imposes a specific duty on all directors to request and evaluate, and a duty on an adviser to furnish, such information as may reasonably be necessary for the directors to evaluate the terms of the adviser's contract. The directors' duty under this provision "is one of the most important fund governance obligations assigned to directors under the Investment Company Act." See Role of Independent Directors of Investment Companies, Investment Company Act Release No. 24082 (proposed Nov. 3, 1999).

15. While Section 15(c) does not define what is "reasonably necessary" to evaluate a contract's terms, the Commission has promulgated various fund filing disclosure requirements to better inform shareholders about a board's evaluation process when approving or renewing an advisory contract. First, in 1994, the Commission adopted the requirement that a fund disclose in its proxy statements the material factors that formed the basis for the board's recommendation that shareholders approve an advisory contract. See Amendments to Proxy Rules for Registered Investment Companies, Investment Company Act Release No. 20614 (Oct. 13, 1994). In 2001, the Commission adopted form amendments requiring funds to provide similar disclosures in their Statements of Additional Information ("SAI"). See Role of Independent Directors of Investment Companies, Investment Company Act Release No. 24816 (Jan. 16, 2001). As noted by the Commission in that adopting release, "[m]utual funds fees and expenses, including advisory fees, are extremely important to shareholders," and therefore "[f]unds are required to provide appropriate detail regarding the board's basis for approving an existing investment advisory contract, including the particular factors forming the basis of this determination." Particularly relevant here, with these new form amendments, the Commission reminded funds in enacting the release "that 'boilerplate' disclosure is not appropriate."

16. In 2004, the Commission again adopted form amendments, which replaced the previous SAI requirements and require that when a fund board approves or renews any advisory contract, the fund's next shareholder report must discuss, in reasonable detail, the material factors and conclusions with respect thereto that formed the basis for the directors' approval or renewal of that contract. See Disclosure Regarding the

Approval of Investment Advisory Contracts by Directors of Investment Companies, Investment Company Act Release No. 26486 (June 30, 2004). In support of these amendments, the Commission reasoned that the visibility of this disclosure to fund shareholders "may encourage funds to provide a meaningful explanation of the board's basis for approving an investment advisory contract," which "in turn, may encourage fund boards to consider investment advisory contracts more carefully."

17. In addition, as part of the 2004 form amendments described in paragraph 16, above, the Commission adopted several enhancements to the existing disclosure requirements to address "concerns regarding the adequacy of review of advisory contracts and management fees by fund boards" with the notion that "[i]ncreased transparency with respect to investment advisory contracts, and fees paid for advisory services, will assist investors in making informed choices among funds and encourage fund boards to engage in vigorous and independent oversight of advisory contracts." Investment Company Act Release No. 26486. Specifically, as to the approval or renewal of an advisory contract, funds must include a discussion in their shareholder reports concerning, at a minimum: (1) the nature, extent, and quality of the services to be provided by the investment adviser; (2) the investment performance of the fund and the investment adviser; (3) the costs of the services to be provided and profits to be realized by the investment adviser and its affiliates from the relationship with the fund; (4) the extent to which economies of scale would be realized as the fund grows; and (5) whether fee levels reflect these economies of scale for the benefit of fund investors. See Form N-1A, Item 27(d)(6)(i). Furthermore, Form N-1A requires that the shareholder report indicate whether the board relied upon fee comparisons with other funds or types of clients in approving the contract and, if so, describe the comparisons that were relied upon and how they assisted the board in concluding that the contract should be approved. *Id.*

18. As noted by the Commission, "[i]t would be difficult for a board to reach a final conclusion as to whether to approve an advisory contract without reaching conclusions as to each material factor." Investment Company Act Release No. 26486. Therefore, the form amendments require a discussion of "how the board evaluated each factor," and indicate that "conclusory statements or a list of factors" will not be considered sufficient disclosure. See Form N-1A, Item 27(d)(6), Instruction No. 2. Thus, the Commission addressed some commenters' views that such specific disclosure "would be useful in ensuring that the discussion has reasonable detail and does not rely on boilerplate disclosure." Investment Company Act Release No. 26486.

19. In connection with a board's Section 15(c) evaluation process, the Commission also amended a fund recordkeeping rule, Rule 31a-2 under the Investment Company Act, which requires that funds retain copies of the written materials that directors considered in approving or renewing an advisory contract. Rule 31a-2(a)(6) under the Investment Company Act. According to the Commission, that requirement was designed "to improve the documentation of a fund board's basis for approving an advisory contract, which would assist [the Commission's] examination staff in determining whether fund directors are fulfilling their fiduciary duties when approving advisory contracts."

See Investment Company Governance, Investment Company Act Release No. 26520 (July 27, 2004) (amending Rule 31a-2).

The Disclosures Included Within Certain Shareholder Reports Regarding the Trustees' Section 15(c) Evaluation Process

20. During the relevant period, the Trustees conducted fifteen board meetings during which they considered whether to approve or renew a total of 113 advisory and 32 sub-advisory contracts in accordance with their duties under Section 15(c) of the Investment Company Act. The board meetings also covered other official business of the Trusts and their series, and typically lasted at least a full day. The number of advisory contracts that the Trustees considered varied with respect to each meeting as did the time for which the Trustees discussed each contract, with more time typically spent on new contracts and less on renewals. Because of the large number of series within the Trusts, the Trustees often had to consider several new contracts and renewals at each board meeting, and at two separate board meetings, the Trustees considered over twenty contracts. The Trustees understood that fund shareholder reports were required to disclose the material factors considered and conclusions reached by them in deciding to approve or renew a fund's advisory contract. In all cases, the Trustees knew that the disclosures required to be contained in the shareholder reports would be prepared by GFS and were subject to the review and approval of the Trust's outside counsel prior to their publication. The Trustees further understood that their meeting minutes should document their consideration of and conclusions reached with respect to such material factors. For each contract consideration, and on the advice of the Trusts' outside counsel, the Trustees requested information from the relevant adviser related to the factors discussed in paragraph 17, above, including information related to fee comparisons. Outside counsel solicited and reviewed the information received in response to these requests for completeness on an adviser-by-adviser basis in advance of each board meeting, and the information was then used by the Trustees to evaluate the terms of the advisory contract.

21. Each board meeting included an individual who was responsible, as the note taker or secretary to the Trusts, for taking notes that would be used to draft the board minutes. The secretary was also responsible for preparing and finalizing the board minutes. Typically, the secretary created the first draft of the minutes with the assistance of various GFS paralegals, who were responsible for providing the secretary with a "bones" draft of the minutes normally within six weeks after the relevant board meeting. The paralegals drafted the "bones" version based on their review of the meeting agenda and use of a minutes template, which included boilerplate language concerning the material factors and conclusions which formed the basis for the Trustees' Section 15(c) approval or renewal of the advisory contracts. These initial drafts were supplemented with details by the Trusts' corporate secretary, and then reviewed for accuracy, revised, and approved by the Trusts' outside counsel who led the Trustees in the Section 15(c) process and participated in each meeting.

22. After the secretary finalized the minutes, and they were reviewed and revised by the Trusts' outside counsel using notes taken at the meeting, the minutes were submitted to the Trustees for their review and final approval typically weeks or months

after the meeting occurred. During the relevant period, the Trustees were advised by the Trusts' outside counsel that "[m]eeting minutes are the official record of the Board meetings and document the fulfillment by the Board of its regulatory responsibilities. Trustees should review the minutes to confirm that they accurately reflect Board discussions." The minutes, as reviewed and approved by the Trustees, were later used by GFS to draft those sections of the applicable fund shareholder reports that included a discussion of the Trustees' Section 15(c) evaluation process. Like the minutes, these fund filing disclosures included, among other things, the boilerplate language concerning the material factors and conclusions which formed the basis for the Trustees' approval or renewal of the advisory contracts.

23. During the relevant period, there were instances where certain series' shareholder report disclosures concerning the Trustees' Section 15(c) evaluation process were materially untrue or misleading, in that the boilerplate disclosures either misrepresented material information considered by the Trustees or omitted material information concerning how the Trustees evaluated certain factors. Examples of such untrue or misleading disclosures included:

a. **Example 1:** In connection with the Trustees' decision to renew an advisory contract, the applicable fund shareholder report disclosed that the adviser "had provided the Board with written materials regarding ... the level of the advisory fees charged compared with the fees charged to comparable mutual funds or accounts," and that the Trustees "discussed the comparison of management fees and total operating expense data and reviewed the Fund's advisory fees and overall expenses compared to a peer group of similarly managed funds," and ultimately concluded that the Fund's advisory fee was "acceptable in light of the quality of the services the Fund currently receives from the Adviser, and the level of fees paid by funds in the peer group." However, these boilerplate statements were materially untrue since the adviser had not provided any advisory fee peer group information to the Trustees for their consideration.

b. **Example 2:** In connection with the Trustees' decision to renew an advisory contract, the applicable fund shareholder report disclosed that the Trustees "discussed the comparison of management fees and total operating expense data and reviewed the Fund's advisory fees and overall expenses compared to a peer group of similarly managed funds.... The Trustees concluded that the Fund's advisory fees and expense ratio were acceptable in light of the quality of the services the Fund currently receives from the Adviser, and the level of fees paid by a peer group of other similarly managed mutual funds of comparable size." However, these boilerplate statements were materially misleading since they implied that the fund was paying fees that were not materially higher than the middle of its peer group range when, in fact, the adviser's approved fee was materially higher than all of the fees of the adviser's selected peer group of 74 funds and nearly double the peer group's mean fee. Therefore, the reference to "the level of fees paid by funds in the selected peer group," without further meaningful discussion about the adviser's comparable fee and other information considered by the Trustees, did not provide current and prospective fund shareholders with all necessary material facts concerning the basis for the Trustees' conclusion that the advisory fee was acceptable.

c. **Example 3:** In connection with the Trustees' decision to approve an advisory contract, the applicable fund shareholder report disclosed that the Trustees "reviewed information regarding fees and expenses of comparable funds and concluded that [the adviser's] advisory fee and expense ratio were acceptable in light of the quality of the services the Fund expected to receive from the Adviser, and the level of fees paid by the funds in the peer group." However, these boilerplate statements were materially misleading since they implied that the fund was paying fees that were not materially higher than the middle of its peer group range when, in fact, the adviser's approved fee was materially higher than all of the fees of the adviser's selected peer group of 17 funds and more than double the peer group's mean fee. Therefore, the reference to "the level of fees paid by funds in the peer group," without further meaningful discussion about the adviser's comparable fee and other information considered by the Trustees, did not provide current and prospective fund shareholders with all necessary material facts concerning the basis for the Trustees' conclusion that the advisory was acceptable.

24. Although not created for public disclosure, the relevant board minutes were intended to summarize the key items addressed during the board meetings, and also formed the basis for the shareholder report disclosures, including the examples referenced in paragraph 23, above. The minutes, as drafted by GFS, reviewed and approved by the Trusts' outside counsel and then reviewed and approved by the Trustees, sometimes contained boilerplate language that was materially untrue or misleading.

The Failure by GFS to Ensure that Certain Series Maintained and Preserved Their Complete Section 15(c) Files

25. During the relevant period, GFS, as the fund administrator to all series of the Trusts, was contractually responsible for ensuring that the series maintained and preserved all documents and other written information that the Trustees considered in approving the series' advisory contracts in accordance with Rule 31a-2(a)(6) under the Investment Company Act. However, in several instances, certain series' Section 15(c) files were deficient and therefore failed to comply with the Rule. For example, on three occasions and at the advisers' request, written financial information provided by the advisers as part of their Section 15(c) submissions was discarded by GFS or returned to the advisers after the board meetings due to the advisers' concerns of confidentiality. Furthermore, on four other occasions, certain series failed to maintain written management fee peer group comparisons as submitted by the advisers. Finally, throughout most of the relevant period, certain series failed to maintain written 15(c) summaries that were prepared by the Trusts' outside counsel to assist the Trustees during their 15(c) analysis.

The Failure by GFS to Ensure that Certain Shareholder Reports
Included All Disclosures Concerning the Trustees' Section 15(c) Evaluation Process

26. As the fund administrator to all series of the Trusts, GFS was also contractually responsible for preparing the series' shareholder reports, including those portions of the reports that included a discussion of the Trustees' Section 15(c) evaluation process as required by Item 27(d)(6) of Form N-1A. However, on ten occasions during the relevant period, GFS failed to ensure that certain shareholder reports included the required discussion of the Trustees' evaluation process....

....

The Trustees Caused Violations of Section 34(b) of the Investment Company Act Certain Series' Shareholder Reports

34. Section 34(b) of the Investment Company Act makes it unlawful for any person to make any untrue statement of a material fact in a document filed or transmitted pursuant to the Investment Company Act or the keeping of which is required pursuant to Section 31(a). The same section makes it unlawful to omit to state from any such document any fact necessary in order to prevent the statements made therein, in light of the circumstances under which they were made, from being materially misleading. As noted in paragraph 20, above, the Trustees knew that fund shareholder reports are required to disclose the material factors considered, and conclusions reached, by the Trustees in deciding to approve or renew a fund's advisory contract. The Trustees further understood that their meeting minutes should document their consideration of, and conclusions reached with respect to, such material factors, and that the "Trustees should review the minutes to confirm that they accurately reflect Board discussions." As described in paragraph 24, above, certain board minutes reviewed and approved by the Trustees contained boilerplate language and materially untrue or misleading statements concerning the material factors and conclusions that formed, at least in part, the basis for the Trustees' renewal or approval of certain advisory contracts. These minutes were then used by GFS to draft the required disclosures within the applicable series' shareholder reports, which also included the materially untrue or misleading disclosures concerning the Trustees' Section 15(c) evaluation process. Accordingly, the Trustees were a cause of those series' violations of Section 34(b) of the Investment Company Act.

The Corresponding Board Minutes

35. Section 31(a) of the Investment Company Act requires registered investment companies to maintain and preserve such records as prescribed by Commission rules and regulations. Rule 31a-1(b)(4) thereunder requires each registered investment company to maintain minute books of directors' meetings. In connection with each meeting, the Trustees understood that their meeting minutes should document their consideration of the material factors considered, and conclusions reached, in deciding to approve or renew a fund's advisory contract, and that the "Trustee should review the minutes to confirm that they accurately reflect Board discussions." Accordingly, the Trustees also caused violations of Section 34(b) of the Investment Company Act

by approving certain board minutes, as noted in paragraph 24, above, that were materially untrue or misleading.

....

GFS Caused Certain Series' Violations of Section 31(a) of the Investment Company Act and Rule 31a-2(a)(6) Thereunder

37. As noted above, Section 31(a) of the Investment Company Act requires registered investment companies to maintain and preserve such records as prescribed by Commission rules and regulations. Rule 31a-2(a)(6) thereunder pertains to the specific record-keeping requirement regarding an investment company's Section 15(c) files. Specifically, the Rule requires each investment company to "[p]reserve for a period of not less than six years ... any documents or other written information considered by the directors of the investment company pursuant to Section 15(c) of the Act in approving the terms or renewal of a contract[.]" As a result of the conduct described in paragraph 25, above, GFS caused certain series' violations of Section 31(a) of the Investment Company Act and Rule 31a-2(a)(6) thereunder by failing to ensure, as the fund administrator, that these series maintained and preserved copies of all documents considered by the Trustees in approving or renewing the advisory contracts to those series. [* * *]

* * *

Notes and Applications

Funds' disclosure requirements regarding approval of advisory agreements. As a matter of policy and a desire for transparency, the SEC has over time required more and more detailed disclosures regarding the board approval processes for advisory agreements. Originally, a prospectus had to note and disclose the name of the adviser and its fee. Gradually, additional details regarding advisory contracts and the investment adviser were added to the disclosure requirements, such as the names and qualifications of the individuals actually managing the fund's assets.

In 2004, the SEC adopted a significant overhaul of disclosures regarding approvals of advisory agreements.[2] As noted in the Adopting Release in 2004,

> Recently, concerns have been raised regarding the adequacy of review of advisory contracts and management fees by fund boards. In particular, the level of fees charged by investment advisers to mutual fund clients, especially in comparison to those charged by the same advisers to pension plans and other institutional clients, has become the subject of debate. In February 2004, the Commission proposed to require enhanced disclosure regarding the board's basis for approving, or recommending that shareholders approve, investment advisory contracts, in order to encourage fair and reasonable fund fees. Increased transparency with respect to investment advisory contracts, and fees paid for advisory services, will assist investors in making in-

---

2. Disclosure Regarding Approval of Investment Advisory Contracts by Directors of Investment Companies, Investment Company Act Release No. 26486, 69 Fed. Reg. 39798 (June 30, 2004) ("Adopting Release").

> formed choices among funds and encourage fund boards to engage in vigorous and independent oversight of advisory contracts. This proposal was part of a larger series of Commission rulemaking initiatives that have sought to improve disclosure to investors concerning fund fees and charges."[3]

To address the perceived concerns, the SEC adopted revisions to the registration forms for investment companies, e.g., Form N-1A (for registration of mutual funds). As implemented, the new forms:

> require fund shareholder reports to discuss, in reasonable detail, the material factors and the conclusions with respect thereto that formed the basis for the board of directors' approval of any investment advisory contract. This requirement applies to shareholder reports of open- and closed-end management investment companies and insurance company managed separate accounts that offer variable annuities ...
>
> We continue to believe ... that including disclosure regarding the board's basis for approving an advisory contract in shareholder reports will provide existing fund shareholders with more timely disclosure of the reasons for the board's approval of an investment advisory contract. The visibility of this disclosure, alongside other current information about a fund, such as investment performance and current period dollars and cents expense disclosure, may encourage funds to provide a meaningful explanation of the board's basis for approving an investment advisory contract. This, in turn, may encourage fund boards to consider investment advisory contracts more carefully and investors to consider more carefully the costs and value of the services rendered by the fund's investment adviser.[4]

The amendments and form changes clarified that a fund's disclosures must include "factors relating to both the board's selection of the investment adviser, and its approval of the advisory fee and any other amounts to be paid under the advisory contract...." In these circumstances, there is perhaps an understandable temptation for funds to offer generic disclosure that addresses the recognized factors that should inform a board's decision, but in a way that does not meaningfully distinguish one fund from another or one renewal from another. Perhaps mindful of this type of outcome, the SEC added specific guidance to the disclosure instructions for registration and proxy statements to forestall boilerplate disclosure: "Conclusory statements or a list of factors will not be considered sufficient disclosure. Relate the factors to the specific circumstances of the Fund and the investment advisory contract for which approval is sought and state how the board evaluated each factor. For example, it is not sufficient to state that the board considered the amount of the investment advisory fee without stating what the board concluded about the amount of the fee and how the amount affected its determination to recommend approval of the contract."[5] Why are fund boards likely to be less than enthusiastic about being fully transparent re-

3. *Id.* at 39799.
4. *Id.* at 39799-800.
5. *Id.* at 39807-809.

garding their review process and how effective are disclosure instructions such as those provided by the SEC in getting funds to be more forthcoming? Are there other ways that the SEC might make the disclosure obligations relating to the renewal process more effective?

12.3 Assignment and Termination of the Advisory Agreement

Like all business relationships, changes must be anticipated. Generally, material amendments to an advisory agreement are subject to the Section 15(a) approval requirements, including both board and shareholder approvals. Non-material amendments, e.g., correcting typographical errors in an agreement, may be made without such approvals. Over time, the SEC has permitted certain other types of material amendments without requiring shareholder assent, through its no-action letter process. A reduction in advisory fees is one example.

The Company Act, under Section 15(a), requires that a fund's advisory agreement provide that it may be terminated at any time on not more than 60 days' written notice to the adviser. In addition, it requires that termination be free of any penalties payable by the fund or its shareholders. In practice, terminations take much longer than 60 days, as the transition from one adviser to another is fraught with details related to management, operations and technical systems that must be planned and executed properly. Wholly apart from the operational obstacles, investment advisers are rarely terminated by a fund.

12.3.1 Assignments under the Company Act

The Company Act seeks to preclude sales of fund advisory relationships or so-called "trafficking" in fund advisory agreements. The regulatory concern relating to trafficking targets situations where the investment adviser could economically benefit by transferring or assigning an investment advisory contract. In its crudest form, this might mean an adviser transferring a contract for a side payment. Such an arrangement would raise obvious fiduciary concerns, because a fiduciary cannot be enriched by trading their client relationships to another. Of course, it is possible to imagine slight variations that have the same practical effect. Suppose an adviser sells ownership of its advisory firm to another at a premium price?

Section 15(a) limits appropriation of such benefits by requiring termination of an advisory agreement automatically upon assignment. "Assignment" is a technical term defined in Section 2(a)(4) of the Company Act that includes any transfer of an advisory agreement from one adviser to another or the transfer of a controlling ownership interest in the adviser. Section 2(a)(9) defines "control" and creates a rebuttable presumption that an interest of more than 25% of an adviser constitutes control of the adviser. Read together, that suggests that any transfer of more than 25% of an adviser's ownership must be carefully examined to determine if it triggers the automatic termination provisions of the adviser's fund advisory contracts. The Advisers Act contains similar, but not identical, assignment provisions and so the concern in the Company Act should not be viewed as unique. Nevertheless, many transactions relating to the adviser, such as a change in partners of an adviser organized as a partnership, may be deemed assignments for purposes of Section 2(a)(4) and 15(a) and therefore warrant special attention.

In connection with a transaction that might trigger a termination of a fund's advisory agreement, the affected adviser will seek board and shareholder approvals before completion of the transaction to make sure that the contracts do not terminate automatically. However, unanticipated situations can arise which make pre-approval impractical or difficult to complete. For example, a rancorous split in the ranks of a closely-held investment adviser or the death of a controlling shareholder. Clearly the prospect of a fund without an adviser in place to replace an outgoing adviser would be intolerable for investors. To address such situations, the SEC adopted Rule 15a-4, which provides that an adviser can serve under an interim agreement for up to 150 calendar days after a terminating event is triggered. The rule facilitates an orderly transition so that there is not a period where an automatic termination is triggered before a replacement adviser is in place. However, the rule contains a variety of conditions designed to protect funds and their shareholders which must be satisfied in order to qualify for the interim contract treatment.

A related concern is sale of an investment advisory firm may occasionally raise questions whether the value paid in the transaction is related to the adviser's participation in lucrative advisory agreements with registered investment companies. This element of value under normal fiduciary principles belongs to the fund and not to the adviser. Nevertheless Congress also recognized that control transactions involving the adviser may advance legitimate business objectives and that it would not necessarily be in the interests of fund investors to prevent or deter any and all sales of control involving advisers. Accordingly, the Company Act was amended in 1975 to provide a statutory safe harbor for the economic benefits received by the adviser to a registered investment company in connection with a sale of the adviser which results in an assignment of fund investment advisory contracts. Under the safe-harbor provision, Section 15(f), the existing adviser may retain the economic benefit arising from the sale of shares provided certain conditions are met: (1) for three years after the transaction, at least 75% of the fund's board of trustees must be independent of both the old and new advisers, and (2) no "unfair burden" may be imposed on the fund for a two year period after the transaction, meaning essentially that the old and new advisers (and affiliated parties) should only receive fees for bona fide advisory or other services. From a policy perspective, the safe harbor attempts to strike a balance between the legitimate incentives of parties in control transactions within the advisory business and protection of the fund and its shareholders from extraneous fees and expenses resulting from opportunistic conduct by the relevant advisory firms.

12.3.2 Removing or Replacing Advisers

Investment advisers are seldom discharged by boards. From a policy perspective, this may appear puzzling. The Company Act appears to encourage such transitions, e.g., the nature and requirements of the 15(c) process and the 60 day termination provision of Section 15(a) support boards' careful evaluation of adviser performance and prompt termination, if desired. Yet, as a practical matter, this rarely happens. From a business and operations perspective, such transitions can be challenging, not to mention disruptive. In addition, there are legal issues posed in any removal situation.

Navellier v. Sletten

262 F.3d 923 (9th Cir. 2001)

[**Textbook Note:** *This decision arose from a suit brought by an investment adviser against independent trustees and professionals who provided advice to the independent trustees in connection with the replacement of an incumbent investment adviser. The attempted replacement was effected by a determination not to renew the existing investment advisory agreement. The record reveals a dysfunctional relationship between the board and the investment adviser and an acrimonious parting of ways. The resulting proxy contest and unsuccessful efforts to obtain permanent shareholder approval for an interim replacement attest to the hurdles faced by a board seeking to replace its incumbent investment adviser. Of course, the case itself concerns collateral claims arising out of this broken relationship.*]

Gould, Circuit Judge. This appeal follows an Investment Company Act of 1940 ("ICA") action seeking to impose personal liability on the independent trustees of a mutual fund for the non-renewal of an investment advisory contract. After a fourteen-day trial, the jury determined that the independent trustees acted within their discretion under the business judgment rule in replacing the investment adviser.

Plaintiffs-Appellants are: (1) shareholders and former shareholders of the Navellier Series Fund ("Fund"); (2) the original investment adviser of the Fund, Navellier Management, Inc. ("NMI"); and (3) Louis Navellier, an interested trustee of the Fund (collectively, "appellants"). Defendants-Appellees are: (1) three former independent trustees of the Fund-Donald Simon, Kenneth Sletten, and Lawrence Bianchi (collectively, "independent trustees"); (2) Roy Adams, counsel for the independent trustees; (3) Massachusetts Financial Services ("MFS"), former investment adviser of the Fund; and (4) Arnold Scott, former trustee of the MFS Series Trust (collectively, "appellees").

Appellants challenge the district court proceedings on numerous grounds, complaining about pre-trial, trial, and post-trial rulings. Sletten cross-appeals both an imposition of sanctions against him and his counsel, and the dismissal of his counterclaim for breach of contract. We reject all of appellants' many claims, uphold the jury verdict exonerating the independent trustees, and affirm the judgment of the district court against appellants. On Sletten's cross-appeal, we affirm dismissal of his counterclaim but grant limited relief, holding that the district court abused its discretion in affirming the imposition of sanctions against cross-appellant Sletten and his counsel.

FACTS AND PROCEDURAL BACKGROUND

On May 15, 1993, Navellier organized the Fund as a Delaware business trust that would invest in an open-ended investment company or mutual fund. Navellier and one of his employees, Jack Drinkwater,[5] served as interested trustees, while Simon, Sletten, and Bianchi served as independent trustees. Sam Kornhauser, Navellier's attorney, was hired as Fund counsel.

On the day the Fund was organized, the Fund entered into an investment advisory agreement with NMI. Under this agreement, NMI provided investment advice and managed the Fund's assets. The initial term of the investment advisory contract was two years, annually renewable if approved by a majority of the independent trustees.

In January 1995, the independent trustees sought independent counsel. In October 1995, they hired Adams, an experienced mutual fund attorney, as independent counsel. Adams advised the independent trustees that, to fulfill their fiduciary obligations to the shareholders of the Fund, it was necessary to obtain certain financial information about NMI in order to conduct their annual review of the investment advisory agreement. Adams also told the independent trustees that he had concern about Kornhauser's abilities. Adams expressed the opinion that Kornhauser should not continue as counsel for the Fund while he remained counsel for NMI, Navellier, and Navellier's other businesses.

At a board of trustees' meeting on April 26, 1996, Navellier presented a motion to the trustees of the Fund to merge the Fund into the Navellier Performance Funds. This merger would have been a tax-free reorganization. The assets of the Fund would have been transferred to a portfolio of the Navellier Performance Funds in exchange for the shares of the Navellier Performance Funds. The merger would have terminated the independent trustees' positions.

The independent trustees deferred consideration of Navellier's merger proposal because they concluded that "further consideration would be premature given that the disinterested Trustees did not have any advance notice or information as to the relative merits of the proposal." The next order of business for the meeting was the annual review of the investment advisory agreement. The independent trustees expressed frustration at being asked to review and approve the investment advisory agreement without having received requested information from Kornhauser or NMI. The independent trustees then voiced their concern as to whether Kornhauser should continue as counsel to the Fund. A contentious discussion ensued, after which Navellier threatened to terminate his relationship with the Fund and left the meeting. The independent trustees then voted to remove Kornhauser as counsel to the Fund.

---

5. In July 1995, Drinkwater resigned as an interested trustee and was replaced by Alan Alpers, another employee of Navellier's.

The independent trustees conditioned their future consideration of the merger proposal on review of certain information concerning the finances of Navellier and his companies. After Navellier refused to provide this information, the independent trustees contacted the Securities and Exchange Commission ("SEC") in an effort to compel Navellier to produce the information. This effort to obtain the SEC's assistance in compelling this information did not succeed. Thereafter, the independent trustees decided to put Navellier's proposed merger to a shareholder vote by way of a proxy prepared by NMI.

Pending resolution of the merger proposal, the independent trustees held a board of trustees meeting on March 13, 1997, and voted not to renew NMI's investment advisory contract, which was scheduled to expire by its terms on March 15, 1997. The independent trustees also voted to hire MFS as the Fund's investment adviser. MFS conditioned its agreement to become investment administrator on assurances that the current trustees would not continue as trustees after the vote of the Fund's shareholders.

Navellier and Alpers filed a complaint on April 9, 1997, seeking to enjoin the independent trustees from removing them as interested trustees. Navellier also requested injunctive relief to block the investment advisory agreement with MFS so NMI could regain its former position as investment adviser.

On April 10, 1997, the independent trustees voted to remove Navellier and Alpers from their positions as interested trustees. According to appellants, the independent trustees undertook this allegedly wrongful act to entrench themselves more completely, to neutralize opposition to their upcoming proxy, and to ratify their decision to hire MFS. The independent trustees then eliminated the two positions formerly held by Navellier and Alpers, reducing the trustees of the Fund.

On May 23, 1997, after the reorganization of the board of trustees, a shareholder vote was held to determine whether MFS should continue as investment adviser to the Fund. The proposal to retain MFS failed, receiving less than the required two-thirds vote of shareholders. Navellier refused to return to the Fund unless the independent trustees released him from liability and agreed to resign as trustees. The independent trustees signed a release, returned management of the Fund to NMI, and resigned.

On February 24, 1998, appellants filed a first amended class action complaint. The amended complaint alleged the following claims: (1) breach of fiduciary duty under the ICA and Delaware law against the independent trustees, MFS, and Scott; (2) breach of fiduciary duty and negligence under California law against Adams; and (3) waste and intentional interference with prospective economic advantage against all defendants.... The district court made several pre-trial rulings, which left for trial only appellants' claims for breach of fiduciary duty and waste against the independent trustees and the independent trustees' counterclaims for indemnification....

Jury trial commenced on June 21, 1999. After a fourteen-day trial, the jury returned a unanimous verdict for the independent trustees on all claims. The district court entered judgment on August 24, 1999.

DISCUSSION

I. Pre-Trial Rulings

A. Dismissal of claims against Adams

....

[T]he district court correctly held that Adams, by advising the independent trustees, did not assume a duty of care to the Fund's shareholders. The district court reasoned that the shareholders were not the intended beneficiaries of Adams' counsel to the independent trustees; the harm alleged by the appellants (i.e., capital gains taxes) was not a foreseeable result of Adams' conduct; the connection between Adams' advice to the independent trustees and the alleged injury was remote and tenuous; no moral blame could be attached to Adams' conduct in advising the independent trustees of their obligations under the law; and strong public policy reasons militated against finding any duty owed by Adams to the shareholders.

We see no sound basis for disagreement with this analysis. Adams was representing the independent trustees. Nothing in that relationship suggested that he owed a duty to the shareholders of the Fund. To imply such a duty would be contrary to the sound policy requiring his undivided loyalty to his clients. We hold that the district court properly dismissed appellants' claims against Adams for breach of fiduciary duty and negligence.

B. Dismissal of ICA claims against MFS and Scott

Appellants contend that the district court erroneously dismissed their claims against MFS and Scott for breach of fiduciary duty under the ICA pursuant to Federal Rule of Civil Procedure 12(b)(6). The district court addressed three theories in dismissing appellants' claims against MFS and Scott for breach of fiduciary duty under the ICA. We address each theory in turn.

1. Fiduciary Duty

The ICA expressly provides that decisions regarding the renewal of investment advisory contracts are within the sole discretion of a fund's independent trustees.

> [I]t shall be unlawful for any registered investment company having a board of directors to ... renew ... any contract or agreement ... whereby a person undertakes regularly to serve or act as investment adviser ... for such company, unless the terms of such contract or agreement and any renewal thereof have been approved by the vote of a majority of directors, *who are not parties to such contract or agreement or interested persons of any such party....*

15 U.S.C. § 80a-15(c) (emphasis added).

MFS is not alleged to have been, and never was, a trustee of the Fund. In fact, MFS did not become the Fund's investment adviser until March 15, 1997, two days after the independent trustees decided not to renew NMI's contract. Further, according to the Declaration of Trust, a trustee must be a natural person. Similarly, the independent trustees did not appoint Scott as a trustee of the Fund until April 13, 1997, nearly one month after the independent trustees voted not to renew NMI's contract.

Additionally, because Scott was an officer and director of MFS, he served as an *interested* trustee of the Fund. By the plain terms of the ICA, interested persons are prohibited from participating in the vote to retain or replace an investment adviser. *See* 15 U.S.C. § 80a-15(c).

The district court properly concluded that neither MFS nor Scott were trustees to the Fund-and therefore did not owe a fiduciary duty to the shareholders-when the independent trustees decided to change investment advisers.

....

3. Control

The district court also properly concluded that MFS and Scott cannot be held liable for breach of fiduciary duty under the ICA on the theory that they "controlled" the independent trustees.

The ICA defines "control" as "the power to exercise a controlling influence over the management or policies of a company, unless such power is solely the result of an official position with such company." 15 U.S.C. § 80a-2(a)(9). MFS and Scott could not have been "control persons" under the ICA, however, because the independent trustees do not fall within the definition of "controlled persons" under the ICA. "A natural person shall be presumed not to be a controlled person within the meaning of this subchapter." 15 U.S.C. § 80a-2(a)(9). This presumption can only be overcome by "a determination to the contrary made by the Commission." *Id.* No such determination has been made by the SEC here. MFS and Scott cannot be held liable for breach of fiduciary duty under a theory of control.

....

III. Jury Instructions

A. ICA instruction

Appellants argue that the district court "committed prejudicial error" by refusing to instruct the jury that, absent an emergency or unforeseen event, section 15 of the ICA requires prior shareholder approval before an investment adviser may be replaced. We disagree with appellants' construction of the ICA and we hold that the district court properly refused to give appellants' requested instruction.

Section 15(a) of the ICA makes it unlawful to serve as an investment adviser except under a contract approved by the shareholders. *See* 15 U.S.C. § 80a-15(a). Recognizing that an unavoidable lapse of time may occur between the end of one contract and the date on which a new contract is approved by a majority of shareholders, the SEC promulgated Rule 15a-4, which provides in pertinent part:

> Notwithstanding section 15(a) of the Act, a person may act as investment adviser for [a fund] pursuant to a written contract which has not been approved by a majority of the outstanding voting securities of such company during the one hundred and twenty day period after the termination of an investment advisory contract by an event (other than an assignment by an investment adviser in connection with which such investment adviser, or a controlling

> person thereof, directly or indirectly receives money or other benefit) described in paragraphs (3) or (4) of section 15(a) of the Act or by the failure to renew such contract....

17 C.F.R. § 270.15a-4.[10] Under the plain language of Rule 15a-4, this exemption is not limited to unforeseeable non-renewals or terminations. As *amicus curiae*, the SEC explains:

> The availability of [Rule 15a-4] is not conditioned on a finding that either of the first two events—the non-renewal or termination of an advisory contract by the fund—was unforeseeable. Rather, under the rule's plain language, the only conditions are that: the interim contract may not last more than 120 days; it must be approved by the directors, including a majority of the independent directors; and the compensation under the contract may not exceed what would have been paid under the most recent contract that was approved by the shareholders. *See* § 17 C.F.R. 270.15a-4(a) and (b).

Appellants argue that appellees' "reliance on Rule 15a-4 as legal grounds for their actions is legally wrong.... Rule 15a-4 is an SEC rule and is not necessarily the law if it does not carry out the intent of the statute (§ 15(a) of the '40 Act)." We disagree with appellants' analysis. As we see it, Rule 15a-4 is fully consistent with Congressional intent, and indeed is reasonably necessary to implement the purposes of the ICA. We see no reason here not to defer to the sensible and informed judgment of the SEC, the agency charged with administering the statute.

Section 6(c) of the ICA grants the SEC broad authority to exempt certain actions from the requirements of the ICA. Section 6(c) of the ICA provides:

> The Commission, by rules and regulations upon its own motion, or by order upon application, may conditionally or unconditionally exempt any person ... or transaction, or any class or classes of persons ... or transactions, from any provisions ... of this subchapter or of any rule or regulation thereunder, if and to the extent that such exemption is necessary or appropriate in the public interest and consistent with the protection of investors and the purposes fairly intended by the policy and provisions of this title.

15 U.S.C. § 80a-6(c). The authorization to exempt any person or transaction from the provisions of the ICA when "necessary or appropriate in the public interest and consistent with the protection of investors" reflects the Congressional intent to entrust certain policy decisions to the SEC.

In determining the appropriate scope of the exemption embodied by Rule 15a-4, the SEC was required to balance two important investor protections in Section 15(a). On the one hand, the shareholder approval requirement ensures that fund investors have the authority to decide whether a particular investment adviser is retained by the fund. On the other hand, granting the trustees the authority to terminate or not renew an existing contract gives them critical oversight. Deciding how to reconcile

---

10. This regulation has since been amended, but we quote the version that governs this case.

these provisions when their policies conflict is precisely the sort of judgment entrusted to the SEC by Congress.

Appellants do not demonstrate that the SEC's promulgation of Rule 15a-4 is inconsistent "with the protection of investors or the purposes fairly intended by the policy and provisions" of the ICA. *See* 15 U.S.C. § 80a-6(c). While Rule 15a-4 permits a brief postponement of the shareholders' right to vote on an advisory contract, it includes additional investor safeguards, such as the requirement that a majority of the independent trustees approve the interim contract and compensation limitations for the interim period.[1]

....

Because appellants' proposed jury instruction is contrary to the plain language of Rule 15a-4, we hold that the district court properly refused to give the proposed instruction. [* * *]

* * *

Notes and Applications

The many lessons of Navellier. The *Navellier* case is interesting at several levels. It certainly provides comfort to independent directors and their advisers that their discretion regarding replacement of an incumbent investment adviser will be insulated from subsequent attack, even if shareholders do not ultimately approve the replacement. But the case also illustrates the practical difficulties faced by independent trustees in making such a determination stick when there is a disagreement between the independent trustees and the incumbent adviser. Wholly apart from the trustees' determination to hire a new adviser, shareholders ultimately must be asked to ratify that determination. How is this required by the statute and why does the statute impose such a requirement? Here, the shareholder vote went against the trustees, even though they managed to obtain more than half the votes cast. Why was this insufficient voting power? Finally, think about the dynamics of the replacement process from the shareholders' perspective. Do shareholders select a fund because they hope that trustees will make wise choices or because they are attracted by the investment adviser? After a dispute breaks out, shareholders of a mutual fund face a decision, and the decision is potentially colored by the fact that the fund's shares are redeemable. Thus, shareholders may either (i) retain share ownership in the fund to cast a vote in a contest that pits the adviser against the independent trustees; or (ii) vote with their feet by redeeming their shares. Once all of the pros and cons are tallied, do you think the outcome (legal and practical) is likely to increase or decrease the willingness to replace an incumbent investment adviser? Do trustees have other options in trying

---

1. 1 Further, contrary to appellants' claim, the independent trustees do not have unbridled discretion for 120 days. In deciding whether to enter into an interim contract, just as in deciding whether to renew or terminate an existing contract, the independent trustees must satisfy their duties as fiduciaries of the fund. These duties are enforceable under the ICA, and include the obligation to inform themselves of material facts and exercise their judgment for the benefit of the fund. *See* 15 U.S.C. § 80a-15(c).

to improve the quality of an investment adviser's performance? If trustees are less willing to replace an adviser, is that likely to embolden the adviser to disregard input from trustees of a fund advised by the adviser?

12.4 Section 36 and Shareholder Litigation against the Adviser under Section 36(b)

While contemporary standards require fund boards to serve essentially as "watchdogs" or checks on management, this was not always true historically. When the Company Act was passed, the process of board oversight with respect to management fees was weaker. Rather, the drafters of the Company Act intentionally excluded any appearance of rate regulation from the Act. David Schenker, Chief Counsel of the SEC's 1930s Investment Trust Study, and one of the draftsmen of the Company Act, testified to Congress in 1940 in favor of the bill promulgating the Company Act, "There is not a single provision in section 15 which even remotely assumes to fix what [advisers] should be paid as compensation.... If [stockholders] want to pay a man a million dollars to manage the fund and if they know they are paying him a million dollars and if they have the right to approve the payment of a million dollars, this bill says that is perfectly all right." In the absence of a federal standard, one must revert to analyzing the corporate or trust principles underlying a fund's entity. In essence, the original terms of the Company Act deferred any discussions of excessive fees to state law principles of corporate waste.

Rapid fund growth during the 1950s and 1960s prompted a rethinking, as well as several studies of fund industry fees and dynamics. After two major studies were issued in the early and mid-1960s, the SEC proposed that the Company Act be amended to require that advisory fees be "reasonable." It also proposed that the SEC and shareholders be entitled to enforce this standard by suing in federal court. It took three years of Congressional hearings to finalize a modernization of the Company Act in 1970, which included two key provisions regarding advisory fees and contracts: Section 15(c) and Section 36(b). New Section 15(c), as noted above, requires fund boards to request from the adviser such information as may be reasonably necessary to evaluate an advisory agreement and its fees. Equally important, Section 36(b), which is discussed in greater detail later in this chapter, imposes on advisers a "fiduciary duty with respect to compensation" they receive from investment companies.

Section 36 in its original form created enforceable statutory fiduciary obligations on directors and officers of registered investment companies. However, Congress expanded the fiduciary zone under Section 36 by imposing on investment advisers a fiduciary obligation with respect to receipt of fees from the registered investment company. In particular, Section 36(b) states that "investment company advisers owe shareholders in investment companies a fiduciary duty with respect to determining and receiving their advisory fees." Although Section 36(b) is also enforceable by the SEC, the section's greatest significance has come in enabling the registered investment company's shareholders to bring private actions for breach of this fiduciary duty directly against advisers on behalf of the fund. *See Daily Income Fund, Inc. v. Fox*, 464 U.S. 523 (1983). The Company Act imposes several statutory requirements related to bringing such actions:

(1) suing shareholders must "own shares at the time the action is initiated and continue to own share throughout the pendency of the litigation";

(2) damages are limited to recovery of advisory fees for one year before the action was brought;

(3) damages are limited "to the actual damages resulting from the breach of fiduciary duty";

(4) the defendant must be either an adviser or an affiliate of the adviser; and

(5) a fund's board approval of an advisory agreement and compensation "shall be given such consideration by the court as is deemed appropriate under all the circumstances."

Fee litigation pursuant to Section 36(b) became widespread in the 1980s. One case—*Gartenberg v. Merrill Lynch Asset Management, Inc.*, 694 F.2d 923 (2d Cir. 1982), *cert. denied*, 461 U.S. 906 (1983)—emerged as the bellwether authority in its articulation of a workable legal standard under Section 36(b), the so-called *Gartenberg* Standard, with an articulation of factors that should govern courts' analyses under that standard. Interestingly, the case involved management fees for a large money market fund managed by an affiliate of the brokerage firm Merrill Lynch. The money market fund was used to facilitate what at the time was a novel cash management feature for brokerage accounts in which brokerage clients were able to earn interest on cash balances in their brokerage account. Twenty-five years later, the Supreme Court was asked to opine on the *Gartenberg* Standard.

Jones v. Harris Associates L.P.

559 U.S. 335 (2010)

[**Textbook Note:** *This decision provides the Supreme Court's definitive interpretation of the appropriate standards governing litigation under Section 36(b) of the Company Act. Federal courts had long adhered to the* Gartenberg *Standard and subsidiary factors enunciated in that decision. Surprisingly, the Seventh Circuit issued a controversial decision explicitly rejecting* Gartenberg, *which is summarized in the Supreme Court's decision, even though no litigant had urged adoption of such a position. The Supreme Court's decision reestablished* Gartenberg *as a guide star for courts and situates* Gartenberg's *analysis in terms of Section 36(b)'s legislative history. In doing so, it also resolved several additional interpretive issues left open by* Gartenberg.]

Justice Alito delivered the opinion of the Court. We consider in this case what a mutual fund shareholder must prove in order to show that a mutual fund investment adviser breached the "fiduciary duty with respect to the receipt of compensation for services" that is imposed by § 36(b) of the Investment Company Act of 1940, 15 U.S.C. § 80a-35(b) (hereinafter § 36(b)).

I

A

The Investment Company Act of 1940 (Act), 54 Stat. 789, 15 U.S.C. § 80a-1 et seq., regulates investment companies, including mutual funds. "A mutual fund is a pool of assets, consisting primarily of [a] portfolio [of] securities, and belonging to the individual investors holding shares in the fund." *Burks v. Lasker*, 441 U.S. 471, 480 (1979). The following arrangements are typical. A separate entity called an investment adviser creates the mutual fund, which may have no employees of its own. See *Kamen v. Kemper Financial Services, Inc.*, 500 U.S. 90 (1991); *Daily Income Fund, Inc. v. Fox*, 464 U.S. 523, 536 (1984); *Burks*, 441 U.S., at 480–481. The adviser selects the fund's directors, manages the fund's investments, and provides other services. See *id.*, at 481. Because of the relationship between a mutual fund and its investment adviser, the fund often "'cannot, as a practical matter sever its relationship with the adviser. Therefore, the forces of arm's-length bargaining do not work in the mutual fund industry in the same manner as they do in other sectors of the American economy.'" *Ibid.* (quoting S.Rep. No. 91-184, p. 5 (1969) (hereinafter S. Rep.)).

"Congress adopted the [Investment Company Act of 1940] because of its concern with the potential for abuse inherent in the structure of investment companies." *Daily Income Fund*, 464 U.S., at 536 (internal quotation marks omitted). Recognizing that the relationship between a fund and its investment adviser was "fraught with potential conflicts of interest," the Act created protections for mutual fund shareholders. *Id.*, at 536–538 (internal quotation marks omitted); *Burks, supra*, at 482–483. Among other things, the Act required that no more than 60 percent of a fund's directors could be affiliated with the adviser and that fees for investment advisers be approved by the directors and the shareholders of the fund. See §§ 10, 15(c), 54 Stat. 806, 813.

The growth of mutual funds in the 1950's and 1960's prompted studies of the 1940 Act's effectiveness in protecting investors. See *Daily Income Fund*, 464 U.S., at 537–538. Studies commissioned or authored by the Securities and Exchange Commission (SEC or Commission) identified problems relating to the independence of investment company boards and the compensation received by investment advisers. See *ibid.* In response to such concerns, Congress amended the Act in 1970 and bolstered shareholder protection in two primary ways.

First, the amendments strengthened the "cornerstone" of the Act's efforts to check conflicts of interest, the independence of mutual fund boards of directors, which negotiate and scrutinize adviser compensation. *Burks, supra*, at 482. The amendments required that no more than 60 percent of a fund's directors be "persons who are interested persons," e.g., that they have no interest in or affiliation with the investment adviser. 15 U.S.C. § 80a-10(a); § 80a-2(a)(19); see also *Daily Income Fund, supra*, at 538. These board members are given "a host of special responsibilities." *Burks*, 441 U.S., at 482–483. In particular, they must "review and approve the contracts of the investment adviser" annually, *id.*, at 483 and a majority of these directors must approve an adviser's compensation, 15 U.S.C. § 80a-15(c). Second, § 36(b), 84 Stat. 1429, of the Act imposed upon investment advisers a "fiduciary duty" with respect to compensation received from a mutual fund, 15 U.S.C. § 80a-35(b), and granted individual investors a private right of action for breach of that duty, *ibid.*

The "fiduciary duty" standard contained in § 36(b) represented a delicate compromise. Prior to the adoption of the 1970 amendments, shareholders challenging investment adviser fees under state law were required to meet "common-law standards of corporate waste, under which an unreasonable or unfair fee might be approved unless the court deemed it 'unconscionable' or 'shocking,' " and "security holders challenging adviser fees under the [Investment Company Act] itself had been required to prove gross abuse of trust." *Daily Income Fund*, 464 U.S., at 540, n. 12. Aiming to give shareholders a stronger remedy, the SEC proposed a provision that would have empowered the Commission to bring actions to challenge a fee that was not "reasonable" and to intervene in any similar action brought by or on behalf of an investment company. *Id.*, at 538. This approach was included in a bill that passed the House. H.R. 9510, 90th Cong., 1st Sess., § 8(d) (1967); see also S. 1659, 90th Cong., 1st Sess., § 8(d) (1967). Industry representatives, however, objected to this proposal, fearing that it "might in essence provide the Commission with ratemaking authority." *Daily Income Fund*, 464 U.S., at 538.

The provision that was ultimately enacted adopted "a different method of testing management compensation," *id.*, at 539 (quoting S.Rep., at 5 (internal quotation marks omitted)), that was more favorable to shareholders than the previously available remedies but that did not permit a compensation agreement to be reviewed in court for "reasonableness." This is the fiduciary duty standard in § 36(b).

B

Petitioners are shareholders in three different mutual funds managed by respondent Harris Associates L.P., an investment adviser. Petitioners filed this action in the Northern District of Illinois pursuant to § 36(b) seeking damages, an injunction, and rescission of advisory agreements between Harris Associates and the mutual funds. The complaint alleged that Harris Associates had violated § 36(b) by charging fees that were "disproportionate to the services rendered" and "not within the range of what would have been negotiated at arm's length in light of all the surrounding circumstances." App. 52.

The District Court granted summary judgment for Harris Associates.... A panel of the Seventh Circuit affirmed based on different reasoning, explicitly "disapprov[ing] the *Gartenberg* approach." 527 F.3d 627, 632 (2008). Looking to trust law, the panel noted that, while a trustee "owes an obligation of candor in negotiation," a trustee, at the time of the creation of a trust, "may negotiate in his own interest and accept what the settlor or governance institution agrees to pay." *Ibid.* (citing Restatement (Second) of Trusts § 242, and Comment f. The panel thus reasoned that "[a] fiduciary duty differs from rate regulation. A fiduciary must make full disclosure and play no tricks but is not subject to a cap on compensation." 527 F.3d, at 632. In the panel's view, the amount of an adviser's compensation would be relevant only if the compensation were "so unusual" as to give rise to an inference "that deceit must have occurred, or that the persons responsible for decision have abdicated." *Ibid.*

The panel argued that this understanding of § 36(b) is consistent with the forces operating in the contemporary mutual fund market. Noting that "[t]oday thousands of mutual funds compete," the panel concluded that "sophisticated investors" shop for the funds that produce the best overall results, "mov[e] their money elsewhere" when fees are "excessive in relation to the results," and thus "create a competitive pressure" that generally keeps fees low. *Id.*, at 633–634. The panel faulted Gartenberg on the ground that it "relies too little on markets." 527 F.3d, at 632. And the panel firmly rejected a comparison between the fees that Harris Associates charged to the funds and the fees that Harris Associates charged other types of clients, observing that "[d]ifferent clients call for different commitments of time" and that costs, such as research, that may benefit several categories of clients "make it hard to draw inferences from fee levels." *Id.*, at 634.

II

A

Since Congress amended the Investment Company Act in 1970, the mutual fund industry has experienced exponential growth. Assets under management increased from $38.2 billion in 1966 to over $9.6 trillion in 2008. The number of mutual fund investors grew from 3.5 million in 1965 to 92 million in 2008, and there are now more than 9,000 open- and closed-end funds.

During this time, the standard for an investment adviser's fiduciary duty has remained an open question in our Court, but, until the Seventh Circuit's decision below, something of a consensus had developed regarding the standard set forth over 25 years ago in *Gartenberg*, supra. The *Gartenberg* standard has been adopted by other federal courts, and "[t]he SEC's regulations have recognized, and formalized, *Gartenberg*-like factors." Brief for United States as Amicus Curiae 23. See 17 CFR § 240.14a-101, Sched. 14A, Item 22, para. (c)(11)(i) (2009); 69 Fed.Reg. 39801, n.31, 39807–39809 (2004). In the present case, both petitioners and respondent generally endorse the *Gartenberg* approach, although they disagree in some respects about its meaning.

In *Gartenberg*, the Second Circuit noted that Congress had not defined what it meant by a "fiduciary duty" with respect to compensation but concluded that "the test is essentially whether the fee schedule represents a charge within the range of what would have been negotiated at arm's-length in the light of all of the surrounding circumstances." 694 F.2d, at 928. The Second Circuit elaborated that, "[t]o be guilty of a violation of § 36(b), ... the adviser-manager must charge a fee that is so disproportionately large that it bears no reasonable relationship to the services rendered and could not have been the product of arm's-length bargaining." *Ibid.* "To make this determination," the Court stated, "all pertinent facts must be weighed," *id.*, at 929, and the Court specifically mentioned "the adviser-manager's cost in providing the service, ... the extent to which the adviser-manager realizes economies of scale as the fund grows larger, and the volume of orders which must be processed by the manager." *Id.*, at

930.[5] Observing that competition among advisers for the business of managing a fund may be "virtually non-existent," the Court rejected the suggestion that "the principal factor to be considered in evaluating a fee's fairness is the price charged by other similar advisers to funds managed by them," although the Court did not suggest that this factor could not be "taken into account." *Id.*, at 929. The Court likewise rejected the "argument that the lower fees charged by investment advisers to large pension funds should be used as a criterion for determining fair advisory fees for money market funds," since a "pension fund does not face the myriad of daily purchases and redemptions throughout the nation which must be handled by [a money market fund]." *Id.*, at 930, n. 3.

B

The meaning of § 36(b)'s reference to "a fiduciary duty with respect to the receipt of compensation for services" is hardly pellucid, but based on the terms of that provision and the role that a shareholder action for breach of that duty plays in the overall structure of the Act, we conclude that *Gartenberg* was correct in its basic formulation of what § 36(b) requires: to face liability under § 36(b), an investment adviser must charge a fee that is so disproportionately large that it bears no reasonable relationship to the services rendered and could not have been the product of arm's length bargaining.

1

We begin with the language of § 36(b). As noted, the Seventh Circuit panel thought that the phrase "fiduciary duty" incorporates a standard taken from the law of trusts. Petitioners agree but maintain that the panel identified the wrong trust-law standard. Instead of the standard that applies when a trustee and a settlor negotiate the trustee's fee at the time of the creation of a trust, petitioners invoke the standard that applies when a trustee seeks compensation after the trust is created. Brief for Petitioners 20–23, 35–37. A compensation agreement reached at that time, they point out, "'will not bind the beneficiary' if either 'the trustee failed to make a full disclosure of all circumstances affecting the agreement' " which he knew or should have known or if the agreement is unfair to the beneficiary. *Id.*, at 23 (quoting Restatement (Second) of Trusts § 242, Comment i). Respondent, on the other hand, contends that the term "fiduciary" is not exclusive to the law of trusts, that the phrase means different things in different contexts, and that there is no reason to believe that § 36(b) incorporates the specific meaning of the term in the law of trusts. Brief for Respondent 34–36.

We find it unnecessary to take sides in this dispute. In *Pepper v. Litton*, 308 U.S. 295(1939), we discussed the meaning of the concept of fiduciary duty in a context

---

5. Other factors cited by the *Gartenberg* court include (1) the nature and quality of the services provided to the fund and shareholders; (2) the profitability of the fund to the adviser; (3) any "fall-out financial benefits," those collateral benefits that accrue to the adviser because of its relationship with the mutual fund; (4) comparative fee structure (meaning a comparison of the fees with those paid by similar funds); and (5) the independence, expertise, care, and conscientiousness of the board in evaluating adviser compensation. 694 F.2d, at 929-932 (internal quotation marks omitted).

that is analogous to that presented here, and we also looked to trust law. At issue in *Pepper* was whether a bankruptcy court could disallow a dominant or controlling shareholder's claim for compensation against a bankrupt corporation. Dominant or controlling shareholders, we held, are "fiduciar[ies]" whose "powers are powers [held] in trust." *Id.*, at 306. We then explained:

> "Their dealings with the corporation are subjected to rigorous scrutiny and where any of their contracts or engagements with the corporation is challenged the burden is on the director or stockholder not only to prove the good faith of the transaction but also to show its inherent fairness from the viewpoint of the corporation and those interested therein.... *The essence of the test is whether or not under all the circumstances the transaction carries the earmarks of an arm's length bargain.* If it does not, equity will set it aside." *Id.*, at 306–307 (emphasis added; footnote omitted); see also *Geddes v. Anaconda Copper Mining Co.*, 254 U.S. 590, 599 (1921) (standard of fiduciary duty for interested directors).

We believe that this formulation expresses the meaning of the phrase "fiduciary duty" in § 36(b), 84 Stat. 1429. The Investment Company Act modifies this duty in a significant way: it shifts the burden of proof from the fiduciary to the party claiming breach, 15 U.S.C. § 80a-35(b)(1), to show that the fee is outside the range that arm's-length bargaining would produce.

The *Gartenberg* approach fully incorporates this understanding of the fiduciary duty as set out in *Pepper* and reflects § 36(b)(1)'s imposition of the burden on the plaintiff. As noted, *Gartenberg* insists that all relevant circumstances be taken into account, see 694 F.2d, at 929, as does § 36(b)(2), 84 Stat. 1429 ("[A]pproval by the board of directors ... shall be given such consideration by the court as is deemed appropriate *under all the circumstances*" (emphasis added)). And *Gartenberg* uses the range of fees that might result from arm's-length bargaining as the benchmark for reviewing challenged fees.

Gartenberg's approach also reflects § 36(b)'s place in the statutory scheme and, in particular, its relationship to the other protections that the Act affords investors.

Under the Act, scrutiny of investment adviser compensation by a fully informed mutual fund board is the "cornerstone of the ... effort to control conflicts of interest within mutual funds." *Burks*, 441 U.S., at 482. The Act interposes disinterested directors as "independent watchdogs" of the relationship between a mutual fund and its adviser. *Id.*, at 484 (internal quotation marks omitted). To provide these directors with the information needed to judge whether an adviser's compensation is excessive, the Act requires advisers to furnish all information "reasonably ... necessary to evaluate the terms" of the adviser's contract, 15 U.S.C. § 80a-15(c), and gives the SEC the authority to enforce that requirement. See § 80a-41. Board scrutiny of adviser compensation and shareholder suits under § 36(b), 84 Stat. 1429, are mutually reinforcing but independent mechanisms for controlling conflicts. See *Daily Income Fund*, 464 U.S., at 541 (Congress intended for § 36(b) suits and directorial approval of adviser contracts to act as "independent checks on excessive fees"); *Kamen*, 500 U.S., at 108 ("Congress added § 36(b) to the [Act] in 1970 because it concluded that the shareholders should not have to rely solely on the fund's directors to assure reasonable adviser fees, notwithstanding the increased disinterestedness of the board" (internal quotation marks omitted)).

In recognition of the role of the disinterested directors, the Act instructs courts to give board approval of an adviser's compensation "such consideration ... as is deemed appropriate under all the circumstances." § 80a-35(b)(2). Cf. *Burks*, 441 U.S., at 485 ("[I]t would have been paradoxical for Congress to have been willing to rely largely upon [boards of directors as] 'watchdogs' to protect shareholder interests and yet, where the 'watchdogs' have done precisely that, require that they be totally muzzled").

From this formulation, two inferences may be drawn. First, a measure of deference to a board's judgment may be appropriate in some instances. Second, the appropriate measure of deference varies depending on the circumstances.

Gartenberg heeds these precepts. *Gartenberg* advises that "the expertise of the independent trustees of a fund, whether they are fully informed about all facts bearing on the [investment adviser's] service and fee, and the extent of care and conscientiousness with which they perform their duties are important factors to be considered in deciding whether they and the [investment adviser] are guilty of a breach of fiduciary duty in violation of § 36(b)." 694 F.2d, at 930.

III

While both parties in this case endorse the basic *Gartenberg* approach, they disagree on several important questions that warrant discussion.

The first concerns comparisons between the fees that an adviser charges a captive mutual fund and the fees that it charges its independent clients. As noted, the *Gartenberg* court rejected a comparison between the fees that the adviser in that case charged a money market fund and the fees that it charged a pension fund. 694 F.2d, at 930, n. 3 (noting the "[t]he nature and extent of the services required by each type of fund differ sharply"). Petitioners contend that such a comparison is appropriate, Brief for Petitioners 30–31, but respondent disagrees. Brief for Respondent 38–44. Since the Act requires consideration of all relevant factors, 15 U.S.C. § 80a-35(b)(2); see also § 80a-15(c), we do not think that there can be any categorical rule regarding the comparisons of the fees charged different types of clients. See *Daily Income Fund, supra*, at 537 (discussing concern with investment advisers' practice of charging higher fees to mutual funds than to their other clients). Instead, courts may give such comparisons the weight that they merit in light of the similarities and differences between the services that the clients in question require, but courts must be wary of inapt comparisons. As the panel below noted, there may be significant differences between the services provided by an investment adviser to a mutual fund and those it provides to a pension fund which are attributable to the greater frequency of shareholder redemptions in a mutual fund, the higher turnover of mutual fund assets, the more burdensome regulatory and legal obligations, and higher marketing costs. 527 F.3d, at 634 ("Different clients call for different commitments of time"). If the services rendered are sufficiently different that a comparison is not probative, then courts must reject such a comparison. Even if the services provided and fees charged to an independent fund are relevant, courts should be mindful that the Act does not necessarily ensure fee parity between mutual funds and institutional clients contrary to petitioners' contentions. See *id.*, at 631. ("Plaintiffs maintain that a fiduciary may charge its controlled clients no more than its independent clients").[8]

By the same token, courts should not rely too heavily on comparisons with fees charged to mutual funds by other advisers. These comparisons are problematic because these fees, like those challenged, may not be the product of negotiations conducted at arm's length. See 537 F.3d, at 731–732 (opinion dissenting from denial of rehearing en banc); *Gartenberg, supra*, at 929 ("Competition between money market funds for shareholder business does not support an inference that competition must therefore also exist between [investment advisers] for fund business. The former may be vigorous even though the latter is virtually non-existent").

Finally, a court's evaluation of an investment adviser's fiduciary duty must take into account both procedure and substance. See 15 U.S.C. § 80a-35(b)(2) (requiring deference to board's consideration "as is deemed appropriate under all the circumstances"); cf. *Daily Income Fund*, 464 U.S., at 541 ("Congress intended security holder and SEC actions under § 36(b), on the one hand, and directorial approval of adviser contracts, on the other, to act as independent checks on excessive fees"). Where a board's process for negotiating and reviewing investment-adviser compensation is robust, a reviewing court should afford commensurate deference to the outcome of the bargaining process. See *Burks*, 441 U.S., at 484 (unaffiliated directors serve as "independent watchdogs"). Thus, if the disinterested directors considered the relevant factors, their decision to approve a particular fee agreement is entitled to considerable weight, even if a court might weigh the factors differently. Cf. *id.*, at 485. This is not to deny that a fee may be excessive even if it was negotiated by a board in possession of all relevant information, but such a determination must be based on evidence that the fee "is so disproportionately large that it bears no reasonable relationship to the services rendered and could not have been the product of arm's-length bargaining." *Gartenberg, supra*, at 928.

In contrast, where the board's process was deficient or the adviser withheld important information, the court must take a more rigorous look at the outcome. When an investment adviser fails to disclose material information to the board, greater

8. Comparisons with fees charged to institutional clients, therefore, will not "doo[m] [a]ny [f]und to [t]rial." Brief for Respondent 49; see also *Strougo v. BEA Assocs.*, 188 F.Supp.2d 373, 384 (S.D.N.Y.2002) (suggesting that fee comparisons, where permitted, might produce a triable issue). First, plaintiffs bear the burden in showing that fees are beyond the range of arm's-length bargaining. § 80a-35(b)(1). Second, a showing of relevance requires courts to assess any disparity in fees in light of the different markets for advisory services. Only where plaintiffs have shown a large disparity in fees that cannot be explained by the different services in addition to other evidence that the fee is outside the arm's-length range will trial be appropriate. Cf. App. to Pet. for Cert. 30a; see also *In re AllianceBernstein Mut. Fund Excessive Fee Litigation*, No. 04 Civ. 4885(SWK), 2006 WL 1520222, *2 (S.D.N.Y., May 31, 2006) (citing report finding that fee differential resulted from different services and different liabilities assumed).

scrutiny is justified because the withheld information might have hampered the board's ability to function as "an independent check upon the management." *Burks, supra*, at 484 (internal quotation marks omitted). "Section 36(b) is sharply focused on the question of whether the fees themselves were excessive." *Migdal v. Rowe Price-Fleming Int'l, Inc.*, 248 F.3d 321, 328 (C.A.4 2001); see also 15 U.S.C. § 80a-35(b) (imposing a "fiduciary duty with respect to the *receipt of compensation* for services, or of payments of a material nature" (emphasis added)). But an adviser's compliance or noncompliance with its disclosure obligations is a factor that must be considered in calibrating the degree of deference that is due a board's decision to approve an adviser's fees.

It is also important to note that the standard for fiduciary breach under § 36(b) does not call for judicial second-guessing of informed board decisions. See *Daily Income Fund, supra*, at 538; see also *Burks*, 441 U.S., at 483 ("Congress consciously chose to address the conflict-of-interest problem through the Act's independent-directors section, rather than through more drastic remedies"). "[P]otential conflicts [of interests] may justify some restraints upon the unfettered discretion of even disinterested mutual fund directors, particularly in their transactions with the investment adviser," but they do not suggest that a court may supplant the judgment of disinterested directors apprised of all relevant information, without additional evidence that the fee exceeds the arm's-length range. *Id.*, at 481. In reviewing compensation under § 36(b), the Act does not require courts to engage in a precise calculation of fees representative of arm's-length bargaining. See 527 F.3d, at 633 ("Judicial price-setting does not accompany fiduciary duties"). As recounted above, Congress rejected a "reasonableness" requirement that was criticized as charging the courts with rate-setting responsibilities. See *Daily Income Fund, supra*, at 538–540. Congress' approach recognizes that courts are not well suited to make such precise calculations. Cf. *General Motors Corp. v. Tracy*, 519 U.S. 278, 308 (1997) ("[T]he Court is institutionally unsuited to gather the facts upon which economic predictions can be made, and professionally untrained to make them"); *Verizon Communications Inc. v. FCC*, 535 U.S. 467, 539 (2002); see also *Concord v. Boston Edison Co.*, 915 F.2d 17, 25 (CA1 1990) (opinion for the court by Breyer, C.J.) ("[H]ow is a judge or jury to determine a 'fair price'?"). *Gartenberg*'s "so disproportionately large" standard, 694 F.2d, at 928, reflects this congressional choice to "rely largely upon [independent director] 'watchdogs' to protect shareholders interests." *Burks, supra*, at 485.

By focusing almost entirely on the element of disclosure, the Seventh Circuit panel erred. See 527 F.3d, at 632 (An investment adviser "must make full disclosure and play no tricks but is not subject to a cap on compensation"). The *Gartenberg* standard, which the panel rejected, may lack sharp analytical clarity, but we believe that it accurately reflects the compromise that is embodied in § 36(b), and it has provided a workable standard for nearly three decades. The debate between the Seventh Circuit panel and the dissent from the denial of rehearing regarding today's mutual fund market is a matter for Congress, not the courts. [***]

* * *

Green v. Fund Asset Management, L.P.

286 F.3d 682 (3d Cir. 2002)

[**Textbook Note:** *This appellate decision addresses another aspect of Section 36(b). Essentially, it asks the following question: does that statutory provision provide redress for potential conflicts of interest as well as conflicts of interest that have actually resulted in injuries to the beneficiary shareholders? This case requires the reader to understand the nature of the underlying potential conflict of interest in addition to why the court concludes that a potential conflict by itself is insufficient to state a claim under Section 36(b).*]

Ward, District Judge *(sitting by designation)*

.... I. Background

Plaintiffs, shareholders in seven closed-end, publicly-traded municipal investment funds (the "Funds"), brought suit against the Funds and their investment advisors, Fund Asset Management, L.P. ("FAM") and Merrill Lynch Asset Management, L.P. ("MLAM"), claiming that defendants had violated their fiduciary duties under the ICA and state law.

The Funds at issue invest in long-term, tax-exempt municipal bonds. In order to increase the overall yield to shareholders, the Funds' advisors seek to maximize the number of high-yield, long-term bonds in the Funds' portfolios through the use of leverage. The advisors raise capital to buy additional long-term bonds by selling shares of preferred stock. Investors who buy preferred stock receive tax-exempt monthly dividends based on short-term interest rates, typically two and one-half to four percent. Because the long-term investments purchased by the Funds with the proceeds from the sale of preferred shares normally pay higher rates of return than the Funds are obligated to pay to preferred shareholders, the yield to common shareholders is increased. All of the tasks associated with the sale of preferred stock as well as the overall management of the Funds are handled by FAM and MLAM. For their services, FAM and MLAM receive an advisory fee of one-half of one percent of the Funds' average weekly net assets.

Plaintiffs here do not allege that the advisors' compensation was excessive; rather, they allege that because the bonds purchased with the proceeds from the sale of preferred shares are included in the corpus of assets upon which the advisory fee is based, FAM and MLAM have a strong financial incentive to keep the Funds fully leveraged. This incentive, they maintain, creates an actual conflict of interest between the Funds and their advisors that amounts to a per se breach of fiduciary duty under § 36(b). Secondly, plaintiffs allege that the advisors' failure to disclose this conflict of interest adequately in the Funds' prospectuses is a separate actionable breach of fiduciary duty.

... Because the court determined that, even if true, plaintiffs' allegations did not establish a violation of § 36(b), the court entered summary judgment for defendants. This appeal followed.

II. Discussion

Our initial task is to determine whether the district court erred in ruling that a fee arrangement in which a fund's investment advisors have an incentive to maximize leverage in order to increase their advisory fees is not a per se breach of an investment advisor's fiduciary duties under § 36(b) of the ICA. We conclude that the legislative history and the text of § 36(b) make clear that potential conflicts of interest in mutual fund fee arrangements are not per se violations of investment advisors' fiduciary duties: an actual breach must be alleged and proven.

Section 36(b) of the ICA provides that investment company advisors owe shareholders in investment companies a fiduciary duty with respect to determining and receiving their advisory fees. 15 U.S.C. § 80a-35(b) (1997). The legislative history of the section indicates that Congress recognized the conflicts of interest inherent in mutual fund fee arrangements-indeed, this was the impetus for enacting § 36(b). The Senate Report accompanying § 36(b) noted that "[s]ince a typical fund is organized by its investment adviser which provides it with almost all management services and because its shares are bought by investors who rely on that service, a mutual fund cannot, as a practical matter, sever its relationship with the adviser." S. Rep. No. 91-184 (1969), reprinted in 1970 U.S.S.C.A.N. 4897, 4901. The report also stated that "in view of the potential conflicts of interest involved in the setting of these fees, there should be effective means for the courts to act where mutual fund shareholders or the SEC believe there has been a breach of fiduciary duty." *Id.* at 4898 (emphasis added). Section 36(b), Congress believed, "provides an effective method whereby the courts can determine whether there has been a breach of this duty by the adviser." *Id.*

....

The fact that the fiduciary duty imposed by § 36(b) is significantly more circumscribed than common law fiduciary duty doctrines is demonstrated by § 36(b)'s limitations on recovery: under § 36(b), a shareholder may only sue the recipient of the fees; recovery is limited to actual damages resulting from the breach; and damages are not recoverable for any period prior to one year before the action was instituted, in this case before June 21, 1995. 15 U.S.C. § 80a-35(b)(3). Further, the plaintiff has the burden of proving a breach of fiduciary duty, *id.* at § 80a-35(b)(1), in contrast with the common law rule that requires a fiduciary to justify its conduct. See, e.g., *Gartenberg v. Merrill Lynch Asset Mgmt., Inc.*, 528 F.Supp. 1038, 1044 n. 6 (S.D.N.Y.1981), aff'd, 694 F.2d 923 (2d Cir.1982) ("At common law it was incumbent on the fiduciary to justify his transaction with his cestui. Under this statute [§ 36(b)] the burden is reversed.").

....

Our interpretation of both the text and legislative history of § 36(b) mandates that plaintiffs allege and prove an actual breach of fiduciary duty in order to prevail on their claims. Because plaintiffs have not pointed to any instance during the period for which they can recover damages when the advisors improperly failed to de-leverage the Funds in order to maximize their fees and because plaintiffs have not alleged any actual damages they or the Funds suffered as a result of any improper decision by

the Funds' investment advisors, they do not have a cognizable claim under § 36(b). [* * *]

* * *

Notes and Applications

1. *Action on behalf of an investment company—direct versus derivative actions.* The formulation of Section 36(b) is unusual. Other than in an SEC action, it is an action on behalf of the registered investment company brought by a shareholder. But if it is being brought on behalf of the investment company, can the investment company bring such an action? Or alternatively, if the claim is in fact derivative of the company's rights, do shareholders need to comply with the demand requirement found in Fed. R. Civ. P. 23.1 which typically gives the entity's board the ability to control the litigation if it so chooses? The Supreme Court answered no to both questions based on the language of the statute and the overarching design and policy of the Company Act. *See Daily Income Fund, Inc. v. Fox*, 464 U.S. 523 (1982). Why would Congress provide that the action is on behalf of the investment company, but also limit the involvement of the investment company's board? Finally, although the SEC is authorized to bring Section 36(b) actions, it does so only rarely in egregious cases. *See, e.g., SEC v. AMMB Consultant Sendirian Berhad*, SEC Litigation Release No. 22402 (June 27, 2012) (obtaining settlement in a Section 36(b) action for fees obtained by a sub-adviser to a single country (emerging market) closed-end fund in which the sub-adviser actually did nothing; this action and a related one also alleged violations of Section 15(c) by the primary adviser and the sub-adviser).

2. *Relationship between Section 36(b) and Section 15(c) and the* Gartenberg *Factors.* The *Jones* opinion, as supplemented by footnote 5, enumerates the factors that were developed in *Gartenberg* (usually referred to as the *Gartenberg* factors). Unlike its explicit adoption of the *Gartenberg* standard, the Court did not make the factors themselves part of its holding but did acknowledge them as instructive guideposts. The *Gartenberg* factors has long been embraced by most courts. To what extent do each of these factors provide an indication of whether the management fee is excessive? One of the enumerated factors is typically regarded as first among equals: "the independence, expertise, care, and conscientiousness of the board in evaluating adviser compensation," a process-based factor. The importance of process in Section 36(b) litigation has also profoundly shaped the dynamics of the review process associated with advisers' contractual relationships with funds. The adviser has an interest in making the Section 15(c) process constructive. In theory, the better the 15(c) process, the more deference courts will accord to a board's determination with respect to advisory fees. By the same token, the other *Gartenberg* factors are used throughout the fund industry by boards to guide their deliberations in the review process pursuant to Section 15(a) and 15(c).

3. *The public value of Section 36(b) fee litigation.* Beginning in the 1980s, numerous fee cases were brought against investment advisers. However, the number of successful

actions has been fairly small under the *Gartenberg* framework. One commentator has described the net result as a "stunning lack of investor success." Lyman Johnson, *A Fresh Look at Director "Independence": Mutual Fee Litigation and Gartenberg at Twenty-Five*, 61 Vand. L. Rev. 497, 527 (2008). What factors may explain this outcome? Other commentators have questioned a variety of statutory features that limit the effectiveness of such litigation. *See, e.g.*, Quinn Curtis & John Morely, *The Flawed Mechanics of Mutual Fund Fee Litigation*, 32 Yale J. Reg. 1 (2015). At the very least, the commentary and the relatively meager results of litigation pose a question of whether the cause of action, as fashioned, serves a useful public policy purpose.

Investment advisers and boards understandably feel that the costs and benefits of such litigation are questionable at best. One area that has been a source of concern, and indeed the circumstances that gave rise to the litigation in the *Jones* case, has been the fact that investment advisers customarily charge actively managed mutual funds a much higher investment advisory fee than would be charged to manage accounts of institutional investors that are managed with similar investment styles and strategies. This issue had been specifically flagged in the academic literature as potentially problematic. *See* John P. Freeman & Stewart Brown, *Mutual Fund Advisory Fees: The Cost of Conflicts of Interest*, 26 J. Corp. Law 610 (2001). The *Jones* opinion hints at possible justifications for two parallel fee schedules, one for registered investment companies and the other for institutional investors. Are these justifications persuasive or implausible? From the perspective of potential defendants, one of the great concerns is whether the ability of defendants to obtain summary judgment is foreclosed when the record evidences use of dual fee schedules. In footnote 8, the Supreme Court appears to offer defendants some comfort on this score. Does this seem reasonable in the face of concerns regarding dual fee schedules? Finally, in recent years in response to the success of passively-managed mutual funds and the rise of ETFs, market forces have begun to exert a separate significant check on advisory fees, which has given rise to a welcome trend for investors: lower advisory fees across the industry.

4. *And what of Section 36(a)?* Section 36(a) was part of the original Company Act and imposes a fiduciary duty on the officers and directors of the investment company (as well as the investment company's principal underwriter in the case of investment companies that issue redeemable securities). Although the statutory provision expressly authorizes the SEC to bring actions to enforce such obligations, some early appellate cases were willing to recognize an implied private action on behalf of shareholders to bring such claims as well. However, the Supreme Court's implied private action jurisprudence over the last generation has become decidedly less favorable to implying private causes of action. Accordingly, appellate courts have expressly declined to follow those earlier cases at least with respect to Section 36(a). *See, e.g., Laborers' Local 265 Pension Fund v. iShares Trust*, 769 F.3d 399 (6th Cir. 2014), *cert. denied*, 135 S. Ct. 1500 (2015). The SEC typically reserves Section 36(a) actions against officers and directors for egregious misconduct in an official capacity. Are there sound legislative reasons for distinguishing under federal law between private remedies for shareholders against directors and officers and private remedies for shareholders against investment advisers?

12.5 Other Service Provider Agreements and Potential Issues

Since most funds operate as externally managed, they must look to third party service providers for all key services. Chapters 3 and 4 explain the fundamentals of these relationships. For purposes of this discussion, it is important to remember that a fund's board of trustees has responsibility for general oversight of the service providers, including consideration and approval of contracts and fees. Day to day oversight, management and interaction, however, is typically the function of the adviser. Given the potentially substantial fees involved in these relationships, one must always be alert to the potential for conflicts of interest. In addition to investment advisory services, funds require a variety of ancillary services to operate, including distribution, fund accounting, fund administration, custody, transfer agency, and several professional services. When such services are performed by the adviser or an affiliate of the adviser, they generally are subject to the same review standards as advisory agreements in order to protect against conflicts of interest. Services such as auditing and directors' independent counsel must be free from conflicts regarding the sponsor, adviser and distributor.

12.5.1 Affiliated Service Providers

Such conflicts of interest are more prominent when a service provider, such as a transfer agent, is affiliated with the adviser, distributor or sponsor of a fund. In such instances, consideration of the transfer agency agreement and fees should be considered as part of the overall Section 15(a) and (c) consideration process. Among the *Gartenberg* standard elements are the adviser's profitability and the fall-out benefits of the advisory relationship. Thus, in considering the overall service relationships of an adviser and its affiliates, the overall flow of fees and business relationship benefits should be part of the 15(c) due diligence by the board, disclosure by the adviser and approval process of the board. However, shareholder approval of such agreements is not required. Note, until the late 1970s, affiliated service provider arrangements also triggered concerns that they involved affiliated transaction issues under Section 17(d). (Affiliated transactions will be discussed in much greater depth in Chapter 14.) In 1977, the SEC staff laid out its no-action position that no action would be taken if the board makes certain findings in its deliberations, specifically findings designed to ensure that the contracts are fair, reasonable and in the best interests of the fund.

Nonetheless, circumstances have arisen where the board review process has not gone as contemplated by the SEC staff, such as the case of a transfer agent owned by the parent of an investment adviser. The settled administrative action, *In the Matter of Smith Barney Fund Management LLC and Citigroup Global Markets, Inc.*, Investment Advisers Act Release No. 2390 (May 31, 2005), involved the brokerage firm Smith Barney (now part of Morgan Stanley). The Smith Barney Funds' 15(c) process was thwarted by the adviser when it failed to completely disclose a scheme to divert transfer agency fees primarily to an affiliated transfer agent. As a result, the affected funds paid over $100 million in arguably excessive fees to the adviser's affiliate. The summary of the settled administrative action provides a good discussion and analysis:

[***] 1. This is a case about an investment adviser placing its interest in making a profit ahead of the interests of the mutual funds it serves. Investment advisers have a fiduciary duty to act in the best interests of the mutual funds they advise and their shareholders. Mutual funds pay fees for various services provided to the mutual funds, including transfer agent services. Among its duties, the adviser may advise fund boards about the retention of a particular transfer agent and how much to pay for the transfer agent's services. In this case, the Adviser, which serves as investment adviser to the Smith Barney Family of Funds (the "Funds"), recommended the Funds contract with an affiliate of the Adviser, which would perform limited transfer agent services and sub-contract with the Funds' existing transfer agent. The existing transfer agent would perform almost all of the same services it had performed previously, but at deeply discounted rates, permitting the affiliate of the Adviser to keep most of the discount for itself and make a high profit for performing limited work. In making this recommendation, the Adviser misled the boards by omitting material facts, which led the boards to believe that the Adviser's recommendation was made in the Funds' best interests, which was not true. This self-interested proposal permitted the Adviser and its affiliates to profit from the transfer agent function at the expense of the Funds.

2. The Adviser and the asset management operations of Global Markets are part of Citigroup Asset Management ("CAM"), a business unit of Citigroup Inc. ("Citigroup") that provides investment advisory and management services to Citigroup-sponsored funds. In 1997, CAM began a formal study of the transfer agent ("TA") function in anticipation of the expiration of the existing contract between the Funds and First Data Investor Services Group ("First Data"). CAM representatives knew that First Data had been making high profit margins on the TA contract. Instead of using its strong bargaining position to benefit the Funds in the negotiation of a new TA contract, CAM sought to keep for itself much of the profit First Data had been making. In fact, CAM did not pursue or inform the Funds' boards of an offer by First Data to continue to perform all transfer agent services for the Funds at a $25 million annual fee discount.

3. CAM ultimately recommended that the Funds replace First Data with an affiliate of the Adviser. The recommended structure called for the affiliated TA (which is now Citicorp Trust Bank, fsb ("CTB")) ... to contract directly with the Funds as named TA, perform limited functions and sub-contract with First Data for the bulk of the transfer agent services. (CAM referred to First Data as "sub-TA.") Except for a small customer service function that the affiliated TA would undertake, First Data would continue to perform the same work it had performed under the expiring contract, but at a significant discount from the fees it had been charging the Funds—a discount that would start at 33.5% and increase to as much as 60% over the five-year term of the contract. CAM kept the majority of the savings it had negotiated with First Data for itself, and offered the Funds a limited fee reduction through the institution of fee caps.

4. CAM should have first offered these substantial savings to the Funds, as an opportunity belonging to the Funds. At the very least, CAM should have disclosed this opportunity for significant savings to the Funds. CAM did neither. Instead, CAM took this opportunity for itself and then presented a recommendation to the Funds' boards in a memo that gave them the impression that the affiliated TA proposal was the best deal that the Funds could have achieved, which was not true. In presenting its recommendation to the Funds' boards, CAM did not disclose that First Data was to perform almost all of the same work as before, with the affiliated TA taking most of the profit for doing limited work.

5. CAM's recommendation also contained numerous material misrepresentations about the particulars of the arrangement, including the extent of the benefits CAM would realize. Among other things, CAM failed to disclose that it had entered into a side letter agreement (the "Side Letter") with First Data, pursuant to which First Data committed to providing millions of dollars of investment banking and asset management revenue to Citigroup entities (the "Revenue Guarantee").

6. Over the past five years, CTB has received more than $100 million in net fees for operating a small customer service call center and performing limited additional oversight and quality control functions at a total cost of approximately $11 million. [***]

* * *

The fraud was perpetrated against the Smith Barney Funds, and the SEC sanctioned the adviser and its corporate parent for fraud and deceit violations of the Advisers Act (Sections 206(1) and 206(2)). Consider whether violations of the Company Act could have been brought. Also consider whether shareholders could have brought an action pursuant to Section 36(b).

12.5.2 Unaffiliated Service Providers

Even if there is no affiliated relationship with the adviser, a service provider's service agreements with a fund must generally be reviewed and approved by the fund's board. When there is no affiliation with the sponsor, adviser or distributor of the fund, such approval can be made by simple vote of the board, i.e., not the 15(c) and bifurcated vote process for contracts such as the advisory agreement. Nonetheless, agreements for services such as fund administration, accounting, custody, and transfer agency have occasionally been the source of fraudulent or deceptive practices.

Administrative actions against BISYS Fund Services, Inc. ("BISYS") and one of its clients, AmSouth Bank, N.A. ("AmSouth"), provide an illustration of how legitimate fund servicing expenses can become mishandled. In the 1990s, BISYS grew into a large third-party services firm providing fund accounting, fund administration, transfer agency and distribution services to smaller funds and bank-affiliated fund groups.

Because of the regulatory strictures on bank distribution of funds, banks and their affiliates struggled to successfully market their funds. To assist them, beginning in the 1990s, BISYS offered a scheme to bank-affiliated fund advisers which essentially took administrative fees paid to BISYS by funds and allocated them back to banks and their affiliated advisers as marketing budgets and to pay unrelated other client expenses. Between 1999 and 2004, BISYS had 27 such arrangements pursuant to which it paid $230 million to or on behalf of advisers. Generally, the arrangements were governed by undisclosed written or oral side agreements as a means of sharing or reallocating fees, as in the *Smith Barney/Citigroup* case. In the administrative proceeding, BISYS was found to have aided and abetted advisory fraud and deceit violations as well as related investment company violations. *See In the Matter of BISYS Fund Services, Inc.*, Investment Advisers Act Release No. 2554 (Sept. 26, 2006).

An important lesson is that great care must be taken by all service providers—not just advisers—to disclose to the board the full nature of their services and relationship with funds and their affiliates like an adviser or distributor. Not addressed by the SEC is whether the additional fees paid to the advisers or given to them as a marketing budget should have had a collateral impact on the board's deliberations regarding the service provider contract. Another issue that was raised in these proceedings concerned whether marketing and distribution expenses can legitimately be paid out of fund assets (that topic involves Rule 12b-1 and is explored in Chapter 17).

Chapter 13

Fund Registration and Disclosure

Key Ideas: This chapter discusses registration by funds and their securities and the disclosure scheme primarily applicable to mutual funds (i.e., this chapter largely ignores analogous registration and disclosure issues applicable to other types of registered investment companies). The Company Act involves two types of registration: (1) as an investment company, and (2) the investment company's securities. In practice, these two types are closely related, but serve distinct regulatory purposes. Registration of investment companies is the formal process for establishing regulatory oversight over the investment company itself, while registration of offered securities ultimately is the process that ensures fair and adequate disclosure to the investing public regarding fund share purchases.

Registration of fund securities offerings, like the securities offerings of conventional public companies, is governed primarily by the Securities Act of 1933, although disclosure for RICs is also supplemented by provisions of the Company Act. However, unlike most public companies, mutual funds, and ETFs make continuous offerings of their securities. As a result, the SEC has specifically adapted the Securities Act's registration and disclosure requirements to the practical needs of issuers and investors to make the offering and disclosure more functional and useful. Funds also are subject to familiar forms of periodic disclosure, but here too, the relevant disclosure and filing requirements have been adapted to elicit meaningful information from funds and to better serve the needs of investors. Finally, funds are subject to stringent regulation of their marketing and advertising activities in offering shares.

These disclosure and filing requirements are enforced through government sanctions and private damages litigation. Through its administrative and civil enforcement powers, the SEC may seek an expansive range of sanctions against primary and secondary defendants to ensure compliance with the Company Act, Advisers Act, and other securities statutes. In contrast, investor private actions are limited to (1) express civil liability provisions of the Securities Act against a more limited class of statutory defendants, and (2) the general antifraud provisions arising under the Exchange Act that typically will not include the investment adviser, notwithstanding the adviser's substantial role in preparing fund disclosure.

Chapter Contents

13.1 Introduction

Registration of investment companies and their securities are actually two distinct, albeit intertwined, registration concepts. Registration of the investment company is simply the registration of the entity in which the fund is housed and establishes SEC jurisdiction over the fund. Registration of the fund is a prerequisite for publicly-sold funds to engage in the fund business. The other operative type of registration relates to the registration of the fund's offering and sale of securities. Sale of securities to the public is subject to the same expansive regulatory registration and disclosure requirements as applicable to ordinary public company issuers. However, the selling function for funds is at the very core of the fund arrangement: sale of fund securities is the means by which investors provide assets for the fund to manage and those sales constitute the principal way of growing the fund's assets under management. The Securities Act's registration requirement for securities offerings ensures investor access and receipt of mandated disclosures. The SEC has tailored the disclosure requirements for mutual funds to address the information needs of average investors. The relevant SEC requirements give special emphasis to simplification, standardization, and comparability in disclosure. The SEC's regulations also facilitate use of the internet to satisfy disclosure obligations. Because mutual funds are engaged in continuous offerings, mutual fund advertising must comply with restrictions in the Securities Act relating to the registration process. As a result, the SEC has significant authority over advertising by funds. In addition, registered investment companies are subject to a full panoply of periodic disclosure requirements relating to regular shareholder reports, fund portfolio holdings, and proxy voting by funds relating to portfolio holdings.The first half of this chapter provides an introduction to the conceptual and legal features of registration and ongoing disclosure obligations of registered investment companies. These requirements are divided into various component disclosure areas. The remainder of the chapter seeks to address potential liability, remedies, and sanctions for materially false and misleading disclosure in a variety of contexts.

13.2 Registration of Investment Companies and Their Securities Offerings

Registration of investment companies under Section 8 of the Company Act serves two fundamental purposes. First, company registration is necessary to overcome the flat prohibition contained in Section 7(a) of the Company Act against transacting business as an investment company unless registered as such. Second, once registered as an investment company, the company is subject to the SEC's regulatory jurisdiction. Thus, the SEC has the ability to revoke or suspend a registration, conduct examinations, and prevent unilateral de-registration (i.e., withdrawal of registration). The latter provision merely ensures that the SEC does not lose jurisdiction over an investment company while a fund effects an orderly liquidation and cessation of business.

For mutual funds, registration, both as an investment company and of its offering of securities, is accomplished by filing a Form N-1A registration statement. Funds make an initial notice filing of an intent to register (Form N-8A) and (concurrently or shortly after) file a Form N-1A, which is subject to a review and comment process by the SEC staff, a process lasting several weeks to several months. Only after the registration statement goes effective can the fund begin selling its securities to the public. Going effective, as a practical matter, involves the SEC's acquiescence but provides no formal blessing or endorsement. The SEC retains the power to issue a "stop order" to prevent an offering from proceeding, but that power is rarely invoked.

Form N-1A reflects the mandates of Section 8 as to specific content requirements relating to investment company policies, classification as an investment company, investment objectives, capital structure and leverage, concentration of investments, and portfolio turnover. These content requirements identify the nature and basic policies of the investment company. The registration statement must also enumerate "fundamental investment policies," which are changeable only by a vote of shareholders, pursuant to Section 13. These basic requirements ensure that investment companies cannot change the nature of their business overnight or alter fundamental fund investment objectives without an opportunity for shareholder input or regulatory oversight.

Registration of securities offered by the fund serves a broader purpose, namely ensuring fair and adequate disclosure to investors in the offering process. Section 24 of the Company Act mandates that the offering of investment company securities must be registered in accordance with the requirements of the Securities Act as supplemented or modified by the SEC, e.g., to reflect Company Act requirements. Under Section 8(c) of the Company Act, Congress authorized the SEC to adopt a uniform registration form for company and securities offering registration, which the SEC has done for most types of funds as detailed in Table 13A below. The result is a distinct registration process based primarily on the Securities Act requirements but integrating Company Act requirements as well.

In a conventional public company offering, the basic timing requirements and communication restrictions are governed by Securities Act Section 5, subject to modification by SEC rules. Offerings by conventional public companies are typically discrete capital-raising events that continue only until all of the securities being offered are sold. In most public offerings, a company proceeds through a well-established cycle of activities: (1) drafting and filing disclosure materials relating to the offering; (2) disseminating preliminary disclosure materials to the public and engaging in oral marketing efforts; and then (3) selling the registered securities as soon as possible after going effective (i.e., after the SEC has authorized actual sales pursuant to the filed registration statement). The company may use separate subsequent offerings to issue additional securities.

Fund offerings, and in particular mutual funds, differ in several respects from the conventional issuer model for offering securities. Unlike conventional offerings, which are discrete capital raising events, mutual fund offerings are typically continuous in nature (i.e., do not end at some fixed point in time), and the continuous nature of the offering is an intrinsic feature of the fund's business. Fund offerings are the means by which investors commit funds for management by an investment manager (and size of AUM is in turn the basis of determining the adviser's management fees). The bulk of the selling of a fund's securities occurs well after, indeed even years after, the fund originally goes public.

The distinction between discrete and continuous offerings has huge implications under Section 5 of the Securities Act. First, funds' primary offering documents, like a prospectus, must be "evergreen," i.e., the documents' substantive disclosures must be updated regularly to be accurate on a continuous basis. Second, Section 5 imposes significant communication restrictions on issuers during a public offering, restrictions that limit extraneous forms of disclosure by the issuer. In the typical discrete offering by an ordinary corporate issuer, these communication restrictions last only for a limited period of time, only a fraction of the issuer's corporate existence. In contrast, mutual fund offerings typically are continuous and, as a result, the SEC retains significant control over all facets of a mutual fund's ongoing offering communications, including its marketing and advertising materials, because such activities are deemed part of its offering of securities.

The link between AUM and offerings has added significance because mutual funds issue redeemable securities. Thus, mutual funds are always subject to the risk that investors will withdraw (or remove) their assets from the fund. Accordingly, mutual funds typically engage in a continuous public offering not only to increase AUM, but at the very least, to stabilize AUM by selling shares to offset redemptions of shares by those investors who seek to liquidate their investment in the fund.

13.3 Fund Offering Disclosure to Investors

The SEC has customized its approach to securities offerings by funds. The use of different registration forms for different types of funds is the most basic aspect of its attempt to tailor the registration process. The vast majority of registered investment companies are mutual funds or ETFs structured as mutual funds—both in terms of number of issuers and AUM (by trillions and trillions of dollars). Thus, Form N-1A is of unusual practical significance in understanding public offering regulation in the fund industry and is the primary focus of this discussion of registration and disclosure issues. Nevertheless, before turning to mutual fund registration and disclosure in earnest, it is probably worth identifying the different types of investment company registration forms to avoid confusion. See Table 13A below. Each type of form raises its own issues (which would go well beyond the scope of this chapter), but this fact underscores a central practice issue when it comes to fund disclosure: what type of registered investment fund product is being addressed? Although mutual fund issues have an outsized significance in understanding registration and disclosure issues, related issues can arise with other types of funds, especially in the area of misleading disclosure.

Table 13A — Table of SEC Investment Company Registration Forms

Registration Statement Form Number	Purpose/Type of Fund
Form N-8A	Notice of registration for investment companies under the Company Act (note: this form is technically not a registration statement but merely a form that signals initiation of the company registration process).
Form N-1A	Mutual funds (including ETFs structured as mutual funds) — otherwise known as open-ended management investment companies
Form N-2	Closed-end management investment companies
Form N-3	Separate accounts offering variable annuity contracts structured as management investment companies
Form N-4	Separate accounts offering variable annuities structured as unit investment trusts
Form N-5	Small business investment companies
Form N-6	Separate accounts organized as unit investment trusts that offer variable life insurance policies
Form N-8B-2	Unit investment trusts

13.3.1 Mutual Fund Disclosure: Function and Purpose

Before discussing the specific features and disclosure documents involved in a mutual fund offering, it is worthwhile to think about the purposes of disclosure in the mutual fund context. Disclosure, of course, is the cornerstone of investor protection under federal securities law and is intended to ensure that investors have full information before making investment decisions. But this simple formulation overlooks the differences between the purpose of disclosure in the context of mutual funds and in the case of conventional public companies. In the conventional public company context, dissemination of information by the company also affects the market price of the company's securities since investors use the information provided by a company to determine a company's intrinsic value. Of course, actual market price in that context may exceed or be less than the company's intrinsic value and will ultimately be determined by supply and demand for the company's securities in the market. In contrast, disclosure is largely irrelevant to the pricing of mutual fund shares; mutual funds are sold at net asset value (i.e., the fund's true intrinsic value determined by pricing its portfolio of securities). This result follows directly from the fact that mutual fund shares are redeemable: redemption ensures that an investor can always demand the intrinsic value of the shares and issuers will offer additional shares at the same price.

It is worth considering in the abstract what kind of information would be most useful to mutual fund investors. Presumably investors would like to be able to determine whether a particular fund is likely (or at least more likely) to be successful in delivering results in the future that meet the investor's defined goals. This relatively simple formulation of the investor's problem actually conceals complex issues about determining what are successful or reasonable investment goals for an individual investor, and whether an investor will likely be able to make informed predictions regarding the ability of a fund to achieve returns consistent with their reasonable expectations. Should the investor be focused on trying to pick the fund that will deliver the highest returns? How should the investor factor in items such as expenses incurred by investors and risks associated with different fund investments? Is it reasonable for an investor to think that he or she will be successful in identifying funds that are capable of outperforming the market? Is outperforming the market even a rational fund investment strategy? How should investors go about the decision of combining several fund investments in an investment portfolio?

The SEC approach that is described below is squarely grounded in principles of investor choice, while imposing regulatory constraints. The regulatory constraints are designed to eliminate some abuses and promote more informed choices, even if the choices made by investors are not always the best choices. Such an approach is potentially beneficial in two respects. First, average individual investors, if provided reasonable amounts of information, may be more likely to make better investment decisions and be less vulnerable to various types of abusive conduct. Second, if average investors make better decisions, competition among funds will encourage funds to adhere to investment principles that are performance justified (in terms of risk, returns and costs). In a sense, the SEC's policy seeks to move investors in the right direction. Nevertheless, investor behavior is not always well-informed or disciplined, and the marketing practices of some funds may not foster sound investment decisions.

Other policy approaches exist in theory. For example, there could be direct government control of investment and savings alternatives, such that investors would only be able to use government sponsored funds for investment savings. Government could also impose restrictions on investment choices for less sophisticated investors, such as limiting investment choices to broad-based passive investment vehicles (like index funds) that reflect market performance for a given asset class like stocks or bonds. Such paternalistic alternatives are in stark contrast to the prevailing scheme of regulation predicated on investor choice. While the SEC's prevailing regulatory policies are designed to promote more informed decision-making, an investor's actual decisions will nevertheless remain subject to marketing influences that may result in less than rational investment choice. In short, although SEC disclosure policy may enable investors to make more informed decisions, these policies will not guarantee that investors make good decisions.

13.3.2 The Evolution of Mutual Fund Disclosure Policy

The current requirements governing fund disclosure mark the culmination of a long process that has been shaped by two main considerations (i) compliance with the basic statutory securities law requirements governing offerings and periodic reporting and (ii) recognition of unique policy considerations applicable to fund investors. A third factor has also affected this evolution—a willingness by the SEC to experiment with disclosure formats that differ in important respects from the format and manner of offering restrictions applicable to conventional public companies. The resulting disclosure scheme is tailored to improve fund investor decision-making and satisfy fund marketing needs.

Prior to the 1980s, the requirements for fund prospectuses (the core offering document of an issuer's registration statement) were largely based on the model developed for conventional public companies: Under the Securities Act, investors who buy securities in a public offering must receive a comprehensive disclosure document known as the prospectus. In 1983, the SEC elevated simplification as a new goal for fund disclosure in the prospectus-based scheme. Specifically, it determined that the existing statutory prospectus—the core document in the mutual fund's registration statement on Form N-1A—should be bifurcated into a streamlined final prospectus, consisting of the so-called "statutory prospectus" (now Part A of Form N-1A), and a new document called the "statement of additional information" (the "SAI"—now Part B of Form N-1A). Bifurcation proved a key step in implementing the SEC's simplification strategy. Investors were ensured delivery of a shortened statutory prospectus while retaining the right to obtain additional information contained in the fund's SAI. The statutory prospectus continues to contain the most important information for average retail investors, such as disclosure regarding the fund's investment objectives and its historical performance in terms of risk, return, and fees or expenses, and other matters relating to incidence of ownership (such as sales commissions, advisory and other fees, redemption rights, taxes, and contact information). The fund's separate SAI contains additional information (and frequently more detailed, and technical, information) that supplements what is found in the statutory prospectus, such as details on the fund's investment policies and restrictions, brokerage arrangements, service provider contracts, and management of the fund.

In the SEC's view, the shorter prospectus would be more readable and accessible to average retail investors. In this way, simplification helps average investors make more informed decisions in choosing fund investments because average investors would be more likely to read and understand the prospectus. Bifurcation also caused the SEC to focus on other ways to increase the understandability of the statutory prospectus's contents with the knowledge that more detailed information would remain available to investors in the SAI.

Bifurcation as an approach to disclosure, however, entails potential policy problems: in the interests of simplification, is it appropriate to omit material information from the document that investors are most likely to read? And if so, are regulators signaling that certain material information is really not all that material? How should policymakers decide what appears in the primary or most basic document and what appears in the second document? At the very least, bifurcation is premised on the notion that what appears in the primary document is in some way incomplete. This immediately raises the issue of who bears the risk of the incompleteness—issuers or sponsors in terms of potential liability or investors in terms of presumed responsibility for considering all available information?

From a purely legal perspective, the statutory prospectus is the type of prospectus prescribed by Securities Act Section 10(a)(1) for purposes of Securities Act Section 5(b)(2)'s prospectus delivery requirement. The statutory prospectus is the fund's principal SEC-mandated disclosure document for soliciting investors in the bifurcated disclosure scheme. (As we will see, however, other forms of communication can be used to solicit investors as well.) As a Section 10 prospectus, the statutory prospectus has liability implications for purposes of the right of investors to sue for misrepresentations under Securities Act Section 12(a)(2). The other key disclosure document that is part of mutual fund registration statements is the SAI. The SAI, unlike a statutory prospectus, is not a prospectus for purposes of the Securities Act. Accordingly, delivery to investors is not required by Section 5(b)(2). Nevertheless, the SEC requires that it be made available to investors on request. Today the "upon request" limitation is largely irrelevant in practice because funds can make such documents easily accessible to all on the internet.

Two significant aspects of the simplification/bifurcation approach are worth highlighting:

(a) Standardization and comparability in fund disclosure. The contents of the prospectus are more readily understandable for investors because the SEC has increased the standardization of certain types of information and format. This kind of standardized information made it easier for investors to make comparisons among funds.

Fund disclosure in this respect differs somewhat from ordinary public company disclosure. Prospective fund investors frequently focus a limited number of narrow factors when comparing and deciding between different funds in which to invest. In this context, fostering standardization in fund disclosure makes good regulatory sense and assists investors. Standardization of disclosure relates to both substantive information and form of presentation. For example, the SEC mandates use of standardized performance calculation and presentation requirements.

The SEC has imposed forms of quantitative standardization in disclosure in three specific areas, all of which must be set forth in the summary prospectus: fund performance, a risk illustration regarding fund returns, and fund expenses. Fund prospectuses must provide standardized performance figures in which total return is calculated according to established methodologies for 1, 5, and 10 year periods as calculated through the most recently completed quarter (although, since funds use different dates for filing prospectuses, the figures in the 1, 5, and 10 year periods are not entirely comparable across prospectuses). The multiple time slices reduce the ability of funds to selectively choose time periods to their own advantage. In addition, the fund's standardized performance figures must be accompanied by standardized performance figures for an appropriate securities index over the same periods. With standardization, investors (and regulators) can compare funds' performance side by side knowing that such performance should be calculated in a standardized manner using the same formulae over roughly similar time periods.

A fund's risk/return summary also contains a chart representing the fund's performance over each of the 10 preceding years to graphically illustrate (as a proxy for risk) variability of return. The fund must also disclose its best single quarterly performance over the last 10 years, along with its worst single quarterly performance during the same period. Finally, basic fund expenses must be set forth in a tabular summary as a percentage of assets, which includes the management fee, other expenses, and the total annual operating expenses (i.e., the expense ratio). Additionally, the fund must provide a concrete illustration of the hard dollar cost that would be incurred over 10 years by an investor making a $10,000 investment with an assumed constant return over the relevant period. These examples above illustrate how the SEC has tried to encourage simplified quantitative standardization in targeted areas.

Illustration: Disclosure of After-Tax Fund Returns—Standardization with a Grain of Salt

The text emphasizes the role of standardization in performance disclosure. A wrinkle in this area relates to the distinction between performance and after-tax performance. Generally, funds are pass-through tax vehicles (i.e., funds do not retain any net income or gains; instead, shareholders are directly responsible for the income and gains that the fund distributes to them). This fact can lead to widely divergent results in understanding the effect of standardized performance for investors. Suppose Fund 1 and Fund 2 have equivalent standardized performance returns. If Fund 2's performance figures reflect huge potential tax liabilities on investment positions which have greatly appreciated in price, rational investors might be cautious about Fund 2 because the share price does not fully reflect deferred fund tax liability (i.e., the liability that will come due when the fund sells its appreciated fund position). The SEC has adopted disclosure requirements to address this issue, but the mandated standardized figures are inherently imprecise because of the many variables affecting realization of income and taxable gains by the fund and the tax status of individual shareholders. For example, if a fund has offsetting tax losses, the effect of the gains can be minimized. Similarly, some shareholders may hold the fund shares in a tax-sheltered retirement account, in which case the tax on the dividends and distributions will be deferred. In addition, if the shareholder sells appreciated fund shares before capital appreciation is realized by the fund and paid out to the shareholder, then the liquidating shareholder will not be liable for the unrealized gains. As a result, the after-tax results are not a reliable indicator of the investor's potential return but merely signals to the investor of such potential returns and that there are potential issues associated with tax liability arising from the fund's investment positions.

(b) Incorporation by reference. Bifurcation and more pronounced forms of layered disclosure discussed below rely heavily on the concept known as "incorporation by reference". Incorporation by reference potentially enables an issuer to modify or supplement disclosure contained in a shorter document, such as the statutory prospectus, by referring in the shorter document to more comprehensive disclosure found in other disclosure documents. For example, if disclosure in a SAI is incorporated by reference into the statutory prospectus, the disclosure in the SAI is deemed to supplement the disclosure provided in the statutory prospectus as if it were stated in the prospectus in determining whether the prospectus disclosure itself is misleading or incomplete.

Incorporation by reference provides issuers with a workable legal solution to liability concerns under the Securities Act arising from the omission of material information. Streamlined disclosure is at risk of being potentially misleading because the shorter format may omit boilerplate disclaimers or excessive qualifications. Incorporation by reference gets around this problem by allowing the issuer to provide concise disclosure while alerting the investor to additional disclosure that may be relevant or more comprehensive. Removing potential liability stemming from incomplete or omitted disclosure eliminates a major concern of issuers and increases their willingness to use abbreviated disclosure. Absent liability concerns, issuers (for reasons of economy in delivery and effectiveness of communication) and average investors (for reasons of readability) likely prefer using solicitation documents that do not have excessive boilerplate language and are less voluminous.

Incorporation by reference creates an offsetting potential liability for funds. Disclosure incorporated by reference into a prospectus means that the incorporated disclosure itself will be subject to the strict liability standard for material misleading disclosure found in Section 12(a)(2) of the Securities Act. Thus, although incorporation by reference to supplement fund disclosure minimizes liability from being potentially misleading, it correspondingly expands the zone of disclosure liability to encompass possibly misleading disclosure contained in the incorporated document.

As a policy matter, incorporation by reference raises concerns that investors do not necessarily consult the disclosure incorporated by reference and thus may be informationally shortchanged. Put simply, disclosure incorporated by reference will not be as informative for average investors as if the incorporated information had appeared directly in the incorporating document, unless the investor actually reviews the document from which the disclosure was incorporated. The court's decision in *White v. Melton*, 757 F. Supp. 267 (S.D.N.Y. 1991), illustrates the potential problem. There, investors claimed that they were misled by disclosure contained in the statutory prospectus relating to a non-obvious method of computing the contingent deferred sales charge involving an exchange of funds within the same fund family. The issue was fully explained in the fund's SAI which the investor had not consulted. The court held the investor could not recover because the source of confusion had been adequately disclosed to investors in the fund's prospectus by referencing the SAI's fuller disclosure and the incorporation by reference was all that the SEC required with respect to required prospectus disclosure relating to sales charges.

While incorporation by reference creates tension between the goal of simplifying disclosure for investors to make disclosure more readable and the goal of providing investors with comprehensive disclosure, funds do not have unlimited discretion in availing themselves of incorporation by reference. First, the SEC expressly mandates that the prospectus must contain certain essential information. Thus, disclosure incorporated by reference can only supplement the essential disclosure mandated by the SEC: it cannot entirely displace or supersede the required disclosure. Second, funds may use incorporation by reference only to incorporate information from enumerated disclosure documents, such as the SAI, and not to introduce information omitted entirely from established disclosure documents.

13.3.3 The Current Approach to Layered Disclosure and Its Components

In 2009, the SEC overhauled its bifurcation disclosure strategy. This new approach, known as layered disclosure, represents a significant extension of the SEC's original bifurcation approach to simplification by employing the capabilities of the internet to support a range of disclosure options for investors. Essentially, the layered disclosure approach affords funds and their shareholders a wider range of disclosure options. The centerpiece of the SEC layered disclosure initiative is its introduction of a new prospectus document—the "summary prospectus". The purpose of the summary prospectus is to provide an even more simplified, abbreviated, and standardized presentation for average retail investors. The summary prospectus has two possible uses. First, the contents of the summary prospectus must be made available to all investors in the forepart of the statutory prospectus. Second, it may be used as a self-contained soliciting document for investors independently of the statutory prospectus. The most important condition is internet accessibility for investors on the fund's or fund sponsor's website of the fund's statutory prospectus, SAI, and most recent fund annual or semi-annual report to shareholders (discussed below). The prescribed disclosure in the summary prospectus, which cannot be enlarged or omitted, consists of identifying information and seven key items that must be presented in a standardized sequence. The contents of the summary prospectus are set forth in Securities Act Rule 498 and Form N-1A. As noted, the summary prospectus can be used in isolation as a soliciting document, but in any event, the summary prospectus must appear in the front part of the separate and more complete statutory prospectus.

The SEC's layered disclosure approach offers investors disclosure in several formats with each format offering differing amounts of detail. This approach enabled the SEC to embrace use of an extremely simplified document for many investors. The SEC concluded that it is better to have simplified and readable documents for average investors, because average investors are more likely to read such documents. The highly simplified document is effective, because it allows less sophisticated, average retail investors to focus on the most salient features of the investment decision, in lieu of requiring such investors to slog through detailed documents that might exceed their patience and understanding.

At the same time, the SEC preserved the ability of regulators to obtain comprehensive disclosure from funds and retained (perhaps even enhanced) investors' electronic access to comprehensive forms of disclosure. Whether the right policy balance has been struck is of course a contestable issue, but it is important to understand that the debate between simplification and comprehensiveness is more about how to balance these policy objectives rather than whether funds should provide comprehensive forms of disclosure in the first place. An additional, separate policy debate relates to the volume and specificity of disclosure requirements, with predictable positions from the SEC (more is necessary in order for investors to have access to disclosure that is fully comprehensive) and industry (less is sufficient for the needs of investors and more is too costly).

The layered disclosure initiative also underscores the significance of the internet in understanding how offering disclosure operates in practice. The internet has fundamentally altered the method by which funds and investors interact, and these changes have significantly affected the way in which fund disclosure operates. First, and most obviously, fund documents are easily accessible to investors electronically. For the diligent and motivated investor, electronic accessibility to fund documents makes a greater variety of the issuer's documents readily available. However, the average fund investor may not be diligent. As a result, mere ease of access does not always translate into actual review or familiarity with the mandated disclosure documents (i.e., there is little guarantee that investors will actually open and read the electronic documents). By the same token, however, there is no assurance that physical delivery of printed prospectuses will cause investors to read those documents.

During the early stages of the internet, the SEC confronted this basic tension between ease of electronic access and possible adverse effects on willingness to read documents. In addressing statutorily prescribed delivery obligations, such as Securities Act Section 5(b)(2), the SEC concluded that as long as documents were electronically available to investors and the investor consented to accept delivery of the document by those means, then electronic delivery would be equated with physical delivery in determining whether delivery had occurred.

Delivery of a prospectus by the internet had another useful dimension for funds in terms of complying with statutory communication restrictions. Although the internet greatly increased the technological capability of funds to communicate directly with prospective investors in terms of sales literature and other forms of issuer-sponsored content, such forms of communication faced a significant legal impediment. Ordinarily such communications would be barred because of concerns that the communication might supplant the prospectus. Under a second SEC interpretive position known as the envelope theory, however, the SEC permitted such communications as long as a statutory prospectus was available with any sales materials.

To understand this result, it is necessary to understand the practical effect of Section 5 of the Securities Act in restricting the availability of material marketing securities to investors, including website content. The Securities Act's free-writing prohibition (Section 5(b)(1)) generally prohibits an issuer from soliciting investors through advertisements or sale literature (i.e., informal types of prospectuses), unless the advertisement is itself a prospectus or the sales literature is accompanied by (or preceded by delivery of) a statutory prospectus (i.e., a prospectus compliant with Section 10(a)). Since mutual funds are typically engaged in a continuous offering of their shares, the free-writing prohibition means that use of marketing and sales literature is ordinarily subject to severe legal constraint. Accordingly, marketing content and sales literature on a fund website ordinarily would run afoul of the free-writing prohibition.

However, sales literature physically accompanied or preceded by a statutory prospectus is not deemed to be an impermissible form of communication. (Technically, the sales literature would otherwise be treated as a non-compliant soliciting prospectus under Securities Act Section 2(a)(10).) Under the envelope theory, the SEC concluded, for interpretive purposes, that a website providing access to a prospectus along with marketing content is essentially no different than an envelope containing both sales literature and a statutory prospectus. Just as the sales literature is deemed not to be a prospectus when physically delivered in the same envelope as a statutory prospectus, featuring marketing content on a fund website, which also offers ready access to a fund prospectus, will not violate the free-writing prohibition.

A website, however, is not entirely analogous to an envelope merely containing paper versions of sales literature and a prospectus. First, websites are a potentially supercharged source of marketing content that may contain visually-appealing graphics and even interactive planning tools. In contrast, prospectuses mandated by the SEC tend to be plain, text-laden formats. Average investors might opt for deftly crafted marketing materials over the rather plain SEC documents in navigating a fund's website, and herein lies a policy issue. Because funds (or other market professionals such a broker-dealers) control the electronic channels by which mandated disclosure is delivered (i.e., websites), funds or market professionals are in a position to favorably frame for investors the presentation of sales and marketing literature that accompanies mandated electronic disclosure, subject to some constraints on advertising and marketing materials. In theory, this result might cause investors to rely less on SEC-mandated documents in favor of issuer-generated presentation formats. Even though the two formats exist side-by-side on the issuer's website, the way access is structured and graphical disparities in presentation can dictate widely different utilization of the two formats. This phenomenon creates a risk of what one of the authors has referred to as "substituted" disclosure[1]—namely investors may gravitate toward and rely on content shaped by funds and market professionals, albeit subject to minimum presentation standards mandated either by the SEC or FINRA.

As an aside, not only are funds and average investors more likely to engage in direct communications through the internet, but investors have access to more comparative information from third-party sources about fund selection. The internet as an independent source of relevant comparative information will make diligent investors (and not necessarily the investors who are the most sophisticated) better informed than they would be otherwise. In a sense, this democratizing feature of the internet at least partially offsets the risk of fund-sponsored, substituted disclosure.

13.4 Fund Advertising

In addition to restrictions on delivery of sales and advertising literature on the internet, the SEC has grappled with a number of other issues affecting the use of sales and advertising literature involving rules that permit advertising prospectuses suitable for publication, content requirements and advertising review by regulators. As noted, from a legal perspective, mutual funds cannot use mass marketing materials, such as newspaper advertisements, other than a prospectus unless the materials are (1) accompanied by delivery of a statutory prospectus (not feasible in the case of mass publication), or (2) themselves either a prospectus compliant with Securities Act Section 10 or not deemed to be a prospectus at all. As noted, fund websites afford considerable latitude in the presentation of marketing materials because such platforms routinely carry links to the statutory prospectus, which satisfies the first exception. To fit within the second exception, two different forms of advertising are permitted

1. Joseph A. Franco, *A Consumer Protection Approach to Mutual Fund Disclosure and the Limits of Simplification*, 15 Stan. L.J. 1 (2009).

under SEC rules: (1) advertisements that conform to Securities Act Rule 482 which are deemed Section 10(b) compliant prospectuses; and (2) generic advertisements permitted and not deemed to be prospectuses under Securities Act Rule 135a.

13.4.1 Securities Act Rule 482

Funds regularly utilize advertisements that comply with Securities Act Rule 482, which enables funds to use stand-alone "advertising prospectuses" under certain conditions, to advertise their shares. These advertisements may appear in publications such as newspapers for purposes of marketing to the investing public and may contain performance information. Rule 482 requires the use of cautionary legends (e.g., most famously that, "past performance does not guarantee future results"), appropriate formatting, and the use of standardized performance results for 1, 5, and 10 year periods if performance figures are used. The release below gives an overview of the rule in its current form.

Amendments to Investment Company Advertising Rules

Securities Act Release No. 8294 (Sept. 29, 2003)

[**Textbook Note:** *This reading is an excerpt from the adopting release discussing major amendments to the advertising rules applicable to investment companies. It covers a number of issues that the amendments were designed to address with the existing rules. To some extent, it presumes familiarity with the existing framework grounded primarily in Securities Act Rule 482, since the amendments build on that framework. This excerpt focuses only on certain features that have continuing significance in understanding basic themes relating to the advertising rules. At the outset, it is important to remember that virtually all mutual fund advertising is subject to the freewriting prohibition found in Section 5(b)(1) of the Securities Act. As a result, substantive forms of advertising will invariably constitute a prospectus, and the only permissible form of advertising prospectus must conform to SEC rules. The issues discussed in this excerpt relate to a very legalistic issue regarding the "substance of which" requirement that underscores some of the wrinkles associated with the Securities Act's freewriting prohibition. A second set of issues relates to the potential for advertising to mislead investors even when the advertisement complies with the literal terms of Rule 482. The excerpt addresses this issue in at least three respects: (i) the absence of safe harbors from fraud prohibitions even when a communication is otherwise permissible under the offering restrictions, (ii) the need for current information even when the rule does not mandate its presentation, and (iii) the importance of balance in presenting information permitted under the rules.*]

[***] I. Introduction and Background

Like most issuers of securities, when an investment company ("fund") offers its shares to the public, its promotional efforts become subject to the advertising restrictions of the Securities Act. Congress imposed these restrictions so that investors would base their investment decisions on the full disclosures contained in the "statutory prospectus," which Congress intended to be the primary selling document. The advertising restrictions of the Securities Act cause special problems for many investment companies, particularly for open-end management investment companies ("mutual funds") and other investment companies that continuously offer and sell their shares. For these funds, the advertising restrictions apply continuously because the offering process, in effect, is continuous.

In recognition of these problems, the Commission has adopted special advertising rules for investment companies. The most important of these is rule 482 under the Securities Act, which permits investment companies to advertise investment performance data, as well as other information. Rule 482 advertisements are "prospectuses" under section 10(b) of the Securities Act (so-called "omitting prospectuses"), which means that, historically, they could only contain information the "substance of which" is included in the statutory prospectus.

...

II. Discussion

A. Eliminating the "Substance of Which" Requirement from Rule 482 ...

We are adopting, as proposed, the amendment removing the requirement that a rule 482 advertisement contain only information the "substance of which" is included in the statutory prospectus. This amendment implements section 24(g) of the Investment Company Act, added by NSMIA, which directs the Commission to adopt rules or regulations that permit registered investment companies to use prospectuses that (i) include information the substance of which is not included in the statutory prospectus, and (ii) are deemed to be permitted by section 10(b) of the Securities Act. Eliminating this requirement will permit investment companies to include up-to-date information in rule 482 advertisements, such as information about current economic conditions that normally would not be included in a fund's prospectus. The amendment also will permit funds to eliminate certain information from the statutory prospectus, such as boilerplate disclosure about the methods used to calculate performance in fund advertising, that clutters the statutory prospectus and obscures other important information. As a result, investors should receive better, more understandable, and more timely information in both the statutory prospectus and fund advertisements. In addition, the costs of regulatory compliance should be reduced for funds and, ultimately, for investors.

Elimination of the "substance of which" requirement from rule 482 should not diminish investor protection. The "substance of which" requirement is a technical requirement that does not, in itself, prevent misleading statements because it does not require an advertisement to use the same words as the statutory prospectus or prohibit the use of advertising techniques that are not included in the statutory prospectus. Importantly, rule 482 advertisements, as "prospectuses," will remain subject to liability under section 12(a)(2) of the Securities Act and the antifraud provisions of the federal securities laws. Also, rule 482 advertisements, as section 10(b) prospectuses under the Securities Act, are subject to the summary suspension provisions of section 10(b), which permit the Commission to suspend the use of a materially false or misleading prospectus. In addition, fund advertising materials must continue to be filed with [FINRA] or the Commission, and FINRA rules relating to fund advertising will continue to apply.[5] Finally, we are adopting additional amendments to rule 482 to reinforce antifraud protections, particularly in the area of fund performance....

... We believe that investor protection will be increased if fund advertisements including this information are subject to rule 482 and, as a result, to liability under section 12(a)(2) of the Securities Act.[20]

B. Applicability of Antifraud Provisions to Fund Advertising

We are adopting, with modifications suggested by the commenters, amendments to the fund advertising rules that are intended to reemphasize that fund advertisements are subject to the antifraud provisions of the federal securities laws. When we initially proposed rule 482 in 1977, we indicated that rule 482 advertisements would be subject to section 12(a)(2) of the Securities Act and the antifraud provisions of the federal securities laws. Since then, we have reiterated that compliance with the "four corners" of rule 482 does not alter the fact that funds, underwriters, and dealers are subject to the antifraud provisions of the federal securities laws with respect to fund advertisements.[22]

---

5. Section 24(b) of the Investment Company Act [15 U.S.C. 80a-24(b)] requires the filing with the Commission of "any advertisement, pamphlet, circular, form letter, or other sales literature" for any registered investment company other than a closed-end fund. Rule 24b-3 under the Investment Company Act [17 C.F.R. § 270.24b-3] relieves funds of the obligation to file advertisements and other sales materials with the Commission if those materials are filed with [FINRA]....

20. Because a rule 482 advertisement is a prospectus under section 10(b) of the Securities Act, a rule 482 advertisement is subject to section 12(a)(2) of the Securities Act [15 U.S.C. 77*l*(a)(2)], which imposes liability for materially false or misleading statements in a prospectus or oral communication, subject to a reasonable care defense. An action under section 12(a)(2) does not require proof of scienter (*i.e.*, an intent to defraud investors), *e.g.*, *Wigand v. Flo-Tek, Inc.*, 609 F.2d 1028, 1034 (2d Cir. 1979), or investor reliance on a misleading statement or omission, *e.g.*, *MidAmerica Fed. S. & L. Assoc. v. Shearson/American Express, Inc.*, 886 F.2d 1249, 1256 (10th Cir. 1989); *Sanders v. John Nuveen & Co.*, 619 F.2d 1222, 1225 (7th Cir. 1980), *cert. denied*, 450 U.S. 1005 (1981). In contrast, antifraud claims by investors under section 10(b) of the Securities Exchange Act of 1934 ("Exchange Act") [15 U.S.C. 78j(b)] require proof of scienter and investor reliance. Under either type of claim, however, the plaintiff must establish that the misrepresentation or omission is material. Rule 134 advertisements are subject to the antifraud provisions under the federal securities laws but do not create liability under section 12(a)(2) of the Securities Act because rule 134 advertisements are not considered "prospectuses." Rule 134 was adopted under section 2(a)(10)(b) of the Securities Act [15 U.S.C. 77b(a)(10)(b)], which excepts certain communications from the definition of "prospectus."

22. Investment Company Act Release No. 16245 (Feb. 2, 1988) [53 F.R. 3868, 3878 n. 51 (Feb. 10, 1988)]. *See also* Investment Company Act Release No. 24832 (Jan. 18, 2001) [66 F.R. 9002, 9008 (Feb. 5, 2001)] (compliance with rule 482 is not a safe harbor from antifraud liability); Investment Company Act Release No. 15315 (Sept. 17, 1986) [51 F.R. 34384, 34391 (Sept. 26, 1986)] (in proposing amendments to rule 482 to require the inclusion of a legend on advertisements, Commission stated that it was "not suggesting that the legend information contains all the material information necessary to prevent an ad from being misleading ... [and] that whoever sponsors the ad, be it the fund, the underwriter, or the dealer, bears the primary responsibility for assuring that the ad is not false or misleading"); 1977 Advertising Proposing Release, *supra* note 13 [omitted], 42 F.R. at 30380 (advertisements made pursuant to rule 434d (subsequently renumbered as rule 482) would be subject to the antifraud provisions of the securities laws); *In the Matter of The Dreyfus Corporation and Michael*

To emphasize this principle, we are adding a note to newly adopted paragraph (a) of rule 482 that states that an advertisement that complies with rule 482 does not relieve the fund, underwriter, or dealer of any obligations with respect to the advertisement under the antifraud provisions of the federal securities laws. We also are adding a similar note to the introductory paragraph of rule 34b-1 under the Investment Company Act with respect to supplemental sales literature. These notes include cross-references to rule 156 under the Securities Act, which provides guidance about the factors to be weighed in determining whether statements, representations, illustrations, and descriptions contained in fund advertisements and sales literature are misleading.

As proposed, the language of the notes to rules 482 and 34b-1 would have stated that compliance with the rules does not relieve the fund, underwriter, or dealer of the obligation to "ensure" that the advertisement is not false or misleading. One commenter objected to the use of the term "ensure," stating that it could potentially expand the responsibility of funds, underwriters, and dealers because it might imply that they are guarantors of the accuracy of statements contained in advertisements. Our proposal incorporated language, including the term "ensure," similar to that used in an existing note to paragraph (a)(3) of rule 482, and we did not intend to alter existing standards of liability. In order to address the commenter's concern, however, we have revised the language of the note to remove the term "ensure" and clarify that compliance with rules 482 and 34b-1 does not relieve the fund, underwriter, or dealer of any obligations with respect to the advertisement under the antifraud provisions of the federal securities laws. This change is intended to clarify that the scope of a fund's, underwriter's, or dealer's obligations under the antifraud provisions is drawn from the federal securities laws and relevant precedents and not from the language of rule 482 or 34b-1 itself.

Two commenters urged the Commission to confirm in the adopting release that, notwithstanding the note to rule 482(a), performance information in a rule 482 advertisement (as opposed to other disclosures included in the advertisement) will not be deemed to be false or misleading if it (i) is computed in accordance with the methodology required by the rule; and (ii) complies with the currentness requirements of the rule. We disagree with this position. An advertisement that complies with rule 482 will be deemed to be an "omitting prospectus" under section 10(b) of the Securities Act for the purposes of section 5(b)(1) of the Securities Act.[25] Rule 482, however, is not a safe harbor from antifraud liability for any information included in a rule 482

L. Schonberg, Investment Advisers Act Release No. 1870 (May 10, 2000) (advertisements that comply with rule 482 are subject to the general antifraud provisions of the securities laws).

25. Section 5(b)(1) of the Securities Act [15 U.S.C. 77e(b)(1)] makes it unlawful to use interstate commerce to transmit any prospectus relating to a security with respect to which a registration statement has been filed unless the prospectus meets the requirements of section 10 of the Securities Act. Section 10(b) of the Securities Act [15 U.S.C. 77j(b)] permits the Commission to adopt rules that provide for a prospectus that "omits in part" or "summarizes" information contained in the statutory prospectus. Rule 482 was adopted under the authority of section 10(b) of the Securities Act.

advertisement, including performance information complying with the requirements of the rule.

In addition, we are amending rule 156 to provide further guidance regarding the factors to be weighed in considering whether a statement involving a material fact in investment company sales materials is or might be misleading. As discussed in the Proposing Release, we are concerned that the advertisement of past performance without an adequate explanation of other facts may create unrealistic investor expectations or even mislead potential investors. For that reason, we are modifying the language of rule 156 to state more explicitly that portrayals of past income, gain, or growth of assets may be misleading where the portrayals omit explanations, qualifications, limitations, or other statements necessary or appropriate to make these portrayals of past performance not misleading. This language is intended to address our concerns with fund performance advertisements that do not provide adequate disclosure: (i) of unusual circumstances that have contributed to fund performance; (ii) that more current performance may be lower than advertised performance; or (iii) that would permit an investor to evaluate the significance of performance that is based on selective dates. We remind funds and their underwriters and dealers, however, that this language would address other circumstances that we have not specifically enumerated and that each fund, and its underwriters and dealers, is responsible for analyzing the facts and circumstances concerning its advertisements and determining whether its advertisements may be misleading.

C. Enhanced Disclosure under Rule 482

We are adopting, with modifications to address commenters' concerns, additional amendments to rule 482 that will require enhanced disclosure of certain information designed to encourage advertisements that convey balanced information to prospective investors. Our amendments require that funds that advertise performance information make available to investors total returns that are current to the most recent month-end. They also require that fund advertisements include improved narrative information and present explanatory information more prominently.

Availability of Month-End Performance Information

Currently, rule 482(g) requires all performance data contained in any mutual fund advertisement to be as of the most recent practicable date, provided that any advertisement containing total return quotations is considered to have complied with the requirement if the total return quotations are current to the most recent calendar quarter ended prior to submission of the advertisement for publication. We are adopting a second condition for a fund advertisement to be considered to have complied with the requirement of rule 482 that performance be as of the most recent practicable date. Specifically, total return quotations current to the most recent month-end, and available to investors within seven business days of the most recent month-end, must be provided at a toll-free or collect telephone number or on a website, unless the advertisement contains total return quotations that are current to the most recent month ended seven business days prior to the date of use of the advertisement. As a result, investors who are provided advertisements highlighting a fund's performance should have ready access to performance data that is current to the most recent month-end and will not be forced to rely on performance data that may be more than three months old at the time of use by the investor....

Improved Narrative Disclosure

Advertising that focused on extraordinary fund performance during 1999-2000 led to increasing concerns that some funds, when advertising their performance, may resort to techniques that create unrealistic investor expectations or may mislead potential investors. These concerns have arisen again with the recent improvement in market performance, as commentators have noted an increase in advertisements highlighting favorable short-term performance. To address these concerns, we are adopting, with modifications to address concerns raised by commenters, changes to the narrative disclosure that is required to accompany performance advertisements. These changes are intended to help investors understand the limitations of past performance data and enhance their ability to obtain updated performance information. In particular, these amendments will require funds to include the following information in rule 482 advertisements that contain performance data: (i) a statement that past performance does not guarantee future results; (ii) a statement that current performance may be lower or higher than the performance data quoted; and (iii) a toll-free or collect telephone number or a website where an investor may obtain performance data current to the most recent month-end, unless the advertisement includes total return quotations current to the most recent month ended seven business days prior to the date of use.....

...

We are also adopting, with modifications suggested by a commenter, an amendment to rule 482 that would direct prospective investors' attention to a fund's charges and expenses. As proposed, the amendment would have required a fund to note in its rule 482 advertisement that information about charges and expenses is included in the statutory prospectus. As adopted, the rule would require rule 482 advertisements to include a statement that advises an investor to consider the fund's investment objectives, risks, and charges and expenses carefully before investing; explains that the prospectus contains this and other information about the investment company; identifies a source from which an investor may obtain a prospectus; and states that the prospectus should be read carefully before investing. We were persuaded by a commenter's argument that the proposed required disclosures, while helpful, would not adequately direct investors' attention to the important factors that they should consider. We agree with the commenter that investors should consider a fund's objectives and risks, and its charges and expenses, before investing because these factors will directly affect future returns. We are concerned that the many fund advertisements highlighting performance have focused investors' attention on fund returns and that investors may be overlooking other important fund features, particularly charges and expenses, that may diminish a fund's returns.

...

Presentation of Explanatory Information

We are adopting, with modifications suggested by commenters, requirements that funds present certain information in their rule 482 advertisements more prominently. These prominence requirements are designed to prevent advertisements from marginalizing or minimizing the presentation of the required disclosure. The amendments will require print advertisements to present required narrative disclosures in a type size at least as large as and of a style different from, but at least as prominent as, that used in the major portion of the advertisement. This requirement will apply to the required narrative disclosures about the prospectus and the performance data. The amendments will also provide an exception to this requirement, which was suggested by a commenter; *i.e.*, when performance data is presented in a type size smaller than that of the major portion of the advertisement, the required narrative disclosure pertaining to the performance data may appear in a type size no smaller than that of the performance data. We were persuaded that, in such cases, presenting the required performance-related narrative disclosure in a type size larger than that of the performance data itself may be distracting.

...

In addition, we are adopting, as proposed, a requirement that the narrative disclosures that specifically relate to fund performance be presented in close proximity to the performance data in both print and radio and television advertisements. In a print advertisement, this information also would be required to appear in the body of the advertisement and not in a footnote. Rule 482 currently requires that performance advertisements identify the dates during which quoted performance occurred. We are adopting, as proposed, a requirement that this information be adjacent to, and have no less prominence than, the performance quotation itself. These proximity requirements are intended to help investors more readily find information necessary to understand and evaluate the performance data shown, and to remind investors of the limitations of performance data.

While the newly adopted prominence and proximity requirements apply only to certain information expressly required by rule 482, we wish to emphasize that the purpose of these requirements is to encourage fair and balanced advertisements. In that regard, we encourage funds and their underwriters and dealers to review their advertisements to ensure that the format of all the information in an advertisement results in a fair and balanced presentation. For example, an advertisement that hypes extraordinary performance but contains only footnote disclosure of unusual circumstances that have contributed to fund performance may not result in a fair and balanced presentation. [***]

* * *

13.4.2 Rule 135a Generic Advertising

Another widely used form of advertising by funds is a so-called "generic advertisement" pursuant to Rule 135a. Generic advertisements are advertisements that do not specifically refer to an investment company or its securities; rather, they provide information about investment company securities generally or types of investment objectives and styles of investment companies. Such advertisements or sales materials are not prospectuses for purposes of Securities Act Section 5. However, such advertisements may identify an investment adviser or broker-dealer where additional information relating to funds can be obtained. Generic advertising is permissible because it is not a prospectus of any sort, i.e., it is not a written offer of fund securities. Nevertheless, with the rise of fund families, such ads can be used to push investor traffic to fund family websites where, as noted, the fund family has significant latitude in placing marketing materials. Used in this way, generic advertising may have a useful marketing purpose, but will seldom be a source of liability.

13.4.3 The Role of FINRA and Advertising Review

The self-regulatory organization for broker-dealers, FINRA, plays an integral role in overseeing advertising for registered investment companies. Although FINRA has no direct oversight of registered funds, a fund's principal underwriter (which frequently may be an affiliate of the fund's investment adviser) will be a registered broker-dealer and, thus, subject to FINRA rules. In addition, Company Act Section 24(b) requires that advertisements and sales literature for mutual funds or unit investment trusts be filed with the SEC. To avoid the resources required to review such materials, the SEC by rule (Company Act Rule 24b-3) deems such materials when filed with FINRA (which separately "provides standards for the investment company advertising practices of its members") as discharging the Section 24(b) filing obligation. As a practical matter, FINRA oversees the bulk of all reviews relating to advertising and sales literature to ensure that such materials do not contain unsupported or exaggerated assertions.

In addition to its advertising review requirements, FINRA enforces rules that affect the content of sales materials disseminated to the public. Under FINRA Rule 2210, relating to communications with the public, broker-dealers face more stringent restrictions in disseminating sales materials containing information about an adviser's related performance in managing other funds or private accounts with similar investment objectives than imposed by the SEC in terms of what can be included in a statutory prospectus. FINRA Rule 2212 contains specific guidelines regarding the use of fund ratings of third-party ratings services, such as Morningstar and Lipper, in sales materials to prevent misleading characterization of such ratings. Thus, for example, FINRA requires that a fund using ratings in an advertisement also disclose the size of the pool of funds against which a particular fund is rated and the relevant time period over which the rated fund was evaluated.

13.5 Disclosure Obligations Pursuant to Periodic Reporting Requirements

Funds file periodic reports like conventional public companies, but, pursuant to Company Act Section 30, Congress gave the SEC considerable regulatory latitude in modifying and expanding the periodic reporting requirements found in the Securities Exchange Act. Below, the periodic requirements for mutual funds, which are generally applicable to ETFs as well, are used to illustrate these requirements. Other types of investment companies may have slightly different features.

13.5.1 Shareholder and Other Reports

Mutual funds provide reports to their shareholders semi-annually (usually referred to as the semi-annual and annual shareholder reports) in lieu of periodic reports prepared by conventional public companies. The shareholder reports provide extensive financial information about the fund's assets, liabilities, and operations during the relevant accounting period. The annual report also provides detailed fund information, such as (1) Management's Discussion of Fund Performance (MFDP), which is a narrative disclosure about the fund's performance and the factors that materially affected the fund's performance; and (2) extended narrative disclosure regarding the basis for the trustees' approval of the investment advisory agreement (although this latter disclosure, depending on timing issues, could be in the semi-annual report). In addition, the annual report provides a concrete illustration of fund performance. Fund performance is illustrated for a hypothetical investment of $10,000 in the fund over the preceding 10 fiscal years and compared to the performance of a suitable broad-based index. Both the annual and semi-annual report must provide a table illustrating both actual fund expenses incurred semi-annually in dollars for an investor investing $1,000, and an analogous hypothetical calculation based on the firm's expense ratio, assuming a 5 percent annual return. The financial statements contained in these reports and a review of the adequacy of internal controls must be certified by the fund's principal operating officers on Form N-CSR, to ensure compliance with financial integrity policies under the securities laws applicable to periodic reports generally.

The annual and semi-annual reports must also contain a schedule of fund portfolio holdings. This requirement is supplemented by an additional requirement that schedules of fund portfolio holdings be filed with the SEC regularly. Formerly, the SEC required that the disclosure be quarterly—on Form N-Q at the end of the first and third fiscal quarters on a delayed basis as well as annually and semi-annually. In 2016, the SEC eliminated this regime and replaced it with more frequent reports on a new form, Form N-Port. N-Port must be filed monthly on a 30 day delayed basis with the SEC and must be supplemented with financial metrics, including metrics relating to exposure and sensitivity to market risk and certain types of securities activities. Only the portfolio holdings at quarterly intervals will be made available to the public by the SEC on a delayed 60 day basis. Disclosure of portfolio holdings raise issues uniquely affecting the operation of investment companies. Active investment managers regularly voice concerns that such disclosure adversely affects implementation of investment strategies since the market is more aware of what specific fund holdings are. In addition, disclosure may lead to a phenomenon of "window dressing" where portfolio managers may feel the need to spruce up a portfolio in conjunction with disclosure deadlines to avoid adverse fallout from having a portfolio that contains investments that are publicly perceived as unwise or to garner favorable views by adding investment positions that have experienced recent market success. Such information may well be useful to investors, but at the same time, it raises the possibility that disclosure can affect portfolio selection and strategies.

Finally, the SEC requires disclosure of (i) proxy voting policies and procedures in the fund's annual shareholder report and (ii) factors that shape fund voting policies. This disclosure requirement is an objective corollary to the rule-based conduct standard relating to advisers' duty to maintain policies and procedures regarding how the adviser decides to exercise voting rights with respect to portfolio holdings (i.e., the votes attached to stock—voting of client securities and to make clients aware of those practices (Advisers Act Rule 206(4)-6)). Essentially, in the investment company context, this obligation is extended to the fund's shareholders. A separate annual filing with the SEC (on Form N-PX) detailing the fund's actual voting record is also required. This filing must also be made available to shareholders, which is typically done on the fund's website.

Like portfolio holdings disclosure, disclosure of a fund's proxy voting record raises conflicting policy considerations. Since voting power of securities held by the fund is an aspect of the fund's ownership of securities on behalf of fund shareholders, advisers should be accountable for the manner in which they exercise voting discretion. At the same time, public disclosure of a fund's voting record may cause certain shareholders to exert pressure on advisers regarding the voting positions of the fund. Such concerns have been raised with respect to union and public pension funds that typically take vocal roles in matters of shareholder advocacy.

The SEC traditionally gathered semi-annually "census" information regarding funds such as, that is, information identifying fund location, personnel involved in operating the fund, and AUM. That regime was altered in 2016 with a new annual reporting regime on Form N-CEN (replacing Form N-SAR). The basic types of information have remained unchanged. The SEC, however, has updated the reporting requirements to eliminate redundancy in some areas while providing new information in other areas.

13.5.2 Fund Proxy Materials

Distinct from mandated disclosures of funds is the need for funds to occasionally solicit their shareholders' votes on certain matters. Registered funds are subject to the same proxy requirements as ordinary public companies in soliciting proxies for meeting votes (Company Act Section 20 and Rule 20a-1), but as a practical matter, these requirements are less relevant for registered investment companies than for the typical public company. Unlike public companies which prepare proxy statements annually to solicit proxies from their shareholders in connection with the election of directors and the appointment of an independent auditor, annual votes by the shareholders of registered investment companies are relatively rare. As discussed in Chapter 11, this is because business entity laws frequently permit fund directors to remain in office for many years without a shareholder vote unless a shareholder vote happens to be triggered by a Company Act requirement. As a result, the instances involving shareholder votes are not regular and may not be required for years at a time. Events that will trigger the need for a shareholder meeting, and therefore a need for a proxy solicitation, are worth noting. Material changes to the investment advisory agreements, such as a new investment adviser, would require a proxy solicitation as would a merger of the fund into another fund. In addition, over time, a fund will eventually have to hold a shareholder vote to elect replacement trustees for retiring trustees. Such a requirement is triggered if the appointment of a new trustee would result in less than two-thirds of the board's trustees not having been elected by shareholders.

13.5.3 The Annual Disclosure Cycle for a Typical Mutual Fund

While the process above describes the offering and periodic requirements applicable to a typical mutual fund, the requirements tend to work on an integrated basis over an annual cycle. Remember, mutual funds offer securities continually, and so their registration obligations are ongoing. These obligations become part of the annual cycle associated with periodic reporting. Thus, in effect, the combined offering and periodic disclosure provides a full picture of the fund and its operations. The coordination of the ongoing disclosure requirements requires an orderly calendar system to ensure timely registration and disclosure compliance. In Table 13B below, we provide a sample compliance schedule to provide some practical insight into the rhythm of this process.

13.6 Misleading Disclosure by Registered Investment Companies

The securities laws contain numerous provisions that create liability for, or subject to sanction, materially misleading information or omissions. The express civil liability provisions of the Securities Act—specifically Section 11 (relating to materially false or misleading statements in a registration statement) and Section 12 (relating to materially false or misleading statements in a prospectus)—apply to offerings of securities by registered investment funds. These provisions, however, have particularly broad application to mutual funds, since all mutual fund shares are sold as part of a continuous public offering and, thus, the sales are tied to the accuracy of disclosures contained in the fund's registration statement and prospectus. In addition, the general antifraud provision Rule 10b-5 under Section 10 of the Securities Exchange Act applies to all purchase and sales of fund securities, including redemptions.

13.6.1 Misleading Performance Disclosure

Fund sponsors use fund performance results when investors are likely to view such information positively. Accurate standardized performance information does not eliminate the problem of misleading performance disclosure. Performance disclosure

Table 13B: Sample annual disclosure cycle for mutual fund with fiscal year ending September 30. [The SEC is in the process of transitioning from Form N-SAR and Form N-Q to Forms N-CEN and N-PORT, respectively. Form N-SAR was rescinded as of June 1, 2018 and Form N-PORT will be phased in through 2020.]

Fund Filing or Disclosure Requirement	Purpose	Timing
Updated Registration Statement on Form N-1A **1. Updated final prospectus, including updated summary prospectus.** **2. Updated SAI** **3. Part C — updated exhibits (filed only)**	Update information in the fund's prospectus and SAI. New investors and existing shareholders typically will receive a copy of the new prospectus and the updated documents are available to all shareholders and prospective investors. (Updated exhibits, such as key contracts, are publicly available to investors.)	Annual update within 120 days of end of fund's fiscal year. *[In our sample case of a fiscal year ending September 30, no later than January 28]*
Shareholder reports (annual and semi-annual)	This is the basic form of periodic financial disclosure (quarterly reports generally are not used).	Must be sent to shareholders within 60 days of the semi-annual and annual reporting periods *[In our example, no later than May 30 (semi-annual report) and no later than November 29 (annual report)]*
Form N-CSR	Filing containing certifications of the fund's shareholder reports and financial statements by its principal executive officer (PEO) and principal financial officer (PFO)	Filing must be made within 10 days of sending shareholder reports to shareholders. *[In our sample, no later than 10 days from the end of May (semi-annual report) and 10 days after the end of November (annual report)]*
Form N-PORT **[replacing old Form N-Q]**	Filing of portfolio holdings monthly with the SEC along with other financial metrics. The portfolio holding will be made public quarterly.	Filing must be within 30 days of the end of the month and the portfolio holdings will be made public quarterly 60 days after the end of the quarter. *[In our sample, portfolio holdings will be available to the public no later than the end of February (as of Dec. 31), the end of May (as of March 31), the end of August (as of June 30), and the end of November (as of Sept. 30)].*
Form N-PX	Discloses fund's proxy voting record (i.e., how the fund voted its portfolio holdings when they solicited proxies) for the 12 month period ending June 30	No later than August 31 for the most recently ended voting year.
Form N-CEN **[replaced old Form N-SAR]**	Form on which funds report a wide variety of census and statistical information to the SEC regarding a fund's organization, service providers, etc. This SEC filing should not be confused with the shareholder reports sent to investors.	File within 75 days after fiscal year-end *[In our example, no later than December 14 for a fund with a Sept. 30 fiscal year-end]*

must be understood in the broader disclosure context in which it operates. Specifically, fund sponsors exercise considerable discretion over the context of performance disclosure. While the requirements relating to standardized performance figures, whether in a statutory prospectus, a Rule 482 prospectus or sales literature subject to Company Act Rule 34b-1, are clear, a number of additional factors affect the presentation of performance information. For example, fund sponsors choose which funds to advertise and when. In extreme cases, fund sponsors eliminate funds with poor performance records either by liquidating the fund or merging the fund into another fund. The sponsor's discretion over how and when funds are marketed creates a filtering bias. Understandably, fund sponsors will market those funds which happen to be doing well relative to other funds and in terms of market conditions. For example, when oil prices are up, energy funds might be featured. If a particular fund is outperforming peers, then its adviser or sponsor may decide that fund's performance will be trumpeted. The filtering bias stems from the fact that the fund sponsor is selectively highlighting favorable outcomes to investors, while average investors lack practical means of determining the relevant size of the pool from which the favorable outcomes are derived. What appears to be a decisive illustration of intrinsic success when presented on a selective basis may actually be nothing more than the effect of random variation in outcomes (i.e., pure luck!).

A similar source of distortion can arise in aggregate performance figures, even when it appears that an observer has access to the performance of a broad pool of funds. Fund sponsors directly control the elimination of poorly performing funds either through liquidation or merger into a more successful fund. Not surprisingly, less successful funds are the most likely candidates for elimination. The ability of fund sponsors to eliminate poorly performing funds creates an inherent survivorship bias over time, meaning that funds with better performance results are likely overrepresented in the pool of surviving funds as fund sponsors carefully cull poorly performing funds (and their performance records) from the pool of continuing funds.

In the Matter of Van Kampen Investment Advisory Corp.

Investment Company Act Release No. 23996 (Sept. 8, 1999)

[**Textbook Note:** *This settled administrative proceeding arose out of allegedly misleading disclosure regarding a fund as it transitioned from its incubation stage to its sale to the general public. It is not uncommon for sponsors to launch a fund to build some sort of performance track record before offering the fund's shares to the public. This early stage is referred to as the "incubation stage." There are several issues posed by incubation. First, are presumably successful results (assuming sponsors would choose not to launch funds that had only poor results) indicative of managerial skills or merely luck? Second, even assuming that a fund's performance reflects skillful management, will the strategies that worked so well in the incubation period be easy to replicate after the fund is sold broadly? After all, a fund may grow many, many fold between its initial incubation period and its operation as a fund marketed to and widely held by the public. In particular, there is a direct issue of whether a particular investment* *strategy is scalable (i.e., will an investment strategy that worked when a fund is smaller work as effectively when the fund is larger by many multiples?). The issue of scalability underlies the SEC's findings here.*]

[***] Respondents

A. Van Kampen Advisory, a Delaware corporation headquartered in Oakbrook, Illinois, has been incorporated and registered with the Commission as an investment adviser from 1982 through the present. Van Kampen Advisory is a wholly owned subsidiary of Van Kampen Investments Inc. (Van Kampen Investments). At all relevant times, Van Kampen Advisory was the investment adviser for, among others, the Van Kampen Growth Fund (Growth Fund).

B. Sachtleben, age 57 and a resident of Houston, Texas, was, at all relevant times, an associated person of Van Kampen Advisory. He served as the Chief Investment Officer for Equity Investments (Chief Investment Officer) for Van Kampen Advisory and its predecessor company from October 1987 through approximately June 1998, when he retired. He also served as Vice-President of the Growth Fund during the relevant period. As Chief Investment Officer, Sachtleben supervised, among others, Van Kampen Advisory's portfolio managers, research personnel, and trading staff in Houston.

Related Entities

C. Van Kampen Growth Fund was an incubator fund that began operations on December 27, 1995, as a new diversified series of the Van Kampen Equity Trust, an investment company registered with the Commission.[2]

D. Van Kampen Funds Inc., formerly Van Kampen Distributors Inc. (Van Kampen Distributors), a broker-dealer registered with the Commission, is the Growth Fund's principal underwriter. In February 1997, Van Kampen Distributors prepared and distributed sales literature on behalf of the Growth Fund concerning its opening to public investors. Van Kampen Distributors is a wholly owned subsidiary of Van Kampen Investments.

Facts

The Growth Fund's Incubation

E. From its inception on or about December 27, 1995 to on or about February 3, 1997, the Growth Fund was an incubator fund whose shares were generally not available to the public for investment. Van Kampen and persons affiliated with Van Kampen provided seed money for the Growth Fund. During most of 1996, the Growth Fund had net assets of $200,000 to $380,000. The portfolio manager, under Sachtleben's supervision, invested the Growth Fund's assets in various securities with, among other things, the goal of establishing a performance track record to be used in marketing the fund to the public.

F. During its incubation period, the Growth Fund's Class A shares achieved, without adjusting for the applicable sales load, a 61.99% one-year total return as of December

2. The term "incubator fund" commonly refers to investment vehicles not generally available to the public created by a sponsor for the purpose of establishing a performance track record and testing investment techniques prior to being offered to the public.

31, 1996. The Growth Fund was reported to be the best-performing fund in 1996 for its category and a full 20 percentage points ahead of the second-best performing fund based on calculations by Lipper Analytical Services (Lipper). More than 50% of the Growth Fund's 1996 return was attributable to securities it acquired for investment through 31 hot initial public offerings.[3] Although the Growth Fund only purchased 100 to 400 shares in each hot IPO, those IPO shares had a magnified impact on the Growth Fund's return because of its small asset base.

G. During the last quarter of 1996, senior management of Van Kampen Advisory and Van Kampen Distributors decided to market the fund to the general public, in part, as a result of the Growth Fund's performance. The Board of Trustees (Trustees) for the Growth Fund, which was required to approve the opening of any fund for public investment, was scheduled to consider the opening of the Growth Fund at its quarterly board meeting in late January 1997.

The Street Article

H. On or shortly after January 7, 1997, Sachtleben received a copy of a December 31, 1996 article published in *The Street*, an internet publication, which, among other things, questioned the "phenomenal" gains of the Growth Fund and the possible use of hot IPOs to bolster its performance. The article highlighted concerns associated with small funds advertising impressive one-year returns as they go public without disclosing the source of such returns, thus unrealistically raising investor expectations. The article further stated that Van Kampen Advisory could have given "a small fund like Growth a spectacular return by allocating hot initial public offerings to the fund.... Because the fund is so small, any one-shot gains will make a big difference in performance."

The IPO Impact Study

I. In mid-January 1997, shortly after he received the Street Article, Sachtleben directed one of the employees under his supervision to conduct a study to determine the impact of IPOs on the Growth Fund's 1996 performance. The IPO impact study eliminated the effect of the Growth Fund's initial gains from IPOs by assuming that the IPO purchases were made on the secondary market at the higher, post-IPO, price. The results of the study, dated January 21, 1997, showed that the impact of IPOs accounted for approximately one-third of the Growth Fund's 1996 return.[4]

The January 1997 Board of Trustees Meeting

J. Sachtleben and others made presentations regarding the Growth Fund's 1996 performance at the quarterly Board of Trustees meeting on January 23 and 24, 1997,

3. Hot IPOs generally refer to securities that trade at a premium over their initial public offering price immediately after the initial public offering.

4. However, while the study did not make these calculations, the actual gains from the Growth Fund's IPO shares accounted for more than 50% of the Growth Fund's 1996 return. The actual gains on the IPO shares derived from the difference between the IPO prices paid and the prices at which Van Kampen Advisory sold those shares or the value of the shares it held as of December 31, 1996.

at which the public offering of the Growth Fund was approved. However, Sachtleben did not tell the Trustees that he had initiated a study to determine the impact of IPOs on the Growth Fund's 1996 performance. The results of the study were not discussed at the Board of Trustees Meeting.

Omissions of Material Facts Concerning the Growth Fund's Performance

K. From February 3, 1997 to March 14, 1997, the Growth Fund was open to the public for investment. During that period, the number of shareholders increased from 14 to 14,883 and the Growth Fund raised approximately $109 million from sales of its shares. The Growth Fund's net assets increased from $1.1 million to $110.1 million.

L. While the Growth Fund was open to the public for investment, Van Kampen Distributors disseminated an advertisement to the public called a "Fact Card." The Fact Card prominently displayed the Growth Fund's 61.99% return and its #1 Lipper ranking, but did not disclose that IPOs had a large impact on the Growth Fund's 1996 return. Sachtleben, in his capacity as Chief Investment Officer for Van Kampen Advisory and as an officer of the Growth Fund, was responsible for providing information about the Growth Fund, including the IPO impact, to the Trustees of the Growth Fund and senior officers of Van Kampen Advisory and Van Kampen Distributors. Sachtleben knew that the Growth Fund's performance figures would be used in the Growth Fund's advertising, but he did not tell the Trustees or the senior officers that he had initiated an IPO impact study or the results of the impact study, which reflected that IPOs had a large impact on the Growth Fund's performance.

M. The Fact Card also contained the following disclaimers: "The Fund's adviser believes the Fund was managed substantially the same as if the Fund had opened for investment to all public investors. No assurance can be given, however, that the Fund's investment performance would have been the same during the period if the Fund had been broadly distributed." These statements were also included in the Growth Fund's December 31, 1996 semi-annual report and in its prospectus. These statements failed to mention that a large portion of the Growth Fund's return was attributable to its investments in IPOs.

N. The Growth Fund's December 31, 1996, semi-annual report, which was filed with the Commission on February 28, 1997, failed to include any information regarding the impact on performance from the hot IPO investments. The Growth Fund's December 31, 1996, semi-annual report, which Sachtleben reviewed and signed, reported, among other things, that the Growth Fund achieved a 61.99% total return for 1996. Despite Sachtleben's having the results of the IPO impact study, the semi-annual report attributed this performance to investment in technology, financial services, and health care sectors, which were "some of the best performing [sectors]," and gave examples of four securities that posted large gains during the last six months. None of those securities were IPO securities. In addition, the Growth Fund's semi-annual report included a shareholder letter which discussed the 1996 IPO market generally along with other economic developments. The report gave no indication that the Growth Fund had in any way participated in the IPO market that year. Because information about the impact of IPOs on the Growth Fund's performance would have significantly altered the total mix of information available to investors, this omission made the statements about the Growth Fund's performance in the semi-annual report materially misleading.

O. As a result of the lack of disclosure by Sachtleben to the Trustees of the Growth Fund and senior officers of Van Kampen Advisory and Van Kampen Distributors, none of the fund's communications to potential shareholders or current shareholders (e.g., the Fact Card, prospectus and semi-annual report) at the time of the fund's dissemination of its first year performance returns included information regarding the large impact of IPOs on the Growth Fund's performance.

P. Pursuant to Section 31(a) of the Investment Company Act, and Rule 31a-2(a)(3) thereunder, Van Kampen Equity Trust maintained the Fact Card in its files as sales literature intended for distribution to prospective investors. In addition, Van Kampen Equity Trust filed the Growth Fund's December 31, 1996, semi-annual report with the Commission on February 28, 1997, without disclosing the large impact that IPOs had on the Growth Fund's 1996 return.

Other Public Statements Attributed to Van Kampen

Q. Statements in the press attributed to representatives of Van Kampen Distributors and Van Kampen Advisory indicated that there were a limited number of IPOs in the Growth Fund during 1996 and they did not greatly affect the fund's performance. These statements included: "It's not as if the [Growth F]und has had a bunch of hot IPOs;" and "the performance of the [Growth Fund] last year was not greatly influenced by investments in initial public offerings." Given these statements made in the press and the information available to the public in the Fact Card, prospectus and semi-annual report, investors had no reasonable basis to conclude that the Growth Fund's 1996 performance was largely impacted by investments in IPOs.

Violations

R. Under the facts and circumstances of this case, disclosure that a large portion of the Growth Fund's return was attributable to its investments in IPOs would have been material to an investor's decision whether to invest in the Growth Fund, particularly in light of the fact that, given the growth in the fund's total assets, it was questionable whether the fund could continue to experience, by investing in hot IPOs, substantially similar performance as the fund had previously experienced. Based on the foregoing, Van Kampen Advisory willfully violated and Sachtleben caused and willfully aided and abetted Van Kampen Advisory's violation of Section 206(2) of the Advisers Act. As part of the conduct described in paragraphs III.E. through III.Q. above, Van Kampen Advisory and Sachtleben omitted to state material facts to its client, the Growth Fund, Growth Fund shareholders, and prospective shareholders concerning the impact of hot IPOs on the Growth Fund's 1996 performance.

S. As part of the conduct described in paragraphs III.K. through III.Q. above, Van Kampen Advisory and Sachtleben caused and willfully aided and abetted Van Kampen Equity Trust's violations of Section 34(b) of the Investment Company Act which prohibits the filing, transmitting, or keeping of registration statements, applications, reports, accounts, records, or other documents required to be kept under section 31(a) of the Investment Company Act that omit to state facts necessary in order to prevent the statements made in those documents, in the light of the circumstances under which they were made, from being materially misleading. [***]

* * *

Notes and Applications

Related performance. Related performance is a term used to describe the performance results obtained by a fund's investment adviser in managing another fund or account with similar investment objectives and strategies. Information about related performance is arguably relevant to investors in assessing the skills of investment advisers in managing comparable portfolios. Related performance may be the sole relevant performance information regarding an investment adviser when a new fund is formed. In addition, an investment adviser wants to share related performance information when it evidences past managerial success. On the other hand, such information would almost surely be omitted when unfavorable; there is no requirement or incentive to share it.

Controversy surrounds related performance because of the perceived potential for investment advisers to mislead. How can investors evaluate whether the accompanying circumstances of the related fund are actually analogous to the subject fund and therefor providing a reliable benchmark for assessing managerial acumen? Moreover, suppose an investment adviser has many different examples of related fund performance. How can investors ensure that the adviser did not cherry-pick the related performance, omitting disappointing results? Finally, how should prospective investors in a fund even assess the relevance of related performance?

Through a series of no-action letters in the 1990s, the SEC staff determined that related performance information could be included in prospectuses or sales materials. Specifically, the staff of the SEC has addressed four types of related performance in the context of public funds: (1) predecessor performance (where an investment adviser seeks to provide performance information about a fund or account before its conversion into a registered fund, similar to the *Van Kampen* action);[2] (2) private account performance (where an investment adviser seeks to provide performance information about related private accounts or funds similar to the registered fund);[3] (3) clone or mirror fund performance (where an investment adviser seeks to provide performance

2. MassMutual Institution Funds, SEC No-Action Letter, 1995 WL 611558 (Sep. 28, 1995) (enabling investment adviser to include predecessor performance in sales material and prospectus).

3. *See* GE Funds, SEC No-Action Letter, 1997 WL 50053 (Feb. 7, 1997) (authorizing new fund's advertisement of institutional account performance under same manager); Nichols-Applegate Mutual Funds II, SEC No-Action Letter, 1997 WL 50052 (Feb. 7, 1997) (condoning usage of private account performance in advertisements and supplemental sales materials for public fund); Nichols-Applegate Mutual Funds I, SEC No-Action Letter, 1996 WL 450350 (Aug. 6, 1996) (advising no enforcement would result from adviser's usage of related performance in prospectus).

information from managing a fund with identical objectives and strategies, which the subject fund was modeled after);[4] and (4) related manager performance (where a portfolio manager seeks to use performance information from managing another fund with similar objectives).[5]

Nevertheless, use of related performance disclosure is subject to important limitations. Specifically, such disclosure (1) has to be appropriately qualified about differences in circumstances and context; (2) is not appropriate if the related performance involved selective use of such information; and (3) should not give undue prominence to the related performance results in a way that could confuse or mislead investors as to the distinction between fund performance and related performance. In short, the SEC appeared to take the view that investors should make up their own minds about the significance of related performance if the underlying facts are fully explained.

In contrast, FINRA has been more guarded in allowing advisers to use related performance in marketing materials to retail investors, although it has exercised greater flexibility in the case of materials given to institutional investors.[6] Surprisingly, FINRA has openly criticized the SEC's approach to related manager performance because performance in the two contexts may arise from sharply differing investment circumstances and, therefor, inclusion of such results could be misleading for investors.

13.6.2 Misleading Disclosure Regarding Strategies and Risk

In addition to performance disclosure, fund disclosure about strategies and risk is a fertile area for potential misstatements. If a fund's performance uncharacteristically stumbles badly, an immediate question is whether investors understood the risk entailed by the fund's investment strategy when they purchased the fund's shares. To be sure, there are two powerful psychological forces in play: investor overconfidence at the time of investment (i.e., investors focus on the upside prospects of their decision) and a strong hindsight bias (i.e., when things actually turn out bad, investors want to know why they were not given greater warning, even if at the time of investment, the risk was known but the chances of an adverse outcome seemed remote). Investing is inherently risky, and disclosure must draw a delicate balance between both the potential rewards and losses from a particular investment strategy. The risk that disclosure will be found deficient is particularly pronounced when adverse investment consequences result from an investment strategy that deviates from the fund's stated investment strategy.

---

4. *See* ITT Hartford Mutual Funds, SEC No-Action Letter, 1997 WL 50054 (Feb. 7, 1997) (permitting inclusion of insurance fund performance in sales literature for cloned public fund).

5. *See* Bramwell Growth Fund, SEC No-Action Letter, 1996 WL 450346 (Aug. 7, 1996) (allowing manager to incorporate previous fund's performance into prospectus considering similar "objectives, policies, and strategies").

6. *See NASD Regulation Request for Comment 97-47*, FINRA (August 1997), http://www.finra.org/industry/notices/97-47; *FINRA Interpretive Letter to Edward P. Macdonald, Hartford Distributors, LLC*, FINRA (May 12, 2015), http://www.finra.org/industry/interpretive-letters/may-12-2015-1200am.

In the Matter of Charles Schwab Investment Management

Investment Company Act Release No. 29552 (Jan. 11, 2011)

[**Textbook Note:** *This settled administrative proceeding arose out of the significant losses in an ultrashort bond fund that invested significantly in mortgage-backed securities. The fund was marketed as a slightly more risky alternative to a money market fund. In the 2008 Financial Crisis, the fund performed miserably in light of its allegedly low-risk profile. Indeed, the fund's investment profile became progressively more risky as the Crisis approached with inadequate notice to investors of this change. In addition, certain investors, but not others, received selective disclosure of material non-public information regarding the fund's performance. The SEC's administrative action catalogues the legal deficiencies with this form of deficient risk disclosure and selective disclosure of material non-public information.*]

[***]Summary

4. These proceedings arise out of the offer, sale, and management of the Schwab YieldPlus Fund (the "Fund" or "YieldPlus Fund"), a fixed-income mutual fund managed by Charles Schwab Investment Management and marketed and distributed by Charles Schwab & Co., Inc., which suffered a significant decline during the credit crisis of 2007-2008. Respondents: (1) offered and sold the Fund as a cash alternative without adequately disclosing the differences between the Fund and the cash investments with which it was compared, which misled investors; (2) deviated from the Fund's concentration policy when it invested more than 25% of Fund assets in non-agency mortgage-backed securities without obtaining a shareholder vote as required by statute; (3) made inaccurate statements concerning the Fund while its NAV declined; and (4) failed to establish and implement internal controls reasonably designed to prevent the misuse of material nonpublic information....

Respondents

5. **Charles Schwab Investment Management, Inc. ("CSIM")** is a San Francisco-based, wholly-owned subsidiary of the Charles Schwab Corporation. CSIM was incorporated in Delaware in October 1989 and has been a registered investment adviser since January 25, 1990. CSIM manages the assets of registered and unregistered investment companies, including the Fund and other Schwab-branded mutual funds.

6. **Charles Schwab & Co., Inc. ("CS&Co.")** serves as the distributor and transfer agent for the Fund. CS&Co. is a registered broker-dealer, transfer agent, and investment adviser. Various CS&Co. employees, including the product development and management group responsible for marketing the YieldPlus Fund and other Schwab funds, provided services to CSIM and the Fund. CS&Co. is a wholly-owned subsidiary of Schwab Holdings, Inc., which in turn is a wholly-owned subsidiary of the Charles Schwab Corporation. CS&Co. was incorporated in California in 1971.

7. **Schwab Investments** is a no-load, open-end management investment company organized as a Massachusetts business trust and is organized as a series investment

company registered under the Investment Company Act as of October 26, 1990. The YieldPlus Fund and the Schwab Total Bond Market Fund are series issued by Schwab Investments.

Other Relevant Entities

8. **Charles Schwab Corporation ("CSC")** is a publicly traded corporation organized under the laws of Delaware and headquartered in San Francisco, California. CSC's securities are registered under Section 12(b) of the Exchange Act and are listed on the New York Stock Exchange. CSC is the parent company of CSIM and CS&Co.

9. **Schwab YieldPlus Fund ("YieldPlus Fund" or the "Fund")** is a series of Schwab Investments and an open-end fund organized as a Massachusetts business trust registered under the Investment Company Act. The Fund is managed by CSIM. The YieldPlus Fund had two classes of securities, Investor Shares and Select Shares.

10. **Schwab Total Bond Market Fund ("Total Bond Fund")** is a series of Schwab Investments and an open-end fund organized as a Massachusetts business trust registered under the Investment Company Act. The Total Bond Fund is managed by CSIM.

Background

11. The YieldPlus Fund, formed in 1999, is an ultra-short bond fund[3] that, until mid-2008, primarily invested in mortgage-backed securities ("MBS"), asset-backed securities, and corporate bonds. As recited in its prospectus, the Fund's investment objective is to seek "high current income with minimal changes in share price." The YieldPlus Fund's assets grew significantly after its formation, becoming CSIM's largest variable net asset value ("NAV") fund in 2006. At its peak in 2007, the YieldPlus Fund had $13.5 billion in assets and over 200,000 accounts, making it the largest ultra-short bond fund in the category. For several years, the Fund was one of the best performing funds in the ultra-short category, first earning a 5-star Morningstar rating in late 2004 for its 3-year performance.

12. The Fund suffered a significant decline during the credit crisis of 2007-2008 that led to declines in some bond valuations. During an eight-month period, the Fund's NAV dropped 28% and its assets under management fell from $13.5 billion to $1.8 billion due to redemptions and declining asset values.

Offer and Sale of the YieldPlus Fund

13. From at least 2006 to 2008, CSIM and CS&Co. described the Fund as a cash "alternative" that generated a higher yield with slightly higher risk than a money market

---

3. Ultra-short bond funds are fixed-income funds with durations usually less than one year. Unlike maturity, duration is not a measurement of time; instead, duration is a ratio that reflects a fund's sensitivity to interest rate changes. Ultra-short bond funds generally maintain short durations by investing in fixed income securities with short-term maturities and by using interest rate hedging strategies. See generally http://www.sec.gov/investor/pubs/ultra-short_bond_funds.htm. YieldPlus owned many long-maturity bonds, but the Fund used an interest rate hedging strategy to maintain a low duration and preserve its classification as an ultra-short fund.

fund. Some communications emphasized that the Fund's NAV "may fluctuate minimally." Others stated that the NAV "would fluctuate" but noted that it had fluctuated by only pennies in recent years. The Fund had experienced some volatility from its inception in 1999 through 2002, and then fluctuated by pennies during the next several years. Nevertheless, the statements were misleading because the YieldPlus Fund was not slightly riskier than money market funds, CDs and other cash alternatives to which it was compared. Investments in the Fund are not insured, as are CDs, and the maturity and credit quality of the Fund's securities were significantly different than those of a money market fund. Although the Fund's prospectus informed investors that the Fund was not a money market fund and better explained the differences among these investments, the disclosure was insufficient to remedy the misleading statements and omissions in the offer and sale of the Fund.

14. In 2004, the NASD raised concerns with CS&Co. about advertisements that compared the YieldPlus Fund to money market funds without adequate disclosure of the differences between the products. In response to the NASD's concerns, CS&Co. added the word "slightly" to the advertisements, stating that the Fund was "designed to provide a higher yield with slightly higher risks than a money market fund but with less risk than a long-term bond fund." CS&Co. also added, in some advertisements, a statement that the Fund's "investment value will fluctuate and shares, when redeemed, may be worth more or less than original cost." In its advertisements and other communications, however, it continued to describe the Fund as a cash alternative and did not highlight the differences between the Fund and a money market fund.

15. In 2006, a Commission staff examination included a statement that YieldPlus Fund sales materials did not include balanced disclosure and could mislead investors because they compared the Fund to money market funds without describing the differences between these two investments. Commission staff communicated the conclusion to Schwab Investments, CSIM and CS&Co. In response, CSIM and CS&Co. added additional disclosure in the Fund's prospectus about the differences between the YieldPlus Fund and money market funds but did not include the additional disclosure in its advertisements and other sales communications until after the Fund's NAV began to decline in 2007.

16. In 2006, a group of high-level executives for CSC and its related entities, referred to as the "Cash Council," held a series of meetings about the many cash alternative products across their operating businesses. Products addressed in the meetings included accounts at Schwab Bank, sweep money market funds, purchased money market funds, and CDs. The Council asked one of its members, and his product placement group at CS&Co., to recommend an "attractive yield product" to be marketed with cash products. They identified the YieldPlus Fund. Following that recommendation, the Council sought to "[m]ake it easier to see information about Yield Plus [sic] on the web, including links to it from pages where we talk about cash and information about it that includes consistently up to date SEC Yield info," and to highlight the Fund's recent limited NAV fluctuation. As a result, various links and content were added to Schwab's website, which typically characterized the Fund as a long-term cash alter-

native even though it had previously been marketed with short-term and long-term bond funds.

17. Some CS&Co. registered representatives also described the YieldPlus Fund as a cash alternative with minimal price fluctuation when discussing the Fund with investors. Periodically, representatives called customers with fixed-income investments coming due, such as maturing CDs, and highlighted the YieldPlus Fund as an option for investing the proceeds. They emphasized what they described as the Fund's historically narrow NAV fluctuation, and minimized its potential for volatility.

18. As a result of the above, Respondents failed to adequately inform investors about (1) the risks associated with investing in the YieldPlus Fund and (2) the differences between the Fund and other investments.

Understating the Fund's Weighted Average Maturity

19. A fund's weighted average maturity ("WAM") is a measurement of the average length of time until the underlying bonds in a portfolio mature. WAM can be used by investors to evaluate the riskiness of a product; among similar funds, those with a longer WAM generally involve more risk. A fund's duration is different than WAM; duration is a mathematical measure of a fund's sensitivity to interest rate risk, but is not a measurement of time. For the relevant period, the YieldPlus Fund's duration was a lower number than its WAM.

20. Between February 2006 and September 2007, in some communications with investors, Schwab substituted the Fund's duration for its WAM, in some instances without noting the change. The resulting understatement appeared in sales and marketing materials and one Commission filing, a Form N-CSR Annual Report dated August 31, 2007. In other communications provided to investors during the same period, Respondents reported the Fund's correct WAM. These included various semi-annual and annual reports, which were filed with the Commission and sent to shareholders, and quarterly fact sheets that were posted on Schwab's public website.

21. In early 2006, the YieldPlus Fund's WAM increased significantly to over one to two years in length because of a change in the calculation method used by CSIM's new fund accountant. Investors noticed the change. CSIM and CS&Co. then listed the Fund's duration in place of its WAM in the sales materials, including tables that listed statistics for all Schwab's funds and, internal daily reports. Schwab did not replace WAM with duration for any other fund.

22. In some communications, CS&Co. and CSIM noted the replacement with a footnote indicating that duration, not WAM, was listed. However, in tables on the Schwab.com website, one Commission filing, and two issues of *On Investing* magazine, CS&Co. and CSIM did not include the footnote. As a result, for eighteen months, the website indicated that the average maturity of the Fund's bonds was six months when the Fund's WAM actually ranged from at least 1.3 to 2.2 years.

23. In addition, the duration number that Respondents listed was not accurate. Although the Fund's duration fluctuated from 0.4 to 0.6, CS&Co. and CSIM hard-coded

the number "0.5" into some tables and documents instead of updating the information on a daily basis. This inaccurately suggested that the Fund's duration (or WAM, when the footnote was omitted) was constant rather than variable.

Deviations From the Bond Funds' Concentration Policy

24. Section 8 of the Investment Company Act requires that funds' registration statements contain a recital of certain investment policies, including a policy regarding concentration of investments in particular industries. Under Section 13(a)(3) of the Investment Company Act, once a fund recites a concentration policy, it must obtain shareholder approval to "deviate from its policy in respect of concentration of investments in any particular industry or group of industries as recited in its registration statement...."

25. To comply with Section 8 of the Investment Company Act, Schwab Investments recited a single concentration policy for the taxable bond funds, including the YieldPlus Fund and the Total Bond Fund. The funds stated in their registration statement that they would not concentrate in any industry. They defined concentration as investing more than 25% of their assets in an industry. Before August 2006, the concentration policy specifically stated: "Based on characteristics of mortgage-backed securities, each fund has identified mortgage-backed securities issued by private lenders and not guaranteed by the U.S. government agencies or instrumentalities as a separate industry for purposes of a fund's concentration policy." Because they identified nonagency MBS as an industry, the YieldPlus Fund and the Total Bond Fund could not invest more than 25% of their assets in non-agency MBS without obtaining shareholder approval under Section 13(a).

26. By early 2006, under CSIM's direction, the YieldPlus Fund deviated from the concentration policy by investing more than 25% of Fund assets in non-agency MBS. Before September 2006, Respondents inconsistently classified several securities in filings with the Commission. If those securities had been consistently treated as MBS, Fund filings would have reflected the deviation from its concentration policy by approximately 2-3% of the Fund's assets. In addition, the Fund also exceeded the concentration limit because it excluded certain categories of non-agency MBS, such as commercial MBS, when it calculated its investment in non-agency MBS.

27. In mid-2006, the Fund increased investments in non-agency MBS because of, among other things, the Fund's portfolio managers' concerns about increasing corporate buy-out activity and the credit risks associated with corporate bonds. In August 2006, CSIM requested that the Schwab Investments board of trustees change the concentration policy to reclassify non-agency MBS such that it would not be an industry to allow more than 25% of Fund assets to be invested in non-agency MBS. Without the shareholder approval required by statute, the board of trustees voted on August 29, 2006, to approve the change. The YieldPlus Fund's investment in non-agency MBS increased after the purported change to 50% of assets in the Fund's portfolio, with nearly all of the MBS being rated AAA. By at least October 2006, the Total Bond Fund also invested more than 25% of its assets in non-agency MBS.

28. Schwab Investments did not follow the required procedure for disclosing the purported change to its registration statement. On September 1, 2006, it filed a Form 497 amending the taxable bond funds' prospectus, but not its registration statement as required by the Investment Company Act. In November 2006, Schwab Investments filed an amendment to its registration statement that reflected the purported change to the concentration policy. Amendments involving material changes, such as a change to a fund's concentration policy, must be filed on Form 485A, which typically are reviewed by Commission staff and become effective after 60 days. Schwab Investments, however, filed the amendment on Form 485B, with certifications that the filing did not contain any material changes. Filings on Form 485B typically are effective immediately and not reviewed by Commission staff. Schwab Investments should have filed on Form 485A.

Misrepresentations During the Fund's Decline

29. As the credit crisis unfolded and bond valuations declined in the summer of 2007, the Fund's NAV began to decline and many investors redeemed their holdings. Unlike money market funds, which can rely on maturing securities to generate cash, only $675 million, representing 6% of the Fund's over $11.2 million in assets, were scheduled to mature within the next six months. As a result, the Fund had to sell assets in a depressed market to raise cash to meet redemptions.

30. As the NAV declined, CSIM and CS&Co. held a series of conference calls and issued written materials to investors, independent investment advisers, and CS&Co. registered representatives. CS&Co. representatives also spoke with many individual customers. In these communications, CSIM and CS&Co. expressed confidence in the Fund; urged investors to have a patient, long-term perspective; and emphasized that most of the Fund's NAV decline represented unrealized, rather than realized, losses.

31. During the decline, CSIM and CS&Co. made a number of material misstatements and omissions concerning the Fund. For example, during two prescheduled conference calls in August 2007, the Fund's then-lead portfolio manager ("Lead Portfolio Manager"), who also was CSIM's Chief Investment Officer for Fixed Income, understated the Fund's redemptions at the time. During the first two weeks of August, investors redeemed almost $1.2 billion from the Fund, or approximately 10% of Fund assets. During this same two-week period, the YieldPlus Fund sold over $2.1 billion in portfolio securities—16% of assets—to raise cash to meet redemptions. The Lead Portfolio Manager monitored redemption levels throughout each day and reviewed a detailed summary each evening. During this time period, on August 8, 2007, another Fund portfolio manager sent an email to the Lead Portfolio Manager, the President of CSIM and others saying "we need flows to stabiliz[e]." On August 11, 2007, the Lead Portfolio Manager sent an email to the President of CSIM saying "[i]f the Advisor community starts to bail out, who [sic] has been stable to this point, we will be in trouble." On Sunday, August 12, 2007, the Lead Portfolio manager sent an email regarding his deletion of information about the Fund's holdings and assets under management information from a Q&A for the Schwab website. In the email, he said, "I don't want anyone to sense that we are having outflows."

32. On August 14, 2007, the Lead Portfolio Manager held a conference call with registered investment advisers to discuss the Fund. During the question and answer portion of the call, an adviser asked him, "how expensive have your redemptions been since the decline?" During his response, the Lead Portfolio Manager said that some advisers had purchased more shares, and "we've got very, very, very slight negative flows over the course of the last week or two." Two days later, on August 16, 2007, the Lead Portfolio Manager held a conference call with CS&Co. registered representatives. In that call, a representative asked "what are the net outflows of the Schwab Yield Plus fund to date?" During his answer, the Lead Portfolio Manager said, "[i]t's not that much.... So outflows have been minimal." These statements were false and misleading. The Fund's outflows, which already had required over $2 billion in asset sales to that point, were not "very, very, very slight" or "minimal." After the conference calls, some CS&Co. representatives communicated the Lead Portfolio Manager's comments to Fund investors.

33. Another example involves a November 2007 internal memorandum that circulated a set of talking points. CSIM and CS&Co. prepared and circulated the talking points to assist CS&Co. representatives in responding to questions about the Fund. Both the President of CSIM and the Lead Portfolio Manager reviewed, and the President approved, the talking points document, which repeated the positive theme, stating, among other things, that "[t]he portfolio management team has confidence in the Fund's strategy" and that "[d]espite the recent spike in bond market volatility, history suggests this is a temporary condition." The talking points document was inconsistent with contemporaneous internal emails discussing the Fund that were sent by the portfolio manager responsible for providing daily updates to management. In one email, a YieldPlus Fund portfolio manager reported to the Lead Portfolio Manager, the President of CSIM, and other senior executives that raising cash "was like pulling teeth" and that "[l]iquidity is AWFUL.... period." In a second email, the same portfolio manager reported to the Lead Portfolio Manager that "it[']s not better today and likely won't be for some time." In a third email, he reported to the executives that "we are hostage to the market at this point and can't improve the NAV." In light of the Fund's holdings, and the market conditions at the time, CSIM and CS&Co.'s statements were incomplete and misleading.

34. CSIM and CS&Co. made other inaccurate statements and omissions. These included statements that: (1) the Fund was selling securities to raise cash to capitalize on purchasing opportunities in the current market environment and to meet redemptions, when meeting redemptions was the motivation for the sales; and (2) the Fund had a short maturity structure that had mitigated the price erosion experienced by some of the Fund's peers.

Redemptions by Schwab-Related Funds and Individuals

35. Although CS&Co. and CSIM's policies broadly prohibited trading on the basis of material nonpublic information, those entities did not have adequate policies and procedures to prevent the misuse of material nonpublic information about the Fund, taking into consideration the nature of their businesses. For example, CSIM and CS&Co. did not have policies in place to review redemptions of Fund shares by all Schwab-

related personnel and funds for compliance with the general policy. Moreover, although certain people (such as the Fund's own portfolio managers) had to obtain pre-approval for personal trades of the Fund's shares, individuals whose responsibilities provided them with material nonpublic information about the Fund had no preapproval obligations. CSIM and CS&Co. also failed to maintain appropriate information barriers concerning nonpublic and potentially material Fund information. Finally, CSIM and CS&Co. had no specific policies and procedures governing redemptions by portfolio managers who advised Schwab funds of funds. As a result, several Schwab-related funds and individuals were free under CSIM and CS&Co.'s policies and procedures to redeem their own investments in the Fund during the Fund's decline.

36. One instance involved Schwab Charitable, a 501(c)(3) public benefit corporation that is not a subsidiary of CSC. On March 5, 2008, Schwab Charitable's Investment Oversight Committee voted to recommend to its board that the fund redeem its $91 million investment in the YieldPlus Fund due to the Fund's poor performance. The recommendation was scheduled for discussion and vote by the Charitable Fund's board on March 12, 2008, at its next scheduled meeting. On March 7, 2008, however, the fund's Chief Operating Officer ("COO") unilaterally decided to redeem the fund's entire investment before the board approved the decision. Prior to the redemption, the COO had received an email from CSIM that contained a mix of public and nonpublic information regarding the Fund and its recent decline. The email was forwarded to the COO by a CS&Co. employee who had no business reason for receiving it but was a member of Charitable's Investment Oversight Committee.

37. A second instance involved redemptions in March 2008 by the Schwab Target Date Funds, which are CSIM-managed, fund-of-fund mutual funds with primarily retail investors. The Target Date Funds' senior portfolio manager served as CSIM's Chief Investment Officer for Equities ("CIO-Equities"). The CIO-Equities had access to two potential sources of nonpublic information regarding the Fund when he accelerated the Target Date Funds' redemptions of their YieldPlus investments. First, he participated in internal meetings between CSIM's President and his direct reports. During these meetings, the Lead Portfolio Manager and other executives discussed the YieldPlus Fund, including nonpublic information about the Fund's redemption levels and plans to satisfy redemptions. Second, the CIO-Equities was a member of Charitable's Investment Oversight Committee, and in that capacity learned that Schwab Charitable intended to redeem its YieldPlus Fund investment. The CIO-Equities informed the CSIM President of his intention to redeem and the CSIM President approved the redemption.

Violations

38. Schwab Investments deviated from the bond funds' concentration policy without obtaining shareholder approval when the YieldPlus Fund and the Total Bond Fund invested more than 25% of their assets in non-agency MBS. Accordingly, Schwab Investments willfully violated Section 13(a) of the Investment Company Act. *See In re Charles Schwab Corp. Secs. Litig.*, 2010 WL 1261705 (N.D. Cal. March 30, 2010) (investing more than 25% in non-agency MBS required shareholder vote). CSIM willfully aided and abetted

and caused the violations when it directed the investments in MBS in excess of the YieldPlus Fund's 25% limit, proposed the change to the funds' concentration policy, and directed the Total Bond Fund's investment of over one-third of assets in non-agency MBS.

39. CSIM and CS&Co. willfully violated anti-fraud provisions of the Securities Act, Sections 17(a)(2) and (3), when, as described above, they: (1) made materially misleading statements and omissions about the Fund and its risk before the Fund's NAV declined; (2) made materially misleading statements and omissions during the Fund's NAV decline; and (3) materially understated the Fund's WAM from February 2006 to September 2007 in certain communications.

40. CSIM also willfully violated Section 206(4) and Rule 206(4)-8 of the Advisers Act by materially misstating the Fund's WAM and by making materially false and misleading statements about the Fund during its decline.

41. CSIM and CS&Co. willfully aided and abetted and caused violations of Section 34(b) of the Investment Company Act. CSIM and CS&Co. provided substantial assistance to persons making the misstatements and omissions detailed above that appeared in sales materials filed with NASD or FINRA and, consequently, with the Commission. CSIM and CS&Co. also willfully aided and abetted and caused violations of Section 34(b) of the Investment Company Act by providing substantial assistance regarding (1) a Form N-CSR Annual Report dated August 31, 2007, misstating the Fund's WAM; (2) a Registration Statement stating that the YieldPlus Fund would not invest more than 25% of its assets in non-agency MBS at a time when the Fund exceeded that concentration limitation; and (3) a Form 485B falsely certifying that it contained no material changes when it included the unauthorized change to the funds' concentration policy.

42. CSIM and CS&Co.'s policies and procedures were not reasonably designed, given the nature of their business, to prevent the misuse of material nonpublic information about the Fund by Schwab-related personnel and funds. Accordingly, CSIM and CS&Co. willfully violated Sections 204A of the Advisers Act and 15(g) (formerly Section 15(f)) of the Exchange Act, respectively. [***]

* * *

Notes and Applications

1. *Misleading adviser disclosure regarding funds in times of stress.* The *Schwab Investment Management* administrative action echoes some of the themes addressed in the *State Street Bank and Trust* action discussed in Chapter 9. That action, like *Schwab*, arose out of the events surrounding the 2008 Global Financial Crisis. In both situations, the SEC sanctioned the money managers for disclosure that unduly minimized the potential consequences of market turmoil on the funds from market events and, in each case, the adviser provided affiliated fund investors material information selectively that influenced those investors' decisions to redeem. The Securities Act violations in each case were similar. However, the *Schwab* matter presented a wider range of sanctionable violations because the SEC was also able to draw on the Advisers Act, the Company Act, and the rules thereunder. Remember in the *State Street Bank*

matter, neither of those statutes were directly applicable because State Street, as a bank, was not acting as an investment adviser under the Advisers Act, nor were the affected funds registered investment companies under the Company Act.

2. *Failure to identify material changes in riskiness of a sub-adviser's investment strategies.* In another settled administrative action arising out of the 2008 Financial Crisis, *In the Matter of Claymore Advisors, LLC*, Investment Company Act Release No. 30308 (Dec. 19, 2012), the SEC addressed a fund's disclosure regarding an unusual complicated investment strategy that went awry leading to the collapse of a closed-end fund in the 2008 Financial Crisis. The fund's collapse, while a regrettable event for investors, is not itself a violation of the Company Act; it is merely a disastrous investment outcome. Nevertheless questions arose regarding the fund's disclosure regarding its disastrous investment strategy. Essentially, immediately before the Financial Crisis, the fund's sub-adviser made huge investment bets that the stock market would likely not fall by much in the foreseeable future nor experience unusual volatility, which were diametrically opposed to what actually happened in the Financial Crisis. The investment positions involved esoteric derivatives strategies. One involved so-called "put contracts" which obligated the fund to guarantee a fixed value for S&P 500 options contracts and the other involved so-called "short swap variance" whereby the fund entered into swap contracts in which it was obligated to make payments that increased in magnitude with market volatility in return for a stream of fixed payments. These intricate and extremely risky investment strategies were not sufficiently disclosed to the fund's investors either in terms of updates to the registration statements or in shareholder reports. There was an added layer of complexity to the enforcement proceedings because the fatal investment strategies were implemented by the fund's sub-adviser. Thus, although the SEC separately sanctioned the sub-adviser (*Fiduciary Asset Management, LLC*, Investment Company Release No. 30309 (Dec. 12, 2012)), the SEC also determined that Claymore Advisors, the fund's investment advisor, should be sanctioned for failing to monitor the fund's disclosure by and relating to the sub-adviser and its strategies.

The theme of adviser liability for disclosure violations having their source in sub-adviser disclosure misconduct is not limited to disclosure relating to risk and strategies. The SEC has applied the same reasoning in imposing sanctions on an adviser for a sub-adviser's misrepresentations as to historical performance that was communicated by the adviser to clients. *See Virtus Investment Advisers, Inc.*, Investment Advisers Act Release No. 4266 (Nov. 16, 2015).

* * *

Just as disclosure about strategies may be materially misleading if the disclosure causes investors to make inaccurate inferences about the likely factors influencing future performance, so too disclosure about risk may be materially misleading if it causes investors to make inaccurate inferences about the types and likelihood of risk that particular investment strategies may entail. Disclosure about risk is perhaps even more difficult, because it is inherently forward-looking and is inherently contingent on unknown factors. Obviously, a flawed investment strategy may fail if it is improperly formulated, but its failure may also reveal that the investment strategies were inherently riskier than represented. In hindsight, investors and managers may disagree whether a particular disappointing outcome resulted from a fully disclosed strategy that turned out to be ill-suited for market events, or because the strategy was misrepresented.

Olkey v. Hyperion 1999 Term Trust, Inc.

98 F.3d 2 (2d Cir. 1996)

[**Textbook Note:** *The court decision below shows how a strategy with poor results may be viewed differently from a disclosure perspective in hindsight. The majority decision gives significant leeway to the adviser and imposes significant responsibility on investors to evaluate proposed strategies, whereas the dissent seeks to impose a more exacting standard on advisers and requires that risk disclosure provide investors with greater clarity in order to dismiss private securities law actions.*]

Parker, Circuit Judge:

Plaintiffs Marilyn Olkey et al., a group of investors, brought a class action against Hyperion 1999 Term Trust, Inc. et al. seeking damages for fraud in issuing and using prospectuses to market mortgage-backed securities, in violation of Sections 11, 12(2), and 15 of the Securities Act of 1933 ("the 1933 Act"), 15 U.S.C. §§77k(a), 77*l*(2), and 77*o*; and Sections 10(b) and 20(a) of the Securities Exchange Act of 1934 ("the 1934 Act"), 15 U.S.C. §78j(b), SEC Rule 10b-5, 17 C.F.R. §240.10b-5, and 15 U.S.C. §78t(a)....

I. BACKGROUND

The plaintiffs are a group of more than twenty investors who purchased common stock in three investment companies—Hyperion 1997 Term Trust, Inc., Hyperion 1999 Term Trust, Inc., and Hyperion 2002 Term Trust, Inc. (collectively, "the Trusts"). The investors sue on behalf of themselves and a class of similarly situated investors. The class period extends from June 1992 when the registration statement for Hyperion 1999 became effective and the initial public offering commenced, until October 1993, the date on which the defendants announced that each Hyperion Trust was reducing its dividend. The defendants include the Trusts, Hyperion Capital Management, which served as the investment advisor and administrator of the Trusts, individuals who served as officers or directors of the Trusts or Hyperion Capital, and nine underwriters who participated in the Hyperion offerings.

The Trusts are closed-end investment companies, so they are not obligated to redeem shares bought by investors; investors must resell their shares on the secondary market. The Trusts were formed to invest primarily in mortgage-backed securities. The securities comprising the Trusts included interest-only strips (IOs) of mortgages, which tend to go up with interest rates, and mortgage-backed securities, which tend to go down when interest rates go up. IOs and mortgage-backed securities were intended to balance each other, to serve as a hedge against interest rate changes. Interest rates subsequently declined to historic lows, and the value of the trusts declined.

The plaintiffs alleged that the prospectuses misled investors by indicating that securities would be selected to achieve a balance such that, as interest rates rose and fell, the value and earnings of the Trusts would remain stable. The plaintiffs contended that this was a misrepresentation because the defendants actually invested in a combination of securities which required rising interest rates to succeed. The plaintiffs further alleged that the defendants failed to disclose the limitations of their hedging strategy, namely, its vulnerability to decreasing interest rates, and that therefore the prospectuses and registration statements misrepresented both the investment strategy of the trust and the risks involved. Finally, the plaintiffs claimed that the defendants misrepresented the riskiness of the Trusts in the presentations, known as roadshows, which they gave to potential brokers.

The plaintiffs offer the following argument: The Trusts were based upon a failed bet that interest rates would rise. The riskiness of this bet was disproportionate to the level of return promised to investors; promised profits were small in comparison to the risk and potential size of losses. This bet was not disclosed to investors. If it had been disclosed, the investors would not have bought shares in the trust because no reasonable investor would accept low return for high risk. The cautionary language in the prospectuses is too general and generic to have alerted investors of the actual risks they faced and should therefore be ignored as boilerplate. These warnings do not mention risk to capital, to the total value of the portfolio rather than merely components of it. Read as a whole, each prospectus gave the false impression of an attempt to pursue a balanced strategy to minimize risk. In fact, the Trusts speculated on high interest rates. The roadshows compounded the false impression of balance and safety.

II. DISCUSSION

It is undisputed that the prospectuses must be read "as a whole," *see, e.g., McMahan & Co. v. Wherehouse Entertainment, Inc.,* 900 F.2d 576, 579 (2d Cir.1990), *cert. denied,* 501 U.S. 1249 (1991). It is further undisputed that the "central issue ... is not whether the particular statements, taken separately, were literally true, but whether defendants' representations, taken together and in context, would have misl[ed] a reasonable investor about the nature of the [securities]," *id.* A prospectus will violate federal securities laws if it does not disclose "material objective factual matters," or buries those matters beneath other information, or treats them cavalierly. *Pincus, [Meyer Pincus & Assocs., P.C. v. Oppenheimer & Co.,]* 936 F.2d at 762 [(2d Cir. 1991)].

The prospectuses included the following assurances of balancing:

> [T]he Adviser believes that it will be able to manage the composition of the Trust's portfolio in such a manner that any decreases in the value of securities as a result of changes in interest rates will be offset by increases in the value of other securities whose value moves in the opposite direction in response to changes in interest rates, thereby avoiding the realization of capital losses which are not offset by capital gains over the life of the Trust....

Prospectus for Hyperion 1997 Term Trust, Inc., at 19 (Oct. 23, 1992) ("1997"); Prospectus for Hyperion 1999 Term Trust, Inc., at 16 (June 18, 1992) ("1999"); Prospectus for Hyperion 2002 Term Trust, Inc., at 19 (Oct. 23, 1992) ("2002").

> The Trust's investment in IOs, when combined with other instruments in the Trust's portfolio, is expected to aid the Trust in its attempt to preserve capital. The values of IOs tend to increase in response to changes in interest rates when the values of these other Mortgage-Backed Securities and of Zero Coupon Securities are decreasing, and to decrease when the values of such other instruments are increasing. While the Adviser has no control over changes in levels of interest rates, it has designed the initial composition of the Trust's portfolio and will manage the portfolio on an ongoing basis in an attempt to minimize the impact of changes in interest rates on the net asset value of the portfolio.

1997 at 4; 1999 at 4; 2002 at 4. *See* 1997 at 8-9; 1999 at 6-7; 2002 at 8. Despite these assurances of hedging, we agree with the district court, 1995 WL 422480, at *7, that the prospectuses when read in their entirety are not overly sanguine but instead "bespeak caution," *Pincus*, 936 F.2d at 763; *Luce* [*v. Edelstein*], 802 F.2d at 56 [(2d Cir. 1986)]. The assurances were balanced by extensive cautionary language. The plaintiffs seek to have all of the cautionary language disregarded as boilerplate, but it is too prominent and specific to be disregarded. The prospectuses warn investors of exactly the risk the plaintiffs claim was not disclosed. A reasonable investor could not have read the prospectuses without realizing that, despite the use of balancing in an attempt to minimize the impact of fluctuating interest rates, a significant downturn in interest rates could decrease the value of the Trusts and decrease earnings. The prospectuses included the following warnings about mortgage-backed securities:

> The investment characteristics of Mortgage-Backed Securities differ from traditional debt securities.... These differences can result in significantly greater price and yield volatility than is the case with traditional debt securities. As a result, if the Trust purchases Mortgage-Backed Securities at a premium, a prepayment rate that is faster than expected will reduce both the market value and yield to maturity from that which was anticipated....

1997 at 7-8; 1999 at 6; 2002 at 7.

> Because of the effect that changes in interest rates may have on prepayment rates, changes in interest rates may have a greater effect on the value of Mortgage-Backed Securities than is the case with more traditional fixed income securities.

1997 at 9; 1999 at 7; 2002 at 8-9.

> Amounts available for reinvestment by the Trust are likely to be greater during a period of declining interest rates due to increased prepayments and, as a result, likely to be reinvested at lower interest rates than during a period of rising interest rates. Most Mortgage-Backed Securities in which the Trust may invest, like other fixed income securities, tend to decrease in value as a result

> of increases in interest rates but may benefit less than other fixed income securities from declining interest rates because of the risk of prepayment.

1997 at 13; 1999 at 10; 2002 at 13. In a section set apart under the heading "Risk Factors," the prospectuses even suggested the possibility of precisely the scenario that occurred—namely, interest rates fell, and, because prepayments increased significantly and because of the Trusts' use of leverage, the Mortgage-Backed Securities were an insufficient hedge against the decline in value of the IO strips:

> A significant decline in interest rates could lead to a significant decrease in the Trust's net income and dividends.... [T]he Trust may be unable to distribute at least $10.00 per share ... on [its termination date].... The market prices of [most mortgage-backed securities] may be more sensitive to changes in interest rates than traditional fixed income securities. While the Trust will seek to minimize the impact of such volatility on the net asset value of the Trust's assets, there can be no assurance it will achieve this result. In addition, in the case of an IO, prepayment of the underlying mortgages may result in the Trust's not recouping a portion of its initial purchase price in addition to the loss of interest income.... To the extent that the Trust utilizes leverage, the impact ... of volatility on the Trust's income and net asset value will be magnified.

1997 at 13-14; 1999 at 10-11; 2002 at 13-14 (paragraph headings omitted). *See* 1997 at 32; 1999 at 28; 2002 at 31. The prospectuses stated the intent to use leverage and noted that leverage would "exaggerate the decline in the net asset value or market price of the Shares." 1997 at 13; 1999 at 10; 2002 at 13. *See also* 1997 at 33-34; 1999 at 29-30; 2002 at 33.

The prospectuses repeatedly warned of risk to the entire portfolio:

> [T]he market value of the Trust's portfolio ... [is] dependant on market forces not in the control of the Adviser.

1997 at 9; 1999 at 7; 2002 at 9.

> [T]he Trust may be unable to distribute to its shareholders at the end of the Trust's term an amount equal to at least $10.00 for each Share then outstanding.

1997 at 19; 1999 at 16; 2002 at 19.

> No assurance can be given that the Trust will achieve its investment objectives, and the Trust may return less than $10.00 per Share. A significant decline in interest rates could lead to a significant decrease in the Trust's net income and dividends while a significant rise in interest rates could lead to only a moderate increase in the Trust's net income and dividends. Changes in interest rates will also lead to changes in the Trust's net asset value.

1997 at 2; 1999 at 2; 2002 at 2.

The second sentence of this passage—positioned on the second page of each prospectus such that no reasonable reader could miss it—unequivocally states that a drop in interest rates could significantly reduce net income and dividends. The next sentence by itself is vague—it does not state whether changes in interest rates could reduce net asset value, only that they will change net asset value. But the juxtaposition of the two sentences creates an unmistakable inference that a drop in interest rates could decrease net asset value. The two sentences combined elaborate the first sentence by spelling out the condition under which the Trusts could fail to return the investor's money—a significant drop in interest rates.

As stated above, the complaint alleges that investors were misled into believing that their investment would be balanced to remain stable as interest rates rose and fell, when in fact there was an undisclosed bias toward rising interest rates. (The plaintiffs cite, as if it were a smoking gun, the defendants' post-offering report stating that the Trusts were designed "with a bias toward a rising interest rate environment," Hyperion 1999 Term Trust Semi-Annual Report (May 31, 1993).) The complaint also alleges failure to disclose the risk that falling interest rates could diminish asset value and dividends. The passages quoted above dispose of both of these allegations. While we agree that the prospectuses contain no specific statement that there was a bias in favor of rising interest rates, we find that the prospectuses implicitly and clearly communicated such a bias.

Reasonable investors in the Trusts would hope to preserve capital and earn income. They were informed that the nature of the investment was such that fluctuating interest rates could affect the investment's value. They were told that different types of securities would be affected differently by rising or falling rates and that hedging would be used to minimize those effects. And they were told that a significant decline in interest rates could lead to significant decreases in income and asset values while significant rate increases could lead to only moderate increases in income and asset value. Thus, they were told that the value of losses if rates dropped could exceed the value of profits if rates rose. The *only* way reasonable investors would then invest in the Trusts would be if they believed that the probability of rates rising exceeded the probability of interest rates dropping.

This is the very bias which plaintiffs claim was not disclosed. Reasonable investors would have to be aware that they were risking low returns and erosion of capital if there was a significant drop in interest rates, which is precisely what occurred. Any reasonable investor would have to conclude that the investment objectives could only be achieved here if interest rates rose more than they fell. No reasonable investor could have relied on perfect balancing because that was not promised.

The dissent believes that this claim should proceed because the fund managers failed to disclose the fact that they were betting on rising interest rates and, therefore, "invested disproportionately in instruments that would benefit from rising rates." 98 F.3d at 9. But, the dissent also acknowledges, as it must, that if all that the plaintiffs are claiming is that the fund managers turned out to be "less skillful at balancing their portfolios than the investors hoped[,] ... their suit would be properly dismissed." 98 F.3d at 11. In fact, that is exactly what is being claimed here.

As the dissent indicates, the appellants "do not claim that no balancing occurred; clearly there was some diversification in the portfolios." The prospectuses reveal that a combination of mortgage-backed investments and IO strips were used in an attempt to minimize the impact of interest rate fluctuations. However, the appellants say too much emphasis was placed on IOs because the investment managers believed that interest rates would likely rise.

Every attempt at balancing, of course, must necessarily involve the selection of a mix of investments based in part upon an assessment of what might happen with interest rates; attempting to balance investments in interest-rate sensitive securities without taking prospective rates into account would surely be foolhardy. The plaintiffs are displeased that the fund managers made what turned out to be the wrong assumptions about interest rates while attempting to balance the portfolio. This is not something upon which a fraud claim can be based. Disclosure of the specific reasons for making the investment choices that were made is not required by the Securities laws. The risks involved, in the event that incorrect choices were made or interest rates fell, were appropriately and fully disclosed.

Despite that, plaintiffs now claim that balancing was not as skillfully done as it should have been. They claim that another set of investment choices should have been made, based upon a different conception of what interest rates would likely do. It is hardly a sound argument, as the dissent suggests, 98 F.3d at 12, to say that some other unspecified income funds performed better. That is only to say in hindsight that the managers of those funds turned out to be more skillful in their predictions.

It should also be noted that the alleged undisclosed bias had no direct relationship to the losses claimed to have been incurred. The losses resulted from an extraordinary drop in interest rates. The plaintiffs claim that the failure to disclose the bias toward rising rates masked the fact that this was a high risk/low return investment that they would not have purchased if they had known. The risk, however, was that interest rates would fall or not rise more than they fell. That risk was fully and explicitly disclosed. Therefore, there is no causal relationship between losses claimed to have been suffered and any risk factor not clearly disclosed in the prospectuses....

Since a reasonable investor could have found the promise of moderate returns attractive despite the risk of substantial losses, there is no reason to dismiss the extensive and detailed cautionary language of the prospectuses as boilerplate. That language fully disclosed the risk of investment and was specific enough to warrant a reasonable investor's attention. This court has found language more general than that found in the Hyperion prospectuses to be sufficiently specific to warrant a Rule 12(b)(6) dismissal of a Rule 10b-5 claim. In *Luce*, the offering materials merely warned that potential benefits were "necessarily speculative," that "no assurance could be given that [they] would be realized," and "actual results may vary [materially] from the predictions." 802 F.2d at 56 (original brackets omitted). The *Luce* plaintiffs alleged that the defendants promised profits without warning that profits were not guaranteed, while the instant plaintiffs allege the defendants promised a secure investment without warning that preservation of capital was not guaranteed. Both plaintiffs' claims founder on the face of the offering materials.

Made cognizant by the Hyperion prospectuses of the risk posed by declining interest rates, reasonable investors purchased shares of the Trusts in the failed expectation that interest rates would rise. Their expectations were not deceptively manipulated but were simply unmet. The prospectuses contained no material misstatements or omissions of fact, and the plaintiffs fail to state a claim under either the 1933 or 1934 Acts, or under common law fraud.

Jon O. Newman, Chief Judge, dissenting:

I respectfully dissent. This stock fraud claim alleges that the issuers of closed-end funds, formed to invest primarily in mortgage-backed securities, represented that the portfolios would be "balanced," *i.e.*, invested in debt instruments that respond in opposite directions to fluctuations in interest rates, and failed to disclose that the fund managers were in fact betting heavily on rising interest rates and invested disproportionately in instruments that would benefit from rising rates.[1] During the class period, interest rates declined 1.3 percentage points, contrary to the managers' expectation of a rise, and the three funds lost 8.5 percent, 10.5 percent, and nearly 25 percent, respectively, of their net asset values—an outcome that *Barron's* described as "far and away the worst showing of any closed-end bond fund." Complaint ¶ 16. It is undisputed that several months after the prospectuses were issued and the appellants' investments were made, the chairman and chief executive officer of the issuer of the funds disclosed in a report to shareholders that the initial portfolio of one of the funds was designed "with a bias toward a rising interest rate environment."

The Court affirms the dismissal of the complaint for failure to state a claim on the ground that the allegedly undisclosed bias in favor of rising interest rates was in fact disclosed. Though the Court acknowledges that "the prospectuses contain no specific statement that there was a bias in favor of rising interest rates," 98 F.3d at 7, the Court nevertheless concludes that the prospectuses "implicitly and clearly communicated

---

1. Normally, the value of mortgage-backed securities decrease when interest rates increase, and rise when interest rates decline. These effects are enhanced by the change in the rate at which mortgagors elect to pay off their mortgages. When interest rates rise, the pay-off rate declines, and holders of mortgage-backed securities have, in effect, lengthened maturities on average and thereby reduced value. When interest rates decline, the mortgage pay-off rate rises, and holders of mortgage-backed securities have, in effect, shortened maturities on average, received back principal sooner than anticipated, and thereby enhanced value. One way of balancing a portfolio of mortgage-backed securities in order to lessen the effect of interest rate fluctuations is to purchase interest-only securities ("IO strips")—securities that entitle the holder to the interest payments of a mortgage, but no principal payments. IO strips respond to interest rate fluctuations in opposite directions from mortgage-backed securities (both those that entitle the holder to receive principal and interest and those that entitle the holder to receive only principal). Thus, the value of IO strips increases when interest rates rise and decreases when interest rates decline. The funds in this case included significant amounts of IO strips in anticipation of rising interest rates. Some IO strips were purchased with borrowed funds, and this leveraging accentuated the adverse impact of the decline in interest rates that occurred.

such a bias." *Id.* As evidence, the Court points to a passage in the prospectuses that disclosed that the decrease in net income and dividends that could result from a significant decline in interest rates could be greater than the increase in net income and dividends that could result from a significant rise in interest rates.[2] ...

To assert, especially in the absence of evidence, that the purchasers of the Hyperion funds bought in the expectation of rising rates is a proposition at least unsupported and in all likelihood unsupportable. It is possible that a few of the purchasers expected a slight increase in interest rates. Others who bought might have expected a slight decrease in interest rates. Regardless of their expectations as to rates, the repeated assurances that the funds would be "balanced" entitled all of them to believe that the funds would be so structured as to be relatively insulated from any significant rate movements.

The fixed-income securities market uses the term "convexity" to describe the degree to which the values of securities are subject to interest rate fluctuations. The term applies primarily to mortgage-backed securities with components of principal and interest. A security that decreases in value in a rising interest rate environment to a greater extent than it increases in value in a declining interest rate environment is said to have "negative convexity." Conversely, a security that increases in value in a declining interest rate environment to a greater extent than it decreases in value in a rising interest rate environment is said to have "positive convexity." A fund sold as "balanced" can reasonably be expected to try to select securities so that the fund's net convexity approaches zero. If a fund elects not to aim for as much balance as it can achieve and instead bets on a pronounced change in interest rates, it can be so structured (using significant amounts of IO strips) that its overall value will increase with a rise in interest rates or decrease with declining interest rates. That is what happened with the Hyperion funds. But a "balanced" fund, even one that acknowledges the possibility that significant rate decreases could harm more than significant rate increases could benefit, is still expected to structure the portfolio so that the net convexity is very slight. If the fund managers are secretly betting so heavily on rising interest rates by such a significant inclusion of leveraged IO strips that an interest rate decline will cause substantial decreases, they must say so. Their acknowledgement of the possible differing consequences of significantly decreasing and increasing rates does not reveal that their investment strategy is contrary to what would reasonably be expected of a "balanced" fund.

Of course, the investors in such funds have no valid stock fraud claim if fund managers turn out to be less skillful at balancing their portfolios than the investors hoped; if that is all that the appellants in this case were claiming, their suit would be properly

2. The key sentence states, "A significant decline in interest rates could lead to a significant decrease in the Trust's net income and dividends while a significant rise in interest rates could lead to only a moderate increase in the Trust's net income and dividends." Prospectus for Hyperion 1997 Term Trust, Inc. at 2. Identical statements were contained in the prospectuses for the 1999 and 2002 funds.

dismissed. But they are not alleging unsuccessful balancing. Their claim is that the fund managers misrepresented when they announced their intention to try to balance the funds to an extent that would insulate against significant rate fluctuations, yet planned, from the outset and thereafter, to structure the portfolios in a way that would yield benefits only if their undisclosed bet on rising interest rates was successful.

The Court asserts that the prospectuses warn investors of exactly the risk the plaintiffs claim was not disclosed. A reasonable investor could not have read the prospectuses without realizing that, despite the use of balancing in an attempt to minimize the impact of fluctuating interest rates, a significant downturn in interest rates could decrease the value of the Trusts and decrease earnings. 98 F.3d at 5 (footnote omitted). This assertion misconceives the risk on which this suit is based. The appellants are not suing because of the disclosed risk that if interest rates declined, asset values would decline. They are suing because of the undisclosed risk that the fund managers would structure the initial portfolios and make investment decisions thereafter by selecting securities that would respond significantly to rate fluctuations that the managers believed, but did not disclose, would be rate rises. The investors accepted the risk that interest rates might decline and that imperfect balancing might cost them some money. They did not accept the risk that a fund, sold as being balanced in order to minimize the effects of interest rate fluctuations, would in fact be deliberately tilted so heavily in the expectation of rising interest rates that a decline in interest rates would incur devastating losses.

It is no answer to suggest that the funds were "balanced" in that they contained some securities whose values would move in opposite directions in response to interest rate fluctuations. Appellants do not claim that no balancing occurred; clearly, there was some diversification in the portfolios. The claim is that whatever balancing occurred was undertaken, initially and thereafter, on the undisclosed prediction by the fund managers that interest rates would rise. The fact that some mortgage-backed securities and some IO strips were included in the portfolios indicates only that some diversification occurred. The significant losses occurred because of the undisclosed fact that the fund managers, betting heavily on rising interest rates, purchased on a highly leveraged basis a quantity of IO strips of particular rates and maturities to such an extent that interest rate declines proved devastating.

It may well be, as the majority suggests, that portfolio managers of funds claimed to be balanced must inevitably make some predictions about future interest rates. Since it is unlikely that interest rates will remain completely static for any significant period of time, a manager of a balanced portfolio probably makes some prediction of the likely near-term direction of rates. But the whole point of balancing is to structure a portfolio so as to minimize the effects of any interest fluctuations, whether interest rate declines or rises are expected. Even a manager who believes that rates will rise will try to live up to the promise of a balanced fund by selecting a group of securities of low net convexity to guard against the risk of significant loss from rate fluctuations in either direction.

It cannot be maintained that what happened here is simply the inevitable inability of fund managers to balance as skillfully as might have been hoped. The other fixed-income funds that claimed to be balanced survived the modest interest decline that devastated the Hyperion funds. The Hyperion funds ended disastrously not because the managers lacked skill in balancing, but because they bet their investors' money so heavily on rising rates. They were free to market a fund on that basis and invite investments from those who were also willing to bet heavily on rising interest rates. But they were not free to bet heavily on rising rates and conceal this critical fact from their investors. [***]

13.6.3 Who Is Responsible and Who Is Liable for Investment Company Disclosure?

The examples of false and misleading disclosure above focus on what it means to be misleading. A related issue that entails its own conceptual problems concerning who may be held liable for misleading statements. In practice, fund advisers and fund counsel typically shoulder primary responsibility for drafting fund disclosure. In SEC civil enforcement actions or administrative proceedings, a broad class of individuals may be sanctioned for their individual roles in contributing to the misleading disclosure. Thus, the fund may be liable, but so too may the investment adviser, board of trustees, supervisory personnel and/or compliance officers, and if not directly, as aiders and abettors or as persons causing violations or as responsible supervisory or compliance personnel. The SEC can seek sanctions for disclosure violations arising under the Company Act, Advisers Act, Securities Act, and Securities Exchange Act for a whole panoply of possible violations.

In contrast, liability in private actions for damages is limited to a smaller class of potential defendants consisting of (i) primary defendants (or controlling persons) in fraud actions, (ii) persons signing or named in a registration statement (e.g., Form N-1A) or other prescribed statutory parties in actions under Section 11 of the Securities Act (an express private cause of action for misleading statements contained in a registration statement), and (iii) statutory sellers in actions under Section 12 of the Securities Act (an express private cause of action for materially misleading statements in a prospectus). The primary defendant category in private fraud action may lead to seemingly strange results as reflected in the Supreme Court's decision below—the party drafting the deficient disclosure may not face private damages liability. In the context of funds, this result is at least ironic: the investment adviser and its affiliates may be primarily involved in drafting fund disclosure that is subsequently determined to be materially misleading, but those persons will generally not be liable in a private action for their role in drafting the disclosure.

Janus Capital Group, Inc. v. First Derivative Traders

564 U.S. 135 (2011)

[**Textbook Note:** *This Supreme Court decision reflected a broader issue of liability for misrepresentation in connection with private securities law liability for fraudulent misrepresentations under Rule 10b-5. Over a series of decisions* *beginning in 1995, the Supreme Court eliminated aiding and abetting liability in private actions under Rule 10b-5, and in two subsequent decisions (*Stoneridge Investment Partners, LLC v. Scientific-Atlanta, Inc.*, 552 U.S. 148 (2008), and this case), a divided Supreme Court sought to limit recharacterization of what it perceived as aiding-and-abetting conduct as coming within the ambit of primary liability (which would thereby enable private plaintiffs to sue the named participant for fraud). This issue has special resonance in the area of investment companies and pooled investment vehicles generally, because the contractually affiliated investment adviser typically prepares all disclosure documents subject to final (or ultimate) board approval. In this case, the Supreme Court squarely addressed whether the investment adviser could be liable in a private action, no matter how misleading the fund disclosure that it prepared, provided the investment adviser merely drafts the disclosure in the name of the fund without any authorial attribution to the adviser itself.*]

Justice Thomas delivered the opinion of the Court.

This case requires us to determine whether Janus Capital Management LLC (JCM), a mutual fund investment adviser, can be held liable in a private action under Securities and Exchange Commission (SEC) Rule 10b–5 for false statements included in its client mutual funds' prospectuses. Rule 10b–5 prohibits "mak[ing] any untrue statement of a material fact" in connection with the purchase or sale of securities. 17 CFR § 240.10b–5 (2010). We conclude that JCM cannot be held liable because it did not make the statements in the prospectuses.

I

Janus Capital Group, Inc. (JCG), is a publicly traded company that created the Janus family of mutual funds. These mutual funds are organized in a Massachusetts business trust, the Janus Investment Fund. Janus Investment Fund retained JCG's wholly owned subsidiary, JCM, to be its investment adviser and administrator. JCG and JCM are the petitioners here.

Although JCG created Janus Investment Fund, Janus Investment Fund is a separate legal entity owned entirely by mutual fund investors. Janus Investment Fund has no assets apart from those owned by the investors. JCM provides Janus Investment Fund with investment advisory services, which include "the management and administrative services necessary for the operation of [Janus] Fun[d]," App. 225a, but the two entities maintain legal independence. At all times relevant to this case, all of the officers of Janus Investment Fund were also officers of JCM, but only one member of Janus Investment Fund's board of trustees was associated with JCM. This is more independence than is required: By statute, up to 60 percent of the board of a mutual fund may be composed of "interested persons." See 54 Stat. 806, as amended, 15 U.S.C. § 80a–10(a); see also 15 U.S.C. § 80a– 2(a)(19) (2009 ed. and Feb. 2011 Supp.) (defining "interested person").

As the securities laws require, Janus Investment Fund issued prospectuses describing the investment strategy and operations of its mutual funds to investors. See 15 U.S.C. §§ 77b(a)(10), 77e(b)(2), 80a–8(b), 80a–2(a)(31), 80a–29(a)–(b). The prospectuses for several funds represented that the funds were not suitable for market timing and can be read to suggest that JCM would implement policies to curb the practice. For example, the Janus Mercury Fund prospectus dated February 25, 2002, stated that the fund was "not intended for market timing or excessive trading" and represented that it "may reject any purchase request ... if it believes that any combination of trading activity is attributable to market timing or is otherwise excessive or potentially disruptive to the Fund." App. 141a. Although market timing is legal, it harms other investors in the mutual fund.

II

We granted certiorari to address whether JCM can be held liable in a private action under Rule 10b–5 for false statements included in Janus Investment Fund's prospectuses. Under Rule 10b–5, it is unlawful for "any person, directly or indirectly, ... [t]o make any untrue statement of a material fact" in connection with the purchase or sale of securities. 17 CFR § 240.10b–5(b). To be liable, therefore, JCM must have "made" the material misstatements in the prospectuses. We hold that it did not.

A...

1

One "makes" a statement by stating it....

For purposes of Rule 10b–5, the maker of a statement is the person or entity with ultimate authority over the statement, including its content and whether and how to communicate it. Without control, a person or entity can merely suggest what to say, not "make" a statement in its own right. One who prepares or publishes a statement on behalf of another is not its maker. And in the ordinary case, attribution within a statement or implicit from surrounding circumstances is strong evidence that a statement was made by—and only by—the party to whom it is attributed. This rule might best be exemplified by the relationship between a speechwriter and a speaker. Even when a speechwriter drafts a speech, the content is entirely within the control of the person who delivers it. And it is the speaker who takes credit—or blame—for what is ultimately said.

2

The Government contends that "make" should be defined as "create." Brief for United States as Amicus Curiae 14–15 (citing Webster's New International Dictionary 1485 (2d ed.1958) (defining "make" as "[t]o cause to exist, appear, or occur")). This definition, although perhaps appropriate when "make" is directed at an object unassociated with a verb (e.g., "to make a chair"), fails to capture its meaning when directed at an object expressing the action of a verb.

Adopting the Government's definition of "make" would also lead to results inconsistent with our precedent. The Government's definition would permit private plaintiffs to sue a person who "provides the false or misleading information that another person then puts into the statement." Brief for United States as Amicus Curiae 13.... We see no reason to treat participating in the drafting of a false statement differently from engaging in deceptive transactions, when each is merely an undisclosed act preceding the decision of an independent entity to make a public statement.

For its part, [Plaintiff] suggests that the "well-recognized and uniquely close relationship between a mutual fund and its investment adviser" should inform our decision. Brief for Respondent 21. It suggests that an investment adviser should generally be understood to be the "maker" of statements by its client mutual fund, like a playwright whose lines are delivered by an actor. We decline this invitation to disregard the corporate form. Although First Derivative and its amici persuasively argue that investment advisers exercise significant influence over their client funds, see *Jones v. Harris Associates L.P.*, 559 U.S. 335, ——, (2010), it is undisputed that the corporate formalities were observed here. JCM and Janus Investment Fund remain legally separate entities, and Janus Investment Fund's board of trustees was more independent than the statute requires. 15 U.S.C. § 80a–10. Any reapportionment of liability in the securities industry in light of the close relationship between investment advisers and mutual funds is properly the responsibility of Congress and not the courts....

B

Under this rule, JCM did not "make" any of the statements in the Janus Investment Fund prospectuses; Janus Investment Fund did. Only Janus Investment Fund — not JCM — bears the statutory obligation to file the prospectuses with the SEC. 15 U.S.C. §§ 77e(b)(2), 80a–8(b), 80a–29(a)–(b); see also 17 CFR § 230.497 (imposing requirements on "investment companies").... There is no allegation that JCM in fact filed the prospectuses and falsely attributed them to Janus Investment Fund. Nor did anything on the face of the prospectuses indicate that any statements therein came from JCM rather than Janus Investment Fund — a legally independent entity with its own board of trustees.

[Plaintiff] suggests that both JCM and Janus Investment Fund might have "made" the misleading statements within the meaning of Rule 10b–5 because JCM was significantly involved in preparing the prospectuses. But this assistance, subject to the ultimate control of Janus Investment Fund, does not mean that JCM "made" any statements in the prospectuses. Although JCM, like a speechwriter, may have assisted Janus Investment Fund with crafting what Janus Investment Fund said in the prospectuses, JCM itself did not "make" those statements for purposes of Rule 10b–5.

* * *

The statements in the Janus Investment Fund prospectuses were made by Janus Investment Fund, not by JCM. Accordingly, First Derivative has not stated a claim against JCM under Rule 10b–5. The judgment of the United States Court of Appeals for the Fourth Circuit is reversed.

Justice Breyer, with whom Justice Ginsburg, Justice Sotomayor, and Justice Kagan join, dissenting.

This case involves a private Securities and Exchange Commission (SEC) Rule 10b–5 action brought by a group of investors against Janus Capital Group, Inc., and Janus

Capital Management LLC (Janus Management), a firm that acted as an investment adviser to a family of mutual funds (collectively, the Janus Fund or Fund). The investors claim that Janus Management knowingly made materially false or misleading statements that appeared in prospectuses issued by the Janus Fund. They say that they relied upon those statements, and that they suffered resulting economic harm.

Janus Management and the Janus Fund are closely related. Each of the Fund's officers is a Janus Management employee. Janus Management, acting through those employees (and other of its employees), manages the purchase, sale, redemption, and distribution of the Fund's investments. Janus Management prepares, modifies, and implements the Janus Fund's long-term strategies. And Janus Management, acting through those employees, carries out the Fund's daily activities.

Rule 10b–5 says in relevant part that it is unlawful for "any person, directly or indirectly ... *[t]o make* any untrue statement of a material fact" in connection with the purchase or sale of securities. 17 CFR § 240.10b–5(b) (2010) (emphasis added). See also 15 U.S.C. § 78j(b) (§ 10(b) of the Securities Exchange Act of 1934). The specific legal question before us is whether Janus Management can be held responsible under the Rule for having "ma[d]e" certain false statements about the Janus Fund's activities. The statements in question appear in the Janus Fund's prospectuses.

The Court holds that only the Janus Fund, not Janus Management, could have "ma[d]e" those statements. The majority points out that the Janus Fund's board of trustees has "ultimate authority" over the content of the statements in a Fund prospectus. And in the majority's view, only "the person or entity with ultimate authority over the statement, including its content and whether and how to communicate it" can "make" a statement within the terms of Rule 10b–5.

In my view, however, the majority has incorrectly interpreted the Rule's word "make." Neither common English nor this Court's earlier cases limit the scope of that word to those with "ultimate authority" over a statement's content. To the contrary, both language and case law indicate that, depending upon the circumstances, a management company, a board of trustees, individual company officers, or others, separately or together, might "make" statements contained in a firm's prospectus—even if a board of directors has ultimate content-related responsibility. And the circumstances here are such that a court could find that Janus Management made the statements in question. [***]

* * *

Notes and Applications

1. *Adviser primary liability for fund misrepresentations. Janus Capital* posed the issue of adviser liability for fund disclosure in a somewhat strained procedural posture. The plaintiff class consisted of shareholders of Janus Capital, a publicly-traded company that owned the adviser. The Janus Capital's shareholder class contended that they were misled by disclosure contained in a mutual fund prospectus drafted by the adviser and disseminated by the Janus Investment Fund, a registered investment com-

pany. The adviser's role, according to the Court, even if deliberate and wholly responsible, precluded primary liability under Rule 10b-5 and at most could only rise to the level of aiding and abetting, for which, liability for damages was foreclosed.

Suppose, however, fund shareholders sought to sue the adviser for fraudulent disclosure that the adviser had drafted for the fund and which the fund had disseminated to investors. Could the fund shareholders assert such a securities fraud claim? Based on *Janus Capital*, the answer is emphatically no. The result turns entirely on the role of the adviser in the fund's disclosure. Even though the adviser is almost certainly the most knowledgeable and active participant in drafting fund disclosure, it is not the party, in the Supreme Court language, with "ultimate authority" in making the disclosure and, hence, not a party that can be held primarily liable. Rather, the person is no more than an aider and abettor for which there is no liability in a private securities fraud action for damages. The *Janus Capital* Court did not address the issue of adviser liability under the control person liability provisions of the Exchange Act. Arguably, an adviser could be held liable under the express private action for damages under Section 18 of the Exchange Act which creates such a cause of action against persons who "make or cause to be made" misleading statements in documents filed with the SEC. However, that cause of action would appear to be of negligible significance in the case of mutual funds, since Section 18 actions are limited to misstatements affecting the price at which a security is bought or sold. Why would this be unavailing to shareholders of a mutual fund?

This does not mean that the SEC lacks the ability to sanction advisers for their role in fund disclosure. The SEC can bring civil or administrative actions for aiding and abetting and seek sanctions for a wider range of violations under the Advisers Act and the Company Act (the latter solely on a theory of secondary liability) for which there is no private action for damages. Interestingly, a sharply divided SEC has indicated its belief that primary liability under Rule 10b-5 for fraud is not foreclosed by *Janus Capital* in actions for schemes to defraud rather than misrepresentation, but such a view would appear contestable, to say the least. *See In re John P. Flannery*, Securities Act Release No. 9689 (Dec. 14, 2014) (in a 3-2 decision advancing a novel reading of *Janus Capital*'s scope under Rule 10b-5 and Securities Act Sections 17(a)(2) & (3)), *rev'd on other grounds*, 810 F.3d 1 (1st Cir. 2015).

2. *Fund liability for misrepresentations drafted by the adviser.* A natural question arising from *Janus Capital* is the potential liability of the fund for fraud. The fund in many circumstances will be liable under the express civil remedy provisions of Sections 11 and 12(a)(2) of the Securities Act because those provisions do not require a finding of scienter (i.e., a culpable state of mind). What about liability under Exchange Act Rule 10b-5, where scienter is a required element? On first blush, this might be challenging, since the Court's "ultimate authority" standard identifies the fund and its board as the makers of the statements set forth in fund documents, and frequently the board's independent trustees will lack the requisite scienter. Nevertheless, nothing in *Janus Capital* prevents application of traditional principles

by which scienter might be attributed to the fund from the scienter of its agents which would likely encompass the mental state of the adviser and its personnel.

3. *Allocation of liability between the adviser and the fund by contract.* The final dangling liability issue arising out of *Janus Capital* is what the fund should do vis-à-vis the adviser. After all, misleading disclosure may cause the fund to be liable for damages while the adviser, arguably the most culpable party, skirts free of civil liability. The fund's board, and especially its independent trustees, if sufficiently concerned by the allocation of liability for fund disclosure, can push back contractually. How might a fund board use an indemnification agreement to insulate the fund from liability caused by disclosure drafted by the adviser? Wholly apart from the financial contribution derived from such an agreement, how would such an agreement serve to align the interests of the fund and its adviser?

Chapter 14

Section 17 and the Affiliated Transaction Prohibitions

Key Ideas: Section 17 of the Company Act imposes significant prohibitions on affiliated persons with respect to transactions involving an affiliated investment company. This chapter examines the three primary transaction prohibitions: (i) with respect to *principal* transactions with a registered investment company or a company that it controls (Section 17(a)); (ii) with respect to *joint* transactions with a registered investment company or a company that it controls (Section 17(d) and Rule 17d-1); and (iii) with respect to *affiliate compensation* received in connection with a transaction on behalf of the investment company from a source other than the investment company (as well as receipt of excessive commissions by a broker acting for or with respect to a registered investment company) (Section 17(e)). In each case, it is necessary to understand (a) the nature of the specific transaction prohibition and (b) the transaction participants covered. Indeed, the class of transaction participants subject to the particular transaction restriction determines the scope of the prohibition in question. The prohibitions, as noted, rely heavily on affiliation under the Act's definition of "affiliated person." Moreover, since the principal and joint transaction prohibitions extend the relevant prohibitions to "affiliates of affiliates," the analysis of affiliation is both critical and often intricate. The SEC retains broad power to exempt (or permit) transactions prohibited under either Sections 17(a) and (d) or the rules thereunder through exemptive rules, exemptive orders and interpretatively through no-action letters. Investment companies widely rely on some or all of the exemptive rules relating to Section 17(a). These rules are carefully tailored, making it important to strictly adhere to requirements and conditions governing eligibility and application. While joint transactions may appear more benign than principal transactions, they raise similar conflict of interest concerns. Finally, the prohibition on affiliates' receipt of compensation from others with respect to activities on behalf of investment companies combats yet another form of conflict of interest. While Section 17 also contains other requirements, the transaction prohibitions are of paramount significance because they broadly constrain how affiliates of investment companies interact with investment companies and correspondingly act as a constraint on company conduct itself.

Chapter Contents

14.1 Introduction

In its legislative findings that serve as a preamble to the Company Act (Section 1(b)(2)), Congress declared that "the national public interest and the interest of investors are adversely affected ... when investment companies are organized, operated, managed, or their portfolio securities selected, in the interests of directors, officers, investment advisers, depositors, or affiliated persons thereof." That finding addresses some of the most common abuses by investment companies in the pre-Company Act era. Section 17 directly responds to these legislative findings. The section imposes strict prohibitions involving transactions or arrangements between an investment company, i.e., a fund (including companies controlled by the investment company) and the investment company's affiliates or affiliates of those affiliates. It also imposes other prohibitions regarding receipt of third-party compensation by affiliates in connection with transactions in which the affiliate acts for the investment company and authorizes the SEC to impose prohibitions on arrangements in which the affiliated persons' economic interests are not fully aligned with the affiliated investment company. The statute also provides a robust framework for exemptive relief from the SEC, either by rule or order. The exemptive overlay on Section 17 adds significant nuance in understanding the relevant prohibitions. This chapter explores the dual aspects of Section 17, its prohibitions and exemptive relief from those prohibitions.

14.2 The Concept of Affiliation in the Affiliated Transaction Prohibitions

The affiliated transaction prohibitions are triggered in part by the concept of affiliation and more specifically the statutorily defined term *affiliated person* of an investment company and (the doubly complicated) phrase of "affiliated person of such a person," which is commonly termed "an affiliate of an affiliate."[1] Because the prohibitions require that one of the transaction participants falls within one of two tiers of affiliation, a threshold issue involves understanding application of the concept of affiliation, which is addressed below. However, before turning to the technical features of such relationships, it is important to underscore the central purpose tied to the Company Act's focus on affiliation: affiliated relationships trigger statutory hurdles because of the conflict in economic interests between the affiliated person and the fund. By focusing on different aspects of an affiliated person's relationship with the fund, the statute implicitly recognizes that such relationships may cause actors to act in ways that diverge from the best interests of fund investors. At the same time, although the statute requires closer scrutiny of affiliated relationships in the affairs of the fund, it also creates mechanisms whereby an investment company may pursue such arrangements where such arrangements advance the interests of fund investors.

In classifying affiliation relationships, it is common to distinguish between so-called "first-tier affiliates" ("affiliated persons" of the investment company) and "second-tier" affiliates (or "affiliates of affiliates"). Either form of affiliation may trigger transaction prohibitions, but the latter entails an added level of abstraction that can present complications in application. The lynchpin of the analysis is the definition of affiliated person found in Section 2(a)(3) which enumerates six categories of affiliates which in turn implicate other definitions under the Act. Specifically, an affiliate of another person (whether an affiliate of the investment company or an affiliate of such an affiliated person) means:

> (A) any person directly or indirectly owning, controlling, or holding with power to vote, 5 per centum or more of the outstanding voting securities of such other person;
>
> (B) any person 5 per centum or more of whose outstanding voting securities are directly or indirectly owned, controlled, or held with power to vote, by such other person;
>
> (C) any person directly or indirectly controlling, controlled by, or under common control with, such other person;
>
> (D) any officer, director, partner, copartner, or employee of such other person;
>
> (E) if such other person is an investment company, any investment adviser thereof or any member of an advisory board thereof; and
>
> (F) if such other person is an unincorporated investment company not having a board of directors, the depositor thereof.

1. The relevant statutory language also encompasses transactions with promoters and principal underwriters and their affiliates. For the sake of simplicity, this chapter focuses exclusively on affiliated persons of the investment company and their affiliates, but a similar kind of analysis needs to be performed with respect to promoters and principal underwriters and their affiliates.

The main parts of the definition are fairly straightforward. Most of the enumerated categories identify instances of one-way affiliation, meaning the affiliated person is an affiliate of the investment company (or so-called "first-tier affiliates"), but the investment company is not an affiliate of the affiliated person. So, for example, a director of an investment company is an affiliate of the investment company, but the investment company is not an affiliate of the director.

Categories (A) and (B), when read together, and category (C) incorporate the broader notion of two-way affiliation. The affiliated person is not only an affiliate of the other person, but the other person is itself an affiliate of the affiliated person. For example, if an investment company owns at least 5% of a company, the investment company is an affiliate of the other company pursuant to category (A), and the other company is an affiliate of the investment company pursuant to category (B). As discussed below, two-way affiliation has the potential to increase the web of affiliated relationships.

Two additional points should be highlighted. First, not only is it important to recognize circumstances where affiliation exists, but conversely, also to recognize circumstances where seemingly related entities are not true statutory affiliates. For example, a director of a registered fund is by definition an affiliate of the registered fund. The same director may also be a director of a non-financial public company and, therefore, would be an affiliate of that company as well. Nevertheless, although the two companies—the registered fund and the non-financial public company—share an affiliate (i.e., the director), the companies are not themselves affiliates or even affiliates of affiliates by virtue of sharing a common director. Board membership is a form of one way affiliation and, therefore, does not make two entities with a common director affiliates-of-affiliates, merely by virtue of the common director.

Second, and of great practical significance, registered funds that share a common investment adviser are affiliates of one another. A common investment adviser exercises effective control over the investment portfolio of each fund. Although being an investment adviser is a form of one-way affiliation and, thus, would not result in the funds being affiliates of an affiliate, both funds are under common control of the investment adviser. As a result, the funds in a fund family are deemed affiliates of one another. This result makes intuitive sense, because the investment adviser is in a position to direct the financial affairs of the fund and would be in a position theoretically to benefit one fund at the expense of another.

To some extent, affiliation is easier to grasp diagrammatically. One-way affiliation is typically indicated by an arrow pointing from the affiliate toward the entity with whom the affiliate is affiliated, while two-way affiliation is typically indicated by an arrow that points both ways. This method makes it easy to determine whether a purported affiliate of an affiliate of an investment company is in fact one. The purported affiliate of an affiliate must be linked to the investment company by two arrows leading toward the investment company from the purported affiliate of an affiliate: first, pointing from the affiliate of the affiliate toward the affiliate and then from the affiliate to the investment company. These basic concepts are illustrated in the series of accompanying Figures below.

The easiest affiliation concept to illustrate is one-way affiliation. Certain enumerated persons are affiliates of the investment company, but the investment company is not an affiliate of the enumerated persons.

Figure 14A — One-way affiliation

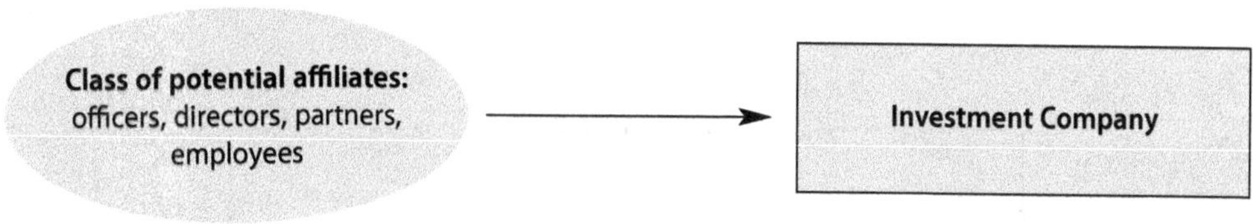

Two-way affiliation stands in contrast to first-tier affiliation. A registered investment company that has a two-way affiliate will also be an affiliate of that affiliate.

Figure 14B — Two-way affiliation: each entity is an affiliate of the other (in this case by virtue of shareholder's 5% ownership in the investment company)

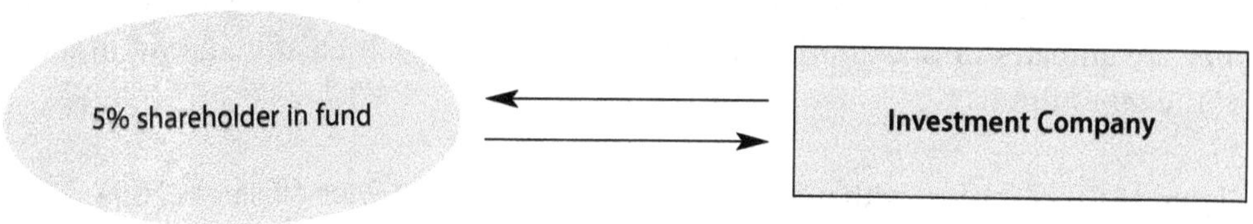

Two-way affiliations greatly increase the potential for affiliation relationships to give rise to second-tier affiliation whereby an affiliate is also an affiliate of an affiliate.

Figure 14C — Affiliate of an affiliate: controlling shareholder of the investment adviser is an affiliate of an affiliate of the investment company

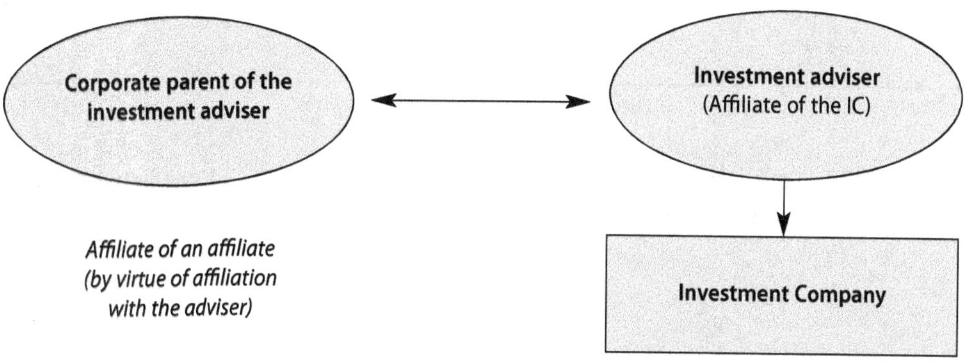

Just because two entities share a common affiliate does not mean either entity is an affiliate of an affiliate of the other. The reason is that the common affiliate may share only a one-way affiliation with each entity so that the entities are not affiliates of the common affiliate, thereby precluding either entity from being an affiliate of an affiliate of the other.

Figure 14D — Affiliates with a common affiliate (common director): but public company is <u>not</u> an affiliate of an affiliate of the investment company

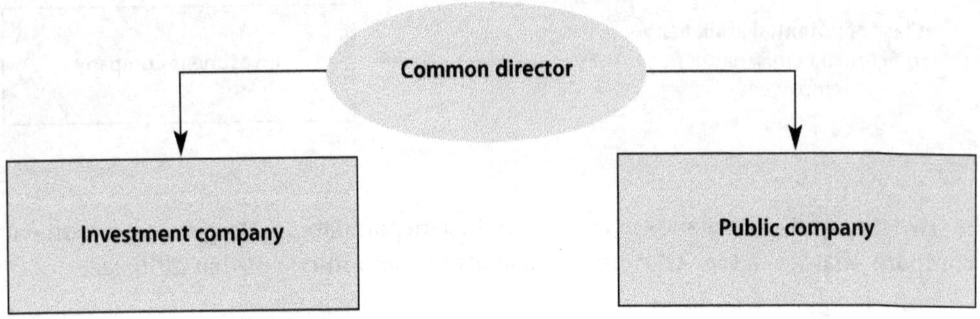

One well recognized affiliation category are funds that share a common adviser. In such cases, the two funds are deemed affiliates of one another. Moreover, since they are affiliates of one another, affiliates of one fund will be affiliates of affiliates of the other fund.

Figure 14E — Affiliates with a common adviser: Funds 1 and 2 are affiliates of one another

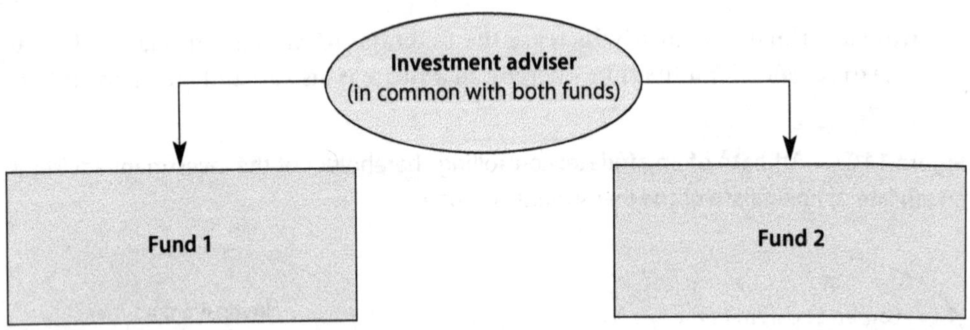

These basic affiliation relationships will make it possible to better navigate application of the prohibitions discussed in subsequent sections.

14.3 The Prohibition on Affiliates Regarding Principal Transactions

This section focuses on the prohibition on principal transactions by affiliates with the fund, perhaps the most intuitive of the affiliate transaction prohibitions. To further break down the complexity of this subject, it is best to begin with a discussion of the prohibition itself and then follow up with the topic of exemptions from the prohibition. Exemptions are permitted both by SEC orders, with respect to specific applications for exemptive relief, and by rule, with respect to entire classes of transactions provided the registrant satisfies the rule's requisite conditions. These twin aspects—the prohibition and exemptions—are examined sequentially.

14.3.1 The Prohibition

Section 17(a) imposes a *per se* prohibition on affiliated persons (first- or second-tier affiliates) of a registered investment company engaging in so-called principal transactions with the corresponding registered investment company (or another protected participant). The prohibited transactions encompass (i) the sale or purchase of securities or other assets; or (ii) transactions in which securities or assets are borrowed from or lent to a registered investment company or protected participant. The motivation behind the prohibition is fairly obvious: direct dealings between an affiliate (or an affiliate of an affiliate) and the fund involve conflicts of interest in which the affiliate may advance its economic interests at the expense of the fund or protected participant. Imagine for a moment the problem of allowing a fund's investment adviser to buy securities from or sell securities to the fund that it manages (i.e., the fund for which the adviser makes all investment decisions). An unscrupulous adviser might be inclined to overcharge the fund for securities held by the adviser and buy securities from the fund's securities portfolio at a discount price. Such obvious forms of self-interest are inherently abusive and represent the very kind of conduct that the prohibition is intended to prevent.

Just as affiliation is easier to understand with diagrams, it may help to illustrate the principal transaction prohibition diagrammatically. However, it is useful to note from the outset a common mistake among novices in applying the prohibition. The prohibition relates only to transactions between a first- or second-tier affiliate on the one hand and an investment company on the other. It does not apply to transactions between mere affiliates. Section 17(a) simply does not purport to regulate activities of affiliates in which a RIC or a RIC-controlled entity is not a counterparty. With that, consider the following illustrations that may or may not trigger the prohibition.

The first illustration (Figure 14F) demonstrates an obvious situation in which the transaction is prohibited. Suppose the investment adviser to the Alpha Fund, Upright Advisers, arranges to sell shares of Blue Chip Technologies from its own investment account to the investment portfolio of Alpha Fund. Under these facts, Upright, an affiliate of Alpha Fund, is selling from its own account to Alpha Fund, whose investment decisions are controlled by Upright. Clearly this is a prohibited affiliated principal transaction: an affiliate (Upright Advisers) is selling a security (shares of Blue Chip) to a registered investment company (Alpha Fund) with which the affiliate is affiliated.

Figure 14F — Violation of principle transaction prohibition: affiliate sale to investment company

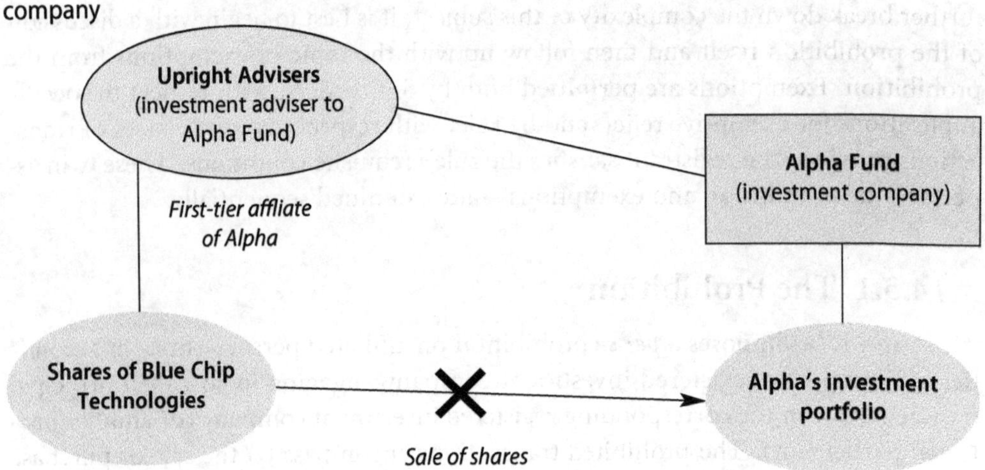

The prohibition on selling securities applies equally to affiliates of affiliates selling or, for that matter, buying securities or property from a registered investment company with which they are affiliated. Thus, taking the example above, if Upright Advisers' corporate parent, Upright Parent Inc., held the shares of Blue Chip Technologies, it would similarly be prohibited from selling the shares to Alpha Fund as reflected below in Figure 14G.

Figure 14G — Violation of principle transaction prohibition: affiliate of an affiliate sale to investment company

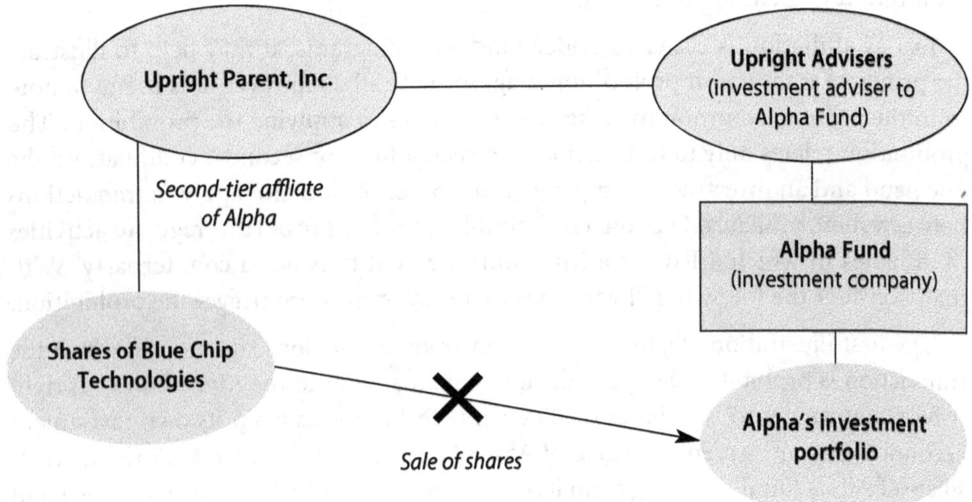

What about transactions among affiliates of a registered investment fund? The language of Section 17(a) does not address such transactions, although, as noted above, it is often easy to fall into a trap thinking that such transactions are among those covered under the rule. Using the example from above in Figure 14F, but altering the facts just slightly, suppose Alpha Fund owns 5.5% of the common stock of Enigma Enterprises. Also in this illustration, further suppose that Upright Advisers wants to sell the shares it owns of Blue Chip Technologies to Enigma Enterprises. This transaction does not involve a transaction with Alpha Fund nor an entity controlled by Alpha Fund and, therefore, is outside the scope of Section 17(a). In short, this proposed sales transaction, among affiliates of Alpha Fund, raises no issue under Section 17(a).

Figure 14H — No violation of principle transaction prohibition: sales transactions between affiliates of a registered investment company

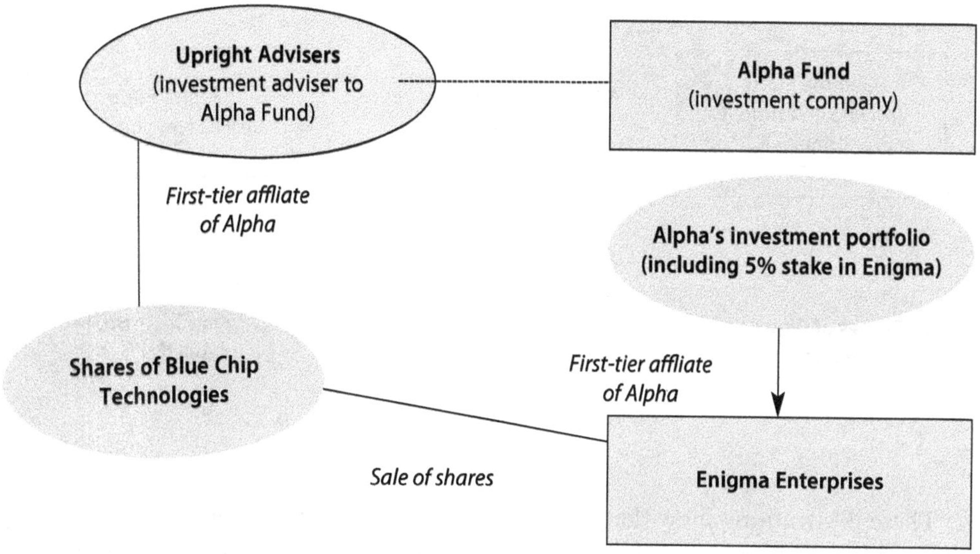

Finally, Figure 14I, addresses a similar situation—the sale of securities between funds managed by the same (that is, a common) investment adviser. This is a common scenario for any fund family. This illustration assumes that Upright Advisers also manages a private investment fund (such as a collective trust) called Gamma Fund, and Upright proposes to sell the shares of Blue Chip Technologies held by Gamma to Alpha. There are several plausible motivations behind a transaction of this nature. The funds might be managed by different portfolio managers of Upright Advisers who seek different risk/reward characteristics in owning Blue Chip. Hence, one fund might be willing to sell while the other buys. Selling between the two funds might allow for savings on brokerage costs. Nevertheless, Gamma would clearly violate Section 17(a) in selling the shares to Alpha Fund because Alpha is a registered investment company and Gamma is an affiliate of Alpha. Notice that, in this case, Alpha Fund's purchase from Gamma would not violate Section 17(a), because Gamma itself is not a registered investment company. Finally, Upright Advisers' trading advice probably violates Section 203 of the Advisers Act and Upright would likely be sanctioned for "causing" Gamma's violation of Section 17(a). As exemplified throughout the next section, under certain conditions, a sale of securities among two registered investment companies managed by the same investment adviser may qualify for a rule exemption to Section 17(a) which is not applicable here, because Gamma is not a registered investment fund.

Figure 141 — Violation of principle transaction prohibition: sales transactions between affiliated funds

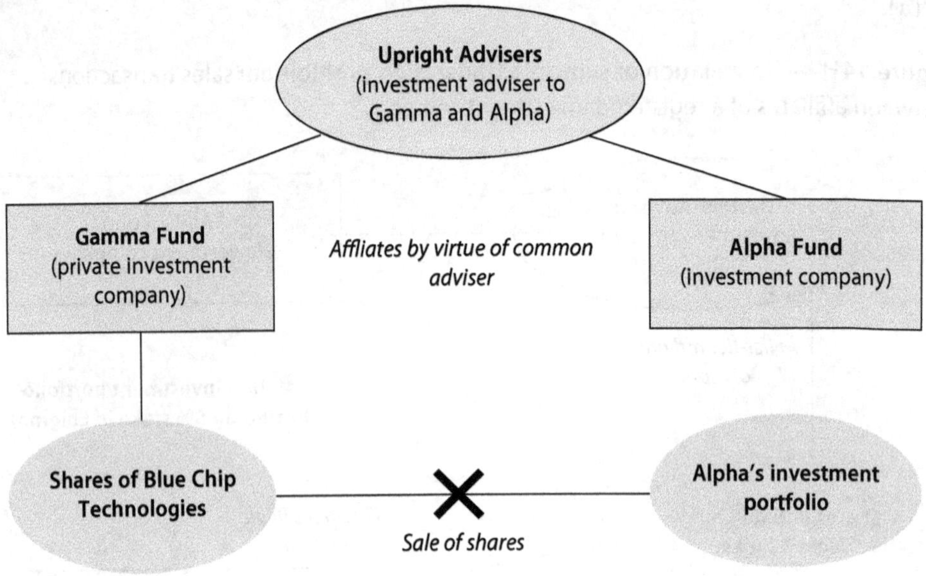

These illustrations show that diagrams can be extremely useful in understanding the application of Section 17(a). The real world offers practical life examples that are somewhat more subtle. The box below illustrates an expense reimbursement cap and the lurking potential for unwittingly triggering a Section 17(a) prohibition.

Illustration: Expense reimbursement caps that create a receivable between the investment adviser and the RIC

Expense reimbursement caps are widely used throughout the mutual fund industry. As the name implies, an expense reimbursement cap is an agreement almost invariably between the sponsoring investment adviser and the fund, in which the investment adviser agrees to pay all fund annual expenses that exceed a pre-determined expense ratio. Thus, if expenses for a fund are projected to be 0.99% (or 99 basis points), the investment adviser may agree to cover the funds' expenses in excess of 75 basis points. The investment adviser is most likely to make such an agreement if the fund is small and, thus, the expense ratio may be abnormally large as certain fixed costs of operating the fund are spread over a relatively small AUM base. The investment adviser may believe that an abnormally large expense ratio will discourage fund growth, as cost-sensitive investors may shun the fund. In this vein, an expense reimbursement cap is a typically viewed as an expression of confidence by the investment adviser in its ability to nurture the growth of the fund to a sufficient AUM level that will bring the expense ratio into line with industry norms. So far, the expense reimbursement cap appears wholly unremarkable. But now let us suppose that as a result of the expense reimbursement cap, the fund is owed over $200,000 at the end of the year from the investment adviser for unreimbursed expenses covered by the expense reimbursement cap. The $200,000 debt is, in effect, money borrowed by the investment adviser (an affiliate of the fund) from the fund and as such runs afoul of Section 17(a)'s prohibition on affiliate principal transactions—in this case taking a loan from the fund. See *In re Vector Index Funds Inc.*, Investment Company Act Release. No. 22055 (July 8, 1996). How should a fund and its board handle such situations to avoid a future unpaid receivable? Can the board insist on assurances of financial ability to satisfy financial obligations arising under an expense reimbursement cap?

14.3.2 Exemptive Orders and Exemptive Rules

Under Section 17(b), Congress authorized the SEC to issue exemptions by order for transactions that would otherwise violate Section 17(a), where the Commission determined (i) that the terms of the transaction were "fair and reasonable" and "did not involve overreaching" by the affiliated person and (ii) that the proposed transaction was consistent with the purposes of the Act and the investment policies of the affected registered investment company. Exemptive orders constitute a major avenue for routinely obtaining relief from the broad prohibition set forth in Section 17(a) on affiliate principal transactions. Thus, by enacting Section 17(b) simultaneously with Section 17(a), Congress demonstrated that it understood the potential overbreadth of Section 17(a): not all principal transactions involving affiliates are inherently bad for a fund. Nevertheless, Congress structured Section 17(a) as a strong default rule, i.e., that under the Section's bright-line prohibition, principal transactions involving affiliates are either flatly prohibited, or at the very least, require approval by the SEC.

Section 17(b) enables adversely affected funds to secure relief from Section 17(a)'s potential overbreadth; however, Section 17(a)'s prohibition can only be overcome by affirmative findings made by the Commission that the proposed transaction does not raise the type of concerns that Congress sought to guard against in the principal transaction prohibition. Despite this restrictive scheme, Section 17(b) orders are well-established forms of relief.

Over time, the Commission recognized that Section 17(a)'s overbreadth was problematic to whole classes of transactions that did not raise concerns. For example, suppose a registered fund makes a *pro rata* distribution to its shareholders (i.e., distributes a dividend). Some of the dividend recipients could easily be affiliates who owned shares in the fund. Obviously, a dividend does not present concerns of overreaching, even though fund property is obtained by an affiliate, because all shareholders (affiliates and non-affiliates alike) are treated the same. The SEC decided to address such situations by different means than Section 17(b). Rather than requiring potentially thousands of applications for exemptive relief, the SEC used its general exemptive authority under Company Act Section 6(c) to exempt entire classes of transactions. Such exemptive rules are self-effectuating, meaning parties relying on the rule do not have to seek specific relief from the SEC, but can act in reliance on the exemptive rule in engaging in certain transactions. In the case of dividends, for example, the relevant exemptive rule—Rule 17a-5 (technically framed as an interpretation of the terms purchase and sale rather than an exemption)—excludes *pro rata* distributions from the meaning of purchases or sales for purposes of Section 17(a). Altogether, the SEC has enacted ten exemptive rules that apply to different classes of transactions. Some of the rules are relied upon more frequently than others.

It does not make sense to go through each rule in detail. Rather than go through each exemptive rule, special attention will be given for purposes of illustration to one such rule: Rule 17a-7. The rule authorizes cross-sales of securities among funds in the same fund family, provided certain conditions are met. The cross-trading exemption is commonly used by fund families, but it is important to underscore another aspect of this rule and other exemptive rules. Just because a rule exists to cover a particular class of transactions does not mean that the transaction is automatically exempt from Section 17(a). Rather the participants in the transaction must ensure that they satisfy the rule's conditions. If not, then the transaction will not be exempt (i.e., it will violate Section 17(a)). The only other avenue of recourse to complete a prohibited transaction that does not satisfy the conditions of an exemptive rule is to seek an exemptive order pursuant to Section 17(b). Accordingly, and for reasons explained below, funds typically have written policies and procedures that govern the process that the funds will use before relying on an exemptive rule. The administrative order below illustrates how this two-step process—(i) reliance on an exemptive rule and (ii) ensuring compliance with the rule's conditions—can prove problematic in practice.

In the Matter of Back Bay Advisors, L.P.

Investment Advisers Act Release No. 2070 (Oct. 25, 2002)

[**Text note:** *This settled administrative proceeding arose from conduct in which an adviser engaged in the mistaken belief that Rule 17a-7 automatically permitted cross-sales between funds with a common investment adviser without* *first considering whether the proposed transactions were eligible for exemptive treatment, and whether the manner in which the cross-sales were effected fully complied with the terms of the exemptive rule. Needless to say, relying on an exemptive rule for which a transaction does not comply will almost guarantee that the transaction will violate the principal transaction prohibition found in Section 17(a). The findings illustrate two important points about exemptive rules: the party relying on the exemptive rule must be certain that the rule is applicable to the proposed transaction, and, in operating under an exemptive rule, the parties must adhere to the rule's conditions.*]

[***]A. RESPONDENT

Back Bay was, at all relevant times, registered with the Commission as an investment adviser pursuant to Section 203(c) of the Advisers Act (File No. 801-27694) with its principal place of business in Boston, Massachusetts. In December 1999, the firm had approximately $5 billion under management. At all relevant times, the firm invested in fixed income securities on behalf of insurance company portfolios and pension and retirement plans, among others. Back Bay originated in 1986 as a subsidiary of The New England Mutual Life Insurance Company ("The New England"). In 1996, Metropolitan Life Insurance Company ("MetLife") acquired The New England. As of August 1996 and at all relevant times thereafter, Back Bay was a wholly-owned subsidiary of Nvest Companies L.P. ("Nvest"), whose managing general partner, Nvest Corporation, was an indirect wholly-owned subsidiary of MetLife. On June 29, 2001, Back Bay ceased managing assets and, on July 9, 2001, withdrew its registration by filing a Form ADV-W with the Commission.

B. RELEVANT ENTITY

Back Bay Total Return Bond Fund (the "Back Bay Bond Fund") was at all relevant times an open-end mutual fund created for institutional clients. The fund commenced sales on December 22, 1997 (File No. 811-8339) and was liquidated on June 29, 2001. Back Bay was the fund's adviser throughout the life of the fund.

C. FACTS

1. Summary

This matter involves Back Bay Advisors, L.P., a registered investment adviser that engaged in violations with respect to prohibited affiliated transactions, including false statements or omissions to clients, alteration of records, and record keeping requirements. Back Bay also failed reasonably to supervise employees with a view toward preventing violations of the federal securities laws. Between 1994 and 1999, Back Bay effected certain trades between its clients—known as "cross trades"—in violation of Sections 17(a)(1) and (2) of the Investment Company Act, which generally prohibit any affiliated person of a registered investment company, or any affiliated person of such affiliated person, acting as principal, from engaging in transactions with the registered investment company. Back Bay's violative affiliated transactions consisted of: (i) cross trades between an investment company client and an account of Back Bay's indirect parent; and (ii) cross trades between Back Bay's investment company clients. Back Bay also made multiple false statements and omissions to clients about those affiliated transactions largely because its internal records did not properly reflect their existence. Back Bay also willfully violated the record keeping provisions of the Investment Company Act and Advisers Act when, shortly before the Commission's regulation staff came on-site to conduct a routine examination in early December 1999, the firm's chief investment officer (the "CIO") told a Back Bay trader to add information to the firm's completed cross trade tickets that would reflect "competitive levels," that is, market bid and ask prices cited by dealers that Back Bay obtained when canvassing the market. The trader thereupon wrote prices on the tickets that reflected merely an estimate of what the competitive levels were at the time of the trades. This rendered these tickets materially inaccurate by implying that the levels had actually been obtained while Back Bay canvassed the market when in fact they were not. Back Bay's violations occurred in part because the firm failed to develop an adequate supervisory system as it increased its business. Accordingly, Back Bay willfully violated Sections 204, 206(1), and 206(2) of the Advisers Act and Rule 204-2(a)(3) thereunder and Section 34(a) of the Investment Company Act and willfully aided and abetted violations of Sections 17(a) and 34(b) of the Investment Company Act....

2. Background

From its inception in 1986 through 1999, Back Bay managed portfolios on behalf of the insurance companies with which it was affiliated, initially The New England and, beginning in 1996, MetLife. Between 1997 and 1999, Back Bay managed three accounts on behalf of MetLife (the "MetLife Accounts") under the CIO's oversight. Back Bay also served as subadviser to two families of retail mutual funds (collectively, the "New England Retail Funds"). In the mid-1990s, Back Bay began expanding its client base by marketing itself to institutional investors such as corporate retirement accounts. By the fall of 1999, Back Bay's institutional assets under management exceeded $2 billion. The Back Bay Bond Fund, an institutional mutual fund which the firm created and launched in late 1997, was managed by a portfolio manager under the oversight of the CIO.

3. Violative Cross Trades

Between 1994 and 1999, Back Bay effected two types of violative affiliated transactions. First, Back Bay effected 65 transactions between the MetLife Accounts on one hand and the adviser's investment company clients on the other, most frequently the Back Bay Bond Fund. Second, Back Bay effected numerous cross trades between its investment company clients.

As discussed in the Legal Analysis below, Sections 17(a)(1) and (2) of the Investment Company Act prohibit any affiliated person, or promoter of, or principal underwriter for a registered investment company, or any affiliated person of such affiliated person, promoter, or principal underwriter, acting as principal, from engaging in certain transactions with such registered investment company, unless the Commission grants an order under Section 17(b) of the Investment Company Act exempting the transaction from the provisions of Section 17(a).[2] Rule 17a-7 exempts from the prohibitions of Sections 17(a)(1) and (2) a purchase or sale transaction between: (i) two registered investment companies, or (ii) "a registered investment company and a person [that] is an affiliated person of such registered investment company (or affiliated person of such person) *solely* by reason of having a common investment adviser or investment advisers that are affiliated persons of each other, common directors, and/or common officers." The exemption provided by the rule is subject to certain conditions, set forth in the rule, intended to ensure that the exempted transaction is fair to both parties.

Back Bay's personnel were ignorant of the applicable statutory requirements and instead followed their own practices for cross trading. They were generally unaware that, as discussed in the Legal Analysis below, cross trades between the MetLife Accounts on one hand and Back Bay's investment company clients on the other were altogether prohibited. Likewise, they were unaware that cross trades between the adviser's investment company clients violated Sections 17(a)(1) and (2) unless the trades conformed to Rule 17a-7's specific provisions governing, among other things, price determination. Instead, to arrive at a price for its cross trades, Back Bay traders estimated the midpoint between the bids and the asks for a given bond based upon their knowledge of the market and general communications with brokers. With an estimated mid-market price in mind, the traders engaged a broker and dictated the price at which the cross trade was to be executed. The prices Back Bay obtained for its clients using its method therefore differed from those which the firm would have arrived at under Rule 17a-7. Further, as part of the process, Back Bay paid an incremental markup for the broker's services, thereby failing to conform to the requirements of Rule 17a-7, which is available only when a brokerage fee (except a customary transfer fee) or other remuneration is not charged. By not following Rule 17a-7, Back Bay caused cross trades between its investment company clients to be effected at prices other than the prices mandated by the rule. If the firm had followed Rule 17a-7, no fees would have been paid. The gross improper costs and expenses incurred by Back Bay's clients for the transactions that could have qualified for Rule 17a-7's exemption was over $200,000.

Back Bay's cross trading violations occurred in part because of its poor compliance controls. The firm's practice for detecting Rule 17a-7 transactions consisted of distrib-

---

2. Section 2(a)(3) of the Investment Company Act defines an "affiliated person" to include "(A) any person directly or indirectly owning, controlling, or holding with power to vote, 5 per centum or more of the outstanding voting securities of such other person; (B) any person 5 per centum or more of whose outstanding voting securities are directly or indirectly owned, controlled, or held with power to vote, by such other person; (C) any person directly or indirectly controlling, controlled by, or under common control with, such other person; (D) any officer, director, partner, copartner, or employee of such other person; [and] (E) if such other person is an investment company, any investment adviser thereof or any member of an advisory board thereof...." Section 2(a)(9) of the Investment Company Act defines "control" as the "power to exercise a controlling influence over the management or policies of a company, unless such power is solely the result of an official position with such company.... Any person who owns beneficially, either directly or through one or more controlled companies, more than 25 per centum of the voting securities of a company shall be presumed to control such company."

uting quarterly compliance forms to portfolio managers on which they were required to indicate with a check mark whether their funds had engaged in any Rule 17a-7 transactions in the preceding quarter. Back Bay never trained its CIO, compliance officer, portfolio managers or any of its other personnel about affiliated transactions. The closest the firm came to educating employees was its practice of periodically distributing a compliance guide to some of its investment staff. However, Back Bay took no efforts to ensure that its staff actually consulted the manual. Some personnel, including the CIO, could not recall ever referring to it. The firm incorrectly assumed that its personnel were familiar with the relevant rules. The portfolio managers who effected cross trades repeatedly indicated on the quarterly compliance questionnaires that no such transactions had occurred. Back Bay had no policies or procedures in place to test the accuracy of those responses. As a result, Back Bay never caught any of the errors and they persisted for years.

4. Back Bay's False Statements and Omissions to Clients Concerning Cross Trading

Back Bay failed to disclose to its investment company clients its practice of cross trading between affiliates because Back Bay's employees misunderstood the relevant statutory provisions and did not report that such trades had occurred. Those clients (the New England Retail Funds and the Back Bay Bond Fund) had each furnished Back Bay with procedures by which Back Bay was supposed to effect Rule 17a-7 transactions. These procedures tracked the language of Rule 17a-7 itself and expressly required Back Bay to report Rule 17a-7 transactions to its investment company clients each quarter. For the New England Retail Funds, Back Bay's compliance officer handled the reporting process, which he did by repeating the information that portfolio managers had provided to him. Since the portfolio managers never identified any Rule 17a-7 transactions on the quarterly compliance reports, in the compliance officer's subsequent representations to the New England Retail Funds, he incorrectly stated that there were no Rule 17a-7 transactions to report. As for the Back Bay Bond Fund, the responsibility of reporting Rule 17a-7 transactions to the client rested with the CIO. The CIO periodically conferred with the secretary of the Fund but, on each occasion, failed to identify any affiliated or Rule 17a-7 transactions.

By virtue of Back Bay's false statements and omissions, the boards of each client investment company did not approve any such transactions or keep records of Rule 17a-7 transactions, which they must do to comply with Rule 17a-7. As a further consequence, Back Bay's investment company clients filed Forms N-SAR incorrectly stating that they did not engage in affiliated transactions.

5. Cross Trading Records

On November 24, 1999, the Commission's regulation staff informed Back Bay by letter of its intent to commence a routine exam in the first week of December 1999. Back Bay was provided with a list of records subject to examination, including documents related to the firm's cross trading. Back Bay distributed a copy of the list to the CIO, among others. As Back Bay and its counsel prepared for the exam, they realized that Back Bay had been effecting cross trades that were not compliant with Rule 17a-7's pricing method of averaging the highest bid and lowest offer. Back Bay and its counsel thereupon attempted to determine what prices the firm would have reached if it in fact had followed Rule 17a-7's specific pricing method.

On November 30, 1999, the CIO directed a trader to add information to the firm's completed cross trade tickets dating back to July 1998 (the same time period referenced by the Commission staff's letter to Back Bay). Specifically, he directed the trader to place "competitive levels" on the tickets, *i.e.*, prices that dealers offered to either buy or sell the bonds that Back Bay had cross traded. In carrying out the task, the trader obtained the firm's original trade tickets and began reviewing them. The trader reviewed trade tickets covering the period October through December 1998 and added competitive levels to ten order tickets concerning cross trades. The prices the trader added, however, were simply estimates of what the competitive levels were on the dates of the trades, based on a working knowledge of the industry and the trader's memory of where those bonds had been trading. The prices the trader added had not actually been obtained by the firm when canvassing the market. The trader stopped doing the task after a portfolio manager advised that writing on original trade tickets was improper. Subsequently, the trader brought the matter to the attention of the firm's CEO, who immediately contacted counsel. Shortly thereafter, Back Bay notified the Commission's regulation staff of the matter.

D. LEGAL ANALYSIS

1. Affiliated Transactions in Violation of Sections 17(a)(1) and (2) of the Investment Company Act Arising Out of Cross Trades

Sections 17(a)(1) and (2) of the Investment Company Act prohibit an affiliated person of a registered investment company, or an affiliated person of such affiliated person, acting as principal, from knowingly selling a security to, or purchasing a security from, the investment company, unless the Commission grants an order under Section 17(b) of the Investment Company Act exempting the transaction from the provisions of Section 17(a). However, Rule 17a-7 sets forth an exemption to Section 17(a)'s general prohibition. To be eligible for the Rule 17a-7 exemption, the transaction must be between two registered investment companies or between an investment company and a person that is an affiliated person of such investment company (or affiliated person of such person) solely by reason of having a common investment adviser. A condition of that exemption is that the trade must be effected at the "current market price," which, for most bonds, is defined as the average of the highest current independent bid and lowest current independent offer determined on the basis of reasonable inquiry. See Rule 17a-7(b)(4). No brokerage commission, fee (except customary transfer fees) or other remuneration may be paid in connection with the transaction. See Rule 17a-7(d). To meet Rule 17a-7's exemption, the board of directors of any investment company involved in the trade must adopt procedures for eligible affiliated transactions and determine at least quarterly that all such transactions complied with those procedures. See Rule 17a-7(e). The investment company is also required to keep records of the terms of all Rule 17a-7 transactions. See Rule 17a-7(g).[6]

In the present case, the violations of Section 17(a)(1) and (2) fall into two general categories: (1) affiliated transactions that were ineligible for Rule 17a-7 altogether, and (2) transactions that may have been exempt from the statutory prohibitions if Back Bay had complied with Rule 17a-7's conditions, but were not exempt because Back Bay failed to execute the trades in accordance with the rule. The first category consists of cross trades between the accounts of Back Bay's indirect parent, MetLife, and various Back Bay investment company clients. MetLife's control of Back Bay made it an affiliated person of Back Bay and an affiliated person of an affiliated person with respect to Back Bay's registered investment company clients. Since Rule 17a-7's exemption only applies where the affiliation between the trading parties is based solely on having a common investment adviser, the cross trades between the MetLife Accounts and Back Bay's investment company clients were altogether ineligible for Rule 17a-7's exemption and therefore violated Sections 17(a)(1) and (2).

The second category of transactions that violated Sections 17(a)(1) and (2) consists of all of Back Bay's other cross trades between investment companies advised by Back Bay. For these cross trades, the trading parties were affiliated solely by having a common investment adviser and therefore could have been exempt under Rule 17a-7 if Back Bay had followed the provisions of the rule. However, in each instance, Back Bay failed to adhere the transactions to the provisions of Rule 17a-7. Significantly, for each of these cross trades, Back Bay did not execute trades at the "current market price" because its traders did not use the average between the highest current bid and lowest current offer determined on the basis of reasonable inquiry. Instead, Back Bay estimated mid-market prices, without regard to the requirements of Rule 17a-7. In addition, Back Bay paid brokerage markups in connection with a majority of these cross trades, in contravention of the Rule 17a-7(d) requirement that no brokerage fee or other remuneration may be paid in connection with the transaction. These cross trade violations caused over $200,000 in gross improper costs and expenses to clients. Further, certain of Back Bay's investment company clients failed to keep records of cross trading as required by then-Rule 17a-7(f) (now Rule 17a-7(g)) because Back Bay failed to inform them of the cross trades. Finally, the boards of those investment companies (which were also not informed about the cross trading) did not determine that the Rule 17a-7 transactions were effected in accordance with the boards' procedures, as required by Rule 17a-7(e).

Based on the two above-described categories of cross trades, Back Bay willfully aided and abetted violations of Sections 17(a)(1) and (2) of the Investment Company Act.[7] [***]

* * *

---

6. Rule 17a-7(g) was formerly Rule 17a-7(f).

7. Back Bay is charged with aiding and abetting—as opposed to directly violating Sections 17(a)(1) and (2) of the Investment Company Act—because Sections 17(a)(1) and (2) apply directly to the party that trades with the registered investment company, not the adviser that effects the trade.

Notes and Applications

1. *Money market funds and the Principal Transaction Prohibition.* Money market funds have been a source of Section 17(a) problems for which the SEC has provided exemptive relief in two instances. Many principal transactions exemptive rules involve situations where the principal transaction either does not entail a material conflict of interest or risk any significant effect on a fund. Rule 17a-9 raises a slightly different possibility: suppose the adviser wants to help out the investment company to its own economic detriment. In other words, what if in certain circumstances, an affiliate (such as an adviser) decides to essentially bail-out the investment company from an investment that caused the fund to lose money (or as they say in the industry, an investment that "goes south"). Such a situation can have special pertinence to money market funds. Prior to 2015, money market funds uniformly adhered to a special fund pricing methodology, known as stable net asset value pricing. With stable NAV pricing, the fund will seek to maintain a stable net asset value of $1.00 per share and any variation in asset value is returned to shareholders as interest in most cases. This feature of money market funds allows them to function in most respects like interest-bearing bank accounts, except of course if the money market fund loses a significant amount of money and can no longer maintain the $1.00 stable net asset value. One way that money market funds avoid this risk of "breaking the buck" is to invest in super-safe instruments with short maturities. However, the unexpected can still occur. Given the reputational importance for money market funds of maintaining a stable NAV, advisers have often been willing to step in and buy problem assets from a fund at their original cost, even if the value of those investments have become impaired. Of course, this is a situation which could be described as the adviser doing the fund a favor in buying back devalued assets at a premium. Eventually the SEC decided to give rule-based exemptive relief for such purchases (Rule 17a-9), rather than requiring the adviser to make a Section 17(b) application to permit purchases of securities held in the money market fund's investment portfolio aimed at shoring up the fund's fixed $1.00 net asset value. Does this appear consistent with the legislative purpose behind Section 17(a)? What statutory support, if any, is there for such a view? Are there any potential downsides to such an exemptive rule from the investor protection perspective? Note: In 2015, the SEC significantly amended the money market fund rule—Rule 2a-7—and the amendment limited the class of money market funds that can use stable net value pricing. Nevertheless, exemptive Rule 17a-9 remains in effect.

2. *Fund-of-funds.* A second principal transaction exemptive rule relating to money market funds arises from so-called fund-of-funds situations within a single fund complex. A fund in a fund complex might want to invest in another fund in the complex. For example, one fund's investment of cash surpluses could be invested in an affiliated money market fund as a method of maximizing the return on overnight cash positions in the first fund's investment portfolio. Such investments would pose problems under the Company Act's anti-pyramiding provisions (found in Company Act Section 12), but for the fund-of-funds exemptive rules. Investment of one fund in an affiliated fund, as opposed to by the affiliated investment adviser, would not

appear to come within any statutory exceptions contained in Section 17(a) for purchase of fund shares. Accordingly in addition to any Section 12 problem (where rule-based exemptive relief may be available), there is also a Section 17(a) issue. Absent an exemptive order pursuant to Section 17(b) or an exemptive rule promulgated in connection with Section 17(a), such transactions would run afoul of the principal transaction prohibition in Section 17(a). However, the SEC has provided exemptive rule relief for Section 17(a) as well for the purchase of money market fund shares by an affiliated fund. However, rather that codify the rule as a conventional "17a-__" rule, the SEC included the exemptive relief with respect to Section 17(a) in the fund-of-fund rules, specifically Rule 12d-1. Thus, this is the rare example of a situation where an exemptive 17(a) rule is codified somewhere besides the "17a-__" series of rules.

14.4 The Joint Transaction Prohibition

The Company Act deals with the issue of joint transactions involving the participation of the investment company and an affiliated person or an affiliate of an affiliate as both analogous, but at the same time, different from the Act's treatment of principal transactions. Principal transactions are subject to a strict regime in which such transactions are prohibited unless exempted by rule or order. Unlike principal transactions where the investment company is dealing directly with (i.e., across the table from) an affiliated person, a joint transaction arises when the investment company and the affiliated person jointly participate in a transaction. In most cases, this means that they are on the same side of the table but participate in a transaction on slightly different terms or that some sort of conflict of interest exists, arising out of their parallel activities.

Section 17(d) governs such joint transactions and does not prohibit them *per se.* Rather, Congress gave the SEC rulemaking authority to formulate appropriate policies. It appears that Congress recognized that joint transactions presented a similar potential for conflict of interests as principal transactions, but that joint transactions implicated a wide range of joint arrangements between an investment company and its affiliated persons that argued against such a strict statutory presumption. Aside from certain obvious regulatory exclusions such as an investment company's investment advisory contract with an adviser, the SEC adopted a rule—Rule 17d-1—that prohibits transactions in which the fund and the affiliate or affiliate of the affiliate participate in a transaction jointly. The following readings illustrate interpretive issues relating to the rule. In the first, it did not appear to the participants that they were engaged in a joint transaction, while in the other reading the transactions appear nominally joint but the SEC staff was careful to explain why, under the facts and circumstances, they would not be treated as a joint transaction.

14.4.1 What Is a Joint Transaction under Rule 17d-1?

Section 17(d) is not a self-effectuating statute, rather it is a grant of rulemaking authority to the SEC. In other words, it was not possible to violate Section 17(d) until the SEC adopted a rule or rules proscribing specific conduct. As noted in the next decision, the SEC did not actually adopt a rule effectuating the purposes of Section 17(d) until many years after the Company Act's enactment. Arguably, the rule exceeded the scope of the authorizing statutory provision which itself was less than clear regarding what types of joint conduct were suspect. Rule 17d-1 under the Company Act was drafted to sweep in most types of joint arrangements. The rule prohibits all such transactions unless prior approval is obtained from the SEC. In theory, all joint arrangements (other than those expressly excluded by rule) are subject to pre-approval by the SEC. The principal difficult is understanding what constitutes a joint arrangement triggering the rule pre-approval process.

SEC v. Talley Industries, Inc.,

399 F.2d 396 (2d Cir. 1968), *cert. denied*, 393 U.S. 1015 (1969)

[**Text note:** *This decision provides a definitive interpretation of the concept of a joint transaction for purposes of Company Act Section17(d) and Rule 17d-1. In doing so, it illustrates one important feature of "jointness," namely it does not require an express agreement. The decision finds the requisite "jointness" from another feature present under the facts and circumstances.*]

Friendly, Circuit Judge:

[* * *] Defendant Talley Industries, Inc. (hereafter Industries) is an 'affiliated person' of defendant American Investors Fund, Inc. (hereafter Fund), a registered investment company, by virtue of Fund's owning 9% Of Industries' voting shares, see § 2(a)(3)(B). As a result of discussions between Franz G. Talley, president of Industries, a company having a net worth of some $10 million, and Michael Kimelman, a partner in the brokerage firm of M. Kimelman & Co., in which Kimelman advanced General Time Corporation, a much larger corporation, as a candidate for acquisition by a merger with Industries, Talley gave Kimelman an order under which he bought 24,800 shares of general Time for Industries on December 26 and 27, 1967; the price was around $23 or $24 per share. This was only some 1% of the outstanding stock of General Time, a long way from what Talley thought would be needed to afford a prospect of success if he should decide to go forward with an acquisition or merger proposal.

On December 29, 1967, Talley telephoned Fund's office, and ultimately spoke to George A. Chestnutt, Jr., president of Fund and of Chestnutt Corporation, its investment adviser. Talley told him that Industries had bought stock in a certain company which he viewed as a possible merger candidate and that he had in mind that Fund also might wish to buy some stock. Chestnutt broke off the conversation to consult his counsel. The latter advised that Fund could follow Talley's suggestion so long as it 'maintained complete independence in our acquisition of stock and didn't make any promises of arrangements' as to voting, disposition or otherwise. Chestnutt relayed this to Talley, who accepted Fund's proceeding in this manner. Talley then named the company, saying he thought it a good investment that might become better under a more aggressive management. He indicated that Industries intended to buy more

General Time stock in the market, with an eye toward a merger; Chestnutt got the impression that Talley was thinking of terms that would yield around $45 in Industries securities for each share of General Time. Talley proposed that Kimelman get in touch with Chestnutt; the latter, after telling Talley that 10% of the General Time stock would be his legal limit, said he would study his own data on the company, would like to see Kimelman, and would think the whole thing over. Shortly thereafter Industries bought 42,000 shares of General Time.

Kimelman visited Chestnutt on January 3. Next day Chestnutt determined that Fund should take a position in General Time. He was motivated both by study of the company's earnings and by a belief that if Industries sought a merger, the stock would rise as a result of that offer or of others it might stimulate. On January 5 Fund placed an order with Kimelman for 205,000 shares, subsequently increased to 210,000, just under Fund's 10% Limit, on a 'not-held' basis, i.e., with the time of execution at the broker's discretion. Chestnutt reported this to Talley.

Chestnutt maintained close supervision of Kimelman's purchases, insisting that on days when Kimmelman had 'not held' orders from other customers, shares should be allocated so as not to favor another customer over Fund. Industries was also making some purchases of General Time through Kimelman but at least on one occasion agreed to forego allocation and accept the most expensive shares. By February 15 Fund had acquired 210,000 shares at an average cost of $28.49 per share.

During the first week of January 1968, Talley discussed the situation including his initial conversation with Chestnutt, with his counsel, who did not mention § 17(d). After some backing and filling unnecessary to recount, Industries resumed purchases of General Time toward the end of January. Talley talked to Chestnutt four or five times during January and reported how many shares he thought 'were being acquired by the Kimelmans and himself and his friends and so on.' He would give Chestnutt percentage figures of what 'we have' and these rather obviously included the holdings of Fund. On February 5 Industries sold 40,000 shares to Donald Harrington, a friend of Talley's, who later increased his holdings to 104,500 Shares. Finding that the record date for General Time's annual meeting was March 1, somewhat earlier than he had believed, and that Industries' own holding were only some 52,000 shares, about 2 1/2% of the stock as against the 10% He considered necessary for a meaningful merger proposal, Talley made a special bid on the advice of his investment bankers, Smith, Barney & Co., and against that of Chestnutt who thought this would drive the price up and would not get Industries the amount of stock it wanted. The bid, on February 19, 1968, was for 200,000 shares at 36 1/2. General Time denounced this as 'grossly inadequate' and said it had a higher offer, on a tax-free basis, from another company. Only 66,437 shares were acquired.

On the afternoon of February 19, a meeting was held at Smith, Barney & Co. at the instance of the management of General Time. Talley proposed a merger and said 'We and our associates own about a third of the stock'—a figure which included Fund's holdings. Later that evening the management sent word to Talley it had decided to fight. Industries, which then owned 118,537 shares, about 5 1/2% of the total, went back into the market and quickly bought another 139,400 shares at prices ranging from 41 1/2 to 43 1/2. This brought its holdings to 257,937 shares, about 12 1/2%, at an average cost of $36.76 per share.

... On [April 12], Chestnutt was asked whether he would consider an offer for Fund's holdings in General Time from Del Coleman, president of Seeburg Corporation having its headquarters in Illinois. He countered by saying that he would be 'down in front of the SEC testifying on the General Time situation next week, probably Tuesday' and might have to reveal anything that was said. Coleman first drew back but then asked whether Chestnutt would entertain a cash offer of $40 a share. Chestnutt replied that he would have to compare this with what anyone else might offer.[2]

April 13 saw the announcement of a plan to merge General Time and Seeburg Corporation, 'contingent upon the continuation of General Time's present management.' The details appeared on April 15. Chestnutt found the terms 'shockingly unattractive'; he thought they would work out at not more than $28 per share of General Time as against a current market of $35. This, according to Chestnutt, was what made him decide to vote Fund's shares for the Committee's nominees and against the management.

The SEC hearings were held April 16, 17, and 18, oral argument was had before the Commission on April 19, and the Commission issued a Memorandum Opinion and Order that afternoon. Concluding that Industries and Fund had entered into and carried out a joint arrangement under § 17(d), that application for approval should have been made under Rule 17d-1, and that there was 'no warrant for granting retroactive approval of the transactions effected in such violation,' the Commission denied the application.

On April 22 ... the stockholders met, the ballots were cast, and the meeting was adjourned to May 3 so that the inspectors could count the votes and certify the result. Preliminary reports indicate a victory for Industries' slate, although by a margin considerably less than the shares voted by Fund.

On May 1, the SEC began this action in the District Court for the Southern District of New York. Asserting violation of § 17(d) and Rule 17d-1 by Industries and Fund, the complaint sought temporary and permanent relief enjoining further acquisition of General Time stock, requiring Industries and Fund to withdraw any votes cast at the stockholders' meeting, enjoining the voting of such shares for nominees proposed by Industries or for any merger with Industries, and enjoining future violations by Industries and Fund. The parties agreed that the court should order the trial to be advanced and consolidated with the hearing on the application for a preliminary injunction, see F.R.Civ.P. 65(a)(2). After trial Judge Wyatt delivered an opinion directing dismissal of the complaint, this appeal followed, and we have given it expedited treat-

2. Chestnutt also testified that a representative of Seeburg said, 'You just name a price between 35 and 50 and we will talk business.' Chestnutt named no price because he didn't feel 'in a position to make such an offer without talking to counsel.' Counsel advised that a sale at a premium might present a problem under *Perlman v. Feldmann*, 219 F.2d 173 (2 Cir.), *cert. denied*, 349 U.S. 952 (1955).

ment. Meanwhile the stockholders' meeting of General Time has been adjourned at first by stipulation and later by a stay issued by this court.

II.

The first issue is whether the SEC may lawfully conclude that when an affiliated person and a registered investment company engage in a plan to achieve together a substantial stock position in another company, they can have effected 'any transaction in which such registered company * * * is a joint or a joint and several participant' with the affiliate even though there is no legally binding agreement between them; we postpone the related issue whether if that proposition be affirmed, the facts here sufficiently disclose such a plan.

Little purpose would be achieved by tried-eye scrutiny of the word 'transaction.' This is not a technical term; 'transact' means 'To prosecute negotiations; to carry on business; to have dealings.... ' Webster's New International Dictionary (2d ed.) 2688. If any investment company and an affiliate agreed that each would buy 20% Of the stock of a third company and would not sell without the other's consent, the case would evidently come within § 17(d), and it would be altogether immaterial whether 'transaction' was read to refer to each purchase or the entire course of dealing or both. The real issue concerns the phrase 'is a joint or a joint and several participant.'[5]

We begin by conceding that, on a quick reading, such black-letter words call up an image of situations where there is a considerable degree of common understanding. Industries argues, in a conspicuously able brief, that this conclusion in reinforced by § 12(a)(2) which forbids any registered investment company, in contravention of Commission rules, regulations or orders, 'to participate on a joint or a joint and several basis in any trading account in securities...,' this rather obviously contemplating a situation where definite legal obligations are fixed. Against this, however, § 17(d) must have been intended to reach situations not already covered by § 12(a). Furthermore any idea that § 17(d) is limited to the typical joint venture in which each of the parties has a fractional share is negated by the point that its very bite is to limit or prevent participation by the investment company 'on a basis different from or less advantageous than that' of the affiliated person.

We find it hard to believe that a Congress which has declared 'that the national public interest and the interest of investors are adversely affected * * * when investment companies are organized, operated, managed, or their portfolio securities are selected, in the interest of directors, officers, investment advisers, depositors, or other affiliated persons thereof * * * rather than in the interest of all classes of such companies' security holders,' § 1(b)(2), meant 'a joint or a joint and several participant' to be read in light

5. We thus find it unnecessary to discuss the issue, much debated by the parties, whether the SEC went beyond the statute when it added the words in Rule 17d-1(a), 'in connection with, any joint enterprise or other joint arrangement or profit-sharing plan. * * *' In defining these terms subdivision (c) requires that the affiliate and the investment company 'have a joint or a joint and several participation' or—not here contended—'share in the profits of such enterprise or undertaking.' Hence, as to this case the critical question under the Rule is the same as under the statute.

of common law concepts of jointness. The need for a liberal construction in order to effectuate the statutory purpose would be clearer if, for example, Industries had been an affiliate because of its holding of 5% Or more of the voting securities of Fund, § 2(a)(3)(A), rather than the reverse. Yet if 'joint' embraces a loose kind of combination in cases of the former type where the case for a liberal construction is strong, as held by Judge Nordbye with respect to directors in *SEC v. Midwest Technical Development Corp.*, CCH Fed.Sec.L.Reptr. P91,252 (D.Minn.1963), it must also do that here where the case is less so[6]—and this even though the strict letter of the statutory command is limited to the affiliate. Moreover, Congress could have thought that downstream affiliation also involved some danger that the investment company's stockholders might be put upon for the benefit of other stockholders of the affiliate. 'Joint' can mean not only 'joined' or 'united' but 'combined.' Webster's New International Dictionary (2d ed.) 1339....

Even on that view, however, some element of 'combination' is required. Industries forcefully contends this to be negated, particularly by Chestnutt's statement to Talley before Fund had even decided to make purchases of General Time. But here Industries encounters the Commission's decision to the contrary....

Our summary of the facts shows there was substantial evidence here. While no one has cast doubt on the veracity of Chestnutt's testimony as to his initial conversation with Talley, this did not preclude the Commission's drawing a contrary inference of intention from what the parties actually did. Indeed developments may well have brought Industries and Fund into a 'combination' not clearly envisioned by either at the outset; war and the threat of war have always been powerful forgers of alliances. The Commission was justified in using its knowledge of the unspoken customs of the business world to conclude that, after Chestnutt had seen Industries spend over $8,300,000 in acquiring the 205,837 shares purchased in the special offer and on February 21 and 23, he was no longer a completely free agent as to the 210,000 shares Fund had purchased, on Talley's recommendation, for about 70% of that price. Experienced business men must have known at the outset that such a situation might arise....

III.

The other serious issue of construction is whether, in seeking to implement § 17(d) by a general requirement of advance application and approval, Rule 17d-1 exceeds the authority granted by Congress. Industries contends that the power conferred by § 17(d) was to prescribe substantive rules and regulations 'for the purpose of limiting or preventing participation by such registered or controlled company on a basis dif-

6. *SEC v. Sterling Precision Corporation, supra*, 2 Cir., 393 F.2d 214, does not support the view that the same language can be read one way in the case of upstream and an-other way in the case of downstream affiliation. We there declined to expand the word 'purchase' in § 17(a)(2) to include a redemption by a downstream affiliate of its securities held by the investment company when a 'sale' to the investment company of securities of the investment company held by an affiliate, whether downstream or up-stream, admitted by the SEC to include a redemption, had been expressly excluded by Congress in § 17(a)(1).

ferent from or less advantageous than that of such other participant'; that the Commission has prescribed none but rather has unlawfully insisted on advance application and approval in every case; that the transaction thus must be deemed lawful since no valid rule or regulation prohibited it; or, at the very least, that it should be upheld because Industries did not acquire General Time stock 'on a basis different from or less advantageous than that of' Fund. The issue must be considered in light of the general power conferred on the SEC by § 38(a) 'to make, issue, amend, and rescind such rules and regulations and such orders as are necessary or appropriate to the exercise of the powers conferred upon the Commission elsewhere in this subchapter.... '

Here again, while initial reaction may favor Industries' contention, reflection sustains the Commission's view. The varieties in which participation by an investment company may be 'different from or less advantageous than that' of an affiliate are infinite. The Commission could well have concluded that an attempt to specify these might fail to accomplish the Congressional purpose in some instances and in others accomplish more than Congress desired, and that the only effective method of regulation was to require advance disclosure and individual decision, at least until a pattern emerged, cf. note 7 [omitted]. Furthermore, as the Commission points out in brief, the public notice and opportunity for interested persons to come forward provided by the application procedure may lead to the development of significant facts that would not otherwise have been disclosed.

Industries mounts a counter-argument based on legislative history. It tells us that the Senate version of what became the Investment Company Act, S. 3580, 76th Cong.3d Sess. (1940), included as § 17(a)(4) a flat prohibition against affiliated persons' effecting transactions in which an investment company was a joint or a joint and several participant; relief would have been obtainable, as is now the case with respect to § 17(a)(1), (2) and (3), by application for an exemption under § 17(b). The change to the final version in which such transactions are condemned only insofar as they violate a particular standard, to be further specified in rules issued by the SEC, thus contra-indicates an intention that the Commission may req uire advance application and approval in all instances. While this is a possible inference, it is equally likely that Congress meant only that such transactions should be governed only by the standard limned in § 17(d) rather than the much more general ones of § 17(b). We thus do not find the legislative history so compelling as to warrant a conclusion that Congress meant to deny the SEC power to utilize a method of regulation it had successfully used in other areas.

IV.

Our reversal of the judgment dismissing the complaint does not imply any belief on our part that the SEC is entitled to the drastic relief sought.... The objective of § 17(d) of the Investment Company Act is to prevent affiliated persons from injuring the interests of stockholders of registered investment companies by causing the company to participate 'on a basis different from or less advantageous than that of such other participant.' On the face of things that has not happened here up to this time, and the objective for a court of equity must be to insure that it does not happen in the future. The judgment dismissing the complaint is reversed, with directions to the District Court to proceed promptly to formulate an injunction consistent with this opinion. The stay of the reconvening of the annual meeting of General Time will remain in effect until such injunction is issued.

* * *

The situation in *Talley* demonstrates the breadth of the joint transaction prohibition. The practitioner must be sensitive to not only actual arrangements but implicit understandings. As *Talley* makes clear, formal agreements are not necessary to establish the type of combination subject to regulatory scrutiny.

14.4.2 The Case of Aggregated Orders and Allocating Trades

While clearly the SEC has sought an active role in policing joint arrangements, the rule has the potential to be over-inclusive. Is it always feasible for the SEC to police every conceivable joint arrangement involving affiliates? Presumably there are joint arrangements whose effect is beneficial for all participants and probably benign.

SMC Capital, Inc.,

SEC No-Action Letter (pub. avail. Sept. 5, 1995)

[**Text note:** *This staff no-action letter addresses a common trading practice that is potentially problematic under Rule 17d-1, namely the aggregation of trades on behalf of multiple advisory clients (such as multiple mutual funds or a collection of mutual funds and separate accounts). It is hardly surprising that a money manager will seek to implement securities selection determinations across the accounts of more than one client. The adviser faces a dilemma in trying to figure out how to sequence the trades (i.e., do I try to buy for Fund A or Fund B first given that the first trade may influence the subsequent market price?). An obvious solution is to aggregate trades of all clients and then reallocate them at a common price among various client accounts. This letter discusses whether this practice, invariably, is subject to Rule 17d-1and hints at circumstances where it might not but also signals circumstances where aggregation is problematic, thereby requiring SEC pre-approval under Rule 17d-1.*]

By letter dated July 11, 1995, you request our assurance that we would not recommend enforcement action to the Commission under section 17(d) of the Investment Company Act of 1940 ("Investment Company Act") or rule 17d-1 thereunder, or section 206 of the Investment Advisers Act of 1940 ("Advisers Act"), if SMC Capital, Inc. ("SMC"), a registered investment adviser, aggregates orders for the purchase or sale of securities on behalf of its clients, as more fully described in your letter.

You state that SMC provides investment advice to a number of different types of clients, including individuals, employee benefit plans, registered investment companies, private investment limited partnerships excepted from the definition of "investment company" under section 3(c)(1) of the Investment Company Act, and insurance company investment accounts. Employees and principals of SMC invest in certain collective investment vehicles advised by SMC.

You state that larger orders for the purchase or sale of securities generally may be executed at lower commission costs on a per-share and per-dollar basis than smaller orders. SMC believes it is obligated to seek the best possible execution of all trades for all its clients, including those clients in which persons associated with SMC are among the investors, by engaging in the aggregation of orders.[2] You also state that, if orders are aggregated in accordance with the standards outlined in your letter, the risk that any particular client would be or could be systematically advantaged or disadvantaged would be minimized.

Proposed Aggregation of Orders

Specifically, SMC proposes to aggregate client orders as follows:

1. Policies for the aggregation of transactions will be fully disclosed in SMC's Form ADV and separately to SMC's existing clients and the broker-dealers through which such orders are placed;[3]

2. SMC will not aggregate transactions unless it believes that aggregation is consistent with its duty to seek best execution (which includes the duty to seek best price) for its clients and is consistent with the terms of SMC's investment advisory agreement with each client for which trades are being aggregated;

3. No advisory client will be favored over any other client; each client that participates in an aggregated order will participate at the average share price for all SMC's transactions in that security on a given business day, with transaction costs shared pro rata based on each client's participation in the transaction;

4. SMC will prepare, before entering an aggregated order, a written statement (the "Allocation Statement") specifying the participating client accounts and how it intends to allocate the order among those clients;

5. If the aggregated order is filled in its entirety, it will be allocated among clients in accordance with the Allocation Statement; if the order is partially filled, it will be allocated pro rata based on the Allocation Statement;

6. Notwithstanding the foregoing, the order may be allocated on a basis different from that specified in the Allocation Statement if all client accounts receive fair and equitable treatment and the reason for the different allocation is explained in writing

---

2. We note that an adviser would not violate its duty to seek best execution merely by failing to aggregate orders for client accounts. The adviser should, however, disclose to its clients that it will not aggregate and the potential consequences of the failure to aggregate. *See In re Mark Bailey*, Investment Advisers Act Release No. 1105, 40 SEC Docket 432 (Feb. 24, 1988).

3. Your letter states that the policies for the aggregation of transactions will be submitted to and approved by the board of directors of any registered investment company for which transactions will be aggregated.

and is approved in writing by SMC's compliance officer no later than one hour after the opening of the markets on the trading day following the day the order was executed;[5]

7. SMC's books and records will separately reflect, for each client account the orders of which are aggregated, the securities held by, and bought and sold for, that account;

8. Funds and securities of clients whose orders are aggregated will be deposited with one or more banks or broker-dealers, and neither the clients' cash nor their securities will be held collectively any longer than is necessary to settle the purchase or sale in question on a delivery versus payment basis; cash or securities held collectively for clients will be delivered out to the custodian bank or broker-dealer as soon as practicable following the settlement;

9. SMC will receive no additional compensation or remuneration of any kind as a result of the proposed aggregation; and

10. Individual investment advice and treatment will be accorded to each advisory client.

... You state that SMC has procedures and mechanisms in place that are reasonably designed to implement its aggregation policies.

Analysis

Section 17(d) of the Investment Company Act provides that the Commission may adopt rules restricting participation by registered investment companies in joint transactions with affiliated persons for the purpose of preventing or limiting participation by such a company on a basis different from or less advantageous than that of any other participant. Rule 17d-1, in relevant part, provides that no affiliated person of a registered investment company, and no affiliated person of an affiliated person, may participate in any joint enterprise, arrangement, or profit-sharing plan, as defined in the rule, without first obtaining an exemptive order from the Commission. Your letter raises issues under section 17(d) because SMC proposes to aggregate orders on behalf of registered investment company clients and other advisory clients in which persons associated with SMC have invested, or other clients that may be affiliated persons of the registered investment company, or affiliated persons of such persons.

---

5. For example, it may be appropriate to deviate from the Allocation Statement when, subsequent to entering the trade but before the final allocation, SMC determines that the security in question would be unsuitable for one of the clients designated in the Allocation Statement. You also represent that if an aggregated purchase or sale order is partially executed and allocated on a basis different from that specified in the Allocation Statement, no client that is benefitted by the different allocation may effect any purchase or sale, for a reasonable period following the execution of the aggregated order, that would result in its receiving or selling more shares than the number of shares it would have received or sold had the aggregated order been fully executed.

Some element of combination or profit motive must generally be present for section 17(d) and rule 17d–1 to apply.[8] You maintain that the aggregation of orders alone does not constitute a combination or enterprise conducted for the purpose of making a profit. A pattern of aggregating trades on behalf of certain clients, you contend, results only from a commonality of investment objectives, not from any motive or purpose related to the execution of the orders. In the alternative, you state that because all of SMC's clients will participate on equal terms, the proposed aggregation of trades need not be prohibited in order to effectuate the policies underlying section 17(d).

We agree that the mere aggregation of orders for advisory clients, including a registered investment company, would not violate section 17(d), provided that the investment company participates on terms no less advantageous than those of any other participant. If a portfolio manager allocates trades in such a way as to disadvantage a registered investment company, however, a joint enterprise or arrangement raising the concerns section 17(d) was designed to address may result.[10]

We would not recommend enforcement action to the Commission under section 17(d) or rule 17d-1 thereunder if SMC engages in the practice of aggregating orders for the purchase or sale of securities on behalf of investment companies and other clients (including clients in which SMC or persons associated with SMC may have an interest), subject to the representations made in your letter and the telephone conversations.[11] Nor would we recommend enforcement action to the Commission under section 206 of the Advisers Act if SMC engages in the proposed aggregation of orders in a manner consistent with seeking best execution.... Section 206 imposes a fiduciary duty on an investment adviser to act in the utmost good faith with respect to its clients, and to provide full and fair disclosure of all material facts.13 Consistent with its fiduciary duties, SMC will allocate trades on an equitable basis with respect to both its investment

8. *In re Steadman Security Corp.*, 1974-75 Fed.Sec.L.Rep. (CCH) ¶ 80,038 at 84,848 (Dec. 20, 1974) (rule 17d-1 "is concerned with joint enterprises or joint arrangements that are in the nature of a joint venture, i.e., that involve the element of seeking to realize a profit or gain through the investment of funds."); *SEC v. Talley Indust., Inc.*, 399 F.2d 396, 403 (2d Cir.1968), cert. denied, 393 U.S. 1015 (1969) (while section 17(d) is not limited to the typical joint venture, "some element of 'combination' is required").

10. *In re Kemper Financial Services, Inc.*, Investment Advisers Act Release No. 1387, Fed.Sec.L.Rep. (CCH) ¶ 85,237 (Oct. 20, 1993). The anti-fraud provisions of the federal securities laws also would apply to transactions that were allocated in order to benefit certain clients over others. In particular, section 17(j) of the Investment Company Act and rule 17j-1(a) thereunder, in relevant part, generally prohibit any affiliated person of a registered investment company, in connection with the purchase or sale by such person of a security held or to be acquired by such registered investment company, from defrauding such registered investment company. Therefore, these provisions prohibit fraudulent practices in connection with aggregated trades in which an investment company and affiliated persons of the investment company participate. See also section 206 of the Advisers Act.

11. SMC states that it will allocate trades at an average price and, if not completely filled, on a pro rata basis. Although you have not asked us to express an opinion on any other allocation method, we note that there may be other allocation methods that advisers can use without violating section 17(d) or section 206.

company and non-investment company clients. Our position with respect to section 206 is based particularly on the following representations: (1) the practice of aggregating orders will be fully disclosed in SMC's Form ADV and separately to SMC's existing clients, and (2) no advisory client, including those clients in which SMC or persons associated with SMC have a direct or indirect beneficial interest, will be favored by SMC over any other client and each client who participates in an aggregated order will participate at the average share price with all transaction costs shared on a pro rata basis.

Because this position is based on the facts and representations made in your letter and the telephone conversations noted above, you should note that any different facts or circumstances might require a different conclusion.[15]

* * *

Notes and Applications

Trade aggregation and negotiated private placements. The *SMC Capital* no-action letter represents a mildly surprising, but perhaps understandable, interpretive result: trade aggregation need not always result in triggering Rule 17d-1, even if persons affiliated with SMC are investors of the funds trading side-by-side with other funds in the aggregated order. Thinking back to the language in *Talley*, aggregation entails an element of "combination," yet the staff concludes that the requisite form of combination for purposes of Rule 17d-1 is not present. Clearly, parallel investment decisions among affiliated funds is not sufficient to show a combination constituting a joint enterprise based on *Talley*. However, aggregating trades, and especially where the adviser may have an economic interest in the transactions, goes considerably beyond mere parallel trading. The staff nevertheless concluded that the answer is still "No," as in the established trade aggregation interpretive position.

The staff offers a legal rationale for its position, but it also appears shaped by pragmatic considerations. Why would the staff seek to exclude most kinds of trade aggregation from the rule's pre-approval requirement? If an adviser chose not to aggregate trades, how would an adviser arrange for execution of nearly simultaneous orders in the same securities from different funds within a fund family? The *SMC* letter contains a variety of conditions. What purpose do they serve with respect to the concerns that motivated Section 17(d) and Rule 17d-1?

The SMC Capital letter expressly declined to address "privately placed securities" in its no-action relief. Not surprisingly, two subsequent related letters explored this unresolved issue. *See Massachusetts Mutual Life Insurance Company*, SEC No Action Letter (pub. avail. June 7, 2000), and *Massachusetts Mutual Life Insurance Company*, SEC No Action Letter (pub. avail. July 28, 2000). The application of the result in the *SMC Capital* letter to negotiated private placements entailed a significantly more difficult issue. As the staff observed:

---

15. Your letter does not request relief with respect to the aggregation of orders involving privately placed securities, and therefore we express no opinion with respect to the aggregation of such securities.

> Aggregated orders for the purchase or sale of private placement securities may involve a conflict of interest between an investment company and an affiliated person of the investment company. A conflict of interest may arise if an affiliated person has both a material pecuniary incentive and the ability to cause the investment company to participate with it in an aggregated transaction. For example, an investment adviser may be interested in participating in an offering of private placement securities but may not be able to participate in the offering if the ability to receive a portion of the offering depends on the size of the purchase order and the adviser's order is too small. As a result, the adviser would have the incentive to aggregate its order with the orders of others. In that circumstance, the adviser would have the material pecuniary incentive and the ability to cause an investment company client to participate with it in an aggregated purchase of the private placement securities, even though the investment company's participation may not be in its best interests.

The staff's no-action determination in these letters hinged on two important aspects: (i) an adviser's material pecuniary interest in the transaction because of its economic interest in one or more participants in the private placement transaction; and (ii) the private placement might involve negotiation by the adviser of one or more terms of the private placement transaction. From the staff's perspective, the conflict of interest coupled with the adviser's negotiating role in a negotiated private placement could rise to the level of a combination driven by a conflicted profit motive and, therefore, implicate Rule 17d-1. Nevertheless, the staff extended its no-action position in *SMC Capital* to limited negotiated private placement contexts where the adviser proposed to negotiate no term of the transaction other than price and to adhere to conditions that would insure that the investment company participated on terms no less advantageous than any other participant in the negotiated private placement transaction. Assuming that *SMC Capital* is a correct interpretation, does the staff's logic with respect to private placements appear compelling legally, pragmatically, or both?

14.5 The Prohibition with Respect to Affiliate Compensation

Section 17(e) addresses another aspect of the potential conflict of interests between affiliated persons (and affiliates of affiliates) and a registered investment company, or alternatively, between a broker acting for a registered investment company and the registered investment company. Affiliated persons (or affiliates of affiliates) who are acting as agents for a registered investment company are potentially subject to divided loyalties if compensated by a third party in connection with the purchase or sale of property to the registered investment company. The affiliated person may no longer exert the same level of diligence on behalf of the fund when compensated by another, presumably one whose interests diverge from those of the fund. This potential conflict is even more direct for a broker when acting on behalf of a fund in the execution of trade.

Section 17(e) has two operative prohibitory provisions. Section 17(e)(1) addresses affiliated persons (and affiliates of affiliates) acting as agents for a fund. Section 17(e)(2) addresses brokers acting on behalf of a fund in the purchase or sale of fund securities. The two readings below deal exclusively with the first provision, since in each case, the participants charged with the violations were acting as agents of the fund. The first case involves traders on the trading desk of a fund complex, and the second case involves a portfolio manager of a fund. Note the difference in compensation in the two actions. In the first, the compensation is directly tied to activities on behalf of the fund by adviser personnel. In the second action, the compensation to the portfolio manager has a seemingly more attenuated relationship to the day-to-day operations of the fund.

In the Matter of Fidelity Management & Research Company

Investment Advisers Act Release No. 2713 (May 5, 2008)

[**Text note:** *This settled administrative proceeding made headlines in the financial press (e.g., was front-page news in the Wall Street Journal). The legal analysis itself is fairly straightforward. The scope of the breach in the firm's gifts and entertainment policy and the virtually routine way in which the firm's trading desk interacted with brokers who were all too willing to lavish such gifts in return for trades is eye-opening. The lesson is fairly direct: anything other than* de minimis *gifts from brokers executing fund trades is clearly out-of-bounds. Although the administrative action (as edited) primarily focuses on the Section 17(e) aspects of the misconduct, the order's findings also suggest avenues for sanctioning conduct of employees of advisers of institutional clients or unregistered pooled investment vehicles. After the* Fidelity *order, industry customs and practices changed, and gifts, travel and entertainment to employees are closely monitored.*]

[***] Summary

16. During the period from at least January 2002 through October 2004, two Fidelity senior executives (DeSano and Grenier) and ten Fidelity equity traders (Beran, Bruderman, Burnieika, Burns, Donovan, Driscoll, Harris, Horan, Pascucci and Smith) in aggregate accepted approximately $1.6 million worth of travel, entertainment and gifts from brokerage firms that sought and obtained orders to buy or sell securities on behalf of Fidelity's advisory clients. In addition, Lynch requested and received tickets to events from two equity traders, who obtained those tickets from brokers. Those brokerage firms each received millions of dollars in commission revenue for handling orders from Fidelity's advisory clients' accounts. DeSano and the traders in aggregate accepted from brokers dozens of expensive trips, frequently by private jet, including excursions to the Super Bowl, family vacations to Bermuda, Nantucket and the Caribbean, golf outings at exclusive clubs in Florida and South Carolina, weekends in Las Vegas, lodging at fine hotels, and even an extravagant, three-day bachelor party for Bruderman in Miami. Brokers also provided the Fidelity executives and traders with gifts including premium tickets to the World Series, the U.S. Open, Wimbledon, Rolling

Stones concerts, and dozens of other sporting events and concerts. In addition, certain traders accepted illegal drugs from brokers and one trader's illegal gambling was facilitated by a broker.

17. The ten traders allowed the receipt of travel, entertainment and gifts to influence their selection of brokers to handle transactions for Fidelity's clients. As one trader commented to another, "Word is out that order flow is for sale." In addition, certain traders routinely sent transactions to brokers who were members of their families or brokers with whom they had a romantic relationship.

18. DeSano, who supervised Fidelity's equity trading operations, personally accepted travel, entertainment and gifts from brokers who sought and obtained securities transactions for Fidelity's clients. He solicited tickets from brokers for himself and to satisfy requests from his supervisor, Grenier. He accompanied certain traders on several trips by private jet paid for by brokers, including attending part of Bruderman's bachelor party in Miami, and traders told him about some of the other private jet trips and tickets they received from brokers. He also knew that certain traders directed transactions to brokers who were members of their family or with whom they had a romantic relationship. Nevertheless, DeSano failed to monitor the traders' receipt of travel, entertainment and gifts in any systematic way and failed to take reasonable steps to ensure that they were seeking best execution or complying with Fidelity's policy concerning its employees' receipt of gifts and gratuities.

19. Under Section 17(e)(1) of the Investment Company Act, affiliated persons of a registered investment company, such as Fidelity executives and traders, are prohibited from accepting "from any source any compensation (other than a regular salary or wages from such registered company) for the purchase or sale of any property" of the investment company. The objective of Section 17(e)(1) is to prevent persons affiliated with registered investment companies from having conflicts of interest impair their judgment and loyalty. A violation of Section 17(e)(1) of the Investment Company Act is complete upon receipt of the compensation. During the Relevant Period, two Fidelity executives (DeSano and Grenier) and ten Fidelity traders (Beran, Bruderman, Burnieika, Burns, Donovan, Driscoll, Harris, Horan, Pascucci and Smith) received compensation in violation of Section 17(e)(1) of the Investment Company Act in the form of travel, entertainment and gifts paid for by brokers who sought and obtained from those traders securities transactions for Fidelity's clients. In addition, another Fidelity executive (Lynch) caused two Fidelity traders' violations of Section 17(e)(1). Fidelity failed to adopt and implement a system of controls sufficient to detect, deter, and prevent the receipt by these executives and traders of travel, entertainment and gifts paid for by brokers as described herein. As a result, Fidelity failed reasonably to supervise the executives and traders, within the meaning of Section 203(e)(6) of the Advisers Act, with a view to preventing their violations of Section 17(e)(1) of the Investment Company Act.

20. Under Section 206 of the Advisers Act, an investment adviser has a fiduciary duty to seek best execution for its clients' securities transactions—that is, to seek the most favorable terms reasonably available under the circumstances. In determining

whether an adviser is seeking best execution, the key criterion is whether the adviser selects the transaction which "represents the best qualitative execution for the managed account." During the Relevant Period, Fidelity allowed certain employees' receipt of travel, entertainment and gifts and certain employees' family or romantic relationships to enter into the selection of brokers. Accordingly, Fidelity willfully violated Section 206(2) of the Advisers Act, resulting in the substantial possibility of higher execution costs for Fidelity's advisory clients.

21. Under Section 206 of the Advisers Act, an investment adviser has a fiduciary duty to disclose all material conflicts of interest to its advisory clients. During the Relevant Period, Fidelity failed to disclose to its advisory clients the conflicts of interest arising from the receipt by certain Fidelity executives and traders of travel, entertainment and gifts from, and certain traders' family and romantic relationships with, brokers who sought and obtained securities transactions for Fidelity's clients, and failed to disclose that such travel, entertainment, gifts and relationships became additional factors in the traders' selection of brokers. Accordingly, Fidelity willfully violated Section 206(2) of the Advisers Act.

22. Under Sections 204, 206 and 207 of the Advisers Act and Rule 204-1 thereunder and Section 34(b) of the Investment Company Act, an investment adviser may not make materially false and misleading statements in public disclosure documents, such as an investment adviser's Form ADV and a registered investment company's prospectus and statement of additional information ("SAI"). During the Relevant Period, Fidelity's Forms ADV and the SAIs which it prepared for the Fidelity Funds stated that Fidelity selected brokers for its clients' transactions based on an itemized list of factors but failed to include the additional significant factors considered by certain traders—their receipt of travel, entertainment and gifts from brokers and their family or romantic relationships with brokers. As a result, Fidelity willfully violated Sections 204, 206(2) and 207 of the Advisers Act and Rule 204-1 thereunder and Section 34(b) of the Investment Company Act.

23. On behalf of Fidelity, DeSano made presentations to committees of the trustees of the Fidelity Funds in which he too identified the factors that Fidelity used in selecting brokers. DeSano also told the trustees that Fidelity required brokers to compete for its brokerage business based on the quality of their trade execution. Those statements were false and misleading because DeSano failed to disclose (1) that certain Fidelity traders selected brokers for Fidelity's business based on additional significant factors of which he was aware—travel, entertainment and gifts from brokers and family or romantic relationships with brokers, and (2) that brokers competed for Fidelity's business based on those additional factors as well. As a result, Fidelity willfully violated Section 206(2) of the Advisers Act.

24. Under Section 204 of the Advisers Act and Rule 204-2 thereunder, an investment adviser is required to make and keep true, accurate and current books and records relating to its investment advisory business, including originals or copies of certain documents reflecting its communications with brokerage firms relating to the placing or execution of orders to purchase or sell securities. During the Relevant Period, Fidelity

traders used an electronic messaging network supplied by Bloomberg L.P. ("Bloomberg") to communicate with brokers. Fidelity failed to make and keep true, accurate, and current originals or copies of such messages. As a result, Fidelity willfully violated Section 204 of the Advisers Act and Rules 204-2(a)(7)(iii) and 204-2(g)thereunder.

Background on Fidelity's Equity Trading Desk

25. Fidelity manages one of the largest mutual fund complexes in the United States. Fidelity equity traders buy and sell millions of shares of stock every day for the Fidelity Funds and other institutional clients. As an investment adviser, Fidelity has a fiduciary duty to seek best execution for its clients' securities transactions and to disclose to its clients all material facts concerning conflicts of interest.

26. The Fidelity Funds and certain of Fidelity's other institutional clients' accounts are managed by portfolio managers who make investment decisions on their behalf. The portfolio managers send their orders to equity traders, who are responsible for selecting brokers to handle the transactions. During the Relevant Period, the Equity Trading Desk bought and sold more than 73 billion shares of equity securities (nearly 26 billion shares per year) with a total principal of more than $1.4 trillion (nearly $500 billion per year). Fidelity's equity trading generated more than $2.3 billion in commissions (over $800 million per year) paid to brokerage firms by Fidelity's clients, including the Fidelity Funds.

27. During the Relevant Period, FMR Co.'s equity trading operations employed nearly sixty people, including 33 traders (seven "primary" traders and 26 "sector" traders). Under DeSano's supervision, the traders had broad discretion to select brokerage firms to handle securities transactions. The primary limitation was that the traders could only select from a list of approximately 100 firms that had been formally approved by Fidelity.

Fidelity Executives and Traders Received Travel, Entertainment and Gifts from Brokers Seeking and Obtaining Securities Transactions for Fidelity's Clients

Overview

28. During the Relevant Period, two Fidelity senior executives (DeSano and Grenier) and ten Fidelity equity traders (Beran, Bruderman, Burnieika, Burns, Donovan, Driscoll, Harris, Horan, Pascucci and Smith) in aggregate accepted approximately $1.6 million worth of travel, entertainment and gifts from brokerage firms that sought and obtained orders to buy or sell securities on behalf of Fidelity's advisory clients. In addition, Lynch requested and received tickets to events from two equity traders, who obtained those tickets from brokers. Brokers took DeSano and/or certain traders, sometimes in groups, on more than thirty trips to such destinations as the Super Bowl, Las Vegas, Florida, the Caribbean, and Nantucket. These excursions sometimes included travel by private jet, lodging at fancy resorts, entry to exclusive golf courses, tickets to major sporting events, limousine service, expensive dinners, other amenities such as spa services, and, for certain traders, adult entertainment and illegal drugs. Bruderman even organized, and brokers paid for, his own extravagant, three-day bachelor party

in Miami, part of which DeSano attended and which cost brokers approximately $160,000.

29. One brokerage firm seeking and obtaining Fidelity's business, Jefferies & Co., Inc. ("Jefferies"), gave one of its brokers, Kevin W. Quinn, a travel and entertainment budget of $1.5 million per year. From that budget, Quinn entertained DeSano and several Fidelity traders, primarily by taking them on weekend excursions by private jet. For example, Quinn organized an annual trip he called the "Fall Classic," which included private jet travel, exclusive golf outings, lodging at expensive resorts, and other activities. During the November 2002 Fall Classic, for example, Quinn took DeSano, Bruderman and Harris by private jet to Las Vegas. Quinn provided accommodations at the Bellagio Hotel, several thousand dollars worth of golf merchandise, a private band, meals, golf, and entertainment at a nearby strip club. The group continued by private jet to Cabo San Lucas, Mexico, where Quinn provided accommodations in villas at the Esperanza Hotel, meals, more golf, and other entertainment. Jefferies paid approximately $200,000 for the expenses incurred on this trip.

30. Brokers other than Quinn also took Fidelity traders on a variety of trips. For example, each year during the Relevant Period, various brokers took several Fidelity traders to the Super Bowl. Brokers often provided the traders with travel by private jet, lodging at expensive hotels, admission to exclusive pre-game parties, tickets to the Super Bowl, golf greens fees, limousines, and other lavish entertainment. Even when they did not provide private jets, brokers often took traders on trips to Las Vegas and on golf weekends to Florida and other warm-weather locations, usually paying for the traders' lodging and meals and sometimes paying for other travel expenses such as commercial airfare.

31. On more than twenty other occasions, brokers made a private jet available for personal use by DeSano and/or certain traders (and at times, their families), without accompanying the Fidelity employee on the trip. Some of the private jet trips were short (such as weekend excursions to Nantucket), but others were quite long (such as flights to Florida and the Caribbean) and cost brokers up to $50,000 or more per trip.

32. Besides the trips, brokers provided to the Fidelity employees identified herein a total of approximately 900 tickets for some of the best seats to more than 270 sporting events, concerts, and other events, none of which the broker attended with the recipient. The events included the World Series, prominent tennis tournaments (Wimbledon, the U.S. Open, and the French Open), Broadway shows, concerts by nationally-known performers (such as the Rolling Stones and Bruce Springsteen), and dozens of sporting events, including baseball, basketball, football and hockey playoff and regular season games.

33. Most of the tickets were for premium or exclusive seats (such as luxury boxes or seats close to the stage, court or field). Brokers frequently provided multiple tickets to the event, so that the recipient could bring his family or friends. The tickets often cost the brokers hundreds of dollars each, and tickets to special events such as playoff games often cost them more than $1,000 each.

34. In addition, brokers sent certain traders expensive wine (including cases that cost from $1,000 to $7,700 each delivered straight to their homes), and other costly items such as entry to a racing school (over $5,000) and a humidor filled with cigars (approximately $1,300).

....

Violation of Section 17(e)(1) of the Investment Company Act

48. Under Section 17(e)(1) of the Investment Company Act, affiliated persons of a registered investment company, such as Fidelity executives and traders, are prohibited from accepting "from any source any compensation (other than a regular salary or wages from such registered company) for the purchase or sale of any property" of the investment company.

49. During the Relevant Period, two Fidelity executives (DeSano and Grenier) and ten Fidelity traders (Beran, Bruderman, Burnieika, Burns, Donovan, Driscoll, Harris, Horan, Pascucci and Smith) received compensation in violation of Section 17(e)(1) of the Investment Company Act in the form of travel, entertainment and gifts paid for by brokers who sought and obtained from the traders securities transactions for the Fidelity Funds. In addition, another Fidelity executive (Lynch) caused two Fidelity traders to receive compensation in violation of Section 17(e)(1) of the Investment Company Act.

....

Fidelity Failed to Seek Best Execution for its Clients' Securities Transactions Because the Traders Allowed the Receipt of Travel, Entertainment and Gifts from Brokers, and Familial and Romantic Relationships with Brokers, to Influence Their Selection of Brokers

The Traders Sent Securities Transactions to Brokers from Whom They Received Travel, Entertainment and Gifts

63. The receipt by ten equity traders, by DeSano (the traders' supervisor) and by Grenier (DeSano's supervisor) of travel, entertainment and gifts from brokers who sought and obtained securities transactions from Fidelity created a material conflict of interest that influenced the traders' selection of brokers to execute securities transactions on behalf of Fidelity's clients. In addition, Lynch (senior officer of FMR and FMR Co. and trustee of the Fidelity Funds) solicited and received tickets to sporting and entertainment events from two members of the Fidelity Equity Trading Desk, who in turn solicited those tickets from brokers who sought and obtained securities transactions from Fidelity, resulting in a material conflict of interest that influenced those traders' selection of brokers to execute securities transactions on behalf of Fidelity's clients.

....

Fidelity's Breach of Fiduciary Duty Resulted in the Substantial Possibility of Higher Execution Costs to its Advisory Clients

85. As set forth above, Fidelity breached its fiduciary duty to its advisory clients, including the Fidelity Funds, in several respects. First, as described herein Fidelity allowed

certain executives' and traders' receipt of travel, entertainment and gifts from brokers and certain traders' family or romantic relationships with brokers to influence its selection of brokers to handle its clients' transactions, resulting in the substantial possibility of higher execution costs to Fidelity's advisory clients. Second, it failed to disclose to its clients the conflict of interest arising from its executives' and traders' receipt of travel, entertainment and gifts from brokers and certain traders' family or romantic relationships with brokers. Finally, it made materially false and misleading statements in public disclosure documents and to the Fidelity Funds' trustees about the factors considered in the selection of brokers.

86. After being informed that some equity traders had accepted travel, entertainment and gifts from some brokers, the independent trustees of the Fidelity Funds retained a former federal judge, then an attorney at a prominent national law firm, to conduct an independent assessment of the adverse impact on the Fidelity Funds, if any, resulting from trades initiated by some Fidelity traders in recognition of improper travel, entertainment and gifts. The attorney was assisted by a team of economic consultants. The attorney submitted his report to the independent trustees in November 2006. (A copy of the final report is available on the SEC Web site.)

87. The report to the independent trustees concluded that "Fidelity clearly breached its duty to the Fidelity Funds to ensure that its traders acted solely for the benefit of the Funds." The report found that, while "it is impossible to 'prove' statistically that the traders' receipt of TEGG [travel, entertainment, gifts and gratuities] did or did not result in excessive execution costs for the Funds, ... both logic and contemporaneous evidence suggest that there is a substantial possibility that the traders' acceptance of TEGG could have resulted in higher execution costs for the Funds." The report further noted that "the question to be answered here is not whether the Funds were in fact harmed by the traders' receipt of TEGG, but how the Trustees should respond to the traders' breach of fiduciary duty that put the Funds in harm's way."

88. The report recommended that the independent trustees seek payment from Fidelity to the Fidelity Funds in the amount of $40.7 million for potential harm to the Fidelity Funds in order "to ensure with reasonable confidence that the Funds do not end up being undercompensated for the improper conduct that indisputably took place." Using the same methodology, the report recommended that a payment of approximately $10.2 million for potential harm be made to non-Fund advisory clients of FMR LLC's affiliates. In addition, the report recommended that Fidelity pay $8.2 million for reimbursement of Fund expenses incurred in connection with the independent trustees' investigation, and $4.5 million of interest through November 30, 2006.

89. During the course of his 14-month investigation, the independent trustees monitored the work of the attorney, heard reports from him and his economic consultants and heard presentations from Fidelity and its economic consultant. After reviewing the attorney's final report, on December 14, 2006, the independent trustees issued their report and conclusions. (A copy of the independent trustees' report and conclusions is available on the SEC Web site.)

90. The independent trustees' report accepted the attorney's final report. The independent trustees' report concluded that, "in spite of the absence of proof that the Funds experienced diminished execution quality as a result of traders' receipt of improper TEGG, the conduct at issue was serious, is worthy of redress and, as [the attorney] concluded, any uncertainty should be resolved in favor of the Funds." The independent trustees determined that it would be "appropriate" for Fidelity to pay the Fidelity Funds $42 million plus interest and expenses. [***]

* * *

The *Fidelity* matter evidences pervasive conduct to curry the good favor of money managers responsible for placing trades generating millions of dollars. As noted, the case led to a major rethinking of compliance policies with respect to travel, entertainment and gifts (or sometimes referred to as TEG) throughout the industry. One of the interesting aspects of the investigation was the inability to quantify the harm done to the affected funds in the Fidelity family. Does this mean that there was no harm? Is there any explanation of how the board arrived at the $42 million figure as reimbursement? Prior to news breaking of significant abuses in 2005, the Wall Street Journal had run a laudatory story concerning the efficiency of Fidelity's DeSano in reining in brokerage costs. *See* Kate Kelly & John Heckinger, *How Fidelity's Trading Chief Pinches Pennies on Wall Street*, Wall St. J. (electronic ed. Oct. 12, 2004). Could DeSano have been doing a great job for Fidelity and still receiving gifts from those who wished to do business with Fidelity? The answer may reveal different shades of gray.

United States v. Ostrander

999 F.2d 27 (2d Cir. 1993)

[**Text note:** *This is an appeal from criminal convictions obtained against a portfolio manager of a mutual fund who managed pension funds as well. The excerpt below explores one of Ostrander's convictions and the meaning of the critical concept of "compensation," a term found in Section 17(e)(1). A similar analysis is used by the court in discussing a related term "things of value" relevant to another of Ostrander's convictions, namely misconduct in managing pension funds. In this case, Ostrander seized an opportunity that was not available to her funds. The court's analysis seeks to reconciles Section 17(e)(1)'s prohibition with the concept of benefit of value.*]

Winter, Circuit Judge:

Patricia Ostrander was charged with two counts of accepting unlawful "compensation" or a "thing of value" from a source other than her employer in connection with the performance of her duties as a portfolio manager, *see* 15 U.S.C. § 80a-17(e), 18 U.S.C. § 1954, and one count of failing to report a personal investment to her employer, *see* 15 U.S.C. § 80a-17(j), 17 C.F.R. § 270.17j-1. After an eight-day trial, the jury convicted Ostrander on all three counts. Judge Owen sentenced her to concurrent terms of two months' imprisonment. We affirm.

BACKGROUND

Most of the pertinent events occurred during 1985 and 1986. When all permissible inferences are drawn in favor of the government, the evidence showed the following. Ostrander was a portfolio manager for Fidelity Management Research and Fidelity Management Trust Company (collectively "Fidelity"), investment advisors registered with the Securities and Exchange Commission, from 1970 to 1987. As a manager of Fidelity's funds, Ostrander purchased hundreds of millions of dollars worth of securities from Drexel Burnham Lambert, Inc. ("Drexel").

During early 1985, Kohlberg Kravis Roberts & Co. ("KKR"), a firm specializing in leveraged-buyouts ("LBOs"), decided upon an LBO of Storer Communications, Inc. ("Storer"). KKR hired Drexel to underwrite the securities for the financial transactions. The publicly offered securities included zero coupon bonds, debenture bonds paying fifteen percent per annum, and preferred stock. The preferred stock "paid-in-kind," meaning that it paid dividends of preferred stock rather than cash. It was the most junior of the securities and the most difficult of the securities to sell.

In addition to these publicly offered securities, 67,840,000 warrants were created. Their holders were entitled to exchange each warrant for one share of common stock in the Storer holding company at an exercise price of $2.05. The warrants represented thirty-two percent of the Storer holding company's common stock. They were described as "equity sweeteners" or "equity kickers" because they were designed to assist in the sale of the debentures and preferred stock. Drexel thus told KKR that they would be offered for private sale only to those institutions who had purchased zero coupon bonds, debentures, or preferred stock. This intent also was stated in the prospectus. Thereafter, the head of Drexel's High Yield Bond Department, Michael Milken, falsely indicated to KKR that the warrant price was too high and that potential bond or stock purchasers were "balking" at a price of fourteen cents per warrant. The warrants then were sold for seven cents each and offered only to a few select investors, including Drexel employees. Many of these Drexel employees kept the warrants in partnerships, one of which was MacPherson Investment Partners L.P.

On behalf of Fidelity, Ostrander attended a Drexel roadshow on October 28, 1985. She agreed to purchase for Fidelity Storer securities issued pursuant to the LBO. On December 5, 1985, KKR executed the Storer LBO. On behalf of Fidelity, Ostrander purchased $10 million of the zero coupon bonds, $26 million of the preferred stock (ten percent of the preferred stock offering), and $59 million of the fifteen percent senior subordinated debentures.

During late December 1985, Drexel's Michael Milken offered Ostrander the opportunity to invest her personal funds in MacPherson Investment Partners L.P., a partnership holding some of the Storer warrants. She was not alone. Sixty-five percent of MacPherson was owned by fiduciaries for institutions that purchased other securities issued in the Storer LBO. Ostrander invested $13,200 in MacPherson (paying approximately nine cents per warrant) during January 1986. When purchased, the warrants were highly speculative, and no witnesses were able to value them even as of late December 1985. KKR sold Storer's stations and cable systems at the top of the market in 1987 and 1988 and realized a profit that surpassed prior expectations. The value of Ostrander's $13,200 investment grew to roughly $750,000.

On October 11, 1991, Ostrander was indicted on three counts. Count One charged her with accepting unlawful compensation in connection with her purchases or sales of securities for registered investment companies that she managed as an affiliated person in violation of 15 U.S.C. § 80a-17(e).... Judge Owen sentenced Ostrander to concurrent terms of two months' imprisonment and to a $100,000 fine.

DISCUSSION

On appeal, Ostrander challenges the conviction on four grounds: (1) an erroneous jury charge stating that the opportunity to purchase the warrants was "a thing of value" even though the actual value of the warrants was not proven, (2) insufficient evidence, (3) erroneous evidentiary rulings, and (4) a claim that Count Three does not allege a crime.

Section 17(e) of the Investment Companies Act makes it unlawful for an "affiliated person" of a registered investment company, acting as its agent, to accept "from any source any compensation (other than a regular salary or wages from such registered company) for the purchase or sale" of property, including securities, by such investment company. 15 U.S.C. § 80a-17(e). Section 1954 of Title 18 prohibits administrators, officers, and employees of employee welfare benefit plans or employee pension benefit plans from receiving "any fee, kickback, commission, gift, loan, money, or thing of value because of or with intent to be influenced with respect to, any of [her] actions, decisions, or other duties relating to" the plan. 18 U.S.C. § 1954.

Ostrander challenges the trial court's instruction that the "opportunity" to purchase the warrants might constitute a violation of Section 17(e) and [the provision governing portfolio management of pension funds] even though there was no proof that the warrants were purchased at a price below their market value. The challenged instruction is set out in full in the margin.[1]

---

1. The challenged instruction stated:

Compensation is anything of benefit or anything of value, whether directly or indirectly received. It may take several forms and is not limited to money or tangible things with an identifiable commercial price tag....

To prove that compensation was received the government must prove that what Mrs. Ostrander received constituted something of value at the time she received it. You need not concern yourselves with finding a precise value in the marketplace. But you may look to the value the recipient here, Mrs. Ostrander, placed on the thing at the time she received it. In other words, the value of something can well be judged and set by the desire of that recipient to have the thing and depends upon that individual and all the circumstances surrounding its receipt.

On this issue you may consider whether or not the defendant herself attached a value to the opportunity to purchase MacPherson and, if she did, whether the value she placed on it was materially above the price being asked to pay for it. Here the defendant contends that MacPherson ... had all of the attendant risks and therefore was not a thing of value as defined. The government, on the other hand, contends that the mere opportunity to invest in MacPherson was itself compensation or a thing of value because the MacPherson interests were by their nature scarce or available to only a few individuals....

Specifically, Ostrander argues that Counts One and Two require proof of receipt of "compensation" or a "thing of value" for a price less than its market value. She argues that the judge charged on a faulty legal theory in stating that "you [jurors] need not concern yourself with finding [the warrants'] precise value in the marketplace." We disagree.

In *United States v. Deutsch,* 451 F.2d 98 (2d Cir.1971), *cert. denied,* 404 U.S. 1019 (1972), the case upon which Ostrander primarily relies, we upheld a trial court's definition of the term compensation as a "benefit or thing of value [including] being granted an opportunity to purchase securities at a discounted price." *Id.* at 114. Our holding that this kind of benefit was included among "things of value" did not limit that definition to securities sold at a discount. In fact, the panel stated that the instructions "were more favorable" to Deutsch than necessary. *Id.* at 115. "He was entitled to an instruction merely that the jury could not convict without being persuaded beyond a reasonable doubt that the agreement to buy [the note] was made with the knowledge that it constituted something of value." *Id.*

....

Without irony, she also contends that the warrants had no value and that the judge erred by instructing the jury to "look to the value [she] placed on the thing at the time she received it." We disagree. First, the warrants had value, if for no other reason because numerous investment professionals, including Drexel employees and fiduciaries for investors, were willing to, and did, purchase them. *See* [*United States v.*] *Williams,* 705 F.2d at 623 [(2d Cir. 1983)]. Indeed, the "they-had-no-value" argument rings particularly hollow from one who actually paid value and then made a profit of nearly $750,000 on an investment of $13,200. Second, the instruction was proper according to our decision in *Williams,* which upheld an instruction "to focus on the value that the defendants subjectively attached to the items received." *Id.*

The jury might easily have found that the warrants were compensation for her past and future purchases of securities from Drexel for Fidelity. She had purchased on behalf of Fidelity large blocs of the securities offered in the LBO, including ten percent of the preferred, the most difficult securities of the package to sell. We are unpersuaded by her argument that, because she purchased no Storer bonds after agreeing to buy the warrants, the jury could not as a matter of law find a connection to her purchase of the Storer securities or to potential future purchases from Drexel of securities in other companies.[2] [***]

It is sufficient that the government prove that the compensation at issue here, namely, the opportunity to invest in MacPherson, was connected to the sale of securities to the funds she managed or, in other words, that it was given and received by her in appreciation of past or in anticipation of future conduct by her.

2. Because we reject Ostrander's theory that the payment of a fair market value for the warrants was a defense, we need not consider her two related arguments: (i) she was deprived of presenting her defense that she did not know that the warrants may have been sold below their market value; if the law does not recognize a legal argument as a valid defense, the court has no duty to instruct the jury on that argument; (ii) the government lacked sufficient evidence that the warrants were sold below their actual value; that is not an element of the crime and thus need not be proven.

* * *

Having read *Ostrander*, explain the basis for the government's implicit view that Ostrander had received an unlawful benefit by virtue of her role as a portfolio manager. In other words, what is the risk that the government seeks to address by seeking to hold Ostrander criminally liable? Criminal punishment may seem severe in what might be viewed as an instance of victimless crime. However, Ostrander had the misfortune to be connected with probably the biggest white collar criminal investigation at the time involving Michael Milken. The investigation culminated not only in his criminal guilty plea, but also in the bankruptcy of a large old-line investment bank, Drexel Burnham and Lambert.

Notes and Applications

A brief note on soft dollars. Advisers frequently seek out arrangements with brokers in which a portion of the trading commissions generated by advisers in trading on behalf of advisory clients is rebated to the adviser by the broker-dealer in the form of credits that can later be used by the adviser to obtain research and brokerage services. The rebated credits are known as "soft dollars," and such arrangements are governed by a specific statutory safe harbor (Securities Exchange Act Section 28(e) and regulatory interpretations regarding the safe harbor's scope). Absent the safe harbor, such practices would arguably violate the adviser's common law fiduciary duties of best execution and accounting for profits or benefits earned by the adviser in acting on behalf of its client. Moreover, in the case of soft dollars obtained in trading on behalf of a registered investment company, the adviser would violate the literal terms of Company Action Section 17(e)(1) (i.e., the receipt of side benefits from a third party in connection with managing the RIC's assets). Even aside from the Company Act's prohibition on affiliate compensation, such arrangements would implicate Advisers Act Section 206(2)'s prohibition of undisclosed conflicts of interest, including the failure to obtain best execution or the receipt of side benefits in acting on behalf of the fiduciary's client.

Notwithstanding these concerns, soft dollar arrangements that comply with the conditions of the safe harbor found in Exchange Act Section 28(e) are permitted. The safe harbor provision was enacted in 1975 as part of the deregulation of brokerage commissions. Concerns arose that deregulating commissions would supplant the then-existing model of brokerage in which investment banks provided extensive research to customers as part of providing customers with brokerage services. One possibility was that brokers would compete for advisers' business solely in terms of quality of execution and size of commission. Section 28(e)'s safe harbor made clear that advisers could pay higher commissions in return for research and other brokerage services "reasonable in relation to [their] value" to the adviser's clients generally. The provision was drafted narrowly to exclude things like gifts and entertainment to advisers. Nevertheless, such arrangements are estimated to account for billions of dollars in commissions on the trillions of dollars in securities transactions of registered investment companies.

Over the years, the provision has been a source of interpretive problems in terms of what are legitimate research and brokerage services as opposed to benefits that might reduce an adviser's overhead or general costs of doing business and has triggered enforcement actions when an adviser's conduct did not come within the safe harbor. Essentially, soft dollars make a wide variety of bundled brokerage arrangements possible ranging from combined execution and proprietary research from the execution provider to execution coupled with credits to obtain third-party proprietary research (frequently effectuated through so-called client commission arrangements or "CCAs"). The Commission's current evolved guidance in this area is set forth in *Commission Guidance Regarding Client Commission Practices under Section 28(e) of the Securities Exchange Act of 1934*, Investment Company Act Release No. 54165, 71 FR 41978 (July 24, 2006). For contrasting views of soft dollar practices, compare D. Bruce Johnsen, *The SEC's 2006 Soft Dollar Guidance: Law and Economics*, 30 Cardozo L. Rev. 1545 (2009) (critical of SEC attempts to restrict such practices), with John C. Bogle, *The End of "Soft Dollars,"* 65 No. 2 Fin. Anal. J. 48 (2009) (advocating their elimination).

Effective 2018, the European Union has adopted a far more stringent approach to such arrangements as part of the revised Markets in Financial Instruments Directive (colloquially referred to as MiFID II). *See* Commission Delegated Directive of Apr. 7, 2015 supplementing Directive 2014/65/EU with regard to the *Safeguarding of Financial Instruments and Funds Belonging to Clients, Product Governance Obligations and the Rules Applicable to the Provision or Reception of Fees, Commissions or Any Monetary or Non-Monetary Benefits*, Recital 24, art. 21(1), C (2016) 2031 final (July 4, 2016).

14.6 The Affiliated Underwriting Prohibition under Section 10 and Other Aspects of Section 17

There is another Company Act affiliated transaction prohibition found in Section 10 instead of Section 17. Section 10(f) prohibits a fund from purchasing securities in an offering if any member of the underwriting syndicate during the offering is affiliated with a syndicate member. Historically, the affiliated underwriting prohibition had a compelling basis. It flowed directly from Congressional concerns that underwriters would use fund portfolios as dumping grounds for selling securities in offerings that proved difficult to place in the broader market. Nevertheless, Congress recognized that a strict prohibition on purchases of all offerings involving an affiliated principal underwriter might foreclose funds from some investment opportunities. Accordingly, the SEC was given the power to exempt transactions from the affiliated underwriting prohibition. Keeping in mind the overriding policy objectives of prohibiting dumping practices, the SEC adopted Rule 10f-3 as an exemptive rule that permits a fund to purchase securities in an affiliated underwriting transaction where the purchases meet conditions suggesting that the success of the offering is not dependent on the fund's participation as a purchaser. Today, the affiliated underwriting prohibition is not a significant hurdle for the vast majority of public or municipal security offerings.

Nevertheless, compliance issues can arise for multi-adviser and multi-line financial service firms, especially with respect to purchases in foreign securities offerings where existing exemptions may not extend.

Section 17 also addresses other transactions raising conflict of interest issues with affiliates. Most significantly, Section 17 deals with custodial arrangements relating to investment company securities, an issue that is touched on in this text in connection with requirements applicable to advisers generally under the Advisers Act. The Company Act adds additional requirements regarding custody of assets of RICs. In addition, Section 17 contains a broad grant of rulemaking authority that enables the SEC to adopt rules and regulations relating to codes of ethics and fraudulent, deceptive or manipulative practices by affiliated persons of the investment adviser or principal underwriter in connection with transactions involving securities held by or to be acquired by registered investment companies. Chapter 15 discusses the SEC's invocation of this rulemaking authority to directly regulate the personal trading activities of funds' advisory personnel as well as the policies and procedures of funds in addressing personal trading activities.

Chapter 15

Ethics and Compliance for Funds and Advisers

Key Ideas: Congress has empowered the SEC to adopt regulations that affirmatively require investment companies and investment advisers to establish a robust infrastructure of compliance and ethics policies and procedures. Regulatory requirements have become increasingly stringent over the last several decades, and it is possible to say that compliance policies and procedures and their implementation touch every aspect of fund operations and the activities of advisory firms.

In 1970, Congress authorized the SEC to adopt rules regulating personal securities trading of portfolio managers of registered investment companies and other affiliated fund service provider personnel which the SEC finally did in 1980 with the adoption of Company Act Rule 17j-1. Among its requirements, the rule required funds to adopt codes of ethics to address personal securities trading and trade reporting by so-called "access" persons of the fund. Fund codes of ethics are administered by the fund under the guidance and oversight of fund trustees. Some years later, the SEC adopted a parallel provision under the Advisers Act, Rule 204A-1, which was designed to accomplish similar objectives more broadly among advisers and not merely advisers advising registered investment companies.

Over time, many funds and advisers widely embraced the use of compliance policies and procedures as a best practice in addition to codes of ethics. However, in 2004, in the face of a massive scandal in the fund industry, the SEC adopted comprehensive compliance requirements for advisers and funds, Advisers Act Rules 206(4)-7 and Company Act Rule 38(a)-1, respectively. The compliance rules require advisers, funds and their service providers to adopt and administer written policies and procedures designed to ensure compliance with federal securities law administered by chief compliance officers ("CCO's"). As a result, the CCO function has assumed great importance in the asset management industry, not to mention the financial services industry generally. A fund's board must exercise oversight of compliance at the fund itself, and engage in a process to evaluate the compliance capabilities of key service providers to the fund. The various affirmative obligations can lead to enforcement liability for funds and advisers when abusive, or even problematic, conduct goes undetected or is not dealt with proactively.

Chapter Contents

15.1 Introduction

As noted in earlier chapters, the Company Act was drafted to provide protections for regulated investment companies and their shareholders from the abuses highlighted in the studies and reports which led up to the promulgation of the Act. Amendments and rulemaking since 1940 have added to these protections and a better understanding of the risks of abuse, but a key challenge remains: "Who is best situated to guard against the abuses and enforce needed protections?" At one level, it's the regulators, primarily the SEC and FINRA. But the role of regulators is invariably after-the-fact and periodic at best. In reality, it is the duty of the board of trustees, management, and chief compliance officers to set the tone and provide critical continuing day-to-day oversight of fund and adviser operations.

Several chapters of this textbook have already discussed key areas implicating compliance duties. Chapters 7, 8, and 9 dealt with conduct and disclosures issues affecting advisers, including fund advisers, and chapters 13, 14, and 16 deal with the issues of disclosure, prohibited affiliate transactions, and pricing, all of which raise fund compliance concerns. This chapter narrows the focus to ethics and compliance issues, i.e., on how and what funds and advisers need to do proactively to curb and address potentially abusive conduct. The key regulatory steps in this have been to mandate creation of a compliance infrastructure involving written policies and procedures and to require the designation of a chief compliance officer to maintain, enforce, and evaluate those policies internally. The chapter begins with codes of ethics specifically designed to address personal securities trading by fund and adviser personnel. It then turns to the more encompassing topic of compliance policies and procedures and the role of compliance officers in developing, maintaining, and enforcing them. Finally, the chapter discusses the important duties that have been placed on fund boards to oversee the compliance programs.

15.2 Codes of Ethics and Personal Securities Trading Policies

Imagine the temptation of the portfolio manager who has developed a "hot" new investment theme: how can she or he profit from it personally when also investing for clients and funds? Of course, it is always possible the both the fund and the individual can mutually profit without interfering with each other. However, in some cases, there is bound to be a tension in terms of timing (e.g., does the person trade for the fund first and his own account second?) or in terms of a limited opportunity that cannot be mutually shared. Fund portfolio managers, advisers, and their staff face this ethical challenge daily. Funds, as clients, face this issue from another perspective: are their service providers, most notably, the adviser and portfolio managers, taking advantage of fund opportunities either by means of appropriating limited opportunities or in front running a fund's investment trading decisions?

By now, conflicts of interest should be a familiar theme to the reader. Personal trading by advisory personnel raises the specter of potential conflicts of interest. Personal trading is a particularly nettlesome area, because in many circumstances it may not be problematic for portfolio managers and other personnel of a fund, adviser, or service provider, while at other times it will be. For an investment adviser or portfolio manager, it is almost natural that the investment information and ideas that are relevant in managing a client's portfolio would also be relevant to the adviser or manager's personal trading decisions. Although not prohibited, personal trading is regulated both by internal policies and procedures, as well as by law.

Congress enacted Section 17(j) of the Company Act specifically to provide the SEC the power to address concerns about personal trading and investing by fund insiders in the portfolio securities of the fund. Concerns were first voiced regarding such trading activities in the 1960s. In 1980, after lengthy consideration and some controversy, the SEC adopted Rule 17j-1 to prohibit "fraudulent, deceptive or manipulative acts" by fund personnel and their advisers and principal underwriters in connection with their personal trading activities with respect to securities held or to be acquired by the fund. The SEC recognized that fund organizations had varying needs and operations. As a result, the final rule took a measured and flexible approach toward regulation.

15.2.1 Section 17(j) and Rule 17j-1: Codes of Ethics for Funds

Section 17(j) makes it unlawful for funds and certain affiliated persons of the funds to engage in activities addressed in rules that the SEC adopts to regulate personal investment activities of fund insiders. Under the current version of Rule 17j-1, regulated investment companies (RICs) and advisers are required to adopt codes of ethics and personal investment trading policies for their personnel. Such policies are generally referred collectively as "codes of ethics," although their coverage may be broader than an attempt to discourage opportunistic trading as required by Rule 17j-1. For example, codes may also govern other aspects of ethical behavior, and may address other conflicts of interest. However, investment activities of fund personnel is the core legally mandated principle for codes of ethics.

Rule 17j-1 imposes four key requirements: every RIC and each of its investment advisers and its principal underwriter must adopt:

- A written code of ethics approved by the fund's board designed to prevent their "access persons" from engaging in fraudulent, deceptive, or manipulative conduct "in connection with the purchase or sale, directly or indirectly by the person of a security held or to be acquired by the Fund";
- A recordkeeping and reporting scheme with respect to personal trading of access persons;
- Procedures reasonably designed to prevent violations of each respective code; and
- Certification requirements pursuant to which each organization certifies to the fund board that the codes are in place.

The rule contains several key definitions. The important definition of *access persons* describes the persons to whom the fund's code must apply and who are subject to reporting obligations. In general terms, the definition extends to fund directors, officers, and personnel who have information about fund portfolio transactions; to investment adviser directors, officers, partners and investment advisory staff; and to principal underwriter directors, officers, and partners who have information about fund portfolio transactions. The definition is described in greater detail in the readings below and, of course, in the rule.

The rule applies to trading in *covered securities*, which relates generally only to securities as defined under the Company Act. The rule's requirements do not extend to money market securities and instruments nor to shares of open-end funds. More importantly, there is a timing limitation relevant to what constitutes covered securities: securities are covered if they are held by the fund or have been or are under consideration for purchase within the last 15 days. That means, for example, a personal securities transaction in a stock is covered if the stock was purchased by the fund three days ago.

The rule has several operational and administrative requirements, among them requirements for adoption and periodic review of the code of ethics; disclosure of the code and its provisions; preclearance, monitoring, and reporting of securities transactions; and resolving and reporting violations of the code of ethics.

In 1999, the SEC significantly amended Rule 17j-1 for the first time. Notably, the SEC continued to believe that a flat prohibition on personal trading activities of fund and adviser personnel was not warranted. However, the rule was significantly tightened in other respects.

Personal Investment Activities of Investment Company Personnel

Investment Company Act Release No. 23958 (Aug. 27, 1999)

[**Textbook note:** *As explained in the SEC's adopting release, the amendments to Rule 17j-1 required enhanced oversight by funds of personal trading activities of fund access persons. In addition to expanding recordkeeping and reporting obligations, the amendments for the first time affirmatively required the fund board's involvement in administering the code of ethics. Moreover, for the first time, the SEC imposed pre-clearance requirements on certain types of trading activities. The latter recommendation addressed conduct which the industry's influential trade industry association, the Investment Company Institute, had been identified as problematic by its member funds.*]

[***] I. Executive Summary

The Commission is adopting amendments to rule 17j-1 under the Investment Company Act. Rule 17j-1 addresses conflicts of interest between registered investment company ("fund") personnel (such as portfolio managers) and their funds that may arise when these persons buy or sell securities for their own accounts ("personal investment activities").

Rule 17j-1 prohibits fraudulent, deceptive or manipulative acts by fund personnel in connection with their personal transactions in securities held or to be acquired by the fund. The rule also contains requirements that are designed to prevent fraud, including (i) requiring funds and their investment advisers and principal underwriters (collectively, "rule 17j-1 organizations") to adopt a code of ethics ("code") containing provisions reasonably necessary to prevent fraudulent, deceptive or manipulative acts and (ii) requiring certain persons to report their personal securities transactions to their rule 17j-1 organization.

The amendments to rule 17j-1 are designed to improve the regulation of personal investment activities in two respects. First, the amendments enhance fund directors' oversight of personal investment activities by requiring that a fund's board, including a majority of independent directors on the board, approve the fund's code and the code of any investment adviser or principal underwriter of the fund. Second, the amendments assist the management of rule 17j-1 organizations in monitoring compliance with the rule. The amendments require initial and annual holdings reports from access persons, as well as review of reports on personal trading by compliance personnel. The amendments also require the fund or its investment adviser to review and preapprove any investment in an initial public offering ("IPO") or a limited offering (such as a private placement) by personnel who participate in managing the fund's portfolio ("investment personnel"). In addition, amendments to the disclosure forms under the Securities Act of 1933 and the Investment Company Act will make information about a rule 17j-1 organization's policies concerning personal investment activities available to the public in the fund's registration statement.

II. Background

Section 17(j) of the Investment Company Act prohibits any affiliated person of a rule 17j-1 organization from engaging in fraudulent trading activities that violate rules adopted by the Commission.[2] Section 17(j) authorizes the Commission to adopt rules to define or prevent fraudulent activities. Under this authority, the Commission adopted rule 17j-1 in 1980. Rule 17j-1 prohibits fund personnel from engaging in fraud in connection with personal transactions in securities held or to be acquired by the fund. In addition, the rule requires every rule 17j-1 organization to adopt a code of ethics designed to prevent "access persons"[5] from engaging in fraud, and requires that the organization use reasonable diligence and institute procedures reasonably necessary to prevent violations of its code of ethics. The rule also requires an access person to report personal securities transactions to his or her rule 17j-1 organization at least quarterly....

III. Discussion

A. Codes of Ethics

Codes of ethics are an important part of a rule 17j-1 organization's efforts to prevent fraud resulting from personal trading in securities by its employees. When the Commission adopted rule 17j-1 in 1980, it stated that the "introduction and tailoring of ethical restraints on the behavior of persons associated with an investment company can best be left in the first instance to the directors of the investment company." Comments on the rule proposals confirmed that a "one size fits all" approach to these codes would not be more effective in preventing fraudulent personal trading practices, and would be unnecessarily burdensome, particularly for smaller rule 17j-1 organizations.

Although rule 17j-1 does not specify the provisions that a code of ethics must contain, funds can take several steps to anticipate and avoid problems resulting from conflicts of interest.

....

2. An "affiliated person" of a rule 17j-1 organization includes: (i) any officer, director, partner, copartner, or employee of the rule 17j-1 organization? (ii) any person directly or indirectly controlling, controlled by, or under common control with the rule 17j-1 organization? (iii) any person owning five percent of the rule 17j-1 organization's voting securities? and (iv) any person in which the rule 17j-1 organization owns five percent or more of the voting securities.

5. Rule 17j-1 defines "access person" to include: (i) any director, officer, or general partner of a fund or of a fund's investment adviser, or any employee of a fund or of a fund's investment adviser who, in connection with his or her regular functions or duties, participates in the selection of a fund's portfolio securities or who has access to information regarding a fund's future purchases or sales of portfolio securities? or (ii) any director, officer, or general partner of a principal underwriter who, in the ordinary course of business, makes, participates in or obtains information regarding, the purchase or sale of securities for the fund for which the principal underwriter acts, or whose functions or duties in the ordinary course of business relate to the making of any recommendation to the fund regarding the purchase or sale of securities. Amended rule 17j-1(a)(1). The term "principal underwriter" is defined in section 2(a)(29) of the Act.

B. Role of Fund Boards

1. Approval of Code of Ethics

Rule 17j-1 requires each rule 17j-1 organization to adopt a code of ethics, but does not currently specify a role for a fund's board of directors with respect to the codes. We proposed that a majority of a fund's board, including a majority of independent directors, be required to approve the fund's code and review the codes of any investment adviser or principal underwriter to the fund.

Commenters generally supported increasing board oversight of codes of ethics, and we are adopting the provision, with certain modifications. As suggested by one commenter, the amended rule requires that instead of *reviewing* the code of an investment adviser and principal underwriter, the board must *approve* the code and any material changes. In addition, the Commission is clarifying that the board must approve the code when the fund initially engages the investment adviser or principal underwriter (rather than upon each contract renewal). If an investment adviser or principal underwriter makes a material change to its code of ethics, the board has six months in which to approve the material change. Under amended rule 17j-1, a fund's board must base its approval of a code of ethics, or a material change to a code of ethics, upon a determination that the code contains provisions reasonably necessary to prevent access persons from violating the antifraud provision of the rule. [21] ... [W]e continue to believe that a basic issue for each board of directors is whether the code should permit personal trading by personnel of a rule 17j-1 organization. This issue is relevant for each organization covered by the rule and is too important for a board to ignore.

2. Annual Issues and Certification Report

The board's involvement in the personal investment policies applicable to the fund should not end after the board's initial approval of a code. Continued oversight of the personal investment policies applicable to the fund is in the interest of shareholders because it subjects these policies to independent, objective analysis by the "watchdog" for fund shareholders. Therefore, we are adopting, as proposed, amendments that require each rule 17j-1 organization to report periodically to the board on issues raised under its code of ethics. Under the amended rule, the management of a rule 17j-1 organization, at least once a year, must provide the fund's board a written report that (i) describes issues that arose during the previous year under the code of ethics or procedures applicable to the rule 17j-1 organization, including, but not limited to, information about material code or procedure violations and sanctions imposed in re-

---

21. The codes of ethics of some rule 17j-1 organizations only recite general principles, and the procedures (rather than the codes) of these organizations contain the specific restrictions, prohibitions, or requirements concerning an access person's personal investment activities. Under amended rule 17j-1, the board must approve a code based on its determination that the *code* contains provisions reasonably necessary to prevent access persons from violating the antifraud provisions of the rule. If a board can make this determination only if it takes into consideration the procedures, then the code must incorporate, or the board must explicitly approve, those procedures, as well as any subsequent material changes to those procedures.

sponse to those material violations and (ii) certifies to the fund's board that the rule 17j-1 organization has adopted procedures reasonably necessary to prevent its access persons from violating its code of ethics.

The issues and certification report is designed to give the board an opportunity to evaluate the effectiveness of codes of ethics and procedures and the manner in which they have been implemented. We expect a fund's board to examine the report carefully, and thus the amended rule requires that the board "consider" the report. Upon receipt and consideration of a report, a fund board may determine that it is necessary to amend the fund's code or procedures, or to suggest to an investment adviser or principal underwriter that it consider amending its code or procedures....

D. Preapproval of Investments in IPOs and Private Placements

... Most individuals rarely have a chance to invest in IPOs, particularly "hot issue" IPOs, shares of which usually are reserved for institutional investors, or wealthy individual customers with large brokerage accounts. As the ICI Advisory Group Report commented, the opportunity for investment personnel to purchase IPO shares presents a "clear potential for conflict between the interests of the individual and the fund." The purchase of IPO shares by investment personnel may raise questions as to whether the investment is an undisclosed reward for directing fund business to the underwriter or issuer,[53] whether the individual is misappropriating an opportunity that should have been offered to the fund,[54] and whether the individual's future investment decisions for the fund will be based solely on the best interests of the fund's shareholders.

Purchases by investment personnel of securities in private placements or other limited offerings ("private placements") may raise similar conflicts because the opportunity to invest in the private placement may be a reward for past business deals. In some cases, the conflict may occur later when the issuer of the privately placed security is considering making a public offering.[57]

To ensure that the potential conflicts associated with these investments can be addressed before they arise, the amendments we are adopting require that investment

53. See, e.g., U.S. v. Ostrander, 999 F.2d 27 (2d Cir. 1993) (affirming conviction of portfolio manager, who purchased privately offered warrants of company whose securities she acquired for the fund, for accepting unlawful compensation for fund's purchase of property in violation of the Investment Company Act).

54. See, e.g., In the Matter of Ronald V. Speaker and Janus Capital Corporation, Investment Company Act Release No. 22461 (Jan. 13, 1997) (investment adviser made $16,000 profit on same day purchase and sale of debentures in which fund could have invested, and failed to disclose transactions to the fund or obtain prior consent of the fund (or a disinterested employee authorized to waive the opportunity on the fund's behalf)).

57. A fund portfolio manager who has invested in the private placement may have an opportunity to increase the value of his or her investment by causing the fund to invest in the public offering and contribute to its success. See ICI Advisory Group Report, supra note 9, at 33-34 (citing John Accola, Firms, Fund Exec Ties "Normal," Rocky Mountain News, Jan. 18, 1994, at 38A).

personnel obtain approval from their fund or adviser before directly or indirectly acquiring any beneficial ownership in securities in an IPO or private placement. The amendments do not prohibit these investments because we recognize that there may be situations in which investment in these offerings does not raise the types of conflicts that the rule is designed to address. In some circumstances, an investment opportunity clearly may be available to investment personnel for reasons other than the individual's position with the fund. The fund or adviser therefore could determine that, based on the particular nature of the offering[59] or the particular facts of the purchase,[60] the investment would create no material conflict. In other circumstances, the investment may raise only potential conflicts from which the fund and its investors can be protected. Because the portfolio manager's fund or investment adviser is in the best position to evaluate whether an investment in an IPO or limited offering creates or may create a conflict of interest, the amendments permit that organization to protect the fund by determining whether to approve the proposed investment.

The Commission expects that a fund or investment adviser, in fulfilling its preclearance responsibilities, will assign appropriate compliance personnel to carefully review each request for approval.[62] We also expect that the fund or adviser will use its judgment to distinguish between serious conflicts that must be avoided and those less serious conflicts that the organization can monitor and manage consistent with the protection of the fund and its investors.[63] In addition, in order to further encourage careful monitoring of potential conflicts, amended rule 17j-1 requires funds and advisers to retain a record of the approval of, and rationale supporting, any direct or indirect acquisition by investment personnel of a beneficial interest in securities in an IPO or private placement. These records also should assist compliance personnel and Commission staff in detecting illegal trading activities by fund personnel.

---

59. A portfolio manager, for example, may have an opportunity to invest in an IPO of the fund adviser as a result of his or her service as an employee of the adviser, in an IPO of a mutual insurance company as a result of his or her ownership of a life insurance policy, or in an IPO of a spinoff company as a result of his or her ownership of stock in the company that spins off the issuer. In each case (and other similar cases), a fund or adviser could determine that the portfolio manager's access to the IPO did not result from his or her position with the fund.

60. For example, a portfolio manager's purchase of privately offered securities issued by a small family business that is unlikely to make a public offering in the future would likely not raise a material conflict if the portfolio manager's fund is prohibited from investing in private placements. Similarly, an investment in an IPO in which all shares are allocated to investors on a non-discriminatory basis may not raise a material conflict....

62. We expect that funds and advisers will review these proposed investments on a case-by-case basis, except for those circumstances in which advance general approval may be appropriate because it is clear that conflicts are very unlikely to arise due to the nature of the opportunity for investing in the IPO or private placement. See supra text accompanying notes 59-60. The fund's inability to invest in the securities would not be a basis for concluding generally that the conflicts are unlikely to arise. See text accompanying note 53 supra.

63. Some conflicts of interest must be reported to the fund's board of directors under rule 17j-1. See supra note 25; amended rule 17j-1(c)(2)(ii) (annual issues and certification report requirement).

The application of the preclearance provision is limited to certain "investment personnel." The term is defined in rule 17j-1 to include portfolio managers and other employees of the fund or its investment adviser who participate in making investment recommendations to the fund, and persons in a control relationship to the fund who obtain information about investment recommendations made to the fund. These persons are involved in investment decisions for the fund and thus have significant opportunities to influence fund decisions that may benefit them personally. [***]

* * *

Notes and Applications

1. *Analyzing Rule 17j-1 in practice: Access Persons.* One of the challenges in regulating personal securities transactions and applying codes of ethics, is to whom should they apply? Rule 17j-1 provides a complex definition for access person. The definition of access person is qualified but encompasses a range of people. It is fundamentally directed towards people who know something about or have the ability to control the fund's investments. There is a distinction in the rule between reporting requirements applicable to access persons of advisers versus those for principal underwriters. Why do you think lesser requirements apply to the access persons of principal underwriters?

2. *Use of code of ethics vs. a prohibition of personal portfolio trading.* A key feature of Rule 17j-1 is that the SEC has not sought to prohibit personal portfolio trading. Why not? Wouldn't it be simpler to just ban all trading of advisory personnel? Consider the implications of such a ban. One implication is that RIC portfolio managers might change jobs to be free of strict prohibitions on personal trading, for example, move to unregistered funds such as hedge funds. Why should registered funds care?

3. *Analyzing Rule 17j-1 in practice: Preclearance.* A practical application of Rule 17j-1 is the "preclearance requirement." Put simply, preclearance requires affected individuals to seek pre-approval of their proposed personal securities transactions. Funds and advisers may have a variety of lists of securities in which access persons may not trade, which are generally securities which the fund is trading or considering trading or securities with respect to which it has inside information. These lists are often called "black lists" or "gray lists." When a request for preclearance is made, the compliance staff checks the appropriate list to determine whether to permit a trade. If a security is on the black list, then personal trading of it is generally denied, although some funds have *de minimis* exceptions if it's clear that a trade would have no impact on the security's price, e.g., buying 100 shares of IBM which has millions of shares outstanding. What are the implications for portfolio analysts or managers: do they like to have to preclear their trades? The Rule itself requires preclearance only in a limited number of circumstances. Why were those situations singled out? Moreover, while the Rule only requires mandatory preclearance in a limited number of situations, firms remain free to impose broader preclearance requirements. What are the pros and cons of imposing preclearance requirements that cover a broader range of securities in a firm's code of ethics?

* * *

Rule 17j-1 contains additional provisions that may subject any affiliated person of the fund (i.e., that reach beyond access persons) to liability for fraudulent or deceptive conduct in connection with personal trading with respect to securities held or to be acquired by the fund, even absent any violation of the fund's code of ethics.

In the Matter of Ronald V. Speaker

Investment Company Act Release No. 22461 (Jan. 13, 1997)

[**Textbook note:** *The* Speaker *case illustrates this latter aspect of Rule 17j-1 and clearly shows that compliance with a code of ethics alone does not insulate affiliated persons from all forms of potential liability in connection with personal trading activities. In this case, the fund adviser and fund group had codes of ethics and compliance policies, and there was no allegation that Speaker's conduct violated the applicable code of ethics. Note that Janus Capital afforded its portfolio managers some convenient trading privileges with respect to their personal trading accounts.*]

[***] A. The Respondents

Since 1978, Janus [Capital Corporation] has been registered with the Commission as an investment adviser ... pursuant to Section 203(c) of the Advisers Act. Janus has its headquarters in Denver, Colorado.

Janus acts as an investment adviser to several registered mutual funds.

Speaker is an employee of Janus and is an executive vice-president of a registered mutual fund ("the fund") for which Janus is the investment adviser. He has been the portfolio manager for the fund since December 1991 and is responsible for making investment decisions for the fund, including the purchase and sale of securities. At the time of the trades at issue the fund's prospectus generally disclosed that portfolio managers such as Speaker may engage in personal trading of securities.

B. Speaker's Trading Activities

On January 12, 1993, Speaker, in his capacity as the portfolio manager for the fund, was contacted by an institutional salesman for a broker-dealer who offered the opportunity to purchase Time Warner 9 1/8% Debentures due 2013 (debentures) at a certain offering price. Speaker rejected the offer on behalf of the fund. Later that day he learned of a bid from another broker-dealer for the debentures at a price higher than the price he was previously offered. This opportunity to profit by buying and shortly thereafter selling the debentures was one of limited availability.

While purchasing and selling the same securities on the same day would have been a deviation from the fund's normal method of investing, the fund was legally and financially able to take advantage of this opportunity. Without disclosing his conflict of interest to, and obtaining the prior consent of the fund (or a disinterested Janus employee authorized to waive this opportunity on the fund's behalf), Speaker personally purchased $10 million of the debentures in two transactions and shortly thereafter sold the debentures that same day for a total profit of $16,000.

Speaker purchased and sold the debentures through a private trading account that he maintained through Janus at a Denver bank. Speaker was able to purchase the $10 million of debentures because Janus had authorized him to use its institutional clearing account for the settlement of his personal trades which was administered by the Denver bank on a Delivery versus Payment or Receipt versus Payment basis. Speaker then paid for his purchases of the $10 million of debentures with proceeds from his offsetting sales.

C. Speaker's Violations of the Securities Laws

Speaker as the portfolio manager for the fund is a fiduciary. Investment advisers and their associated persons, as fiduciaries, are under the highest obligation to avoid conflicts of interest with their clients by disclosing personal trading practices that may affect their recommendations. *Securities and Exchange Commission v. Capital Gains Research Bureau, Inc.*, 375 U.S. 180, 194-197 (1963). Portfolio managers generally may not engage in personal trading that presents a conflict with the interests of their clients absent full disclosure and consent from the clients. See, Prevention of Certain Unlawful Activities, IC Act Rel. No. 11421 (October 31, 1980) (adopting Rule 17j-1 under the provisions of Section 17(j) of the IC Act).... An investor seeking the advice of a registered investment adviser must ... be permitted to evaluate such overlapping motivations, through appropriate disclosure, in deciding whether an adviser is serving two masters or only one, especially ... if one of the masters happens to be economic self-interest. *United States v. Mississippi Valley Co.*, 364 U.S. 520, 549 (1961); ... *Capital Gains*, 375 U.S. at 196.

....

Speaker breached his fiduciary duty to the fund by taking the investment opportunity in the debentures without disclosing the opportunity to, and obtaining the prior consent of the fund (or a disinterested Janus employee authorized to waive this opportunity on the fund's behalf). Speaker thereby willfully violated Sections 206(1) and (2) of the Advisers Act; Section 17(j) of the IC Act and Rule 17j-1(a) thereunder;[2] Section 10(b) and Rule 10b-5 thereunder of the Exchange Act.

2. As an affiliated person of Janus, the investment adviser to the fund which was a portfolio of a registered investment company, Speaker was prohibited by Rule 17j-1(a) from engaging in certain conduct in connection with his purchase or sale of any "security held or to be acquired" by the fund. Rule 17j-1(e)(6) defines a "security held or to be acquired" by a registered investment company as including any security which, within the most recent 15 days, "is being or has been considered by such company or its investment adviser for purchase by such company" (emphasis added). Speaker rejected the offer to acquire the debentures for the fund and thereby "considered" acquiring them for the fund before purchasing them for himself. His later purchase within 15 days of "considering" the purchase for the fund without disclosing the trades to the fund and obtaining the prior consent of the fund, or of a disinterested Janus employee authorized to waive this opportunity on the fund's behalf violated Section 17(j)of the IC Act and Rule 17j-1(a) thereunder.

D. Janus' Supervision of Speaker

At the time of Speaker's trades Janus required its employees, including Speaker, to provide it with complete information regarding their personal trades. After Speaker's trades occurred they were reviewed by Janus' Compliance Department primarily for conflicts with trading activity by the fund. After reviewing Speaker's trades Janus took no further action. Janus had no mechanism for disclosing the trades to the fund and obtaining the prior consent of the fund, or of a disinterested Janus employee authorized to waive this opportunity on the fund's behalf. [***]

* * *

Notes and Applications

1. *Is it fraud?* The Section 206(2) violation requires merely a finding of an undisclosed conflict of interest, which seems beyond dispute under the facts presented. However, the SEC also found violations of fraud requirements—Rule 206(1) of the Advisers Act and Section 10(b) and Rule 10b-5 of the Exchange Act—and such violations require scienter (i.e., a culpable state of mind on the part of the respondent). Arguably, Speaker appears harshly punished for conduct that does not appear invidious. After all, in all likelihood, no disinterested Janus officer would have approved a one-off day-trade by the fund of the sort offered to Speaker. Thus, Speaker's view in that regard was probably perfectly valid. In addition, Speaker disclosed his trading in a timely fashion after it was completed. Nevertheless, the SEC was deeply disturbed by Speaker's conduct and its implications in other contexts. If Janus was not hurt by Speaker's conduct, in what sense were Speaker's actions arguably fraudulent?

2. *Ostrander case—Failure to comply with firm's code of ethics reporting requirements.* The 1993 Appeals Court decision in the *Ostrander* case included in Chapter 14 highlighted the fact that Rule 17j-1 could be enforced criminally. Recall that Ostrander, a portfolio manager for Fidelity mutual funds, was convicted of violating Section 17(e) of the Company Act based on her receipt of illegal compensation in connection with a Fidelity fund investment in certain securities. In addition, however, Ostrander failed to report the securities transactions, as required, under Fidelity's existing code of ethics and its reporting requirements. The court explained, "Any payment to a portfolio manager intended to induce the purchase of a firm's securities on behalf of an investment company easily qualifies as a 'fraudulent, deceptive or manipulative' act 'in connection with' the investment company's acquisition of securities, whether or not the payment consists of an opportunity to purchase securities in a different firm.... The regulation in question [Rule 17j-1], which requires portfolio managers to report to their companies their interests in various securities, is a prophylactic measure reasonably related to the enforcement of Section 17(j).... Ostrander's failure to report her interest in MacPherson [the stock which generated a huge profit for her] was thus [a violation of the rule]."

15.2.2 Rule 204A-1: Codes of Ethics for Advisers

In 2004, the SEC extended code of ethics requirements to investment advisers in the wake of major industry scandals. Of course, advisers managing registered funds were already covered by Rule 17j-1's provisions and requirements as to those funds. However, that left a large group of advisers who didn't advise registered funds, including those who managed only separately managed accounts and hedge funds. Reflecting on-going turmoil in the industry, the SEC adopted Rule 204A-1 shortly after adopting rules covering compliance policies and procedures at funds and investment advisers. The rule was intended to be the Advisers Act version of Rule 17j-1, albeit adapted to the varied businesses and circumstances of advisers. Rule 17j-1 was also updated at that time to conform it to the changes made by Rule 204A-1.

Investment Adviser Codes of Ethics

Investment Advisers Act Release No. 2256 (July 2, 2004)

[**Textbook note:** *In this adopting release for Rule 204A-1, the SEC emphasizes the need for advisers and their personnel to observe fiduciary principles. The release then highlights key provisions of Rule 204A-1, which parallel in many ways Rule 17j-1, but are distinct in light of the differences between adviser business models and fund operations. Significantly, the release also addresses the misuse of inside information, which since 1988 has been the subject of requirements for written policies and procedures under Section 204A of the Advisers Act. This approach evidences an analogous, but fundamentally different, statutory authority for the SEC's parallel rulemaking under Advisers Act.*]

[***] Executive Summary

The Commission is adopting new rule 204A-1 under the Advisers Act to require registered investment advisers to adopt codes of ethics. The rule requires an adviser's code of ethics to set forth standards of conduct and require compliance with federal securities laws. Codes of ethics must also address personal trading: they must require advisers' personnel to report their personal securities holdings and transactions, including those in affiliated mutual funds, and must require personnel to obtain pre-approval of certain investments. The Commission is amending the Advisers Act recordkeeping rule to require advisers to keep copies of their codes of ethics and records relating to the code. The Commission is also amending the client disclosure requirements under Part II of Form ADV to require advisers to describe their codes of ethics to clients.

....

I. BACKGROUND

In January of this year [2004], we proposed to require every adviser registered with us to adopt and enforce a written code of ethics applicable to its supervised persons. Our proposal was designed to prevent fraud by reinforcing fiduciary principles that must govern the conduct of advisory firms and their personnel. The proposal was part of a package of regulatory initiatives with which we have responded to a number of recent enforcement actions against advisers or their personnel alleging violations of their fiduciary obligations to clients, including mutual fund clients.

Advisers' codes would be required to contain provisions reminding employees of their obligations to clients as well as provisions requiring reporting of personal securities transactions and holdings. In order to ensure that advisers' employees are made aware of their firms' standards, advisers would have to obtain (and keep) a written acknowledgement from each supervised person confirming that he or she received a copy of the code of ethics and any amendments. While the code of ethics would have to contain certain minimum provisions, our proposal left advisers with substantial flexibility to design individualized codes that would best fit the structure, size and nature of their advisory businesses.

....

II. DISCUSSION

....

A. Standards of Conduct and Compliance with Laws

Rule 204A-1 requires each adviser's code of ethics to set forth a standard of business conduct that the adviser requires of all its supervised persons. The rule does not require the adviser to adopt a particular standard, but the standard chosen must reflect the adviser's fiduciary obligations and those of its supervised persons, and must require compliance with the federal securities laws.

This provision, which we are adopting as proposed, establishes only a minimum requirement. Advisers are free to set higher standards for their employees, such as those established by professional or trade groups. Of course, any other code adopted for use must meet the minimum requirements of the rule, or be supplemented to meet the minimum requirements.

We urge advisers to take great care and thought in preparing their codes of ethics, which should be more than a compliance manual. Rather, a code of ethics should set out ideals for ethical conduct premised on fundamental principals of openness, integrity, honesty and trust. A good code of ethics should effectively convey to employees the value the advisory firm places on ethical conduct, and should challenge employees to live up not only to the letter of the law, but also to the ideals of the organization.

...

B. Protection of Material Nonpublic Information

We proposed to require codes of ethics to prevent access to material nonpublic information about the adviser's securities recommendations, and client securities holdings and transactions by individuals who do not need the information to perform their duties. Commenters supported our objective of controlling access to information as a first line of defense against misuse, but noted that it may be impractical to segregate employees, particularly in smaller firms that have limited office space. We are not requiring this provision in the code of ethics, but remind advisers that they must maintain and enforce policies and procedures to prevent the misuse of material nonpublic information, which we believe includes misuse of material nonpublic information about the adviser's securities recommendations, and client securities holdings and transactions. Advisers' duty of care also requires that they safeguard this sensitive information. Advisers should carefully consider how to control dissemination of sensitive information both within their organizations and outside them.

C. Personal Securities Trading

Each adviser's code of ethics must require an adviser's "access persons" to periodically report their personal securities transactions and holdings to the adviser's chief compliance officer or other designated persons. The code of ethics must also require the adviser to review those reports. Reviewing these reports will allow advisers as well as the Commission's examination staff to identify improper trades or patterns of trading by access persons. The reports are modeled largely on those required by rule 17j-1 under the Company Act....

....

1. Personal Trading Procedures

As discussed in more detail below, while rule 204A-1 requires advisers' codes of ethics to contain provisions requiring access persons to report securities transactions and holdings, it does not require advisers to adopt many of the detailed prophylactic measures common to many codes. Commenters agreed with this approach, which we took to accommodate the vast differences among advisory firms registered with us and the variety of risks associated with employee securities transactions. Advisory firms that have already adopted codes of ethics, however, commonly include many of the following elements, or address the following issues, which we believe that all advisers should consider in crafting their own procedures for employees' personal securities trading.

- Prior written approval before access persons can place a personal securities transaction ("preclearance").
- Maintenance of lists of issuers of securities that the advisory firm is analyzing or recommending for client transactions, and prohibitions on personal trading in securities of those issuers.
- Maintenance of "restricted lists" of issuers about which the advisory firm has inside information, and prohibitions on any trading (personal or for clients) in securities of those issuers.
- "Blackout periods" when client securities trades are being placed or recommendations are being made and access persons are not permitted to place personal securities transactions.
- Reminders that investment opportunities must be offered first to clients before the adviser or its employees may act on them, and procedures to implement this principle.

- Prohibitions or restrictions on "short-swing" trading and market timing.
- Requirements to trade only through certain brokers, or limitations on the number of brokerage accounts permitted.
- Requirements to provide the adviser with duplicate trade confirmations and account statements.
- Procedures for assigning new securities analyses to employees whose personal holdings do not present apparent conflicts of interest. [***]

* * *

Notes and Applications

Protection of material non-public information ("inside information") vs. regulation of personal securities transactions. What is the connection between the abuse of material non-public information, i.e., inside information, and personal securities transactions? Section 204A was designed to augment the insider trading regulations found under other federal securities law provisions, like Rule 10b-5 under the Exchange Act. Investment advisers and their staff often receive or become privy to material non-public information (from outside sources). For example, a portfolio manager may accidentally receive confidential financial information when interviewing a company officer as part of the manager's research. Or adviser personnel may receive tips from companies and industry sources. A 2016 settlement in an SEC administrative proceeding provided some insight into issues faced by large advisers with hedge funds which scour industry for information. The case, *In the Matter of Federated Global Investment Management Corp.*, Investment Advisers Act Rel. No. 4401 (May 27, 2016), involved gaps in the adviser's compliance program. The adviser, which had inside information policies and procedures, used consultants to provide portfolio analytical and research services. However, the policies and procedures only covered internal adviser staff, not consultants, resulting in the compliance gap. In this case, a consultant provided portfolio trading advice and recommendations related to the pharmaceutical and biotechnology industries. While providing such services, he served on the boards of several such companies, where he had access to inside information.

Congress's enactment of Advisers Act Section 204A anticipated such hazards. The section requires covered advisers to adopt, maintain and enforce written policies and procedures reasonably designed to prevent the misuse of inside information under the federal securities laws.

The potentially misused material non-public information that serves as a basis for Rule 204A-1 is of a different sort. It is information generated by the adviser itself, and the Rule is intended to prevent misuse of that information in connection with the personal investment activities of adviser personnel. In other words, the Rule gets at the same concerns that motivated Rule 17j-1, which is first and foremost one of conflict of interest. In the case of Rule 17j-1, the intent is to protect the funds from abusive personal securities trading by such personnel while in the case of Rule 204A-1, the intent is to protect the adviser's clients, and to a lesser extent, the investing public who may suffer an adverse collateral effect from unmonitored trading of advisory personnel.

15.3 Mandating Compliance Policies and Procedures by Regulation

The role and need for adviser and fund compliance programs and officers have grown almost exponentially in the last two decades. Until the early 2000s, advisers and funds were not required to implement comprehensive compliance policies and procedures. Certain rules such as Rule 17j-1 and Section 204A required policies and procedures, but in general, the Company Act and Advisers Act and their regulations did not require documentation of a broad set of compliance policies and procedures. In addition, the SEC used the books and records requirements of the Advisers Act and Company Act in enforcement actions as a means of encouraging a comprehensive set of compliance policies and procedures. However, it wasn't until the 2003 scandals involving dozens of funds and advisers in a scheme to defraud funds with market-timing and late-trading that the SEC acted to implement compliance requirements. In response to heavy public and Congressional condemnation for failure to have such requirements, the SEC hastily adopted Rule 206(4)-7 under the Advisers Act and Rule 38(a)-1 under the Company Act. The reading below illustrates the turmoil in the industry at the time and the need for such requirements.

Compliance Programs of Investment Companies and Investment Advisers

Investment Advisers Act Release No. 2204 (December 24, 2003)

[**Textbook Note:** *Rule 206(4)-7 under the Advisers Act and, and the even more comprehensive Rule 38a-1 under the Company Act, were hurriedly proposed and adopted in the furor after the market-timing and late-trading scandals discussed in Chapter 16. In this Adopting Release, the SEC discussed the rules' chief features. The rules specifically require written compliance policies and procedures for advisers and funds. The rules also require funds and investment advisers to designate chief compliance officers ("CCOs"). This role (and the direct personal liability which it entails) was intended to precisely locate within the regulated entity the primary responsibility for development, updating, monitoring, and enforcement of compliance policies and procedures. Until that time, it was regarded as a "best practice" to have compliance policies and procedures, but it was not mandated. The implementation of these rules has had a profound effect on how advisers and funds approach their compliance obligations and how the SEC oversees advisers and funds. Notably, the rules give the SEC additional enforcement capabilities, i.e., the ability to cite failures to adopt written policies and procedures which are reasonably designed to prevent violation of the federal securities law, even in the absence of any violation of substantive legal requirements.*]

[***] **Summary:** The Securities and Exchange Commission is adopting new rules under the Investment Company Act of 1940 and the Investment Advisers Act of 1940 that require each investment company and investment adviser registered with the Commission to adopt and implement written policies and procedures reasonably designed to prevent violation of the federal securities laws, review those policies and procedures annually for their adequacy and the effectiveness of their implementation, and designate a chief compliance officer to be responsible for administering the policies and procedures. In the case of an investment company, the chief compliance officer will report directly to the fund board. These rules are designed to protect investors by ensuring that all funds and advisers have internal programs to enhance compliance with the federal securities laws....

I. Background

Earlier this year the Commission proposed rules that would require investment companies ("funds") and investment advisers to adopt written compliance procedures, review the adequacy of those procedures annually, and designate a chief compliance officer responsible for their administration. We proposed the rules because it is critically important for funds and advisers to have strong systems of controls in place to prevent violations of the federal securities laws and to protect the interests of shareholders and clients. The proposed rules were designed to foster, among other things, improved compliance by clarifying the compliance obligations of fund management and to strengthen the hand of fund boards and compliance personnel when dealing with them.

In recent months, the Commission and state securities authorities have discovered unlawful conduct involving a number of fund advisers, broker-dealers, and other service providers that confirms the need for these rules. Fund advisory or distributor personnel have engaged in, or actively assisted others in engaging in, inappropriate market timing, late trading of fund shares, and the misuse of material, nonpublic information about fund portfolios. These personnel, including in some cases senior executives of fund advisers, have placed their personal interests or the business interests of the fund adviser ahead of the interests of fund shareholders, thus breaching their fiduciary obligations to the funds involved and their shareholders. These individuals have harmed the funds, their management organizations, and the confidence of fund investors.

Our response to these events is twofold. First, we are conducting an intensive investigation of funds, advisers, broker-dealers, and others.[7] We will aggressively pursue

7. To date, we have brought 10 enforcement actions. *See SEC v. Mutuals.com, Inc.*, Civil Action No. 303 CV 2912D (N.D. Tex. Dec. 4, 2003) (alleging that dually registered broker-dealer and investment adviser, three of its executives, and two affiliated broker-dealers assisted institutional brokerage customers and advisory clients in carrying out and concealing thousands of market timing trades and illegal late trades in shares of hundreds of mutual funds)? *SEC v. Invesco Funds Group*, Civil Action No. 03N2421 (PAC) (D. Colo. Dec. 2, 2003) (alleging that investment adviser, with approval of its president and chief executive officer, entered into market timing arrangements with more than sixty broker dealers, hedge funds, and advisers without disclosing these arrangements to the affected mutual funds' independent directors or shareholders)? *SEC v. Security Trust Company*, Civil Action No. 032323 (D. Ariz. Nov. 24, 2003) (alleging that unregistered financial intermediary and three of its senior executives facilitated and participated in late trading and market timing schemes by a group

and punish those who have violated the federal securities laws and breached their fiduciary obligations to clients. When appropriate, we will actively work with other federal law enforcement authorities and state authorities to see that the full weight of the law is brought to bear against those who have betrayed mutual funds and fund investors. Second, we will review all of our rules to determine what changes may be required to prevent this type of conduct.

....

II. Discussion

The Commission is adopting new rule 206(4)-7 under the Advisers Act and new rule 38a-1 under the Investment Company Act. The new rules require each registered investment adviser and each fund to adopt and implement compliance programs that conform to the new rules. Failure of an adviser or fund to have adequate compliance policies and procedures in place will constitute a violation of our rules independent of any other securities law violation. The new rules will thus permit the Commission to address the failure of an adviser or fund to have in place adequate compliance controls, before that failure has a chance to harm clients or investors.

A. Adoption and Implementation of Policies and Procedures

1. Investment Advisers

Under rule 206(4)-7, it is unlawful for an investment adviser registered with the Commission to provide investment advice unless the adviser has adopted and implemented written policies and procedures reasonably designed to prevent violation of the Advisers Act by the adviser or any of its supervised persons.[10] The rule requires advisers to consider their fiduciary and regulatory obligations under the Advisers Act and to formalize policies and procedures to address them. Commenters generally supported these new requirements, but some expressed concerns for how they would be applied to smaller advisers. The Commission is sensitive to the burdens

---

of related hedge funds)? *SEC v. Pilgrim*, Civil Action No. 03CV6341 (E.D. Penn. filed Nov. 20, 2003) (alleging that investment adviser and two senior executives permitted a hedge fund, in which one of the executives had a substantial financial interest, to engage in repeated short-term trading of several mutual funds and that one of the executives provided nonpublic portfolio information to a broker-dealer, which passed it on to its customers)? *SEC v. Druffner*, Civil Action No. 0312154RCL (D. Mass. Nov. 4, 2003) (alleging that five brokers, with the assistance of their branch office manager, evaded attempts to restrict their trading and conducted thousands of market timing trades in numerous mutual funds)? *SEC v. Scott*, Civil Action No. 0312082EFH (D. Mass. filed Oct. 28, 2003) (alleging that two senior investment executives of an investment adviser engaged in repeated short-term trading in their personal accounts of funds over which they had investment decision-making responsibility and about which they had access to nonpublic information)? *In re Sihpol, Administrative Proceeding* No. 311261 (Sept. 16, 2003) (charging former broker with playing a key role in enabling certain hedge fund customers to engage in late trading in shares of funds).... A number of state actions are also pending.

10. Rule 206(4)7(a). *See also* section 202(a)(25) of the Advisers Act [15 U.S.C. 80b2(a)(25)] (defining "supervised person" as "any partner, officer, director (or other person occupying a similar status or performing similar functions), or employee of an investment adviser, or other person who provides investment advice on behalf of the investment adviser and is subject to the supervision and control of the investment adviser").

the rule may impose upon smaller advisory firms. The rule requires only that the policies and procedures be *reasonably* designed to prevent violation of the Advisers Act, and thus need only encompass compliance considerations relevant to the operations of the adviser. We would expect smaller advisory firms without conflicting business interests to require much simpler policies and procedures than larger firms that, for example, have multiple potential conflicts as a result of their other lines of business or their affiliations with other financial service firms. The preparation of these simpler policies and procedures and their administration should be much less burdensome.

Rule 206(4)-7 does not enumerate specific elements that advisers must include in their policies and procedures.[14] Commenters agreed with our assessment that funds and advisers are too varied in their operations for the rules to impose of a single set of universally applicable required elements. Each adviser should adopt policies and procedures that take into consideration the nature of that firm's operations. The policies and procedures should be designed to prevent violations from occurring, detect violations that have occurred,[15] and correct promptly any violations that have occurred. Each adviser, in designing its policies and procedures, should first identify conflicts and other compliance factors creating risk exposure for the firm and its clients in light of the firm's particular operations, and then design policies and procedures that address those risks. We expect that an adviser's policies and procedures, at a minimum, should address the following issues to the extent that they are relevant to that adviser:

- Portfolio management processes, including allocation of investment opportunities among clients and consistency of portfolios with clients' investment objectives, disclosures by the adviser, and applicable regulatory restrictions;

---

14. Advisers already are subject to requirements to maintain written compliance policies and procedures in certain areas. The new rules do not alter those requirements. *See, e.g.*, Investment Company Act rule 17j-1(c)(1) [17 CFR 70.17j-1(c)(1)] (requiring each investment adviser and principal underwriter of a fund to "adopt a written code of ethics containing provisions reasonably necessary to prevent" certain persons affiliated with the fund, its investment adviser or its principal underwriter from engaging in certain fraudulent, manipulative, and deceptive actions with respect tothe fund)? Advisers Act rule 206(4)-6 [17 CFR 275.206(4)-6] (requiring investment advisers to adopt and implement written policies and procedures reasonably designed to ensure that the adviser votes securities in the best interest of clients)? Advisers Act section 204A [15 U.S.C. 80b-4a] (requiring each adviser registered with us to have written policies and procedures reasonably designed to prevent the misuse of material nonpublic information by the adviser or persons associated with the adviser)? Regulation SP ("Privacy of Consumer Financial Information") [17 CFR Part 248.30] (requiring investment advisers to "adopt policies and procedures that address administrative, technical, and physical safeguards for the protection of customer records and information").

15. Where appropriate, advisers' policies and procedures should employ, among other methods of detection, compliance tests that analyze information over time in order to identify unusual patterns, including, for example, an analysis of the quality of brokerage executions (for the purpose of evaluating the adviser's fulfillment of its duty of best execution), or an analysis of the portfolio turnover rate (to determine whether portfolio managers are overtrading securities), or an analysis of the comparative performance of similarly managed accounts (to detect favoritism, misallocation of investment opportunities, or other breaches of fiduciary responsibilities).

- Trading practices, including procedures by which the adviser satisfies its best execution obligation, uses client brokerage to obtain research and other services ("soft dollar arrangements"), and allocates aggregated trades among clients;
- Proprietary trading of the adviser and personal trading activities of supervised persons;
- The accuracy of disclosures made to investors, clients, and regulators, including account statements and advertisements;
- Safeguarding of client assets from conversion or inappropriate use by advisory personnel;
- The accurate creation of required records and their maintenance in a manner that secures them from unauthorized alteration or use and protects them from untimely destruction;
- Marketing advisory services, including the use of solicitors;
- Processes to value client holdings and assess fees based on those valuations;
- Safeguards for the privacy protection of client records and information; and
- Business continuity plans;[22]

Rule 206(4)-7 does not require advisers to consolidate all compliance policies and procedures into a single document. Nor does it require advisers to memorialize every action that must be taken in order to remain in compliance with the Advisers Act. In some cases, it may be enough for the compliance policies and procedures to allocate responsibility within the organization for the timely performance of many obligations, such as the filing or updating of required forms.

2. Investment Companies

Rule 38a-1 requires fund boards to adopt written policies and procedures reasonably designed to prevent the fund from violating the federal securities laws. The procedures must provide for the oversight of compliance by the fund's advisers, principal underwriters, administrators, and transfer agents (collectively, "service providers") through which the fund conducts its activities.

a. Service Providers. Most of the operations of funds are carried out by service providers, which have their own compliance policies and procedures. Commenters pointed out that the proposed rule appeared to require a fund to adopt, as its own, the policies and procedures of its service providers. The final rule requires fund boards to approve the policies and procedures of fund service providers, and requires the fund's policies and procedures to include provisions for the fund to oversee compliance by its service providers.

---

22. We believe that an adviser's fiduciary obligation to its clients includes the obligation to take steps to protect the clients' interests from being placed at risk as a result of the adviser's inability to provide advisory services after, for example, a natural disaster or, in the case of some smaller firms, the death of the owner or key personnel. The clients of an adviser that is engaged in the active management of their assets would ordinarily be placed at risk if the adviser ceased operations.

Rule 38a-1 provides fund complexes with flexibility so that each complex may apply the rule in a manner best suited to its organization. A fund complex could, for example, adopt compliance policies and procedures that encompass the activities of the funds, the adviser and affiliated underwriters and transfer agents, while approving the policies and procedures of other service providers, such as sub-advisers, over which it has oversight responsibility under the rule. Another fund complex could adopt policies and procedures that would cover solely activities of the funds, and could approve the policies and procedures of each of its service providers.

b. Board Approval. Rule 38a-1 requires a fund's board, including a majority of its independent directors, to approve the policies and procedures of the fund and each of its service providers. The approval must be based on a finding by the board that the policies and procedures are reasonably designed to prevent violation of the federal securities laws by the fund and its service providers.

Some commenters expressed concern that the rule would require directors to review lengthy compliance manuals and devote considerable time at each meeting to approving numerous amendments. Directors may satisfy their obligations under the rule by reviewing summaries of compliance programs prepared by the chief compliance officer, legal counsel or other persons familiar with the compliance programs. The summaries should familiarize directors with the salient features of the programs (including programs of service providers) and provide them with a good understanding of how the compliance programs address particularly significant compliance risks.

In considering whether to approve a fund's or service provider's compliance policies and procedures, boards should consider the nature of the fund's exposure to compliance failures. In the case of a money market fund, for example, the board should consider whether the policies and procedures sufficiently address the fund's compliance with rule 2a-7 [which lays out specialized valuation, share pricing and other procedures for such funds]. Boards should also consider the adequacy of the policies and procedures in light of their recent compliance experiences, which may demonstrate weaknesses in the fund or service provider's compliance programs. We urge boards to also consider best practices used by other fund complexes, and to consult with fund counsel (and independent directors with their counsel), compliance specialists and other experts familiar with compliance practices successfully employed by similar funds or service providers.

The Commission understands that, in some cases, the fund may employ the services of a service provider that is not an affiliated person of the fund, such as a transfer agent or administrator, and that provides similar services to a large number of funds. In such cases, it may be impractical for the fund or its compliance officer to directly review all of the service provider's policies and procedures. In such cases, we will consider a fund's policies and procedures to have satisfied the requirements of this rule if the fund uses a third-party report on the service provider's procedures instead of the procedures themselves when the board is evaluating whether to approve the service provider's compliance program. The third-party report must describe the service provider's compliance program as it relates to the types of services provided to the fund, discuss the types of compliance risks material to the fund, and assess the adequacy of the service provider's compliance controls.

c. Policies and Procedures. Funds' or their advisers' policies and procedures should address the issues we identified for investment advisers above. In addition, we expect policies and procedures of funds (or fund service providers) to cover certain other critical areas. In light of our recent enforcement actions against a number of fund managers and service providers, we are taking this opportunity to review the application of these policies and procedures to several important areas of compliance with the federal securities laws by funds and their service providers.

• *Pricing of portfolio securities and fund shares.* The Investment Company Act requires funds to sell and redeem their shares at prices based on their current net asset value, and to pay redemption proceeds promptly. The Investment Company Act requires funds to calculate their net asset values using the market value of their portfolio securities when market quotations for those securities are "readily available," and, when a market quotation for a portfolio security is not readily available, by using the fair value of that security, as determined in good faith by the fund's board. These pricing requirements are critical to ensuring fund shares are purchased and redeemed at fair prices and that shareholder interests are not diluted.... Accordingly, rule 38a-1 requires funds to adopt policies and procedures that require the fund to monitor for circumstances that may necessitate the use of fair value prices? establish criteria for determining when market quotations are no longer reliable for a particular portfolio security? provide a methodology or methodologies by which the fund determines the current fair value of the portfolio security? and regularly review the appropriateness and accuracy of the method used in valuing securities, and make any necessary adjustments.

• *Processing of Fund Shares.* Our rules require forward pricing of fund shares. An investor submitting a purchase order or redemption request must receive the price next calculated after receipt of the purchase order or redemption request. Accordingly, rule 38a-1 requires that a fund have in place procedures that segregate investor orders received before the fund prices its shares (which will receive that day's price) from those that were received after the fund prices its shares (which will receive the following day's price). Because fund purchase and redemption orders are ultimately transmitted to transfer agents engaged by the fund, we have expanded the service providers covered by the rule to include transfer agents.

Many funds today have contractual provisions with transfer agents and other intermediaries that obligate those parties to segregate orders received by time of receipt in order to prevent "late trading" based on a previously determined price. Reliance on those contractual provisions alone would be insufficient to meet the requirements of the new rule. Funds should not only approve and periodically review the policies and procedures of transfer agents, as required by the rule, but should also take affirmative steps to protect themselves and their shareholders against late trading by obtaining assurances that those policies and procedures are effectively administered.

• *Identification of Affiliated Persons.* To prevent self-dealing and overreaching by persons in a position to take advantage of the fund, the Investment Company Act prohibits funds from entering into certain transactions with affiliated persons. Funds should have policies and procedures in place to identify these persons and to prevent unlawful transactions with them.

• *Protection of Nonpublic Information.* The federal securities laws prohibit insider trading, and section 204A of the Advisers Act requires advisers (including advisers to funds) to establish, maintain, and enforce written policies and procedures reasonably designed to prevent the adviser or any of its associated persons from misusing material, nonpublic information. Fund advisers should incorporate their section 204A policies into the policies required by rule 38a-1. These policies typically include prohibitions against trading portfolio securities on the basis of information acquired by analysts or portfolio managers employed by the investment adviser. A fund's compliance policies and procedures should also address other potential misuses of nonpublic information, including the disclosure to third parties of material information about the fund's portfolio, its trading strategies, or pending transactions, and the purchase or sale of fund shares by advisory personnel based on material, nonpublic information about the fund's portfolio.

• *Compliance with Fund Governance Requirements.* A fund's board plays an important role in overseeing fund activities to ensure that they are being conducted for the benefit of the fund and its shareholders. Fund boards, among other things, are tasked with approving the fund's advisory contracts, underwriting agreements, and distribution plans. The Investment Company Act requires that fund boards of directors be elected by fund shareholders, and that a certain percentage be "independent directors." To rely on many of our exemptive rules, independent directors must constitute a majority of the board, must be selected and nominated by other independent directors, and if they hire legal counsel, that counsel must be an independent legal counsel.

The consequences of failing to meet the Investment Company Act's governance requirements are severe. Therefore, a fund's policies and procedures should be designed to guard against, among other things, an improperly constituted board, the failure of the board to properly consider matters entrusted to it, and the failure of the board to request and consider information required by the Investment Company Act from the fund adviser and other service providers.

B. Annual Review

1. Investment Advisers

Rule 206(4)-7 requires each registered adviser to review its policies and procedures annually to determine their adequacy and the effectiveness of their implementation.... Although the rule requires only annual reviews, advisers should consider the need for interim reviews in response to significant compliance events, changes in business arrangements, and regulatory developments.

2. Investment Companies

Similarly, rule 38a-1 requires a fund to review its policies and procedures, as well as those of its service providers, annually. The rule does not require a fund board to

conduct the review? the board would, however, have the benefit of the review in the report submitted by the compliance officer....

C. Chief Compliance Officer

1. Investment Advisers

Rule 206(4)-7 requires each adviser registered with the Commission to designate a chief compliance officer to administer its compliance policies and procedures. An adviser's chief compliance officer should be competent and knowledgeable regarding the Advisers Act and should be empowered with full responsibility and authority to develop and enforce appropriate policies and procedures for the firm.[73] Thus, the compliance officer should have a position of sufficient seniority and authority within the organization to compel others to adhere to the compliance policies and procedures.

2. Investment Companies

Rule 38a-1 requires each fund to appoint a chief compliance officer who is responsible for administering the fund's policies and procedures approved by the board under the rule. A fund's chief compliance officer should be competent and knowledgeable regarding the federal securities laws and should be empowered with full responsibility and authority to develop and enforce appropriate policies and procedures for the fund. The chief compliance officer of a fund, like the chief compliance officer of an investment adviser, should have sufficient seniority and authority to compel others to adhere to the compliance policies and procedures.

The rule contains several provisions, some of which were not included in our proposal, designed to promote the independence of the chief compliance officer from the management of the fund. First, the chief compliance officer will serve in her position at the pleasure of the fund's board of directors, which can remove her if it loses confidence in her effectiveness. The fund board (including a majority of independent directors) must approve the designation of the chief compliance officer, and must approve her compensation (or any changes in her compensation). The board (including a majority of the independent directors) can remove the chief compliance officer from her responsibilities at any time, and can prevent the adviser or another service provider from doing so.

Second, the chief compliance officer will report directly to the board of directors. She must annually furnish the board with a written report on the operation of the fund's policies and procedures and those of its service providers. The report must ad-

73. Having the title of chief compliance officer does not, in and of itself, carry supervisory responsibilities. Thus, a chief compliance officer appointed in accordance with rule 206(4)-7 (or rule 38a-1) would not necessarily be subject to a sanction by us for failure to supervise other advisory personnel. A compliance officer who does have supervisory responsibilities can continue to rely on the defense provided for in section 203(e)(6) of the Advisers Act [15 USC 80b3(e)(6)]. Section 203(e)(6) provides that a person shall not be deemed to have failed to reasonably supervise another person if: (i) the adviser had adopted procedures reasonably designed to prevent and detect violations of the federal securities laws? (ii) the adviser had a system in place for applying the procedures? and (iii) the supervising person had reasonably discharged his supervisory responsibilities in accordance with the procedures and had no reason to believe the supervised person was not complying with the procedures.

dress, at a minimum: (i) the operation of the policies and procedures of the fund and each service provider since the last report, (ii) any material changes to the policies and procedures since the last report, (iii) any recommendations for material changes to the policies and procedures as a result of the annual review, and (iv) any material compliance matters since the date of the last report. We have added a definition of the term "material compliance matter" to the rule, to clarify that the report should inform the board of those compliance matters about which the fund's board reasonably needs to know in order to oversee fund compliance.[84]

Third, we are requiring that the chief compliance officer meet in executive session with the independent directors at least once each year, without anyone else (such as fund management or interested directors) present. The executive session creates an opportunity for the chief compliance officer and the independent directors to speak freely about any sensitive compliance issues of concern to any of them, including any reservations about the cooperativeness or compliance practices of fund management.

Fourth, we have added a provision to protect the chief compliance officer from undue influence by fund service providers seeking to conceal their or others' noncompliance with the federal securities laws. Rule 38a-1 prohibits the fund's officers, directors, employees or its adviser, principal underwriter, or any person acting under the direction of these persons, from directly or indirectly taking any action to coerce, manipulate, mislead or fraudulently influence the fund's chief compliance officer in the performance of her responsibilities under the rule.

The appointment of a chief compliance officer with overall responsibility for management of a fund complex's compliance program is a key element of the investor protections we are today adopting. Some commenters representing fund management companies urged us to permit funds to continue to use multiple compliance managers employed by different service providers, rely on the policies of the fund service providers, and omit the requirement that fund boards approve the compliance officer. These commenters would have us maintain funds' current approach to compliance management. Current practices, however, balkanize responsibility for fund compliance and isolate fund boards from compliance personnel, thus impeding boards' abilities to exercise their oversight responsibilities effectively. We decline to accept current practices, which we believe have contributed to the serious compliance lapses that are now the subject of our enforcement actions.

We have observed that executives at service providers have overruled their own compliance personnel because of business considerations. For example, some fund advisers have continued to permit investors with whom they had other business relationships to engage in harmful market timing in fund shares after compliance per-

84. Rule 38a-1(e)(2). Serious compliance issues must, of course, always be brought to the board's attention promptly, and cannot be delayed until an annual report. In addition, individual compliance matters that, taken in isolation, may not be material may collectively suggest a material compliance matter, such as a material weakness in the compliance programs of the fund or its service providers. *See, e.g.*, Personal Investment Activities of Investment Company Personnel, Investment Company Act Release No. 23958, at n. 25 (Aug. 20, 1999) [64 FR 46821 (Aug. 27, 1999)].

sonnel and portfolio managers brought the market timing activity to their attention. These compliance personnel may not have had access to fund directors or, having been overruled by their own management, may have felt they were not in a position to approach the board.

To address these concerns, rule 38a-1 provides fund boards with direct access to a single person with overall compliance responsibility for the fund who answers directly to the board. The rule provides the board with a powerful tool to exercise its oversight responsibilities over fund compliance matters. The new rule also strengthens the hand of compliance personnel by establishing a direct line of reporting to fund boards that is not controlled by management. We have observed that compliance failures have occurred when a fund service provider has denied information to the fund's board, or has been less than forthright, because the service provider viewed full disclosure as detrimental to its own interests. Under the new rule, the chief compliance officer will be responsible for keeping the board apprised of significant compliance events at the fund or its service providers and for advising the board of needed changes in the fund's compliance program....

We expect that a fund's chief compliance officer will often be employed by the fund's investment adviser or administrator.[88] We are not adopting a requirement that the chief compliance officer be employed by only the fund because we believe that such a provision would actually weaken her effectiveness. Funds today typically have no employees, and delegate management and administrative functions, including the compliance function, to one or more service providers. If we were to preclude the chief compliance officer from being an employee of an adviser or any other service provider, she would be divorced from all fund operations. The adviser's chief compliance officer would continue to administer the adviser's compliance programs, and the role of the fund's chief compliance officer would be limited to oversight of the service providers' compliance policies and providing advice to the board on their operation. As a result, the fund's chief compliance officer would be almost entirely dependent on information filtered through the senior management of the fund's adviser rather than, for example, information received directly from a trading desk. Moreover, fund management would be unlikely to consult with an "outside" compliance officer on a prospective business decision to ascertain the compliance implications.

We recognize, however, that a chief compliance officer who is an employee of the fund's investment adviser might be conflicted in her duties, and that the investment adviser's business interests might discourage the adviser from making forthright disclosure to fund directors of its compliance failures. The rule, as adopted, is designed to address these concerns by requiring a fund's chief compliance officer to report directly to the board. The board, and the board alone, can discharge the officer if she fails to live up to the position. Thus, a chief compliance officer who fails to fully inform

88. Indeed, she is likely to be the chief compliance officer of that organization inasmuch as the duties of the positions will have significant overlap. Alternatively, the chief compliance officer of the fund may be another member of the adviser or administrator's legal or compliance departments.

the board of a material compliance failure, or who fails to aggressively pursue non-compliance within the service provider, would risk her position. She would also risk her career, because it would be unlikely for another board of directors to approve such a person as chief compliance officer.

[Note: Rule 17j-1 contains additional provisions that may subject any affiliated person of the fund (i.e., that reach beyond access persons) to direct liability for fraudulent or lesser forms of deceptive conduct in connection with personal trading with respect to securities held or to be acquired by the fund, even absent any violation of the fund's code of ethics.]

The chief compliance officer, in exercising her responsibilities under the rule, will oversee the fund's service providers, which will have their own compliance officials. A chief compliance officer should diligently administer this oversight responsibility by taking steps to assure herself that each service provider has implemented effective compliance policies and procedures administered by competent personnel. The chief compliance officer should be familiar with each service provider's operations and understand those aspects of their operations that expose the fund to compliance risks. She should maintain an active working relationship with each service provider's compliance personnel. Arrangements with the service provider should provide the fund's chief compliance officer with direct access to these personnel, and should provide the compliance officer with periodic reports and special reports in the event of compliance problems. In addition, the fund's contracts with its service providers might also require service providers to certify periodically that they are in compliance with applicable federal securities laws, or could provide for third-party audits arranged by the fund to evaluate the effectiveness of the service provider's compliance controls. The chief compliance officer could conduct (or hire third parties to conduct) statistical analyses of a service provider's performance of its duties to detect potential compliance failures. [***]

* * *

Notes and Applications

Prevent, detect, correct. In a very real sense, those three words express the essence of the compliance rules. As noted in the release, "The policies and procedures should be designed to *prevent* violations from occurring, *detect* violations that have occurred, and *correct* promptly any violations that have occurred." (*emphasis added*). Both at the time of adoption and in the years since, the SEC has repeatedly emphasized the importance of all three aspects to a comprehensive compliance program. Ideally, a compliance program is constantly evolving and improving in light of changing facts and circumstances, including industry practice.

In addition, it is important to note the expansive compliance scope of Company Act Rule 38a-1 relative to Advisers Act Rule 206(4)-7. The Advisers Act rule relates solely to the compliance policies and procedures of the adviser. In contrast, Rule 38a-1 imposes an obligation on the fund's CCO to evaluate not only the fund's compliance and procedures, but also the compliance policies and procedures of most of its third-party service providers. By the same token, the fund's board (and a majority of its independent board members) must approve not only the fund's policies and procedures, but also the compliance policies and procedures of most of its third-party service providers.

15.3.1 Adequacy of Compliance Policies and Procedures in Practice

The idea of evolving sophistication in tailoring compliance programs has a regulatory corollary: evolving compliance norms. Since implementation of the new rules, the SEC has found a variety of situations where advisers and funds have nonetheless not properly prepared and implemented compliance policies and procedures. When originally adopted, the compliance rules were frequently enforced in situations where the adviser simply lacked any compliance policies or procedures. Another common situation arose where advisers had boilerplate compliance manuals that did not mesh with or correspond to the type of substantive compliance challenges faced by them in their actual day-to-day operations. The following case is illustrative of the need for such policies and procedures to address conduct that is potentially problematic.

In the Matter of Structured Portfolio Management, L.L.C.

Investment Advisers Act Release No. 3906 (Aug. 28, 2014)

[**Textbook note:** *This administrative order settled a SEC investigation and proceeding regarding a hedge fund adviser's failure to properly implement written policies and procedures reasonably designed to detect and prevent potentially improper securities trade allocations. Interestingly, in this case, the SEC did not attempt to show that there had in fact been improper trade allocations, but merely that the absence of adequate policies and procedures in that regard tainted certain disclosure policies and procedures of the affected hedge funds. In addition, the case illustrates the broadened scope of the SEC's oversight of hedge funds and their managers under the mandate of compliance policies and procedures and its use of the compliance rule as an enforcement tool.*]

[***] Summary

1. This matter concerns compliance failures by hedge fund adviser Portfolio Management and its affiliated advisers, SPM Jr. and SPM IV (collectively, "SPM"). SPM failed to adopt and implement written compliance policies and procedures reasonably designed to prevent violations of the Advisers Act, as required by Section 206(4) of the Advisers Act and Rule 206(4)-7 thereunder, concerning trade allocation and the review of investor disclosures.

2. The compliance failures are the result of a disclosed, but inadequately addressed, conflict of interest wherein SPM allowed a trader to trade the same securities across three SPM-advised hedge funds. This conflict of interest presented the possibility for the trader to engage in improper allocations from February 2006 through February 2009. Despite SPM's recognition of the conflict and its awareness of internal concerns

regarding trade allocations, SPM failed to adopt and implement written policies and procedures reasonably designed to detect and prevent improper trade allocations. In addition, SPM failed to adopt and implement written policies and procedures reasonably designed to prevent inaccurate disclosures concerning its funds and their investment strategies.

Respondents

3. **Structured Portfolio Management, L.L.C. ("Portfolio Management")** is a Delaware limited liability company located in Stamford, Connecticut. Portfolio Management was formed in February 1997 and advises the Structured Servicing Holdings Master Fund, L.P. Portfolio Management has been registered as an investment adviser with the Commission since April 2000.

4. **SPM Jr., L.L.C. ("SPM Jr.")** is a Delaware limited liability company located in Stamford, Connecticut. SPM Jr. was formed in January 2003 and advised the Parmenides Master Fund, L.P. During the relevant time period, Portfolio Management owned approximately 90% of SPM Jr. SPM Jr. was registered as an investment adviser with the Commission from April 2003 through January 2013.

5. **SPM IV, L.L.C. ("SPM IV")** is a Delaware limited liability company located in Stamford, Connecticut. SPM IV was formed in May 2005 and advised the Aqueous Master Fund, L.P. During the relevant time period, Portfolio Management owned approximately 44% of SPM IV. SPM IV was registered as an investment adviser with the Commission from June 2005 through April 2009.

Other Relevant Entities

6. **Structured Servicing Holdings Master Fund, L.P. ("SSH")** is a Delaware limited partnership that was formed in July 2001 and was advised by Portfolio Management during the relevant time period.

7. **Parmenides Master Fund, L.P. ("Parmenides")** was a Delaware limited partnership that was formed in January 2003 and was advised by SPM Jr. during the relevant time period.

8. **Aqueous Master Fund, L.P. ("Aqueous")** was a Delaware limited partnership that was formed in September 2005 and was advised by SPM IV during the relevant time period.

Facts

A. Background

9. Portfolio Management was formed in 1997 and registered with the Commission as an investment adviser in 2000. During the relevant time period, Portfolio Management advised hedge fund SSH and had a 90% ownership interest in affiliated adviser SPM Jr., which advised hedge fund Parmenides.

10. SSH and Parmenides invested in mortgage-related securities, including collateralized mortgage obligations, mortgage-backed securities ("MBS"), and interest-only

bonds. These securities were subject to interest rate risk, which was hedged by trading a variety of liquid securities, including U.S. Treasury securities ("Treasuries").

11. SSH and Parmenides had separate portfolio managers who traded each fund's core mortgage-related securities holdings. A third trader (hereinafter, "Hedge Trader") was responsible for hedging interest rate risk for both SSH and Parmenides.

12. In 2005, the principals of Portfolio Management formed Aqueous, a new, highly liquid fund that sought to provide excess returns by investing in a wide range of financial assets drawn principally from the U.S. residential and commercial mortgage markets, and including Treasuries and other securities. They created SPM IV to advise it.

13. Aqueous was launched in February 2006 and the Hedge Trader was appointed as its portfolio manager and trader. Aqueous received seed capital from SSH and Parmenides, which were consistently among the largest investors in Aqueous.

B. SPM Failed to Adopt and Implement Policies and Procedures Reasonably Designed to Prevent Improper Trade Allocations

The Potential Conflict

14. After being named Aqueous' portfolio manager and trader, the Hedge Trader continued to trade the hedge positions for SSH and Parmenides. When trading for Aqueous, the Hedge Trader's sole responsibility was to make a profit. In contrast, when trading for SSH and Parmenides, his main responsibility was to hedge interest rate risk.

15. On an average day, the Hedge Trader traded Treasuries to hedge SSH's and Parmenides' core holdings in mortgage-related securities. He also traded the same Treasuries in Aqueous as part of its core holdings; however, those trades were for much smaller quantities and occurred much less frequently. When the Hedge Trader traded the same Treasuries across all three funds, a potential conflict of interest existed concerning how to allocate the trades among the three funds. SPM recognized and disclosed this potential conflict at Aqueous' inception but did not modify or update its written policies and procedures.

16. Portfolio Management, SPM Jr., and SPM IV were subject to the same set of compliance policies and procedures (or "Compliance Manual"). The Compliance Manual, which was created in consultation with an external consultant, stated that SPM traders would seek to allocate trades in a fair and equitable manner in light of the investment objectives and strategies of SPM's funds and other factors.

17. SPM's Compliance Manual also contained trade confirmation procedures. Pursuant to these procedures, upon executing a trade, the trader was required to complete a trade blotter identifying, among other information, the following: (i) the name of the fund purchasing or selling the security; (ii) a description of the security traded; (iii) the amount of securities traded; (iv) the price at which the trade was executed; and (v) the counterparty. On a daily basis, a member of the operations staff was required to obtain the blotter, review it, and enter all of the information into SPM's proprietary trade management system.

18. Although SPM required its traders to identify upon trade execution the fund for which the securities were traded, it did not institute any additional procedures after the creation of Aqueous to confirm that traders actually did so. Trade blotters were provided to, or collected by, the operations department on a sporadic basis throughout the day without any way of determining when the trader had identified the fund for which the securities were traded in relation to the time that the trade was executed.

Concerns Raised

19. In August 2006, internal concerns were raised as to whether Aqueous was receiving more favorable execution prices than SSH and Parmenides when trading the same Treasury security on the same day.

20. The internal concerns were based on a review of the funds' trading data for the time period April to August 2006, which showed that when Aqueous, SSH, and Parmenides each purchased the same Treasury security on the same day, Aqueous consistently bought at a lower price than the other two funds. Likewise, when all three funds sold the same Treasury security on the same day, Aqueous consistently sold at a higher price than SSH and Parmenides. After these concerns were raised, SPM removed the Hedge Trader from trading on behalf of SSH and Parmenides while he was trading for Aqueous. For approximately six months, the Hedge Trader traded solely for Aqueous.

21. In January 2007, SPM lifted the Hedge Trader's trading restriction and allowed him to resume trading for all three funds. While SPM took certain steps to address the earlier concerns as part of the decision to allow the Hedge Trader to resume executing trades for SSH and Parmenides, it did not amend its written policies and procedures to address the potential for conflicts. Instead, SPM simply instructed its traders to provide trade blotters to the operations department more frequently throughout the day and tasked a junior compliance officer with ensuring that trade blotters were provided in a timely manner.

22. These oral instructions regarding the trade blotters were not accompanied by anything in writing and no additional guidance was provided to the traders or to the junior compliance officer. For example, while traders were required to provide blotters to the operations department more frequently, there was no written guidance concerning when the blotter needed to be provided in relation to when the trade was placed. Further, SPM did not provide the junior compliance officer with any written procedures to ensure that blotters were provided in a timely manner. In November 2008, while the junior compliance officer was on vacation and there was no one assigned to carry out those responsibilities, SPM raised concerns that traders were not properly allocating their trades by fund at the time of execution.

23. During SPM's annual compliance review in November 2008, an independent firm separately raised trade allocation concerns.

24. In January 2009, concerns regarding trade allocations were again raised internally. These concerns were based on a statistical analysis that claimed Aqueous' trading performance was aberrational for the time period September 2007 through January

2009. In response to these concerns, SPM hired outside counsel to conduct a review of SPM's trade allocations. The review was inconclusive as to whether trades were or were not allocated improperly.

25. While SPM's compliance manual required traders to identify the fund for which the securities were being traded upon execution, this requirement alone was not sufficient for preventing improper trade allocations. Despite being aware of concerns about improper trade allocations, SPM failed to adopt and implement written policies and procedures reasonably designed to prevent improper trade allocations.

26. In March 2009, SPM closed the Aqueous fund.

C. SPM Failed to Adopt and Implement Written Policies and Procedures to Adequately Review Investor Disclosures

27. SPM failed to adopt and implement written policies and procedures reasonably designed to prevent inaccurate disclosures to current and prospective investors regarding the trading and investment strategy of Aqueous.

28. Aqueous' investment objective was to provide excess returns by investing in a wide range of financial assets drawn principally from the U.S. residential and commercial mortgage markets. The fund's private placement memorandum disclosed that Aqueous would invest primarily in MBS, including Fannie Maes and Freddie Macs, but that it also might invest in Treasuries and other liquid securities.

29. From Aqueous' inception in February 2006 until mid-2007, the fund traded highly liquid MBS and Treasuries as set forth in its offering documents. Over time, however, Aqueous stopped trading MBS and began almost exclusively to day-trade Treasuries. While Aqueous continued to maintain a highly liquid investment strategy, SPM failed to disclose that it was doing so by day-trading Treasuries and continued to represent that it was primarily trading mortgage-related securities.

30. In contrast to these disclosures, Aqueous had not been trading mortgage-related securities. From September 2007 through February 2009, Aqueous had made only two trades that were not trades in Treasuries.

31. SPM did not adopt and implement written policies and procedures reasonably designed to prevent inaccurate investor disclosures. As a result of not adopting and implementing reasonably designed policies and procedures, SPM did not adequately review Aqueous' offering documents and other investor disclosures on a regular basis to determine whether they were inaccurate.

Violations

32. Section 206(4) of the Advisers Act and Rule 206(4)-7 thereunder require registered investment advisers to adopt and implement written policies and procedures reasonably designed to prevent violations of the Advisers Act and its rules.

33. SPM willfully violated Section 206(4) of the Advisers Act and Rule 206(4)-7 thereunder by failing to adopt and implement written policies and procedures reasonably

designed to prevent improper trade allocations and to prevent inaccurate disclosures in its offering and marketing materials. [***]

* * *

Notes and Applications

1. *Key phrase: "reasonably designed."* This case demonstrates clearly how merely having a compliance manual is insufficient to comply with the law. As a matter of fact, the advisers did have compliance manuals which included trade allocation procedures. The point is that the policies and procedures need to be *effective.* When there's an error, fraud or other failure, it is quite easy for the SEC to assert that the policy and/or procedures weren't effective or "reasonably designed" to prevent the cited failure of compliance with federal securities law.

2. *Rules 38a-1 and 206(4)-7 may provide a basis for stand-alone enforcement claims.* The compliance rules in a sense overlay the other substantive provisions of the Company and Adviser Acts. As a result, it has made it much easier for the SEC to bring enforcement actions when evidence of substantive violations are weak, but the conduct revealed is troubling. With the adoption of the compliance rules, lapses or failures of compliance became violations of the compliance rules and, thus, actionable alone. However, as evidenced by administrative proceedings excerpted in the text, a violation of a substantive provision typically is paired with a finding of deficient compliance policies and procedures.

3. *Disclosure vs. compliance.* Note that the SPM settlement was in actuality a case about compliance policies and procedures relating to fund disclosure. The order clearly conveys concerns about trade allocation among the funds but does not assert claims for trade misallocations. At the same time, consider why the SEC didn't bring a case for disclosure omissions or misstatements. (Two hints: (i) recall that the disclosure requirements for registered investment companies are different than for hedge funds; and (ii) was any disclosure false when made or was the concern merely disclosure that was not updated?)

15.3.2 The Role of Fund Chief Compliance Officers

In the SEC's view, perhaps the most important player in the compliance program is the Chief Compliance Officer ("CCO"). The readings above have highlighted the need for CCOs and the important roles they play in the implementation and administration of compliance programs, including codes of ethics. Critically for funds, the CCO is one of the few, if not only, fund employees. As such, the CCO has a certain independence and reports directly to the fund board. The trustees in turn rely on the CCO as their "eyes and ears" with respect to the many aspects of fund operations and most critically those involving conflicts of interest. The following case illustrates the challenges and risks faced by a CCO.

In the Matter of BlackRock Advisors, LLC

Investment Advisers Act Release No. 4065 (April 20, 2015)

[**Textbook note:** *The perceived implications of this administrative proceeding continue to reverberate in the investment management industry. It is notable for its censure and sanctioning of the BlackRock CCO, along with the implication that CCOs are broadly responsible for funds' compliance policies and procedures. As here, the relevant CCO responsibility may not be externally imposed, but rather may stem from a fund's own policies and procedures. That distinction has great importance for CCOs and how compliance policies are drafted. In addition, the order is notable for the fact that the funds' portfolio manager was not censured or fined.*]

[***] Summary

1. This matter concerns investment adviser BlackRock's failure to disclose a conflict of interest involving the outside business activity of one of its portfolio managers. Daniel J. Rice, III was a well-known, long-standing top-performing energy sector portfolio manager. Rice joined BlackRock in 2005 and managed BlackRock energy-focused registered funds, private funds, and separate accounts. In 2007, Rice founded Rice Energy, L.P.—a Rice family-owned-and-operated oil and natural gas production company. Rice was the general partner of Rice Energy and personally invested approximately $50 million in the company. Rice's three sons were the CEO, CFO, and VP of Geology of Rice Energy. In February 2010, Rice Energy formed a joint venture with Alpha Natural Resources, Inc. ("ANR"), a publicly-traded coal company held in the BlackRock funds and accounts managed by Rice. By June 30, 2011, ANR stock was the largest holding (9.4%) in the Rice-managed $1.7 billion BlackRock Energy & Resources Portfolio, primarily as a result of ANR acquiring two other public companies held in that portfolio. BlackRock knew of Rice's involvement with and investment in Rice Energy as well as the joint venture with ANR, but failed to disclose Rice's conflict of interest to the BlackRock funds' boards of directors or to BlackRock advisory clients.

2. BlackRock also failed to adopt and implement written compliance policies and procedures reasonably designed to prevent violations of the Advisers Act and the rules thereunder, as required by Section 206(4) of the Advisers Act and Rule 206(4)-7 thereunder, concerning the outside activities of its employees, including how they should be assessed and monitored for conflict purposes, and when an employee's outside activity should be disclosed to the BlackRock funds' board of directors or to BlackRock advisory clients. BlackRock's chief compliance officer ("CCO"), Bartholomew A. Battista, caused BlackRock's compliance-related violations.

3. BlackRock and Battista also caused the registered funds' failure to have the funds' chief compliance officer report to the funds' boards of directors—in violation of Rule 38a-1(a)(4)(iii)(B) under the Investment Company Act of 1940—Rice's violations of BlackRock's private investment policy. BlackRock and Battista knew about Rice's violations, and knew or should have known that they were not reported to the funds' boards.

Respondents

4. **BlackRock Advisors, LLC**, a Delaware limited liability company headquartered in Wilmington, Delaware, is an investment adviser registered with the Commission. According to its Form ADV filed in June 2014, BlackRock has assets under management of approximately $452 billion. BlackRock is a subsidiary of BlackRock, Inc., an investment management firm with assets under management of approximately $4.3 trillion as of December 31, 2013.

5. **Bartholomew A. Battista,** age 56 and a resident of Sicklerville, New Jersey, was the CCO of BlackRock during the relevant period. Battista joined BlackRock in 1998.

Other Relevant Individual and Entities

6. **Daniel J. Rice III** was a managing director at BlackRock and a co-portfolio manager of approximately $4.5 billion in energy sector assets held in BlackRock registered and private funds as well as separately managed accounts. Rice joined BlackRock in January 2005 and separated from the firm in December 2012.

7. **Rice Energy, LP ("Rice Energy")** was a Delaware limited partnership headquartered in Canonsburg, PA. Rice Energy was founded by Rice in February 2007. During the relevant period, Rice Energy was a Rice family-owned-and-operated oil and gas exploration and production company that focused on drilling oil and natural gas wells. In January 2014, Rice Energy, Inc., a Rice Energy affiliate, completed its $1 billion initial public offering of 50 million shares of common stock, at a price of $21 per share (NYSE: RICE).

Facts

A. Rice's Outside Business Activity Created a Conflict of Interest at BlackRock

8. In late 2004, BlackRock recruited Rice to join BlackRock. Rice joined BlackRock in January 2005 as a managing director and co-portfolio manager of energy sector assets held in BlackRock registered funds, private funds, and separately managed accounts. As an incentive to join the company, BlackRock agreed to pay Rice a portion of the annual investment advisory fees earned on the Rice-managed funds and separate accounts — as a result, Rice was one of BlackRock's most highly compensated portfolio managers.

9. In December 2006 and while employed at BlackRock, Rice formed and funded the Rice Energy Irrevocable Trust (the "Rice Energy Trust") to hold interests in "Rice Energy," which referred to energy companies that Rice intended to create in the future and be managed by his adult children. Rice funded the trust with approximately $2.4 million in gifts as well as $23.5 million in term loans.

10. In February 2007 and while employed at BlackRock, Rice formed Rice Energy, Rice Energy Management, LLC ("REM"), and a Rice Energy drilling subsidiary. In February 2008, Rice formed another Rice Energy drilling subsidiary, Rice Drilling B, LLC ("Rice Drilling B"). Rice was the 100% owner of REM, which was the sole general partner of Rice Energy. Due to his ownership interest, Rice had the ability to exercise broad power

Figure 15A

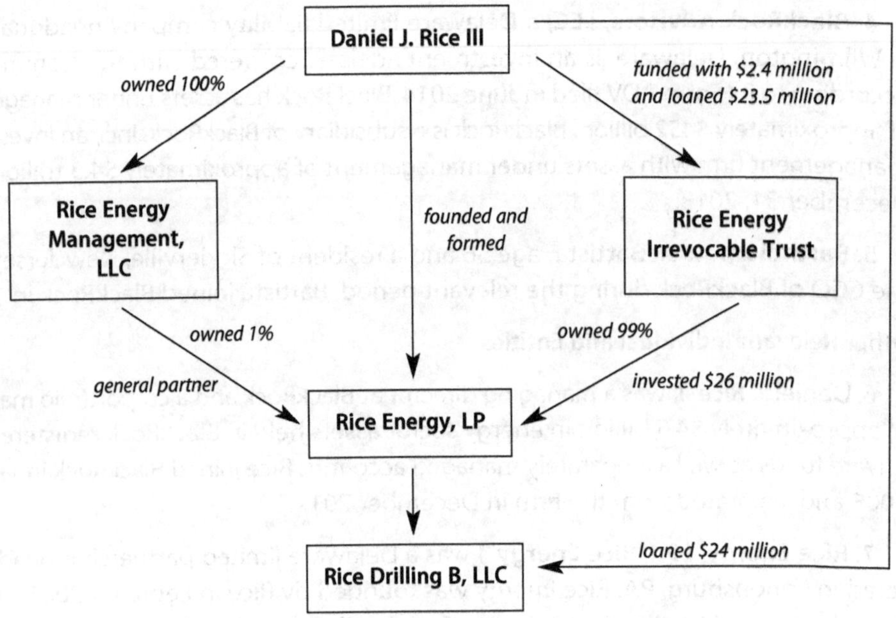

and authority over Rice Energy. Through REM, Rice was not only the general partner of Rice Energy, but he also owned 1% of Rice Energy, and the remaining 99% was owned by the Rice Energy Trust.

11. Between 2007 and mid-2010, Rice had invested in and loaned to Rice Energy a total of approximately $50 million.

12. Rice's three sons, who were Rice Energy's Chief Executive Officer, Chief Financial Officer, and Vice President of Geology, routinely shared information regarding Rice Energy operational issues with Rice, and sought and received direction and advice from Rice. Rice also was a manager at two Rice Energy drilling subsidiaries, including Rice Drilling B. Rice and his sons exercised their power and authority to manage the business and affairs of the companies and made decisions on their behalf.

13. Rice used his BlackRock email address for Rice Energy related communications during which Rice discussed the company. For example, Rice used his industry connections to solicit business partnerships through which Rice Energy would gain access to land on which to drill.

14. During Rice's tenure as a BlackRock portfolio manager, Rice Energy solicited a joint venture with Foundation Coal, a public company held in the Rice-managed funds and separate accounts. In mid-2008, Rice Energy started exploring a potential joint venture, and by early 2009 substantive discussions between the two companies had begun, but final plans were placed on hold until after the merger of Foundation Coal and ANR was completed in July 2009. Shortly after the merger, Rice formed a third Rice Energy drilling subsidiary to hold Rice Energy's interest in its anticipated joint venture with ANR. In October 2009, Rice—in his role as general partner and on behalf of Rice Energy—signed a letter of intent to form the joint venture with ANR. In Feb-

ruary 2010, Rice Energy finalized the joint venture with ANR.

15. By the end of the first quarter of 2010 and after the formation of the joint venture with ANR, the Rice-managed funds and separate accounts together held over two million shares of ANR stock, with the largest fund—the $1.2 billion BlackRock Energy & Resources Portfolio—maintaining a 3.5% position in ANR, making it one of the fund's top ten largest holdings. By the end of the second quarter of 2011 and after ANR acquired Massey Energy, a second public company already held in the Rice-managed funds and separate accounts, the number of shares held in ANR stock increased to over eight million, with the largest fund—the $1.7 billion BlackRock Energy & Resources Portfolio—maintaining a 9.4% position in ANR, making it the fund's largest holding.

B. BlackRock Approved Rice's Outside Business Activity

16. By no later than January 2007, BlackRock learned that Rice had formed and funded the Rice Energy Trust in violation of BlackRock's private investment policy. By at least that time, certain BlackRock senior executives, including Battista, were told that Rice intended to form and fund Rice Energy. BlackRock's Legal and Compliance Department, including Battista, reviewed and discussed the matter and allowed Rice to form Rice Energy. BlackRock concluded that it did not see any conflict of interest with regard to Rice Energy. By no later than January 2010, BlackRock learned that Rice had made additional loans of approximately $14 million to a Rice Energy subsidiary in violation of BlackRock's private investment policy.

17. BlackRock did not report the formation or funding of the Rice Energy Trust or Rice Energy to the boards of directors of the Rice-managed registered funds or to advisory clients. BlackRock also did not advise the funds' boards of Rice's violations of BlackRock's private investment policy. BlackRock did not monitor or reassess Rice's outside business activity and the conflicts associated therewith between January 2007 and January 2010.

18. In January 2010, Rice told BlackRock that he wanted to serve on the board of directors of the joint venture between Rice Energy and ANR. At that time, BlackRock's Legal and Compliance Department did not recall its review of Rice Energy in early 2007. Incorrectly believing this was the first time it was learning about Rice Energy, BlackRock's Legal and Compliance Department conducted several fact-gathering discussions with Rice that resulted in a February 2010 memorandum addressed to Rice ("February 2010 memorandum").

19. Because the Rice-managed funds and separate accounts held ANR stock, the February 2010 memorandum stated the following with respect to conflicts:

> There are potential conflicts of interest in entering joint ventures with companies that you hold in your BlackRock client portfolios and funds. By participating in a personal joint venture with an issuer that you invest in on behalf of your clients, you may create the appearance of a conflict, with respect to whose interests are being placed first (yours or the client's). Additionally, by investing with a company that you hold in your portfolios you raise the con-

cern that you may have access to ANR specific information which you could use for your benefit instead of for your client's.

20. Despite BlackRock's acknowledgement of potential conflicts of interest and the concern that Rice may have access to ANR-specific information that Rice could use for his personal benefit to the detriment of his clients, BlackRock allowed Rice to continue his involvement with and financial investment in Rice Energy while continuing to serve as a BlackRock portfolio manager. As stated in the February 2010 memorandum, to which Rice agreed, BlackRock further allowed Rice to continue managing the ANR stock positions held in the Rice-managed funds and separate accounts, provided that he: (i) not participate in any decisions with respect to the joint venture; (ii) not become a board member of the joint venture; (iii) not receive material information about the joint venture that could restrict Rice's ability to trade in ANR; and (iv) pre-clear with BlackRock any future Rice Energy-related board seats intended to be taken by Rice. BlackRock did not provide any disclosure about Rice Energy or the February 2010 memorandum to the funds' boards or to advisory clients.

21. BlackRock did not follow-up with Rice about Rice Energy thereafter. Instead, BlackRock expected Rice to report back to BlackRock. BlackRock did not monitor or initiate any reassessment of Rice's involvement with Rice Energy. BlackRock did not verify whether certain steps specified in its February 2010 memorandum were taken by Rice, such as removing references to BlackRock from the Rice Energy website—and, ultimately, those references were not removed until after the June 2012 press articles about Rice's involvement with Rice Energy raised questions about the related conflicts of interest.

22. From time to time, Rice discussed other Rice Energy matters with certain BlackRock senior executives. For example, in May 2010 BlackRock approved Rice's sale of certain of his personal securities holdings so that he could make a $10 million loan to Rice Energy. In another instance, in May 2011 Rice received approval from a senior executive in BlackRock's Legal and Compliance Department to participate in a private placement debt offering by Rice Drilling B. The Rice Drilling B private placement memo (the "PPM") described Rice's role at Rice Energy—namely, as founder and managing general partner, as well as co-manager with his son of Rice Drilling B—and his role as managing director and portfolio manager at BlackRock. Rice also made the opening remarks on the offering's internet video roadshow used to solicit potential investors and stated his affiliation with Rice Energy and BlackRock, although at the direction of the BlackRock senior executive, Rice also noted that BlackRock did not have an equity interest or an implied interest in Rice Energy. In December 2011, Rice also notified certain BlackRock senior executives that, in connection with an investment by a private equity family of funds in Rice Energy, Rice's prior loans to a Rice Energy subsidiary would be converted to a direct equity interest in a newly formed Rice Energy subsidiary.

C. BlackRock Breached Its Fiduciary Duty by Failing to Disclose the Conflict of Interest

23. BlackRock did not inform the boards of directors of the Rice-managed registered funds or advisory clients about Rice's involvement with and investment in Rice Energy.

Although senior executives in BlackRock's Legal and Compliance Department considered the disclosure issue in privileged communications, no disclosure was made. On June 1, 2012, The Wall Street Journal published the first of three articles detailing Rice's connection to Rice Energy, and his simultaneous role as an energy sector portfolio manager at BlackRock.

24. As an investment adviser, BlackRock has a fiduciary duty to exercise the utmost good faith in dealing with its clients—including to fully and fairly disclose all material facts and to employ reasonable care to avoid misleading its clients. It is the client, not the investment adviser, who is entitled to determine whether a conflict of interest might cause a portfolio manager—consciously or unconsciously—to render advice that is not disinterested.

25. BlackRock breached its fiduciary duty by failing to disclose to the funds' boards and advisory clients the conflict of interest created when BlackRock permitted Rice to form, invest, and participate in an energy company while Rice was also managing several billion dollars in energy sector assets held in BlackRock funds and separate accounts. The conflict of interest became more acute once Rice Energy finalized its joint venture with ANR, as the Rice-managed funds and separate accounts held significant positions in ANR stock.

D. BlackRock Failed to Adopt and Implement Policies and Procedures Regarding Outside Activities

26. BlackRock did not have any written policies and procedures regarding the outside activities of its employees. BlackRock only required pre-approval for an employee to serve on a board of directors and had a general conflicts of interest provision in its Code of Business Conduct and Ethics ("Code") that addressed conflicts or potential conflicts that could arise from the personal activities or interests of BlackRock employees. Pursuant to the Code, BlackRock required all conflicts and potential conflicts to be reported to a supervisor, manager, or a member of BlackRock's Legal and Compliance Department.

27. BlackRock failed, however, to adopt and implement policies and procedures that addressed how the outside activities of BlackRock employees were to be assessed for conflicts purposes, as well as who was responsible for deciding whether the outside activity should be permitted.

28. BlackRock also failed to adopt and implement policies and procedures to monitor those employees with BlackRock-approved outside activities, so that BlackRock would stay informed about any changes in the employee's outside activity and re-evaluate it, if necessary.

29. As BlackRock's CCO, Battista was responsible for the design and implementation of BlackRock's written policies and procedures reasonably designed to prevent violations of the Advisers Act and its rules. Battista knew and approved of numerous outside activities engaged in by BlackRock employees (including Rice), but did not recommend written policies and procedures to assess and monitor those outside activities and to

disclose conflicts of interest to the funds' boards and to advisory clients. As such, Battista caused BlackRock's failure to adopt and implement these policies and procedures.

30. In January 2013, BlackRock subsequently adopted new written policies and procedures addressing the outside activities of BlackRock employees.

E. Respondents Caused the Funds' Failure to Report Rice's Policy Violations to the Funds' Boards of Directors

31. BlackRock had a private investment policy that, among other things, required employees to receive BlackRock's approval before making any private investments.

32. Rice violated BlackRock's private investment policy by not obtaining pre-approval to: (i) form and fund the Rice Energy Trust; and (ii) make approximately $14 million in loans to a Rice Energy subsidiary.

33. BlackRock and Battista knew about Rice's violations of its private investment policy, and also knew or should have known that these violations were "material compliance matters" under Rule 38a-1 and, hence, were required to be reported to the boards of directors of the Rice-managed registered funds. BlackRock and Battista also knew or should have known that the funds did not, in fact, report Rice's violations to the funds' boards.

Violations

34. As a result of the conduct described above, BlackRock willfully violated Section 206(2) of the Advisers Act, which prohibits an investment adviser from engaging in any transaction, practice, or course of business which operates as a fraud or deceit upon a client or prospective client. BlackRock breached its fiduciary duty by failing to disclose a conflict of interest—namely Rice's involvement with and investment in Rice Energy—to the BlackRock funds' boards of directors or to advisory clients.

35. As a result of the conduct described above, BlackRock willfully violated Section 206(4) of the Advisers Act and Rule 206(4)-7 thereunder by failing to adopt and implement written policies and procedures reasonably designed to prevent violations of the Advisers Act and its rules. BlackRock failed to adopt and implement written policies and procedures to assess and monitor the outside activities of its employees and to disclose conflicts of interest to the funds' boards and to advisory clients. Battista caused BlackRock's compliance-related violations.

36. As a result of the conduct described above, BlackRock and Battista caused certain BlackRock funds' violations of Rule 38a-1(a) under the Investment Company Act. Rule 38a-1(a)(4)(iii)(B) requires registered investment companies, through their chief compliance officer, to provide a written report at least annually to the fund's board of directors that addresses each material compliance matter that occurred since the date of the last report. Rule 38a-1, in pertinent part, defines a "material compliance matter" as any compliance matter about which the fund's board of directors would reasonably need to know to oversee fund compliance, and that involves, without limitation, a violation of the policies and procedures of its investment adviser. BlackRock and Battista

caused the failures by certain BlackRock funds to report all material compliance matters—namely Rice's violations of BlackRock's private investment policy—to their boards of directors. [***]

* * *

Notes and Applications

1. *Compliance officers.* A key aspect of this case is the role and responsibility of Bautista, the CCO. The rules not only require the appointment of someone to serve as a CCO but expose that person to liability for failing to discharge his or her responsibilities. The SEC notes that Bautista "was responsible for the design and implementation of BlackRock's written policies and procedures...." With pre-clearance of outside activities included in BlackRock's policies and procedures, the SEC asserted that there should have also been policies and procedures for how such outside activities are assessed regarding conflicts of interest, including monitoring of the approved activities. The SEC holds Bautista responsible for the series of lapses in monitoring and oversight of Rice's activities, even after BlackRock and Rice agreed to a common approach. Clearly, the CCO of a large complex like BlackRock wouldn't handle the details of the monitoring and reporting necessary in this situation. However, he or she is responsible for ensuring the effectiveness of policies and procedures, especially, as here, where a "material compliance matter" had arisen. At the very least, the CCO must alert ultimate decision-makers of the existence of deficiencies in policies or procedures or problems encountered in applying them.

2. *Disclosure as a potential cure.* Note paragraph 24 of the settlement. What role could disclosure have played in this case? Among the roles, as the SEC notes, it would give the client the ability to decide whether a conflict of interest is troublesome to it. And, if it is, the client can choose to object to the arrangement or, in theory, terminate its agreement with BlackRock. If the ultimate decision-maker gives its *de facto* consent to the arrangement when acting in a fiduciary capacity, such as a fund board, then the board assumes responsibility for that decision.

3. *Board oversight.* In the *BlackRock* case, the SEC focused in part on the failure to inform the RICs' boards of a "material compliance matter," i.e., Rice's outside activities and the various related impacts and conflicts. The SEC's finding only serves to highlight the role and importance of board oversight in Company Act Rule 38a-1. As noted above, board acquiescence in such an arrangement could well have posed an issue as to whether the board or boards in question properly discharged their oversight obligations. This textbook excerpts two SEC administrative orders in in which the SEC sanctions boards for deficient oversight of fund affairs under Rule 38a-1. In *In the Matter of Northern Lights Compliance Services, LLC, et al.*, Investment Company Act Release No. 30502 (May 2, 2013) (discussed in Chapter 12), the SEC did not cite a violation of fiduciary duties under Section 15(c), the area of substantive concern, but rather for the funds' trustees' failure to ensure adequate compliance processes. In the other directors case, *In the Matter of J. Kenneth Alderman, CPA, et. al.*, Invest-

ment Company Release No. 30557 (June 13, 2013) (discussed in Chapter 16), the SEC sanctioned the board in connection with manifest violations of the SEC's pricing rule in calculating the NAV of several funds as a failure of the board's oversight of compliance obligations under Rule 38a-1. Taken together these cases signal the power and importance of having reasonably designed and implemented compliance policies and procedures and the need for robust board engagement in that oversight process.

4. *How to do it right.* In 2014, Rice began serving as the primary portfolio manager for energy sector strategies at GRT Capital Partners, a Boston-based hedge fund company with about $885 million in assets under management. In what sense did this create a conflict that required BlackRock to take steps? The SEC's concern does not appear to be of the sort implicated by Company Act Rule 17j-1 or Advisers Act Rule 204A-1, e.g., that Rice had information about securities held or to be acquired by BlackRock funds that Rice would use to benefit his family's energy company. Instead, the SEC focused on his "outside activity" with his family business as a conflict of interest that BlackRock's policies and procedures should have detected and disclosed to BlackRock's clients, funds, and their boards. How should have BlackRock handled this situation?

5. *Codes of conduct compared to codes of ethics.* Many companies and funds have implemented codes of conduct to govern and oversee employees' activities beyond the use of inside information and personal securities trading. Generally, such codes of conduct can address a broad range of issues from outside activities like working for other companies to dress codes to use of company computers and phones. Section 406 of the Sarbanes-Oxley Act—the provision requiring public companies, including RICs, to disclose whether or not they have a code of ethics for senior financial officers—spurred adoption of such corporate codes by funds and advisers wholly apart from the requirements of Company Act Rule 17j-1 or Advisers Act Rule 204A-1. As articulated in the Sarbanes-Oxley Act provision, such codes can address whether such senior financial officers have any "actual or apparent conflicts of interest between personal and professional relationships" and how such conflicts are resolved. As a practical matter, most RICs adopt an appropriate code of ethics for Sarbanes-Oxley purposes, either separate from their 17j-1 code or integrated into it, at the very least to avoid the need to disclose and explain why they have not done so, but also recognizing the positive effect that codes of conduct have, especially in an environment that demands comprehensive compliance policies and procedures.

Chapter 16

Pricing of Fund Shares and Valuation of Assets

Key Ideas: Most registered funds issue redeemable shares (i.e., mutual funds, UITs and, with respect to creation units, ETFs). As a result, funds must determine the net asset value ("NAV") of their shares (i.e., the value of the fund's assets less accrued liabilities, all divided by the number of shares outstanding). The NAV will determine the price at which shares are redeemed and new shares are issued. Determining fund NAV has consistently been one of the most challenging operational issues for funds and their service providers. There are two major obstacles relating to the NAV calculation: (i) the timing of the NAV calculation; and (ii) the pricing or valuation of the fund's underlying securities positions.

The timing issue concerns when NAV is calculated (i.e., the price at which shares will be redeemed or the price at which new fund shares will be sold). Pursuant to Company Act Rule 22c-1, the SEC mandates a forward-pricing regime (i.e., transaction prices are based on the daily NAV calculated after the order is received) pursuant to which most funds (i.e., mutual funds and ETFs) calculate their NAVs once each business day at the close of U.S. trading. Notwithstanding Rule 22c-1's forward-pricing regime, the mutual fund industry experienced a massive pricing scandal involving so-called late trading and market timing strategies. In the wake of the scandal, Rule 22c-1 was further tightened.

The second "pricing" issue is one of methodology used to accurately value portfolio securities. Accurate valuation of the securities in a portfolio is integral to NAV calculation. Issues affecting valuation of the fund's underlying securities portfolio can cause inaccurate NAVs and lead to mispricing of the fund's shares (i.e., fund shares are not being redeemed or issued at the correct price). Mispricing in turn harms either purchasers or sellers of a fund's shares, depending on whether the price is too high or too low. Company Act Rule 2a-4 mandates one of two methodologies in pricing portfolio securities: market quotations, when readily available, and otherwise, fair value determinations in accordance with board approved policies and procedures. Fair valuing in times of market stress has been a recurrent source of problems for funds and fund boards.

Chapter Contents

16.1 Introduction

Among the most important and challenging operations for most funds and their service providers is the accurate and timely calculation of "net asset value" ("NAV"). NAV constitutes the price that the fund will use to redeem shares and at which new fund shares will be sold. As discussed in Chapter 4, the daily process is complex, but over 10,000 mutual funds, as well as several thousand ETFs, accomplish this task daily in the U.S. Closed-end funds are not required to make the calculation daily, but most do. Even private funds, such as private equity funds and hedge funds, need to determine their NAVs periodically to effectuate redemptions or buy-ins. At the core of each day's calculation is determining the value of the fund's securities portfolio. Since the values of securities owned by the fund fluctuate daily, this task requires pricing each and every securities position in the fund's portfolio, and then using those figures to generate a value for the fund's entire portfolio. To complete its calculation, the fund will net out liabilities accrued on a given day, and, after determining net assets, will then divide the net asset figure by the shares outstanding to determine a per share NAV.

This chapter explores the two most important issues connected to this calculation. First, when redeeming or issuing fund shares, which NAV should be used—the last determined NAV or the next determined NAV? Put more concretely, should the price at which fund shares are redeemed or issued be based on the NAV from yesterday (backward pricing) or the NAV at the end of the day (forward pricing)? The regulatory answer, as reflected in Rule 22c-1, is the latter rather than the former. Indeed, a forward-pricing regime is necessary to prevent flagrant abuses that would otherwise harm average investors in any fund. While Rule 22c-1 was intended to curb systemic pricing abuses, a scandal in the fund industry came to light in 2003 which showed that savvy and unscrupulous traders, aided and abetted by investment advisory personnel, were able to engage in late trading and market timing to the disadvantage of funds' shareholders. This episode revealed weaknesses in the rule which the SEC subsequently addressed.

Second, in determining NAV, how should funds go about valuing the securities in their investment portfolios? Mispricing of portfolio securities will lead to errors in calculating the fund NAV. As a result, valuations that systematically underprice (or more typically, overprice) the value of the fund's portfolio positions will adversely affect the fund and most shareholders (in terms of diluting share value). The Company Act and the rules thereunder require fund pricing and NAV calculation methodologies that are designed to achieve accuracy in pricing of a fund's securities portfolio and in determining a fund's NAV.

16.2 The Timing Issue

16.2.1 Forward vs. Backward Pricing; Rule 22c-1

The NAV of open-end funds (i.e., mutual funds) determines the price at which investors purchase and redeem their shares. NAV is also very relevant to shareholders of closed-end funds and exchange-traded funds. The NAV provides an objective benchmark of the intrinsic value of the fund's shares and provides an obvious reference point for evaluating the relevant price in purchasing or selling the shares of closed-end funds or ETFs. In the case of mutual fund shares, certain sales charges and commissions may be added to the NAV to constitute the "offering price" for load funds or classes of shares. In some instances, certain redemption fees may be deducted from the NAV to determine the proceeds owed to sellers of shares.

Until 1968, funds used the "backward pricing" methodology. Purchases and sales of shares were made at the most recently calculated NAV. Backward pricing was potentially appealing to investors because it allowed them to fix the primary terms of any transaction when placing an order to buy or sell: the price per share, the number of shares and the transaction cost or proceeds. However, as demonstrated in Chapter 4, using such a methodology creates opportunity for arbitrage between the price of shares based on yesterday's close and today's end-of-day expected price. Thus, an investor who knows the NAV (determined the previous afternoon) and trades today, aware that the value of portfolio securities has gone up, will be able to purchase fund shares at a discount (based on the substantial likelihood that the fund's NAV will be higher than yesterday when calculated at the end of the day). In such a transaction, the investor's discount comes at the expense of existing shareholders; the fund, by selling shares at a discount, effectively transfers value from existing shareholders (in the form of diluting the value of the shares of existing fund shareholders) to the new investor.

Rule 22c-1 was promulgated in 1968 to address the perceived unfairness to purchasers and seller of shares in transacting at prices not reflective of current NAV and the potential dilution suffered by existing shareholders. Under Rule 22c-1, funds are required to use "forward pricing," that is, funds use, and investors receive, a price for purchases or sales of shares which is based on the next calculated NAV. Mutual funds and ETFs calculate their NAVs daily as of the close of securities markets in the United States (currently 4 p.m. East Coast time). Since the price for mutual funds is not known until the end of the day, investors buying or selling mutual fund shares can either fix the number of shares to be bought or sold or the total transaction value when placing the order. The final terms, however, will only become known at the end of the day when the transaction price is finally fixed with the calculation of the end-of-day NAV.

Pricing of Redeemable Securities for Distribution, Redemption and Repurchase, etc.

Investment Company Act Release No. 5519 (Oct. 16. 1968)

[**Textbook note:** *The adopting Release for Rule 22c-1 reflects the SEC's twin concerns relating to pricing: unfairness to purchasers and seller of shares and dilution of existing shareholders. The last paragraph highlights the timing practices observed by the SEC in the 1960s. Clearly, backward pricing, if unchecked, had deleterious effects on funds and non-trading shareholders.*]

[* * *] Section 22(c) of the Investment Company Act, by reference to Section 22(a) of the Investment Company Act, authorizes the Commission to make rules and regulations applicable to principal underwriters of, and dealers in, the redeemable securities of registered investment companies "for the purpose of eliminating or reducing so far as reasonably practicable any dilution of the value of other outstanding securities of such company or any other result of such purchase, redemption, or sale which is unfair to holders of such other outstanding securities." Such rules and regulations are authorized with respect to, among other things, the time for computing the minimum price at which any redeemable security issued by an investment company may be purchased from such company and the maximum price at which such security may be sold to such company or at which such security may be surrendered to such company for redemption....

One purpose of Rule 22c-l ... is to eliminate or reduce so far as reasonably practicable any dilution of the value of outstanding redeemable securities of registered investment companies through (i) the sale of such securities at a price below their net asset value or (ii) the redemption or repurchase of such securities at a price above their net asset value. Dilution through the sale of redeemable securities at a price below their net asset value may occur, for example, through the practice of selling securities for a certain period of time at a price based upon a previously established net asset value. This practice permits a potential investor to take advantage of an upswing in the market and an accompanying increase in the net asset value of investment company shares by purchasing such shares at a price which does not reflect the increase. An investor may be encouraged to purchase securities in this manner by the practice of announcing the next sale price in advance of the time at which it becomes effective, thereby enabling the investor to time his purchase so as to obtain investment company securities at the lower of two known prices. Based upon its experience in the administration of the Investment Company Act, the Commission believes that such practices have the effect of diluting the value of outstanding redeemable securities of registered investment companies.

Another purpose of Rule 22c-l ... is to eliminate or reduce so far as reasonably practicable other results, aside from dilution, which arise from the sale, redemption, or repurchase of securities of registered investment companies and which are unfair to the holders of such outstanding securities. The Commission believes that the practice of selling securities for a certain period of time, at a price based upon a previously established net asset value, encourages speculative trading practices which so compromise registered investment companies as to be unfair to the holders of their outstanding securities. This pricing practice allows speculators to buy large blocks of such securities under circumstances where the net asset value of the securities has increased but where the increase in value is not reflected in the price. The speculators hold such securities until the next net asset value is determined and then redeem them at large profits. These speculative trading practices 'can seriously interfere with the management of registered investment companies to the extent that (i) management may hesitate to invest what it believes to be speculators' money and (ii) management may have to effect untimely liquidations when speculators redeem their securities. Based upon its experience in the administration of the Investment Company Act, the Commission believes that such practices cause unfair results to the holders of outstanding securities of registered investment companies. Rule 22c-l ... prohibits any registered investment company issuing any redeemable security; any person designated in such issuer's prospectus as authorized to consummate transactions in any such security; and any principal underwriter of, or dealer in, any such security from selling, redeeming, or repurchasing any such security except at a price determined in accordance with the provisions of the rule.... The rule ... requires that the price be based on the current net asset value of such security which is next computed after receipt of a tender of such security for redemption or of an order to purchase or sell such security. Current net asset value is defined by the rule to be that computed on each day during which the New York Stock Exchange is open for trading, not less frequently than once daily as of the time of the close of trading on such Exchange. The effect of the rule ... is to prohibit the practice of selling securities for a certain period of time at a price based on a previously established net asset value. [***]

* * *

16.2.2 Market Timing and Late Trading

The adoption of forward pricing was supposed to eliminate "gaming" NAV calculations, a practice which unfairly rewarded trading strategies of savvy purchasers and sellers at the expense of other investors. However, as funds traded more and more categories of securities (such as international securities and junk bonds), and as computerized trading systems developed, the issues of fairness and opportunism reemerged, culminating in a full-scale scandal in 2003. Although the forward-pricing regime instituted by Rule 22c-1 was intended to thwart timing arbitrage trading strategies, the regime was nevertheless vulnerable to two forms of risks: (1) risk of circumvention as it became increasingly difficult for funds to monitor the time when trades were actually placed with intermediaries during the trading day, creating late trading opportunities; and (2) risk of a different type of arbitrage known as market timing, trading toward the end of the day (but not after the close of trading) based on predictable systematic biases in calculating NAV at certain funds after the close. These matters came to a head in 2003 with the revelation of pervasive abuses of both types. The net result was dozens of enforcement actions against fund advisers and service providers, rewriting of regulations for funds and advisers, and a fair amount of industry soul-searching.

"Late trading" involved practices where some investors were routinely allowed to enter purchase or sale orders for shares *after* the NAV calculation cut-off time, i.e., after 4 pm. In some cases, this was done with the target fund's complicity and in other cases it was facilitated by poorly policed procedures relating to processing orders from securities intermediaries, such as broker-dealers or transfer agents. These trading opportunities enabled investors to game the pricing processes in exactly the ways the SEC had identified in 1968 and prohibited in Rule 22c-1. Such investors could use earnings announcements and other news released after the NAV calculation to determine with a high degree of certainty whether a fund's NAV, when next computed the following day, would likely be up or down and, thus, know whether purchases or sales of fund shares executed after hours might yield a favorable trading opportunity. Late trading thus was nothing more than a brazen effort to evade the requirements of Rule 22c-1.

"Market timing" reflects another form of unfair practice. In this case, certain funds are vulnerable to known pricing inefficiencies (i.e., systematic bias in reported prices of certain classes of securities in calculating NAV whose bias is predictable based on market events). Select investors allowed by funds to make rapid purchases and sales of fund shares with orders placed just before the end of the day benefited by exploiting these known pricing inefficiencies. In some cases, traders were assisted by receipt of material non-public information relating to the targeted fund's portfolio composition by the investment adviser's personnel. Firms frequently boasted that they had policies and procedures to prevent market timing, when actually they facilitated such trading to the detriment of other shareholders in the fund. As noted by the SEC in a footnote in its 2005 Adopting Release of amendments to Rule 22c-1: "Market timing, while not illegal per se, can harm other fund shareholders because (a) it can dilute the value of their shares, if the market timer is exploiting pricing inefficiencies, (b) it can disrupt the management of the fund's investment portfolio, and (c) it can cause the targeted fund to incur costs borne by other shareholders to accommodate the market timer's frequent buying and selling of shares." In short, while market timing does not violate Rule 22c-1, it is nevertheless harmful to the interests of long-term fund shareholders, and as discussed below, may implicate conduct that violates the securities law provisions.

In the Matter of Invesco Funds Group, Inc.

Investment Company Act Release 26629 (Oct. 8, 2004)

[**Textbook note:** *This settlement of a SEC action provides a detailed description of the way in which both large investors gained preferences with funds and how advisers and distributors facilitated market-timing schemes during the scandal. Interestingly, portfolio managers in this matter internally complained about what they perceived was going on, which indicates that fund personnel viewed the activities from differing institutional perspectives. The scheme itself implicated a wide variety of violations other than the pricing rule itself: Sections 206(1) and 206(2) of the Advisers Act regarding fraud and breach of fiduciary duties;*

Section 17(d) and Rule 17d-1 regarding joint transactions; and Section 34(b) regarding disclosures.]

[***] OVERVIEW

1. This is a proceeding against IFG, AIM Advisors, and ADI based on market timing agreements that allowed certain individuals and entities to make frequent trades in the Invesco Funds advised by IFG and AIM Mutual Funds advised by AIM Advisors. Market timing includes (a) frequent buying and selling of shares of the same mutual fund or (b) buying or selling mutual fund shares in order to exploit inefficiencies in mutual fund pricing.

Market timing, while not illegal per se, can harm other mutual fund shareholders because it can dilute the value of their shares, if the market timer is exploiting pricing inefficiencies, or disrupt the management of the mutual fund's investment portfolio and can cause the targeted mutual fund to incur costs borne by other shareholders to accommodate frequent buying and selling of shares by the market timer.

RESPONDENTS AND RELATED ENTITY

2. AMVESCAP PLC is a United Kingdom holding company whose American Depository Receipts trade on the New York Stock Exchange. IFG, AIM Advisors and ADI are now, and at all times relevant to this Order were, wholly-owned subsidiaries of AMVESCAP.

3. IFG, a Delaware corporation headquartered in Denver, and its predecessors have been registered with the Commission as investment advisers since 1957. During the time period relevant to this Order, IFG served as an investment adviser to eight registered open-ended investment companies, consisting of over forty-five series or mutual funds ("Invesco Funds"). AIM Advisors began assuming responsibility for serving as investment adviser to the Invesco Funds in 2003. IFG intends to voluntarily withdraw its registration with the Commission as an investment adviser as soon as it is practicable. On December 2, 2003, the Commission filed an action against IFG and its former chief executive officer ("CEO") in federal district court in connection with the matters described herein. SEC v. IFG et al., Civil Action No. 03N2421 (PAC).

4. AIM Advisors, a Delaware corporation headquartered in Houston, has been registered with the Commission as an investment adviser since November 1976. In 2003 and 2004, but after the conduct that is the subject of this order, the Invesco and AIM fund complexes became fully integrated and are now overseen by a single board of directors. AIM Advisors currently serves as an investment adviser to 14 registered open-ended investment companies, consisting of approximately eighty-seven series or mutual funds ("AIM Funds"). Five of these registered investment companies were a part of the Invesco complex, and the individual series within these registered investment companies continue to carry the Invesco name.

5. ADI, a Delaware corporation headquartered in Houston, has been registered with the Commission as a broker-dealer since February 1977. ADI is the primary distributor and principal underwriter for AIM Funds.

FACTS

IFG Overview

6. IFG entered into negotiated, but undisclosed, market timing agreements with over 40 individuals and entities (the "market timers" or "timers") which allowed them to "market time" certain Invesco Funds, while representing to other shareholders that it did not permit frequent trading in those funds.

7. Under the agreements, which existed from at least 2001 through July 2003, IFG permitted the market timers to make excessive exchanges and redemptions totaling approximately $58 billion in select Invesco Funds. Some of the timing agreements were entered into with the understanding that the market timer would make long-term investments, so-called "sticky assets," in certain non-timed Invesco Funds. IFG also tolerated market-timing activities by other shareholders with whom it did not have timing agreements from at least 2000 through July 2003 (the "relevant time period.").

8. The market timing agreements financially benefited IFG in that IFG realized additional advisory fees from the timed funds and sticky assets under its management. Because IFG had reason to believe that the assets brought to the Invesco Funds under the market timing agreements, while serving to increase IFG's advisory fees, could be traded in a manner detrimental to the Invesco Funds, IFG had a conflict of interest with the Invesco Funds. IFG failed to disclose the conflict of interest to the board of directors and shareholders of the affected Invesco Funds, thereby breaching IFG's fiduciary duty to the Invesco Funds.

9. The market timing agreements were also inconsistent with the disclosures made in the Invesco Funds' prospectuses. The prospectuses stated that shareholders could make up to four exchanges out of each fund per twelve-month period. The market timing agreements provided for more than the disclosed number of exchanges. Furthermore, while the prospectuses also disclosed that each fund reserved the right to modify the exchange policy if such a modification was determined to be in the best interests of the fund, IFG failed to make a determination that each proposed market timing agreement was in the best interest of the fund before entering into the agreement. In the aggregate, the market timing trades made under the agreements were detrimental to the Invesco Funds' shareholders for the reasons set forth in paragraph 1 above.

IFG's Market Timing Agreements

10. During the relevant time period, IFG experienced a dramatic and prolonged decline in its assets under management. IFG entered into the market timing agreements to lessen this decline.

11. At their height, the market timers held over $1 billion of the assets invested in the Invesco Funds, and during the relevant time period, made excessive exchanges and redemptions totaling approximately $58 billion. Frequent trading by investors who timed the Invesco Funds caused dilution to the affected funds.

12. IFG, through its CEO, established an internal organizational structure by which it entered into agreements with market timers. In most cases, the head of what was known as IFG's "market timing desk" would receive proposals from investors seeking to market time the Invesco Funds. After obtaining information from an investor about its proposed frequent trading model, the head of the market timing desk would then orally present that proposal to IFG's chief investment officer ("CIO"). The CIO then approved or rejected the proposed agreement. By design, none of the market timing agreements was reduced to writing.

13. Furthermore, IFG's commission structure for its salespeople provided for a separate and distinct payout for investments made in the Invesco Funds pursuant to the market timing agreements. Although this commission payout was lower than the payout for ordinary long-term investments, the fact that commission payouts on market timing investments were separately designated shows that IFG institutionalized the practice of entering into market timing agreements. Furthermore, this commission structure created an incentive for salespeople to bring market timing proposals to IFG, and the commission structure had that effect. Members of IFG's senior management knew about and approved this structure.

14. On several occasions, issues arose within IFG relating to the harmful and disruptive trading activities of the market timers. Primarily in response to complaints made by Invesco Fund managers, IFG's CEO, CIO, national sales manager, and the head of the market timing desk met to respond to the complaints while continuing the operation of IFG's market timing program.

15. With all market timers, IFG required that they keep their timed monies within the Invesco Fund complex when exchanging out of a fund approved for timing. With some market timers, IFG also required that they maintain sticky assets within the Invesco Fund complex in exchange for their ability to engage in frequent trading. IFG received additional fees from these assets under management.

16. IFG knew that the assets brought to the Invesco Funds under the market timing agreements, while serving to increase IFG's advisory fees, could be traded in a manner detrimental to the Invesco Funds, thereby placing IFG in a conflict of interest situation with the Invesco Funds. IFG breached its fiduciary duty to the Invesco Funds subject to the timing agreements by failing to disclose this conflict of interest to the board of directors of the Invesco Funds or to the Invesco Fund shareholders and obtain the board members' consent to the agreements.

IFG's Largest Timer

17. According to an internal memorandum, between August 2001 and February 2003, IFG's single largest timer, Canary Capital Partners LLC ("Canary"), was permitted to make up to 52 exchanges per year within ten Invesco Funds, with a total trading capacity of $304 million in those funds.

18. In February 2003, IFG's CIO informed other members of IFG's senior management that Canary's market timing activities were negatively affecting his ability to manage a particular Invesco Fund and costing that fund's "legitimate" shareholders. Due to

these activities, the CIO and another IFG fund manager recommended that IFG terminate Canary's market timing privileges. However, rather than terminating its relationship with Canary, IFG simply reduced Canary's timing capacity and confined Canary's trading activities to five particular Invesco Funds. Thereafter, Canary continued to make frequent trades in these funds until July 2003.

19. During 2002, IFG also introduced Canary to Invesco's European offshore fund complex. IFG did so with the knowledge and understanding that Canary intended to market time the offshore complex's funds, and that IFG would receive additional fees as a result of this agreement. Ultimately, IFG assisted the offshore complex in negotiating a final agreement with Canary, and IFG subsequently received various fees for Canary's trading activities in the offshore funds.

The Invesco Funds' Prospectuses Prohibited Market Timing and Frequent Trading in the Funds at the Same Time IFG Allowed Investors to Market Time the Funds

20. During the same period that IFG entered into agreements with market timers, the prospectuses for the Invesco Funds represented that IFG discouraged frequent trading by investors by attempting to limit the number of exchanges a shareholder could make in each Invesco Fund. To that end, these prospectuses disclosed that shareholders could "make up to four exchanges out of each fund per twelve-month period." The prospectuses further disclosed that "[e]ach Fund reserves the right to reject any exchange request, or to modify or terminate the exchange policy, if it is in the best interests of the Fund."

21. IFG prepared these prospectuses, provided them to shareholders and prospective shareholders in the Invesco Funds, and filed registration statements containing these prospectuses with the Commission.

22. IFG knew that its agreements with market timers were inconsistent with the Invesco Funds' prospectus disclosure. Specifically, IFG knew that the market timers were being allowed to make more than four exchanges out of certain Invesco Funds in a twelve-month period. IFG also knew that a determination that each proposed market timing agreement was in the best interest of the fund was not being made before it entered into the agreement. In fact, IFG knew that the timing activities were harming the Invesco Funds and their shareholders.

23. IFG also knew that its agreements with market timers were inconsistent with earlier representations IFG had made to the Invesco Funds' board of directors about how IFG would discourage market timing activities within the Invesco Funds. Specifically, in 1997, IFG represented to the board that IFG would strictly enforce the prospectus language by allowing a maximum of four exchanges or redemptions by an investor in an Invesco Fund over a twelvemonth period. Despite this representation, IFG subsequently entered into agreements with market timers without informing the board of IFG's unilateral change to the Invesco Funds' market timing policy.

24. Furthermore, in or about January 2003, the attorney who served as IFG's chief compliance officer prepared a memorandum concerning IFG's market timing activities. In the memorandum, the chief compliance officer discussed how IFG's tolerance of

market timers might not be in the best interests of the Invesco Funds and their shareholders, and explained a number of the potentially detrimental effects of market timing, including the portfolio managers' increased need for cash positions, lower returns in the timed funds, capital gain taxes unfairly paid by long-term shareholders, and negative impacts to the portfolio managers' abilities to carry out their investment strategies. Ultimately, the chief compliance officer recommended that IFG either enforce the existing prospectus language, modify the prospectus language to disclose IFG's actual practices, or adopt a new policy to limit market timing. The chief compliance officer gave the memorandum to IFG's CEO in January 2003. IFG's CEO did not circulate the chief compliance officer's memorandum to the board of directors of the Invesco Funds, nor did he follow any of the chief compliance officer's recommendations.

IFG Tolerated Frequent Trading by Investors With Whom It Did Not Have a Specific Agreement

25. In addition to entering into the market timing agreements described above in paragraphs 10 through 19, IFG typically did not take action to restrict the trading of Invesco Fund shareholders whom IFG knew were trading in excess of the four-exchange limit set forth in the Invesco Funds' prospectuses. The frequent trading by these shareholders also resulted in substantial dilution in the affected Invesco Funds....

VIOLATIONS

46. As a result of the conduct described above, IFG ... willfully violated Sections 206(1) and 206(2) of the Advisers Act in that, while each acted as an investment adviser, it employed devices, schemes, or artifices to defraud clients or prospective clients, and engaged in transactions, practices, or courses of business which operated or would operate as a fraud or deceit upon clients or prospective clients. Specifically, IFG and AIM Advisors entered into market timing agreements, which created a conflict of interest that IFG ... knowingly or recklessly failed to disclose to the board of directors or shareholders of their respective funds, and which were inconsistent with the funds' prospectus disclosures....

48. As a result of the conduct described above, IFG [and other named advisors and affiliates], each an affiliated person of its respective timed funds, willfully violated Section 17(d) of the Investment Company Act and Rule 17d-1 thereunder, in that, while acting as a principal, each participated in and effected transactions in connection with joint arrangements in which their respective funds were participants without filing an application with the Commission and obtaining a Commission order approving the transactions.

49. As a result of the conduct described above, IFG ... willfully violated Section 34(b) of the Investment Company Act in that each made an untrue statement of material fact in a registration statement, application, report, account, record, or other document filed or transmitted pursuant to the Investment Company Act, or omitted to state therein any fact necessary in order to prevent the statements made therein, in the light of the circumstances under which they were made, from being materially misleading. [***]

* * *

The 2003 market-timing and late-trading scandal, exemplified by the *Invesco* action, revealed pervasive problems in the fund industry at many levels. In response to these revelations, the SEC adopted significant new compliance policies and procedures initiatives under the Company and Adviser Act rules (discussed in Chapter 15) and governance initiatives (discussed in Chapter 11). To directly address the trading practices which had come to light in the scandal and which were designed to frustrate the purpose and spirit of Rule 22c-1, the SEC adopted Rule 22c-2 relating to redemption fees.

Mutual Fund Redemption Fees

Investment Company Act Release No. 26782 (March 18, 2005)

[**Textbook note:** *As explained in the SEC adopting release below, Rule 22c-2 enables, and indeed, requires fund boards to consider adopting redemption fees to deter market timing. It is important to understand how redemption fees reduce the opportunity to realize quick trading profits. In addition, the SEC required funds to tighten up procedures in dealing with intermediaries and processing trades. The SEC's approach in this area attempts to balance between features that encourage ease of purchase and redeemability of fund shares while reducing the opportunities for market timing or late trading.*]

[***] I. Background

Investors in mutual funds can redeem their shares on each business day and, by law, must receive their pro rata share of the fund's net assets. This redemption right makes funds attractive to fund investors, most of whom are long-term investors, because it provides ready access to their money if they should need it. The redemption right also makes funds attractive to a small group of investors who use funds to implement short-term trading strategies, such as market timing, by making frequent purchases and redemptions in order to capture small gains. Most fund shareholders, however, are not active traders of their shares.

Excessive trading in mutual funds occurs at the expense of long-term investors, diluting the value their shares. It may disrupt the management of a fund's portfolio and raise the fund's transaction costs because the fund manager must either hold extra cash or sell investments at inopportune times to meet redemptions. Frequent trading also may result in unwanted taxable capital gains for the remaining fund shareholders. Funds have taken steps to deter excessive trading or have sought reimbursement from traders for the costs of their excessive transactions.[9]

These steps frequently include establishing market timing policies that prevent shareholders from making frequent exchanges among funds, and imposing a redemp-

---

9. Some of the approaches that funds have adopted include: (i) restricting exchange privileges, including delaying both the redemption and purchase sides of an exchange; (ii) limiting the number of trades within a specified period; (iii) delaying the payment of proceeds from redemptions for up to seven days (the maximum delay permitted under section 22(e) of the Act); (iv) satisfying redemption

tion fee — a small fee at the time a shareholder redeems shares, typically a short time after purchasing them.[10]

Many funds, however, have been unable to effectively enforce their market timing policies or impose redemption fees on the accounts of investors who purchase fund shares through broker-dealers, banks, insurance companies, and retirement plan administrators ("intermediaries"). These shareholdings frequently are identified in the books of the fund (or its transfer agent) in the name of the intermediary, rather than in the name of the fund shareholder. Many intermediaries controlling these so-called "omnibus accounts" have provided the fund with insufficient information for the fund to apply redemption fees. Because of this lack of information, today many funds choose not to apply redemption fees, or are unable to enforce their policies against market timing with respect to shares held through these omnibus accounts. As a result, those shareholders have often been beyond the reach of fund directors' efforts to protect the fund and its shareholders from the harmful effects of short-term trading. A number of the market timing abuses identified through our investigations reveal that certain shareholders were concealing abusive market timing trades through omnibus accounts.

Last year we proposed to address the widespread problem of short-term trading in fund shares by requiring funds to impose a redemption fee of two percent of the amount redeemed on shares held for five business days or less. Under our proposal funds also would have had to require that intermediaries provide them weekly information about transactions of beneficial owners of shares held in omnibus accounts controlled by intermediaries. Our rule proposal was intended to reimburse the funds for the costs of short-term trading and to discourage short-term trading of fund shares by reducing the profitability of the trades.

II. Discussion

... Although many commenters, including fund management companies, supported the proposal, most commenters objected to a rule that would *mandate* a redemption fee. Many were concerned that the redemption fee would inadvertently apply to harmless transactions such as account rebalancings or redemptions after recent periodic contributions. In contrast one commenter urged that, if we were to adopt a mandatory fee, we require that the fee be imposed on *all* short-term redemptions so that it would be easy to implement, while others argued for a variety of exceptions under which a redemption fee would not apply. Still others urged that we permit redemption fees greater than two percent.

---

requests in-kind; and (v) identifying market timers and restricting their trading or barring them from the fund....

10. ... Funds' use of redemption fees is not new. We noted the use of redemption fees by funds in a 1966 report to Congress. Report of the Securities and Exchange Commission on the Public Policy Implications of Investment Company Growth, H.R. Rep. No. 89-2337, at 58, n.156 (1966) ("Redemption fees serve two purposes: (1) they tend to deter speculation in the fund's shares; and (2) they cover the fund's administrative costs in connection with the redemption.").

We continue to believe, and the weight of evidence submitted by commenters suggests, that redemption fees, together with effective valuation procedures, can be an effective means to protect funds and fund shareholders by requiring that short-term traders compensate funds for the costs that may result from frequent trading. Commenters persuaded us, however, that a mandatory fixed redemption fee imposed by Commission rule is not the best way to achieve our goals. Some funds may not have costs that warrant imposing any redemption fee; others may have lower costs and could protect their shareholders by imposing a redemption fee of less than two percent. Boards of directors, as several commenters suggested, are better positioned to determine whether the fund needs a redemption fee and, if so, the amount of the fee. We agree and have decided not to adopt a mandatory redemption fee.

Instead of requiring that each fund impose a redemption fee, the rule we are today adopting authorizes fund directors to impose a redemption fee of up to two percent of the amount redeemed when they determine that a fee is in their fund's best interest.[22] It permits each board to take steps it concludes are necessary to protect its investors, and provides the board flexibility to tailor the redemption fee to meet the needs of the fund. As a result of our adoption of this rule, which is described in more detail below, the staff no-action positions concerning redemption fees have terminated.

We also are adopting a requirement that each fund enter into written agreements with its financial intermediaries, including those holding shares in omnibus accounts, providing the fund with access to information about transactions by fund shareholders. This information will permit funds to better enforce their market timing policies. The agreement also must contain a provision requiring the intermediary to execute the fund's instructions to restrict or prohibit further purchases or exchanges by any shareholder identified by the fund as having engaged in trading that violates the fund's market timing policies.

A. Redemption Fees

Rule 22c-2 requires that each fund's board of directors (including a majority of independent directors) either (i) approve a redemption fee that in its judgment is necessary or appropriate to recoup costs the fund may incur as a result of redemptions, or to otherwise eliminate or reduce dilution of the fund's outstanding securities, or (ii) determine that imposition of a redemption fee is not necessary or appropriate. The rule thus requires each board before the compliance date to at least consider implementing a redemption fee program to counter short-term trading.

---

22. Rule 22c-2 prohibits a fund from redeeming shares within seven days after the share purchase unless the fund meets three conditions. *See* rule 22c-2(a). First, the board of directors must either (i) approve a redemption fee, or (ii) determine that imposition of a redemption fee is either not necessary or not appropriate. Second, the fund (or its principal underwriter) must enter into a written agreement with each financial intermediary under which the intermediary agrees to (i) provide, at the fund's request, identity and transaction information about shareholders who hold their shares through an account with the intermediary, and (ii) execute instructions from the fund to restrict or prohibit future purchases or exchanges. Third, the fund must maintain a copy of each written agreement with a financial intermediary for six years.

The proceeds of the redemption fee, in all cases, must be paid to the fund itself. The redemption fee is designed to reconcile conflicts between shareholders who would use the fund as a short-term trading vehicle, and those making long-term investments who would otherwise bear the costs imposed on the fund by short-term traders. Directors may impose the fee to offset the costs of short-term trading in fund shares, and/or to discourage market timing and other types of short-term trading strategies.

The redemption fee may not exceed two percent of the amount redeemed. Some commenters called for us to permit higher redemption fees because such fees may be more effective at preventing abusive market timing transactions. We believe that a higher redemption fee could harm ordinary shareholders who make an unexpected redemption as a result of a financial emergency. Moreover, it would in our judgment impose an undue restriction on the redeemability of shares required by the Act. The two percent limit is designed to strike a balance between two competing goals of the Commission—preserving the redeemability of mutual fund shares while reducing or eliminating the ability of shareholders who rapidly trade their shares to profit at the expense of their fellow shareholders.[30] Funds have, and should utilize, additional tools to prevent abusive market timing transactions.

Directors may set a redemption fee of less than two percent under rule 22c-2. Unlike the approach taken by certain funds in the past, the amount of the redemption fee approved by directors need not be tied to the administrative and processing costs associated with redeeming fund shares. By adopting rule 22c-2, we now are permitting redemption fees to be based on the judgment of the fund and its board rather than on a strict assessment of administrative and processing costs, which can be difficult to estimate and may vary from period to period. Under rule 22c-2, a fund board setting the amount of the redemption fee could, for example, take into consideration indirect costs to the fund that arise from short-term trading of fund shares, such as liquidity costs, *i.e.*, the cost of investing a greater portion of the fund's portfolio in cash or cash items than would otherwise be necessary.

Rule 22c-2 authorizes the board to approve a redemption fee on shares redeemed within seven or more calendar days after the shares were purchased. Thus, the rule permits a fund board that adopts a redemption fee to determine, in its judgment, whether a period longer than seven calendar days is necessary or appropriate for the fund to protect its shareholders. This determination could, for example, include considerations as to whether different combinations of holding periods and redemption fee levels are appropriate for different funds that do not have the same vulnerability to market timing.

30. We also are using our exemptive authority under section 6(c) of the Act in adopting rule 22c-2. By adopting the rule, we are providing an exemption from the Act's requirement that investors redeeming shares of a mutual fund must receive their pro rata net asset value of their shares (section 2(a)(32) of the Act [15 U.S.C. § 80a-2(a)(32)] and from the Act's prohibition against the issuance of a senior security. Shares not subject to the redemption fee could be considered to be a senior security, in violation of section 18(f)(1) of the Act [15 U.S.C. § 80a-18(f)(1)] (prohibiting a fund from issuing a security that has priority over other securities with regard to distribution of assets).

B. Shareholder Transaction Information

Rule 22c-2 also requires funds to enter into written agreements with their intermediaries under which the intermediaries must, upon request, provide funds with certain shareholder identity and trading information. This requirement will enable funds to obtain the information that they need to monitor the frequency of short-term trading in omnibus accounts and enforce their market timing policies.

Many commenters opposed our proposal, which would have required financial intermediaries to deliver identification and transaction information each week. Commenters argued that weekly delivery and receipt of the information would be costly and burdensome for funds and financial intermediaries.... The rule we are adopting makes funds responsible for determining when they need a financial intermediary's assistance in monitoring and enforcing fund market timing policies....

(1) *Fund Responsibilities.* Rule 22c-2 requires that each fund (or its principal underwriter), regardless of whether it imposes a redemption fee, enter into a written agreement with each of its financial intermediaries under which each intermediary must provide the fund, upon request, information about the identity of shareholders and about their transactions in fund shares. Funds can use this information to monitor trading and identify shareholders in omnibus accounts engaged in frequent trading that is inconsistent with fund market timing policies. Funds have flexibility to request information periodically, or when circumstances suggest that a financial intermediary is not assessing redemption fees or that abusive market timing activity is occurring.[48] Access to this trading information provides funds (and their chief compliance officers) an important new tool to monitor trading activity in order to detect market timing and to assure consistent enforcement of their market timing policies. We expect funds that are susceptible to market timing will use it regularly.

(2) *Financial Intermediaries.* Rule 22c-2 also requires the agreement with financial intermediaries to contain a provision under which the intermediary agrees to execute the fund's instructions to restrict or prohibit further purchases or exchanges by a specific shareholder (as identified by the fund) who has engaged in trading that violates the fund's market timing policies. We have included this provision in response to comments regarding the difficulty of applying fund market timing restrictions to shares redeemed through omnibus accounts. Intermediaries currently may not enforce funds' market timing restrictions on their customers because, as one commenter explained, it is not in the intermediary's interest to do so. Accordingly, even if funds receive shareholder trading information, as another commenter pointed out, it will have little prac-

---

48. Under the rule, a fund that does not impose a redemption fee may nonetheless request the transactional information from its intermediaries. In some cases, such funds may wish to access this information to determine whether a redemption fee is necessary. In addition, intermediaries may have agreed to enforce a fund's market timing policies, or have established procedures designed to preclude violations of the fund's trading policies. In these circumstances, a fund may not need to exercise its rights under the contract. Funds could contract with financial intermediaries for the period of time that intermediaries would have to retain the shareholder information for transmission to the fund.

tical value if the fund is unable to prevail upon the intermediary to enforce its market timing policies. The requirement in the final rule that the written agreement provide for the intermediary to execute the fund's instructions should address these concerns. [* * *]

* * *

Notes and Applications

1. *The purpose of redemption fees.* It is important to be clear regarding the purpose of redemption fees as provided in the rule and the general orientation of the statute. Does the rule require the imposition of redemption fees? Why not? Can a board, if it so decides, impose redemption fees on its shareholders without limitation? Again, from a policy perspective, why not? What is the motivation between the rule's attempt to balance between the selective imposition of redemption fees and the general regulatory policy prohibiting redemption fees? Sections 22(c) and (e) are instructive.

2. *How should boards make decisions regarding redemption fees?* The amendments imposed new responsibilities on boards. The amendments suggest that the suitability of redemption fees may depend on the facts and circumstances of each fund and especially funds' investment strategies. What kind of funds are likely to benefit most from the institution of redemption fees, and for what types of funds would redemption fees make little sense? Should a board document its rationale in determining whether to impose a redemption fee (or perhaps even more importantly, in determining not to impose redemption fees)?

3. *A rule that mandates a "hard close" versus a rule that mandates an information sharing scheme?* The amendments also address a more technical issue regarding the processing of orders to purchase and sell fund shares. Another approach that was considered, and ultimately rejected, was to force funds to impose a hard close, meaning that the fund's transfer agent would have to receive the order no later than a fixed point in time during the day (e.g., 4 p.m. Eastern Standard Time). Why do you think the SEC, in response to industry requests, agreed to permit a complex system of gathering shareholder transaction information rather than imposing a hard close on the fund's receipt of customer orders?

16.3 Valuation Methodology Issue and Rule 2a-4

The timing of the NAV calculation frames a central consideration in understanding pricing issues, but is separate from the issues related to performing the calculation. The central issue in NAV calculation concerns how to value a fund's portfolio securities, which requires a fund to determine the current value of each individual security held by the fund, on a daily basis. Company Act Rule 2a-4 requires funds to use one of two methodologies. When readily available, funds must use market quotations, such as stock market quotes, to value their securities. When a market quotation is not readily available, then the fund must use the fair value of such security, as determined in good faith by the fund's board of directors. In practice, the board oversees the pricing process by approving procedures for fair valuation and periodically reviewing fair valuations made by fund personnel. As a result, a fund must initially determine whether market quotations are in fact readily available, and this determination requires some consideration of the facts and circumstances, even when quotations of some sort appear to be available. Unlike market quotations, a fair value determination is not always bright lined and may require the exercise of professional judgement. The following reading provides an introduction to the challenges of determining which method is appropriate. It also demonstrates what operative standards govern the fair valuation process, which has consistently been among the most challenging operational issues for funds and their service providers.

Investment Company Institute re: Valuation Issues (First Letter)

SEC Staff Interpretive Guidance Letter (December 8, 1999)

[**Textbook note:** *This letter from the SEC's Division of Investment Management provided guidance regarding issues that have specifically arisen regarding the pricing of funds with securities of international issuers in the wake of market interruptions in the relevant foreign markets. While drafted with an eye to those circumstances, the staff's letter provides general guidance regarding the need to use fair value pricing and the role of the board in overseeing pricing procedures.*]

[***] We discuss below three issues relating to funds' responsibilities for pricing portfolio securities. First, we clarify that market quotations for portfolio securities are not readily available when the exchanges or markets on which those securities trade do not open for trading for the entire day, and that funds, accordingly, must price those securities based on their fair value ("fair value price"). Second, we provide additional guidance regarding the process of fair value pricing, and describe certain factors that funds should consider when fair value pricing portfolio securities. Finally, we discuss the obligations of fund boards of directors ("boards") for fair value pricing securities, and discuss measures that boards may take when discharging those responsibilities....

Availability of Market Quotations

The 1940 Act requires mutual funds to value their portfolio securities by using the market value of the securities when market quotations for the securities are "readily available." When market quotations are not readily available, the 1940 Act requires fund boards to determine, in good faith, the fair value of the securities. These pricing requirements are critical to ensuring that the prices at which fund shares are purchased and redeemed are fair, and do not result in dilution of shareholder interests or other harm to shareholders.

When the exchange or market on which a security is traded does not open for trading for an entire trading day, and no other market prices are available, we believe that market quotations for that security are no longer "readily available." In such instances, funds holding securities traded on the closed exchange or market must fair value price those securities. For example, following September's earthquake in Taiwan, the Taiwan Stock Exchange ("TSE") was closed for a number of days. We believe that under these circumstances, market prices for securities traded on the TSE were not "readily available" and that funds holding such securities were required to use fair value prices in determining NAV. In anticipation of circumstances such as these, funds should consider adopting procedures that are designed to alert the board and fund management to conditions that may necessitate fair value pricing of portfolio securities.

Fair Value Pricing

... The Commission has stated that, as a general principle, the fair value of a portfolio security is the price which the fund might reasonably expect to receive upon its current sale. Ascertaining fair value requires a determination of the amount that an arm's-length buyer, under the circumstances, would currently pay for the security. Fair value cannot be based on what a buyer might pay at some later time, such as when the market ultimately recognizes the security's true value as currently perceived by the portfolio manager. Funds also may not fair value price portfolio securities at prices which are not achievable on a current basis on the belief that the fund would not currently need to sell those securities. Thus, bond or similar funds generally may not fair value price portfolio securities at par based on the expectation that the funds will hold those securities until maturity, if the funds could not receive par value upon the current sale of those securities.

This is not to say that fair value pricing is an inelastic concept.... Instead, the Commission adopted a more flexible standard which requires fund directors to "satisfy themselves that all appropriate factors relevant to the value of securities for which market quotations are not readily available have been considered and to determine the method of arriving at the fair value of each such security." ... Whether a factor is "appropriate," and whether a particular indication of value is available, depends upon the particular facts and circumstances of the situation. Thus, during emergency situations, fund boards should evaluate as many relevant factors as they are able to under the circumstances.

... While we believe that an analysis of the value of the investment itself continues to be of primary importance in determining fair value, we also believe that in many situations fund boards may need to incorporate other, external sources of information in their fair value determinations. Information derived from world financial markets and various financial products, which can assist in establishing the value of portfolio securities or can provide indications as to the value of securities comparable to those in the portfolio, may be useful for fair value pricing in certain circumstances.

The following list of factors that fund boards may need to consider, if relevant, when fair value pricing portfolio securities is merely illustrative, and is not intended to preclude a board's consideration of any other factors. The factors include: the value of other financial instruments, including derivative securities, traded on other markets or among dealers; trading volumes on markets, exchanges, or among dealers; values of baskets of securities traded on other markets, exchanges, or among dealers; changes in interest rates; observations from financial institutions; government (domestic or foreign) actions or pronouncements; and other news events. With respect to securities traded on foreign markets, the factors also might include the value of foreign securities traded on other foreign markets, ADR trading, closed-end fund trading, foreign currency exchange activity, and the trading prices of financial products that are tied to baskets of foreign securities....

We believe that a fund board, when fair value pricing portfolio securities in an emergency or other unusual situation, should evaluate the nature and duration of the event and the forces influencing the operation of the financial markets. The board also should evaluate factors relating to the event that precipitated the problem, whether the event is likely to recur, whether the effects of the event are isolated or whether they affect entire markets, countries, or regions. We believe that, at a minimum, fund boards should consider how factors, such as those listed above, or other, similar factors, to the extent relevant, may assist in fair value pricing portfolio securities.

The Board's "Good Faith" Responsibilities

The development of world financial markets and the proliferation of new financial products have both simplified and complicated a board's responsibilities when fair value pricing portfolio securities. Access to information regarding global financial markets, as well as instantaneous communications, are continually raising the amount of current and accurate information in the marketplace. New markets and products, such as those discussed above, provide alternative pricing indicators and benchmarks, which can ease the task of fair value pricing. Conversely, these new sources of information also have increased significantly the number of factors that a mutual fund board may need to evaluate when fair value pricing portfolio securities. This, in turn, provides additional challenges to fund directors, who may have to consider numerous alternatives when making complex decisions under tight time constraints.

We also recognize that different fund boards, or funds in the same complex with different boards, when fair value pricing identical securities, could reasonably arrive at prices that were not the same, consistent with the boards' obligation to fair value price in good faith. We believe that "good faith" is a flexible concept that can accommodate many different considerations, including the incorporation of a variety of sources of information. Finally, we believe that the specific actions that a mutual fund board must take in order to satisfy its good faith obligation under Section 2(a)(41) of the 1940 Act will vary, depending on the nature of the particular fund, the context in which the board must fair value price, and, importantly, the pricing procedures adopted by the board.

... Mutual fund boards, however, typically are only indirectly involved in the day-to-day pricing of a fund's portfolio securities. Most boards fulfill their obligations by reviewing and approving pricing methodologies, which may be formulated by the board, but more typically are recommended and applied by fund management. In reviewing and approving pricing procedures, boards should determine whether those methodologies and procedures are reasonably likely to result in the valuation of securities at prices which the funds could expect to receive upon their current sale. Mutual funds also may use a number of other techniques to minimize the burdens of fair value pricing on their directors. For example, a number of funds delegate certain responsibilities for fair value pricing decisions to a valuation committee. Such committees generally assist the board in developing methodologies by which fair values are to be calculated, and implement the board-approved methodologies on a daytoday basis or as frequently as necessary.

A mutual fund board can take significant steps toward satisfying its good faith obligations prior to an emergency or unusual situation. We believe that, in general, the degree of involvement required of a board during emergencies will depend heavily on the comprehensiveness of the pricing procedures adopted for the fund and the degree of discretion vested in fund management. If, for example, a board has approved comprehensive procedures which provide methodologies for how fund management should fair value price portfolio securities, including procedures which would be appropriate for that particular emergency situation, a board would need to have comparatively little involvement in the valuation process in order to satisfy its good faith obligation. This necessitates, of course, that the board periodically review the appropriateness of the methods used to fair value price portfolio securities and the quality of the prices obtained through these procedures, and that it make changes when appropriate.

When the board has vested a comparatively greater amount of discretion in fund management, or when pricing procedures are relatively vague, we believe that the board's involvement must be greater and more immediate. In these instances, a fund board may be required to evaluate how emergency conditions are affecting the fund's pricing mechanisms, whether the pricing procedures are appropriate, what inquiries fund management is making, and what factors management is considering when making valuation recommendations. Depending on the particular circumstances, the board may need to evaluate how particular portfolio securities are being priced, or, when the fund has limited or no fair value pricing procedures, authorize the specific pricing methodology used.

In any event, given that the fund's board retains oversight responsibility for the valuation of the fund's assets, the board should receive periodic reports from fund management that discuss the functioning of the valuation process and that focus on issues and valuation problems that have arisen. [***]

* * *

Investment Company Institute re: Valuation Issues (Second Letter)

SEC Staff Interpretive Guidance Letter (April 30, 2001)

[**Textbook note:** *In 2001, the SEC's Division of Investment Management provided further elaboration on views expressed in the 1999 Letter, especially relating to the board's duty of good faith. It also discussed in portions not excerpted here regarding when market quotations are not readily available. The Letter also contains a useful practical exhibit illustrating the consequences of not using fair value pricing when there are material pricing events between the closing of a foreign market and the next calculation of NAV in the U.S. based on prevailing prices at the close in New York many hours later. This situation illuminates and shows how errant pricing methodologies may expose the fund to opportunistic investors.*]

[***] B. The Good Faith Requirement

In the 1999 Letter, we discussed the requirement that fund boards must determine, in "good faith," the fair value of portfolio securities for which market quotations are not readily available. We stated our view that the good faith requirement is a flexible concept that can accommodate many different considerations, and that the specific actions that a board must take will vary, depending on the nature of the particular fund, the context in which the board must fair value price, and the pricing procedures adopted by the board.[22]

Since we issued the 1999 Letter, we have been requested to provide additional guidance concerning the good faith requirement. In our view, a board acts in good faith when its fair value determination is the result of a sincere and honest assessment of the amount that the fund might reasonably expect to receive for a security upon its current sale, based upon all of the appropriate factors that are available to the fund. Consistent with the good faith requirement, boards may appoint persons to assist them in determining fair values and to make actual fair value calculations under the boards' direction. See ASR No. 118, *supra* n. 4 [omitted]. See also [the 1999 Letter].[23] Furthermore, we believe that a board acts in good faith when it "continuously review[s] the appropriateness of the method used" in determining the fair value of the fund's portfolio securities. Compliance with the good faith standard generally reflects the directors' faithfulness to the duties of care and loyalty that they owe to the fund.

22. In providing this guidance, we also stated that "different fund boards, or funds in the same complex with different boards, when fair value pricing identical securities, could reasonably arrive at prices that were not the same, consistent with the boards' obligations to fair value price in good faith." See [the 1999 Letter].

23. Consistent with the good faith requirement, boards may appoint persons to assist them in determining fair values and to make actual fair value calculations under the boards' direction. See ASR No. 118, *supra* n. 4. See also [the 1999 Letter].

We believe, however, that a fund board generally would not be acting in good faith if, for example, the board knows or has reason to believe that its fair value determination does not reflect the amount that the fund might reasonably expect to receive for the security upon its current sale. In addition, a fund board generally would not be acting in good faith if it acts with reckless disregard for whether its fair value determination reflects the amount that the fund might reasonably expect to receive for the security upon its current sale. The Commission has instituted several enforcement actions against fund directors under these circumstances.[25] ...

D. The Inappropriate Use of Fair Values when Market Quotations are Readily Available

We also wish to set forth our views on the obligation of funds to value their portfolio securities for which market quotations are readily available. In such circumstances, funds are not permitted to ignore these quotations and fair value price the securities. This would not be consistent with a fund's obligation under the 1940 Act and could result in an incorrect NAV.

We believe that funds must exercise reasonable diligence to obtain market quotations for their portfolio securities before they may properly conclude that market quotations are not readily available. If, for example, a fund obtains market quotations for a portfolio security from one source and determines that they are unreliable, the fund should diligently seek to obtain market quotations from other sources, such as other dealers or other pricing services, before concluding that market quotations are not readily available....

* * *

Example: Fair Value Pricing

The following example illustrates how fair value pricing can safeguard long-term mutual fund investors. It is based entirely on hypothetical facts and does not take any fees into account. All number s have been rounded off.

Assume that two different foreign-stock mutual funds—Fund A and Fund B—both own securities that are traded primarily on the same Asian foreign exchange.

Both funds generally use closing market prices to value their portfolio securities, but Fund B determines the fair value of its portfolio securities if a significant event that would affect the value of those securities occurs after the close of the foreign exchange but before its NAV calculation. Each fund has total assets of $50 million, with 5 million shares outstanding and an NAV of $10 per share.

---

25. In one action, for example, the fund's directors continued to fair value a portfolio security at its last available NASDAQ market quotation for a significant period of time, notwithstanding that the directors knew, among other things, that the security had been de-listed from the NASDAQ, the issuer had experienced continuing losses and repeatedly failed to meet income projections, and actual sales prices during the period were lower than the fair value used by the directors to calculate NAV. *Parnassus Investments, et al.*, Initial Dec. No. 131 (Sept. 3, 1998), initial dec. final (Oct. 8, 1998)....

Day 1: Foreign market declines and investors buy fund shares

On Day 1, the Asian market closes (at 3:00 a.m. Eastern Time) significantly lower, causing the value of the securities held by both funds to decrease approximately 10 percent. During Day 1 in the United States, trading in other instruments (such as financial futures, depositary receipts, exchange-traded funds, and closed-end country funds) indicates a countervailing increase in value of approximately 10 percent, which strongly suggests that stock prices in the Asian market, when it opens, will increase to the same level as before the previous day's decrease. Knowing this, investors buy \$10 million worth of shares of each fund to try to take advantage of potentially undervalued fund shares. At the end of Day 1, Fund A, using the share prices at the close of the Asian market, calculates its NAV at \$9 per share. This is the price at which the investors buy shares of the fund. Fund B's NAV remains at \$10 per share because, using fair value pricing, Fund B took into account the likely increase in share prices in the Asian market by evaluating the trading in other instruments.

Day 2: Foreign market recovers and investors redeem their shares

On Day 2, the Asian market rebounds to equal its original level before Day 1. The market closes on Day 2 at this level. The valuation of the securities in Fund A, using closing market prices, increases and offsets the losses from the previous day. The valuation of the securities in Fund B remains the same as it was at the end of Day 1.

Result: Investors profit at expense of long-term investors in Fund A

If the investors who bought fund shares on Day 1 redeem their shares on Day 2, the investors who bought shares of Fund A (which used closing market prices) have a profit of \$911,110, which reflects their purchase of undervalued fund shares at \$9 per share on Day 1. This profit is at the expense of long-term investors in Fund A, whose share value is reduced by \$0.18 per share (even though the value of the fund's underlying assets is unchanged). This \$0.18 represents profits taken by the short-term, redeeming investors. By contrast, the investors who bought shares of Fund B (which used fair value pricing) break even, because the value at which they redeem their shares on Day 2, \$10 per share, is the same as the value at which they bought the shares on Day 1. The share value of long-term investors of Fund B also remains the same, and there is no loss to these investors.

The chart below illustrates this hypothetical example:

	Beginning	Day 1	Day 2	After Redemption by Investors
Fund A				
Closing Market Prices				
Total Assets	$50 mil.	$45 mil.[1]	$60 million[2]	$49.09 mil.[3]
Fund Shares	5 million	5 Million	6.11 million[4]	5 million
Net Asset Value[5]	**$10/share**	**$9/share**	**$9.82/share**	**$9.82/share**
Profit taken by Investors				**$911,110[6]**
Loss to long-term Investors				**$911,110**
Fund B				
Fair Value Pricing				
Total Assets	$50 mil.	$50 mil.[7]	$60 mil.[8]	$50 mil.[9]
Fund Shares	5 million	5 Million	6 million[10]	5 million
Net Asset Value[5]	**$10/share**	**$10/share**	**$10/share**	**$10/share**
Profit taken by Investors				**0**
Loss to long-term Investors				**0**

[***]

* * *

Notes and Applications

1. *The inputs used in fair valuation.* The accounting literature provides some additional insight into fair valuation of assets. FASB's Accounting Standards Codification

---

1. Total assets ($50 million) minus decrease in value of approximately 10 percent of securities held by the fund ($5 million).

2. Day 1 total assets ($45 million) plus increase in value of approximately 10 percent of securities held by the fund ($5 million) plus amount invested by investors ($10 million).

3. Day 2 total assets ($60 million) minus amount of assets redeemed by investors ($10.91 million = 1.11 million shares invested at $9.82 per share).

4. Day 1 fund shares outstanding (5 million) plus shares issued to investors (1.11 million = $10 million divided by $9 per share).

5. NAV = total assets divided by number of fund shares.

6. Beginning total assets ($50 million) minus total assets after redemption by investors ($49.09 million).

7. Total assets ($50 million) minus decrease in value of approximately 10 percent of securities held by the fund ($5 million) plus likely increase in value of approximately 10 percent of securities held by the fund under fair value pricing ($5 million).

8. Day 1 total assets ($50 million) plus amount invested by investors ($10 million).

9. Day 2 total assets ($60 million) minus amount of assets redeemed by investors ($10 million = 1 million shares invested at $10 per share).

10. Day 1 fund shares outstanding (5 million) plus shares issued to investors (1 million = $10 million divided by $10 per share).

820 on Fair Value Measurements and Disclosure distinguishes between the types of information "inputs" in fair value measurements for financial accounting purposes. Specifically, the FASB's fair value hierarchy distinguishes between three categories of inputs. Level 1 inputs are those related to quoted prices in active markets for those assets and, when available, should be accorded the highest priority in valuation in much the same way prescribed by Company Act Rule 2a-4. Use of Level 2 and 3 inputs accords with what the SEC means when fair valuing securities. Level 2 inputs are "inputs other than quoted prices included within Level 1 that are observable ... either directly or indirectly." Level 3 inputs, which encompass use of observable and non-observable inputs, represent the least favored class of inputs because such inputs inherently introduce an element of subjectivity into the valuation process.

These various types of inputs may come into play in pricing fund portfolio positions. Securities traded on active markets are valued in terms of Level 1 inputs. Bond issues that may go many days without trading and derivative contracts that are not traded on exchange markets, such as swaps, would involve valuation using Level 2 inputs, i.e., valuations derived from observable inputs. For example, in the case of bonds, valuation might involve a pricing service using a value derived from pricing matrices based on trading values of comparable bond issues, while in the case of swaps, a contract's imputed value might be derived from calculating the contract returns based on changing prices, rates, or returns, with respect to the assets referenced in the swap agreement. Restricted securities of start-up companies (i.e., privately-placed securities prior to any public offering) may represent an example of valuation requiring the use of Level 3 inputs. In such a case, valuation would entail a combination of observable and non-observable inputs to come up with an appropriate valuation, such as off-exchange secondary transactions, valuation of comparable firms whose securities are publicly traded, and analyst assessments of comparability of the metrics underlying a private company with those of publicly traded companies.

2. *Restricted securities.* Fund valuation of restricted securities, which would include privately-placed securities of a public company or private company securities, has received some attention recently in the financial press with the proliferation of so-called "unicorns," private start-up companies with valuations exceeding $1 billion, such as (at least as of 2018) Uber or Airbnb and formerly including Dropbox and Spotify until they went public in 2018. Private companies with large market capitalizations are potentially attractive holdings for funds, but are subject to much greater pricing uncertainty. For an informative case study of fund investment in and holdings of private securities by Fidelity Magellan Fund, see Jeff Schwartz, *Should Mutual Funds Invest in Startups? A Case Study of Magellan Fund's Investments in Unicorns (and Other Startups) and the Regulatory Implications*, 95 N. Car. L. Rev. 1341 (2017). Notwithstanding current requirements, Prof. Schwartz is skeptical of the regulatory status quo and specifically questions the adequacy of disclosure to investors regarding these investments and possible fluctuations in their value. During the case study, Magellan's average AUM was about $15 billion. Between mid-2012 and the first quarter of 2016, it made investments totaling $134 million in start-ups. What are the likely pros and cons of additional investor disclosure in this context?

One issue, not relevant to the Magellan situation, is the risk of illiquidity associated with restricted securities. As discussed below, at the end of the chapter, portfolio liquidity can represent a concern closely related to pricing. Thinly traded or illiquid securities are particularly difficult to value, because a sudden need for liquidity will make it difficult for the fund to realize fair value for those securities in times of market stress, the very time when investors are most likely to redeem their fund shares. Regulatory concerns associated with valuation of illiquid securities are not a new phenomenon. In one case, an investment manager systematically undervalued illiquid securities, which if fairly valued, would have shown that the funds under management held portfolios with illiquid positions exceeding 15% of each portfolio's value, which at the time exceeded disclosed prudential position limits on illiquid securities. *See In the Matter of Garrett Van Waggoner*, et al., Investment Advisers Act Release No. 2281 (Aug. 26, 2004). Today, as discussed below, these limits on illiquidity are now mandatory under Company Act Rule 22e-4. *Van Waggoner* is the rare case where an investment adviser committed pricing violations by understating portfolio value. Are understatements of portfolio value as harmful to an investor (or the same group of investors) as overstatements? Explain.

16.4 Pricing Problems in Practice

The *Invesco* case, previously discussed, provides a thorough description of how unscrupulous industry participants manipulated the pricing system to their favor and disadvantaged other investors. Apart from such blatant fraud, the pricing and valuation processes are fraught with potential for error and mispricing. Unless such mispricing is promptly and properly corrected, some investors may be hurt while others gain. In addition, there have been numerous instances where fund managers and service providers manipulated the pricing process. This has often been in hopes of concealing a poor investment decision or a seemingly temporary market drop, only to watch the markets thwart their intentions and make things much worse. In such situations, a portfolio manager may find himself or herself accused of fraud and may drag the fund's board and adviser's supervisory and compliance personnel into the pricing problem. The following cases explore these types of situations.

16.4.1 Pricing Decisions and Procedures

All funds routinely follow pricing policies in calculating the value of their securities portfolios on a daily basis. In cases where securities trade in markets with readily accessible quotations, there is no room for judgment. However, many securities held by funds do not have readily accessible market quotations, including fixed income instruments, some derivatives, and privately-placed securities. As discussed above, such securities must be priced using fair pricing policies, approved by the board. It is entirely possible that fund policies may give an erroneous value and usually there is an exceptions procedure that will allow a Valuation Committee or others at the fund to override the price derived using the routine policy (which is called a "price override"). Price overrides can entail their own set of problems if they are improper or inaccurate and may also create the opportunity for deliberate pricing errors by, for example, a portfolio manager who may seek to hide poor performance. In times of market stress, there is incredible pressure to price according to one's belief about long-term prospects rather than to reflect the dynamics of possible temporary market upheaval, which of course is antithetical to fund's pricing obligations.

In the Matter of Mitchell Hutchins Asset Management Inc.

Investment Company Act Release No. 22805 (Sept. 2, 1997)

[**Textbook note:** *This settled SEC administrative proceeding illustrates the problem of pricing overrides and pricing errors and how funds try to manage these conflicting demands. In this action, these problems arose not only from an apparently rogue portfolio manager, but a wholly deficient supervisory structure relating to pricing. The combination completely compromised the fund's pricing integrity. Interestingly, the pricing problems appeared to be incidental to actions by the portfolio manager which were inconsistent with the represented fund objectives and resulted from attempts to obscure the anomalous investment decisions of the portfolio manager.*]

[* * *] Respondent

... MITCHELL HUTCHINS is a broker-dealer registered under the Exchange Act and an investment adviser registered under the Advisers Act. It is wholly owned by PaineWebber Inc. ("PaineWebber"), a registered broker-dealer. Mitchell Hutchins serves as the investment adviser and administrator of the PaineWebber Short-Term U.S. Government Income Fund. Mitchell Hutchins also acts as the distributor of each class of the Fund's shares.

Other Relevant Entity

THE PAINEWEBBER SHORT-TERM U.S. GOVERNMENT INCOME FUND (the "Fund"), a diversified series of an open-end, management investment company, commenced operations on May 3, 1993.[2] The Fund's assets totaled approximately $1.7 billion as of November 30, 1993, and approximately $1 billion as of May 31, 1994.

C. Summary

This proceeding involves Mitchell Hutchins' management of the PaineWebber Short-Term U.S. Government Income Fund, which the firm marketed as a higher-yield and somewhat higher-risk alternative to money market funds and bank certificates of deposit. The prospectus disclosed that the Fund's investment objective was to achieve the highest level of income consistent with preservation of capital and low volatility of net asset value ("NAV"). The appendix to the prospectus also disclosed that the Fund had "no present intention" of investing in certain classes of interest only ("IO") and principal only ("PO") stripped mortgage-backed securities ("SMBS").

2. The Fund later was renamed The Paine Webber Low Duration U.S. Government Income Fund.

Mitchell Hutchins violated the antifraud provisions of the federal securities laws because it marketed the Fund as a low-volatility investment, when ultimately it was not. Contrary to the Fund's investment objective and "no present intention" statement, the Fund began investing in certain inappropriate IO and PO securities in the fall of 1993. For the next seven months, Mitchell Hutchins failed to review the securities purchased by the Fund's portfolio manager or to otherwise ensure that the Fund's investments were consistent with the prospectus and other public disclosures.In fact, Mitchell Hutchins recklessly disregarded certain indications that might have led it to discover the portfolio manager's improper conduct in pricing and managing the Fund's securities portfolio. When interest rates increased sharply beginning in February 1994, the Fund incurred significant losses, performing well below comparable funds.

D. Mitchell Hutchins' Disclosures and Representations

The Fund was offered and sold to the public using a prospectus and other documents prepared by Mitchell Hutchins. The prospectus stated that "[t]he Fund's investment objective is to achieve the highest level of income consistent with the preservation of capital and low volatility of net asset value." In addition, the prospectus disclosed that the Fund would invest in U.S. Government securities, including mortgage-backed securities. The appendix to the prospectus said that the Fund had "no present intention" of investing in certain mortgage-backed securities — IO and PO strips of collateralized mortgage obligations ("CMOs") that were not planned amortization class bonds ("non-PAC IOs and POs").[3]

Mitchell Hutchins also prepared and disseminated to PaineWebber's retail sales force marketing materials containing a number of false and misleading statements about the Fund and its expected performance. For example, certain of these materials stated that an investment in the Fund carried somewhat more risk than an investment in a money market fund or a certificate of deposit, but investors could expect returns of 1.5% to 2% more than a money market investment. Based on the performance of a "hypothetical portfolio" prepared by Mitchell Hutchins for marketing purposes,[4] certain marketing materials also stated that a 100 basis point increase in interest rates would cause the Fund's NAV to decrease by only $.02 per share, while a 200 basis point increase would cause the NAV to decrease by only $.04 per share. Finally, certain marketing materials also stated that the Fund would not invest in IOs, POs, or deriv-

3. IOs and POs with prepayment protection, or "PAC bonds," are designed to provide relatively predictable payments according to an established schedule, provided that prepayments on the underlying mortgage assets fall within a certain range (i.e., as long as early pay-offs by mortgagors fall within certain parameters.) Non-PAC IOs and POs, on the other hand, are significantly more volatile because, among other things, they lack prepayment protection and absorb the effects of changes in prepayments for PAC classes. The Fund's prospectus stated that non-PAC IOs and POs "are extremely sensitive to the rate of principal payments (including pre-payments) on the underlying [m]ortgage [a]ssets."

4. Created before any securities were purchased for the Fund's actual portfolio, the "hypothetical portfolio" showed the Fund's anticipated volatility in response to interest rate changes.

atives, or engage in option writing or leverage transactions.[5] In selling the Fund's shares to the investing public, oral representations were made to certain customers based on these marketing materials.

E. The Fund Invested in Certain IO and PO Securities That Were Inconsistent With the Fund's Prospectus Disclosures

In September 1993, Mitchell Hutchins hired a person to act as the Fund's co-portfolio manager, with day-to-day responsibility for managing the Fund's investments (the "portfolio manager"). At that time, the portfolio manager's supervisor and another senior co-portfolio manager told him that IOs and POs without PAC protection were not permitted in the Fund.

Despite these instructions, on September 30, 1993, the portfolio manager purchased a non-PAC PO for more than $15 million. That security was inconsistent with both the prospectus' "no present intention" statement and the Fund's low-volatility investment objective. Thereafter, between September 30, 1993, and February 14, 1994, he bought a total of six non-PAC POs and three non-PAC inverse IOs for an aggregate purchase price of more than $162 million. By February 1994, non-PAC IOs and POs constituted approximately 6% of the Fund's portfolio. During October 1993 through January 1994, the portfolio manager purchased five PAC inverse IOs for a total purchase price of more than $34 million. The PAC inverse IOs also were inconsistent with the Fund's investment objective.[6]

In addition, in March 1994, the portfolio manager purchased two "structured floater" securities for a total purchase price of approximately $203 million. These complex, interest-rate sensitive securities were created by bundling together IO, PO and other components (some lacking PAC protection) of various mortgage transactions. When the portfolio manager purchased the two structured floaters, his supervisor was not aware of the existence of non-PAC IOs and POs and inverse floaters in the portfolio. As a result, these two structured floaters were purchased without adequate consideration of how they might impact the Fund's overall portfolio.

For the first three quarters after its inception, the Fund showed a strong performance. For example, for the period January 1 through March 31, 1994, the A shares, B shares, and D shares ranked 2, 9, and 7, respectively, out of 103 comparable funds.

When interest rates increased sharply in the first half of 1994, however, the Fund incurred significant losses. For example, the Fund's NAV fell $0.21 per share from March 31 to June 30, 1994, placing the Fund's performance among the bottom four of 105 comparable funds during the second quarter of 1994.

---

5. These statements in the marketing materials were inconsistent with disclosures in the prospectus. For example, the prospectus provided that the Fund could purchase certain derivatives (including PAC IOs and POs, which were purchased from its inception), could write options (which it did starting in January 1994), and could enter into leverage transactions.

6. Inverse IOs generally are more volatile than other IO securities because of their extreme sensitivity to interest rate fluctuations. Inverse IOs, which may be either PAC or non-PAC, vary inversely with the London interbank offered rate ("LIBOR").

F. Mitchell Hutchins Failed to Ensure That the Fund's Investments Were Consistent With Disclosures in the Prospectus and Certain Marketing Materials

Until late April 1994, Mitchell Hutchins failed adequately to monitor the Fund's purchases of securities to ensure adherence to the "no present intention" statement and to have a reasonable basis for continuing to characterize the Fund as a low-volatility investment. No one in a supervisory role reviewed the contents of the Fund's securities portfolio to determine consistency with the "no present intention" statement. Other than reviewing aggregate duration calculations, Mitchell Hutchins did not test the Fund's portfolio to determine whether it would perform in the manner described in the marketing materials. While Mitchell Hutchins required portfolio managers to complete a monthly checklist indicating adherence to investment restrictions and limitations, no form was completed for this Fund during the first eleven months of its operation.

When Mitchell Hutchins prepared an amendment to the Fund's prospectus, effective as of April 1, 1994, it failed to make reasonable efforts to determine whether the Fund was adhering to the "no present intention" statement and the low-volatility investment objective.

G. Certain Fund Securities Frequently Were Mispriced

Furthermore, certain of the Fund's portfolio securities frequently were mispriced. The Fund's prospectus and statement of additional information ("SAI") described the method it would use to value portfolio securities. The Fund's SAI disclosed that it would value its portfolio securities based on their current market value where market quotations were readily available. Where market quotations were not readily available, or did not adequately reflect, in Mitchell Hutchins' judgment, a security's "fair value," the SAI said that portfolio securities would be valued based on appraisals received from a pricing service or appraisals based on information provided by recognized dealers in those or similar securities. Finally, in the absence of any of the foregoing market indicators, the SAI stated that portfolio securities would be "valued at fair value as determined in good faith by or under the direction of the Trust's board of trustees."

The Fund's portfolio was valued as of the end of each business day. The Fund received from its custodian bank (the "custodian") a daily report of prices for each of the portfolio securities where dealer quotations could be obtained; these prices, in turn, provided the principal basis for the daily calculation of the Fund's NAV. Pursuant to the Fund's stated valuation method, the custodian-provided prices, in most instances, reflected quotations received from a pricing service or from a dealer (usually the dealer that sold the security to Mitchell Hutchins). Consistent with the firm's procedures, the Fund's day-to-day portfolio manager could substitute his own price for a custodian-provided price if he determined that the latter did not adequately reflect a security's "fair value." However, Mitchell Hutchins had no written procedures to guide portfolio managers in making those pricing determinations.

Prior to the time the portfolio manager assumed day-to-day responsibility for managing the Fund, price overrides were relatively infrequent. By contrast, during his tenure at the Fund from October 1993 through April 1994, the portfolio manager frequently overrode prices provided by the custodian, altering the prices of approximately 5 to 25 securities on many days. On more than 40 occasions, the portfolio manager overrode custodian-provided prices for a particular security for more than a two-week period. Moreover, the portfolio manager overrode custodian provided prices for two of the non-PAC securities for almost the entire time they were held by the Fund.[7]

The portfolio manager overrode custodian-provided prices with prices he derived based on his own method, which did not take into account whether the securities currently could be sold at the prices he calculated. The portfolio manager kept no documentation to support his calculations.

When the portfolio manager overrode custodian-provided prices, in most cases, he replaced them with higher prices. For example, from November 29, 1993, to April 22, 1994, he overrode at least 17 securities in the Fund's portfolio, including non-PAC IOs and POs and PAC inverse IOs, by amounts ranging from approximately 9% to 62% higher than the available dealer quotations.

Because the Fund's NAV is a function of the value of its securities portfolio, the portfolio manager's overrides caused the Fund's NAV to be overstated. For example, following the increase in interest rates during February through April 1994, the portfolio manager overrode custodian-provided prices for a substantial number of securities, resulting in inflation of the Fund's NAV by more than $0.01 per share for a total of 36 days during the period from March 1 to April 25, 1994. The portfolio manager's overrides had the effect of obscuring the volatile effect of the non-PAC IOs and POs and inverse IOs on the Fund's NAV. This, in turn, had the effect of obscuring his purchases of those securities.

Instead of reviewing the actual securities purchased by the portfolio manager, the portfolio manager's supervisor relied on his reported allocation of portfolio securities among various broad classes (e.g., IOs, POs, pass-throughs, etc.), which did not indicate the presence of non-PAC IOs and POs. In monitoring the Fund's volatility, the supervisor relied principally on daily reports of NAV calculated out to five decimal places (the accuracy of which depended on the portfolio manager's accurate valuation of portfolio securities) and on his calculation of aggregate duration, which measures the percentage change in the portfolio's value in response to specified changes in interest rates. By failing to have in place a process to review the support for these aggregate indicators, Mitchell Hutchins failed to detect the portfolio manager's conduct.

7. On September 30, 1993, the portfolio manager purchased the first non-PAC PO; he subsequently overrode custodian-provided prices for that security from October 18 until January 25. 1994, when he sold it. He purchased a non-PAC IO on October 20 1993, and overrode its custodian-provided prices every day from November 2, 1993, through February 14, 1994, when he sold it.

H. Mitchell Hutchins Did Not Adequately Monitor the Portfolio Manager's Conduct

During this period, there was an indication that could have alerted Mitchell Hutchins to the portfolio manager's conduct in purchasing and pricing the Fund's portfolio securities. In November 1993, a Mitchell Hutchins chief investment officer ("CIO"), who reviewed and initialed price overrides in several funds administered by the firm, reported to the then-general counsel that the portfolio manager's overrides were "persistent" and "high" in number. The CIO also reported that the portfolio manager's override documentation precluded a substantive review of his overrides because, among other things, it did not precisely identify the securities at issue. The then-general counsel thereafter brought this matter to the attention of Mitchell Hutchins' president.

Four months following the CIO's report, in late March 1994, there was a meeting at Mitchell Hutchins (involving, among others, the CIO, the then general counsel and the portfolio manager's supervisor) to discuss price overrides. Following this meeting, the CIO refused to initial any additional overrides processed by the Fund's portfolio manager. Mitchell Hutchins did not investigate the portfolio manager's override practices until a month later.

I. Mitchell Hutchins' Discovery of the Portfolio Manager's Improper Conduct and Its Response

... [In late April 1994], Mitchell Hutchins contacted Commission staff concerning the problems with the Fund and the firm's possible purchase of securities from the Fund.[8] Thereafter, Mitchell Hutchins purchased certain IOs and POs from the Fund and paid Fund investors $33 million, which was the amount estimated by the firm as the losses associated with those securities, thereby settling two related class action lawsuits. The firm replaced the firm's president and all persons with direct involvement for the Fund's management and supervision, including the portfolio manager and his supervisor, and revised certain of its policies and procedures. In addition, Mitchell Hutchins paid $145 million to purchase from the Fund certain IO and PO securities and certain structured floater securities.

Legal Analysis

Mitchell Hutchins Violated Section 17(a) of the Securities Act, Section 10(b) of the Exchange Act and Rule 10b-5 Thereunder, and Sections 206(1) and (2) of the Advisers Act.

Section 17(a) of the Securities Act makes it unlawful, in the offer or sale of securities, (1) to employ any device, scheme or artifice to defraud, or (2) to obtain money or property by means of any untrue statement of material fact or any omission to state a material fact necessary to make the statements made, in light of the circumstances in which they were made, not misleading, or (3) to engage in any transaction, practice, or course of business that operates as a fraud or deceit upon a purchaser. Section

8. The staff ultimately issued a no-action letter indicating that it would not object to the purchase of the securities from the fund under Section 17(a) of the Investment Company Act.

10(b) of the Exchange Act and Rule 10b-5 thereunder make it unlawful to employ any device, scheme or artifice to defraud in connection with the purchase or sale of securities. Section 206(1) of the Advisers Act makes it unlawful for an investment adviser to employ any device, scheme or artifice to defraud any client or prospective client. Section 206(2) makes it unlawful for an investment adviser to engage in any transaction, practice, or course of business that operates as a fraud or deceit upon any client.

Mitchell Hutchins willfully violated each of the foregoing antifraud provisions. The portfolio manager purchased non-PAC IOs and POs that rendered materially false and misleading the "no present intention" statement in the Fund's prospectus. These securities together with certain other securities purchased by the portfolio manager also rendered materially false and misleading the characterization of the Fund as a low-volatility investment. [***].

* * *

In the Matter of UBS Global Asset Management (Americas) Inc.

Investment Company Act Release No. 29920 (January 17, 2012)

[**Textbook note:** *This settled administrative proceeding reveals a different manifestation of the pricing problem. UBS Asset Management reflected sophisticated pricing and policies procedures that still malfunctioned in times of unusual market stress. Although the procedures malfunctioned, they also ultimately led to the discovery of the problem within a relatively short period of time. Nevertheless, pricing procedures have to work on a daily basis in times of market stress. Note, unlike the* Mitchell Hutchins *case, UBS Asset Management was also sanctioned for a compliance policies violation given the intervening implementation of Rule 38a-1, and the SEC also found that the lapses by UBS contributed to the affected funds' Rule 22c-1 violations. Although* Mitchell Hutchins *involved more egregious misconduct,* UBS *underscores that the SEC fifteen years later appears less tolerant of breakdowns in pricing policies and procedure.*]

[***] Summary

1. This proceeding concerns the misstatement of the Net Asset Values ("NAVs") of certain registered investment companies (the "Funds") managed by UBSGAM. UBSGAM failed to cause certain fixed-income securities in the portfolios of the Funds to be valued in accordance with the Funds' fair valuation procedures. UBSGAM's failure to properly fair value these securities resulted in a misstatement of the NAVs of the Funds.

2. In June 2008, UBSGAM purchased approximately 54 fixed-income securities from various broker-dealers for the Funds ("the Securities") for an aggregate purchase price of approximately $22 million. Most of the Securities were part of subordinated tranches of non-agency mortgage-backed securities. Non-agency mortgage-backed securities are issued by private institutions; their underlying collateral generally consists of mortgages which do not conform to the requirements (size, documentation, loan-to-value

ratios, etc.) for inclusion in mortgage-backed securities guaranteed or issued by Ginnie Mae, Fannie Mae or Freddie Mac. The Securities also included asset-backed securities and collateralized debt obligations. These securities were not listed or sold on any exchange, and there was not an active market for them.

3. Upon the Funds' purchases of the Securities, all but six of the Securities were valued at prices in excess of the transaction prices. The majority of the Securities were valued at prices at least 100% higher than the transaction prices.

4. The Securities were valued during this period using valuations provided by broker-dealers or a third-party pricing service (the "Pricing Sources") that did not appear to take into account the prices at which the Funds had purchased the Securities.

5. UBSGAM did not fair value the Securities until it held a meeting of the Global Valuation Committee ("GVC") on June 30, 2008, more than two weeks after UBSGAM began receiving reports ("Price Tolerance Reports") identifying the discrepancies between the purchase prices and the valuation of the Securities based on the Pricing Sources.

6. By initially using the valuations provided by the Pricing Sources instead of the transaction prices, the Funds did not follow their own written valuation procedures. These procedures required the Securities to be valued at the transaction price until UBSGAM received a response to a price challenge based on the discrepancy identified in the Price Tolerance Report or the GVC made a fair value determination. The procedures provided that the transaction price could be used for up to five business days until a decision would need to be made as to the fair value. By failing to implement these procedures, the Funds violated Rule 38a-1 under the Investment Company Act and UBSGAM aided and abetted and caused the violations.

7. Because the Funds did not properly or timely fair value the Securities, the NAVs of the Funds were misstated between one cent and ten cents per share for several days in June 2008. Consequently, the Funds sold, purchased, and redeemed their shares based on inaccurately high NAVs on those days. The Funds thus violated Rule 22c-1 adopted pursuant to Section 22(c) of the Investment Company Act. UBSGAM aided and abetted and caused the Funds' violations of Rule 22c-1 under the Investment Company Act.

Respondent

8. **UBS Global Asset Management (Americas), Inc.,** is a registered investment adviser incorporated in Delaware and currently headquartered in New York. At the time of the transactions at issue, UBSGAM was headquartered in Chicago, Illinois. UBSGAM served as an investment adviser to the Funds during the period of the transactions described herein.

The Funds' Stated Valuation Procedures

9. Rule 22c-1 under the Investment Company Act prohibits selling, redeeming, or repurchasing any redeemable security except at a price based on the current net asset value of such security. Under Section 2(a)(41)(B) of the Investment Company Act, registered investment companies must use: (1) market values for portfolio securities with

readily available market quotations; and (2) fair value for all other portfolio assets, as determined in good faith by the board of directors.

10. The Boards of the Funds established the methodologies to be used for valuing the Funds' assets and delegated the responsibility for implementing those methodologies to UBSGAM. UBSGAM appointed the GVC to carry out its valuation responsibilities pursuant to a list of Price Sources for each type of securities ("Pricing Hierarchies"). In general, where broker-dealers supplied market quotes on mortgage-backed securities that were more than three percent different from the prices supplied by the designated third-party pricing vendor, UBSGAM used the broker-dealer price for valuation purposes in lieu of the prices supplied by the third-party vendor. For most of the Securities, the GVC designated a particular broker-dealer to provide daily market quotes. The GVC designated a third-party pricing vendor the remainder of the Securities. The Boards reviewed the GVC's valuations for the purposes of either ratifying or adjusting the GVC's decisions.

11. The Funds' valuation procedures provided for various exceptions and deviations from valuations received from the designated Pricing Sources.

12. One exception provided that whenever the difference between the transaction price for a security and the Pricing Source valuation (referred to in the Funds' procedures as the "vendor price") was three percent or more: Fund Treasury will have the Funds'/Accounts' custodian(s) go with the 'Trade Price' until a response is received in regards to the price challenge or until a fair market price can be determined. Using the 'Trade Price' to value the security can be used for up to five (5) business days until a decision will need to be made in terms of fair valuing the security. During the five (5) day period, the Valuation Committee can advise the Funds'/Accounts' custodian to switch back to the vendor price if it is deemed appropriate. If no decision is made by the end of the 5th business day then the Valuation Committee shall make a valuation determination.

13. The procedures thus required the Funds to use the transaction price (referred to by UBSGAM as the "trade price") as the value for a security for up to five business days whenever there was a variance of three percent or more between the transaction price and the quote or value obtained from a Pricing Source. The procedures also required that UBSGAM issue a price challenge to request justification from the Pricing Source for the price quoted. After receiving a response to the price challenge, the GVC could revert to the Pricing Source's quote price if justified. If no resolution was reached by the end of five business days after issuance of a Price Tolerance Report, the procedures required the GVC at that point to make a valuation determination.

14. As part of its compliance procedures, UBSGAM conducted automated price checks comparing transaction prices with internal valuations for recently purchased securities, which resulted in the creation of Price Tolerance Reports when the transaction price and quote price for a given security varied by three percent or more. When generated, Price Tolerance Reports were sent to the UBSGAM compliance department for investigation. The Price Tolerance Reports put UBSGAM on notice that

the quotes it received may not accurately reflect the market for the security, and then the GVC was required to follow the above procedures.

The Procedures Actually Used

15. Between June 5 and June 25, 2008, UBSGAM caused the Funds to purchase the Securities from various broker-dealers.

16. Immediately after each purchase and pursuant to the Pricing Hierarchies, UBSGAM began using broker-dealer quotations to price 43 of the Securities; 11 were valued by using third-party vendor pricing services.

17. The quotations received from the broker-dealers for 28 of the 54 Securities were more than 100% higher than the transaction prices and, in some cases, were more than 1,000% higher. Additionally, during this period certain of the broker-dealers' market quotes were stale and were not priced daily. And, in some cases the prices were based on prior month-end prices.

18. The prices supplied by the third-party vendors similarly substantially exceeded the transaction prices.

19. Given the large variance between the transaction prices and prices from the Pricing Sources, Price Tolerance Reports were generated for almost all of the Securities. Certain members of UBSGAM's GVC received the first Price Tolerance Report on June 16, 2008, and received Price Tolerance Reports for most of the remaining Securities as the Funds purchased them.

20. The Securities, however, were not valued at the transaction price, despite the requirement under the procedures.

21. Also in contravention of the Funds' valuation procedures, UBSGAM did not issue challenges to the Pricing Sources for a majority of the Securities that appeared on the Price Tolerance Reports. When UBSGAM did issue challenges, it received responses for only a handful of the Securities. For the remaining Securities, UBSGAM did not follow up with the challenged Pricing Source or make fair value determinations at the end of five business days, as required by the valuation procedures. Instead, UBSGAM continued to use the substantially higher broker-dealer quotes and third-party vendor prices until June 30, 2008, when the GVC finally met to discuss the valuation issues relating to the Securities.

22. At the conclusion of the June 30 meeting, the GVC members decided to fair value the securities at the midpoint between the transaction price and the quote prices from Pricing Sources until they received responses to price challenges. The Boards subsequently ratified this decision.

23. Price challenges were not issued for a majority of the Securities until July 1, 2008, and they were never issued for some Securities.

UBSGAM Caused the Funds to Misstate their NAVs

24. As a result of the conduct described in paragraphs 1 through 23 above, the NAVs of the Funds were misstated between one cent and ten cents for several days during June 2008.

Violations

25. The Funds misstated their NAVs and executed transactions in redeemable securities at prices not based on current net asset values. The Funds thus violated Rule 22c-1 under the Investment Company Act, which prohibits selling, redeeming, or repurchasing any redeemable security except at a price based on the current net asset value of such security. UBSGAM willfully aided and abetted and caused these violations.

26. As described above, the Funds did not adequately implement valuation procedures and thus violated Rule 38a-1 under the Investment Company Act, which requires each registered investment company to adopt and implement written policies and procedures reasonably designed to prevent violations of the federal securities laws by the funds. UBSGAM willfully aided and abetted and caused these violations. [***]

* * *

Notes and Applications

Correcting NAV calculation errors. Miscalculations of NAVs can arise from innocent mistakes (commonly referred to as pricing errors) or from deliberate efforts to use inaccurate prices in valuing underlying portfolio securities. In the latter case, there is little doubt that the culpable party (most likely the adviser) must make the affected fund and its investors whole. In the more common garden variety pricing error, a question arises: what should be done if a fund discovers that past NAV calculations were erroneous? Pricing errors are somewhat different than other types of errors that may affect fund operations. For example, trading errors (such as where the wrong securities are purchased for a fund or where an order for a purchase or sale is improperly sized) are relatively easy to handle, because one-off adjustments can quickly be made to the affected fund. Pricing errors potentially are more difficult to correct. Pricing errors may continue for a period of time in which the fund and investors may be affected through dozens or hundreds of transactions (i.e., every purchase or redemption during the affected period).

At one time, the SEC took a strict position that any error that resulted in more than a penny in NAV was *per se* material for investors, thereby requiring each affected investor be made whole. However, that strict materiality position was specifically rejected by the D.C. Circuit in *SEC v. Steadman*, 967 F.3d 636 (D.C. Cir. 1992). More recently, and although never formally endorsed by the SEC, industry practices have developed whereby pricing errors of over a penny per share should lead the responsible party (most often, the fund adviser but also the fund custodian) to make the fund whole for resulting losses and to make adjustments at the fund shareholder level if the losses exceed the level of anything more than 1% of NAV and possibly if as low as .5% of NAV. In addition, most funds adhere to a *de minimis* error exception and do not compensate shareholders for losses arising from pricing errors of below a certain amount, such as $25 per account. Nevertheless, funds should have explicit policies and procedures governing correction of NAV calculation errors and risk sanction for failing to adhere to those policies and procedures or for providing shareholders with misleading disclosure in connection with a correction event. *See, e.g., Calvert Investment Management, Inc.*, Investment Advisers Act Release No. 4554 (Oct. 18, 2016).

16.4.2 The Role of the Board in Fund Pricing

In 2003, the SEC reached a settlement with the board of directors of the Heartland Funds, which in in 2000 struggled to properly value securities in two fixed-income funds, the Short Duration High-Yield Municipal Fund and the High-Yield Municipal Bond Fund. Similar to both the *Mitchell Hutchins* and *UBS* proceedings, the funds' adviser and service providers struggled with the fair valuation of illiquid bonds in both funds. Even after the pricing problem became apparent, the board attempted to reduce the volatility and appearance of any sudden decrease in values by overriding the prices used for valuing certain securities. This calculated effort to smooth out the eventual decline in the fund price resulted in extended miscalculations and misstatements of the NAV over a sustained period of time. The board's behavior resembled an attempt to manage a difficult situation (a recurrent theme in pricing cases), rather than accurately calculating NAV on a daily basis, as required by the pricing rule. The SEC found that the board was negligent in its oversight of the valuation and pricing process and resulting misstatements in fund documents, and were a cause contributing to the mispricing of the fund's shares.

That case, *In the Matter of Jon D. Hammes*, Investment Company Act Release No. 26290 (Dec. 11, 2003), served notice that board's independent trustees had responsibilities that, if not properly discharged, would result in the imposition of sanctions. For practitioners and fund boards, it emphasized the need for aggressive board action when valuation, pricing and liquidity issues involving fund portfolios are presented to the board. In the following more recent case, the board and its counsel had the benefit of the *Hammes* case and the knowledge that compliance obligations were subject to much closer regulatory scrutiny under Company Act Rule 38a-1.

In the Matter of J. Kenneth Alderman, CPA

Investment Company Act Release No. 30557 (June 13, 2013)

[**Textbook note:** *This settlement arose out of the collapse of several funds managed by Morgan Asset Management, then an affiliate of a large southern brokerage firm, Morgan Keegan & Company. The respondents were the board members of the several funds that suffered enormous drops in NAV when the markets for subprime mortgage-related bonds began to falter in 2007, ultimately culminating in the Financial Crisis of 2008. When the funds' securities started to plummet in value, the portfolio manager believed the values would recover quickly. Accordingly, he overrode the fair valuation process and substituted his assessment of values which proved incorrect. In addition, he acted together with the funds' treasurer to "smooth" or step-down the dramatic daily drops in value over longer periods of time. The result was a distortion in the NAVs and pricing* *of fund shares. In separate settlements, the portfolio manager and treasurer were banned from the industry, and significant civil penalties were imposed on the adviser and distributor. The remaining action below was directed at the fund's board. The SEC's order made a number of findings as to deficiencies by the board. It is noteworthy that although the boards' legal counsel and outside auditor was extremely experienced and aware of the situation, they were not ultimately successful in insulating the board from censure.*]

[***] SUMMARY

1. This matter concerns the eight directors (collectively "the Directors") who all served on the boards of five registered investment companies ("The Funds"). Between at least January 2007 and August 2007 (the "Relevant Period"), significant portions of the Funds' portfolios contained below-investment grade debt securities for which market quotations were not readily available. Some of these securities were backed by subprime mortgages. Under the Investment Company Act, those securities were required to be valued at fair value as determined in good faith by the Directors. In discussing fund directors' statutory fair valuation obligations, the Commission has stated that directors must "determine the method of arriving at the fair value of each such security. To the extent considered necessary, the board may appoint persons to assist them in the determination of such value, and to make the actual calculations pursuant to the board's direction. The board must also, consistent with this responsibility, continuously review the appropriateness of the method used in valuing each issue of security in the company's portfolio." The Directors did not specify a fair valuation methodology pursuant to which the securities were to be fair valued. Nor did they continuously review how each issue of security in the Funds' portfolios were being valued. The Directors delegated their responsibility to determine fair value to the Valuation Committee of the investment adviser to the Funds, but did not provide any meaningful substantive guidance on how those determinations should be made. In addition, they did not learn how fair values were actually being determined. They received only limited information on the factors considered in making fair value determinations and almost no information explaining why fair values were assigned to specific portfolio securities. These failures were particularly significant given that fair valued securities made up the majority—and in most cases upwards of 60%—of the Funds' net asset values ("NAVs") during the Relevant Period.

RESPONDENTS

2. J. Kenneth Alderman, 60 years of age and a resident of Birmingham, Alabama, was an interested director of the Funds beginning in 2003 and during the entire Relevant Period. He is a Certified Public Accountant ("CPA"), licensed in Florida and Alabama, and is a Chartered Financial Analyst.... [**Textbook note:** *The six independent directors had similar qualifications, and the only other director was the chief executive officer of the investment adviser.*]

OTHER RELEVANT ENTITIES

10. Morgan Asset Management, Inc. ('Morgan Asset") is an investment adviser registered with the Commission, and Morgan Keegan & Company, Inc. ("Morgan Keegan")

is a broker-dealer and an investment adviser registered with the Commission. Morgan Asset was headquartered in Birmingham, Alabama while Morgan Keegan was headquartered in Memphis, Tennessee. During the Relevant Period, Morgan Asset served as the investment adviser for the Funds and Morgan Keegan provided accounting services to the Funds through its Fund Accounting group ("Fund Accounting").

OVERVIEW OF THE FUNDS

11. The Funds consisted of five registered investment companies: (i) RMK High Income Fund, Inc.; (ii) RMK Multi-Sector High Income Fund, Inc.; (iii) RMK Strategic Income Fund, Inc.; (iv) RMK Advantage Income Fund, Inc.; and (v) Morgan Keegan Select Fund, Inc. ("Select Fund"). The Select Fund was an open-end company with a fiscal year end of June 30 that contained three open-end series — the Select High Income portfolio, the Select Intermediate Bond portfolio, and the Select Short Term Bond portfolio. The other funds were closed-end funds with a fiscal year end of March 31. The closed-end funds calculated and published daily NAVs, although these were not the basis of transactions in their shares.

12. During the Relevant Period, each Fund had a board of directors that consisted of two interested directors and six independent directors. Respondents Alderman and [another] were the interested directors. [Six other directors] were the independent directors. All of the independent directors sat on each Fund's Audit Committee.

13. As of March 31, 2007, the Funds held securities with a combined net asset value of approximately $3.85 billion. The Funds owned many of the same securities and invested the majority of their total assets in complex securities known as structured products that included collateralized debt obligations, collateralized mortgage obligations, collateralized loan obligations, home-equity loan-backed securities, various types of asset-backed securities, and certificate-backed obligations.

14. The Funds' assets were heavily invested in below-investment grade debt securities, which carried inherent risks such as more frequent and pronounced changes in the perceived creditworthiness of issuers, greater price volatility, reduced liquidity, and the presence of fewer dealers in the market for such securities. Another, particularly relevant characteristic of the Funds' holdings was their significant concentrations in mortgage-backed securities.

15. A significant number of the structured products held by the Funds were subordinated tranches of various securitizations, for which market quotations were not readily available during the Relevant Period. As a result, a large percentage of the Funds' portfolios had to be fair valued as determined in good faith by the Funds' directors in accordance with the requirements of Section 2(a)(41)(B) of the Investment Company Act. As of March 31, 2007, more than 60% of the NAV of each of the four closed-end funds was required to be fair valued. As of June 30, 2007, more than 50% of the NAV of each of the two largest open-end series was required to be fair valued.

RESPONDENTS DELEGATE THEIR VALUATION RESPONSIBILITIES WITH MINIMAL GUIDANCE

16. In the Funds' Policy and Procedure Manual (the "Manual"), the Directors delegated to Morgan Asset "the responsibility for carrying out certain functions relating to the valuation of portfolio securities ... in connection with calculating the NAV per share of the Funds." The Manual also stated that "portfolio securities for which market quotations are readily available are valued at current market value [while] ... [a]ll other portfolio securities will be valued at 'fair value' as determined in good faith by [Morgan Asset] in accordance with the Funds' Valuation Procedures."

17. The Funds' Valuation Procedures within the Manual stated more specifically that "[w]hen price quotations for certain securities are not readily available from the sources noted above [i.e., sources of market prices] or if the available quotations are not believed to be reflective of market value, those securities shall be valued at 'fair value' *as determined in good faith by [Morgan Asset's] Valuation Committee*." [Emphasis added] The Valuation Procedures then listed various general and specific factors, which the Valuation Committee was supposed to consider when making fair value determinations. The "General Factors" listed were "(i) the fundamental analytical data relating to the investment; (ii) the nature and duration of restrictions on disposition of the securities; and (iii) an evaluation of the forces which influence the market in which these securities are purchased and sold." The "Specific Factors" listed were: "(i) type of security; (ii) financial statements of the issuer; (iii) cost at date of purchase (generally used for initial valuation); (iv) size of the Fund's holding; for restricted securities; (v) any discount from market value of restricted securities of the same class at the time of purchase; (vi) the existence of a shelf registration for restricted securities; (vii) information as to any transactions or offers with respect to the security; (viii) special reports prepared by analysts; (ix) the existence of merger proposals, tender offers or similar events affecting the security; and (x) the price and extent of public trading in similar securities of the issuer or comparable companies."

18. Other than listing these factors, which were copied nearly verbatim from ASR 118, the Valuation Procedures provided no meaningful methodology or other specific direction on *how* to make fair value determinations for specific portfolio assets or classes of assets. For example, there was no guidance in the Valuation Procedures on how the listed factors should be interpreted, on whether some of the factors should be weighed more heavily or less heavily than others, or on what specific information qualified as "fundamental analytical data relating to the investments." Additionally, the Valuation Procedures did not specify what valuation methodology should be employed for each type of security or, in the absence of a specified methodology, how to evaluate whether a particular methodology was appropriate or inappropriate. Also, the Valuation Procedures did not include any mechanism for identifying and reviewing fair-valued securities whose prices remained unchanged for weeks, months and even entire quarters.

19. The Directors did not provide any other guidance—either written or oral—on how to determine fair value beyond what was stated in the Valuation Procedures.

20. The "Written Reports of Fair Value Determinations" subsection of the Valuation Procedures contained the only procedures regarding information required to be provided to the Directors. It stated that "[u]pon making a determination as to the fair value of a security, the Valuation Committee shall maintain a written report documenting the manner in which the fair value of a security was determined and the accuracy of the valuation made based on the next reliable public price quotation for that security," and further required that the Valuation Committee create and provide to the Directors for review "[q]uarterly reports listing all securities held by the Fund that were fair valued during the quarter under review, along with explanatory notes for the fair values assigned to the securities." The procedures did not require the Directors to ratify any fair value determinations made by Morgan Asset, and they did not ratify any such determinations.

THE FUNDS' ACTUAL FAIR VALUATION PROCEDURES

21. The Valuation Committee, which consisted of Fund officers and Fund Accounting employees, and which did not include any Directors, was responsible according to the Funds' procedures for overseeing the fair valuation process. In practice, the task of assigning fair values on a daily basis was performed by Fund Accounting, a unit which consisted of Morgan Keegan employees.

22. In determining fair value, Fund Accounting did not use any reasonable analytical method to arrive at fair value. For example, neither Fund Accounting nor the Valuation Committee used a pricing model or made any meaningful effort to analyze future cash flows, or the present values thereof, that a particular bond in the portfolio would likely generate.

23. Under the actual fair valuation process, Fund Accounting typically set a security's initial fair value as its purchase price (its cost) and, thereafter, left that fair value unchanged unless a sale or a price confirmation indicated a more than 5% variance from the previously assigned fair value. In addition, the Portfolio Manager repeatedly contacted Fund Accounting, by email or other means, and provided price adjustments for particular securities. Without any explanation of his basis for such prices, Fund Accounting routinely accepted the prices provided by the Portfolio Manager. Neither the Directors nor Morgan Keegan or Morgan Asset ever provided guidelines by which Fund Accounting or the Valuation Committee should evaluate the reasonableness of such adjustments.

24. Shortly after each month end, Fund Accounting selected and sought price confirmations for a random sample of the Funds' securities that were required to be fair valued, except for March and June when, in connection with annual audits, confirmations were sought by the Funds' independent auditors for 100% of the fair valued securities. The price confirmations were essentially opinions on price from broker-dealers, rather than bids or firm quotes. The price confirmations generally contained disclaimers explicitly making clear that the dealer providing the price confirmation was not offering to buy the security at the stated price. In addition, the price confirmations generally related to month-end prices, but were obtained several weeks after the respective month-ends. Accordingly, they could not have sufficed as the primary valuation

method, given the open-end Fund series' obligation to daily price the securities and the closed-end Funds daily publication of their NAVs.

25. The Valuation Procedures contained a section entitled "Price Override Procedures," which provided that the Adviser could "override prices provided by a pricing service or broker-dealer only when it had a reasonable basis to believe that the price ... does not accurately reflect the fair value of the portfolio security." The section further provided that "the basis for overriding the price shall be documented and provided to the Valuation Committee for its review." Because the Valuation Committee and Fund Accounting interpreted this provision as applying only to broker-dealer quotes (i.e., actual offers to buy or sell), the Valuation Committee was not advised, and could not advise the Directors, as to the basis upon which Fund Accounting chose to ignore the price confirmations.

26. In the event a price confirmation indicated a more than 5% variance from the previously assigned fair value, Fund Accounting effectively allowed the Portfolio Manager to determine the fair value. The Portfolio Manager arbitrarily set values without a reasonable basis and did so in a way that postponed the degree of decline in the NAVs of the Funds which should have occurred during the Relevant Period.

27. Fund Accounting also engaged in smoothing prices (using preplanned daily reductions in value provided by the Portfolio Manager to gradually reduce, over days or weeks, a bond to its current proper valuation).

28. As a result of the foregoing practices, during the Relevant Period, the NAVs of the Funds were inaccurate at least from March 31, 2007 through August 9, 2007. Consequently, the prices at which the open-end series sold, redeemed, and repurchased their shares were also inaccurate.

29. During the Relevant Period, the Directors did not determine what methodology was actually used by Fund Accounting and the Valuation Committee to fair value particular securities or types of securities. The information and reports provided to Directors at their board meetings did not provide sufficient information for the Directors to understand what methodology was being used by Fund Accounting to fair value particular securities. For example, at each quarterly board meeting the Directors received a list of the Funds' portfolio securities that were required to be fair valued and the fair values assigned to each security at quarter end. However, the information provided did not identify the type of security, the basis for a particular assigned fair value, or whether that price had changed from prior quarters.

30. The Directors received at each quarterly board meeting three other documents relating to fair value determinations. The three documents were: (i) a "Report from the Joint Valuation Committee [of the Funds]"; (ii) a "Fair Valuation Form" for each of the Funds; and (iii) "Security Sales" reports for each of the Funds.

31. The *Report from the Joint Valuation Committee* provided in connection with the quarterly board meetings in November 2006, January 2007 and May 2007, said: "The Valuation Committee met three times during the [preceding] calendar quarter[.] ... The values of internally-priced securities were randomly confirmed with third parties

and no material exceptions were noted. The Valuation Committee feels that all securities are being fairly priced and there are no material misstatements." The report did not, however, state how fair values were determined, and gave no details on how fair valued securities, which it referred to as "internally-priced securities," were "randomly confirmed with third parties."

32. Although price confirmations played a significant role in the Funds' fair valuation process, the Directors never established any guidelines regarding the use of price confirmations, such as how frequently they should be requested for any particular type of security, or the selection of broker-dealers used to provide such price confirmations. Nor did the Directors require any review to identify those securities for which no price confirmation had been obtained for a particular length of time.

33. The *"Fair Valuation Form"* was received quarterly by the Directors for each of the Funds. That form contained, next to the words "Basis/Source/Method For Determining Price Used," the recurring phrase: "[i]nternal matrix based on actual dealer prices and/or Treasury spread relationships provided by dealers." There was no explanation of the "internal matrix" and no indication of what was meant by the terms "actual dealer prices" or "Treasury spread relationships provided by dealers." Contrary to the statements in the Fair Valuation Form, the internal matrix was only used to price a small percentage (for example, approximately 12% of the securities held by the four closed-end Funds) that were required to be fair valued as of March 31, 2007. The Directors were unaware as to how the matrix operated.

34. Meaningful "explanatory notes for the fair values assigned to the securities" were not presented, quarterly or otherwise, to the Directors, despite the fact that the Valuation Procedures required that the Directors receive them on a quarterly basis. Furthermore, the Directors never followed up to request that such explanatory notes or any other specific information regarding the basis for the values assigned be provided to them. Although the Portfolio Manager's price adjustments were purportedly based on information obtained by the Portfolio Manager from other traders and although the Board-approved Valuation Procedures required the Valuation Committee to present the Board with explanatory notes for all fair-valued securities, the Valuation Committee never identified to the Directors the bonds for which values were assigned based upon the price adjustments. Nor did the Directors require Fund Accounting or the Valuation Committee to identify those instances where the portfolio manager's price adjustment varied materially from a confirmation.

35. The *"Security Sales"* report for the Funds listed information about the securities sold in each Fund in the preceding quarter, including: (1) par value sold; (2) sales price; (3) the previous day's assigned price; (4) whether it was priced externally or internally, *i.e.*, fair valued; (5) the resulting variance; and (6) the impact on the Fund.

36. The Security Sales report included no information about securities that *had not been sold*—a significant limitation given the fact that securities that were required to be fair valued constituted a majority of Fund assets and most of those securities were not sold during the first six months of calendar 2007. For example, although approximately 290 securities were fair valued for substantially all of the period between No-

vember 2006 and July 31, 2007, only 24 of those securities were sold during that period.

37. The absence of information about potentially stale prices further limited the Directors' ability to (a) review carefully the findings of the Valuation Committee and, (b) satisfy themselves that all relevant factors had been considered. Indeed, the prices of many securities remained relatively unchanged for prolonged periods during the Relevant Period. This information would have been particularly valuable given the increasingly turbulent market conditions during the Relevant Period and the Funds' admonition in their filings that the prices for many of the securities in the portfolio could be volatile.

38. Outside counsel advised the Directors in connection with the adoption of the written Valuation Procedures. Further, during the Relevant Period, independent auditors audited the financial statements for the closed-end funds for the fiscal year ended March 31, 2007 and the open-end fund's financial statements for the fiscal year ended June 30, 2007. During each of these audits, the auditor provided unqualified opinions and advised the Directors that the Valuation Procedures were appropriate and reasonable.

39. These audits did not provide the Directors with sufficient information about the valuation methodologies actually employed by Fund Accounting and the Valuation Committee to satisfy the Directors' obligations. The auditors were not retained to opine on the Funds' internal controls and in fact, advised the Directors that the auditors' "consideration will not be sufficient to enable us to provide assurances on the effectiveness of internal control over financial reporting." As a result, the auditors did not advise the Directors in any meaningful detail as to what pricing methodologies were actually being employed.

RESPONSIBILITIES OF THE BOARD

40. Funds are required to adopt and implement policies and procedures reasonably designed to prevent violations of the securities laws, including policies and procedures concerning a fund's determination of the fair value of portfolio securities. It is a responsibility of a fund's board to ensure that the fund fulfills these obligations, particularly with respect to policies and procedures concerning the determination of fair value....

In 1970, the Commission issued guidance on various questions relating to the accounting by registered investment companies for investment securities, including the valuation of such securities. The Commission emphasized that it is the responsibility of a fund's board of directors to determine fair values and cautioned that, while a board may enlist the assistance of individuals who are not board members, it remains the board's duty to establish the fair value methodology to be used and to continuously review *both* the appropriateness of the methods used in valuing each issue of security and the valuation findings resulting from such methods. Specifically, the Commission stated:

[I]t is incumbent upon the Board of Directors to satisfy themselves that all appropriate factors relevant to the value of securities for which market quotations are not readily available have been considered and to determine the method of arriving at the fair value of each such security. To the extent considered necessary, the board may appoint persons to assist them in the determination of such value, and to make the actual calculations pursuant to the board's direction. The board must also, consistent with this responsibility, continuously review the appropriateness of the method used in valuing each issue of security in the company's portfolio. The directors must recognize their responsibilities in this matter and whenever technical assistance is requested from individuals who are not directors, the findings of such individuals must be carefully reviewed by the directors in order to satisfy themselves that the resulting valuations are fair.

The Commission repeated essentially the same guidance in a 1984 Report of Investigation Pursuant to Section 21(a) of the Exchange Act relating to Seaboard Associates ("*Seaboard*"). Finding fault with a registered fund's board of directors that had not properly fair valued oil and gas royalty interests, the Commission wrote:

> While the Commission recognizes the difficulties inherent in the valuation of [such] interests, directors have an affirmative responsibility to keep informed of developments which materially affect those assets not having a readily ascertainable market value.... Consistent with this responsibility, the directors of a registered investment company must continuously review the appropriateness of the method used in valuing the asset not having a readily ascertainable market value.

In ASR 118 and *Seaboard*, the Commission clearly stated that the ultimate responsibility for determining fair value lies with a fund's directors, and that this responsibility cannot be delegated away. And while directors may assign to a separate valuation committee the task of calculating fair values pursuant to board-approved valuation methodologies, "each director retains responsibility to be involved in the valuation process and may not passively rely on securities valuations provided by such a committee."

41. In connection with determining fair values, the Directors did not calculate the valuations themselves, and neither established clear and specific valuation methodologies nor followed up their general guidance to review and approve the actual methodologies used and the resulting valuations. Instead, they approved policies generally describing the factors to be considered but failed to determine what was actually being done to implement those policies. As a result, Fund Accounting implemented deficient procedures, effectively allowing the Portfolio Manager to determine valuations without a reasonable basis. In this regard, the Directors failed to exercise their responsibilities with regard to the adoption and implementation by the Funds of procedures reasonably designed to prevent violations of the federal securities laws.

These failures were particularly significant given that fair-valued securities made up a substantial percentage of the portfolios of each of the Funds — specifically between 64% and 68% of the value of all securities in the closed-end Funds and between 28% and 64% of the value of all securities in the portfolios of the open-end series as of March 31, 2007.

VIOLATIONS

42. As a result of the conduct described above, Respondents caused the Funds' violations of Rule 38a-1 under the Investment Company Act. That rule requires that registered investment companies adopt and implement written policies and proce-

dures reasonably designed to prevent violation of the federal securities laws by the fund, including policies and procedures that provide for the oversight of compliance by the fund's investment adviser. [***]

* * *

Notes and Applications

1. *What's a board supposed to do?* The conclusion in the *Alderman* proceeding is emphatic: the board did not do what it was supposed to have done. However, the specific lessons for boards are perhaps harder to discern. Consider which of the following courses of action the order seems to endorse, and with respect to each possibility, consider how feasible such an approach would be:

- The board should meet daily to evaluate pricing of fund portfolio securities;
- The board should sparingly delegate out duties to service providers relating to pricing;
- The board should establish detailed pricing policies and procedures to govern all pricing determinations and be fully conversant in the suitability of each policy and procedure used by the fund;
- The board should delegate, to outside experts, responsibility for formulating policies and procedures to spell out in great detail how pricing determinations should be made;
- The board may rely on experts and delegate some (or many) responsibilities, but must have pricing policies and procedures that generate meaningful feedback to the board so that the board can regularly evaluate the adequacy and reliability of a fund's pricing policies and procedures in their oversight role.

During early 2007, newspaper articles relating to subprime mortgages and securities backed by subprime mortgages began to appear in the mainstream financial press. Indeed, a front-page story in the New York Times trumpeted the looming crisis. *See* Gretchen Morgenson, *Crisis Looms in Mortgages*, N.Y. Times A1 (March 11, 2007). Several days later, a second article in the front of the business section indicated that Morgan Keegan funds were potentially severely impacted by mortgage securities investments. *See* Gretchen Morgenson, *Mutual Funds at Some Risk on Mortgages*, N.Y. Times C1 (March 14, 2007). Several days later, the large investment banking firm, Bears Stearns, collapsed. Should public news reports be a factor that should weigh in evaluating whether the Morgan Keegan board was discharging its pricing responsibilities under the Company Act and its rules?

2. *Redemptions and the issue of liquidity.* In addition to pricing, Section 22 of the Company Act also addresses redemptions by mutual funds (and other investment companies that issue redeemable securities, i.e., not redemptions by closed-end companies, which are dealt with in Section 23). Specifically, Section 22(e) generally prohibits mutual funds from suspending the right of redemption and requires funds to pay redemption proceeds within seven days, subject only to relief obtained by Com-

mission order or statutorily-defined emergencies. The SEC customarily maintained that Section 22's redemption mandate, at the very least, presumed that funds observe prudential liquidity policies with respect to securities portfolio investments. In other words, funds could not, consistent with their obligations pursuant to Section 22, hold excessive portfolio positions in illiquid securities, namely securities whose disposal at prevailing market values was not reasonably practicable. Why would the SEC as a policy matter, link liquidity issues with the fund's obligation to redeem? In 2015, the SEC codified its prudential view of liquidity in Rule 22e-4 by specifically prohibiting a fund's acquisition of additional illiquid securities, if the value of illiquid assets in the portfolio exceed 15% of its total value. In addition, the rule requires the phase-in by funds of procedures to internally classify all assets held in their portfolio in terms of the assets' liquidity and the establishment of internal fund mechanisms for managing portfolio liquidity risk. *See Open-End Fund Liquidity Risk Management Programs; etc.*, Investment Company Act Release No. 31835 (Sept. 22, 2015), 80 Fed. Reg. 62274 (Oct. 15, 2015).ß

Chapter 17

Distribution of Mutual Funds

Key Ideas: Fund distribution concerns the mechanics of selling fund shares to investors. A fund's sale of shares (or distribution) is the primary means of gathering assets under management. As discussed in Chapter 3, AUM directly affects fund viability in terms of economies of scale and the profitability to the adviser of managing the fund. Distribution, however, is a costly activity, and the costs must be borne directly or indirectly either by investors or the adviser. As a result, distribution poses a significant potential conflict of interest in terms of who should pay for it: do funds try to get bigger to benefit shareholders or to benefit the fund's adviser? Because of this inherent conflict of interest, Congress and regulators have imposed extensive requirements relating to how distribution costs are levied. Transparency with respect to costs in terms of sales charges and asset-based fees have also been issues. These limitations take the form of how (i) sales charges are imposed on investors and the amount of those charges; (ii) fund assets are used to pay for distribution, including, in some cases, outright prohibitions on certain distribution practices; and (iii) disclosure is made to investors relating to these distribution activities.

Essentially, sales charges paid by investors fall into two categories: transaction-based charges (i.e., charges paid directly by a purchasing or selling investor) and asset-based fees (i.e., fees paid out of a fund's assets and thus effectively paid by all shareholders of a particular fund class). Asset-based fees paid pursuant to Rule 12b-1, however, are the only permissible source of asset-based fees that may be used to pay some portion of a fund's distribution expenses. Over time, the SEC has permitted the proliferation of different kinds of transaction sales charges and use of different combinations of transaction-based fees in conjunction with Rule 12b-1 fees. Fee structures typically differ among classes of shares within a single fund. The only other direct source of revenue to pay for distribution is the investment adviser (or sponsor), which may pay or subsidize distribution expenses from its own resources.

Finally, regulators have attacked various undisclosed fee practices. Specifically, the SEC has attempted to enhance disclosure requirements both at the broker-dealer level and at the fund level, with the goal of helping investors make appropriate choices for how to pay for their purchase and holding of fund shares.

Chapter Contents

17.1 Introduction

Distribution is a vital concern to both advisers and fund investors. Merely creating a fund provides no assurance that there will be enough investors or assets under management to be economically viable. Because mutual funds and exchange traded funds issue redeemable shares to investors, fund assets can grow or decline on any given day as investor interest in the fund waxes or wanes. As a result, there is a direct connection between distribution activities (i.e., promotion of sales of fund shares) and fund size. For advisers, growing AUM through sales means growing revenues from advisory fees which are calculated as a percentage of AUM annually. In addition, distribution may also lead to economies of scale that reduce the fund's operating costs on a per share base (i.e., the expense ratio). These combined factors mean that the distribution function can be as important to a fund organization as to the adviser managing a fund's assets. Distribution, however, is a costly activity, and those costs must be borne directly or indirectly by investors or the adviser (i.e., there is no free lunch).

At a practical level, both business and regulators focus on two larger issues, though from sharply different perspectives: how should distribution be structured and who will bear the costs of distribution? For the purposes here, the business perspective is presented simply. The expense of distribution from the adviser's perspective represents a cost of doing business in managing a fund's assets. As a matter of self-interest, advisers will advocate distributional methods that maximize accumulation of assets under management in a cost-effective fashion, including in some cases, directly bearing those costs. However, the adviser may advocate arrangements that shift these costs directly or indirectly onto investors.

Chapter 3 introduced the topic of distribution and noted that funds avail themselves of different distribution channels. Different distribution channels directly affect how much is being paid for distribution, who is being compensated and how the costs are borne by the fund, the adviser, or the investor. Such channels are constantly evolving in response to regulatory and market-place changes.

The Company Act contains various limitations relating to the methods by which investors are required to bear the costs of distribution. From a regulatory perspective, these evolving fund distribution practices are fraught with potential conflicts of interest and issues of transparency. This chapter examines these issues in the context of the mechanics of distribution. It then explores the extensive regulatory structures that have developed to protect investors from excessive loads and distribution charges and fees. Finally, the material focuses on the critical role of disclosure to investors and the constant stream of enforcement cases and activities.

17.2 The Mechanics of Distribution

Distribution is the lifeblood of mutual funds. As important as investment management and performance are, the continuing stream of new assets is vital to successful and efficient operation of a fund and the financial health of the fund's investment adviser. This is where distribution comes in. Conceptually, "distribution" encompasses a broad array of sales activities like advertising, and the development of networks and channels, involving firms and personnel (such as brokers), that support sale of fund shares. An integral aspect is the sales charges and fees that are used to pay for these activities.

As has been discussed earlier in this casebook, mutual funds have an open-end structure, meaning that they continually offer their shares to investors and stand ready to redeem shares as well. Fund assets can only grow in two ways: appreciation of the portfolio and net investments (i.e., new share sales exceed redemptions as opposed to net redemptions where redemptions exceed new share sales). A fund which has no sales of new shares will inevitably shrink in size (that is, in AUM), as investors redeem their shares to pay for things like childrens' college tuition, new houses, or retirement. Net growth in AUM is important for fund operations. With such growth, funds may realize economies of scale in their operating expenses and, thus, enjoy reduced expense ratios. In addition, steady or growing AUM typically helps portfolio managers efficiently manage the fund's portfolio since they can avoid selling investments prematurely to meet redemption requests. Generally, growth in AUM benefits a fund's shareholders. However, in some cases, AUM growth may be a detriment, e.g., funds may become so large that they can no longer use their existing investment strategies effectively to achieve their investment objectives. In such situations, fund size may become an obstacle to fund performance.

The role of the distributor (or "principal underwriter") is an important aspect of distribution. A fund's distributor is like the quarterback of the distribution team. As quarterback, the distributor has a variety of choices on how to distribute or sell the fund's shares. As detailed in Chapter 3, the most basic decision relates to selection of distribution channels. As a quick refresher, funds typically use some or all of these distribution channels:

(1) *Direct or No-Load.* As the name implies, the direct or no-load channel involves no intermediaries. Investors can purchase their shares directly from the fund or its distributor without a load or sales charge.

(2) *Intermediary and broker-sold.* The largest channel by far is the intermediary sales channel which encompasses a broad range of intermediaries as described in Chapter 3. Intermediary sales are typically made through brokers, advisers, trust companies, insurance companies and a variety of other intermediaries who generally offer advice and guidance. Significantly, intermediaries must be compensated for their sales efforts in the form of sales charges or transaction fees paid by the investor or asset-based charges paid at the fund level and/or at the investor account level.

(3) *Retirement plans.* Retirement plan sales and relationships have become a huge factor in fund asset gathering. Plans such as IRAs (individual retirement accounts) and employer sponsored retirement plans (such as 401k and 403b plans), have grown enormously since the 1970s when they were first offered. This channel may involve modest loads and fees to plan sponsors, but they tend to be relatively low compared to the intermediary channel. Recently, because of prospective changes in the fiduciary rules applicable to brokers managing or advising retirement accounts, fees and loads have been dropping tremendously in this channel (e.g., to institutional levels).

(4) *Institutional.* While the retail channels discussed above contribute about 90% of fund sales, institutions also are active buyers of funds. Institutional buyers often demand extremely low sales charges or none at all.

Fund underwriting grew out of the old traditions of stock offerings, where underwriters typically engage in diverse lines of securities market activities. Such offerings generally are firm commitment offerings where the underwriter agrees to buy and resell a fixed amount of shares for a fixed price. In contrast, as noted in Chapter 13, most mutual fund offerings are open-ended both as to time and amount of shares (i.e., funds engage in continuous offerings), and shares are sold at NAV which is constantly changing or at an offering price which is based on the NAV plus a sales load. Thus, unlike the typical firm commitment securities offering which is limited to a specific time period, a fund offering is ongoing. In the former situation, underwriters tend to be well-capitalized broker-dealers which are almost invariably independent of the companies whose securities are being sold. In contrast, because fund distributors are engaged in continual selling efforts, these distribution relationships have evolved in industry-specific patterns involving either affiliated relationships or specialized third-party relationships. In the affiliated distribution relationship, the distributor is a corporate affiliate of the adviser, but remains a distinct business entity which separately registers as a broker-dealer. For some funds, e.g., funds too small to have their own affiliated distributors, it is easier or more efficient to hire an independent specialized third party distributor, which performs the distribution functions for multiple funds and their sponsors.

On a day to day basis, distributors are responsible for supervising the marketing and sales activities of their funds. Such activities include advertising, wholesaling and engaging the broad variety of sales intermediaries in contractual relationships for distribution of fund shares. For funds sold with front-end loads, the distributor performs the technical function of collecting the share sale proceeds, processing the loads and remitting the loads to the intermediaries and remaining proceeds to the fund for investment. In addition, distributors process redemptions either by buying back fund shares or facilitating the processing of the redemptions through the fund's transfer agent. For redemptions, redemption fees or back-end loads may be assessed, the processing of which the distributor is responsible.

An inherent conflict of interest resides in this paradigm, however: If fund assets are used to promote sale of fund shares, then it is the fund's adviser, which may be affiliated with the distributor, which stands to benefit from the fees generated by the increased AUM. This conflict pervades much of the discussion regarding fund distribution practices and accounts for one of the central regulatory fault lines relating to distribution: payment of distribution by investors versus payment for distribution from fund assets.

Notes and Applications

Conflicts of interest in distribution. In order to get a handle on the potential conflict of interest at the core of distribution, consider the incentives of the participants in having the fund itself pay for distribution. Presumably, paying the costs of distribution will mean that the fund assets will grow faster and be greater than would be the case if the fund did not spend money on distribution activities. How do a fund and its shareholders benefit from such expenditures? Well, there are certainly reasons that might make such payments advantageous for the interests of investors, e.g., reduced operating costs due to economies of scale. On the flip side, the fund adviser benefits from a fund having more assets. As AUM increases, advisory revenues to the investment manager will also increase. Although clearly both investors and the adviser could benefit from such expenditures by the fund, the danger is that the adviser might have incentives to urge expenditures on distribution that might not be in the best interests of investors so that the assets and fees grow. Clearly, a tension exists in the potential for conflicts of interest in fund payments for distribution.

17.3 The Regulation of Sales Charges Imposed on the Purchase and Sale of Funds with Redeemable Shares

Legal requirements relating to who would bear the costs of fund distribution date back to the enactment of the Company Act in 1940. At that time, distribution costs were either borne by the investment adviser, in whole or in part, or levied as a *sales load* which is defined in Company Act Section 2(a)(35) as the difference between the price of the security to the public and the portion of the proceeds which is received and invested for investors." In other words, a sales load is essentially an up-front or front-end sales commission which is deducted from the total amount of money an investor invests or pays for his/her shares. This was the sole form of shareholder charge statutorily authorized by Congress at the Act's inception. This provision, along with numerous other provisions in the Act, evidence that Congress understood that there would be payments to brokers in connection with the sale of shares. Moreover, the legislative history of the Act shows that Congress also recognized that because mutual funds offer redeemable shares, they would shrink if they did not continuously sell new shares. For its part, the SEC had concerns that mutual funds with small assets or just starting up might be made to bear the costly burden of selling and distributing their shares, building up AUM for the benefit of the adviser or other affiliates.

While the front-end sales load was the cornerstone of mutual fund distribution for nearly 35 years, that began to change in the mid-1970s when funds and their distributors began to experiment with different types of sales charges and fees to pay for distribution. This experimentation required the acquiescence of the SEC through regulatory action or exemptive relief. Most importantly, in 1980, the SEC permitted limited use of fund assets for payment of distribution costs with the enactment of Rule 12b-1, which is discussed in the next section. Later in the 1980s, deferred sales charges and different charges for different classes of shares of funds were developed, as discussed more thoroughly later in this chapter. While it is probably unnecessary to master the ins-and-outs of all these developments, it is useful to understand the multiplicity of legal issues arising from different sales charges and distribution fees. A tabular appendix at the end of this chapter provides a chronology summarizing the parallel developments relating to different types of sales charges and distribution fees.

Mutual Fund Distribution Fees; Confirmations

Investment Company Act Release No. 29367 (July 21, 2010)

[**Textbook note:** *In 2010, the SEC proposed a significant overhaul of distribution fees levied pursuant to Rule 12b-1, which is a common feature of the current distribution landscape and will be discussed further below. The SEC's proposing release, two excerpts of which are featured in this chapter, provides a nice introductory overview to distribution from a contemporary vantage point.*]

[***] I. INTRODUCTION

More than 87 million Americans, representing slightly less than half of all households, own mutual funds. Some investors buy fund shares directly from mutual fund sponsors without paying a sales charge.[7] However, most fund investors buy through intermediaries. These intermediaries include broker-dealers, banks, insurance companies, financial planners, and retirement plans. When investors use intermediaries to buy fund

7. These are referred to as "no-load" funds because no sales charge or "load" is charged in connection with the transaction....

shares, they typically will pay (either directly or indirectly) some form of sales charge or service fees to compensate the intermediaries for the services they provide.[9]

Investors use intermediaries for a variety of reasons. Some want help in selecting a particular fund or building a diversified portfolio of investments. Others like the convenience of holding a variety of financial assets together in the same account and receiving a single comprehensive account statement. A growing number of investors use mutual funds as a way to fund their retirement plans, college savings accounts, annuity or life insurance contracts, or other tax-advantaged investment vehicles, which are often offered by an intermediary. In some cases, investors use an intermediary (and pay sales charges) not necessarily for the services they obtain from the intermediary, but simply to be able to invest in shares of a particular fund that they cannot buy directly (*i.e.*, that are sold only through intermediaries).

There are over 9,000 funds available to investors, offering a variety of investment strategies to suit different investment needs. Investors can select among many types of intermediaries from which they can purchase fund shares, and have choices as to how they pay for the services of those intermediaries. They may pay a "sales load" at the time they purchase shares, or a deferred sales load when they redeem shares, or they may invest in a fund that pays ongoing sales charges on behalf of investors from fund assets, otherwise known as 12b-1 fees.[12] As an alternative, they may choose to invest through an intermediary that deducts fees directly from the investor's account by a separate agreement (*e.g.*, "wrap fee programs"). Whether an investor pays sales charges depends upon the fee structure of the fund in which the investor chooses to invest, and how those sales charges are paid depends upon the "class" of fund shares that the investor selects.

These sales charge arrangements are disclosed in fund prospectuses, and are governed by a combination of statutory provisions and rules adopted by the Commission and the Financial Industry Regulatory Authority, Inc. ("FINRA"), a self-regulatory organization for broker-dealers.[14] These rules have been in place for many years and, as discussed in more detail below, we believe that they may no longer fully reflect the current economic realities of the mutual fund marketplace or best serve the interests of fund investors....

---

9. Although the use of the term "intermediary" in this Release is not limited to registered broker-dealers, receipt of the fees addressed in this Release may, depending on the services provided, require the recipient to register as a broker-dealer or rely on an exception or exemption from broker-dealer registration....

12. We will use the term "12b-1 fees" generally to describe fees that are paid out of fund assets pursuant to a plan adopted under rule 12b-1 ("12b-1 plan").

14. FINRA rules do not apply directly to mutual funds, but to registered broker-dealers that are FINRA members, including the principal underwriters of most funds. Most funds therefore structure their sales loads to meet FINRA rules in order for their shares to be distributed and sold by registered broker-dealers in the United States.

II. BACKGROUND

A. Mutual Fund Sales Charges

When the Investment Company Act was enacted in 1940, investors paid most of the costs of selling and promoting fund shares in the form of a sales charge or sales "load" deducted from the purchase [public offering] price at the time of sale by the fund's principal underwriter (typically the fund's adviser or a close affiliate).[15] The sales load financed brokers' commissions, advertisements, and other sales and promotional activities. Only a limited number of funds, called "no-load" funds, marketed their shares directly to investors without the assistance of a retail broker, and did not charge sales loads.[16] The selling costs of no-load funds (primarily advertising) typically were subsidized by the funds' investment advisers out of their profits.

In the past, fund sales charges generally were much higher than those customarily charged today and raised concerns for Congress and the Commission.[18] The Commission submitted a report to Congress in 1966 concluding that mutual fund sales charges should be lowered.[19] Following this report, Congress amended the Act in 1970 to give rulemaking authority to the National Association of Securities Dealers, Inc. ("NASD") (now FINRA) to prescribe limits to prevent excessive sales loads. Under this authority, in 1975, the NASD adopted a rule placing a ceiling of 8.5 percent on the front-end sales load that a fund distributed by NASD members could charge. Today, few funds impose sales loads that approach the maximum limit, in part because of investor resistance to paying high front-end loads, but also because of the availability of other sources of revenue to pay distribution costs. [***]

* * *

Explanation: Sales Load: Legal Definition versus Conventional Business Usage

To understand what investors are really paying in terms of a sales load requires a bit more explanation. The definition of sales load in Section 2(a)(35) is clear: it is the difference between the price paid by the investor for the shares and the portion of the proceeds that will be invested in the fund for the investor. For most of this text, NAV—the net asset value per share—has been the touchstone of discussions about the fund's share price. However, as noted above, the traditional form of sales load sometimes referred to as a *front-end sales load* is

---

15. ... Principal underwriters typically confine themselves to wholesale transactions and leave the public selling to independent retail dealers under sales agreements, although some underwriters have their own "captive" retail sales organizations.... Although the principal underwriter collects the sales load, for convenience, throughout this Release, we will simply refer to "funds" as imposing sales loads or determining the amount of sales load payable.

16. ... Some funds also charged low sales loads of one to two percent....

18. During the period of 1927-1935, sales loads for broker-sold funds ranged from five to 10 percent, but by 1935 they were often as high as nine to 10 percent....

19. The Commission recommended that sales loads be limited to a statutory maximum of five percent from the prevailing typical load of 9.3 percent....

levied at the time of purchase of shares and paid by the investor with reference to the "price of the security to the public." This is commonly referred to as the *public offering price* or simply *offering price*, which is distinct from the NAV. In short, the offering price = the NAV + sales load.

Here is where the terminology can be downright confusing. The sales load is typically expressed as a *percentage* based on the public offering price of the fund's shares rather than the fund's NAV, e.g., 8.5% of the public offering price or an 8.5% sales load. The fund's public offering price is necessarily greater than the fund's NAV by definition. Therefore, a sales load expressed as a percentage of the public offering price will actually be slightly greater if expressed as a percentage of NAV.

An illustration will make this distinction sharper. If the current NAV is $9.15 per share and front-end sales load is a charge of 8.5% of the offering price, then the public offering price will be $10 per share. In this instance, the 85 cents sales load per share is a front-end sales load actually representing 9.3% of NAV (i.e., the $9.15 invested per share in the fund), a much higher percentage than the widely-used figure of 8.5% of the public offering price. There is no question that the actual amount of the sales load is $0.85, but that amount is always expressed as a percentage of the public offering price (8.5%) by virtue of industry custom rather than as the higher percentage, namely 9.3% of NAV.

As noted earlier, in the mid-1970s, the paradigm of payments for distribution began evolving, a process which continues. As funds, distributors and the SEC explored different ways to pay for distribution, two problems emerged: how to help small funds compete with larger funds and how to help no-load and low cost funds compete with load funds? Industry lobbying regarding these issues led to development of Rule 12b-1 and the ability to use of fund assets to pay for distribution. Predictably, there were competitive responses in the industry. Rule 12b-1 fees (and other changes to advertising rules) meant that low cost and small funds could invest more resources in distribution without using front-end sales loads which have built-in disincentives for prospective investors (remember, prospective investors can lose as much as 5–8.5% off the top of their investment just for the privilege of investing in a fund). Funds that relied on front-end sales load (and thus on a broker-dealer network to sell shares) understandably perceived a need to reconfigure how their own sales loads were levied. Specifically, those funds sought permission to use *deferred sales charges* which refers to any type of load arrangement that defers levying sales loads until after purchase, either in installments over time or when shareholders redeem their shares. For an investor, such deferred sales charges means that all of his or her money is invested in a fund, just like with a no-load fund; however, a load may be assessed on sale, unlike no-load funds. This confers a competitive advantage for funds with such deferred sales charges, since they look like no-loads up front, and the brokers and advisers selling such funds may be compensated for their efforts, unlike with no-load funds. Many funds received exemptive relief from the SEC in the 1980s to adopt deferred sales loads.

In 1988, the SEC proposed Company Act Rule 6c-10—an exemptive rule—which authorized deferred sales loads without the need for an exemptive order. Although the rule itself was not finally adopted until 1995, the SEC routinely granted exemptive relief to funds in the intervening years before its final adoption. The rule specifically addressed several types of deferred sales load arrangements: (i) a pure *deferred sales load* which is a one-time charge levied at the time a shareholder redeems her or his shares; (ii) a *contingent deferred sales load* which is a deferred sales load which declines in a stepwise fashion the longer that the shareholder holds the fund shares and actually disappears altogether after some point in time, such as the fifth anniversary after the purchase of shares (assuming no redemption occurs); and (iii) an *installment* or *spread load* which is a smaller load imposed in annual installments and is not contingent on redemption.

The fact that the SEC needed to adopt an exemptive rule to authorize imposition of deferred sales loads is legally significant. It necessarily implied that, absent exemptive relief, imposition of such charges would otherwise violate the Company Act. Indeed, the rule itself indicates that it is intended to exempt mutual funds from the provisions of Sections 2(a)(32), 2(a)(35) and 22(d) of the Company Act. It is worth considering how a deferred sales charge might be inconsistent with each of those provisions.

The first two—Sections 2(a)(32), defining *redeemable security*, and 2(a)(35), defining *sales load*—are statutory definitions. The definition of *sales load*, as discussed above, is a sales charge defined with reference to the public offering price. *Redeemable security* is defined as a security that "upon its presentation to the issuer ... entitle[s the shareholder] ... to receive approximately his or her proportionate share of the issuer's current net assets, or the cash equivalent thereof." Although both definitions appear largely innocuous, they implicitly restrict the ability of funds to impose random levies or charges on shareholders. Sales loads, as used by statute, are imposed at the time of share purchases, whereas a deferred sales load is imposed after purchase of fund shares. In addition, the definition of redeemable security (uniquely relevant to mutual funds, UITs and ETFs) and its use throughout the statute serves to guarantee the shareholders' right to receive their *pro rata* share of fund assets upon redemption, absent some form of regulatory or exemptive relief. Requiring that a security be redeemable would not be of much value to the holder of the security unless the holder were also guaranteed a certain value upon redemption. A deferred sales charge diminishes the value that a securityholder receives upon redemption of the holder's security. Thus, the SEC required exemptive relief to permit a small adjustment to the value received by a securityholder upon redemption, until the adoption of Rule 6c-10 allowed deferred or back-end sales charges subject to the Rule's terms and conditions.

In addition, Rule 6c-10 affords relief from Section 22(d). Section 22 which is captioned "Distribution, redemption and repurchase of redeemable securities." As discussed in Chapter 16 on pricing, Section 22(c) and Rule 22c-1 thereunder essentially require that, for purposes of sale, redemption and repurchase, the price of a mutual fund's "redeemable security" be based on the fund's current (next computed) NAV.

Section 22(b) addresses another facet of sale charges, namely the potential need for limits on the size of sales charges. Congress never gave the SEC the power directly to regulate sales charges. However, Section 22(b) provides FINRA with the authority to regulate reasonable compensation of brokers through sales charges on fund shares which is discussed below. Section 22(d) addresses a different issue relating to distribution and indeed is the principal means by which the SEC exercised control over distribution when the Company Act was enacted.

Section 22(d) of the Act requires a mutual fund, its principal underwriter/distributor, and any dealer in redeemable securities issued by the fund to sell the shares only at a current public offering price described in the fund's prospectus. This requirement is often called the *retail price maintenance requirement.* The retail price maintenance requirement effectively establishes a rigid pricing structure and precludes the development of a secondary market for fund shares. In addition, it undoubtedly contributed to the specialized nature of underwriting and distribution involving mutual funds where the underwriter/distributor frequently is affiliated with the investment adviser. Critically, the inclusion of Section 22(d) in the Act gave advisers and distributors control of the distribution process for mutual fund shares.

Such control was important to the fund industry in that it enabled advisers and distributors to set sales load schedules without fear of uncontrolled sales and resales of fund shares, e.g., in a secondary market. Without the retail price maintenance requirement, it would be possible for brokers to buy and sell a fund's shares without levying the sales load, thus depriving distributors of significant income. With the public offering price as the base price, the sales load component of the offering price was essentially "fixed" by Section 22(d), precluding competition by brokers with respect to sales charges. By doing so, Section 22(d) effectively provided that sales charges associated with fund shares would be insulated from the usual antitrust principles favored by U.S. law. This unusual result does not appear to have been extensively considered when the fund industry proposed the inclusion of what developed into Section 22(d) in the Company Act.

The legislative history of Section 22(d) is sparse and has been the subject of much industry, academic, and SEC discussion. The SEC has concluded and stated that the Section was included in the Company Act to address three aspects of fund distribution. First, it precluded the potential for abusive trading that resulted from the "backward pricing" of shares that prevailed in 1940. Without the Section, insiders like the distributor or fund employees could have been able to buy shares without a load today at yesterday's asset valuation (because of backwards pricing). If the asset values rose today, the insider could have purchased today for the lower and sold tomorrow at today's higher value for an immediate and riskless gain. Such trades would also be dilutive, as the gains are made at the cost of investors remaining in the fund. Second, Section 22(d) precluded the development of a secondary market for fund shares as noted above. Third, the Section precluded discrimination or preferential pricing amongst investors.

In the decades since the passage of the Company Act, there has been continual evolution of fund share pricing, distribution methods and sales compensation. A notable change occurred in 1968 with the adoption of "forward pricing" of fund shares, which addressed a key abuse that Section 22(d) was intended to address, i.e., the dilutive trading by insiders. As a result, in the absence of Congressional repeal of Section 22(d), since the 1970s, the SEC has followed an administrative program approach to promote gradual introduction of limited forms of retail price competition. Most notably, the adoption of Rule 22d-1 in 1985 opened the door for the creation of multi-class load structures since it allows the sales of redeemable securities "at prices that reflect scheduled variations in, or elimination of, the sales load." Funds quickly sought exemptive relief to create such multi-class structures based on variations of sales loads. In 1995, the SEC codified such relief in an exemptive rule, Rule 18f-3, which provides exemption from certain provisions of the Company Act designed to prevent creation of securities senior in rights to others within the same fund. In short, Rules 22d-1 and 18f-3 together enabled funds to sell shares in the same fund with varying load and fee structures through the introduction of different classes of shares. Combined with the ability to pay fund asset based distribution fees or expenses under 1980's Rule 12b-1, the effect has been to permit a broadening variety of ways to pay for distribution, from front-end sales loads to deferred sales loads to 12b-1 fees.

Notes and Applications

"Clean Shares." The latest step in the evolution of distribution has led mutual funds to completing the full circle back to pre-Company Act practices in a way: transferring to brokers and other intermediaries the ability to charge brokerage commissions for fund share transactions, rather than applying loads or other fund derived compensation. In early 2017, the sponsor of a large fund family received no-action relief from the SEC to offer a class of shares that unbundles distribution costs from investment management and operational costs of mutual funds. In other words, such "clean shares" will be offered without any front-end load, deferred sales charge, or other asset-based fees for sales or distribution, i.e., no built-in commission, loads or 12b-1 fees. Clean shares may be offered and sold only by brokers who are acting as agents on behalf of their customers. As compensation for such services, the brokers may charge a transaction commission as they might do for buying and selling of stock. In addition, at the fund level, certain transfer agency and shareholder servicing costs may be reduced or eliminated for these types of shares. *See Capital Group*, SEC No-Action Letter (January 11, 2017).

Conceptually, the no-action letter relief addresses a nuanced distinction between the role of brokers as agents of customers versus dealers for funds and their distributors. However, the import of that distinction is to eliminate any concerns arising under Section 22(d). In its letter, the SEC notes, "By its terms, section 22(d)'s restrictions do not apply to a broker, as that term is defined in the 1940 Act. In a report to the Senate Committee on Banking, Housing, and Urban Affairs in November 1974, we considered policy arguments in support of permitting brokers to make reasonable charges for services rendered in connection with the purchase of no-load mutual fund shares. We distinguished these intermediary-imposed fees from mutual fund-imposed sales loads that are a component of the fund's public offering price, noting that 'if the broker's charge is not required by the fund, no part of it is received by the fund, and it is something over which the fund has no control, it may be viewed as being separate and apart from the price of fund shares ... in order to compensate [the broker] for certain services not offered by the fund. These characteristics distinguish such a charge from a sales load which is not only retained in part by the fund underwriter, but is mandated by the fund to cover the cost of the selling effort which is an integral part of the fund's distribution system.' " In contrast, the concern was that receipt of some form of load or compensation from the fund or its distributor would make a broker-dealer a dealer under the Company Act, which means essentially acting as a principal rather than strictly as an agent of a customer.

As noted above, Section 22(d) was designed to address several abuses in the pricing and sale of fund shares. By completely stripping shares of distribution charges, clean shares arguably eliminate such concerns. Mutual fund share sales become strictly a matter of the agency relationship between a broker and its customers. The mutual fund and its distributor become simply vendors in this relationship. The only remaining potential conflict of interest is the fund's investment adviser's interest in having the assets under management grow so that advisory fees can grow. In this light, the SEC was able to provide no-action relief.

One might ask why fund distributors would want to give up the load and fee structures? The answer is quite simple: the evolving regulatory and competitive landscape for broker-dealers. In the spring of 2017, the Department of Labor began implementation of rule changes (which were later vacated by the courts) for broker-dealers advising retirement accounts, requiring such brokers to act in the best interests, essentially as fiduciaries, of their customers. Previously, brokers had to provide only advice suitable to the customer and his/her needs. The heightened standard of care created a potential need for fund share classes where the brokers have no financial interest in selling one fund versus another, e.g., by receiving better load or 12b-1 payments. Clean shares were viewed as one potential solution to address such need. In 2018, the Department of Labor abandoned its attempts to implement such rules after several adverse court decisions. Although the DOL's abandonment of its rule eliminated the immediate need for clean shares, it remains to be seen whether clean shares will prove desirable to the fund industry for other reasons.

17.4 Rule 12b-1 and Restrictions on Use of Fund Assets to Pay for Distribution

The costs of distribution and marketing can be paid only in three ways: (1) by the investor, directly, in the form of loads, commissions and service fees; (2) by the investor, indirectly, in the form of higher fund fees; and/or (3) by the fund's advisor, distributor or other affiliate. While sales loads are the traditional means of paying for distribution, this section examines fund payments for distribution and marketing, and restrictions on such payments.

As noted above, in 1980, the SEC adopted Rule 12b-1 to permit funds to pay fees, costs and expenses, out of fund assets, for distribution, marketing and advertising (collectively called "distribution activities" in this text). Since then, plans created pursuant to Rule 12b-1 ("12b-1 plans") have facilitated such payments but also raised several challenging new issues. Analytically, the first question to ask is whether fund assets are being used to pay for distribution activities, including advertising and marketing? If such payments are made outside the terms of a 12b-1 plan or agreement, then they are prohibited. If payments are made pursuant to a 12b-1 plan, the next analytical question is whether the payments are truly in support of distribution activities? Misclassification of expenses and payments is a problem for the industry. For example, funds and their investment advisers have frequently gotten into trouble by using 12b-1 fees to pay for expenses not directly connected with fund distribution activities. One area where this distinction must be drawn carefully is that of shareholder servicing activities, i.e., differentiating activities intended to procure additional share sales versus addressing existing shareholder needs to retain such investors. The next reading and the "Fund Supermarket Letter: SEC to ICI," included below, goes into some detail on this issue. However, before going into the complexities of Rule 12b-1, it is important to understand its backstory.

Section 12(b) states in pertinent part:

> It shall be unlawful for any registered open-end company ... to act as a distributor of securities of which it is the issuer, except through an underwriter, in contravention of such rules and regulations as the Commission may prescribe....

In connection with enactment of the Company Act, the SEC's Chief Counsel at the time, David Schenker, characterized the purpose of Section 12(b) as a way to protect funds "against excessive sales, promotion expenses, and so forth." Section 12(b) does not expressly prohibit funds from underwriting their own securities; rather it was structured to prohibit funds merely from doing so in contravention of SEC rules. Nevertheless for some 40 years, the SEC declined to adopt rules under Section 12(b), and registered investment companies declined to act as underwriters for their funds or to pay for distribution activities directly. For decades, the SEC staff's position was that use of fund assets to pay for distribution activities was prohibited. In 1980, the SEC made such a prohibition explicit as part of Rule 12b-1, and then used the Rule to lay out the conditions under which it would permit use of fund assets to support distribution activities. The adoption of Rule 12b-1 changed the dynamics of fund distribution not merely in authorizing the payment of fund asset-based fees and expenses for distribution activities, but in sparking the introduction of a wide array of sales charges other than front-end sales loads. Its limitations and scope continue to shape the way the fund industry structures distribution activities.

Rule 12b-1 plans permit funds to pay for distribution out of their assets, typically through a fee assessed at the fund level similar to advisory fees, i.e., a fund pays a certain percentage of AUM annually or a fixed fee irrespective of the distributor's costs of selling a fund's shares. Such plans are known as *compensation plans*, and plan payments are not tied to the share price nor to share purchases. In addition, some 12b-1 plans are designed to pay certain distribution related costs such as advertising and marketing, i.e., only the actual expenses are paid, but not a set fee.

To be implemented, 12b-1 agreements and plans need to be adopted by the fund's board and shareholders. Approval requirements mirror the ones for approval of advisory agreements given the potential conflicts of interest for the adviser and distributor. Generally, a 12b-1 agreement and plan is developed when a fund is created and registered, in which case, the board and shareholder approvals are accomplished prior to the fund being offered publicly. If the agreement and plan is amended once the fund is public, then such changes must be submitted to the fund's shareholders for approval. A 12b-1 agreement spells out the terms of the agreement between the fund and distributor. The 12b-1 plan, which is often integrated into the agreement, details the operative provisions of the 12b-1 agreement, including the types of distribution costs and expenses that are covered.

Mutual Fund Distribution Fees; Confirmations

Investment Company Act Release No. 29367 (July 21, 2010)

[**Textbook note:** *As noted earlier, the 2010 Proposing Release proposed a fundamental overhaul of Rule 12b-1 because the Rule has operated in ways that were not intended at the time of its adoption. The Release provides both an excellent overview of the Rule's history and the concerns that have emerged regarding the operation of Rule 12b-1 plans. The SEC never implemented this rule proposal, but the questions posed in the release are worthy of consideration and serve to raise the fundamental issues of who should pay for distribution and how those payments should be structured.*]

[***] B. Adoption of Rule 12b-1

The ... Commission adopted rule 12b-1 in 1980. As described in more detail below, rule 12b-1 permits a fund to use fund assets to pay broker-dealers and others for providing services that are primarily intended to result in the sale of the fund's shares. The Commission adopted rule 12b-1 under its authority in section 12(b) of the Investment Company Act, which authorizes the Commission to regulate the distribution activities of funds that act as distributors of their own securities. Section 12(b) was designed to protect funds from being charged excessive sales and promotional expenses. The requirements of the rule are intended, in part, to address the conflicts of interest between a fund and its investment adviser that arise when a fund bears its own distribution expenses.[27]

27. When a fund pays promotional costs, the fund's investment adviser or distributor is relieved from bearing the expense itself, and the adviser benefits further if the fund's expenditures result in the growth of the fund's assets and a related increase in advisory fees (because an adviser's fees typically are based on a percentage of fund assets). However, commentators have noted that the benefits to existing fund shareholders from these expenditures may be "speculative at best."

The Commission's adoption of rule 12b-1 arose in the context of two significant developments in the mutual fund market that occurred during the 1970s. First, many funds experienced a prolonged period of net redemptions (i.e., redemptions exceeded new sales), which reduced the amount of fund assets. Fund company representatives asserted that using fund assets to fuel the sale of fund shares could benefit fund shareholders by increasing economies of scale and reducing fund expense ratios. The second was the development of money market funds and no-load fund groups, including internally managed funds, which did not charge sales loads but required a source of revenue to support their direct selling efforts. By offering a less expensive way for many investors to become fund shareholders, no-load funds promised to introduce greater price competition in the sale of mutual funds to retail investors, which might lower sales loads for all investors.

Before the rule's adoption, the Commission generally had opposed the use of fund assets for the purpose of financing the distribution of mutual fund shares, noting that existing shareholders of a fund "often derive little or no benefit from the sale of new shares." After engaging in a thorough review of the public policy and legal implications of permitting funds to bear these types of expenses, which included a public hearing and two requests for public comment, the Commission ultimately decided that there may be circumstances in which it would be appropriate for a fund to bear its own distribution expenses.

The Commission remained concerned, however, about the inherent conflicts of interest on the part of the fund adviser. Therefore, in crafting the conditions of the rule, we sought to minimize the role of the adviser and its affiliates in establishing both the amount and uses of fund assets to support distribution. As adopted, the rule required the fund's board of directors, and in particular its independent directors, to play a key role in deciding the level of the fund's distribution charges and how the revenue would be spent.

Rule 12b-1 requires that, before using fund assets to pay for distribution expenses, a fund must adopt a written plan (a "rule 12b-1 plan") describing all material aspects of the proposed financing of distribution, which must contain provisions similar to several of those the Act requires for advisory contracts between the fund and its investment adviser. The rule 12b-1 plan must be approved initially by the fund's board of directors as a whole, and separately by the "independent" directors. If the plan is adopted after the sale of fund shares to the general public, it also must be approved initially by a vote of at least a majority of the fund's voting securities.

The rule does not restrict the amounts of the fees that may be approved under the plan. It also does not specify all of the activities that are "primarily intended to result in the sale of shares" and therefore may be paid by a fund only according to a rule 12b-1 plan. Nor does it specifically prohibit a fund from paying for non-distribution expenses under a rule 12b-1 plan. Instead of limits or restrictions, the rule requires directors (including a majority of the independent directors) to conclude, in exercising their reasonable business judgment and in light of their fiduciary duties, that there is a reasonable likelihood that the plan will benefit both the fund and its shareholders.

The directors have a duty to request and evaluate as much information as is reasonably necessary for the directors to make an informed business decision. The rule also requires any person authorized to direct payments under the plan or any related agreement (such as the fund's underwriter) to provide quarterly reports to the board of directors of all amounts expended under the plan and the purposes for which the expenditures were made. The fund's board of directors (including a majority of the independent directors) must decide each year whether to re-approve the plan based on the same considerations as required initially to adopt the plan. Any material increases in the amounts paid under the plan must be approved by the fund's board, the fund's independent directors, and the fund's shareholders.

In the 1980 Adopting Release, the Commission provided a list of nine factors that were intended to provide guidance to directors in considering whether the use of fund assets for distribution would benefit the fund and its shareholders. The factors included: (i) the need for independent counsel or experts to assist the board; (ii) the "problems" or "circumstances" that make the plan necessary or appropriate; (iii) the causes of such problems or circumstances; (iv) how the plan would address the problems; (v) the merits of possible alternatives; (vi) the interrelationships between the plan and distributors; (vii) the possible benefits of the plan to other persons relative to the benefits to the fund; (viii) the effect of the plan on existing shareholders; and (ix) in deciding whether to continue a plan, whether the plan has produced the anticipated benefits to the fund and its shareholders.

The rule was intended to allow fund boards some latitude to exercise their reasonable business judgment to authorize the distribution arrangements and continue them from year to year as circumstances warranted. The annual re-approval requirement and the factors enumerated in our adopting release reflected an expectation that a fund would use the rule in order to address particular distribution problems, such as periods of net redemption. The rule was also designed to allow distribution arrangements to evolve. However, the rule ultimately resulted in distribution practices that we did not originally anticipate, as described below....

....

2. Enhanced Disclosure

Over the years, the Commission has taken several steps designed to improve investor understanding of 12b-1 fees and the impact they have on fund expenses and investor returns. We required funds to include a fee table in the prospectus identifying, among other things, the amount of any 12b-1 fee paid. As part of the 1992 amendments to the NASD [now called FINRA] sales charge rule, we also approved a new provision prohibiting registered broker-dealers from describing funds as "no-load" funds if the funds charged 12b-1 fees greater than 25 basis points. We amended our proxy rules to require funds to better describe material facts to shareholders when requesting approval of a rule 12b-1 plan or an amendment to the plan. Through our Web site, we have also provided investors with information and tools designed to enhance their understanding of the fees and distribution expenses they pay as a consequence of owning mutual funds.

D. The Current Role of 12b-1 Fees

Rule 12b-1 plans continue to play a significant role in paying for fund distribution costs. The majority of funds have adopted rule 12b-1 plans, which paid a total of $9.5 billion in 12b-1 fees in 2009 (down from a high of $13.3 billion in 12b-1 fees in 2007).

There has been a trend in fund class share ownership away from those that impose the highest sales loads and 12b-1 fees. In recent years, no-load share classes have attracted more net new cash flow than load share classes. According to Investment Company Institute ("ICI") figures, in 2009, $323 billion flowed into no-load share classes of long-term mutual funds, while in comparison, load share classes only received $39 billion in net new cash flow....

Although more investors appear to be investing in no-load funds and share classes, these statistics do not reflect a trend away from using intermediaries. According to the ICI, 80 percent of investors who own funds outside of a retirement plan use an intermediary that provides professional financial assistance ("financial advisor"). Of those investors, almost half own funds purchased solely through financial advisors, while the rest own funds purchased through financial advisors as well as directly from fund companies, mutual fund supermarkets, or discount brokers.[96] The data suggest a growing predominance of no-load or load-waived classes in funds that traditionally were sold with a load. In these circumstances, investors do not pay a sales load, but pay distribution expenses through a separate fee arranged between the intermediary and the investor, and/or through the payment of ongoing "service fees."

A significant use of 12b-1 fees today is for what is typically characterized as "services" provided to investors after the sale by the broker-dealers and other intermediaries who sell the fund. According to the Investment Company Institute, more than half of all 12b-1 fees paid by funds are used for this purpose, with broker-dealers and bank trust departments being the primary recipients. Under the NASD sales charge rule discussed above, up to 25 basis points of fund assets annually may be paid to members as a "service fee."

Amounts deducted from assets in excess of a service fee are typically charged to support the fund's distribution efforts and operate as an alternative to a front-end sales load. These 12b-1 fees, which are used to pay the selling costs of B and C share classes, are "asset-based sales charges" under the NASD sales charge caps and are limited to a maximum of 75 basis points of fund assets, annually, as discussed above.

A common use of 12b-1 fees is to pay for the fund to be included on third-party platforms for purchasing mutual funds, such as employer-sponsored retirement plans and fund supermarkets. Supermarkets and retirement plans have become major av-

96. ... Mutual fund supermarkets, which are sponsored by brokerage firms, "permit investors to purchase and hold a broad range of funds from many different fund sponsors through a single brokerage account." Robert C. Pozen, The Mutual Fund Business (2d ed. 2002), at 304. The primary benefit of this "one-stop shopping venue" is simplicity: an investor can buy funds from different fund families and receive all of their statements in a single report. Discount brokers allow investors to trade securities at a lower commission rate but provide less individualized service.

enues by which investors purchase mutual funds. They have assumed many of the recordkeeping and ongoing servicing and support functions for shareholders that funds otherwise would perform, and these are often paid for, at least partially, through 12b-1 fees. Under the NASD sales charge rule, no-load funds are able to compensate discount brokers and supermarkets for the costs of servicing shareholders in those channels through asset-based fees of up to 25 basis points annually of the value of fund shares that are held in the intermediary's client accounts. Funds that are offered as investment options in defined contribution retirement plans also may pay 12b-1 fees (often 50 basis points or more annually) to the plan administrator to offset some of the costs of servicing shareholders (and perhaps other participants) who invest through those plans.

A minor use of 12b-1 fees is to pay expenses of the fund's principal underwriter and for advertising and promotions. Although this was one of the main purposes for which 12b-1 plans originally were intended, in recent years, only about two percent of 12b-1 fees have been used to pay these types of expenses. [***]

* * *

Notes and Applications

The prohibition on directed brokerage. In the 2003–2004 market timing and late-trading scandal era, a form of distribution payments in guise was discovered: directed brokerage. Under a *directed brokerage* arrangement, a mutual fund's adviser directs execution of the fund's securities transactions to certain brokers in return for certain additional services and payments, including distribution. This raises an inherent conflict of interest question: Is the adviser and/or its affiliates avoiding having to pay for distribution expenses by directing fund brokerage? Conceptually, the securities transaction commissions or costs that a fund pays are the fund's assets. Why? Simply because it is money paid by the fund. When used in part to pay for other services including distribution, funds and advisers need to consider the benefits and purposes of such services.

As a result of the scandal and the discovery of directed brokerage payments for distribution, in 2004, the SEC amended Rule 12b-1 (see Rule 12b-1(h)) to prohibit the explicit or informal linkage of distribution of fund shares to portfolio execution commissions and fees. However, merely because a broker or dealer markets fund shares to its retail customers does not mean that it is prohibited from executing portfolio transactions on behalf of the fund or the fund from using the broker or dealer. However, before directing portfolio transactions of a fund to a broker or dealer that also sells the fund's shares to retail customers, the fund must implement policies and procedures that ensure against potential conflicts of interest in directing brokerage transaction to such brokers or dealers.

17.5 FINRA Caps on Sales Charges and Different Charges for Different Classes

Congress never actually gave the SEC the direct power to set sales charge rates, notwithstanding the significant requirements administered by the SEC relating to payment of distribution and marketing expenses, and SEC authority with respect to disclosure of sales charges. In the absence of explicit rate regulation, until 1970, load funds often charged up to 8.5% of the public offering price as a sales load for the purchase of fund shares. However, in 1970, Congress amended the Exchange and Company Acts to give the FINRA (then known as the NASD) rate setting authority on sales loads. Recall that FINRA is a self-regulatory organization charged with overseeing registered broker-dealers. Given that brokers are the primary intermediaries for distribution of fund shares, FINRA is a key regulator with respect to fund sales. FINRA maintains a substantial manual of its Rules, which used to be known as its Rules of Conduct. However, the SEC oversees FINRA and has the authority to approve or reject FINRA's rulemaking. So, curiously, the SEC does have indirect oversight of the rate setting. Consider whether you think this is an inefficient or inappropriate allocation of power by the government? Is there a better way to do it?

After being given the authority, FINRA acted to establish ceilings on funds' sales loads and 12b-1 sales charges. First, in 1975, FINRA capped front-end sales load charges at 8.5%. Later, as Rule 12b-1 plans proliferated and funds and fees grew in size, FINRA studied the collective impact of all types of sales loads, asset-based charges and 12b-1 fees. In 1992, FINRA amended its Rules for its member broker-dealers to bar excessive fee structures, under Rule 2341(d) (formerly 2830(d)).

The caps on direct sales charges and asset-based sales charges imposed in 1992 are still in effect, capping the annual amount of asset-based sales charges (basically 12b-1 fees) to 0.75% of fund assets. Additionally, funds with such asset-based sales charges are limited to a maximum of 6.25% of new gross share sales on the total sales charges applied, including asset-based, front-end, and deferred or contingent sales charges. A higher cap of 7.25% is permitted for funds that do not pay asset-based fees. This blend of caps initially created an accounting nightmare for brokerage firms, as it requires them to keep a running tally of all sales charges and fees imposed on funds. The caps have become even more complex with the addition of "shareholder servicing fees" designed to compensate brokers for their work in assisting existing shareholders of funds, in contrast to facilitating the sale of fund shares. Under the FINRA cap structure, such service fees are limited to 0.25% annually.

Partly in response to regulatory developments and partly as a result of industry competition and innovation, funds and their sponsors developed a variety of fund share classes which can be confusing to investors. Such share classes are designed to mix and match the various load and fee alternatives and to address different distribution channels. See the share class explanation box below.

Given the complexity of the requirements relating to sales charges and distribution fees, ample opportunity has developed for ambiguity regarding the meaning and significance of various terms. For example, when you see the expression no-load, what does that suggest to you? For most, it suggests that there is no sales charge or distribution fees. In reality, this is not true in the arcane world of fund loads and fees. At the time the FINRA rules were being discussed, a major point of contention was the definition of "no-load funds." Traditionally, no-load meant that a fund levied no sales charges for sale of fund shares. After the adoption of Rule 12b-1, a number of no-load funds adopted 12b-1 plans to provide for shareholder servicing, and in part to pay for listing on fund supermarket platforms which we explore in detail below. The controversy between pure no-load funds and those sporting service fees was settled by FINRA's rulemaking which defined no-load as funds with 12b-1 fees up to 0.25%.

If no-load traditionally meant a fund without a sales charge or load, how then is it appropriate for FINRA to permit funds to charge up to 0.25% 12b-1 fees and still be called no-load funds? The reasoning is not immediately intuitive, but it is rational. In 1992, the SEC approved a rule change by FINRA implementing this approach. In doing so, the SEC and FINRA recognized that the expenses of funds with low 12b-1 fees tend to more closely resemble those of funds with no sales loads or 12b-1 fees. They determined that, by not permitting low 12b-1 fee funds to call themselves no-load would make it difficult for investors to differentiate low 12b-1 fee funds, which use such fees to finance advertising and other promotional activities, from funds that use higher 12b-1 fees as an alternative to front-end sales charges. *See generally Self-Regulatory Organizations, National Association of Securities Dealers, Inc., Order Approving Proposed Rule Change Relating to the Limitation of Asset-Based Sales Charges as Imposed by Investment Companies*, Exchange Act Release No. 30897 (July 7, 1992).

Explanation: Class Is in Session—-Understanding the A, B and Cs of Fund Classes

As discussed earlier, a single mutual fund may offer more than one class of its shares to investors. Each class represents an interest in the mutual fund's portfolio, but is differentiated from other classes by different fees and expenses, primarily representing payments for distribution. While the industry has not completely agreed on standardization of class definitions, the following are common:

- *Class A shares:* are offered with the traditional front-end load or sales charge, which is paid at the time of purchase. A 12b-1 fee may also be assessed on Class A shares.
- *Class B shares:* are often called "spread load" or "back-end load" shares because the sales charges are spread over time. Instead of a front-end load or sales charge, investors pay a deferred sales load which may decline the longer shares are held, in which case it's called a "contingent deferred sales load (or charge)" ("CDSL" or "CDSC"). Typically, the CDSL declines to zero after year 6 or 7, at which point the Class B shares usually convert automatically to Class A shares. Finally, Class B shares may also be subject to an annual 12b-1 fee of up to 1.0%.

- *Class C shares:* represent a "level load" class for which the deferred sales load is fixed (does not decline with time) and is applied only to redemptions occurring within the first year after purchase. Like Class B, Class C shares may also be subject to an annual 12b-1 fee of up to 1.0%. Finally, Class C shares don't convert to another class.
- *Class I shares:* are "institutional" class shares. They may be sold with no-load or low loads. Typically, investors must invest at least $500,000 to purchase such shares. There are rarely 12b-1 fees associated with Class I shares.
- *Class R shares:* are "retirement" class shares, offered and sold to qualified retirement account holders only. They also sport lower fees and loads: R share classes of mutual funds generally do not have a load (i.e., front-end load, back-end load or level load), but they do have 12b-1 fees that typically range from 0.25% to 0.50%.
- *Class T shares:* for brokers who don't want to sell clean shares (see below), Class T shares are shares which were designed for brokerage channels, including self-directed brokerage channels and supermarket platforms. This type of class garnered significant interest in advance of the now vacated DOL fiduciary standard for brokererage retirment accounts which was to have been implemented in 2017-18. To eliminate certain types of favoritism amongst fund shares based on loads and fees, brokers selling T shares would offer only funds with similar load and 12b-1 fee structures.
- *Clean shares:* charge only management fees and operational expenses. Clean shares don't include any payments or charges for sales loads, distribution charges or 12b-1 fees levied by the fund or its distributor. They were developed in response to the changing fiduciary standards noted earlier and the growth in popularity of ETFs, which trade on stock exchanges and are subject to commissions or brokerage fees applicable to their purchase and sale. In addition, clean shares provide a T shares alternative to brokers, who can sell such shares to clients by charging their own transaction fees or commission, wholly apart from fee structures traditionally used by funds and their distributors. Fund families have labeled clean shares with all sorts of designations, e.g., Class F, P and Z, and made access to them limited to purchases only through brokers agreeing to serve in an agent capacity for their customers.

Fund distributors can mix and match the various types of class and fee structures to meet the needs of the many distribution channels used by their funds. For example, some funds offer over a dozen share classes.

Notes and Applications

1. *Considering what's best for investors.* Putting it all together, it's clear that investors and their advisers, brokers and other investment counselors face a myriad of choices. Different types of sales charges will have differing economic consequences for different investors. Factors that investors should consider include:

a. How long the investor expects to hold the shares;

b. How much the investor intends to invest;

c. Total expenses associated with owning each class of shares;

d. Whether the investor qualifies for any reduction or waiver of sales charges, e.g., quantity discounts or eligibility for retirement share class purchases;

e. Whether the investor intends to take distributions from the investment in the near future, e.g., that may influence the decision regarding a class with a contingent or deferred sales load; and

f. Availability to the investor of certain share classes, e.g., retirement investors may be eligible for retirement class shares and institutional class shares are only available to large or institutional investors.

Clearly, the importance of presenting the available alternatives is critical to assist investors in selecting their method of paying the advice and assistance of a broker or financial adviser. Discussed later in this chapter is the issue of disclosure and related sales abuses.

2. *What's the better deal for investors? A practical illustration.* Consider three retail investors' perspectives—Juan, Ellen, and Anaya. Delta Funds offer three classes of shares: Class A shares with a 5% sales load paid at the time of purchase; Class B shares with a deferred sales load of 5% if sold before one year and which declines by 1% per year on the anniversary date of the purchase until it is 0% after holding the shares for five years; and Class C shares which have a 1% contingent deferred sales charge which is eliminated one year after purchase but such shares also have a 1% annual 12b-1 fee. For this illustration, Classes A and B have no 12b-1 fees. Further suppose that each of our investors buys $10,000 worth of Delta Fund shares with Juan purchasing Class A shares, Ellen Class B shares and Anaya Class C shares.

First, consider: How much did each investor pay in sales charges when they invested? How much of their money actually went to work as an investment? And how many shares do they get?

- Juan: bought Class A shares with a 5% sales load. Remember, that the load is calculated as a percentage of the offering price per share. Thus, the 5% load is equivalent to 5.26% of the net amount invested (in terms of NAV): $10,000 x 5% = $500 in sales load paid, leaving $9,500 invested. At a $10 NAV, that means Juan holds 950 shares.

- Ellen: bought Class B shares with a deferred sales load and no front-end sales load. Thus, she paid $0 as a sales load but may be subject to the deferred sales load. Her full $10,000 was invested. At a $10 NAV, that means Ellen holds 1,000 shares.

- Anaya: bought Class C shares, also with a deferred sales load. Like Ellen, she paid $0 initially but is subject to the deferred sales charge during the first year should she redeem. Her full $10,000 was invested. At $10 NAV, that means Anaya holds 1,000 shares.

Now, consider several different scenarios and the effects on each of the investors.

a. Scenario 1: Each investor owns their shares for exactly six months and then sells them at the NAV of $11 a share, before application of the impact of any 12b-1 fees.
   - Juan: holding 950 Class A shares, with no deferred sales load, he receives $10,450.
   - Ellen: holding 1,000 Class B shares, subject to a 5% deferred sales load for sales during the first year, her shares are worth $11,000 before the sales charges of $550, thus, returning $10,450 to her.
   - Anaya: the Class C shares she holds are subject to the 12b-1 fee of 1% per year and, thus, all else being equal in terms of fees and costs amongst the share classes, the NAV will be slightly less than for the Class A and B shares. For simplicity, assume that half the 1% fee has been accrued to the Class C shares. As a result, their NAV will be approximately $10.95. Anaya's holding of 1,000 Class C shares, subject to the 1% contingent deferred sales charge for the first year, her shares are worth $10,950 before the sales charges of $110 are applied; thus, returning $10,840 to her.

b. Scenario 2: Each investor holds their shares for three years and a day and then sells them at the NAV of $13 a share for Classes A and B and approximately $12.61 for Class C shares after applying the annual 1% 12b-1 fee (for simplicity the 12b-1 fee was calculated as 3%; in reality, the calculation is more complex under fund accounting rules).
   - Juan: holding 950 Class A shares, with no deferred sales load, he receives $12,350.
   - Ellen: holding 1,000 Class B shares, subject to a declining deferred sales load for sales during the first five years, her deferred sales charge is 2% (during the fourth year of holding shares) and her shares are worth $13,000 before the sales charges of $260, thus, returning $12,470 to her.
   - Anaya: holding 1,000 Class C shares, has no deferred sales load, which applied only during the first year. However, her shares were subject to the 12b-1 fee and, thus, she receives only $12.61 NAV for those shares, resulting in net proceeds of $12,610 to her.

c. Scenario 3: Each investor owns their shares for seven years and then sells them at the NAV of $15 a share for Classes A and B and approximately $13.95 for Class C shares, after applying the annual 1% 12b-1 fee (for simplicity the 12b-1 fee was calculated as 7%; in reality, the calculation is more complex under fund accounting rules).
   - Juan: holding 950 Class A shares, with no deferred sales load, he receives $14,250.

- Ellen: holding 1,000 Class B shares, subject to a declining deferred sales load for sales during the first five years, her deferred sales charge is now 0% and her shares are worth $15,000.
- Anaya: holding 1,000 Class C shares, has no deferred sales load, which applied only during the first year. However, her shares were subject to the 12b-1 fee and, thus, she receives only $13.95 NAV for those shares, resulting in net proceeds of $13,950 to her.

Given these scenarios, which class of shares would you want to purchase? How does your investment time horizon impact your decision? What if you do not know the likely time horizon of your investment at the outset? Are there other factors that you would consider in deciding which share class to purchase? Finally, consider the role of alternatives like clean share classes and ETFs as alternatives for an investor: What should the investor do?

Generally, if you are a self-directed investor, your best alternative is to select no-load funds, clean shares if available or ETFs. For most investors, needing assistance in fund selection, it is a more difficult choice based on the factors noted in the section above, and hopefully the broker or adviser will provide good, honest advice.

17.6 Fund Supermarkets and the Problem of Distribution in Guise

In the early 1990s, discount brokers (led by firms like Charles Schwab) began offering funds the opportunity to list on the brokers' platforms for easy trading by investors. The design concept is quite simple: A supermarket of funds. Each such platform may contain hundreds of unrelated funds from which investors can choose from and pay a small transaction fee. Some programs offer no transaction fee funds which can be purchased without any sales charges or transaction fees. For investors, the fund supermarket structure offers the opportunity to buy a wide variety of funds without maintaining accounts with different fund families. Instead, using a single account maintained with a brokerage sponsoring a fund supermarket, investors can buy and sell the shares of many different funds and hold them in that one brokerage account. Life is much simpler for investors in dealing with one brokerage account rather than multiple fund accounts, and the popularity of fund supermarkets attests to their obvious appeal.

Mechanically, the broker is the nominal fund shareholder in a fund supermarket arrangement, and on its books, the broker reflects the investors' ownership of various funds. In effect, the broker, acting as sub-transfer agent, creates a "sub-transfer agency" relationship with its customers holding their shares in an omnibus account for benefit of all investors investing through the broker. The fees charged for fund supermarkets payable by funds and/or their adviser or distributor started quite small in the early 1990s, usually less than 0.25% annually, guided by the early model of 0.25% 12b-1 fees. But in time, the fees grew appreciably, almost doubling, and thus exceeding that threshold of many Rule 12b-1 plans. As a result, a portion of the supermarket fee either has to be classified as a non-distribution expense, i.e., for shareholder servicing, to permit its payment with fund assets or the supermarket fee has to be absorbed in part in a revenue sharing arrangement where a fund's adviser agrees to share part of its advisory fee revenues with the broker. The proper categorization and attribution of fees and expenses associated with fund supermarkets has become a significant compliance and regulatory issue.

Investment Company Institute re: Fund Supermarkets

SEC Staff Interpretive Guidance Letter (October 30, 1998)

[**Textbook note:** *In 1998, the SEC made public a letter addressed to the Investment Company Institute, the fund industry's trade association, to provide the industry with the SEC's insights and guidance based on its examination of the emerging use of fund supermarkets, which had exploded in popularity over the decade. This letter, which is known as the "Fund Supermarket Letter," provides guidance on the SEC's views of what is and isn't proper in making payments to supermarket brokers and platforms. In essence, it's a pronouncement of the Division of Investment Management's views on payment of distribution costs and expenses out of fund assets relating to inclusion on a supermarket platform. The problem addressed in the letter is the allocation of costs for a fund's participation in a supermarket platform for distribution expenses (payable only out of Rule 12b-1 plan proceeds) and non-distribution expenses (freely payable from fund assets, including its Rule 12b-1 plan). The issue has proved vexing for funds as the costs are not transparent and are not always easily classified and has resulted in additional guidance from the SEC to address the concern of* de facto *distribution payments in the guise of payments for non-distribution services (so called "distribution in guise.")*.]

[***] We are writing to you to outline the views of the Division of Investment Management on certain legal issues arising from the participation of mutual funds in "fund supermarkets." As you know, fund supermarkets are an increasingly popular means through which investors can buy and redeem shares of mutual funds. As of late last year, approximately $79 billion had been invested in mutual funds through no-transaction-fee fund supermarkets, an increase of over 750% during the prior five years.

In a typical fund supermarket, the sponsor of the program—a broker-dealer or other institution—makes available various services to a participating fund and its shareholders. The sponsor offers a menu of services including: establishing, maintaining, and processing changes in shareholder accounts; 'communicating with shareholders; preparing account statements and confirmations; and providing distribution services on behalf of, or with, the fund. For the services that it provides, the sponsor charges the participating fund a fee that is calculated on the basis of the amount of assets of the fund's shareholders that is held through the program. The fee is paid by the fund, its investment adviser, an affiliate of the adviser, or a combination of all three entities.

....

In the Division's view, payments of fees for participating in fund supermarkets may be made pursuant to or outside of rule 12b-1 plans, depending on the purpose of the payments and the party making the payment. Whether a fund's payment of part or all of a supermarket fee must be made pursuant to a rule 12b-1 plan depends on an analysis of the purpose for which the payment. is made. The determination of the purpose of the payment must be made by the fund's board of directors and requires careful' consideration and monitoring.

....

Fund Supermarkets

Beginning in 1992, several broker-dealers introduced a new method for investors to purchase and redeem mutual fund shares: the fund supermarket. A fund supermarket is a program offered by a broker-dealer or other financial institution through which its customers may purchase- and redeem a variety of funds, with or without paying transaction fees.

The sponsor of a fund supermarket usually charges a fee to the participating fund if the sponsor does not charge transaction fees to its customers. The fee generally ranges from .25% to .40% annually of the average net asset value of the shares of' the fund held by the sponsor's customers. This fee compensates the sponsor for permitting the fund to participate in the fund supermarket and for providing the services used by the fund. These services can include certain administrative services to customers who purchase shares of the fund,[3] and certain distribution services for the fund.[4]

Fund supermarkets have become quite popular with investors, as they provide investors with the ability to consolidate their fund holdings at different fund complexes in a single brokerage account and to receive a consolidated brokerage statement

3. In a typical fund supermarket, the sponsor offers various administrative services to its customers such as: sub-accounting; shareholder account set up and maintenance; shareholder assistance; transaction processing and settlement; preparation and distribution of account statements and transaction confirmations; payment of fund distributions; and distribution of prospectuses. If the customers invested directly in a fund instead of investing through the fund supermarket, the fund typically would pay its service providers for providing these administrative services to the customers.

4. Fund supermarkets differ from more traditional distribution channels in that sponsors of fund supermarkets typically do not solicit their customers to buy shares of any particular funds. Although the sponsors typically distribute prospectuses and other information for the funds that participate in the fund supermarkets, the sponsors typically make no recommendations about individual funds; they merely provide their customers with marketing and sales information for funds participating in the supermarkets. Many sponsors include marketing materials with proxy materials and other mailings to fund shareholders, a practice that provides a fund's adviser with the opportunity to "cross sell" other investment products to fund shareholders. Many sponsors also make discount advertising space available to a participating fund if the advertisement includes the telephone number of the sponsor's sales staff, rather than the fund's telephone number, for inquiries. Some sponsors conduct conferences for fee-based investment advisers to which the sponsors provide recordkeeping services. At these conferences, the sponsors allow participating funds to make presentations to the advisers about the appropriateness of the funds for the advisers' clients.

listing all fund holdings.[5] The amount of assets invested in funds through fund supermarkets has increased significantly over the past few years. Many funds currently participate in fund supermarkets, and many financial institutions currently sponsor fund supermarkets.

[The Letter then explained the results of an extensive examination performed by the SEC's Office of Compliance, Inspections and Examinations and the basics of Rule 12b-1 and 12b-1 plans before continuing as follows.]

As noted above, many of the funds that were examined by OCIE treat all or part of the fund supermarket fee as a distribution expense and pay the fee out of their own assets pursuant to their rule 12b-1 plans. Some funds pay a portion of the fund supermarket fee out of their own assets, but not pursuant to a rule 12b-1 plan, and some of their advisers or the advisers' affiliates pay the remainder of the fee. Whether payments of fund supermarket fees must be made pursuant to rule 12b-1 primarily depends on (a) whether the payments are being made for services that are primarily intended to result in the sale of the fund's shares, and (b) whether the fund or another party is making some or all of the payments.

A. Payment of Fees bv Funds Pursuant to Rule 12b-1 Plans

When a fund participates in a fund supermarket primarily to sell its shares to investors, at least part of the fee must be considered to be compensation paid to the sponsor for providing distribution services, i.e., services primarily intended to result in the sale of the fund's shares. In such a case, the part of the fee paid for distribution may be paid by the fund only pursuant to a rule 12b-1 plan.

If a fund has adopted, a rule 12b-1 plan, then the fund may pay for distribution expenses to the extent permitted under its plan.[14] A fund that pays all of its fund supermarket fee pursuant to a rule 12b-1 plan need not determine which portion of the fee is primarily for distribution services or which portion is primarily for administrative services.

B. Payment of Fees by Funds Outside of Rule 12b-1 Plans

If a fund has not adopted a rule 12b-1 plan, then it cannot use fund assets to pay for services that are primarily intended to result in the sale of the fund's shares. Thus, any portion of the supermarket fee that is primarily for distribution services cannot be paid out of the fund's assets. A fund that has not adopted a rule 12b-1 plan, however, may use its assets to pay a fund supermarket sponsor for services that the fund's board has determined to be non-distribution services.

---

5. The sponsor of a fund supermarket usually holds the fund shares of each fund in which its customers invest in an omnibus account on behalf of the customers, *i.e.*, the sponsor is the shareholder of record.

14. The fund may do so regardless of whether its payment of the fees is intended to compensate the sponsor, in whole or in part, for providing non-distribution services. The Commission previously has stated that funds may pay for non-distribution expenses pursuant to rule 12b-1 plans ... (when proposing amendments to rule 12b-1, the Commission stated that "rule 12b-1 does not specifically prohibit the payment of non-distribution expenses under a 12b-1 plan ...").... Funds, however, are not required to pay for non-distribution services pursuant to rule 12b-1 plans even if the recipient of the payment also is involved in the distribution of fund shares.

C. Payment of Fees by Funds' Investment Advisers

If a fund's investment adviser makes distribution-related payments out of its own resources, rule 12b-1 generally would not apply because the payments are not being made out of fund assets. Thus, if a fund's investment adviser pays all of the fund supermarket fee, or the portion of the fee that is for services that are primarily intended to result in the sale of fund shares, rule 12b-1 generally would not apply.

Rule 12b-1 could apply, however, in certain cases in which the adviser makes distribution-related payments out of its own resources. As the Commission has stated, "an indirect use of fund assets for distribution would result if any allowance were made in the investment adviser's fee to provide money to finance distribution." Thus, for example, if a fund approved an increase in the advisory fee of its investment adviser so that the adviser could pay for distribution services for the fund, such payments could be made only pursuant to a rule 12b-1 plan. In future examinations, OCIE staff will closely scrutinize any increase in a fund's investment advisory fee that appears to be for the purpose of compensating the fund's investment adviser for paying the fund's supermarket fee.

Role of the Fund's Board of Directors

The board of directors of a fund that participates in a fund supermarket plays a critical role. The board is responsible for determining whether any portion of a fund supermarket fee paid (or to be paid) by the fund is for distribution, *i.e.*, services primarily intended to result in the sale of fund shares. Whether or not any particular payment of a fund supermarket fee by a fund is for distribution services or non-distribution services is primarily a question of fact for the fund's board of directors to determine. This responsibility necessarily entails considering the nature of the services used by the fund or provided to the fund by the supermarket sponsor. The sponsor's characterization of the services that it offers is one factor that the board should consider in making this determination.

....

Conclusion

Rule 12b-1 does not prohibit funds from paying fund supermarket fees in different ways and for different purposes. A fund's board of directors, however, has the responsibility to determine whether any portion of a fund supermarket fee that is directly or indirectly paid by the fund is primarily for distribution and, if so, to ensure that any such payments are made pursuant to a rule 12b-1 plan. [***]

* * *

The issues of shareholder servicing fees and distribution in guise have continued to be a challenge for the SEC and industry. For distributors developing and maintaining their distribution activities, it obviously is critical to know whether an expense fits properly into the distribution, shareholder servicing or another category. In addition, fund boards and service providers must also be sensitive to how expenses and fees are characterized.

Analytically, miscellaneous non-advisory or administrative fees and expenses can be reviewed as follows:

1. Is the fee or expense in any way for distribution and marketing services?
2. If so, what portion of the fee is attributable to distribution and marketing services?
3. The fund may pay the distribution and marketing portion of the fee, but only if there is a fund Rule 12b-1 plan which provides sufficient resources to pay the distribution and marketing portion of the fee.

Here are some examples of fee categorizations:

Distribution expenses: sales loads and commissions, compensation of sales personnel, advertising, sales literature including brochures designed for brokers or investors, and printing and mailing prospectuses and other fund documents to prospective investors. These types of expenses generally qualify for 12b-1 plan purposes, except note that loads and commissions often are paid as front-end loads and not from the 12b-1 fee.

Shareholder servicing expenses: costs of servicing existing shareholders when paid to brokers or intermediaries. These services might include activities like updating shareholders on how their fund is performing, their account balances and redeeming their shares. These are analogous to transfer agency fees and are typically not included as 12b-1 fees or expenses. On the other hand, some shareholder servicing may be more of a distribution nature, e.g., helping investors decide whether to buy more shares of a fund or, perhaps, not to panic and sell their shares in a market correction. In this case, the expenses may be payable from a 12b-1 plan. Either way, these are legitimate fund expenses.

Non-distribution expenses: typical adviser expenses of portfolio management, research, fund administrative expenses (fund accounting, tax, performance analytics, custody, etc.), transfer agency expenses, fund brokerage for transactions, etc. These are not distribution related expenses and, thus, not proper 12b-1 plan expenses.

In 2013, the SEC launched a lengthy industry examination of distribution, focusing on the various types of payments funds make to intermediaries and service providers which sell shares and provide services to shareholders. Fundamentally, the purpose of the exam was to determine if there was widespread covert payment of distribution expenses improperly categorized as shareholder servicing or transfer agency expenses, i.e., "*distribution in guise*." Remember, as discussed above, 10 years earlier, the SEC had to take action to eliminate directed brokerage. This examination included inspections of a number of mutual fund complexes, investment advisers, broker-dealers, and transfer agents. A key target was gray zone expenses, i.e., ones which may or may not be arguably for distribution and one type of shareholder servicing expense that the SEC has dubbed "sub-accounting fees." Such fees are used to compensate service providers for shareholder recordkeeping, sub-transfer agent and other administrative services that intermediaries provide to fund shareholders. Recall that fund transfer agents are responsible for keeping a record of fund shareholders and their shares, as well as responding to shareholder and investor questions, phone calls, mail, redemption requests, and a myriad of other shareholder servicing functions. Often these services are delegated to other firms providing some of these services, including intermediaries in the distribution chain. Hence, the terms *sub-accounting fees* and *sub-accounting services*, describing the services for which such fees are paid.

In 2015, the SEC prosecuted its first distribution in guise case arising from the inspections, settling an administrative action against an adviser and its affiliated distributor for their mismanagement of their funds' 12b-1 plans and related payments that arguably should have paid pursuant to the plans. This case, *In the Matter of First Eagle Investment Management, LLC and FEF Distributors, LLC*, Investment Company Act Release No. 31832 (Sept. 21, 2015), illustrates a situation where distribution in guise arguably arose through administrative oversight. As a result, expenses which might have been legal and appropriate under a 12b-1 plan were deemed to be distribution payments outside such a plan yet paid by the funds. Clearly, the difficulty of proper categorization discussed above is illustrated by this case. The parties had no fraudulent intent, but the challenges of proper expense allocation led to an administrative lapse. As a follow-up to this case, the SEC then issued one of its Guidance Update series in January 2016 to provide funds and their boards and advisers with additional guidance on the treatment of sub-accounting fees *See IM Guidance Update: Mutual Fund Distribution and Sub-Accounting Fees No. 2016-01* (January 2016) (the "Guidance").

The Guidance makes it clear that the SEC expects funds to have compliance "policies and procedures reasonably designed to prevent violations of section 12(b) and Rule 12b-1," which include "policies and procedures for reviewing and identifying any payments that may be for distribution-related services that are not paid through [a Rule 12b-1] plan."

In addition, the Guidance focuses on the role of fund directors as the watchdogs and arbiters of the distribution arrangements. As a result, the Guidance increases the burden and responsibility of boards and of service providers to provide directors with relevant and appropriate information and data to "make an informed judgment as to whether fund-paid fees are being used to pay directly or indirectly for distribution...." The Guidance provides a great deal of detail on specific facts and information that boards should be receiving from intermediaries and service providers. In addition, reflecting the *First Eagle* case facts and others discovered during the SEC's exam program, the Guidance discusses a list of "indicia that a payment may be used to pay for distribution." Clearly, the SEC is trying to assist the industry in differentiating distribution and shareholder servicing expenses from other expenses. The practical effects of the data requirements suggested by the Guidance are still rippling through the industry, and it is likely that over the next few years, new best practices will emerge.

17.7 Disclosure Relating to Distribution Arrangements and the Challenges of Distribution and Sales Conduct Abuses

Various aspects of who pays for what in distribution has been rapidly evolving. Both the business and legal requirements of who and what are charged was discussed above. An equally important topic is what and how investors are told about loads and fees, and even more specifically, who is responsible for this disclosure and to whom and where must it be made?

17.7.1 Fund Purchase and Sale Disclosures

To understand the difficulty of the disclosure issue, it is necessary to understand the multiple levels of the fund sales process. Most investors purchase funds through a broker, financial advisor, investment advisor or other intermediary. Effectively, this is the retail level or so-called "point of sale" of the process: it's where the investor receives information about the fund and the sales loads and fees. The wholesale level is the fund distributor which, as has been described, is responsible for the distribution activities for the fund. Finally, there is the fund itself, often viewed in the industry as the "product." Each of these three levels has its own responsibilities and requirements regarding disclosure.

Starting with fund disclosure documents, i.e., the prospectus and statement of additional information, these must contain extensive disclosures regarding a fund's loads, 12b-1 fees, and other sales charges in addition to investment advisory fees and other expenses. As detailed in Chapter 13, these documents are filed with the SEC and with most state securities commissions. Generally, investors receive such disclosure documents at the time of investment or before they buy shares in a fund.

Fund disclosure documents are formally overseen by fund boards, but generally it is a fund's counsel, adviser or administrator that prepares and files the documents. Closely related to the public disclosures are the information and data conveyed to funds' boards regarding distribution arrangements and contracts. As discussed previously, boards have the responsibility to approve fund distribution agreements, including 12b-1 agreements and plans, and oversee related programs and distribution activities. In addition to providing effective disclosures to fund boards, fund investment advisers also must disclose their fee arrangements in their disclosure documents like Form ADV.

At the wholesale level, the distributor is generally responsible for preparing and/or filing fund advertisements and marketing materials, like brochures on behalf of a fund and subject to the fund board's oversight. Like the fund disclosure documents, such materials must be filed with the appropriate regulator, typically FINRA.

Finally, at the retail or point of sale level, sales intermediaries such as registered investment advisers ("RIAs) and brokers-dealers also have obligations to disclose charges they may apply to purchase and sales transactions in addition to fund level charges. Rule 10b-10 under the Exchange Act articulates general requirements and standards for investment transaction confirmation statements provided to investors. Rule 10b-10 provides in pertinent part that it is "unlawful for any broker or dealer to effect for or with an account of a customer any transaction in, or to induce the purchase or sale by such customer of, any security ... unless such broker or dealer, at or before completion of such transaction, gives or sends to such customer written notification disclosing ... the source and amount of any other remuneration received or to be received by the broker in connection with the transaction...." In practice, brokers comply with this Rule by sending investors a transaction confirmation statement, which may reflect certain transaction fees, and a fund prospectus, which discloses loads, 12b-1 fees, and other generalized distribution expense details.

Adviser, broker or both? It makes a difference. Before exploring the basic disclosure requirements applicable to them, it is important to review the distinctions between RIAs and broker-dealers. By definition RIAs are registered investment advisers, generally under the Advisers Act or under state law, as discussed earlier in this text. RIAs may also be registered as broker-dealers under the Exchange Act and generally with FINRA. When they do so, they are considered to be "dually registered." Broker-dealers, including financial advisers, may be registered only as brokers-dealers or dually registered as investment advisers as well. The distinctions in registration have great legal significance.

Firms and individuals acting solely as broker-dealers have a different standard of care for their customers than investment advisers. As was discussed in earlier chapters, advisers have a fiduciary duty to act in the best interests of their customers. In contrast, brokers are governed by FINRA's Rule 2111, which requires, in part, that a broker-dealer or associated person "have a reasonable basis to believe that a recommended transaction or investment strategy involving a security or securities [including mutual funds] is suitable for the customer, based on the information obtained through the reasonable diligence of the [firm] or [broker or financial adviser] to ascertain the customer's investment profile." This is known as the "*suitability standard*." It is a lesser standard of care.

Rule 2111 requires that, in general, a customer's investment profile should include the customer's age, investment experience, savings, other investments, financial situation and needs, tax status, investment objectives, investment time horizon, liquidity needs and risk tolerance. The Rule, moreover, identifies the three main suitability obligations: (i) "Reasonable-basis obligation" requires a broker to have a reasonable basis to believe, based on reasonable diligence, that a recommended investment or investment strategy is suitable for at least some investors. (ii) "Customer-specific obligation" requires that a broker have a reasonable basis to believe that the recommendation is suitable for a particular customer based on that customer's investment profile. (iii) "Quantitative suitability" requires a broker to have a reasonable basis for believing that a series of recommended transactions, even if suitable when viewed in isolation, are not excessive and unsuitable for the customer when taken together in light of the customer's profile. Finally, certain institutional customers may be exempt from the rule. The key legal issue to note with respect to suitability is how it is distinct from a basic fiduciary duty: Suitability does not require the broker to act in the best interests—to the exclusion of his or her own interests—of the investor.

Why is this distinction important? It relates to what brokers and advisers must be providing to customers in terms of information about the fees and charges related to their fund investments, and, more importantly, the nature of the advice versus sales counseling provided to clients. Acting as a fiduciary, an investment adviser has a duty to be forthcoming regarding fees and expenses of making investments, including buying and selling fund shares. Such disclosures are often presented in the adviser's Form ADV, a portion of which is typically provided to investors when they open an account with the adviser. The ADV should also highlight any potential conflicts of interest that the adviser may have with respect to fund sales and advice. In contrast, brokers, acting under a suitability standard, generally have not been held to a fiduciary level of responsibility and disclosure. As a result, these relationships are fertile territory for financial abuse.

Notes and Applications

An investor's experience. What information does an investor get when he or she is deciding about a fund investment? As noted, the issue of proper disclosures of sales and distribution loads, fees and expenses has two levels: the fund level and the retail/point of sale (investment adviser or broker) level. Many times, though, the fund disclosure documents comprise much of the retail level disclosures.

Consider a situation where an investor named Monica deals with a large brokerage firm as her financial firm. The financial adviser there will likely be registered as a broker. So what fee and expenses disclosures might Monica expect to receive? First, the financial adviser might provide Monica with a fund brochure describing its wonderful performance. Generally, it should be accompanied by at least a summary prospectus, which goes into some detail on fund expenses and fees and provides generalized information on loads and sales charges. Absent further inquiry from Monica, that may be all that she receives in advance. Indeed, in many situations, she may only receive the summary prospectus at the time of her purchase of fund shares or even later when she receives her confirmation of the purchase. Such are the generalized requirements of Rule 10b-10. Only if Monica actively seeks out the statutory prospectus or even the SAI will she receive such documents.

In addition, it is likely that Monica received generalized brokerage firm disclosures when she set up her account. The account set-up forms and contracts typically contain detailed disclosures about the various fees, commissions and charges that may be applied to an account and to transactions. But such information is generalized and not focused on a specific fund purchase or sale. A dually registered financial adviser, as a fiduciary, might feel obligated to provide further information on the type of fund share class he or she recommends for Monica's purchase. But a broker working under the suitability standard has no such obligation. Rather he or she can make the decision based on his/her judgment of what is "suitable" for Monica.

What information would you request when making an investment decision to purchase fund shares?

17.7.2 Distribution and Sales Conduct Abuses

Misconduct related to distribution activities is common, whether deliberate or inadvertent as in the *First Eagle* distribution in guise case discussed earlier. In addition to distribution in guise, there are practices that have led to abuse.

One common abuse is the failure of brokers and advisers to offer or ensure that investors take advantage of quantity purchase discounts many load funds make available. For example, such funds may reduce front-end loads for purchases over $100,000. Such load reduction points are termed *breakpoints*. Often there are multiple levels of such breakpoints, e.g., also at $500,000 and $1 million. Investors who take advantage of such quantity purchase discounts can save substantially on their load costs. Conversely, the financial adviser who offers or points out the fund's breakpoints stands to lose those load dollars. He or she may choose to sell more than one fund at below breakpoint levels to maximize his/her commissions.

The issue of breakpoint abuses first became widely known in the early 2000s after a period of SEC and FINRA examinations focused on mutual fund sales practices, in particular, disclosures made by funds in their documents and by intermediaries such as broker-dealers. This focus resulted in multiple enforcement actions, litigation and regulatory improvements all with the intention of making the "what" and "how" of fund distribution charges and expenses transparent and easy to understand for investors. In addition to finding breakpoint abuses, examiners also found related share class sales abuses, where brokers or advisers put their clients into fund share classes with high combinations of loads and/or 12b-1 fees when the investors were eligible for lower load and fee classes.

A typical and prominent case is one involving the large broker-dealer, Morgan Stanley. *See In the Matter of Morgan Stanley*, Securities Exchange Act Release. No. 48789 (Nov. 17, 2003). Brought in 2003, the SEC in the *Morgan Stanley* administrative proceeding and settlement addressed two types of wrong-doing: First, a program for institutional favoritism where Morgan Stanley, its Financial Advisers ("FAs"), and staff were financially incented to favor certain funds over others. The favored funds paid additional (often undisclosed) compensation to gain priority in sales recommendations, a form of shelf space arrangements, which are discussed more below. Arguably, this presents a conflict of interest for the brokerage firm and its sales staff. Second, Morgan Stanley's FAs routinely sold higher cost load/commission share classes to investors without properly disclosing their practices, e.g., by not disclosing applicable commission breakpoints. This practice is a clear abuse of the FA function which is regarded by some as a form of fiduciary, although legally many FAs need only comply with the suitability standard.

Morgan Stanley's funds offered extensive quantity discounts or breakpoints: For example, in 2000, the firm offered over than 60 mutual funds in its Morgan Stanley Funds family. Most of these funds offered four classes of shares, A, B, C and D. The Class A shares were subject to a front-end sales load of 5.25% on investments up to $25,000. The load was reduced to 4.75% for investments between $25,000 and $49,999. An investment between $50,000 and $99,999 would receive a reduced load of 4%.

Over $100,000 up to $249,999, the load was reduced to 3%. Further reductions applied to larger investments. Each incremental reduction in load is referred to as a "breakpoint." Class A shares also had to pay a 12b-1 fee of 0.25% annually.

Other classes, like class B, had differing sales charge schemes. Morgan Stanley's Class B shares charged no up-front load. Instead, they were subjected to a declining contingent deferred sales charge ("CDSC") starting at 5% in year one and declining to 1% in year six, with no CDSC after that. Class B shares offered no breakpoints and had to pay a 12b-1 fee of 1% yearly. Morgan Stanley FA's received additional incentives for sales of class B shares.

Class B shares could be advantageous for certain investors. But for large investors, e.g., investing over $100,000, with the intention of holding shares longer than six years, it was more advantageous to buy Class A shares with a reduced breakpoint load and lower 12b-1 fee. Nonetheless many such investors were sold the Class B shares.

The SEC found that thousands of sales of fund shares were made without disclosure of the breakpoints nor of the differing advantages and disadvantages of the various classes available. It was clear that the conflicts of interest presented by the differing compensation schemes and class breakpoints skewed share sales towards higher payouts for Financial Advisers.

Unlike many of the cases included in this casebook, this action was brought under the Securities Act and the Exchange Act, not the Company Act. This highlights the fact that brokers are subject to Exchange Act and FINRA regulation and generally not the Company Act for their broker-dealer operations. In this case, the funds may have had compliant disclosure documents, e.g., prospectuses, SAIs, sales literature and financial statements, for general purposes, but they were insufficient with respect to disclosing these types of relationships.

As a result of the administrative proceeding, Morgan Stanley had to revamp its compliance functions, make investors whole and pay a fine of $25 million. Morgan Stanley was one of many brokerage firms to engage in such sales tactics. Others were similarly investigated and censured. And these cases prompted the 2004 enactment of fund disclosure enhancements and the proposal of new Exchange Act point of sale disclosure requirements, which the industry successfully forestalled.

To bolster disclosures made at the time of sale by the broker, the SEC in 2004 proposed two new rules under the Exchange Act to create a sales confirmation/disclosure regime specifically for funds and separate from the general broker confirmation rule, Rule 10b-10. If ever adopted, the rules would require broker-dealers to provide their customers with specific, targeted information regarding the purchase/sale costs of mutual funds transactions and the conflicts of interest that arise from the distribution of mutual fund shares. The rules would require disclosure at two key times: first, at the time or point of sale, and second, in the transaction confirmation for a completed transaction.

While those rules have yet to be finalized, another rulemaking, which was promulgated in 2004, made revisions to Form N-1A, the mutual fund registration statement. *See Final Rule: Disclosure of Breakpoint Discounts by Mutual Funds*, Investment Company Act Release. No. IC-26464 (June 7, 2004). The SEC's adoption of amendments to Form N-1A required mutual funds to provide enhanced and detailed disclosures regarding breakpoint or quantity discounts on front-end sales loads. Under the amendments, a mutual fund is required to describe in its prospectus any arrangements that result in breakpoints in sales loads and to provide a brief summary of shareholder eligibility requirements. These disclosure requirements were intended to address the situation where brokers, dealers, advisers and other distribution intermediaries failed to disclose breakpoints which could have advantaged investors by reducing their sales loads if they invested enough money to reach a breakpoint. As the SEC noted in its release, "these proposed amendments ... are intended to assist investors in understanding the breakpoint opportunities available to them, and to alert investors as to the information that they may need to provide to funds and broker-dealers to take full advantage of all available breakpoint discounts. The amendments also should help broker-dealers to access information about available breakpoint discounts."

Another version of share class sales abuse relates to 12b-1 classes. Representative is the case of *In the Matter of Cadaret, Grant & Co., Inc.*, Investment Advisers Act Rel. No. 4736 (August 1, 2017). The Cadaret firm is a Syracuse, NY regional broker-dealer. It settled fraud charges, under Advisers Act sections 206(2) and 206(4) related to 12b-1 share class abuses. As noted in the release, "[F]rom at least 2011 to 2016, Cadaret invested advisory clients in mutual fund share classes with 12b-1 fees instead of lower-fee share classes of the same funds that were available without 12b-1 fees. In its capacity as a broker-dealer, Cadaret received at least $1.93 million in 12b-1 fees for investing clients in the higher-fee share classes. Cadaret failed to disclose in its Forms ADV or otherwise that it had a conflict of interest concerning mutual fund share classes." In short, Caderet advisers sold their clients the higher fee funds so that the firm and its advisers could receive higher 12b-1 fee payments.

As you consider these cases, consider whether the 2004 proposed revisions to the Exchange Act confirmation requirements, i.e., essentially enhancing Rule 10b-10, would have ameliorated these situations. Would the hypothetical investor, Monica, have chosen a different, lower fee class had she received specific, targeted information regarding the purchase/sale costs of mutual funds transactions and the conflicts of interest? Also, recall the hypothetical class selections examples earlier in this chapter: What choices did you make? Clearly, what is the better deal for an investor may diverge financially from the interests of the broker or adviser.

Another form of sales practices abuse arose from the manner of funding *shelf space arrangements*, the practice of advisers' paying a broker or adviser to promote sales of funds of an adviser. The term originated in the practices of retail stores, like bookstores or groceries, where shelf space is the allocation of physical, linear shelf space for certain products and providing space on high visibility shelves such as those at the end of an aisle or entrance to a store. Similarly, fund advisers and distributors have resorted to paying retailers or fund shares, like brokers or advisers, to secure privileges such as higher listings in lists of funds available or for brokers to pay higher compensation for sales of certain funds.

To compensate the broker for such arrangements, advisers and distributors have used various mechanisms. Cleanest and least controversial is direct payments to intermediaries by fund advisers or distributors. Direct payments from the adviser or distributor is not a prohibited practice. Closely related are "revenue sharing arrangements" whereby an adviser might share part of the additional advisory fees derived from the additional assets under management resulting from the fund shares sold by the broker or financial planner. Recall that under Section 12, the Company Act prohibits a fund from acting as its own distributor. Where a part of the advisory fee is explicitly used to pay for distribution, there is an argument that the revenue sharing arrangements may be in contravention of such provisions. However, the SEC has consistently treated such payments as being derived from the adviser's revenues or profits and not from the fund's assets. Another approach, now prohibited, was the use of the brokerage commissions paid by funds for their portfolio transactions. Recall that Rule 12b-1 was amended to explicitly prohibit use of directed brokerage to support shelf space payments after a series of shelf space disclosure cases in the early 2000s.

A representative fund adviser case from the time is *In the Matter of Massachusetts Financial Services Company* ("*MFS*") Investment Company Act Release. No. 26409 (March 31, 2004), a settled administrative action. MFS, a well-known Boston investment adviser, set up a program to essentially buy shelf space for its funds paid for with brokerage commissions incurred in connection with the purchase and sale of securities for the portfolios of various funds managed by MFS. This specific practice, as noted above, was subsequently addressed with amendments to Rule 12b-1 found in subsection (h). Although the use of directed brokerage arrangements in this fashion is prohibited, it is important to remember that shelf space arrangements themselves are not unlawful if properly funded. In the *MFS* matter, notwithstanding the absence of a specific prohibition (augmented with an affirmative requirement for policies and procedures governing any brokerage directed to a broker or dealer that is selling fund shares), the SEC attacked the practice based on disclosure deficiencies that accompanied the arrangements. MFS's use of fund brokerage to pay fund distribution expenses that arguably should have been borne by the adviser or distributor resulted in an inherent conflict of interest that should have been disclosed. MFS failed to make appropriate and adequate disclosures of the shelf space payment scheme to both the funds' boards and to the investing public. Such disclosure lapses deceived both the funds' boards and public investors, and violated Section 206(2) of the Advisers Act. In the absence of a clear conflict of interest, the adviser's disclosure obligations in connection with shelf space arrangements are less clear. Nevertheless, investors arguably should be alerted to such payments by the adviser in the fund disclosure documents.

Note that the *MFS* case involved only an investment adviser, but recall that disclosure of fund information and sales compensation always involves multiple levels. The following case illustrates the shelf space issue from the broker-dealer perspective.

In the Matter of Edward D. Jones & Co., L.P.

Exchange Act Release No. 50910 (December 22, 2004)

[**Textbook note:** *This proceeding involved a fund sales program, but focused on the liability of a participating broker-dealer under the Securities Act and the Exchange Act, rather than the conduct of the investment adviser under the Advisers Act. Edward Jones, a large national brokerage firm, operated a well-structured program to encourage its brokers to sell funds from a list of recommended or preferred fund families. In exchange for such preferential treatment, Edward Jones negotiated "revenue sharing" arrangements under which it received a portion of the advisory fees earned by the funds' advisers and other forms of consideration. The broker-dealer (and its sales representatives) failed to provide customers with adequate disclosure regarding fund sales programs, and the deficiencies resulted in sanctions under Exchange Act Rule 10b-10 and other provisions.*]

[***] 2. Edward Jones is one of the largest sellers of brokerage-sold mutual funds in the United States.... Edward Jones' customers hold onto their investments for a lengthier period of time than customers at other broker-dealers. Edward Jones has selling agreements with approximately 240 mutual fund families which permit its IRs to sell at least 1,930 different mutual funds.

3. Prior to the late 1980s, Edward Jones had internally designated certain of the mutual fund families with which it had selling agreements as "recommended." In the late 1980s, Edward Jones approached certain of those mutual fund families ("Preferred Families") with which it had longstanding relationships and sought to obtain revenue sharing from them. Edward Jones set an internal revenue sharing target of 25% of the advisory fees earned by those mutual fund families on the mutual fund assets purchased or held by Edward Jones' customers, plus in most instances sought an equity interest in their advisers or distributors.

The Preferred Mutual Fund Family Program

4. By the early 1990s, six mutual fund families had agreed to make revenue sharing payments to Edward Jones. Between 1993 and 1996, Edward Jones removed one of these fund families and added two new fund families to the list of Preferred Families, raising the total number of Preferred Families to seven.

5. Each of these fund families agreed to make revenue sharing payments to Edward Jones in varying amounts up to and in several cases meeting Edward Jones' target of 25% of the advisory fees for assets purchased or held by Edward Jones' customers. These fees were calculated in various ways and by various measures, including: a flat fee determined by the fund family based on the total fund assets held by Edward Jones' customers; 7.5 to 10 basis points of average fund assets held by Edward Jones' customers in a given year; 12.5 basis points on the gross sales of a Preferred Families' mutual funds made by Edward Jones to its customers in a given year; or 25% of the advisory fee attributable to the average assets of certain Preferred Families' mutual funds held by Edward Jones' customers in a given year. One of the Preferred Families

also agreed to provide Edward Jones an equity interest of at least 5% in the distributor of its mutual funds if Edward Jones reached a certain threshold of sales of its mutual funds, this was later changed to profit participation.

6. Revenue sharing was a material factor, among others, in the selection of at least two of the Preferred Families. Revenue sharing was also a material factor, among others, with respect to the retention of fund families as Preferred Families. Edward Jones periodically sought to negotiate additional revenue sharing payments from its Preferred Families.

7. Edward Jones' revenue sharing agreements with the Preferred Families are and have been highly profitable to Edward Jones. Between 1999 and the present, the firm has collected tens of millions of dollars in revenue sharing payments from the Preferred Families each year. Most of these payments have been paid directly to Edward Jones from the assets of the advisers or distributors associated with the Preferred Families. However, for a portion of this time period, Edward Jones also accepted millions of dollars in directed brokerage commissions ... from three of the Preferred Families for distribution of mutual fund shares. In these instances, the advisers of these Preferred Families instructed the brokerage firm executing portfolio transactions for their mutual funds to ... direct a portion of the commissions for the transactions to Edward Jones. These directed brokerage payments ceased in 2003.

8. Edward Jones' distributed 11% to 12% of its net income, which includes net revenue sharing, to its limited partners and 10% to 12% of its net income to its subordinated limited partners each year and the residual is distributed to the general partners. Thus, the majority of any revenue sharing received by Edward Jones, after operating expenses, was distributed to the firm's general partners, some of whom make decisions regarding which mutual fund families become "Preferred Families" and others of whom are Edward Jones IRs who recommend the Preferred Families to their customers. During 2003 alone, the revenue sharing received by Edward Jones was equivalent to 33% of the net income of Edward Jones' parent holding company, Jones Financial.

9. Out of the approximately 240 mutual fund families with which Edward Jones has selling agreements, only the seven Preferred Families make revenue sharing payments to Edward Jones. These payments are in addition to standard sales loads, commissions, Rule 12b-1 fees, expense reimbursements and sub-transfer-agent fees for maintaining customer account information. Edward Jones does not receive any revenue sharing payments from any non-preferred mutual fund families. Historically, 95% to 98% of Edward Jones' sales of mutual fund shares have been sales of the Preferred Families.

10. Edward Jones and its partners have a financial incentive to internally promote the sales of mutual funds from the Preferred Families over other mutual funds that its IRs can sell. Edward Jones promoted to IRs the existence of revenue sharing by the Preferred Families and encouraged IRs on a case-by-case basis to consider revenue sharing in making recommendations to their customers to purchase certain mutual funds.

11. For example, during the relevant time period, Edward Jones' Director of Mutual Fund Marketing described his "greatest contribution to the Firm's bottom line" as "the

Department's ability to continue the focus on selling preferred fund families and the subsequent leverage this gives us to negotiate revenue sharing programs with vendors." He also represented to the IRs that Edward Jones directly passes the revenue sharing income along to the "IRs who did the work to get the money in the first place."

12. During the "rollouts" of the two newest Preferred Families, a general partner of the firm also made broadcast presentations to IRs throughout the country further extolling the benefits the IRs receive from the revenue sharing agreements negotiated with these Preferred Families.

13. At least one newsletter distributed by an Edward Jones regional leader conveyed this message by describing how "[r]evenue sharing can contribute large benefits to the firm in terms of profit and bonus." In a January 2000 regional newsletter, a regional leader further promoted the sales of mutual funds from Preferred Families that provide revenue sharing payments over those that do not provide revenue sharing by describing how, over a ten year period, an IR would receive an additional $256,369 in profit from the sales of such mutual funds. During regional and other meetings, another of Edward Jones' regional leaders, who was also a general partner, encouraged IRs in his region to sell the mutual funds of one Preferred Family over the funds of another Preferred Family that paid less revenue sharing.

14. Edward Jones' IRs receive credits for the amount of revenue sharing that Edward Jones receives from the IRs' proportionate sales and customer holdings of funds from the Preferred Families. These credits were not directly paid to IRs, but were applied as a separate line item to the profit and loss statements ("P&Ls") prepared for each IR's office. These P&Ls are distributed monthly to the IRs and track their profitability to the firm. An IR's profitability to the firm determines whether the IR is successful at Edward Jones and is used as a factor in determining whether the IR will be considered for status as a limited partner. In addition, three times per year, Edward Jones' IRs are eligible to receive bonuses based, in part, on their overall profitability which is impacted by their revenue sharing credits. For an IR to receive a bonus in any of Edward Jones' three annual bonus periods, both the firm and the particular IR's office must be profitable during the period. In addition, if an IR has worked for Edward Jones for more than 30 months, the IR also needs to make at least $4,000 in profits to become eligible for a bonus. Edward Jones' top-producing IRs have received as much as an additional $5,000 per bonus period as the part of their bonuses based directly on revenue sharing payments attributable to the IRs' sales and customer holdings of funds from the Preferred Families to their retail customers.

15. Edward Jones further offers "diversification contest" trips to its IRs two times each year. During these contests, the IRs can qualify for a trip by earning points based on, among other things, their sales of mutual funds. Once an IR earns a specific number of points, the IR "wins" a trip. Although the IRs generally can earn contest points for selling any mutual funds or other investment product, for a ninety-day period in the fall of 2002, Edward Jones only gave mutual fund contest points for the sale of a subset of mutual funds from the Preferred Families. One or more of the Preferred Families always participate in the sponsorship of the diversification trips and make one short

training presentation for the IRs during each trip. Sponsorship of these trips and other meetings provide the Preferred Families with exclusive access to and visibility with the IRs.

16. The Preferred Families receive certain benefits not otherwise available to non-preferred families. First, Edward Jones exclusively promotes the seven Preferred Families on its public website and exclusively provides links to the Preferred Families' websites on Edward Jones' internal computer system accessible only to its IRs. Second, Edward Jones exclusively lists the Preferred Families in sales literature and newsletters provided to its customers. Third, Edward Jones provides its IRs with research on only the seven Preferred Families and maintains a "Preferred Funds List" containing the names of approximately 110 mutual funds within the Preferred Families that Edward Jones' Product Review department recommends for sale to Edward Jones' retail customers. Only funds from the seven Preferred Families are considered for inclusion on this list. The Product Review department does not review any mutual funds from fund families that are not Preferred Families for this "Preferred Funds List." Fourth, Edward Jones uses only the Preferred Families as examples in its internal training sessions for new IRs and only invites representatives from the Preferred Families to make presentations at these training sessions. Finally, Edward Jones facilitates exclusive direct access for the Preferred Families to its IRs for the dissemination of marketing materials and to answer IRs' questions regarding the funds offered by the Preferred Families.

Edward Jones Did Not Disclose Its Financial Incentives To Sell Mutual Funds From The Preferred Families

17. The mutual fund section of Edward Jones' public website lists only the seven Preferred Families and provides links to only the Preferred Families' websites. In addition, since approximately 1997, Edward Jones has claimed on its public website that it focuses on the seven Preferred Families because: "With nearly 11,000 mutual funds available, it can be difficult to know which fund(s) to pick. That's why at Edward Jones, we focus on seven preferred mutual fund families that share our same commitment to service, long-term investment objectives, and long-term performance."

18. During the same time period, Edward Jones did not disclose on its website or in any other written document that it prepared, the revenue sharing, directed brokerage payments and other payments received from the Preferred Families for distribution of mutual fund shares as described above. Edward Jones also did not disclose the dimensions of the potential financial conflict created by these payments.

19. Edward Jones and its IRs do not orally disclose to customers the revenue sharing, directed brokerage or other payments received by Edward Jones in connection with the distribution of mutual fund shares or the potential conflict of interest such payments create.

20. Instead, Edward Jones claimed to rely on language contained in the Preferred Families' prospectuses and Statements of Additional Information ("SAIs") to disclose rev-

enue sharing arrangements. At all relevant times, Edward Jones required its IRs to provide customers with a prospectus at the point-of-sale or with the confirmation of sale of any mutual fund; however, the firm did not require its IRs to provide and IRs did not provide customers with copies of SAIs unless a customer specifically requested a copy.

21. Many of the Preferred Families' prospectuses and SAIs fail to disclose adequate information about the source and the amount of the revenue sharing payments to Edward Jones and the dimensions of the resulting potential conflicts of interest. Although the Preferred Families' prospectuses and SAIs contained various disclosures concerning payments to broker-dealers distributing their funds, few of these disclosures adequately described Edward Jones' potential conflict of interest. [* * *]

* * *

Notes and Applications

What level and type of disclosure is adequate for an investor? That essential question has long been the basis for debate in the industry. On the one hand, the U.S. securities laws are disclosure based, meaning that the idea is to give investors full and adequate disclosure of all facts material to their investment decisions. On the other hand, the SEC and FINRA appear to feel an obligation to protect investors as well, but the only real means of doing so is disclosure based.

Consider a hypothetical investor named Monica. If she were an Edward Jones customer, what information would she have received when buying fund shares? According to the case, basically she would have received a confirmation consistent with Rule 10b-10 and the fund prospectus at the point of sale. Having received those documents at the time of purchase, would Monica have known or been alerted to the conflicts of interest and incentives created to sell her shares of funds from the "Preferred Families?" Perhaps she would, but only if Monica studied the prospectus and the SAI, which she would have had to request. Probably not, though, as the SEC noted that many of the preferred funds' prospectuses and SAIs failed to fully disclose the types and nature of payments being made to Edward Jones.

So, if you were to design an approach to help investors understand what they are paying as fees, loads and commissions—and their sources—how would you design it? Would you require pre-purchase disclosure? How detailed? Finally, it has been widely noted that investors are fairly apathetic about disclosure documents and investment decisions. Do you think there are ways to overcome such apathy?

* * *

Distribution is a fundamental issue for advisers and fund boards of directors and directly affects the interests of fund shareholders. These issues are vital to fund viability, and also implicate the business interests of advisers. Given these cross-currents, significant regulatory limitations are in place that shape distribution practices. While the distribution process is affected by complex commercial arrangements that operate in the background, ultimately these arrangements must be in the interests of fund investors. Moreover, individual investors must be treated fairly by market professionals and fully informed of how these arrangements affect their economic interests.

Table 17A — Sales Charges and Distribution Fee Developments Chronology

1940	**Enactment of the Investment Company Act with statutory features affecting distribution:** • Section 2(a)(32) — Definition of Redeemable Security • Section 2(a)(35) — Definition of Sales Load • Section 12(b) — rulemaking grant which was always interpreted as a bar to self-distribution of shares by funds or the payment of distribution of expenses from fund assets. • Section 15(b) — requiring funds to have a written agreement specifying fees for principal underwriter. • Section 18(b) — prohibiting mutual funds from issuing multiple classes of shares. • Section 22(b) — general prohibition on grossly excessive sales loads by mutual funds as determined by national securities associations (subsequently amended in 1970). • Section 22(d) — requirement that mutual fund shares be sold at a fixed offering price
1940-1960	Most funds are load funds sold through broker-dealers. Some no-load fund marketed directly to investors through principal underwriter.
1960-1980	SEC causes issuance of two studies – the Wharton Study (1962) and the Public Policy Implications of Investment Company Growth Report (1966) – which raise issues regarding adequacy of regulation of sales loads. No-load funds grow in popularity, but most fund shares are still sold with loads through brokers.
Section 12(b) and Rule 12b-1	
1980	Rule 12b-1 is adopted, in part to assist small funds and no-load funds compete with other financial services by assessing a fund a small fee to support distribution.
1980s	Widespread adoption of 12b-1 fees with many exceeding 0.25%. SEC grants permission to combine 12b-1 fees with contingent deferred sales charges ("CDSCs"); see Rule 6c-10, below.
2004	SEC adopts amendment to Rule 12b-1 prohibiting funds from paying for distribution with brokerage commissions of the fund's portfolio ("directed brokerage").
2010	SEC proposes first major overhaul of Rule 12b-1 and distribution principles. The new framework, which the SEC failed to adopt, would have largely repealed Rule 12b-1, replacing it with new Rule 12b-2.

Section 22(d)	
1985	Rule 22d-1 adopted: permits sales of redeemable securities with varying sales loads.
2017	SEC issues no-action letter interpreting 22(d) as permitting a dealer (but not a broker) to charge its own transaction fees and charges for purchases and sales of mutual fund shares that have been stripped of all fund and distributor level fees, loads and charges, including 12b-1 fees and most transfer agency expenses. Such share classes are called "clean shares."
Rule 6c-10	
1988	SEC proposes Rule 6c-10 permitting funds to impose contingent deferred sales charges. The proposal ratifies prior SEC exemptive relief positions and leads to routine exemptive relief regarding such sales charges.
1995	SEC finally adopts Rule 6c-10 largely as proposed.
1996	SEC amends Rule 6c-10 to expand the list of permissible forms of deferred sales loads.
2010	In conjunction with a proposed overhaul of Rule 12b-1, the SEC proposes amendments to Rule 6c-10 which were never adopted. Rule 6c-10 would have been amended to permit "ongoing sales charges."
Rule 18f-3	
1995	The SEC adopted Rule 18f-3, permitting funds to issue multiple classes of shares.

Chapter 18

Exchange-Traded Funds

Key Ideas: Exchange-traded funds ("ETFs") are a hybrid type of investment company that has enjoyed enormous success in gathering assets under management in recent years. As previously noted, ETFs have features similar to open-end funds and other features similar to closed-end funds. They are typically structured as open-end funds. However, unlike the typical open-end funds, the redeemable securities issued by ETFs (known as creation units) are redeemable only in large bulk units by authorized participants. The authorized participants divide the large creation units into fractional undivided interests (shares) in the fund, and it is these fund shares that are traded on stock exchanges by investors. The dual structure of ETFs—redeemable creation units and exchange-traded shares—enables intraday trading of fund shares by investors and maintains a mechanism whereby the shares are unlikely to trade at a price significantly different from the redeemable value of the creation units. Exchange-traded funds have enjoyed enormous popularity and rapid growth since their introduction in the early 1990s. Over time, two fundamentally different categories of ETFs have arisen. The most common type of ETFs are passively managed and index-based. The other category, though much smaller in number and AUM, are actively-managed ETFs. Like passively-managed ETFs, actively-managed ETFs have portfolios that are publicly transparent. Proposals for actively-managed ETFs with nontransparent portfolios have emerged, but are controversial. From a legal perspective, ETFs present challenging issues under the Company Act, and these issues depend on the type of ETF. When enacted, the Company Act did not contemplate ETFs, but through innovative forms of exemptive relief and safeguards, the funds' unique structures have been reconciled with the requirements of the Company Act. The SEC is on the verge of adopting a rule that will serve to codify regulation of broad classes of ETFs.

Chapter Contents

18.1 Introduction and a Brief History of ETFs

The textbook's preceding chapters have largely focused on conventional mutual funds as the quintessential type of registered investment company. For a generation or more, conventional mutual funds represented well over 95% of the assets managed by registered investment companies, but the industry appears to be in the process of a monumental change. The change is tied to the advent of a new hybrid type of registered investment company, exchange-traded funds ("ETFs"). ETFs now represent roughly 15% of the assets managed in the registered investment company space. Moreover, in terms of flow of funds, ETFs actually outpace conventional mutual funds in gathering new assets.

The milestones in this change are relatively well-defined. In 1990, the SEC approved exemptive relief for a new type of hybrid product known as The SuperTrust.[1] The product was the brainchild of an investment advisory firm interested in quantitative investment strategies. The firm was widely associated with portfolio insurance and program trading in the 1980s.[2] Portfolio insurance traditionally connoted downside protection for a long securities portfolio. The SuperTrust product offered an efficient way to secure portfolio insurance, but could also be used to implement other strategies to cover short positions as well. The structure of the SuperTrust product contained the basic features of what we know today as exchange-traded funds, most notably the ability to trade a basket of securities in one security, but the product itself proved too complex and unwieldy, and as a result, it was not successful in garnering sufficient market acceptance.

In 1992, the SEC approved exemptive relief for what today is commonly regarded as the first successful U.S. ETF—State Street Bank's Standard & Poors Depositary Receipts ("SPDR"). This fund, which trades under the ticker SPY, was organized as a unit investment trust (rather than as an open-end, registered investment company)

1. One of the authors of this text has provided a detailed history of The SuperTrust. *See* Letter from Karl-Otto Hartmann, Co-Founder and Editor of www.40Act.com, *Re: Release No. 34-75165 Request for Comment on Exchange-Traded Products* (August 16, 2015), https://www.sec.gov/comments/s7-11-15/s71115-12.pdf.

2. Portfolio insurance and program trading are sophisticated strategies that use market basket trading, along with options and commodities futures trading, to improve money managers' investment results when compared to just buying and holding securities portfolios. Portfolio insurance was initially implicated in a seemingly inexplicable volatility in securities markets throughout October 1987 and a precipitous price decline on October 19, *see generally* Division of Market Regulation, U.S. Securities and Exchange Commission, The October 1987 Market Break (February 1988), but the finding has been disputed by others.

and currently holds roughly $200 billion AUM. According to State Street Global Advisors, SPY was "the most liquid and actively traded security in the world" in 2016.

While the first ETFs were organized as UITs, that structure is not common today. In 1996, the SEC approved exemptive relief and allowed an exchange-traded fund to be organized as an open-end, registered company. Since then, most ETFs have been organized in an open-end structure (i.e., mutual fund). Each ETF trust must secure an exemptive order from the SEC, because the structure and operation is inconsistent with Company Act provisions and the rules thereunder. Each exemptive order invariably contains conditions that are roughly comparable to conditions imposed on other similarly situated ETFs, but the orders usually allow each trust to organize additional ETFs under the same trust structure.

The use of the exemptive process as a primary method of regulation introduces delay and uncertainty into the process of launching an ETF. In the intervening years, the SEC continuously struggled to determine which proposed funds raised novel issues that required additional conditions or, in some cases, that should not be permitted (i.e., cases in which exemptive relief is denied). This chapter provides an introduction into the principal legal issues affecting ETFs and the fund structures that have posed regulatory challenges.

18.2 The Basic Structure—Functional Attributes and the Difference between Index-Based and Actively-Managed Funds

Chapter 2 discussed some of the functional attributes of ETFs. This chapter provides an extended analysis of these functional features and the legal challenges they pose. As previously noted, ETF is a term applied to registered investment companies that are exchange-traded. Accordingly, ETFs must meet the basic definition of an investment company, namely an issuer of securities that primarily engages in the business of investing, reinvesting, and trading securities. Investment vehicles that deal in non-securities, such as commodities, are typically grouped under the broader category of exchange-traded products ("ETPs"), a term that encompasses (i) exchange-traded funds, (ii) non-securities investment vehicles with the same functional attributes, and (iii) "exchange-traded notes," where a bank issues a fixed-income obligation with its return tied to the performance of a securities or non-securities-based index. Other than ETFs, ETPs are not regulated as investment companies but, as discussed below, do come within the ambit of the federal securities laws. This section deals with ETFs at a functional level. The next section addresses the legal challenges associated with ETFs.

18.2.1 Functional Attributes of ETFs

As explained earlier in this chapter, ETFs are essentially conventional mutual funds whose shares trade intraday on securities markets at prices that approximate the fund's

NAV. To achieve these characteristics, the product has a bifurcated structure as shown in Chapter 2. The ETF issues redeemable securities to a limited set of large investors known as authorized participants, and the proceeds (if purchased with cash) are invested in a basket of securities corresponding to the fund's composition. More commonly, however, authorized participants purchase creation units in-kind by exchanging a basket of securities that proportionately mirrors the composition of the ETF portfolio in return for a creation unit. The authorized participants then subdivide their creation units into a pre-established number of shares (typically the sponsor uses increments ranging from 50,000 to 100,000 shares per creation unit). Thus, the ETF itself deals with authorized participants either in issuing or redeeming creation units (which represent an ownership in a creation basket). Authorized participants in turn buy and sell shares of the ETF with investors through trading on the ETF's listing market. Of course, investors may also trade (purchase or sell) shares with other investors in the market.

This dual structure is essential to accomplishing intraday trading of shares at approximate real-time NAV; in practical terms, it provides an arbitrage mechanism between the value of creation units and the value of the underlying basket of securities. Authorized participants will have an incentive to create or redeem creation units as the ETF's market share price exceeds or falls short of the approximate real-time NAV. The arbitrage strategy for an authorized participant is straight forward. Authorized participants will purchase creation units at NAV (and simultaneously sell ETF shares in the market) whenever the price of shares constituting a creation unit exceeds the real-time NAV of the creation basket. By the same token, the authorized participant will buy shares in the open market and redeem creation units for the market basket of securities (while simultaneously selling the market basket of securities in the open market) whenever the market value of the basket exceeds the price of the shares constituting a creation unit. This redemption process will reduce the supply of ETF shares, pushing the price of the ETF shares toward the real-time NAV.

ETFs embody a number of functional features that operate differently than conventional mutual funds. Most obviously, they permit intraday trading of fund shares at prices that reflect pricing information about the market basket's securities. As noted, the intraday trading relies on the arbitrage activity of funds' authorized market participants. In order to make the arbitrage more efficient, ETFs must continuously disseminate pricing that estimate share NAV—known as the Intraday Indicative Value ("IIV")—in 15 second intervals throughout the day. The IIV relies heavily on transparency regarding the composition of each fund's portfolio (market basket).

Second, liquidity operates differently in an ETF than in a conventional mutual fund. In most respects, liquidity is less of a problem for an ETF. Most purchases and redemptions of creation units are done in-kind, with cash adjustments as necessary, meaning the authorized participant either delivers the underlying securities that constitute the market basket (creations) or receives the securities that comprise the market basket (redemptions). As a result, creations or redemptions are typically not affected by the need to purchase the market basket securities on exchanges. However, in times of market stress, the demand for creation or redemption may increase, and the inability to obtain some component market basket securities may disrupt pricing of the ETF or lead to unusual volatility, especially for ETFs that contain thinly traded securities.

The method of distribution for ETFs also fundamentally differs from the methods used by conventional mutual funds. As discussed in previous chapters, mutual funds are sold and redeemed in dedicated channels. Thus, mutual funds (or particular fund share classes) typically are sold through one of several channels: (i) direct-sold or discount brokerage; (ii) broker—or other intermediary—sold; or (iii) retirement accounts. In addition, conventional, actively managed mutual fund shares are seldom held by large institutional investors, because the institutional investor will likely be able to obtain a lower management fee by having a separate account managed directly by the same adviser. As a result, it is not uncommon to see money managers charge one fee to institutional investors and a different fee for managing the same strategy for a mutual fund (and its retail investors). This expense and distribution structure is not easily replicated in the ETF space for funds that enjoy both an institutional and retail shareholder constituency. ETFs charge a uniform management fee and other expenses that cannot discriminate between institutional and retail investors. Thus, a fund in an ETF wrapper makes it possible for a retail shareholder to obtain a lower management fee than the same retail shareholder would obtain in a mutual fund offered in a conventional mutual fund wrapper. For example, sales charges and 12b-1 fees are absent in the case of ETFs. However, because ETF shares are traded on the market, investors do incur commission charges.

Because ETFs bypass traditional mutual fund distribution channels, ETF distribution focuses on direct marketing and advertising to retail investors (i.e., by the ETF sponsor and by retail brokerages) and wholesaling to institutional investors. In addition to potential commission charges earned by brokers, the authorized participant may earn a trading spread in buying and selling shares of the ETF in the market at prices that deviate from their NAV, as previously discussed. Thus, brokerage commissions and trading spreads are the principal source of funding distribution costs in the ETF world.

Finally, ETFs have an attribute frequently touted by financial advisers: tax efficiency. This attribute is an artifact of the tax code and index-based funds. Many index-based funds have a stable underlying portfolio which reduces fund turnover. Moreover, redemptions frequently result in in-kind exchanges that can be used to minimize fund capital gains. Thus, the pass-through tax liability of ETFs to investors is generally much smaller than actively managed mutual funds.

Request for Comment on Exchange-Traded Products

Exchange Act Release No. 75165 (June 12, 2015)

[**Textbook Note:** *In this release, the SEC sought comment on the trading attributes of ETPs (which as noted above is a broader category for viewing exchange traded products and is not limited to exchange-traded registered investment companies*

(ETFs)). While it is unnecessary to address the broader issues of ETPs, the excerpt also summarizes well-known features of ETFs as they operate currently.]

[***]A. Introduction

Exchange-traded products ("ETPs") constitute a diverse class of financial products that seek to provide investors with exposure to financial instruments, financial benchmarks, or investment strategies across a wide range of asset classes. ETP trading occurs on national securities exchanges and other secondary markets that are regulated by the Commission under the Securities Exchange Act of 1934 ("Exchange Act"), making ETPs widely available to market participants, from individual investors to institutional investors, including hedge funds and pension funds.

The Commission approved the listing and trading of shares of the first ETP—the SPDR S&P 500 ETF ("SPY")—in 1992. Since the SPY began trading on January 22, 1993, there has been enormous growth in the number, aggregate market capitalization, and variety of ETPs. The chart below depicts the growth of ETPs, both in number and market capitalization, since 1993.

As reflected in Figure 1 (below), from 2006 to 2013, the total number of ETPs listed and traded as of year end rose by an average of 160 per year, with a net increase of more than 200 in both 2007 and 2011. By comparison, from 1993 to 2005, the total number of ETPs listed and traded as of year end rose by an average of just 17 per year, with a net increase of 60 in 2000. The total market capitalization of ETPs has also grown substantially, nearly doubling since the end of 2009. Much of this growth has been in index-based ETPs.

As of December 31, 2014, there were 1,664 U.S.-listed ETPs, and they had an aggregate market capitalization of just over $2 trillion. Trading in these ETPs makes up a significant portion of secondary-market equities trading. For example, during 2014, trading in U.S.-listed ETPs made up about 16.7% of U.S. equity trading by share volume and 25.7% of U.S. equity trading by dollar volume.

There has also been significant growth in the range of investment strategies that ETPs pursue. These strategies have expanded from exchange-traded funds ("ETFs") that track equity indices (such as the original SPY) to include, among other things: (i) ETPs that track other types of indices (such as those based on fixed-income securities or on derivatives contracts on commodities and currencies); (ii) actively managed ETPs that hold portfolios of equities, fixed-income instruments, foreign securities, commodities, currencies, futures, options, or other over-the-counter or exchange-traded derivatives; (iii) leveraged, inverse, and inverse leveraged ETPs; and (iv) ETPs employing market volatility, hedging, or options-based strategies.

The increasing scope and complexity of ETP investment strategies in recent years have led to an increase in the number and complexity of requests by issuers for exemptive relief under the Exchange Act (to allow ETPs to be offered for sale on exchanges) and in the number and complexity of proposed rule changes filed with the Commission by exchanges seeking to establish listing standards for the securities of new ETPs.

Figure 18A — Aggregate Market Capitalization and Number of ETPs, 1993–2014

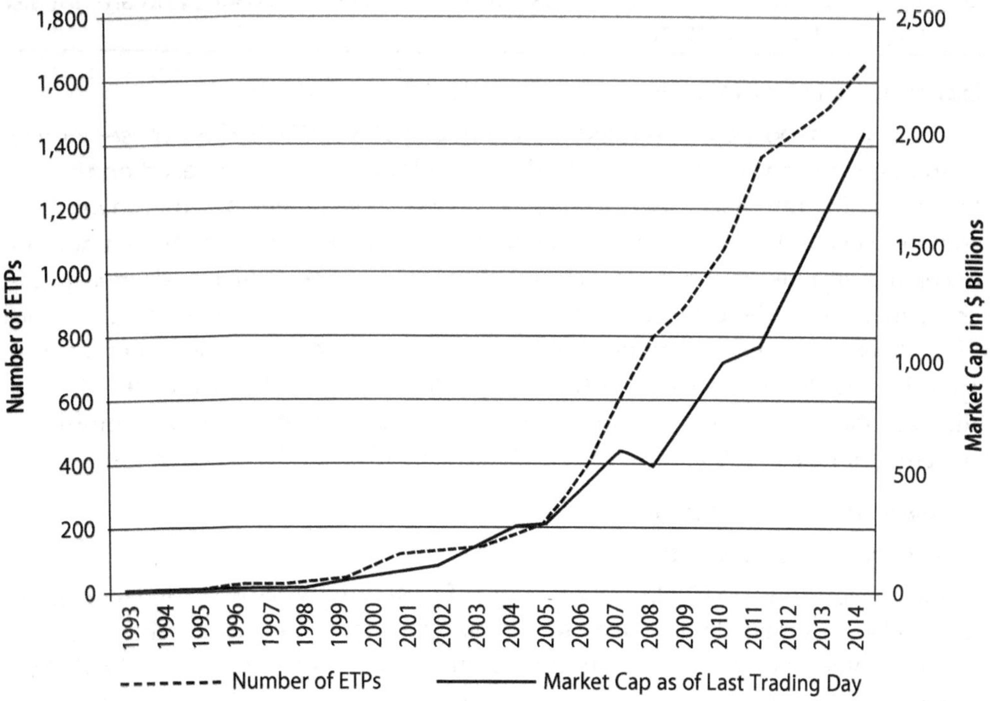

B. The Types of ETPs

Although ETPs constitute a diverse class of financial products, for purposes of this Request for Comment they are classified into three broad categories.

Exchange-Traded Funds (ETFs)

The first, and largest, category comprises ETFs, which are open-end fund vehicles or unit investment trusts that are registered as investment companies under the Investment Company Act of 1940 ("1940 Act"). Like an open-end fund, an ETF pools the assets of multiple investors and invests those assets according to its investment objective and principal investment strategies, and each share of an ETF represents an undivided interest in the underlying assets of the ETF. However, unlike open-end funds—shares of which are purchased or redeemed at the fund's current net asset value ("NAV"), which is typically calculated at the end of the trading day—ETF shares may be bought or sold by investors throughout the day through a broker-dealer at a market-determined price.

Non-1940 Act Pooled Investment Vehicles

The second category comprises ETPs that, generally, are trust or partnership vehicles that are not registered under the 1940 Act because they do not invest primarily in securities. Examples of ETPs in this category include those that physically hold a precious metal or that hold a portfolio of futures or other derivatives contracts on certain commodities or currencies. Offerings of securities issued by ETPs in this second category are registered only under the Securities Act of 1933 ("Securities Act") and are not also registered under the 1940 Act.

Exchange-Traded Notes (ETNs)

The third category comprises exchange-traded notes ("ETNs"). ETNs are senior debt instruments issued by financial institutions, and they pay a return based on the performance of a "reference asset"—an asset, market benchmark, or other investment strategy, such as the return on the S&P 500 Index, the performance of commodities or commodity indices, or the performance of the common stock of an individual public company. Unlike the other two categories of ETPs described above, ETNs are not pooled vehicles, and they do not hold an underlying portfolio of securities, futures, over-the-counter derivatives, or other assets. Offerings of ETNs are registered under the Securities Act, and the performance of the reference assets generally determines the amount owed by the issuer of the ETN to the holder of the ETN at maturity.

C. How Existing ETPs Function

1. Purchases, Sales, Creations, and Redemptions

Most investors in an ETP buy and sell the ETP's securities in the secondary market, at a market-determined price, with other market participants, including other investors, broker-dealers, and market makers, on the other side of the transaction. The ETP securities that are listed for trading on an exchange ("ETP Securities") are either (i) shares issued by the ETP or (ii) in the case of ETNs (which are, as noted above, debt instruments issued by a financial institution), the debt instruments themselves.

Although most investors can buy or sell ETP Securities only in the secondary market through a broker-dealer, certain large market participants, typically broker-dealers, can become authorized participants ("Authorized Participants") with respect to most ETPs. Each Authorized Participant enters into a contractual relationship with the ETP issuer that allows it to engage in purchases and redemptions of ETP Securities directly with that issuer.

For almost all ETPs, the issuance and redemption of ETP Securities operates in essentially the same manner. ETPs generally issue ETP Securities only in large aggregations or blocks (for example, 50,000 ETP shares) called creation units ("Creation Units"). Most ETPs are structured so that an Authorized Participant will purchase a Creation Unit with a portfolio deposit ("Portfolio Deposit"), which is a basket of assets (and sometimes cash) that generally reflects the composition of the ETP's portfolio. The ETP makes public the contents of the Portfolio Deposit before the beginning of the trading day. Because the purchase price of a Creation Unit and its aggregate NAV must be equal, an amount of cash will be exchanged between the Authorized Participant and the ETP at the time of purchase when necessary to balance the value of the Portfolio Deposit with that of the Creation Unit. After purchasing a Creation Unit, an Authorized Participant may hold the ETP Securities or sell (or lend) some or all of them to investors in the secondary market.

Similarly, for most ETPs, when an Authorized Participant wishes to redeem ETP Securities, it presents a Creation Unit to the ETP for redemption and receives in return a redemption basket ("Redemption Basket"), the contents of which are made public by the ETP before the beginning of the trading day. The Redemption Basket (which is usually, but not always, the same as the Portfolio Deposit) typically consists of securities or commodities and a small amount of cash. As with purchases from the ETP, redemptions to the ETP are priced at NAV, and an amount of cash will be exchanged when necessary to balance the value of the Redemption Basket with that of the Creation Unit.

When creation and redemption transactions occur wholly or partly "in kind"—in other words, when securities constituting the ETP's portfolio are exchanged for ETP Securities and vice versa—certain benefits can accrue to the ETP and its investors. In-kind exchanges generally result in lower trading expenses (because securities received or delivered in kind do not need to be purchased or sold in the market by the ETP, thus avoiding brokerage fees) and lower taxable gains to shareholders (because appreciated securities are not sold but are delivered in kind to redeeming Authorized Participants).

2. Arbitrage Between an ETP's Market Price and Its NAV

Because of the creation and redemption mechanisms, most existing ETPs present market participants, including Authorized Participants, market makers, and institutional investors, with opportunities to engage in arbitrage, which generally helps to prevent the market price of ETP Securities from diverging significantly from the value of the ETP's underlying or reference assets. Although most ETPs calculate and disseminate their official NAV only once per day as of the close of regular trading hours, market participants can use other methods during the trading day to calculate or approximate the value of the assets underlying or referenced by a share of an ETP.

For example, exchange listing standards require every currently traded, actively managed ETP to make daily disclosure of its entire portfolio. Current exchange listing standards do not require similar disclosures for index-based ETPs, but the make-up and value of the underlying indices are widely available, and most index-based ETPs, as a matter of practice, make daily disclosure of their portfolios. With this information, market participants can access pricing data about an ETP's portfolio assets and perform their own calculations of the per-share value of that portfolio.

In addition, exchange listing standards require existing ETPs to publicly disseminate during the trading day an intraday indicative value ("IIV"), which is designed to provide investors with information on the value of the investments held by the ETP (or, in the case of an ETN, the reference assets). The IIV is typically calculated and disseminated at least every 15 seconds during the trading day and is typically disseminated over the Consolidated Tape or via an exchange data feed. The IIV may or may not be based on the entire portfolio held by an ETP, and it may or may not be equal to the per-share value of an ETP's underlying portfolio or reference assets.

A simplified example of "riskless" arbitrage will help to clarify how the arbitrage process for existing ETPs is intended to work. If the shares of an ETP that uses an in-kind creation and redemption process begin to trade at a discount to the value of the underlying portfolio at any point during the trading day, arbitrageurs can capture this difference (minus expenses) by: (i) Purchasing ETP Securities in the secondary market in an amount equal to a Creation Unit while simultaneously selling short the securities or commodities in the Redemption Basket; (ii) redeeming the Creation Unit with the ETP at the end-of-day NAV (either as an Authorized Participant or through a relationship with an Authorized Participant), thereby receiving the securities or commodities in the Redemption Basket; and (iii) using the contents of the Redemption Basket to close out the arbitrageur's short position. Purchasing the ETP Securities and selling short the securities or commodities in the Redemption Basket also apply market pressure that tends, all other things being equal, to bring the ETP Security's market price closer to the value of the underlying portfolio assets.

Similarly, if the shares of this same ETP begin to trade at a premium to the value of the underlying portfolio, arbitrageurs may profit by: (i) Selling short the ETP Securities; (ii) purchasing the securities or commodities that make up the Portfolio Deposit; (iii) exchanging the Portfolio Deposit for a Creation Unit through an Authorized Participant; and then (iv) using the ETP Securities in the Creation Unit to close out the short position. Again, the sales of the ETP Securities and the purchases of the contents of the Portfolio Deposit apply market pressure that tends, all other things being equal, to bring the price of the ETP Securities closer to the value of the underlying portfolio assets.

Market participants can also engage in arbitrage activities that do not necessarily require them to engage in creations or redemptions. For example, if a market participant believes that an ETP is overvalued relative to its underlying or reference assets, the market participant may sell ETP Securities; buy the underlying or reference assets; and, if the trading prices move toward parity, close out the positions in both the ETP Securities and the underlying or reference assets. The market participant would thereby realize a profit from the relative movement of those trading prices without engaging in an ETP creation. Similarly, a market participant could buy ETP Securities and sell the underlying or reference assets in an attempt to profit when an ETP Security is trading at a discount to its underlying or reference assets. As discussed above, the trading of an ETP Security and its underlying or reference assets applies market pressure that may bring the prices of the ETP Security and those assets closer together. [***]

18.2.2 The Great Divide between Passively-Managed ETFs and Actively-Managed ETFs

ETFs are frequently classified as either passively-managed (index-based) or actively-managed. The basic difference is that index-based funds seek to match the performance of a benchmark index, while actively-managed funds seek to outperform market benchmarks through investing acumen that relies on proprietary trading strategies. In terms of indices, one of the best-known examples is the S&P 500 index. This index reflects the price performance of 500 of the largest U.S. public-company common shares. The S&P 500 is weighted by issuer market capitalization, and the selection of the 500 issuers incorporates adjustments to make the index more representative of industrial sector composition of the market as a whole (e.g., issuers in technology, energy, financials, consumer goods, etc.). Capitalization weighted indexes merely means that issuer weight in the index is based on size of market capitalization. For example, Apple Inc. is given much greater weight in the index (approximately 3.5%) than a smaller company like Caterpillar Inc. (approximately 0.35%) because Apple is roughly ten times the size of Caterpillar in terms of market capitalization. The largest ETF—the SPDR S&P 500 fund discussed earlier—tracks the performance of the S&P 500 index, and thus, its approximately $200 billion in AUM (as of 2016) reflects the relative weight assigned to particular securities in the index.

Index funds are well-suited for an ETF structure because they do not rely on proprietary trading strategies (proprietary trading strategies typically involve non-transparency and significant managerial investing discretion). As noted above and discussed below, ETFs are more efficient and raise fewer regulatory concerns regarding the arbitrage mechanism when the underlying ETF portfolio is entirely transparent, as is the case with index-based ETFs. Advisers of actively managed funds, on the other hand, typically place a premium on their proprietary investment and trading strategies in selecting portfolio securities and seek to keep these strategies and investments private. This creates fundamental challenges for advisers and funds if the funds' underlying portfolios must be transparent for ETF market listing and trading purposes.

Moreover, index-based strategies are suited to infinite variation and low-cost management fee structures. Index construction can turn on numerous factors. Indexes can be based on different universes of securities (e.g., large cap issuers, small cap issuers, different industrial sectors), different weighting strategies (e.g., market capitalization, equal-weight, fundamental weighting) or different securities selection strategies (based on so-called securities factors or attributes such as beta, momentum, or value). Indexes based on other than simple market capitalization weighting are typically referred to as smart-beta indexes (i.e., strategies that try to achieve enhanced return by picking out indexes that outperform market based indexes). Finally, indexes may also lend themselves to long-short strategies that try to hedge positions by using long positions on securities in tandem with other positions involving sale of borrowed securities (or shorted). The former position is a bet that the particular issuer's securities will increase in value while a short position is a bet that the securities of another issuer will lose value. In addition, index-based ETFs can give a multiple of the performance return on the daily performance of a given index (such as two times (or "2X") the daily performance) through the use of complex strategies that employ derivatives—so-called "leveraged ETFs."

Index-based funds typically use a variety of techniques to achieve their objectives. No index fund can perfectly track the performance of its benchmark index, because the fund must incur transaction costs (e.g., buying and selling securities and administering the fund) to recreate and deliver the investment performance of the index. Thus, index-based funds at best will usually only deliver the investment performance of the index less the transaction costs. In recreating the investment performance of the index, the fund's investment policies elect either to replicate the index or mimic its performance through sampling. Replication entails buying each component security of the index in exactly the right proportion to the index. This approach can be expensive from a transactional cost perspective if the index has many component securities or when some of the component securities are thinly traded. As an alternative, some funds may seek to approximate the return of the index through cost-efficient sampling techniques that use a smaller subset of component index securities, which will very closely approximate the index return rather than incurring the expense of precisely replicating the index.[3]

The SEC first approved the offering of actively-managed ETFs in 2008. Actively-managed ETFs pose different management and trading challenges than index-based ETFs. As noted, index-based ETFs are entirely transparent in terms of their portfolio holdings. As a result, the arbitrage mechanism associated with the pricing of shares and the purchase and redemption of creation units is likely to be fairly efficient. Moreover, the transparency of any fund's holdings does not impair the success of the fund's investment strategies, because those strategies merely try to match a benchmark index rather than outperform it. In contrast, transparency introduces problems for the actively managed ETF. By definition, an actively managed fund is designed to outperform the market-equivalent benchmark, but this goal will be difficult to realize if the implementation of a manager's trading strategy is fully transparent or visible in real time. All competitors will know what the active ETF manager is doing and, as such, competitors have the opportunity to copy the strategy and even trade before the ETF manager can fully execute its own strategy. Some actively managed, fixed-income ETFs have been successful largely because the fixed-income market is so large and the variety of issues is great. However, actively managed equity-based ETFs have been rare. The greatest industry interest in the active-managed arena is in nontransparent, actively-managed ETFs. In this variation of the ETF, a blind trust third-party arrangement is used to restrict direct public transparency, while preserving essential features of established arbitrage pricing mechanism. In 2014, the SEC specifically declined to provide exemptive relief for such a product, but sponsors are seeking to advance alternatives that satisfy the SEC's reservations. Actively-managed ETFs are discussed at greater length later in this chapter.

3. Two other terms are frequently used in connection with indexes. "Rebalancing" refers to the fact that the holdings of the fund portfolio over time will begin to diverge from the index weightings as the price of the portfolio securities change. Index-based funds will establish time periods (such as monthly or quarterly) for rebalancing the portfolio so the fund's portfolio matches the weighting of the index. "Reconstituting" refers to rules-based indices whose underlying component securities change over time. Thus, in a low beta fund that holds the 100 lowest beta stocks in the S&P 500, the membership of the 100 lowest beta stocks will change somewhat over time. The index will be reconstituted at regular intervals to identify the 100 lowest beta stocks. These concepts implicate unique features associated with each index product that fall under the rubric of "index construction." The particulars of any index construction can cause the performance of one index fund to diverge slightly from the performance of funds tracking similar indexes.

18.3 Regulation of ETFs under the Company Act and the Exemptive Process

ETFs do not fit easily within the regulatory scheme of the Company Act and also pose challenges under the Securities Exchange Act. Their structure and operation runs afoul of specific statutory and regulatory requirements. As noted, most ETFs are organized as mutual funds (open-end investment companies). The redemption feature for ETFs—redemption by authorized participants and non-redemption of the ETF shares—is neither consistent with the Company Act's definition of a redeemable security (Section 2(a)(32)) nor compliant with the daily redemption requirement applicable to open-end investment companies (Section 5(a)(1)). Similarly, the offering price of ETF shares and the absence of daily pricing processes violates Company Act requirements (ICA Section 22(d) and Rule 22c-1, respectively). In addition, creation and redemptions can trigger the affiliated transaction prohibition in Company Act Section 17(a). There are other potential violations that are not addressed here, which relate to timely redemptions and holding restrictions on fund shares by other funds.

However, the SEC has recognized that while ETFs operations may violate the letter of certain Company Act provisions and rules, the funds do not necessarily violate the spirit of those provisions. Accordingly, the SEC has used its extensive exemptive authority to provide ETFs with relief from a variety of requirements, subject to conditions ensuring investor protection. No ETF can conduct business without first securing the necessary exemptive relief, which has been the policy since the introduction of ETFs. The SEC routinely grants necessary exemptive relief under the Exchange Act to permit trading of ETF shares. Additionally, the Commission has authorized listings of most types of ETF shares by stock exchanges pursuant to generic listing standards for ETFs. As discussed below, the SEC has explored the possibility of adopting a rule that would have standardized many of the features of its exemptive relief.

Exchange-Traded Funds

Investment Company Act Release No. 33140 (June 28, 2018)

[**Textbook Note:** *In this SEC administrative release, the SEC re-proposed an exemptive rule for ETFs—proposed Rule 6c-11, which was originally proposed in 2008, but never adopted. The purpose of the proposed rule is to standardize the features that are common in individual exemptive orders issued by the SEC for ETFs. Until the rule is adopted, exemptive orders will remain necessary to give ETFs relief from certain statutory and rule-based requirements that would otherwise pose an obstacle to their operation. Indeed exemptive relief will still be required for ETFs not covered by the rule. The proposing release provides an excellent discussion that summarizes the key elements of what is reflected in numerous exemptive orders granted by the SEC over a period twenty-four years. The proposed rule may well be adopted shortly after publication of this textbook.*

I. Introduction

The Commission is proposing rule 6c-11 under the Investment Company Act to permit ETFs that satisfy certain conditions to operate without the expense and delay of obtaining an exemptive order from the Commission under the Act. This rule would modernize the regulatory framework for ETFs to reflect our 26 years of experience with these investment products. It is designed to create a consistent, transparent, and efficient regulatory framework for ETFs and to facilitate greater competition and innovation among ETFs.

The Commission approved the first ETF in 1992. Since then, ETFs registered with us have grown to $3.4 trillion in total net assets. They now account for approximately 15% of total net assets managed by investment companies,[3] and are projected to continue to grow. ETFs currently rely on exemptive orders, which permit them to operate as investment companies under the Act, subject to representations and conditions that have evolved over time. We have granted over 300 of these orders over the last quarter century, resulting in differences in representations and conditions that have led to some variations in the regulatory structure for existing ETFs.

Proposed rule 6c-11 would simplify this regulatory framework by eliminating conditions included within our exemptive orders that we no longer believe are necessary for our exemptive relief and removing historical distinctions between actively managed and index-based ETFs. In connection with the proposed rule, we also propose to rescind certain exemptive orders that have been granted to ETFs and their sponsors. As a result, proposed rule 6c-11 would level the playing field for ETFs that are organized as open-end funds and pursue the same or similar investment strategies. The proposed rule also would assist the Commission with regulating ETFs, as funds covered by the rule would no longer be subject to the varying provisions of exemptive orders granted over time, and instead would be subject to a consistent regulatory framework. Furthermore, creating an efficient regulatory framework for ETFs would allow Commission staff and industry resources to focus the exemptive order process on products that do not fall within the scope of our proposed rule.

In addition, we are proposing certain disclosure amendments to provide additional information to investors who purchase and sell ETF shares in the secondary markets, and to provide investors who purchase UITs with the same disclosures that we propose to require of ETFs organized as open-end funds. The proposed amendments would include new disclosures regarding certain unique costs associated specifically with ETFs, such as the bid-ask spread and premiums and discounts from the ETF's net asset value ("NAV").

---

3. ICI, 2018 Investment Company Fact Book (58th ed., 2018) ("2018 ICI Fact Book"), available at https://www.ici.org/pdf/2018_factbook.pdf, at 96. When the Commission first proposed a rule for ETFs in 2008, aggregate ETF assets were less than 7% of total net assets held by mutual funds. See Exchange-Traded Funds, Investment Company Act Release No. 28193 (Mar. 11, 2008) [73 FR 14618 (Mar. 18, 2008)] ("2008 ETF Proposing Release").

Our proposal takes into account the comments we received in response to our 2008 ETF proposal, which was designed to codify the exemptive relief that had been issued to ETFs at that time. Developments in the ETF industry since the 2008 proposal and interim Commission actions also have informed the parameters of proposed rule 6c-11 and the related disclosure amendments that we are proposing.

A. Overview of Exchange-Traded Funds

ETFs are a type of exchange-traded product ("ETP").[10] ETFs possess characteristics of both mutual funds, which issue redeemable securities, and closed-end funds, which generally issue shares that trade at market-determined prices on a national securities exchange and are not redeemable. Because ETFs have characteristics that distinguish them from the types of investment companies contemplated by the Act, they require exemptions from certain provisions of the Investment Company Act in order to operate. The Commission (and Commission staff under delegated authority) now routinely grants exemptive orders permitting ETFs to operate as investment companies under the Investment Company Act, generally subject to the provisions of the Act applicable to open-end funds (or UITs).[12] These exemptive orders reflect our determination that, based on the factual representations offered by the applicants and the conditions to which the applicants have agreed, the requested relief is necessary or appropriate in the public interest and consistent with the protection of investors and the purposes fairly intended by the policy and provisions of the Investment Company Act. The Commission also has approved the standards of national securities exchanges, under which ETF shares are listed and traded.

As discussed above, ETFs have become an increasingly popular investment vehicle over the last 26 years. They also have become a popular trading tool, making up a significant portion of secondary market equities trading. During the first quarter of 2018, for example, trading in U.S.-listed ETFs made up approximately 18.75% of U.S. equity trading by share volume and 28.2% of U.S. equity trading by dollar volume.

Investors can buy and hold shares of ETFs (sometimes as a core component of a portfolio) or trade them frequently as part of an active trading or hedging strategy. ETF investors can sell ETF shares short, write options on them, and set market, limit, and stop-loss orders on them. Moreover, because certain costs are either absent in

---

10. ETFs are investment companies registered under the Investment Company Act. See 15 U.S.C. 80a-3(a)(1). Other types of ETPs are pooled investment vehicles with shares that trade on a securities exchange, but they are not "investment companies" under the Act because they do not invest primarily in securities. Such ETPs may invest primarily in assets other than securities, such as futures, currencies, or physical commodities (e.g., precious metals). Still other ETPs are not pooled investment vehicles. For example, exchange-traded notes are senior, unsecured, unsubordinated debt securities that are linked to the performance of a market index and trade on securities exchanges.

12. Historically, ETFs have been organized as open-end funds or UITs. See 15 U.S.C. 80a-5(a)(1) (defining the term "open-end company") and 15 U.S.C. 80a-4(2) (defining the term "unit investment trust"). Some fund groups have multiple orders covering different types of ETFs (e.g., one order covering ETFs organized as UITs and another covering ETFs organized as open-end funds or one order covering index-based ETFs and another covering actively managed ETFs).

the ETF structure or are otherwise partially externalized, many ETFs have lower operating expenses than mutual funds.[17] ETFs also may offer certain tax efficiencies compared to other pooled investment vehicles because redemptions from ETFs are often made in kind (that is, by delivering certain assets from the ETF's portfolio, rather than in cash), thereby avoiding the need for the ETF to sell assets and potentially realize capital gains that are distributed to its shareholders.

ETFs today provide investors with a diverse set of investment options. While the first ETFs held portfolios of securities that replicated the component securities of broad-based domestic stock market indexes, some ETFs now track more specialized indexes, including international equity indexes, fixed-income indexes, or indexes focused on particular industry sectors such as telecommunications or healthcare. Some ETFs seek to track highly customized or bespoke indexes, while others seek to provide a level of leveraged or inverse exposure to an index over a fixed period of time. Investors also have the ability to invest in ETFs that do not track a particular index and are actively managed.[20]

B. Operation of Exchange-Traded Funds

An ETF issues shares that can be bought or sold throughout the day in the secondary market at a market-determined price. Like other investment companies, an ETF pools the assets of multiple investors and invests those assets according to its investment objective and principal investment strategies. Each share of an ETF represents an undivided interest in the underlying assets of the ETF. Similar to mutual funds, ETFs continuously offer their shares for sale.

Unlike mutual funds, however, ETFs do not sell or redeem individual shares. Instead, "authorized participants" that have contractual arrangements with the ETF (or its distributor) purchase and redeem ETF shares directly from the ETF in blocks called "creation units." An authorized participant may act as a principal for its own account when purchasing or redeeming creation units from the ETF. Authorized participants also may act as agent for others, such as market makers, proprietary trading firms, hedge funds or other institutional investors, and receive fees for processing creation units on their behalf. Market makers, proprietary trading firms, and hedge funds provide additional liquidity to the ETF market through their trading activity. Institutional investors may engage in primary market transactions with an ETF through an authorized participant as a way to efficiently hedge a portion of their portfolio or balance sheet or to gain exposure to a strategy or asset class.

---

17. For instance, ETFs typically do not bear distribution or shareholder servicing fees. In addition, ETFs that transact on an in-kind basis can execute changes in the ETF's portfolio without incurring brokerage costs, leading to transaction cost savings.

20. An actively managed ETF's investment adviser, like an adviser to any actively managed mutual fund, generally selects securities consistent with the ETF's investment objectives and policies without trying to track the performance of a corresponding index. Actively managed ETFs represent approximately 1.3% of total ETF assets as of September 2017. ...

An authorized participant that purchases a creation unit of ETF shares directly from the ETF deposits with the ETF a "basket" of securities and other assets identified by the ETF that day, and then receives the creation unit of ETF shares in return for those assets. The basket is generally representative of the ETF's portfolio[25] and, together with a cash balancing amount, equal in value to the aggregate NAV of the ETF shares in the creation unit. After purchasing a creation unit, the authorized participant may hold the individual ETF shares, or sell some or all of them in secondary market transactions. Investors then purchase individual ETF shares in the secondary market. The redemption process is the reverse of the purchase process: The authorized participant redeems a creation unit of ETF shares for a basket of securities and other assets.

The combination of the creation and redemption process with secondary market trading in ETF shares provides arbitrage opportunities that are designed to help keep the market price of ETF shares at or close to the NAV per share of the ETF. For example, if ETF shares are trading on national securities exchanges at a "discount" (a price below the NAV per share of the ETF), an authorized participant can purchase ETF shares in secondary market transactions and, after accumulating enough shares to compose a creation unit, redeem them from the ETF in exchange for the more valuable securities in the ETF's redemption basket. The authorized participant's purchase of an ETF's shares on the secondary market, combined with the sale of the ETF's basket assets, may create upward pressure on the price of the ETF shares, downward pressure on the price of the basket assets, or both, bringing the market price of ETF shares and the value of the ETF's portfolio holdings closer together. Alternatively, if ETF shares are trading at a "premium" (a price above the NAV per share of the ETF), the transactions in the arbitrage process are reversed and, when arbitrage is working effectively, keep the market price of the ETF's shares close to its NAV.

Market participants also can engage in arbitrage activity without using the creation or redemption processes. For example, if a market participant believes that an ETF is overvalued relative to its underlying or reference assets (i.e., trading at a premium), the market participant may sell ETF shares short and buy the underlying or reference assets, wait for the trading prices to move toward parity, and then close out the positions in both the ETF shares and the underlying or reference assets to realize a profit from the relative movement of their trading prices. Similarly, a market participant could buy ETF shares and sell the underlying or reference assets short in an attempt to profit when an ETF's shares are trading at a discount to the ETF's underlying or reference assets. As with the creation and redemption process, the trading of an ETF's shares and the ETF's underlying or reference assets may bring the prices of the ETF's shares and its portfolio assets closer together through market pressure.

25. The basket might not reflect a pro rata slice of an ETF's portfolio holdings. Subject to the terms of the applicable exemptive relief, an ETF may substitute other securities or cash in the basket for some (or all) of the ETF's portfolio holdings. Restrictions related to flexibility in baskets have varied over time.

The arbitrage mechanism is important because it provides a means to maintain a close tie between market price and NAV per share of the ETF, thereby helping to ensure ETF investors are treated equitably when buying and selling fund shares. In granting relief under section 6(c) of the Act for ETFs to operate, the Commission has relied on this close tie between what retail investors pay (or receive) in the secondary market and the ETF's approximate NAV to find that the required exemptions are necessary or appropriate in the public interest and consistent with the protection of investors and the purposes fairly intended by the policy and provisions of the Act. Investors also have come to expect that an ETF's market price will maintain a close tie to the ETF's NAV per share, which may lead some investors to view ETFs more favorably than similar closed-end funds. On the other hand, this expectation may lead investors to view ETFs as a less attractive investment option or cause them to sell ETF shares if market price and NAV per share diverge, particularly during periods of market stress.

II. Discussion

Given the growth in the ETF market, ETFs' popularity among retail and institutional investors, and our long experience regulating this investment and trading vehicle, we believe that it is appropriate to propose a rule that would allow most ETFs to operate without first obtaining an exemptive order from the Commission under the Act. We believe that such a rule would create a consistent, transparent and efficient regulatory framework for the regulation of most ETFs and level the playing field for these market participants. Proposed rule 6c-11 includes several conditions designed to address the concerns underlying the relevant statutory provisions and to support a Commission finding that the exemptions necessary to allow ETFs to operate are in the public interest and consistent with the protection of investors and the purposes fairly intended by the policy and provisions of the Act. The proposed conditions are based upon the existing exemptive relief for ETFs, which we believe have served to support an efficient arbitrage mechanism, but reflect several modifications based on our experience regulating this product.

A. Scope of Proposed Rule 6c-11

Proposed rule 6c-11 would define an ETF as a registered open-end management investment company that: (i) Issues (and redeems) creation units to (and from) authorized participants in exchange for a basket and a cash balancing amount (if any); and (ii) issues shares that are listed on a national securities exchange and traded at market-determined prices.[33]

33. ... Under the proposed rule, the term "basket" would be defined to mean the securities, assets, or other positions in exchange for which an ETF issues (or in return for which it redeems) creation units. The term "exchange-traded fund" thus would include ETFs that transact on an in-kind basis, on a cash basis, or both.

1. Organization as Open-End Funds

Proposed rule 6c-11 would be available only to ETFs that are organized as open-end funds. The vast majority of ETFs currently in operation are organized as open-end funds, although the earliest ETFs were organized as UITs ("UIT ETFs"). These early UIT ETFs represent a significant amount of assets within the ETF industry. For example, two of the largest ETFs by total net assets and estimated dollar trading volume (SPDR S&P 500 ETF Trust (SPY) and PowerShares QQQ Trust, Series 1 (QQQ)) are organized as UITs.

A UIT is an investment company organized under a trust indenture or similar instrument that issues redeemable securities, each of which represents an undivided interest in a unit of specified securities. By statute, a UIT is unmanaged and its portfolio is fixed. Substitution of securities may take place only under certain pre-defined circumstances. A UIT does not have a board of directors, corporate officers, or an investment adviser to render advice during the life of the trust. By contrast, ETFs organized as open-end funds are managed by investment advisers and, in addition to replicating an index, can be actively managed or use a "sampling" strategy to track an index. Unlike an ETF structured as a UIT, an open-end fund ETF may participate in securities lending programs and has greater flexibility to reinvest dividends from portfolio securities. ETFs structured as open-end funds also may invest in derivatives, which typically require a degree of management that is not provided for in the UIT structure. As a result, we understand that most ETF sponsors now prefer the open-end fund structure over the UIT structure given the increased investment flexibility the open-end structure affords. Indeed, we have received very few exemptive applications for new UIT ETFs since 2002 and no new UIT ETFs have come to market in that time.

...

While we acknowledge that excluding UIT ETFs would result in a segment of ETF assets that are outside the regulatory framework of proposed rule 6c-11, we do not believe there is a need to include ETF UITs within the scope of the proposed rule given the limited sponsor interest in developing ETFs organized as UITs. In addition, even if we were to include UIT ETFs within the scope of the rule, we believe that the unmanaged nature of the UIT structure would require conditions that differ from the conditions applicable to ETFs organized as open-end funds, requiring a regulatory framework that would be different than our proposed structure for open-end ETFs.... Instead, we believe that UIT ETFs should continue to operate pursuant to their exemptive orders, which include terms and conditions that are appropriately tailored to address the unique features of a UIT..... To the extent that ETF sponsors develop unforeseen, novel UIT ETFs, we believe that the Commission should review such products as part of its exemptive process to determine whether the relief is necessary or appropriate in the public interest and consistent with the protection of investors. We therefore are not proposing to include ETFs structured as UITs within the scope of proposed rule 6c-11.

....

2. Index-Based ETFs and Actively Managed ETFs

Proposed rule 6c-11 would provide exemptions for both index-based ETFs and actively managed ETFs, but would not by its terms establish different requirements based on whether an ETF's investment objective is to seek returns that correspond to the returns of an index. We believe that index-based and actively managed ETFs that comply with the proposed rule's conditions function similarly with respect to operational matters, despite different investment objectives or strategies, and do not present significantly different concerns under the provisions of the Act from which the proposed rule grants relief. For example, both index-based and actively managed ETFs register under the Act, issue and redeem shares in creation unit sizes in exchange for baskets of assets, list on national securities exchanges, and allow investors to trade ETF shares throughout the day at market-determined prices in the secondary market.

....

The actively managed ETF market has grown considerably since 2008. There are now over 200 actively managed ETFs with approximately $45.8 billion in assets. The Commission has observed how actively managed ETFs operate during this time, and has not identified any operational issues that suggest additional conditions for actively managed ETFs are warranted. As noted below, we believe that the arbitrage mechanism for existing actively managed ETFs has worked effectively with small deviations between market price and NAV per share.

We believe that permitting index-based and actively managed open-end ETFs to operate under the proposed rule subject to the same conditions would provide a level playing field among those market participants. Furthermore, we believe that it would be unreasonable to create a meaningful distinction within the rule between index-based and actively managed ETFs given the evolution of indexes over the last decade. The proliferation of highly customized, often methodologically complicated, indexes has blurred the distinction between such products. At the same time, ETF industry practices in areas such as portfolio transparency have converged between these types of funds. We therefore believe that eliminating the regulatory distinction between index-based ETFs and actively managed ETFs would help to provide a more consistent and transparent regulatory framework for ETFs organized as open-end funds. This approach also would be consistent with our regulation of other types of open-end funds, which does not distinguish between actively managed and index-based strategies.

The rule we proposed in 2008 similarly would not have distinguished between index-based ETFs and actively managed ETFs, except in one respect—it would have permitted an index-based ETF to disclose daily the composition of its index in lieu of disclosing its portfolio holdings. However, we believe that distinguishing between index-based ETFs and actively managed ETFs in this manner is no longer necessary given that all ETFs that could rely on the proposed rule currently provide full portfolio transparency.

3. Leveraged ETFs

Although the proposed rule would not distinguish between actively managed ETFs and index-based ETFs in general, it would take a different approach with respect to leveraged ETFs, which are a type of index-based ETF that presents unique considerations. "Leveraged ETFs" refers to ETFs that seek, directly or indirectly, to provide returns that exceed the performance of a market index by a specified multiple or to provide returns that have an inverse relationship to the performance of a market index, over a fixed period of time. A leveraged ETF seeks to amplify the returns of its underlying index or to profit from a decline in the value of its underlying index. It also typically seeks to deliver the targeted return over a short period of time, such as a day. This means that investors holding shares over periods longer than the targeted period may experience performance that is different, and at times substantially different, from the targeted returns. Leveraged ETFs seek to achieve their targeted returns by using financial derivatives. These funds are sometimes referred to as trading tools because they can be used by investors to hedge against or profit from short-term market movements without using margin.

....

... Accordingly, we propose to include a condition that would prevent leveraged ETFs from relying on proposed rule 6c-11. ETFs that seek to provide returns that exceed the performance (or inverse performance) of a market index by a specified multiple over a fixed period could not operate under our proposed rule.

....

B. Exemptive Relief Under Proposed Rule 6c-11

Proposed rule 6c-11 would provide ETFs within the scope of the rule with exemptions from certain provisions of the Act that are necessary to allow ETFs to operate. These exemptions are generally consistent with the relief we have given to ETFs under our exemptive orders. Proposed rule 6c-11 would permit an ETF that meets the conditions of the rule to: (i) Redeem shares only in creation unit aggregations; (ii) permit ETF shares to be purchased and sold at market prices rather than at NAV per share; (iii) engage in in-kind transactions with certain affiliates; and (iv) in certain limited circumstances, pay authorized participants the proceeds from the redemption of shares in more than seven days. As discussed below in section II.C, the exemptions would be subject to certain conditions that are designed to address the concerns underlying the relevant statutory provisions and to support a Commission finding that the exemptions are in the public interest and consistent with the protection of investors and the purposes fairly intended by the policy and provisions of the Act.

1. Treatment of ETF Shares as "Redeemable Securities"

Under proposed rule 6c-11, an ETF, as defined in the rule, would be considered to issue a "redeemable security" within the meaning of section 2(a)(32) of the Act. As discussed above, ETFs have features that distinguish them from both traditional open-end and closed-end funds. A defining feature of open-end funds is that they offer redeemable securities, which allow the holder to receive his or her proportionate share of the fund's NAV per share upon presentation of the security to the issuer. Although individual ETF shares cannot be redeemed, except in limited circumstances, they can be redeemed in creation unit aggregations. Therefore, we believe that ETF shares are most appropriately classified under the proposed rule as redeemable securities within the meaning of section 2(a)(32), and that ETFs should be regulated as open-end funds within the meaning of section 5(a)(1) of the Act.

The arbitrage mechanism that is central to the operation of an ETF (and the conditions in our relief designed to facilitate an effective arbitrage mechanism) serves to keep the market price of ETF shares at or close to the ETF's NAV per share. As a result, even though only authorized participants may redeem creation units directly from the ETF at NAV per share, investors are able to sell their ETF shares on the secondary market at or close to NAV, similar to investors in an open-end fund that redeem their shares directly from the fund at NAV per share. The shares of closed-end funds, on the other hand, generally trade on the secondary market at a discount or premium to NAV.

Our exemptive orders have provided exemptions from sections 2(a)(32) and 5(a)(1) of the Act so that ETFs may register under the Act as open-end funds while issuing shares redeemable in creation units only. Unlike our exemptive orders, however, the proposed rule would not provide an exemption from the definition of "redeemable security" in section 2(a)(32) or from the definition "open-end company" in section 5(a)(1). We believe that it is more appropriate for the proposed rule to address these questions of status by classifying ETF shares as "redeemable securities." Thus, any ETF operating in compliance with the rule's conditions and requirements would meet the definition of open-end company.

....

2. Trading of ETF Shares at Market-Determined Prices

Section 22(d) of the Act, among other things, prohibits investment companies, their principal underwriters, and dealers from selling a redeemable security to the public except at a current public offering price described in the prospectus. Rule 22c-1 generally requires that a dealer selling, redeeming, or repurchasing a redeemable security do so only at a price based on its NAV.[FN110] Together, section 22(d) and rule 22c-1 are designed to: (i) Prevent dilution caused by certain riskless trading practices of principal underwriters and dealers; (ii) prevent unjust discrimination or preferential treatment among investors purchasing and redeeming fund shares; and (iii) preserve an orderly distribution of investment company shares. ETFs seeking to register under the Act obtain exemptions from these provisions because investors may purchase and sell individual ETF shares from and to dealers on the secondary market at market-determined prices (i.e., at prices other than those described in the prospectus or based on NAV). Consistent with our prior exemptive orders, proposed rule 6c-11 would provide exemptions from these provisions.

As discussed above, only authorized participants can purchase and redeem shares directly from an ETF at NAV per share and only in creation unit aggregations. Because authorized participants (and other market participants transacting through an authorized participant) can take advantage of disparities between the market price of ETF shares and NAV per share, they may be in a different position than investors who buy and sell individual ETF shares only on the secondary market. However, if the arbitrage mechanism is functioning effectively, entities taking advantage of these disparities in market price and NAV per share move the market price to a level at or close to the NAV per share of the ETF. The proposed rule would provide exemptions from section 22(d) and rule 22c-1 because we believe this arbitrage mechanism—and the conditions in this rule designed to promote a properly functioning arbitrage mechanism—have adequately addressed, over the significant operating history of ETFs, the potential concerns regarding shareholder dilution and unjust discrimination that these provisions were designed to address.

....

The arbitrage mechanism is the foundation for why retail and other secondary market investors generally can buy and sell ETF shares at prices that are at or close to the prices at which authorized participants are able to buy and redeem shares directly from the ETF at NAV. In the Commission's experience, the deviation between the market price of ETFs and NAV per share, each calculated as of the close of trading each day, generally has been relatively small. For example, during 2016–2017, the closing price of ETFs based on U.S. equity indexes were within 1% of NAV for 97.9% of trading days and within 1% of NAV for actively managed ETFs investing in U.S. equities for 98.5% of trading days. The absolute weighted average of the daily difference between the NAV and market price during a six-month period ending in December 2017 was 0.014% for ETFs based on U.S. equities indexes and 0.074% for actively managed ETFs investing in U.S. equities.[120]

Other types of ETFs have had a somewhat higher deviation between NAV per share and market price. During 2016–2017, the closing price for index-based and actively managed ETFs investing in international equities, for example, were within 1% of NAV for 87.4% and 86.8% of trading days, respectively. Similarly, the absolute weighted average of the daily difference between the NAV and market price during a six-month period ending in December 2017 for index-based and actively managed ETFs investing in U.S. fixed-income securities were 0.067% and 0.068%, respectively. The absolute weighted average of daily difference between NAV per share and market price during the six-month period studied was 0.206% for ETFs based on international equities indexes and 0.390% for actively managed ETFs investing in international equities.

120. An ETF can trade at a premium or discount to its NAV per share on any given day. When taking an average over many days, premiums (which have a positive difference) and discounts (which have a negative difference) may offset each other. Therefore, to calculate deviation from NAV, we use the absolute value of premiums and discounts when calculating weighted average differences to prevent such offsetting.

These numbers represent only broad averages with respect to end-of-day differences, however, and intraday deviations between market price and NAV per share may be greater under certain circumstances. These figures also do not reflect intraday deviations between market prices and the contemporaneous value of the ETF's portfolio. However, one academic paper has shown that deviations between intraday market prices and estimated intraday values for domestic ETFs also were generally small.

The Commission and its staff have observed the operation of the arbitrage mechanism during periods of market stress when the deviation between intraday market prices and the next-calculated NAV per share significantly widened for short periods of time. During periods of extraordinary volatility in the underlying ETF holdings, it may be difficult for authorized participants or market makers to confidently ascribe precise values to an ETF's holdings, thereby making it more difficult to effectively hedge their positions. These market participants may widen their quoted spreads in ETF shares or, in certain cases, may elect not to transact in or quote ETF shares, rather than risk loss.

....

In particular, as discussed in section II.C.6, we are proposing to require ETFs to disclose on their websites the median bid-ask spread for the ETF's most recent fiscal year and certain historical information about the extent and frequency of an ETF's premiums and discounts. This would allow investors to be more aware of this risk when deciding whether to invest in ETFs generally or in a particular ETF. Our proposed amendments to Form N-1A would require additional disclosure regarding ETF trading information and related costs, including information relating to high-end (95th percentile) spread costs.[FN136] We also request comment below on whether there are other ways to calculate premiums and discounts, or other metrics we should consider, to better inform investors about an ETF's history of deviations between intraday market prices and (i) the next-calculated NAV; or (ii) the contemporaneous value of the ETF's portfolio.

....

C. Conditions for Reliance on Proposed Rule 6c-11

Proposed rule 6c-11 would require ETFs to comply with certain conditions that would allow them to operate within the scope of the Act, and that are designed to protect investors and to be consistent with the purposes fairly intended by the policy and provisions of the Act. These conditions are generally consistent with the conditions we have imposed under our exemptive orders, which we believe have effectively accommodated the unique structural and operational features of ETFs while maintaining appropriate protections for ETF investors. The conditions also reflect certain changes to the conditions imposed under our exemptive orders that, based on 26 years of experience regulating ETFs, we believe will improve the overall regulatory framework for these products.

1. Issuance and Redemption of Shares

Proposed rule 6c-11 would include several requirements in the paragraph defining "exchange-traded fund," including a requirement that the ETF issue (and redeem) creation units to (and from) authorized participants in exchange for baskets and a cash balancing amount (if any). As such, the proposed rule would seek to preserve the existing structure, reflected in our ETF exemptive orders, whereby only an authorized participant of an ETF may purchase creation units from (or sell creation units to) the ETF. This requirement is designed to preserve an orderly creation unit issuance and redemption process between ETFs and authorized participants. An orderly creation unit issuance and redemption process is of central importance to the arbitrage mechanism, which forms the basis for several of the proposed rule's exemptive provisions.

The proposed rule would define an authorized participant as a member or participant of a clearing agency registered with the Commission, which has a written agreement with the ETF or one of its service providers that allows the authorized participant to place orders for the purchase and redemption of creation units. This definition differs from the definition of "authorized participant" we recently adopted in connection with Form N-CEN, which, in relevant part, defines the term as a broker-dealer that is also a member of a clearing agency registered with the Commission or a DTC Participant and has a written agreement with the ETF or one of its service providers that allows the authorized participant to place orders to purchase and redeem creation units of the ETF. Our proposed definition also differs from the definition of authorized participant in our ETF exemptive orders and Form N-CEN, because it does not include a specific reference to an authorized participant's participation in DTC since DTC is itself a clearing agency. We believe the definition that we are proposing remains largely consistent with our existing exemptive relief, while eliminating unnecessary terms. As discussed further below, we are proposing a corresponding amendment to Form N-CEN.

The proposed rule would define the term "creation unit" to mean a specified number of ETF shares that the ETF will issue to (or redeem from) an authorized participant in exchange for the deposit (or delivery) of a basket and a cash balancing amount (if any). In their exemptive applications, ETFs have stated that they would establish a specific creation unit size (i.e., a minimum number of shares). Creation unit aggregations may differ among ETFs based on an ETF's investment strategy, the type and availability of the assets in the basket, and the types of authorized participants (and other market participants) that are expected to engage in creation and redemption transactions with the ETF. For example, an ETF tracking a narrowly focused niche strategy may establish a smaller creation unit size than an ETF tracking a broad-based index, such as the S&P 500, in order to facilitate arbitrage. Accordingly, we do not believe it is necessary to mandate a particular maximum or minimum creation unit size for all types of ETFs. This approach is consistent with our 2008 proposal, and commenters who addressed this aspect of the 2008 proposal generally supported it.

....

2. Listing on a National Securities Exchange

Proposed rule 6c-11 defines "exchange-traded fund," in part, to mean a fund that issues shares that are listed on a national securities exchange and traded at market-determined prices. Exchange-listing is one of the fundamental characteristics that distinguishes an ETF from other types of open-end funds (and UITs) and is one reason that ETFs need certain exemptions from the Act and the rules thereunder. The Commission has premised all of its previous exemptive orders on an ETF listing its shares for trading on a national securities exchange. Listing on an exchange provides an organized and continuous trading market for the ETF shares at market-determined prices. Trading on an exchange also is important to a functioning arbitrage mechanism. We proposed a similar condition in 2008 that would have required ETF shares to be approved for listing and trading on a national securities exchange. Commenters on the 2008 proposal generally agreed that listing on an exchange would provide an organized and continuous trading market for the ETF shares.

The proposed definition would require that the ETF's shares be traded at market-determined prices. Like other exchange-traded equity securities, however, we understand that there may be instances where ETF shares simply may not trade for a given period due to a lack of market interest. This proposed requirement is not designed to establish a minimum level of trading volume for ETFs necessary in order to rely on the rule, but rather to distinguish ETFs from other products that are listed on exchanges, but trade at NAV-based prices (i.e., exchange-traded managed funds).

....

3. Intraday Indicative Value

Exchange listing standards include a requirement that an intraday estimate of an ETF's NAV per share (an "intraday indicative value" or "IIV") be widely disseminated at least every 15 seconds during regular trading hours (60 seconds for international ETFs). Our orders also require the dissemination of the IIV, and ETFs have stated in their exemptive applications that an ETF's IIV is useful to investors because it allows them to determine (by comparing the IIV to the market value of the ETF's shares) whether and to what extent the ETF's shares are trading at a premium or discount. We are not proposing, however, to require the dissemination of an ETF's IIV as a condition of the proposed rule. We understand that market makers today typically calculate their own intraday value of an ETF's portfolio with proprietary algorithms that use an ETF's daily portfolio disclosure and available pricing information about the assets held in the ETF's portfolio. We further understand that they generally use the IIV, if at all, as a secondary or tertiary check on the value that their proprietary algorithms generate.

We believe that the IIV is no longer used by market participants when conducting arbitrage trading. In today's fast-moving markets, 15 seconds is likely too long for purposes of efficient market making and could result in poor execution. An ETF's current value changes every time the value of any underlying component of the ETF portfolio changes. Therefore, the IIV for a more frequently traded component security might not effectively take into account the full trading activity for that security, despite being available every 15 seconds. In particularly volatile markets, the dissemination lag of the IIV may not reflect the actual value of the ETF.

The IIV also may not reflect the actual value of an ETF that holds securities that do not trade frequently. For example, the IIV can be stale or inaccurate for ETFs with foreign securities or less liquid debt instruments. For such ETFs, there may be a difference in value between the IIV, which is constructed using the last available market quotations or stale prices, and the ETF's NAV, which uses fair value when market quotations are not readily available. Moreover, because there currently are no uniform methodology requirements, the IIV can be calculated in different, and potentially inconsistent, ways.

....

4. Portfolio Holdings

As discussed above, since the first exemptive order for an ETF, the Commission has relied on the existence of an arbitrage mechanism to keep the market prices of ETF shares at or close to the NAV per share of the ETF. One mechanism that facilitates the arbitrage mechanism is daily portfolio transparency. Portfolio transparency provides authorized participants and other market participants with an important tool to facilitate valuing the ETF's portfolio on an intraday basis, which, in turn, would enable them to assess whether arbitrage opportunities exist. It also provides information necessary to hedge the ETF's portfolio. The ability to hedge is important because market makers generally trade to provide liquidity, balance supply and demand, and profit from arbitrage opportunities (without seeking to profit from taking a directional position in a security). Without the ability to hedge, market makers may widen spreads or be reluctant to make markets because doing so may require taking on greater market risk than the firm is willing to bear. For this reason, to facilitate the ability of market makers to make markets in ETF shares, our exemptive orders have historically required ETFs to provide a certain degree of daily transparency. Furthermore, Commission staff has observed that all ETFs that could rely on the proposed rule currently provide full transparency as a matter of industry market practice.

a. Transparency of Portfolio Holdings

Proposed rule 6c-11 would require an ETF to disclose prominently on its website, which is publicly available and free of charge, the portfolio holdings that will form the basis for each calculation of NAV per share. The portfolio holdings disclosure must be made each business day before the opening of regular trading on the primary listing exchange of the ETF's shares and before the ETF starts accepting orders for the purchase or redemption of creation units. For portfolio transparency to facilitate effective arbitrage, authorized participants or other market participants buying or selling ETF shares, whether on the secondary market or in a primary transaction, should have access to portfolio composition information at the time of the transaction. The proposed rule's timing requirements, therefore, are designed to prevent an ETF from disclosing its portfolio holdings only after the beginning of trading or after the ETF has begun accepting orders for the next business day.

In addition, the proposed rule would require the portfolio holdings that form the basis for the ETF's NAV calculation to be the ETF's portfolio holdings as of the close of business on the prior business day. Changes in an ETF's holdings of portfolio securities would therefore be reflected on a T+1 basis. This condition is consistent with current ETF practices and enables an ETF to disclose at the beginning of the business day the portfolio that will form the basis for the next NAV calculation, helping to facilitate the efficient functioning of the arbitrage process.

....

6. Website Disclosure

There has been a significant increase in the use of the internet as a tool for disseminating information, and we believe that many investors obtain information regarding ETFs on the ETFs' websites. Proposed rule 6c-11 therefore would require ETFs to disclose certain information on their websites as a condition to the rule. As noted above, we believe that the arbitrage mechanism works more efficiently when certain data is publicly available to investors each trading day, and are therefore proposing ETF website disclosures in order to provide transparency of portfolio holdings and baskets. In addition, we are proposing several website disclosure requirements that are designed to provide investors with key metrics to evaluate their investment and trading decisions in a format that is easily accessible and frequently updated. Specifically, the proposed rule would require disclosure regarding: (i) The ETF's NAV per share, market price, and premium or discount, each as of the end of the prior business day; (ii) bid-ask spreads; and (iii) historical information regarding premiums and discounts.

Some of these conditions are based on our exemptive relief, which has required ETFs to disclose on their websites certain information regarding their investments and operations, including quantitative information regarding discounts or premiums at which the ETF's shares trade on the secondary market. Our orders have required ETFs to publicly disclose on their websites: (i) The prior business day's NAV per share; (ii) the market closing price or the midpoint of the bid-ask spread at the time of the calculation of NAV; and (iii) a calculation of the premium or discount of the market closing price or midpoint of the bid-ask spread against NAV per share. Similarly, Form N-1A currently provides an ETF with the option to omit certain historical information regarding premiums and discounts from its prospectus and annual report if the disclosure is provided on its website. Based on our experience overseeing ETFs, we are proposing additional website disclosure requirements that have not been part of our exemptive relief or Form N-1A requirements. We also are requesting comment regarding ways to better inform investors about intraday deviations between an ETF's market price and: (i) NAV per share; (ii) the contemporaneous value of its portfolio; or (iii) both. Each of the proposed website disclosures is discussed below.

a. Daily NAV, Market Price, and Premiums and Discounts

Proposed rule 6c-11(c)(1)(ii) would require ETFs to post on their websites, on each business day, the ETF's current NAV per share, market price, and premium or discount, each as of the end of the prior business day. This disclosure provides investors with a "snapshot" view of the difference between an ETF's NAV per share and market price on a daily basis. It is designed to alert investors to the relationship between NAV per share and the market price of the ETF's shares and that they may sell or purchase ETF shares at prices that do not correspond to NAV of the ETF. It also is designed to allow investors to compare this information across ETFs. For example, an investor using this information likely would notice that ETFs tracking emerging markets tend to have greater premiums or discounts than ETFs tracking broad-based domestic indexes. We believe that daily website disclosure of this information would promote transparency and help investors better understand the risk that an ETF's market price may be higher or lower than the ETF's NAV per share. We further believe that ETF investors use this information today, as ETFs currently provide this website disclosure pursuant to the terms of their exemptive orders.

. . . .

b. Bid-Ask Spread Disclosure

As discussed in more detail below, our proposed amendments to Form N-1A would include new requirements for an ETF to disclose information regarding bid-ask spreads on its website and in its prospectus. Specifically, an ETF would be required to disclose the median bid-ask spread for the ETF's most recent fiscal year. A bid-ask spread is the difference between the highest price a buyer is willing to pay to purchase shares of the ETF (bid) and the lowest price a seller is willing to accept for share of the ETF (ask). The proposed website disclosures are designed to inform investors that they may bear bid-ask spread costs when trading ETFs on the secondary market, which ultimately could impact the overall cost of the investment. We are concerned that investors may not be aware of the impact trading costs may have on their investments in ETFs, and therefore, propose to require ETFs to disclose median bid-ask spread information pursuant to a prescribed methodology that would be set forth in Form N-1A. We believe that this information would provide ETF investors with greater understanding of these costs and would allow investors to compare this information across ETFs. Spread costs for ETFs can vary significantly, and disclosure regarding these costs could aid comparisons of ETFs pursuing similar investment strategies. We believe this information also would allow investors to better understand the costs of investing in an ETF.

We are proposing to require the disclosure of the bid-ask spread information on an ETF's website to provide trading information that can help investors make better informed investment decisions in a format that is easily accessible and relied upon by a growing segment of investors. Given the importance of this information to understanding the total expenses an investor may bear when investing in an ETF, we preliminarily believe that bid-ask spread information also should be included in an

ETF's prospectus. Without this bid-ask spread information, we preliminarily believe the fee and expense information provided in a prospectus may not always provide a complete picture of an investment's true costs and/or allow investors to easily compare prospectus disclosures across certain investment options.

c. Historical Information Regarding Premiums and Discounts

We also are proposing to require that ETFs disclose on their websites historical information about the extent and frequency of an ETF's premiums and discounts. In particular, proposed rule 6c-11(c)(1)(iii) and (iv) would require an ETF to post on its website both a table and line graph showing the ETF's premiums and discounts for the most recently completed calendar year and the most recently completed calendar quarters of the current year. Alternatively, for new ETFs that do not yet have this information, the proposed rule would require the ETF to post this information for the life of the fund.

Currently, an ETF is required to disclose historical premium/discount information in its prospectus by providing tabular disclosure of the number of trading days during the most recently completed calendar year and quarters since that year ended on which the market price of the ETF shares was greater than the ETF's NAV per share and the number of days it was less than the ETF's NAV per share. An ETF currently may omit the disclosure of specific premium/discount information in its prospectus or annual report if the ETF provides the information on its website and discloses in the prospectus or annual report a website address where investors can locate the information. We believe that investors may find this tabular information helpful in understanding how often an ETF trades at a premium or discount and the size of such premiums and discounts and are proposing to require publication of a table on the ETF's website as part of proposed rule 6c-11.

We additionally believe that graphic disclosure could assist some investors with understanding how the arbitrage mechanism performs for an ETF under various market conditions. Depending on a variety of factors, an ETF could have persistent premiums or discounts (or both) from the ETF's NAV. For example, certain classes of ETFs, such as those that invest in less liquid securities, like high-yield bonds, and securities that trade on international markets, have more persistent deviations in ETF share prices from the ETF's NAV. Additionally, for certain types of ETFs, the disclosure may inform investors about the pricing of the ETF's portfolio holdings. ETFs holding foreign securities that are traded on markets that are closed during U.S. trading hours, for example, may have persistent premiums or discounts resulting from this timing differential. In other cases, a persistent deviation between market price and NAV per share could demonstrate inefficiencies in an ETF's arbitrage mechanism.

While past performance cannot predict how an ETF will trade in the future, we believe that it is important that investors, and particularly retail investors, understand that certain classes of ETFs could have a larger and more persistent deviation from NAV, which could result in a higher cost to investors and a potential drag on returns. In addition to alerting secondary market investors that an ETF's NAV per share and market price may differ, these disclosures would provide information regarding the frequency and extent of these deviations. These disclosures thus would help investors understand the value of their investment and could help shape whether they want to invest in a particular ETF.

. . . .

G. Effect of Proposed Rule 6c-11 on Prior Orders

The Commission has authority under the Act to amend or rescind our orders when necessary or appropriate to the exercise of the powers conferred elsewhere in the Act. Pursuant to this authority, we are proposing to amend and rescind the exemptive relief we have issued to ETFs that would be permitted to rely on the proposed rule. Our proposed rescission of orders would specifically be limited to the portions of an ETF's exemptive order that grant relief related to the formation and operation of an ETF and, with the exception of certain master-feeder relief discussed above in section II.F, would not rescind the relief from section 12(d)(1) and sections 17(a)(1) and (a)(2) under the Act related to fund of funds arrangements involving ETFs.

The terms of the exemptive relief granted to ETFs have evolved over time and have resulted in an uneven playing field among ETF complexes, subjecting ETFs that pursue the same or similar investment strategies to different operational requirements. Moreover, many ETF complexes have multiple exemptive orders permitting them to operate ETFs. Some of those orders contain different conditions for relief and different representations by the applicants regarding how the ETFs formed pursuant to the order would operate. Many of those orders also provide relief for future ETFs created pursuant to the terms of a particular exemptive order. As a result, ETF complexes with multiple orders can effectively choose the exemptive relief that would be applicable to a new ETF by selecting what legal entity should form the new ETF series. Moreover, differences in the terms of our various orders have had varying impact on the structure and costs of an ETF. For example, shares of an ETF with a less flexible basket condition in its order could have wider spreads than a similarly situated ETF with more flexible basket compositions. However, investors may not be able to discern the difference between these two ETFs' orders. As we have stated elsewhere in this release, among our goals in proposing rule 6c-11 is to create a consistent, transparent and efficient regulatory framework for many ETFs. We do not believe this goal would be furthered if ETFs that could rely on the rule continue to rely on those orders. [* * *]

. . . .

* * *

Text of SEC's Proposed Rule 16c-11

Exchange-Traded Companies, Investment Company Release No. 33140 (June 28, 2018).

(a) Definitions. For purposes of this section:

Authorized participant means a member or participant of a clearing agency registered with the Commission, which has a written agreement with the exchange-traded fund or one of its service providers that allows the authorized participant to place orders for the purchase and redemption of creation units.

Basket means the securities, assets or other positions in exchange for which an exchange-traded fund issues (or in return for which it redeems) creation units.

Business day means any day the exchange-traded fund is open for business, including any day when it satisfies redemption requests as required by section 22(e) of the Act (15 U.S.C. 80a-22(e)).

Cash balancing amount means an amount of cash to account for any difference between the value of the basket and the net asset value of a creation unit.

Creation unit means a specified number of exchange-traded fund shares that the exchange-traded fund will issue to (or redeem from) an authorized participant in exchange for the deposit (or delivery) of a basket and a cash balancing amount if any.

Custom basket means:

(i) Baskets that are composed of a non-representative selection of the exchange-traded fund's portfolio holdings; or

(ii) Different baskets used in transactions on the same business day.

Exchange-traded fund means a registered open-end management company:

(i) That issues (and redeems) creation units to (and from) authorized participants in exchange for a basket and a cash balancing amount if any; and

(ii) Whose shares are listed on a national securities exchange and traded at market-determined prices.

Exchange-traded fund share means a share of stock issued by an exchange-traded fund.

Foreign investment means any security, asset or other position of the ETF issued by a foreign issuer as that term is defined in § 240.3b-4 of this title, and for which there is no established United States public trading market, as that term is used in 17 CFR 227.201 (Item 201 of Regulation S-K under the Securities Act of 1933).

Market price means:

(i) The official closing price of an exchange-traded fund share; or

(ii) If it more accurately reflects the market value of an exchange-traded fund share at the time as of which the exchange-traded fund calculates current net asset value per share, the price that is the midpoint between the national best bid and national best offer as of that time.

National securities exchange means an exchange that is registered with the Commission under section 6 of the Securities Exchange Act of 1934 (15 U.S.C. 78f).

Portfolio holdings means the securities, assets or other positions held by the exchange-traded fund.

Premium or discount means the positive or negative difference between the market price of an exchange-traded fund share at the time as of which the current net asset value is calculated and the exchange-traded fund's current net asset value per share, expressed as a percentage of the exchange-traded fund share's current net asset value per share.

(b) Application of the Act to Exchange-Traded Funds.

If the conditions of paragraph (c) of this section are satisfied:

(1) Redeemable security. An exchange-traded fund share is considered a "redeemable security" within the meaning of section 2(a)(32) of the Act (15 U.S.C. 80a-2(a)(32)).

(2) Pricing. A dealer in exchange-traded fund shares is exempt from section 22(d) of the Act (15 U.S.C. 80a-22(d)) and §270.22c-1(a) with regard to purchases, sales and repurchases of exchange-traded fund shares at market-determined prices.

(3) Affiliated transactions. (i) A person who is an affiliated person of an exchange-traded fund (or who is an affiliated person of such a person) solely by reason of the circumstances described in paragraphs (b)(3)(i)(A) and (B) of this section is exempt from sections 17(a)(1) and 17(a)(2) of the Act (15 U.S.C. 80a-17(a)(1) and (a)(2)) with regard to the deposit and receipt of baskets:

(A) Holding with the power to vote 5% or more of the exchange-traded fund's shares; or

(B) Holding with the power to vote 5% or more of any investment company that is an affiliated person of the exchange-traded fund.

(4) Postponement of redemptions. If an exchange-traded fund includes a foreign investment in its basket, and if a local market holiday, or series of consecutive holidays, or the extended delivery cycles for transferring foreign investments to redeeming authorized participants prevents timely delivery of the foreign investment in response to a redemption request, the exchange-traded fund is exempt, with respect to the delivery of the foreign investment, from the prohibition in section 22(e) of the Act (15 U.S.C. 80a-22(e)) against postponing the date of satisfaction upon redemption for more than seven days after the tender of a redeemable security if the exchange-traded fund delivers the foreign investment as soon as practicable, but in no event later than 15 days after the tender of the exchange-traded fund shares. The exemption provided in paragraph (b)(4) of this section will expire and no longer be effective on [date ten years from effective date of rule].

(c) Conditions.

(1) Each business day, an exchange-traded fund must disclose prominently on its website, which is publicly available and free of charge:

(i) Before the opening of regular trading on the primary listing exchange of the exchange-traded fund shares and before the exchange-traded fund starts accepting orders for the purchase or redemption of creation units:

(A) The portfolio holdings that will form the basis of the next calculation of current net asset value per share;

(B) A basket applicable to orders for the purchase or redemption of creation units to be priced based on the next calculation of current net asset value; and

(C) The estimated cash balancing amount, if any;

(ii) The exchange-traded fund's current net asset value per share, market price, and premium or discount, each as of the prior business day;

(iii) A table showing the number of days the exchange-traded fund's shares traded at a premium or discount during the most recently completed calendar year and the most recently completed calendar quarters since that year (or the life of the exchange-traded fund, if shorter);

(iv) A line graph showing exchange-traded fund share premiums or discounts for the most recently completed calendar year and the most recently completed calendar quarters since that year (or the life of the exchange-traded fund, if shorter); and

(v) If the exchange-traded fund's premium or discount is greater than 2% for more than seven consecutive trading days, a discussion of the factors that are reasonably believed to have materially contributed to the premium or discount, which must be maintained on the website for at least one year thereafter; and

(vi) The exchange-traded fund must present the description, amount, value and unrealized gain/loss in the manner prescribed within 17 CFR 210.12-12, 210.12-12A, 210.12-13, 210.12-13A, 210.12-13B, 210.12-13C, and 210.12-13D (Article 12 of Regulation S-X) for each portfolio holding or basket asset required to be disclosed pursuant to paragraphs (c)(1)(i) of this section.

(2) An exchange-traded fund must reflect changes in the exchange-traded fund's portfolio holdings in the first calculation of net asset value per share on the first business day following the trade date.

(3) An exchange-traded fund must adopt and implement written policies and procedures that govern the construction of baskets and the process that will be used for the acceptance of baskets; provided, however, if the exchange-traded fund utilizes a custom basket:

(i) These written policies and procedures also must:

(A) Set forth detailed parameters for the construction and acceptance of custom baskets that are in the best interests of the exchange-traded fund and its shareholders, including the process for any revisions to, or deviations from, those parameters; and

(B) Specify the titles or roles of the employees of the exchange-traded fund's investment adviser who are required to review each custom basket for compliance with those parameters.

(4) The exchange-traded fund may not seek, directly or indirectly, to provide returns that exceed the performance of a market index by a specified multiple, or to provide returns that have an inverse relationship to the performance of a market index, over a fixed period of time.

(5) Notwithstanding the definition of exchange-traded fund in paragraph (a) of this section, an exchange-traded fund is not prohibited from selling (or redeeming) individual shares on the day of consummation of a reorganization, merger, conversion or liquidation.

(d) Recordkeeping. The exchange-traded fund must maintain and preserve for a period of not less than five years, the first two years in an easily accessible place:

(1) All written agreements (or copies thereof) between an authorized participant and the exchange-traded fund or one of its service providers that allows the authorized participant to place orders for the purchase or redemption of creation units;

(2) For each basket exchanged with an authorized participant, records setting forth:

(i) The names and quantities of the positions composing the basket exchanged for creation units;

(ii) If applicable, identification of the basket as a custom basket and a record stating that the custom basket complies with policies and procedures that the exchange-traded fund adopted pursuant to paragraph (c)(3)(i) of this section;

(iii) Cash balancing amount, if any; and

(iv) Identity of authorized participant transacting with the exchange-traded fund.

* * *

The proposed rule and the SEC's failure to adopt reveal a difficulty associated with the agency's wariness of ETFs. A rule would undoubtedly diminish the agency's workload and the the regulatory burden faced by ETF sponsors. The failure to adopt the rule may be the lack of urgency associated with the issue by the agency and/or sponsors, a preference for tighter control over the creation of ETFs inherent in the exemptive relief process, or uncertainty or controversy regarding the sufficiency of the proposed conditions. Nevertheless the framework provides a roadmap regarding the SEC's general concerns relating to ETFs. A pervasive theme relates to the health of the arbitrage mechanism underlying ETFs. Why is this issue so important for the SEC? How does that issue relate to transparency?

18.4 Actively-Managed ETFs—Transparent and Nontransparent ETFs

Actively-managed ETFs, as their name implies, use active management strategies rather than passive index-based strategies in managing the ETF's portfolio. Active management seeks to outperform, rather than match, a relevant performance benchmark.[4] The main challenge for actively-managed ETFs is the potential that daily transparency of the fund portfolio, as required for index-based ETFs, would impede execution of many, if not most, kinds of actively managed strategies. Although actively-managed transparent funds were approved in 2008, they have been relatively few in number and have been only marginally successful in gathering assets in most cases. There is only a smattering of large, transparent, actively-managed ETFs, and these isolated examples exist only in the fixed-income space. Most recently, the SEC received pressure to provide exemptive relief to nontransparent ETFs that attempt to preserve the requisite arbitrage link through intricate third-party blind-trust mechanisms.

18.4.1 Transparent Actively-Managed ETFs

Transparency is a significant issue for sponsors of actively-managed ETFs but not for passively-managed ETFs. Why? Transparency concerns real-time knowledge relating to the underlying composition of a fund portfolio. In the case of passively-managed funds, the fund merely tries to match the performance of an index representing the performance of the component securities of the index in accordance with the index weights. Public knowledge of the components of a broad-based index is unlikely to affect trading in the underlying components, since trades executed on behalf of the fund do not reveal new information to the market. However, the same cannot be said about actively-managed funds. Transparency in such circumstances would result in public knowledge of the fund's trading activity which, in turn, might reveal the portfolio manager's active investment ideas. Why might transparency adversely affect an actively-managed ETF? Again, as noted above, why, from the SEC's perspective, is transparency an important feature of ETFs?

18.4.2 Nontransparent Actively-Managed ETFs

The amount of assets gathered by transparent actively-managed ETFs since 2008 is remarkably small compared to the total assets managed by ETFs. As of the beginning of 2018, total AUM of all ETFs exceeded $3 trillion, which constitutes more than a trebling of assets since 2010, and only a fairly small fraction of that AUM represents transparent, actively-managed ETFs. The tepid market response suggests that transparent, actively-managed ETFs are viable products only in limited circumstances. However, on the sponsor side, there is considerable interest in so-called nontransparent, actively-managed ETFs. A nontransparent ETF, as the term is commonly used, would *not* provide daily portfolio transparency as an index-based fund would (i.e., a complete listing of portfolio composition at the outset of every trading day). Such a structure is attractive to sponsors, because it seemly combines the market appeal of ETFs with well-established models of active management, like mutual funds, where the composition of an actively-managed portfolio is not available to the public (and competitors) in real time.

While such a structure is appealing to sponsors, the SEC has declined to approve nontransparent, actively-managed ETFs. The SEC has questioned whether such ETFs would provide an effective arbitrage mechanism that is fair to investors, both in terms of the sale and redemption of creation units and the pricing of ETF shares on securities exchanges.

In lieu of daily portfolio transparency, sponsors have advocated the use of a third-party blind trust that would know the actual composition of the ETF portfolio and publish intraday indicative values (IIVs) for the portfolio in regular intervals, such as every fifteen seconds. Market makers and authorized participants, however, would not have independent models to validate the IIVs, so the arbitrage mechanism would be less robust than the arbitrage mechanism involved with indexed-based funds. The SEC has considered several variations on this approach, but so far has declined to provide exemptive relief. In a particularly notable example, the SEC published a notice of application for exemptive relief that indicated the SEC's intention to deny the request.

Precidian ETFs Trust—Notice of Application

Investment Company Act Release No. 31300 (Oct. 21, 2014)

[**Textbook Note:** *This item is unusual as a procedural matter. The SEC routinely issues Notices of Application in anticipation of granting exemptive relief after reviewing an application for exemptive relief. If the SEC anticipates adverse action with respect to an application, the applicant typically withdraws the application. In this case, the applicant declined to withdraw the request for exemptive relief, and the SEC issued an order indicating its intent to deny the application. The SEC's order singled out the arbitrage blind trust mechanism—a fifteen second delayed IIV dissemination—as the primary basis for its preliminary intent to deny the application for exemptive relief, which it did indeed subsequently deny. The SEC's order specifically noted the following deficiencies in the IIV: (i) "the IIV is stale data"; (ii) "the IIV is not subject to meaningful standards"; (iii) "the IIV would be inaccurate for certain securities and asset classes"; (iv) "IIV inaccuracies can increase ETF tracking error"; and (v) "IIV inaccuracies can increase during periods of market stress or volatility."*]

[***] 36. As discussed above, the Commission preliminarily believes that Applicants have not provided an adequate substitute for portfolio transparency such that the proposed ETFs would consistently trade at or close to NAV. A close tie between market price and NAV per share of the ETF is the foundation for why the prices at which retail investors buy and sell ETF shares are similar to the prices at which Authorized Partic-

ipants are able to buy and redeem shares directly from the ETF at NAV. This close tie between the prices paid by retail investors and Authorized Participants is important because section 22(d) and rule 22c-1 under the Act are designed to require that all fund shareholders be treated equitably when buying and selling their fund shares. In fact, in granting relief from section 22(d) and rule 22c-1 under the Act, the Commission has relied on this close tie between what retail investors pay and what Authorized Participants pay to make the finding that the ETF's shareholders are being treated equitably when buying and selling shares.

37. The lack of portfolio transparency or an adequate substitute for portfolio transparency coupled with a potentially deficient back-up mechanism presents a significant risk that the market prices of ETF shares may materially deviate from the NAV per share of the ETF—particularly in times of market stress when the need for verifiable pricing information becomes more acute. This would be contrary to the foundational principle underlying section 22(d) and rule 22c-1 under the Act—that shareholders be treated equitably—and may, in turn, inflict substantial costs on investors, disrupt orderly trading and damage market confidence in secondary trading of ETFs.

A. Substantial Costs to Investors

38. One of the primary benefits of current ETFs is that investors are generally able to obtain a similar economic experience to investors in traditional open-end funds (*i.e.*, price at or close to NAV), but without certain of the costs associated with such funds (*e.g.*, transfer agency fees). The Commission preliminarily believes the proposed ETFs would not provide either element of this benefit if, as the Commission anticipates, the arbitrage mechanism does not function properly. A breakdown in the arbitrage mechanism could result in material deviations between market price and NAV per share of the ETF. Such deviations can hurt an investor. For example, if an investor places a buy order and the ETF is trading at a premium, this would result in a lower return for the investor as opposed to if the investor had bought the ETF when its prices were at or close to the NAV per share of the ETF or at a discount. As discussed above, the arbitrage mechanism inherent in the ETF structure keeps these differences small.

39. In this regard, the Commission finds it significant that market makers for Applicants expressed some skepticism during meetings with Commission staff that the IIV could be used as the primary pricing signal for ETFs with active management strategies that might involve high portfolio turnover. They indicated that they would likely use the pieces of information provided by the Applicants (IIV, quarterly portfolio holdings disclosure and prospectus disclosure) to construct hedge portfolios using sophisticated algorithms. Their ability to construct hedge portfolios that are generally predictive of the portfolio holdings of the ETF is critical to their management of their exposure to the ETF. If there is a break in the alignment between the market makers' hedge portfolios and the NAV per share of the ETF, the market makers' risk of loss increases. The greater the risk of loss, the more the market makers will seek to cover that risk by quoting wider price spreads of the proposed ETFs. This would result in market prices, at which investors would buy and sell the ETF shares, not being at or close to the NAV per share of the

ETF, which would be contrary to the foundational principle underlying section 22(d) and rule 22c-1 under the Act that shareholders be treated equitably.

40. The Commission preliminarily believes that, even under normal market conditions, market makers could be unable to deconstruct the portfolio holdings of a proposed ETF with sufficient accuracy in order to construct a hedge portfolio that is closely aligned to the NAV per share of the ETF. The proposed disclosures by the Applicants would likely be useful in narrowing down the pool of securities and other assets that may be held by the ETF, but only to a limited extent. For example, prospectus disclosures of general risks and investment objectives provide little quantitative precision about an ETF's assets and risk exposures. The proposed quarterly portfolio disclosures would provide little additional quantitative precision as a result of portfolio turnover, as discussed previously. Consequently, variability would inevitably be introduced into the proposed model. The Commission believes that this may lead to a break in alignment between a market maker's hedge portfolio and the NAV per share of the ETF; this could diminish the market maker's ability to manage its risks, which, in turn, could increase its risk of loss. This greater risk of loss would be reflected in wider bid/ask spreads and result in intraday market prices that deviate from the NAV per share of the ETF, which would be contrary to the foundational principle underlying section 22(d) and rule 22c-1 under the Act that shareholders be treated equitably.

41. The Commission also preliminarily believes that this potential price disparity could be even worse under times of market stress or volatility. Market makers would likely be heavily reliant on sophisticated algorithms to deconstruct the portfolio holdings of the proposed ETF in order to construct the hedge portfolio. During times of market stress or volatility, the Commission believes that reliance on these algorithms would not be sufficient for market making purposes in the proposed ETFs and the correspondence between the hedge portfolio and the NAV per share of the ETF might be expected to lag. This is because the market makers' hedge portfolio may deviate significantly from the actual portfolio of the proposed ETF, resulting in greater intraday market risk to the market maker and a corresponding widening of the bid/ask spread. This would result in market prices, at which investors would buy and sell the ETF shares, not being at or close to the NAV per share of the ETF, which would be contrary to the foundational principle underlying section 22(d) and rule 22c-1 under the Act that shareholders be treated equitably. Accordingly, although some market makers supporting Applicants noted that they should be able to construct hedge portfolios that were closely aligned (and would remain aligned) to the NAV per share of the ETF for the domestic equity ETFs proposed by Applicants, the Commission cannot fully agree with that conclusion.

42. Finally, although Applicants proposed a retail redemption option to address a significant deviation of market price to NAV, as discussed in detail above, the Commission preliminarily believes that this option is not sufficient to protect investors as required by the Act.

B.Potential Disruption of Orderly Trading and Damage to Market Confidence

43. In the absence of sufficient information for market makers to accurately assess the value of the underlying portfolio securities and to make markets in ETF shares at levels that are closely aligned to the NAV per share of the ETF, market makers are likely to trade in proposed ETFs with wide bid/ask spreads and variable premiums/discounts to the NAV per share of the ETF. This would be particularly the case during times of market stress and for active management strategies that might involve high portfolio turnover when there is a greater need for confidence in pricing signals. Under particularly stressful or volatile market conditions, the inability to independently and accurately value an ETF's portfolio assets may cause market makers to withdraw from providing meaningful liquidity, which in turn can lead to the disruption of orderly trading in the ETF. The Commission preliminarily believes that a structure that may lead market makers to make markets in the proposed ETFs at prices that are not closely aligned to the NAV per share of the ETF is not necessary or appropriate in the public interest, nor is it consistent with the protection of investors or with the foundational principle underlying section 22(d) and rule 22c-1 under the Act that shareholders be treated equitably.

44. Further, any breakdown in the pricing or the ability to price the proposed ETF may result in damage to market confidence in secondary trading of ETFs—not just in the proposed product, but in ETFs generally. Investors may exit the ETF market because of a loss of trust, particularly in actively managed ETFs, should the proposed ETFs fail to function in a manner similar to current ETFs. For this additional reason, the Commission preliminarily believes that it is not necessary or appropriate, nor in the public interest or consistent with the protection of investors and the purposes fairly intended by the policy and provisions of the Act, to grant the requested relief. [***]

* * *

Notes and Applications

The next step—secondary trading of mutual funds. In 2014, Eaton Vance successfully applied to the SEC for exemptive relief to permit "exchange-traded managed funds," meaning mutual funds that could trade during the day at prices different from the next determined NAV. Eaton Vance—Notice of Application, Investment Company Act Release No. 31333 (Nov. 6, 2014). The exchange-traded managed fund is a variant of the nontransparent ETF. Like traditional ETFs, investors can intraday trade exchange-traded managed funds (using a mechanism of creation units and authorized participants similar to traditional ETFs), thus providing trading accessibility and liquidity throughout the trading day. Unlike traditional ETF shares, shares of the exchange-traded managed fund are priced during trading at a discount or premium to the "to-be-determined" end of day NAV. Like the nontransparent ETF, the underlying portfolio of the exchange-traded managed fund is not transparent to investors, except on a delayed basis as is the case with any mutual funds. Nevertheless, shareholders would be assured that the transaction price would reflect the end-of-day NAV plus or minus an agreed-to premium or discount. The SEC viewed the exchange-traded managed fund more favorably than nontransparent

ETFs, because each trading transaction would ultimately be based on the NAV of fund shares. At the same time, active strategies would not be impaired by virtually real-time transparency of underlying securities portfolios. The market has been slow to embrace exchange-traded managed funds since the SEC's grant of exemptive relief.

18.5 Other Regulatory Issues Affecting Exchange-Traded Products

Exchange-traded products implicate other regulatory issues under the securities laws. In addition to obvious issues under the Company Act, they also raise issues under the Securities Act and the Exchange Act, which the SEC has addressed through exemptive relief. As noted above, exchange-traded products also encompass fund products that do not hold securities, and therefore are not subject to the Company Act. Nevertheless, such funds must comply with the Securities Act and Exchange Act reporting and disclosure requirements applicable to ordinary public companies. Separately, the SEC has at times noted concerns relating to the heavy reliance of ETFs on derivatives in executing trading strategies and highlighted instances where ETFs may be vulnerable to liquidity concerns in times of unusual market stress. For the most part, the SEC has refrained from raising investor protection concerns with respect to ETFs. One exception to the SEC's general hands-off approach concerns "leveraged ETFs," which have been a source of concern even though the SEC originally approved the requisite exemptive relief permitting leveraged ETFs. Recently, the SEC has signaled renewed concerns and indicated that it may take action to curb the most aggressive kinds of leveraged ETFs, although some space for leveraged ETFs would remain.

Non-Traditional ETFs

FINRA Regulatory Notice 09-31 (June 2009)

[**Textbook Note:** *Both the SEC and FINRA have raised fundamental suitability concerns relating to so-called "leveraged ETFs." The product greatly magnifies returns and losses by a factor of 2 (i.e., 2x) or more. The products' features are easily misunderstood and, therefore, understandably are viewed by regulators as inappropriate for average retail investors. This Regulatory Notice from FINRA cautions member broker-dealers regarding their responsibilities in recommending such products to clients.*]

[***] Background and Discussion

Leveraged ETFs seek to deliver multiples of the performance of the index or benchmark they track. Some leveraged ETFs are "inverse" or "short" funds, meaning that they seek to deliver the opposite of the performance of the index or benchmark they track. Like traditional ETFs, some inverse ETFs track broad indices, some are sector-specific, and still others are linked to commodities or currencies. Inverse ETFs are often marketed as a way for investors to profit from, or at least hedge their exposure to, downward moving markets. Some funds are both short and leveraged, meaning that they seek to achieve a return that is a multiple of the inverse performance of the underlying index. An inverse ETF that tracks the S&P 500, for example, seeks to deliver the inverse of the performance of the S&P 500, while a 2x leveraged inverse S&P 500 ETF seeks to deliver twice the opposite of that index's performance. To accomplish their objectives, leveraged and inverse ETFs pursue a range of investment strategies through the use of swaps, futures contracts and other derivative instruments.

Most leveraged and inverse ETFs "reset" daily, meaning that they are designed to achieve their stated objectives on a daily basis. Due to the effect of compounding, their performance over longer periods of time can differ significantly from the performance (or inverse of the performance) of their underlying index or benchmark during the same period of time. For example, between December 1, 2008, and April 30, 2009:

> The Dow Jones U.S. Oil & Gas Index gained 2 percent, while an ETF seeking to deliver twice the index's daily return fell 6 percent and the related ETF seeking to deliver twice the inverse of the index's daily return fell 26 percent.
>
> An ETF seeking to deliver three times the daily return of the Russell 1000 Financial Services Index fell 53 percent while the index actually gained around 8 percent. The related ETF seeking to deliver three times the inverse of the index's daily return declined by 90 percent over the same period.

This effect can be magnified in volatile markets. Using a two-day example, if the index goes from 100 to close at 101 on the first day and back down to close at 100 on the next day, the two-day return of an inverse ETF will be different than if the index had moved up to close at 110 the first day but then back down to close at 100 on the next day. In the first case with low volatility, the inverse ETF loses 0.02 percent; but in the more volatile scenario the inverse ETF loses 1.82 percent. The effects of mathematical compounding can grow significantly over time, leading to scenarios such as those noted above.

Suitability

[FINRA Rule 2111] requires that, before recommending the purchase, sale or exchange of a security, a firm must have a reasonable basis for believing that the transaction is suitable for the customer to whom the recommendation is made. This analysis has two components. The first is determining whether the product is suitable for any customer, an analysis that requires firms and associated persons to fully understand the products and transactions they recommend. With respect to leveraged and inverse ETFs, this means that a firm must understand the terms and features of the funds, including how they are designed to perform, how they achieve that objective, and the impact that market volatility, the ETF's use of leverage, and the customer's intended holding period will have on their performance.

Once a determination is made that a product is generally suitable for at least some investors, a firm must also determine that the product is suitable for the specific customers to whom it is recommended. This analysis includes making reasonable efforts to obtain information concerning the customer's financial status, tax status, investment objectives and "such other information used or considered to be reasonable by such member or registered representative in making recommendations to the customer." While the customer-specific suitability analysis depends on the investor's particular circumstances, inverse and leveraged ETFs typically are not suitable for retail investors who plan to hold them for more than one trading session, particularly in volatile markets. [***]

* * *

ETFs (and indeed the broader category of ETPs) represent the dynamic developmental edge of product offerings and regulatory challenges at this time. The ability of the SEC to accommodate the development of such hybrid products in the context of the requirements of laws enacted decades ago is a testament to the viability and flexibility of such laws. Although the recent growth and popularity of ETFs is fundamentally altering the structure of the fund and investment management industries, the Company Act and rulemaking authority thereunder appear to provide the means for continued effective regulation.

Index